The Leading Men of
MGM

Books by Jane Ellen Wayne include:

The Golden Girls of MGM: Glamour and Grief
Robert Taylor: The Man with the Perfect Face
Kings of Tragedy
Stanwyck
Cooper's Women
Ava's Men
The Life and Loves of Grace Kelly
Marilyn's Men
Clark Gable: Portrait of a Misfit

The Leading Men of
MGM

Jane Ellen Wayne

CARROLL & GRAF PUBLISHERS
NEW YORK

To Robert Taylor,
in remembrance

The Leading Men of MGM

Carroll & Graf Publishers
An Imprint of Avalon Publishing Group Inc.
245 West 17th Street
11th Floor
New York, NY 10011

AVALON
publishing group incorporated

Library of Congress Cataloging-in-Publication Data is available.

ISBN-10: 0-78671-768-8
ISBN-13: 978-0-78671-768-2

10 9 8 7 6 5 4 3 2 1

Printed in the United States of America
Distributed by Publishers Group West

Contents

Foreword

I am the author of many books about Hollywood celebrities, but reliving the Golden Era in *The Golden Girls of MGM* published in 2002 gave me the greatest pleasure of all. It revolved around the women who, with their virginal images, helped mould Metro-Goldwyn-Mayer. It made sense to follow up with a volume about *The Leading Men of MGM* who remain legends to this day. Their lives were more tragic than those of the girls, but I've yet to figure out why this was so. Did it have something to do with the fact that MGM mogul Louis B. Mayer gave the Boys more freedom? In this regard the public remains fickle. Women represent motherhood. Men represent liberality, not fatherhood. If he commits adultery he's a rascal. If his wife is unfaithful she's a whore.

It was Joan Crawford who said that. Women grow old, men become distinguished. I learned a great deal from Joan. She gave me the key to a good interview: 'Don't ask "if". Ask "why". Let them think you know more than you do.' I did, and it worked like a charm. She also insisted I talk to the technicians, stagehands, doormen, chauffeurs, head waiters and security guards. They saw and heard what others didn't. But their names are unfamiliar outside the hallowed gates of Hollywood so they remain anonymous as requested.

She was also right that the famous reveal nothing. Interviewing them is a waste of time unless you're an autograph hunter. But on the other hand there were the unknown starlets who carried a grudge and were eager to express their resentment. Instead of performing, they stood behind the camera and observed.

The prostitutes were very informative and amusing. Living in luxury, they bore resentment towards no one. A favourite subject of theirs was penis size. It didn't occur to me to inquire, but they talked openly and without vulgarity about it. To them it was amusing. They agreed that, with the exception of Humphrey Bogart, Forrest Tucker and Milton Berle, none of the big stars were 'big' in that sense. Alas, none of the well endowed, other than Frank Sinatra, were on the MGM roster.

West coast MGM publicity chief Howard Strickling gave away few secrets; after a few martinis he loosened up a little but he was still guarded. I had close friends at MGM's parent company, Loews, and they joined us in the bar. Although Howard wanted to help me, he would protect his MGM players to his grave, giving away only what he thought was harmless. He was annoyed, though, that I put his stars on a pedestal, especially Robert Taylor. After Howard's third martini he growled, 'Get with it, girl! Bob was a royal cocksman!' I was delighted to hear that. It gave me more to write about in Taylor's biography.

The MGM Boys were what the public wanted them to be, the publicity department saw to that. Their masculine image was most important. They were wholesome, clean-cut, handsome, kind to their mothers, loyal to their wives and always six feet tall. Mickey Rooney, the perpetual teenager as Andy Hardy, was the single exception.

I remember director George Cukor telling me how beautiful the men were at MGM. They were always well groomed, always had a smile and good posture. 'MGM was pristine,' he remembered. 'Everything and everyone sparkled. The contract players reflected this aura. It was a marvellous place to work. Going home at night was a sad reminder that there was a real and not so pleasant world outside the golden gates of MGM.'

Joan Crawford told me about her leading men, in particular Clark Gable. She almost married him and they had an affair, on and off, for thirty years. When I spoke to Robert Taylor, he remained loyal to Louis B. Mayer. He was one of the last to leave MGM to collect his pension. Unlike the other stars, he was given good films in the fifties and faltered when he had to choose his own. 'I was virtually lost when I left Metro,' he admitted. 'I'd never made my own airline reservations and had to ask someone what to do. It never occurred to me all I had to do was pick up the telephone. You see, everything was taken care of by the studio. Limousines picked you up and were waiting at restaurants and airports. I was going on fifty years old and helpless.'

John Wayne told me that MGM was the elite. 'But I wouldn't be comfortable as one of their contract players,' he said. 'I like to rough it and that wasn't their style. I made a film there and was rather uncomfortable especially if my shoes weren't shined.'

I was fortunate to begin my writing career in 1969 when many of those connected with MGM were still alive. With their help I entered into a glittering world of Hollywood tinsel and glamour that was fading quickly. This became all too apparent as soon as May 1970 when MGM auctioned off their costumes, furniture and props. I did not attend because I dislike funerals. Houses and shops familiar from MGM films were decaying and falling apart. They would soon be demolished and, within months, condominiums would rise from this graveyard of memories.

The Golden Age of Hollywood was over . . .

Jane Ellen Wayne

Introduction

Mischievous misfits. Indiscriminate lovers, closeted homosexuals, spoiled scoundrels, handsome legends . . .

They were the most admired and beloved actors in the history of Hollywood. Under the watchful eye of Metro-Goldwyn-Mayer potentate Louis B. Mayer, they were pampered and protected. They were magnificent creations of this dream factory, moulded, sculptured, glamorised and perfected. 'At MGM, men are men,' Mayer said. They are known not so much for their acting skills as for their own personalities, which were injected into their screen roles – a clever ploy that few of us recognised. When Clark Gable refused to speak with a Southern accent in *Gone With the Wind*, director George Cukor and producer David Selznick complained bitterly. But, as Mayer pointed out, the public were paying to see Clark Gable, and he did not have a Southern accent.

The MGM Boys were told what to do, how to do it and when. There was usually a publicity agent present during interviews which were cut short if the star was not responding intelligently. The studio had invested millions of dollars in their male idols to preserve their sterling reputations and box-office appeal. When they left the MGM building at night Mayer said, 'There go my greatest assets.' But the mighty mogul was always in control. The MGM police force of over eighty officers was on duty 24 hours a day, shielding the stars from avid fans – and from themselves. The MGM police had connections both in the Los Angeles Police Department and in law enforcement agencies in other major cities around the country. City officials were paid well for their cooperation, discretion and silence in cases of disorderly conduct, adultery, drunken misbehaviour, suicide and even murder.

Boze Hadleigh, author of *Hollywood Gays*, asked silent star Billy Haines, 'How did Mayer get to cover up so many things?' Billy replied, 'Company town. Corrupt cops, corrupt D.A.s or assistant D.A.s, people in high places, informants, the newspapers, of course – the press was the easiest to control, and the biggest columnists owed everything to their cooperation and conniving with Mayer and all the other studio skunks.'

It was West coast publicity chief Howard Strickling who did the hard work in concealing a multitude of scandals. The MGM players trusted him completely. And rightfully so, because Howard was often caught in the middle of Mayer's disputes with his male stars, carrying messages diplomatically back and forth. That Strickling got along with everyone so well is a miracle considering the egos involved. How often did he pick up his telephone in the middle of the night to hurriedly get one of the MGM Boys out of trouble and then face the press? The reporters knew the score, but they respected Strickling's explanation. It was always logical. The very fact that he agreed to face suspicious reporters was a pacifier.

Homosexuals were encouraged to marry and have children. In the Golden Era this was proof of their masculinity, and an effective way of squashing rumours about their sexual preferences. Mr. Mayer decided that Keenan Wynn's wife, Evie, would make a perfect and understanding wife for their close friend, Van Johnson, after the all-American boy with the trademark red socks was caught performing in public urinals once too often. Mayer even arranged for the Wynns to divorce so Van could marry Evie. Van's career was saved when they had a daughter, and they remained together for almost twenty years until Van fell in love with a chorus boy.

Silent film idol Billy Haines was a homosexual who was arrested several times for picking up sailors. When Mayer grew tired of covering up these scandalous incidents he demanded that Billy get married. 'But I already have a loving wife,' Haines insisted, referring to his live-in lover, Jimmie Shields. So MGM let his contract run out, and Billy became a very successful interior decorator. When he died many years later, Jimmie committed suicide. According to Joan Crawford, Billy's good friend, 'Billy and Jimmie had the happiest marriage in Hollywood.' She even offered to marry Haines, but he answered that if he were ever to take a wife she would have to be a lesbian.

Then there were the bisexuals, who made up the majority in Tinseltown. As actor Cesar Romero explained, 'The Hollywood actor can enjoy sex with either. Why? Beauty. We had the most beautiful people in the world here. Of both sexes.' But to survive, a homosexual had to play the game and get married.

*

Within the Golden Gates of MGM there was a good deal of hanky-panky going on. Putting the most beautiful men and women in the world under the same roof meant sex was rampant. The actors were not only tempted but compelled to prove themselves. When Goldwyn, Metro and Mayer merged in 1924, their stars convened for a celebration on the front lawn of the new studio. While aircraft flew in formation overhead, brass bands played and executives gave their speeches, the stars were contemplating who they hoped to seduce.

There were no secrets at MGM. It was well known to all who was sleeping with whom – in dressing rooms, on movie sets and in dark corners. Mr. Mayer had so many spies that he too was aware of the trysts. But he understood, and stayed out of it – unless the situation got out of hand. When he found out that Mickey Rooney, his Andy Hardy, was bedding down Norma Shearer, his Marie Antoinette, he called them both into his office and put an end to it. After all, Mickey was the most popular star in the world, the *Andy Hardy* series an American tradition.

Somehow Mayer always knew best. He had a cat house for his stable of male stars so as to prevent them from contracting a social disease or getting a one-night stand pregnant. The MGM hookers were rejected starlets, routinely checked by studio doctors to ensure their cleanliness. They were made up to resemble the great screen beauties – Harlow, Crawford, Garbo, Clara Bow. But the MGM Boys were reluctant to use their facilities. Mayer probably had the rooms bugged, or maybe the girls reported back to him about their impotence and requests for kinky sex. Mayer even closed down a gay bordello because he despised homosexuals. Had he been more tolerant he would have realised the gay crowd needed an outlet to keep them off the streets.

Many contract players hated Mayer for these tactics, but in his defence, his was the biggest and most prestigious movie studio in the world. It's breathtaking to remember the outstanding roster of stars under contract to Metro-Goldwyn-Mayer: Ethel Barrymore, John Barrymore, Lionel Barrymore, Cyd Charisse, Joan Crawford, Arlene Dahl, Marion Davies, Nelson Eddy, Clark Gable, Greta Garbo, Judy Garland, Greer Garson, Stewart Granger, Kathryn Grayson, Jean Harlow, Helen Hayes, Katharine Hepburn, Van Johnson, Gene Kelly, Deborah Kerr, Hedy Lamarr, Peter Lawford, Janet Leigh, Myrna Loy, Jeanette MacDonald, the Marx Brothers, Laurel and Hardy, Donald O'Connor, Eleanor Powell, Debbie Reynolds, Mickey Rooney, Rosalind Russell, Norma Shearer, Frank Sinatra, Red Skelton, James Stewart, Elizabeth Taylor, Robert

Taylor, Spencer Tracy, Lana Turner, Esther Williams and Robert Young. And the list goes on.

Louis Burt Mayer was able to manufacture the backgrounds of his stars to suit their image, but his own roots should not be overlooked. He was born in Russia in 1885 and grew up in a kosher home. Three years later his parents settled in Boston where Louis went into the junk business with his father. He became interested in motion pictures and formed his own production company, which eventually merged with Metro Pictures and Goldwyn Pictures. In 1924, when Metro-Goldwyn-Mayer was born, Louis became the highest-paid individual in the United States.

He was considered the best actor on the MGM lot. On cue he could cry, faint, and foam at the mouth. Mayer considered his stars a 'family' and himself as their 'father'.

Mayer was not known for employing a casting couch but even he had his share of women and, occasionally, fell in love. After his wife had a hysterectomy and claimed she could no longer have sex, he began courting beautiful women like singer Ginny Simms and dancer Ann Miller. Since he revered motherhood, he invited their mothers to join them on dates. When Miss Miller chose her career over him, Mayer attempted suicide at least twice.

He was intimate with diva Jeanette MacDonald, promising to make her a star. Once her name dominated the movie marquees, he ended the affair. Mayer worshipped Greer Garson but put her on a pedestal, not in his bed. Eventually he divorced his mentally unbalanced wife and married a younger woman.

Though Mayer was the man to reckon with, Irving Thalberg had just as much power at MGM in the twenties and thirties. Primarily involved in production, he avoided publicity and chose to work behind the scenes to bring great classics to the screen – and to smooth the ruffled feathers of his stars. He tried desperately to save the careers of the great John Gilbert, who was Greta Garbo's discarded lover, and Billy Haines. Known as the Boy Genius, Irving was the model for F. Scott Fitzgerald's *The Last Tycoon*.

Irving eventually married actress Norma Shearer, who waited patiently for his proposal while he chased the love of his life, actress Constance Talmadge. Like a schoolboy he waited in his car outside her house at night to see who brought her home, but she discarded Irving as a potential husband, since they made love seldom if at all. Embarrassed because he suffered from premature ejaculation, he could not bear to risk humiliation with the sophisticated and passionate Constance. So, when she married, Thalberg called Norma into his office and showed her a tray of diamond rings. She chose the biggest one. Why not? But the passionate Norma would have to forget about great sex until Irving, who had a weak heart, died in 1936 at the age of just 37.

Spencer Tracy, John Barrymore, Robert Walker and John Gilbert were dedicated alcoholics. Tracy, a married Catholic, had affairs with most of his leading ladies. He would disappear for weeks at a time on binges and might have been fired had it not been for Katharine Hepburn, who signed a contract with MGM in 1940 and asked for Spencer to co-star with her in *Woman of the Year*. Mayer knew Hepburn would control Tracy, though he still managed to get into drunken brawls that got Howard Strickling out of bed in the middle of the night. Tracy would destroy hotel rooms and movie sets in drunken rages. When MGM eventually fired him, he wept. The Tracy/Hepburn relationship, no secret in Hollywood, was respected by the press – until Spencer blurted out the truth in an interview. What he didn't say was that there was no sex involved. Tracy, though without a doubt the best actor in Hollywood, was an unmitigated perpetual bastard.

John Barrymore was a great Shakespearean actor who gave up the stage for big money in Hollywood. The grandfather of Drew Barrymore would drink anything from perfume to gasoline if he was deprived of liquor. He was known to expose himself on the movie set and use the ladies' room. But his wicked and amusing sense of humour charmed his co-stars, and women of all ages. When he died his corpse was taken to Errol Flynn's house and propped up on a chair. Flynn walked through the front door, saw his friend, and literally ran for the Hollywood Hills. Even in death, Barrymore had the last laugh.

John Gilbert was humiliated in his first talking film. Maybe his voice was too high or maybe Mayer, who despised him, rigged the sound system, but more than likely his voice simply clashed with his image. The alcoholic Gilbert choked to death on his own tongue at the age of 37.

Robert Walker never got over his wife Jennifer Jones leaving him for producer David O. Selznick. He dated the beautiful Ava Gardner, his co-star in *One Touch of Venus*. When the filming was over, Ava went her own way and Walker became abusive. She had to change her phone number and eventually move. MGM finally sent Walker to the Menninger Clinic for alcoholism and manic depression, but he managed to escape and was arrested for drunken driving. At the age of 32, he was given a shot of sodium amytol during an alcoholic binge and died. Jennifer Jones did rather better. As the wife of producer David O. Selznick, she was able to choose never to wear the same pair of stockings or brassiere more than once.

The handsome Peter Lawford, who spoke with an English accent, had been only ten years old when his nanny introduced him to group sex. Peter had many affairs with women, including Judy Garland and Lana Turner, while his male lovers included Keenan Wynn, Sal Mineo and Van Johnson. Peter, like Robert Walker, enjoyed the company of Nancy Davis, who would later marry Ronald Reagan. Peter said Nancy gave the best head in Hollywood. He was very impressed, but not surprised, when she became First Lady.

Elizabeth Taylor chased Peter, but she did not appeal to him; he said her fat thighs turned him off. In 1954 he married John F. Kennedy's sister, Pat, and bought Louis B. Mayer's beach house in Santa Monica. It was here that Kennedy and Marilyn Monroe had their trysts. Peter enjoyed taking pictures of them making love in the bathtub, a great turn-on for Kennedy.

Lawford suffered from years of drug addiction and died a painful death, blood oozing from every opening in his body. His ashes were interred near the burial place of Marilyn Monroe in Westwood Memorial Park, but they had to be removed four years later because his funeral expenses had not been paid. Peter's remains were finally scattered over the Pacific Ocean.

Director Victor Fleming has been sadly overlooked in Hollywood chronicles, though he directed many outstanding films including *Gone With the Wind*, *The Wizard of Oz* and *Captains Courageous*. Like Irving Thalberg, Fleming preferred to take a back seat and ignored the many honours bestowed on him. Part American Indian, Fleming was tall and broad shouldered, with salt-and-pepper hair and grey eyes. He was also a great lover. According to Clara Bow, Fleming was very well endowed; whenever she was frustrated with another man, she called on Victor to satisfy her.

Among Victor's other conquests were Norma Shearer and Ingrid Bergman, while Judy Garland did her best to seduce him during the filming of *The Wizard of Oz* and giggled incessantly in his company. On one such occasion, Fleming had to slap Judy across the face to diminish her libido.

Most interestingly, Clark Gable idolised Fleming; in fact, he owed his personality to him. Producer Arthur Freed claimed that 'Clark modelled himself on Victor.' A longtime bachelor, Fleming finally married a friend's wife in 1933 after impregnating her. But he continued his womanising, and almost gave everything up for Ingrid Bergman.

Baritone Nelson Eddy, hopelessly and selfishly in love with his operatic co-star Jeanette MacDonald, demanded she give up her career to marry him. His enormous ego simply would not allow him to accept the fact that she was a bigger star than he. Thanks to L.B. Mayer, Jeanette married gay actor Gene Raymond, while Eddy took a wife but was so drunk he couldn't remember the ceremony. Jeanette died a few years before Nelson, whose widow whispered to Raymond at Eddy's funeral, 'Now they can sing together forever.'

One of L.B. Mayer's greatest achievements was Robert Taylor, who had to contend with a 'Pretty Boy' image and has been labelled a homosexual by authors in recent years. Howard Strickling insisted that Taylor was straight, even though he hung out with a theatrical group that was primarily homosexual before he joined the MGM family. And being labelled beautiful didn't help the young kid from Nebraska either. Actor Cesar Romero doubted that Bob was gay but said he was confused and unhappy.

Mayer had a great influence over Taylor, who did what he was told. In 1939 he was forced to marry actress Barbara Stanwyck, but not to cover up his homosexuality; MGM rushed him to the altar after *Photoplay* magazine published an article entitled 'The Unmarried Husbands and Wives', intimating that Bob and Barbara had lived together for three years. 'All I had to say about it was "I do",' Taylor recalled. Those who paint it as a 'lavender' marriage claim that Stanwyck was bisexual and had sexual encounters with Joan Crawford, Marlene Dietrich and Marilyn Monroe.

After Taylor's discharge from the Navy in 1945, he had problems performing in bed with Barbara and consulted a therapist, who dismissed the idea he was gay and instead suggested an affair. It was Ava Gardner who proved to Bob that his problem was Barbara, who was more a mother to him than a wife. When he was making *Quo Vadis* in Rome, word got back to Barbara that he was having an affair. She flew to Italy and nagged him into the truth. 'At least I can get it up with her,' he exclaimed.

Barbara said she would not only file for divorce but bleed him for the rest of his life. Already wealthy in her own right, she collected 15 per cent of his salary to his dying day. Even when she was on her deathbed, friends said Barbara was sure Taylor had 'come for her with love'.

Although Clark Gable was not thought to be a homosexual, he did give himself to gay actor Billy Haines in 1925 when he was desperate for a job as an extra in films. Some insiders claim Clark was also a male gigolo, servicing rich women and influential men. Gable's first wife, a dowdy drama coach thirteen years older than he was, paved his way to the Broadway stage. He got there via Houston where he met a wealthy widow, this time twelve years his senior. When he was offered a play in Los Angeles his second wife joined him.

Clark was soon offered an MGM contract and began an affair with Joan Crawford. L.B. Mayer threatened to ruin both stars if they continued seeing each other. But it was Carole Lombard who stole his heart, though love did not prevent him from having affairs with Lana Turner and Hedy Lamarr. When Carole was killed in a plane crash in 1942, Gable turned to alcohol in his grief, killing a pedestrian when he was drunk behind the wheel of his car. But he was spared by Howard Strickling who was able to cover up the truth, while Mayer found someone else at MGM to claim responsibility and go to jail 'in Gable's place'. Oh, the power! Clark finally found happiness with his fifth wife, Loretta Young, who gave birth to a son after his death from a fatal heart attack in 1960.

Gable had too many love affairs to mention but among his other conquests were Grace Kelly, Louella Parsons and the unattractive writer Adela Rogers St. Johns. When Gable saw a group picture of the MGM girls, he said, 'Aren't they lovely? I've had every one of 'em.' But Carole Lombard had fun when he boasted of his sexual conquests: 'If his cock were an inch shorter he'd be queen of Hollywood,' she remarked to startled friends. Gable was known to bed down any woman if she was breathing. He was not a satisfying lover but he spent a good deal of time trying to prove to himself that he was. 'I gotta keep practisin',' he said.

Frank Sinatra made musicals for MGM in the forties. He danced, he sang and he tried to act. Ignoring the fact that he was a married man with three children, he romanced Lana Turner, Marilyn Maxwell, Marlene Dietrich –

and Ava Gardner, whom he would marry. His blatant affair with Ava prompted Loius B. Mayer to cancel his MGM contract. Mayer called Ava a whore but spared her because she was a hot box-office attraction.

Frank was at his lowest ebb when he was turned down repeatedly for a screen test for the part of Maggio in *From Here to Eternity* at Columbia Pictures. It was Ava who finally convinced mogul Harry Cohn to give her husband a chance, while in return she would be available to make a film for his studio. Frank never knew about the arrangement. But he and Ava, always miserable apart, were equally miserable together so they finally divorced. Frank's ego was so bloated he thought he owned the world. He did own a big chunk of it . . .

The studio system collapsed in the fifties. MGM could no longer afford to pay enormous salaries to their stars so their contracts were not renewed. L.B. Mayer was ousted in 1951, and his successor Dore Schary loathed stars, treating them with little respect. The great MGM contract players packed up their belongings and departed without fanfare. Only Robert Taylor stayed on to collect his pension, and he goes down in history as having the longest unbroken contract in Hollywood history.

Clark Gable's hatred of MGM was so intense that he refused to make another film for them, regardless of how much money they offered. He told his agent, 'Tell them to shove it up their ass!' He left his home studio quietly, refusing to allow friends to give him a farewell party. It was over – and thank God.

Two years after the King of Hollywood drove through the MGM gate for the last time, everyone at the studio rushed to the windows to see a new star drive up to an entrance blocked by the rush of stagehands, technicians, cameramen – and the stars themselves.

Van Johnson admitted that he bowed to the new King. 'It was like royalty,' he said. Who could have predicted that Elvis Presley would replace Clark Gable on the MGM throne?

1

Irving Thalberg

He was F. Scott Fitzgerald's *The Last Tycoon*, and in the movie based on Fitzgerald's unfinished novel, Robert De Niro played the part most effectively. As was his practice, the actor did his homework, researching the life of his character thoroughly. He had to appear rather thin and fragile but have an aura of confidence and depth. De Niro lost so much weight for the role that director Elia Kazan was concerned, at least until he realised his leading man was always equally obsessed with his portrayal of non-fictional characters. While preparing for *The Last Tycoon*, De Niro was filming *Taxi Driver* when he began his strict diet. By the time he started *Tycoon*, few recognised the robust actor. Kazan remarked, 'Bob had never played an executive or intellectual. He'd never played a lover. I had to find that side of him.'

Though the script was weak, De Niro portrayed the brilliant and tragic Hollywood tycoon of the thirties to perfection. In his confrontation with a Communist screenwriter, played by Jack Nicholson, he portrayed a man with morals, uncorrupted by those who would taint the movie industry. De Niro was especially convincing as a man in love with an indifferent woman. With all his fame and money, he wasn't able to win her over, yet he refused to give up.

Soft spoken, Thalberg had a handsome, boyish face that smiled, but rarely laughed. He had a weak heart but forged ahead with optimism and vigour. He had a quiet faith in himself and ignored Hollywood's great admiration for his accomplishments: he was known as 'The Boy Wonder' and 'The Boy Genius'. 'I don't want my name on the screen,' he said, 'because credit is something that should be given to others. If you're in the position to give credit yourself, then you do not need it.'

De Niro's depiction of his character was the only honest aspect of *The Last Tycoon*. Otherwise, the story bears little resemblance to that of the man who created the biggest and most powerful movie studio in the world – the studio that had more stars than than there were in heaven.

3

*

The Academy Awards often bestow the Irving Thalberg Award upon a deserving producer 'for the most consistent high quality of production achievement by an individual producer based on pictures he has personally produced during the preceding year.' Among its recipients over the years have been Darryl F. Zanuck, David O. Selznick, Cecil B. De Mille, Alfred Hitchcock, Billy Wilder, Steven Spielberg, Clint Eastwood and Warren Beatty.

Maybe you've wondered who Irving Thalberg was and why he is considered a Hollywood legend above all the others. That he chose not to brag about his accomplishments and kept his name off the screen credits is one reason why he remains an enigma. We know more about his actress wife, Norma Shearer, on whose career he concentrated on during the last few years before his untimely death. But it was not only her films for which he won acclaim. Among his masterpieces are *The Merry Widow*, *Ben Hur*, *Anna Christie*, *A Free Soul*, *Grand Hotel*, *The Barretts of Wimpole Street*, *China Seas*, *Mutiny on the Bounty*, *A Night at the Opera*, *Romeo and Juliet*, *The Good Earth*, and *Camille*.

Though Thalberg is best known for bringing plays and classic novels to the screen, he also defied film censorship in such films as *Red Headed Woman*, starring the sexy Jean Harlow. By turning the story into a comedy, he got it past the censors. Often Thalberg rewrote scripts and took part in directing his films, and he was the first producer to ask for retakes. Following private previews, he would add or delete portions of his movies. This was a costly process, but one that proved very successful at the box office.

Irving did not marry the love of his life. Though Norma Shearer proved to be a devoted mate, for a long time he carried a torch for the flighty actress Constance Talmadge. It was love at first sight for him and they seemed meant for each other – on the surface, anyway. His usually placid eyes sparkled in her company. After they parted, that sparkle was gone. Possibly he couldn't satisfy Constance sexually. His capacity for making love was limited and he was known to ejaculate prematurely. To perform he needed a patient lover and that was not Constance, whose passion was unlimited. It wasn't until he realised she would never marry him that he turned to Norma. She knew she was second choice, but she was so much in love with Irving, she'd take him any way she could. Losing Constance might have destroyed him, but Irving was used to adversities and setbacks.

Thalberg might have been a playboy like Howard Hughes, but his weak heart prevented him from living the good life. He did see a generous chunk of it, but mostly it was lived vicariously through his rowdy, hard-drinking poker pals, Howard Hawks, Victor Fleming, John Gilbert, Chico Marx and Jack Conway. They talked freely about women, who was sleeping with whom, and who was cheating on whom. Thalberg was keen to know everything that was going on in Hollywood. He talked about movies socially – movies, movies, movies. He lived for his work and though it took a toll on his health, without it he might have died before the age of 37 – seven years more than predicted by heart specialists.

He was born on 30 May 1899 in Brooklyn, New York. Irving Thalberg was a 'blue baby', born with a congenitally defective heart. His mother, Henrietta, devoted her life to Irving and proved to be a very strong influence in his short life. Both she and her husband William were German-Jewish immigrants. Both were anxious to succeed, but he was less ambitious than she. Henrietta had married him on the rebound and though she never admitted it, they were a mismatched couple. William was satisfied to operate a lace importing company at Ninth Street and Fifth Avenue, so Henrietta put all her faith in Irving who, she was determined, would make something of himself. He wanted to be an attorney and she encouraged him.

Though frail, Irving engaged in sports under Henrietta's watchful eye. He was young and unaware of his shortcomings, but she was always on constant vigil. Possibly she felt responsible for his birth defect and sought to overcome it by being alert to his symptoms and willing him to succeed. Despite many absences, Irving graduated from public school as an honour student and enrolled at Brunswick High. When he came down with diphtheria at the age of fourteen, though, doctors pronounced him an invalid for life.

Yet Henrietta was unfaltering in her belief that Irving would get a good education. Because he was so bright, his teachers were willing to tutor him at home. He became an avid reader of great works, plays and novels. He devoured the writings of William James, whose works of philosophy fascinated him. Among Irving's favourites were *Principles of Psychology*, *The Meaning of Truth*, and *Pragmatism*. He considered these bedridden years the foundation of his beliefs and goals.

Irving was well enough to attend school for a year or so before he was stricken with rheumatic fever. Doctors again gave up hope – but not Henrietta, even though she had to accept that Irving could not bear the rigours of law school. Mother and son were equally determined that he would recover. Even when she gave birth to a daughter, Sylvia, she was dedicated to Irving, and he finally gained his high school diploma.

Irving began working as a clerk in his grandfather's department store to earn enough money to pay for night courses in business, shorthand and Spanish at New York University. He then worked for the Hudson Trading Company answering business correspondence. Soon bored, he found a job at the export firm of Taylor, Clapp and Beall, becoming assistant manager. But Thalberg was restless and eventually resigned. He loved the theatre, but flopped when he attempted to become an actor. Henrietta suggested politics, but Irving was no orator.

Undecided as to his path in life, he decided to take time off and spend it with his grandmother in Edgemere on Long Island. Carl Laemmle, head of Universal Studios and a neighbour, had set up a projector on his front porch where he showed his latest movies on a bed sheet. Irving was not only a frequent guest but a critic as well. Laemmle, impressed by the young man's comments, offered him a job as secretary to a senior executive for $35 a week at the Universal headquarters in the Mecca Building on Broadway.

Nineteen-year-old Irving, who was five feet six, towered over 51-year-old Laemmle at five feet two inches. Psychologically, Thalberg felt at ease with the mogul and was eager to learn from him.

A keen observer, Thalberg soon noticed how disorganised his boss was. None of his staff knew what their duties were, and they spent their time running helter skelter with no authority. Laemmle, who commuted between New York and his studio in Los Angeles, was oblivious to this until Irving spelled it out for him.

'Why did Mae Murray and Rudolph Valentino leave Universal?' Thalberg asked.

'They were complaining about money.'

'If you offered your stars lucrative contracts that wouldn't happen,' Irving said.

Laemmle listened and was so impressed with Thalberg that he made him his personal executive secretary. In July 1919, he decided at the last minute to leave for California and asked Irving to join him. Excited and eager, Irving called Henrietta who rushed to Grand Central Station with her son's suitcases. With hugs and kisses, she told him to take care of himself and take the medication she had carefully packed.

Thalberg followed his boss around the studio, making observations and notes. 'You're more disorganised out here than you are in New York,' he commented bluntly. 'No one seems to know what to do.' Laemmle might have been insulted. Instead he opened his eyes, at last, to the existing problems. 'I'm going back to New York, Irving, but you're staying here. I'm making you one of my key executives.'

'That depends on the money, Carl.'

'Sixty-five a week.'

'Have a safe trip.'

Six months later Laemmle returned to Los Angeles. Irving made him a detailed report of mismanagement. Production was a maze of misfits. 'There's no one here to coordinate,' he stressed.

'We're making a profit,' Laemmle pointed out.

'Not nearly as much as other studios. I have the figures. Take a look.'

'I don't have to, Irving. Suppose I made you general manager out here?'

'You already have two studio heads.'

'I'm sure you can handle that,' Laemmle said. 'I'm off to Europe.'

Irving didn't have to handle anyone. They quit, leaving him in charge. Word quickly got around Hollywood that a twenty-year-old was head of Universal Studios. It was unheard of. Just as shocking was his firing of director Erich von Stroheim for going over budget. The two men initially came to blows during *Foolish Wives*. Irving kept a watchful eye on him and saw him spending money foolishly once again during the making of *The Merry-Go-Round*. In the middle of production, Irving told him, 'Universal cannot afford you, Erich. You are being replaced.'

Eric von Stroheim, a big brute who could have picked up Thalberg with one hand and thrown him to the coyotes, threatened to smash his face. Irving told him to 'go ahead'. The younger man's victory was seen in Hollywood as a major success and he was applauded by his peers, though few of them had even been introduced to him as yet. Everyone who was anyone in town was talking about Thalberg – at 22 he was the youngest executive in the movie capital. But still he resented any reference to his age and would always avoid the subject. He did not want to be known for his youth.

Hollywood insiders were also buzzing about Irving's relationship with Laemmle's daughter, Rosabelle, whom he had been dating for several years. He was a regular dinner guest at her home and she was his date at premieres. Rosabelle was an attractive girl whose mother had died when she was young. It was now her task to play hostess for her father, with whom she travelled to Europe occasionally. Irving admired her energy and poise, and when they met in New York he was smitten. At the time however he was a nobody and Rosabelle wasn't interested in getting involved, though she agreed to date him for her father's sake. But she changed her mind when Thalberg took charge of Universal in California. Did she think he was a fool? Naturally she was interested now that he was a success. He considered this a form of snobbery, but nonetheless they dated whenever she was in Hollywood.

Most likely Rosabelle was Irving's first sexual encounter. When they were getting along, their romance was hot and heavy, but they often fought over his dedication to his films and the long hours he worked. Then it was their arguments that were hot and heavy.

During his two years as head of Universal, Irving gained the confidence he needed not to settle for second best. As his mother Henrietta pointed out, Rosabelle was not good enough for him. Rosabelle did not give up the chase, however. And as for Henrietta's influence over Irving, he listened to her advice with respect – and then did exactly what he wanted to do.

Thalberg produced *The Hunchback of Notre Dame*, the movie that made Lon Chaney famous. It was a huge undertaking on film with a budget to match. Laemmle, who was in Germany at the time, was livid that Irving was spending so much money on *Hunchback*. But Thalberg knew what he was doing and the film made a huge profit.

As 1923 approached, he had already personally supervised over a hundred movies in addition to reorganising Universal's internal affairs. Though Laemmle still had great faith in Irving, he resented the wasy he was taking over Universal, Laemmle's pride and joy. Then there was Rosabelle. Laemmle wanted her to marry Thalberg, but the young man was suddenly showing less interest. The two men never discussed this touchy subject, but both were keenly aware of the friction between them. When Laemmle realised not only that Irving was now a powerful man in his own right but that he was not about to marry his daughter, he began telling colleagues of his concerns over Thalberg's health – and the fate of Universal if anything happened to Irving.

When Laemmle offered Irving only a small raise in pay, it was the Boy Wonder's cue to find work elsewhere. Word got around Hollywood quickly and he received an offer from Hal Roach whose speciality was slapstick comedy. But Roach changed his mind when he realised Irving had no experience in comedy. Thalberg turned to Laemmle's attorney, Edwin Loeb, a man he could trust. Loeb arranged for him to meet 38-year-old

Louis B. Mayer, who had his own production company. The two men hit it off, but they did not join forces right away. Instead they spent time together discussing the film business, their personal interests and their goals before finally, on 15 February 1923, they reached an agreement. Thalberg accepted a salary of $600 a week. It was less than he had been making at Universal, but he liked the way Louis B. Mayer Productions on Mission Road operated. It was a small company, but Mayer, like Thalberg, had plans. In turn Thalberg admired this man who had gone broke in the junk business and rented a theatre in Boston, from which he had built his own little empire in Hollywood.

When Laemmle heard that Thalberg had accepted the position of vice-president and production assistant at the Mayer Company, he refused to speak to Mayer for a long time.

Irving was impressed with Mayer, whose humble beginnings had given him little opportunity for success. Likewise, Mayer liked Thalberg, who spoke about his mother's dedication and how devoted he was to her. Mayer believed in motherhood, family values and the American way. He had two daughters and now, he decided, he had the son he always wanted. He was not threatened by Irving's amazing rise to fame as Laemmle had been. With Irving alongside him, he could achieve his goal.

He invited the young man to dinner at his home. But he was not interested in him as a son-in-law. He told his daughters, Irene and Edith, 'Irving has a bad heart and I don't want a young widow in the family. Date him if you wish, but make up your mind to dismiss any deep feelings.' He said he had almost not signed Irving up because his daughters might find him romantically interesting. As Irene recalled,

> Irving very soon came to dinner. It was hard to believe that anyone that modest and boyish could be so important. He had the most engaging manner, but we had been totally unprepared for anyone that good looking. If only he were healthy. My father kept an eye on my sister and me. If he sensed anything amiss, there would be no chance of our seeing Irving again. The evenings he came for dinner were exciting because he and my father exchanged their opinions and ideas, exploring each other's reactions. The growing bond between them was evident. There was confidence, enthusiasm, and affection – all of it mutual. The more there was, the greater was my father's pain at the sentence which hung over Irving's head.

Irving enjoyed the power he had achieved. His waiting room was always full. People often had to wait several days to get in to see him, and it would always be this way. When someone finally got into his office, he would sit at his desk looking over some papers for a minute or two before glancing up in surprise. Once they had his attention, however, he concentrated entirely on the person sitting on the other side of his desk. These habits of his were annoying at times, but he was able to charm anyone into admiration and respect.

Always on the lookout for new talent, he had been interested in a young actress, Norma Shearer. While still at Universal, he contacted her having been impressed by her performance in *The Stealers*. Norma was 21 and not beautiful, with a cast in one eye that made her appear cross-eyed, but she had learned how to make herself attractive. She worked hard at acting and was determined to make something of herself. Like Irving, Norma had a strong and supportive mother who urged her on during difficult times. But after he refused to pay her mother's train fare from New York to Los Angeles, Norma turned Universal down. Hal Roach also approached her, but before her agent had a chance to negotiate, the Mayer Company offered her a contract and agreed to pay for her mother's transportation.

Excited at the anticipation of arriving in Hollywood, Norma spent hours on her hair, her make-up and selecting the right outfit to conceal her unattractive legs. With the aura of a star she disembarked in Pasadena and smiled for the cameras that were not there. In fact, no one was there to greet her. Her mother Edith had done her homework, however, and found a taxi to take them to the inexpensive Hollywood Hotel.

The next morning Norma put on her 'arrival' outfit and headed for the Mayer Company on Mission Road. Still annoyed that no one had greeted her when she arrived, she haughtily introduced herself to the receptionist. A young man suddenly appeared and said, 'We've been expecting you, Miss Shearer.' Assuming he was an office boy, she followed him to an empty office. The young man took his place behind the desk and announced, 'I'm Irving Thalberg.'

Stunned by his youth, Norma wanted to let him know how important she was. 'I've had many offers,' she exclaimed. 'In fact, Universal offered me a lot of money.'

Thalberg smiled. 'Not that much, Miss Shearer.'

'How do you know that?' she snapped.

'Because I was the one who made the offer.'

'Well, Hal Roach was very generous, as well.'

'Not that generous, Miss Shearer. You see, I was with Hal Roach just before I joined Mayer.' He went on to explain that he had admired her in the few films she had made in New York. She would have to make a screen test, but in the meantime the studio would help her find an apartment or house to rent.

Norma's first screen test was a disaster, but a keen cameraman suggested she make another one. Although the second wasn't much better, she finally signed a contract. If Thalberg and Mayer hadn't been so busy negotiating a merger with Metro and Goldwyn Pictures, most likely she would have been on her way back to New York.

It was 1923 when Marcus Loew, owner of the largest movie chain in the country, decided to take over Metro Pictures in order to provide films for his theatres nationwide. Goldwyn Pictures was Loew's next acquisition. Goldwyn's studio was in Culver City, an ideal location, and although Sam Goldwyn was no longer associated with the company, he demanded his name be part of any new merger. Loew then approached Louis B. Mayer, who became first vice-president of the newly formed Metro-Goldwyn-Mayer. Thalberg would be the second, and was given the additional title of 'supervisor of production'.

On 26 April, MGM moved into their Culver City headquarters and the celebration began. The Navy band played while the stars and other guests located their seats. Mayer made a speech promising that MGM's pictures would 'reach a point of perfection never approached by any other company'. Army and Navy planes flew in formation overhead, dropping rose petals on the celebrants. During the ceremony, director Marshall Neilan walked out with his crew. His reason was the tight control exerted by Irving Thalberg.

But Thalberg had other things on his mind that day; his mind dwelled on the production of the epic *Ben Hur* that MGM had inherited from Goldwyn. Filming was taking place in Rome and was out of control. In a memo, he wrote, 'It is almost beyond my conception that such stuff should have passed by people of even moderate intelligence . . . that anyone could have tolerated for one single day, the ill-fitting costumes, the incongruous action, the almost silly and typical European movements of the people; not in my wildest imagination could I have pictured anything that broad.'

Mayer eventually made the arduous trek to Italy and decided to move the entire production to Culver City. Thalberg scrapped everything filmed in Rome and began anew, with Ramon Novarro replacing George Walsh in the lead role. A historical epic like *Ben Hur* was not Irving's forte, but the movie was worth doing right because he knew it would be a classic. Replicas of Italian buildings were erected, including one of the Circus Maximus where the famous chariot race would be shot. Thalberg was on the set every day, testing his strength to the limit. While the famous chariot race scene was being shot, he stood in the middle of the Circus Maximus shouting orders to his staff. During rehearsals for the race Ramon Novarro was nearly killed.

Outwardly calm about the incident, Irving was churning with fear inside. Before rehearsals ended, Irving had a heart attack and collapsed. Doctors could not promise his recovery, and a sobbing Mayer retreated to his office where he remained alone waiting for the fateful phone call. But, when he heard from Henrietta, it was good news. Irving would be all right. Still sobbing, Mayer told her how happy he was that she and William had moved to Los Angeles to be with their son. 'You're worth more than all the doctors in the world,' he said.

'Irving wants to see the rushes of *Ben Hur*,' Henrietta exclaimed. 'He's adamant about it.'

'Is he well enough to come to work?' Mayer asked.

'No, no. He's going to view it on the ceiling over his bed.'

Mayer was stunned, yet thoroughly impressed by Thalberg's ambition even in his weakened condition. But shouldn't he be free of such responsibilities while recuperating? Henrietta exclaimed, 'It's work that's keeping Irving alive.'

Irving was acclaimed for *The Merry Widow* and *The Big Parade*, but his greatest achievement was *Ben Hur*, which he had rescued from disaster despite his heart attack.

Though their personalities differed, Mayer and Thalberg were very much alike in their working habits. They were dedicated to MGM seven days a week. On Sundays Mayer always held a brunch around the pool for his staff. In this relaxing atmosphere, he and Irving were able to talk business without being bothered. They wanted Culver City to be a home to their family of stars, directors and other staff members. Mayer's door was always open to his family. And Thalberg was just as gracious, even though getting into see him might take several days.

Irving worked long hours and admired those who, like him, did not watch the clock. On Christmas Eve 1924 Norma Shearer was working late when she received a phone call from Thalberg, who had seen a light in her dressing room. He had rung simply to wish her a merry Christmas.

Professionally, though, Norma was a thorn in Thalberg's side since she was never satisfied with either her roles or her directors. Irving was known for his ability to placate his stars, but she was stubborn in her efforts to better herself. And to Norma, he was equally stubborn, rarely taking her side. The director is always right, he'd say. You can learn from him, he'd say. Irving frustrated her – but she was falling in love with him and soon made up her mind to marry him.

Meanwhile, though, Norma had her affairs with director Victor Fleming, John Gilbert, Billy Haines and director Monta Bell. She knew, too, all about Irving's women. He was involved with actress Bessie Love, Ziegfeld showgirl and well-known gold-digger Peggy Hopkins Joyce, and Marie Provost, who had been under contract at Universal and went with Irving to MGM. In fact he had played the field, until one sunny Sunday he met actress Constance Talmadge on a yachting party.

For Thalberg it was love at first sight; even Rosabelle Laemmle paled in comparison. But Constance was a flighty playgirl, a cocaine addict and nightclub carouser. Irving, of course, was unable to keep up with her, though he tried – much to the distress of Henrietta, who disapproved of all his showgirl romances. Thalberg was obsessed with Constance. Often he parked in front of her house late at night to find out who brought her home. Much to Irving's relief, it was usually gay Billy Haines and his lover Jimmy Shields. Had Constance returned his affection and married him, there is no doubt he would have died an early death with a smile on his face.

Theirs was an on-and-off relationship anyway, but when she became involved in a highly publicised romance with Allaster MacIntosh, a companion of the Prince of Wales, Irving resumed his romance with Rosabelle – until one night in New York when he was held up at a business meeting.

'I'll send my car for you,' he said, 'and meet you at the party later.'

'I will not attend without an escort,' she exclaimed. 'Either you take me or I won't go.'

Irving hurried home, changed his clothes and picked up Rosabelle, but this was the beginning of the end for her.

Constance Talmadge went on to live a crazy life as an alcoholic. Fearing talkies would ruin her, she retired from films in 1929. After a quick marriage to a wealthy tobacco heir, she married MacIntosh, who had a commission in His Majesty's Horse Guards. But she grew bored of the staid

British aristocrats, got a divorce and married a Detroit department store tycoon. When he grew fat, she married a Wall Street broker who made her a very wealthy widow. She died in 1973.

In July 1925 Norma Shearer was getting ready to leave the studio when she received a call. 'Miss Shearer, this is Mr. Thalberg's secretary. He would like to know if you could attend the premiere of *The Gold Rush* with him this evening.'

'I'd be delighted,' Norma replied. She told her mother that she was sure Irving was listening in on the extension. He picked her up in his black Cadillac limousine and she emerged with him to crowds of cheering people outside the Egyptian Theater. After the premiere, he took her for dinner and dancing at the famous Coconut Grove. At the end of the evening he dropped her off and did not ask for another date.

According to producer-writer Sam Marx, Thalberg was well aware who was sleeping with whom in Hollywood, and that included Norma. He hung out with two of her lovers, John Gilbert and Victor Fleming, as well as hard-drinking directors Jack Conway and Howard Hawks. Marx said, 'I think Irving got a vicarious thrill out of their bawdy stories. He was interested in sex and scandal, the raunchier the better. He was no prude. Had he been a healthy guy, Irving would have been the biggest playboy in town. Knowing Norma was a passionate girl escalated his interest in her. In his company she was prim and proper, he was her boss, after all, and she knew he was in bad health. In her attempt to get him, she made sure he was home early when they were out to impress Henrietta, who was appreciative, but not eager for her son to marry.'

Actress Louise Brooks told of a dinner party she held to which Norma and Irving were invited. 'All the place cards at dinner were books,' she explained. 'In front of Thalberg's place was Dreiser's *Genius*. In front of Norma's place I put *The Difficulty of Getting Married* – she'd been trying and trying. It was so funny because Irving walked right in and saw *Genius* and sat down. But Norma kept walking around. She wouldn't sit down in front of *The Difficulty of Getting Married*. Not at all.'

When Irving finally asked her for a date, Norma told her mother, 'Well, I guess Constance and Rosabelle are busy tonight.'

It was when she was filming *The Student Prince* late one day that she got a call from Thalberg to come to his office. He was sitting at his desk looking at a tray of diamonds. With a weak smile he told her to choose the one she wanted. Norma recalled how she held back the tears and picked out a ring.

When L.B. Mayer went home that night, he excitedly told his family, 'Irving's decided to marry her! There's no risk. Everything will go on as it is. Henrietta's accepted the situation.'

Thalberg wanted to get married and have children. Not knowing how long he would live, it was foolish to wait for Constance whom he still loved. Norma had proven herself a devoted companion while he chased Constance and everyone in Hollywood knew it. He had come to grips with his loss and chosen a woman he could eventually come to love. In later years Norma admitted that Irving had never told her he loved her, though he proved it in many other ways. But for the bride-to-be there would be no more passionate lovemaking. She would have to be as subdued in bed as she was in the parlour. To get what she wanted Norma would have to make sacrifices, and satisfying sex was one of them.

Living with Henrietta was another. It would be a September wedding; to make things more convenient for Irving, Henrietta agreed that he and Norma should spend the summer at their beach house in Santa Monica.

On 29 September 1927, Norma married Irving at his house at 9401 Sunset Boulevard. Though Irving was not a religious man, Norma converted to Judaism so they could be married by a rabbi. She wore a gown of soft, ivory velvet studded with pearls, with a diamond pin, a gift from Irving, on her bodice. L.B. Mayer was best man. While the groom prepared himself for the ceremony, he was having a conference about a new film in which he was planning to star Ramon Novarro.

It's interesting to note that one of Norma's bridesmaids, Irving's former girlfriend Bessie Love, was almost responsible for a Thalberg divorce not long after the wedding. Norma found out that Irving had sent flowers to Bessie on her first day on the set of MGM's pioneer talkie, *Broadway Melody*, and she left him. But after she spent a few days with her mother, the couple made peace.

The newlyweds went to the Del Monte Lodge on the Monterey Peninsula. Irving was a romantic groom but lacked the sexual enthusiasm he had with Peggy Hopkins Joyce, a man-eating tiger. As for Norma, she was content and in love. If her husband carried a torch for Constance Talmadge, that was quite all right. It was the girl who married him who had won the jackpot.

She and Irving settled down to life with Henrietta and William. The only friction occurred over the dinner parties that Norma set up before leaving for the studio in the morning. During the day Henrietta would rearrange the dinner table and alter the menu. Though Norma was put out, she was too interested in her career to be upset for long; and, in defence of Henrietta, she knew how busy Norma was and always tried to ease her burden by taking charge of household matters.

Though no one will argue that Thalberg was indeed the Boy Genius, he was sceptical about sound, and Mayer agreed with him. But they had to admit their mistake when Warner Brothers released their first talkie, *The Jazz Singer*, and it was a smash hit. In fact it was Loew's president Nicholas Schenck who demanded MGM gear up for sound, and the studio's first attempt, *Broadway Melody* of 1929, won an Oscar for Best Picture. Leo the Lion could be heard for the first time, and Bessie Love was nominated for an Academy Award.

Regardless of his weaknesses, Thalberg was still regarded as 'The Boy Genius'. *Vanity Fair* wrote,

> There is a latent spiritual quality about Thalberg. It even survived a business course in Brooklyn. Not strong physically, he gives one the impression of a poet. There is about his eyes a twinkle of mirth and sadness. His fingers are long, sensitive and delicate – the fingers of a Richelieu – or a Machiavelli . . . Thalberg is boyish, kindly and intuitive. He has a quick mentality that runs in narrow grooves. If it were deeper and vaster and more profound, he would be a financial failure in the business of films. To Thalberg all life is a soda fountain. He knows how to mix ingredients that will please the herd on a picnic. He has piled one piece of clay upon another until he has succeeded in building a hill for the commonalty. Upon this hill his co-workers, being lesser people than himself; and more nearsighted, see a mirage which they call genius. It often takes the form of a young man with a sad expression, leading sheep to a withered pasture. Thalberg is the epitome of the common man . . .

Irving resented such articles. Those who worked for him, he insisted, were not 'lesser men' but equals. He surrounded himself with highly intelligent people, such as screenwriter-director Paul Bern whose fetish was prostitutes and hopeless dope addicts, though his interest was in reforming and saving them. Irving did not delve into the personal affairs of his associates – what they did in their spare time was their business. Maybe Irving chuckled, though, when he found out Bern had tried to drown himself in his toilet bowl when 'The Girl Who Was Too Beautiful', Barbara La Marr, turned down his marriage proposal. Bern got stuck in the toilet seat and had to be rescued.

Thalberg came to the defence of several stars whom Mayer disliked intensely. There was Billy Haines, a homosexual who refused to get married, and screen idol John Gilbert, who had a bitter fight with the mogul after referring to his own mother as a whore. Irving was not judgemental. He had a keen understanding of those who became caught up in the evils of Hollywood. It was all too easy and, therefore, only to be expected.

Though Irving might appear prim, he was far from it. Author Roland Flamini wrote in his book, *Thalberg*, that Irving was a cross-dresser. 'Thalberg's thin frame never varied and Norma's dresses fitted him well, as did her shoes. One of their private jokes was to dine together by candlelight wearing each other's clothes, Thalberg in an Adrian creation complete with makeup, Norma wearing one of his suits.'

Billy Haines remembered attending a costume party to which Irving and Norma came dressed in identical outfits. Billy goosed Thalberg. 'Oh,' Billy smiled. 'I thought you were Norma!' Irving swallowed a smile. How many MGM players could get away with goosing the vice-president of production?

Joan Crawford was less fortunate. When she complained to Irving that Norma was getting all the good parts, Joan was demoted to make a B western.

Irving did generally bow to his wife's wishes, but he initially rejected her plea to play the lead in *The Divorcee*. 'You're not sexy enough for the part,' he said. In order to prove otherwise, Norma had a very provocative photo taken of herself lounging on a chaise longue in a revealing gown. Apparently Irving had never noticed this side of Norma. But now she had convinced him, and she won an Oscar for *The Divorcee*.

After a three-month vacation in Europe, Thalberg decided to concentrate on bringing the theatre to the screen. That was what the potential of sound represented to the Boy Wonder, and he enlisted the help of Paul Bern, whom he sent to New York to see all the plays and, hopefully, lure some stage actors to MGM.

It was only a matter of time before Mayer and Thalberg clashed. In 1929, William Fox, head of Fox Movietone Studios, began buying up

Loew's stock. His plan was to gain control of MGM. He made a deal with Nicholas Schenck, who would be paid off with $8 million under the table. However, the stock market crash that year foiled Fox's scheme. Loew's stock dipped to its lowest and Fox was forced to sell it. From then on Mayer referred to Schenck as 'Nick Skunk'.

Thalberg was now making $3000 a week plus 30 per cent of MGM's yearly profits. He suffered heavy losses, though, when the stock market crashed and was suddenly in need of money. Knowing that Schenck would not give Irving a raise, Mayer reduced his own percentage of profits by 10 per cent and gave it to Irving.

Thalberg, still in need of money, accepted $250,000 from Fox and Schenck to stay out of their fracas. Mayer resented the lack of support from his partner, even though he had cut a deal for $1 million from Fox should he gain control of MGM. Once the facts became known, the relationship between Mayer and Thalberg was never the same. Nonetheless, their belief in MGM, their loyalty to the studio's ideals, kept them together. Through it all, they could still work in harmony, 'making beautiful pictures for beautiful people'.

When Norma discovered she was pregnant in 1929, she told Irving they needed a home of their own, and good riddance to Henrietta. So the Thalbergs built a ten-room French provincial beach house in Santa Monica. There were two bedroom suites on either end of the house, two guest suites, a large living and dining room, a library with a concealed movie screen, a nursery and a card room for Irving's poker games, a pool and veranda. The house was one of the first to be equipped with air conditioning. The household staff consisted of a maid, a butler, a chef, and a nurse for Irving Jr, born on 25 August 1930.

Concerned about losing her figure and being off the screen for even a few months, Norma was not eager to have a baby. She did so only for Irving's sake and to have a home of her own, free of Henrietta. She spent very little time with her son other than when they posed for publicity pictures. Irving, on the other hand, found time to play with his son whenever possible.

Thalberg had put Clark Gable under contract despite his protruding ears and awkward demeanour. Gangster films were all the rage in the early thirties and *A Free Soul* proved an excellent vehicle for Gable, the crook who seduces rich girl Norma. The big scene, in which he pushes her around and shoves her on to the couch, was a big hit with moviegoers, many of whom supposed Gable had slapped Shearer. The misconception drew hordes more fans to the box office.

While filming the movie, there were rumours of an affair between the pair. Although it was Thalberg's habit to visit the movie sets of the films he produced, many observers claimed that he was carefully watching his wife act out her passion with womaniser Gable. In fact Irving was concerned about the movie, not the sight of his wife in the arms of another man. He was, too, making sure Gable lived up to his potential. Building a star took thought and effort, and Thalberg knew how to do it.

But there were some miracles he could not perform and one was saving John Gilbert's career. The sound of the silent star's voice in his first talkie had caused moviegoers to snicker. It was even suggested by Hollywood insiders that L.B. Mayer, who hated Gilbert, had deliberately ruined him, though it's more plausible that Gilbert's voice just did not match his image. Whatever the cause, he lost favour at the box office, lost the love of his life, Greta Garbo, became an alcoholic and died at an early age. Nor was Irving able to save the movie career of Billy Haines. While he was on holiday in Europe, Mayer laid the law down to Billy: 'It's either your boyfriend or your MGM contract.' Billy told the mogul to tear up his contract, and went on to greater fame as an interior decorator.

Grand Hotel, a hit Broadway play financed by MGM, was made into a movie starring John and Lionel Barrymore, Joan Crawford, Greta Garbo and Wallace Beery. It won an Academy Award for best picture and remains a Thalberg classic to this day.

Mayer was appalled by Irving's plans to film *Red Headed Woman*, about a girl who sleeps her way to the top. It was to feature the platinum-blonde Jean Harlow, who would don a red wig for the role. This was not a dignified MGM film, he argued, and the thought of Harlow in the starring role was disgusting. She was nothing more than a tart with big breasts, he remarked. Known for the picture *Hell's Angels*, in which she played the girl who asked, 'Do you mind if I slip into something more comfortable?', she did not represent the ideal MGM contract player. But Irving went ahead with his plans, buying Harlow's contract from Howard Hughes for $50,000.

Writer Anita Loos was with Thalberg on the day he met Harlow.

'How did you make out with Hughes?' he asked Jean.

'One day he was eating a cookie and offered me a bite,' she replied.

Thalberg waited for the rest of the story, but Harlow disappointed him. 'Don't underestimate that,' she spoke up. 'The poor guy's so frightened of germs, it could darn near be a proposal.'

'Miss Harlow, do you think you can make people laugh?'

'With me or at me?'

'At you,' he said.

'Why not? People have been laughing at me all my life.'

But when Irving viewed the film, no one laughed. '*Red Headed Woman* is laced with sex,' Irving told Loos, 'so we have to make it a comedy. We'll change the the the opening scene to set the mood.'

The clever Loos wrote a prologue that set the pace – Harlow looks in the mirror and turns to the camera with, 'Gentlemen prefer blondes, do they? Sez who?' Then, shopping in a department store, she tries on a dress. 'Is this dress too tight?' she asks the salesgirl.

'Yes it is,' comes the reply with a scowl.

'Good,' Harlow exclaims. 'I'll take it!'

Despite these changes, *Red Headed Woman* was condemned. The audience laughed, but they were disgusted that the girl, who sleeps with every rich man she meets and tries to kill her husband, gets away with it. The film was banned in Great Britain and denounced by the Catholic Church. MGM was forced to withdraw it, but Harlow became a star.

Thalberg, nonetheless, knew he had defied the censorship code, which he considered outdated and ridiculous. It was in his nature to attempt to anticipate future movie trends. Even if a good message movie lost money, he deemed that the picture had been worth making if it set the pace for future films with the same theme. This was depicted in the film of *The Last Tycoon*: Thalberg, played by Robert De Niro, is not shaken when one of his films loses money. Though the picture has gone over budget, he tells his colleagues he is paving the way for similar movies to be successful in the future. Naturally, they do not agree with him.

Paul Bern, who was dating Jean Harlow, now came up with the idea for *Red Dust*. She would play a prostitute who seduces Gable, who in turn seduces a married woman. Again Mayer protested, but to no avail. Thalberg put his best writers to work on the script and chose his buddy Victor Fleming to direct.

Paul Bern was a short, balding little man with a pot belly – hardly the type who would qualify to become Jean Harlow's husband. Thalberg agreed, but did not interfere when his friend married the platinum blonde. He and Norma attended the wedding at Bern's house on 2 July 1932. Jean was 21 to Bern's 42. Irving did not think the marriage would last, but sexually the idea fascinated him.

According to writer Anita Loos, Thalberg thought of sex as comical rather than dramatic. 'Irving could spot sublimated sex in every human relationship,' she said. 'I told him if he ever made a movie of *Frankenstein*, he'd try to prove he had a mad crush on the monster he created.'

'Why not?' Thalberg exclaimed. 'That old yarn is about due for a new twist.'

Which is exactly what Gene Wilder and Mel Brooks thought in 1974 when they made the very funny *Young Frankenstein*.

But the fun and games would come to an abrupt halt on Labor Day 1932. The Thalbergs were lunching with the Goldwyns at the beach house when Irving received a call from L.B. Mayer. Paul Bern was dead, having apparently committed suicide. Thalberg, in a daze, watched Paul's body being removed from the house. 'What happened?' he asked publicity chief Howard Strickling.

'It seems Paul had a common-law wife who showed up last night. Jean caught them talking at poolside and joked about his having two wives. Then she went to bed, heard a shot and found Paul dead with a gun clutched in his hand. Jean called me first, of course.'

Close to tears, Irving asked, 'Did he leave a suicide note?'

'Mayer found a letter but there's no date on it, something about a silly farce that he hoped she considered a joke. Mayer's going to use it to protect Jean.'

'How?'

'To prove that Paul was impotent. He had the genitalia of a young boy. Possibly he was bisexual.'

'You can't do that to Paul. He doesn't deserve it.'

Mayer interrupted. 'Paul's dead and Jean's alive. Think about that.'

Thalberg was shattered by Bern's death. He attended the funeral and wept, before going into seclusion for several days. Harlow chose to resume filming *Red Dust*, playing the 'bath in a rain barrel' scene in the nude. When the cameras weren't rolling, she stood up and gave the crew a thrill. Very proud of her body, she rubbed ice cubes on her nipples to make them firm.

Quietly, Irving went on with his work, but his suffering was apparent. *Fortune* wrote that Thalberg weighed only 122 pounds even after a good night's sleep, 'but in frantic moments he appears as a pale and flimsy bag of bones held together by concealed bits of string.'

Tired and depressed, Irving was fed up with Mayer's insensitivity. He told Norma he was going to terminate his contract for some peace of mind. Though she dreaded the thought of leaving MGM, Norma agreed to go with him.

Thalberg met with Nicholas Schenck and Mayer, who stormed out of the room in a rage. Schenck, however, was concerned that Irving would be hired by another studio, and he didn't want that to happen. He offered Thalberg 100,000 shares in Loew's at 20 per cent of their market value. The Boy Genius was taken aback. How often before had he fought over money? How often did he have to prove his worth before getting any satisfaction? Yet, now that he sincerely wanted to leave MGM because he was worn out and fed up, he was being handed a plum he couldn't refuse.

Norma was relieved. Though she was married and financially secure, MGM had been her home for nearly ten years. Like Irving, she would be able to make movies at another studio, but not one as glamorous and prestigious. She and Irving discussed the films she would like to do. Both agreed on *Marie Antoinette* but this big production would take a year or so to get underway. Irving wanted her to make *The Barretts of Wimpole Street*, but Norma did not want to play an invalid. Joan Crawford said, 'Norma likes to make love in her movies. She gets her thrills that way.'

Charles Laughton, who played Norma's father in *The Barretts of Wimpole Street*, had discussed with Irving the incestuous relationship between father and daughter in the film. Laughton did it brilliantly, with a twinkle in his eye. Thalberg was anxious to sign him to a contract – but Laughton was gay and knew how Mayer felt about homosexuals. Finally, after long talks with Laughton, Irving was grateful to secure his services for *The Hunchback of Notre Dame* and *Mutiny on the Bounty*.

On 24 December 1932, MGM shut down early for the annual Christmas party, or as Anita Loos referred to it, 'the MGM orgy'. Secretaries, hairdressers, and receptionists sat on the executives' laps. Accompanied by loud music, there was plenty of drinking, kissing and disrobing, while ladies of the night were ushered in the back door. It was a night that many would want to forget; the rest, suffering from memory-dulling hangovers, simply couldn't remember it.

Norma went home early, but Irving stayed on working until his office was invaded by girls who smothered him with kisses. Deciding to celebrate his victory and enjoy some of the fun that was not hard to find, he had more to drink than his usual pre-dinner weak scotch and soda, before leaving for home around eleven o'clock. On Christmas morning Irving had his second heart attack, though it was diagnosed as only a mild coronary and he did not have to be hospitalised. The doctor recommended plenty of bed rest, with no visitors or phone calls. Norma gleefully turned away Mayer and Henrietta alike. By February Thalberg was recuperating nicely and told Norma he'd like to take another European vacation.

While Thalberg was away Mayer hired his son-in-law, David Selznick, to produce films at MGM. Believing he should have been consulted first, Irving felt betrayed. *Variety* indicated he had been replaced during his absence. Norma feared Irving would suffer another attack, but he managed to get through the ordeal. On his way home he stopped off in New York to see Nicholas Schenck who explained the situation. 'We want you to have your own production unit,' he told Irving. 'This will ease the workload and you can concentrate on Norma's projects. Also, you'll report directly to me from now on, not Mayer.'

'He won't like that,' Irving said with a crooked smile.

'That shouldn't concern you so it doesn't concern me,' Schenck responded.

As for David Selznick, Irving was an admirer of his work and even invested in Selznick International Pictures. Thalberg knew Selznick was under extra pressure because he was Mayer's son-in-law. Irene Mayer Selznick claimed that her father wanted David to take over from him when he retired. But that was not how things turned out. Selznick went his own way and would eventually produce the great *Gone With the Wind*, though even then he needed Mayer's permission to use Clark Gable in the role of Rhett Butler.

In October 1934 Norma told Irving she was pregnant again. She dreaded the thought of another child. Always concerned about her appearance, she did not want to be seen in public during her pregnancy, but she was forced into it. Irving, meanwhile, made a point of attending premieres and other Hollywood functions to keep in touch with his peers in the industry.

As predicted by Irving, a daughter, Katharine, was born on 13 June 1935. He had it all now – the perfect family and a production unit of his own. And he had surprised the doctors by reaching the age of 36.

Almost as surprising was Thalberg's interest in the Marx Brothers, whose last movies at Paramount had flopped. When Irving heard about this from his bridge partner, brother Chico, he arranged to view their films. He remembered that Hal Roach had thought he was incapable of making comedies, but he would prove Roach wrong.

Thalberg's sense of timing was always good: he noted that *Duck Soup* was not cued for laughs, while the film was poorly edited. He also felt the brothers' movies lacked another important element: 'You need women in your films. Maybe a romance. Otherwise you'll attract only a male audience.' He had faith in the Marx Brothers, even if Mayer felt they were not good enough for MGM. Irving said the studio's roster of films lacked comedies. And he proved it with *A Night at the Opera*. Allan Jones sang love songs to Kitty Carlisle, while Margaret Dumont was Groucho's foil. Then there was the famous scene in the tiny stateroom that overflows with bodies when Dumont opens the door.

Groucho Marx described the wait to see Thalberg as nerve-racking. He would meet the brothers in his office and then disappear 'for a few minutes'. Hours went by. When Irving finally returned, the Marx Brothers were sitting in front of the fireplace in the nude roasting potatoes. And, to Mayer's distress, Groucho wanted to replace Leo the Lion. To say the least, having the Marx Brothers on the MGM lot was havoc. Irving solved this by sending them on the road with their films.

Thalberg was also busy with *Mutiny on the Bounty*, which was filmed on Catalina Island, off the California coast. Clark Gable, who did not like homosexuals, resented having to work with Charles Laughton, who in turn considered Gable a snob. Irving told Laughton not to look directly into Gable's eyes. 'He might get the wrong impression.' There were production problems and bad weather to contend with as well. Thalberg admitted he should never have done the film, but he changed his mind when he received an Oscar for Best Picture.

Though Norma was now known as 'Queen of the MGM Lot', Irving still wanted her to appear in the kind of pictures he wished to make – highbrow films based on stage plays. However, his choice of *Romeo and Juliet* is still questioned. Norma, over thirty, was too old for the role of Juliet and so was her Romeo, Leslie Howard, who would become famous in his role of Ashley Wilkes in *Gone With the Wind*.

Also in *Romeo and Juliet* was the great John Barrymore as Mercutio. By now Barrymore was a hopeless alcoholic. Unable to remember his lines, he had to use cue cards. During filming he was in a sanitarium, but he regularly disappeared on drunken binges. Thalberg considered replacing him, but Norma insisted he remain in the part since he amused her. In one scene with Romeo, Barrymore began reciting his lines to suit himself: 'He heareth not, he stirreth not, he moveth not . . .' Then a pause and, 'He pisseth not.' Thalberg was called to the set and finally he persuaded Barrymore to say his lines as Shakespeare had written them.

Norma in contrast worked tirelessly, learning Shakespeare and perfecting her Juliet, but at best the film was mediocre.

There were rumours about this time that the Thalbergs were contemplating divorce. Some swore he had a mistress, others said it was preposterous. There were sound reasons for both opinions. Norma was less glamorous than Irving's former girlfriends. She knew how to use her make-up cleverly, but underneath she was unattractive. Her figure, too, lacked sex appeal. She has to be given credit for creating an image that could endure during a love affair, but it was not enough to sustain a marriage. Irving had been very particular about the women he dated and bedded down, vivacious girls like Billie Dove and Constance Talmadge. Though he was wise in his choice of a wife and mother of his children, he still had yearnings.

However, if he wanted great sex, Norma was capable of satisfying him. As for his having a mistress, it seems very unlikely. As his good friend, writer Anita Loos, commented, 'Irving poured his sexual energies into his work.' And when would he find the time, working seven days a week, sometimes into the late hours of the night? Often he came home worn out, with a migraine headache. Norma calmed him down with a mild scotch and soda, listening to his problems and serving him a nourishing dinner that he never finished. Unsure how long he would live, Irving crammed as much as possible into each minute.

Director King Vidor remembered arriving at Thalberg's office for a conference about *Billy the Kid*. They had just begun discussing the script when Irving glanced at his watch. 'Come with me,' he said, walking out of the building to a waiting limousine. They continued the conversation until the car stopped at a funeral parlour. Vidor was so surprised he said nothing, but followed Irving into the chapel where a crowd of celebrities were gathered. He turned to someone and asked, 'Who died?'

'Mabel Normand. Don't you read the newspapers?'

Vidor realised he had been so busy with Thalberg that he wasn't aware of the famous comedienne's death. In a state of shock he listened to the eulogy, until Irving leaned over and muttered, 'Too many murders.'

'She was murdered?' Vidor asked in horror.

'In *Billy The Kid*,' Irving whispered.

On the way back to the studio Vidor tried to digest what he had just been through, Mabel Normand's funeral and the rewriting of a movie script. 'Was Pat Garrett his friend during the last five murders?' Irving asked. He was, in essence, in a world of his own, talking to himself and answering his own questions. When the limo pulled up to his office building, Irving jumped out and said, on the run, 'I'll call you!'

Thalberg admired writers and preferred their company. He could spend months on a script – the rewrites for *Marie Antoinette* took a year. Irving paid his writers well and had formed a special relationship with them. And so it was a shock when he found out they were planning to form the Screen Writers' Guild to improve their working conditions. 'I can't believe it,' Thalberg said. 'Writers are living like kings out here. Why on earth would they want to join a union like coal miners and plumbers?' He called a meeting of the MGM writers at which he voiced his concern. 'If you strike, you'll put hundreds of people out of work. Think of others. We work together for the benefit of all. So if you go ahead with this strike, I will close down the entire plant, with no exception.' As he prepared to leave he exclaimed, 'Make no mistake about it. I mean precisely what I say. I shall close the studio and lock the gates. And that will be the end of productions at Metro-Goldwyn-Mayer. And it will be you – the writers – who will have done it!'

He managed to talk them out of setting up the guild, but ultimately it would prevail.

Thalberg had Mayer's support in this matter, but otherwise the two men were growing further and further apart. Now that Irving had his own production company he no longer had access to the best directors and writers. Mayer, it seems, was trying to take complete control of the studio, selecting films that did not live up to the high standards of MGM. What was he doing in production, anyway? The answer to that one was that David Selznick and Darryl Zanuck had turned down his offer to work for Leo the Lion.

There are no secrets in Hollywood, and it was well known that Mayer envied Irving's talent and popularity. He was disappointed that his partner was still turning out quality films, and had maintained his prestige despite losing overall control of MGM film production. Then there was the fact that Irving, who reported directly to Schenck, had expressed objections about Mayer's choice of films. 'Louis doesn't know the first thing about production,' he told Schenck. 'He is a politician. He knows how to handle dignitaries and has important connections in Washington. But he's not qualified to schedule films and organise them. He should stay in the front office where's he's needed . . . where he belongs.'

Schenck was no fan of Mayer's either, but he liked the way he ran the studio and tried to placate him without mentioning that he and Thalberg had spoken. What lingered in everyone's mind was Irving's health. How much longer could he live? Who would replace him? Schenck surmised that MGM could survive without Thalberg, but not without Mayer.

In the meantime, Irving's films were still of high quality. He was planning *Marie Antoinette*, *The Good Earth* and *Camille*. He didn't have to prove himself. Norma claimed in later years that Irving and Mayer were still loyal to each other. 'We were neighbours on the Santa Monica Beach and often socialised,' she said. 'I always felt that Louis thought of Irving as a son and dreaded the day he would lose him. The pressure was so great on both of them that they often fought bitterly, but with MGM in mind. They were bound to differ and yet they supported each other when a serious matter arose. Sometimes they were both right and then it was difficult.'

Mayer, feeling that people weren't interested in Chinese peasants, objected in particular to *The Good Earth*. He even tried to stop production, but he was overruled by Schenck, who concluded that Mayer simply wanted to turn out a large number of films while Thalberg preferred making fewer films of high quality.

Screenwriter Sam Marx, who had known Irving when he was at Universal, commented,

Mayer wanted to make money, money was his god. Irving often went over budget. He believed in retakes, many of them, until he got what he wanted. He'd preview his films, get the audience's written comments and rewrite scripts, cut out scenes and do them over. He was a perfectionist. His films rarely lost money, but he could be exasperating. The writers and directors were always on call, always subject to long conferences, more retakes and more rewriting. Sometimes he made movies that would not make a profit, but he considered this an experiment. Often he said, "One has to experiment in this business or there's no progress." This did not go over with Mayer or his investors, of course. While Irving thought of the movie business as an art, they considered only the money. I think this was the big difference between Thalberg and Mayer. Still, MGM was a family and, in public, they supported each other. They made a point of being seen together at premieres and so forth. Even though Irving was not involved with as many productions, he was making bigger ones that were more time-consuming. We all thought he was pushing himself too hard, as if he had to prove himself all over again to Mayer and Schenck.

While Thalberg found comfort in his family, Mayer's marriage was dissolving. After his wife's hysterectomy, doctors told her not to have sex, and Margaret obeyed orders. Mayer began spending nights on the town and met a beautiful young actress, Jean Howard, with whom he fell deeply in love. After finding out that she was about to marry agent Charles Feldman, Mayer threatened suicide. He managed to patch things up with Margaret temporarily, but there would be more broken love affairs and more suicide attempts.

Then, on 9 January 1936, John Gilbert died from a heart attack at the age of only 37. He had been forced to sit out his MGM contract without work and felt deeply betrayed. His heavy drinking did not help the situation, nor did being ignored by the love of his life, Greta Garbo. Thalberg was very sad to lose one of his best friends, a man who had acted brilliantly in *The Merry Widow* and *The Big Parade*. At Gilbert's funeral, Irving was appalled when Marlene Dietrich, who had made a final attempt to nurse Gilbert back to health, made her dramatic entrance on the arm of Gary Cooper, only to collapse in tears. 'It was all too over-dramatic,' he commented. 'No need for it.' Irving himself dealt with the death of Gilbert better than expected. Perhaps Dietrich's theatrics had helped him overcome his grief.

While working on *The Good Earth*, Thalberg was planning *Maytime* with Jeanette MacDonald and Nelson Eddy. One of his favourite projects, though, was *Camille*. Because Marguerite Gautier, the Lady of the Camellias, is a courtesan, Irving had to soften her image. 'The idea that a woman with a past can ruin her marriage is old-fashioned,' he explained. 'It's been proven that whores make good wives.' He chose Greta Garbo for the lead role and newcomer Robert Taylor to play her young lover. The casting of Taylor in the role was criticised – he was not an experienced actor yet. 'True,' Irving said, 'but all he has to do is look handsome, which he is, and fawn over Garbo. He can do that.' Garbo was always adamant that there should be no visitors on her movie sets – and that included Thalberg, who always looked in on his productions. So he laughed it off and stayed away.

Camille proved to be Garbo's greatest film. She said, however, 'I never had a problem when I was in public. People didn't bother me until I made *Camille*. After that I had no peace.'

Observers were saying that Irving appeared thin and tired these days. Norma was concerned that he was working too hard, but he ignored suggestions that he should slow down. He was planning *Goodbye, Mr. Chips* and *Pride and Prejudice*. 'Norma will retire after *Marie Antoinette*,' he said. 'Actresses should know when to quit when they pass 35. I plan to form my own production company free of MGM. Loew's will distribute the films.' He was asked if he would take any of the MGM stars with him. 'Norma, of course, and the Marx Brothers,' he replied.

When word got back to Mayer about Irving's future plans, the mogul was furious. Sam Goldwyn was so concerned that he went to see Mayer. When he walked into the office, Goldwyn remarked, 'My God, Louie, one has to hail a cab to get to your desk!'

'And I suppose I'm the Pharaoh.'

'Well, your desk is raised like a throne. It's rather imposing.'

'I'm sure you didn't come here to redecorate my office, Sam.'

'No, I came to talk to you about Irving. Ease up on him, Louie. You'll never find another talent like him. He's a sensitive boy in bad health.'

Mayer said he would take the advice. 'Sam, you're very thoughtful. Why do people hate you so much?'

'Louie, if you were aware of what people thought of you, you wouldn't come to work tomorrow.'

Mayer did ease up on Thalberg, and signed him to a new contract. When that expired he was on his own to make films that would be distributed by Loew's. It was his ultimate dream and now it was becoming reality. Is this one reason why he turned down *Gone With the Wind?* Norma said he liked the book and thought it would make a fine film with Clark Gable as Rhett Butler; on the other hand, he claimed that the reason he had turned down Margaret Mitchell's best-selling novel was 'because no one wants to watch a movie about the Civil War.' But in fact he was tired. Such productions as *Mutiny on the Bounty* had drained him, and he needed all the energy he could muster for *Marie Antoinette*.

Irving and Norma spent the Labor Day weekend of 1936 at their honeymoon retreat, the Del Monte Club on the Monterey Peninsula. As usual Thalberg wanted to mix business with pleasure and invited Mr. and Mrs. Sam Wood, Jack Conway and his wife, Chico Marx, and Mervyn LeRoy and his wife to join them. Irving was anxious to discuss the forthcoming Marx Brothers movie, *A Day at the Races*. He and his friends enjoyed playing bridge on the hotel veranda, but the evenings were cool with a brisk breeze. Norma wanted him to put on a sweater, but he declined; he wanted to be one of the boys and they were in their shirt sleeves.

On Tuesday, 8 September, he returned to work with the sniffles. That night he went to the Hollywood Bowl to watch the rehearsal of Max Reinhardt's *Everyman*, a production to raise money for Jewish charities. Two nights later he and Norma attended the premiere. As one of the sponsors, Irving stood up to accept the applause of twenty thousand people in the audience. The next day he woke up with chills and a high fever. The doctor said he had a throat infection. When Irving did not respond to treatment he suggested flying him to the Mayo Clinic in Rochester, Minnesota, where he could be given sulfonamide drugs that were not available elsewhere. By the time arrangements were made, though, Irving was too ill to make the trip.

On Sunday Thalberg was diagnosed with pneumonia and was unable for the first time to attend MGM's annual picnic, a fun event that included a tug of war between his team and Mayer's. Norma sent a telegram in his name: 'ONLY ILLNESS KEEPS ME FROM BEING WITH YOU.'

Irving's business colleague Bernie Hyman came to see him. 'I'm not going to make it this time,' Thalberg muttered. 'Nearer, my God, to thee . . .'

Among the few visitors allowed was Rosabelle Laemmle. Irving managed a smile for her. It had been rumoured for some time in Hollywood that they had resumed their love affair a few years ago. Close friends said that Norma knew about it and was preparing herself for a divorce. This is mere speculation, but it cannot be dismissed entirely. Perhaps it's why Norma allowed Rosabelle to see Irving when others were turned away.

On Sunday evening Thalberg's condition worsened. Doctors put him in an oxygen tent to aid his laboured breathing and he seemed to rally, but on Monday morning his fever was dangerously high, and he went into a coma. He mumbled, but there were no last words. On 14 September 1936, Irving Thalberg died at 10:15 a.m. The cause of death was lobar pneumonia. Doctors said his heart had withstood the illness even during the high fevers he suffered.

Mayer rushed to Norma's side. With the help of Rabbi Magnin, who had married Irving and Norma, they planned the funeral which, according to Jewish tradition, was to be held two days later. Mayer said he had lost 'the finest friend a man could ever have'. The *New York Times* wrote, '. . . [Thalberg] helped, perhaps more than any other man in Hollywood, to make the motion picture a medium of adult entertainment, and by thousands of theatergoers his talent and vitality will be missed.' The tributes poured in: 'More than any other man he raised the industry to its present world prestige' . . . 'the greatest conceivable loss to the motion picture industry' . . . 'It will be utterly impossible to replace him' . . . 'Irving Thalberg was beyond any question the greatest individual force for fine pictures.' C.A. Lejieune, film critic for the London *Observer*, wrote:

> A temperate man in all his ways of living, in this one respect he was an inveterate gambler. If he believed in a man, or a project, or a story, he would stake everything on his conviction . . . Everyone who worked for Thalberg loved him. He had the quality, rare among showmen, and precious among men, of standing back after an achievement and letting the other fellow take the credit. There was nothing thrustful about Thalberg; he never wanted to be known as a big promoter. He just saw a little further than most of the others, and trusted his vision, and worked like a labourer until it came true . . . In the whole of the film-making world there are perhaps a half-dozen producers whose calligraphy we can identify. Of them all, Thalberg was the most significant, and not alone because he had the resources of the world's most important film company behind him. Genius is an infinite capacity for taking chances, and that genius Thalberg had in full measure. What he also had was a great kindliness, a love for his work, workers, friends and audiences.

On 17 September, the day of the funeral at the B'nai B'rith Synagogue on Wilshire Boulevard, the American flag at MGM was lowered to half mast. A black mourning band was wrapped around the bottom of the flag pole. The busy offices and bustling sound stages were dark. The only activity could be found in the garages where studio limousines emerged to pick up 'more stars than there are in heaven'. The limousines, each flying a black flag of mourning, pulled up in front of the synagogue where a crowd of hundreds waited to get a glimpse of their favourite movie star. Fans might have gasped occasionally, but they mourned quietly, as did those with bowed heads inside the temple. To list them all would be time-consuming, but it's safe to say that everybody who was anybody in Hollywood was there that day. Even Greta Garbo in a black jersey dress was in attendance. Among the ushers were Clark Gable, Douglas Fairbanks Jr, and Moss Hart. Norma Shearer, heavily veiled in black, sat near the altar concealed from the others, accompanied by William Thalberg and an inconsolable Henrietta.

Rabbi Magnin read the many tributes to Irving, along with a wire of sympathy from Franklin D. Roosevelt. The love shared by Norma and Irving, he said, was greater than that of Romeo and Juliet. He intoned the ancient Hebrew ritual for the dead. When Grace Moore sang the Psalm of David, Norma broke down, though she composed herself for the walk up the aisle behind Irving's copper casket covered with gardenias. Twelve limousines made the slow drive to Forest Lawn Memorial Park in Glendale. The MGM police force guarded Norma as she entered the marble pavilion in the Sanctuary of the Benediction. There were truckloads of floral tributes; the biggest was from Louis B. Mayer, gardenias shaped like a throne with a caged white dove suspended from it.

Henrietta collapsed as she was leaving the mausoleum and had to be half-carried to her limousine. On her way home, Norma paid a visit to Sam Goldwyn who was recuperating from an operation.

Mayer was said by some to have remarked to a friend, leaving the funeral, 'Ain't God good to me,' but it's doubtful he would stoop so low. His grief was sincere, and he found peace recollecting with Norma how he and Irving had given birth to Metro-Goldwyn-Mayer. They talked for hours about their hopes and dreams, their success and their differences. Through it all, he said, 'I loved Irving like the son I never had.'

For the first time Thalberg was given credit for one of his films. A few months after his death *The Good Earth* was released with a tribute: 'To the memory of Irving Thalberg, we dedicate this picture – his greatest achievement.' The new administration building was also named after him, while the Motion Picture Academy inaugurated the Irving G. Thalberg Award, to be presented each year to a deserving member of the Academy.

Though Irving had been frail for some time, his death had come suddenly, brought on by a simple head cold. In shock and grieving, Norma faced an uncertain future in films without her husband. She was still under contract to MGM, but not bound to it without Irving. After spending half a million dollars on sets and costumes, MGM wanted to proceed with *Marie Antoinette*, but Norma asked for sixty days to think it over. During this time she paid regular visits to Forest Lawn Cemetery, placing flowers on Irving's marble tomb.

The pressure of the past few weeks finally caught up with Norma. She came down with a serious case of pneumonia and was confined to her bed for several weeks. Stricken with the same illness that took Irving's life, she feared she might join him sooner than expected. But she recovered, and began tackling legal issues. Irving's estate, originally estimated to be $4.5 million, eventually dwindled to $2.5 million and to $1 million after taxes. Also to be taken into account were shares of stock that Mayer refused to acknowledge now that Irving was gone. Norma fought back – and won, by using Mayer's tactics of leaking the news to the press. MGM was not living up to its obligations, she claimed, and pleaded poverty, which got more than a few chuckles in Hollywood. After all, she had stashed away her salary for many years, and that alone was a fortune. Mayer finally turned over to Norma the shares of stock that had belonged to Irving, and offered her $150,000 for each future picture. To mend their rift, he gave Norma a bonus of $900,000 in July 1937.

Marie Antoinette finally went into production and it was beautifully done. One of Norma's co-stars was handsome Tyrone Power, borrowed from 20th Century-Fox. That Norma was trying to seduce him was obvious on set, but he managed to get through the film without incident. He escorted her to the premiere before quietly drifting off to be with his bride-to-be, Annabella.

On the prowl, Norma met thirty-year-old Jimmy Stewart, a newcomer at MGM, at a party. A little tipsy, he told her she was the most beautiful woman he had ever seen. Norma was overwhelmed by the young man. Embarrassed as he was by her attention – he would hide in the back seat of her yellow Rolls-Royce to avoid being seen with the 'Queen of the Lot' – he couldn't get away from her for six weeks.

In 1939 she seduced nineteen-year-old Mickey Rooney. They confined their lovemaking to her elaborate trailer, which had been built for her during *Marie Antoinette*. When Mayer found out, he put an end to it. No one knows what he said to Norma, but it must have been an embarrassment for her. Mickey was Mayer's fair-haired boy and the star of MGM's *Andy Hardy* series, so he got away with it. Mayer told friends Norma was sex-starved, just as Clark Gable had said when he co-starred with her in *Idiot's Delight*. She had been so seductive it was hard for him to resist, but he had remained loyal to Thalberg.

When Norma met actor George Raft at a party in New York, they were attracted to each other instantly, and had sex the night they met. After a jaunt to Europe together, he moved into the beach house with

Norma, where he got along famously with her children. Hollywood was shocked that Irving Thalberg's widow was being seen around town with Raft, who had connections with mobsters Bugsy Siegel and Lucky Luciano. Though he gave a good performance as the coin-crossing hood in *Scarface*, Raft was remembered best for having been a dancing New York gigolo in his younger days.

Mayer chuckled when Norma and George appeared at the Academy Awards ceremony together. It was an ideal situation for Norma – except for the fact that George was a married man. He had been separated from his wife for a long time, but now she wanted half a million dollars and 20 per cent of his earnings as a divorce settlement. Raft couldn't afford it. Hollywood insiders wondered why Norma didn't come up with the money. The answer is simple: Norma had her pride and she was very close with a buck. In October 1941, Raft told the press, 'We had a wonderful romance . . . She is the swellest person I have ever known, and I wish I could tell you that we are going to be married soon.'

Norma retired from films as Greta Garbo did – with a terrible movie. *Cardboard Lover* with Robert Taylor was a dud. Though Norma had never looked lovelier, she refused to play a middle-aged wife with children in *Mrs. Miniver* and *Old Acquaintance*. Unfortunately, Norma refused to accept the fact that she *was* a middle-aged woman with two children. She had no maternal instincts and paid little attention to Irving Jr and Katharine. They were well cared for and attended the best schools, but they lacked any warmth or soothing closeness from their mother.

In June 1942 Norma took her children to Sun Valley, Idaho, where she met Martin Arroungé, a ski instructor twelve years younger than she was. He reminded her of Irving, she said; though taller, he had the same black hair and dark eyes. Norma did the chasing because Martin was what she wanted. According to writer Anita Loos he had a beautiful body and knew how to handle it. He was, she stressed, sexy and romantic. What Loos didn't say was that Arroungé had no money and earned only $150 a week. But on 22 August Norma told the press she and Martin had signed a prenuptial settlement. Claiming that she was not as rich as most people thought, she explained that she had been living off the interest from a lump sum of $1.5 million. As usual, she did not mention her own earnings.

On 23 August 1942, Norma and Martin were married at the church of the Good Shepherd in Beverly Hills. Her wedding ring, with bands of gold welded on either side, was the one Irving had put on her finger fifteen years earlier.

In 1951, L.B. Mayer was forced to resign from MGM. Norma was asked to speak when the Screen Producers' Guild paid tribute to the mogul. With tears in her eyes she thanked Mayer for bringing her 'the happiest days of my life'. To Norma it was the end of a period in Hollywood that Irving Thalberg had helped turn into the Golden Era.

Norma wanted to film F. Scott Fitzgerald's *The Last Tycoon* with Robert Evans as Thalberg. She had seen the young actor poolside at the Beverly Hills Hotel, and was amazed by his resemblance to her late husband. Instead, Evans played Thalberg in *Man of a Thousand Faces*, based on the life of Lon Chaney. She also wrote an autobiography, but couldn't get it published because it gave such a fairy-tale account of her life.

Now that Katharine and Irving Jr were both married, she sold the beach house in 1961 and found a smaller and less pretentious house at 1207 North Sierre Alta Way. Her only servant was a maid who visited every week.

In 1970 Norma suffered recurring panic attacks. Shock treatment helped but caused her to experience memory loss. She began referring to Marti as 'Irving' and would continue to do so until her death. After she attempted suicide by jumping out the window of a high-rise building, Marti saved her life. More shock treatment followed. When her eyesight failed and her weight dropped to eighty pounds, Marti put Norma in the Motion Picture Country House, a retirement home for actors. Her long hair was now white and stringy but she turned away anyone who tried to fuss with her. One visitor said she resembled the imprisoned Marie Antoinette.

On 12 June 1983 Norma Shearer died of bronchial pneumonia. She was interred next to Irving after a private funeral at Forest Lawn Cemetery in Glendale, California. Irving Thalberg Jr died of cancer in 1987 . . .

'Movies aren't made; they're remade.'

– Irving Thalberg

2

Louis B. Mayer

He was an immigrant junk dealer. He didn't know his birth date so he chose 4 July to show his allegiance to America. He was born in Dymer, Russia. His father couldn't remember the original family name; it often changed to survive religious oppression. Like all Jews, the family was confined to a section called the Pale. Only those outside the Pale were allowed to attend school. In America he never got a high school education; instead he helped his father collect junk to sell. A big fan of silent films, he rented a theatre, cleverly invested the profits and formed his own production company.

'Good people make me look good,' he said, and alongside his brilliant assistant, Irving Thalberg, he lived by those words. Together they gave birth to Metro-Goldwyn-Mayer, the greatest motion picture studio in the world. Mayer would tell his family of stars, 'Make it good . . . Make it big . . . Give it class.' His galaxy of stars were his family and he was their father. Their seven-year contracts were strictly enforced, but he spoiled them – not with money, but with the best couturiers, set designers, hairdressers, tailors, vocal and dance instructors, drama coaches, and make-up artists.

He was a bespectacled man with a short, stocky physique; his office, however, reflected a giant with strength, determination and power. Decorated all in white, including sixty feet of plush carpet from the huge walnut doors to his raised crescent-shaped desk, it seemed like sixty miles to intimidated newcomers. That was the idea. He could look them over and judge their endurance.

He had connections in the White House and held the power to make or break a star. Able to cover up their involvement in manslaughter, suicide and murder, he told them when to get married, when to have babies and when to divorce. Often he walked his divas down the church aisle and handed the groom a box of condoms.

He was a strong believer in the American way, apple pie, orange blossoms and motherhood. He made family films and beautiful musicals.

But behind the milk shakes and ginger snaps was a demanding mogul who made more enemies than friends.

Saint or devil? You decide . . .

He began to unbutton her blouse. She gently removed his hand, lovingly but firmly. 'You said I was free,' she whispered.

'You are, but what's wrong with a fuck now and then?'

'What's over is over. It was your decision.'

'I kept my promise and made you a star, Jeanette.'

'Yes, you did and I proved how grateful I was. But now I'm starting a new life with the man I love.'

'Nelson Eddy?' Mayer laughed. 'Don't waste your time with a man you can never marry.'

'We plan to elope to Reno,' Jeanette MacDonald exclaimed.

'You can't do that without my permission.'

'We know that, but we're going to do it, anyway.'

'I can ruin him with the snap of my fingers.'

'Mr. Mayer, Nelson and I have made millions for MGM. You love our musicals. You said so.'

'Baritones are easy to replace.'

'Not Nelson Eddy,' she spoke up.

'We'll see about that,' Mayer growled. 'Now take off your clothes, or shall I do it?'

They struggled like two teenagers until she reminded him she was on a break and had to resume filming. He smiled, motioned to the door and said, 'There's more than one way to get rid of a baritone.'

Jeanette was pale and shaking when she returned to the movie set. Nelson Eddy finally got the truth out of her. 'We can't see each other again,' she told him. 'Mayer made that very clear when he tried to . . .'

'Did he try to seduce you? I thought he broke up the affair.'

As tears filled her eyes, he stormed off the set and into Mayer's office. 'You son-of-a-bitch!'

'What do *you* want?'

'You dirty bastard!'

41

Mayer leaped from behind his desk and raged at Eddy, who grabbed his throat. 'I'm gonna kill you! I swear to God, I'm going to kill you!' Nelson dragged him to an open window, and he might have gone through with it if actor Frank Morgan hadn't interfered. 'Get a hold of yourself, Eddy, and get the hell out of here.'

But Mayer had his revenge, arranging Jeanette's marriage to gay actor Gene Raymond, and ordering Nelson to sing at her wedding.

'What's holding up the ceremony?' Mayer asked the minister.

'I don't know.'

'You'd better tell me! This is no ordinary wedding. Our great director, King Vidor, is marrying our beautiful star, Eleanor Boardman.'

Publicity chief Howard Strickling came over to Mayer and whispered in his ear. 'It's to be a double wedding. John Gilbert and Greta Garbo, but she's not here yet.'

'What?!'

'He insists we wait for her.'

'She's not going to show up,' Mayer barked. 'I know it, you know it and Gilbert knows it.'

'Louie, this is great publicity. It's worth the wait for the great Garbo to marry our most popular matinée idol.'

'It won't happen, Howard.'

The mogul approached Gilbert, who was looking out the window for a glimpse of his bride-to-be. 'We can't wait much longer,' Mayer said.

'Because you don't want it to happen!'

'That's true, but she doesn't either. How often has she left you waiting at the altar?'

'None of your business.'

'Oh, but you're wrong. My stars *are* my business. You belong to me.'

'You're all wet,' Gilbert hissed.

'I'm a realist, but you're not. You're living with Garbo so why not just fuck her and forget about marriage?'

Gilbert turned and pushed him against a bathroom door. When Mayer fell down, Gilbert grabbed him by the throat and banged his head repeatedly on the tile floor. One of Mayer's colleagues broke up the fight. Gilbert was ready to hit him, but Eleanor Boardman grabbed his arm. 'C'mon, John, the ceremony's about to begin.'

Mayer roared, 'You're finished, Gilbert. I'll destroy you if it costs me a million dollars!'

Another wedding guest was Irving Thalberg, vice-president and head of production at MGM. He gave Gilbert his support and a piece of advice. 'You have to be careful with Mayer,' he said. 'You referred to your mother as a whore, remember?'

'But she *was* a whore. I knew more about sex before I was ten than most people do in a lifetime.'

'You know how Mayer feels about mothers.'

'I know now,' Gilbert said. 'He chased me around his office with a knife. I told him if he cut off my penis, I'd still be more of a man than he was.'

'Jack, you have to play the game. Be one of the family,' Thalberg said. 'You're MGM's biggest star.'

'Then I shouldn't have to play any games with that asshole.'

'These are risky times for all of us in the film industry. We're gearing up for sound and everyone's on edge.'

'Talkies don't scare me, Irving, and neither does Mayer. He's hated me from the first.'

'Your mother's a saint, remember? Even if she *was* a whore . . .'

'Right now the only whore I know is Louis Burt Mayer,' Gilbert said, looking again for Garbo. She never showed up.

'You and Joan Crawford are not to see each other again. Is that clear?'

'Not even on the movie set?'

'That's not what I mean and you know it, Clark.'

'Joan and I are in love.'

'There's no such thing in Hollywood,' Mayer exclaimed.

'We plan to be married.'

'What about your wife and her husband?'

'We're both filing for divorce like everyone else in this town.'

'Have you forgotten the morals clause in your contract? I can fire you, and if I do, I'll make sure no other studio hires you, or Joan. You can go back to the lumberyard and she can go back to the laundry.'

'Right now, that sounds pretty good to me.'

'Who would you fuck in the lumberyard, Clark? One of the guys who looks like Billy Haines?'

'Who?'

'Our queer actor who banged you in the men's room at the Beverly Wilshire Hotel.'

'Back to Joan,' Gable said with a red face.

'I know her better than you do. She's a maneater.'

'Not since she met me.'

'But you haven't been faithful to her,' Mayer said with a crooked grin. 'You screw every girl who's breathing, including our Jean Harlow.'

'That's because my wife is a lot older than I am. I could be faithful to Joanie.'

'Sure, like the sun doesn't shine. If you continue this affair with Joan, you're both through.'

'What about Harlow?'

'I haven't caught you with her yet. You should have been as discreet with Joan.'

'You never lose, do you?'

Mayer smiled. 'When I lose, everybody loses.'

As Gable went out the door, Crawford entered. 'My, you're looking good today, Mr. Mayer, but then you always do.'

'Thank you, Joan. Did you bring a hankie with you?'

'I always do. Why?'

'You'll need it, because you and Gable are through.'

'I'm getting a divorce. What's the problem?'

'He and his matronly wife are going to be seen around town from now on. I kept her out of sight because she's too old for him and bad for his image, but rumours are flying about you and him. It has to stop. It will stop.'

'We've worked hard for you, Mr. Mayer. Our reviews are good and . . .'

'Yes, you click on the screen but you're not established stars yet. The public might protest at first, but they're fickle.'

'I've been with you from the start,' Crawford wept.

'You were a flapper and I made you a star. I changed your name and your image. Have you no loyalty?'

'Clark and I are madly in love.'

Mayer shrugged. 'He fucks around and you fuck around. You and Gable are making MGM look like a bordello. You signed a contract to uphold the high standards of this studio so I'm giving you fair warning. The affair is over or you're finished in Hollywood.'

Joan dabbed at her mascara-stained cheeks. 'I have lunch with Mrs. Gable often. We're good friends.'

'I'm sure you'll have a better relationship after you stop seeing her husband.'

Crawford touched up her make-up and shook hands with her boss, who kissed her on the cheek. 'I love you, Joan.'

'I love you, too, Mr. Mayer.'

Joan and Clark continued to see each other on the sly . . .

'June, what a nice surprise. Your sweet face always cheers me up.'

'Mr. Mayer . . . Pops, I want your permission to get married.'

'You're only a baby, June.'

'I'm 22.'

'You don't look a day over sixteen. Who's the lucky man? Van Johnson? Peter Lawford?'

'Pops, you arranged those dates. I adore them but . . .'

'I'd like to marry off Van Johnson.'

'We're very good friends,' June said.

'Ah, but that chemistry can't only be for the camera,' Mayer winked.

'Pops, I want to marry Dick Powell.'

'Who? What? Dick Powell? Out of the question. He's too old for you.'

'I love him, Pops.'

'Junie, just think what this will do to your image . . . the adorable girl-next-door, June Allyson, weds man old enough to be her father.'

'Richard, I call him Richard, was hard to convince. He thinks he's too old for me, too, but I want to marry him.'

'I'm appalled,' Mayer gasped. 'The man has been divorced twice and has two children. Bad, very bad for your virginal image, Junie. I won't allow it.'

'Pops, I'm sorry . . .'

'You're going through with it?'

'Yes, sir.'

'Then you're suspended without pay.'

'I understand,' she said, forcing a pleasant smile.

June Allyson left Mayer's office, a long walk from his crescent desk to the door when your knees are shaking. She had gone all the way downstairs when a thought struck her. She made the long trek back to Mayer's office and approached him again. He assumed, with relief, that she had changed her mind. Going on suspension is not a pleasant experience.

'Pops, you know my father left us when I was a baby.'

'The beast! Yes, I remember, Junie, but I adopted you so forget the ugly past.'

'I have no one to walk me down the aisle. Will you do it?'

Mayer was shocked. Here stood an actress who was officially on suspension, asking him to give her away at her wedding. 'Well, yes, Junie, it would be an honour,' he managed.

In June Allyson's wedding album are pictures of the 'happy' mogul and the newlyweds. He managed a weak smile for the cameras, but was never his jovial self on such gala occasions. The bride went on suspension, anyway, but returned to work not long after the wedding. June and Powell remained married until his death seventeen years later . . .

'Mr. Mayer, I can't support my mother and myself on thirty-five dollars a week,' Robert Taylor said. 'I want you to release me from my contract.'

'Have a seat, Bob. You know, God never saw fit to give me a son. He gave me two beautiful daughters who have been a great joy to me. They're now married to top producers, Dave Selznick and Billy Goetz, who are wonderful husbands. But for some reason, in His infinite wisdom, He never saw fit to give me a son.

'But if he had given me a son, and that son came to me and said, "Dad, I'm working for a wonderful company, Metro-Goldwyn-Mayer, and for a wonderful man, the head of that company, who has my best interests at heart. But he's only giving me thirty-five dollars a week, Dad. Do you think I should ask him for a raise?" Do you know what I'd say to my son, Bob? I'd say, "Son, it's a fine company. It's going to do great things for you – greater things than it has already done. It is going to make you a big star. You'll be famous. That's more important than a little money. Don't ask for a raise now, son." '

When Taylor left the office he ran into his agent who asked, 'Did you get a raise, Bob?'

'No, but I got a father!'

Louis Burt Mayer did not become the highest-paid executive in the United States for no reason. He started out in life with nothing and worked hard for every reward, great and small. Born Lazar Meir in Minsk in 1885, he left Russia with his family at the age of three and settled in St. John, New Brunswick. He went into the junk business with his father. Louis attended school but also roamed the streets looking for tin cans, scrap iron, and bottles. He was known as a ragpicker and pedlar. But it was an honest profession that put food on the table and clothes on his back. His mother, whom he worshipped, sold chickens door to door. Though she couldn't afford one herself, she sometimes put a skimpy chicken in a pot to make soup. Louis gobbled it up and often bragged about his mother's recipe. In later years it was always on the menu in the MGM commissary.

Louis, at eighteen, went off on his own to Boston where he worked in a junk yard. His aunt told him to look up Margaret Shenberg, whose father was a butcher and cantor of the Emerald Street Synagogue. Louis had no experience with girls; his mother had told him to engage in intercourse 'only to have babies'. Margaret, a plump but attractive girl with ivory complexion and black hair, was three years older than Louis and he fell in love with her. They were married on 14 June 1904, five months after he arrived in Boston. On 14 August 1905, a daughter, Edith, was born. Louis was doing well in the junk business by the time Margaret presented him with another daughter, Irene, on 2 April 1907, but his world caved in that year, during a depression that put him out of business. Humiliated, he and Margaret were forced to live with her parents.

Looking for a job, Louis met Joe Mack, the proprietor of a movie theatre, who gave him a job selling and taking tickets and ushering people to their seats. This was a whole new world to the young man who knew only the junk business. A keen observer, he carefully noted the gleeful customers who paid a nickel to see a film. The theatre was actually a nickelodeon, one of many that had opened in 1903, the beginning of the motion picture industry. The owners would buy films from producers for around ten cents a foot, swapping them with other theatre owners. This was the arrangement that developed in later years into the film distribution busines.

Joe Mack was a good connection for Mayer to make. He was the Boston agent for the films of the Miles Brothers, which were primarily comedies and scenic pictures. Mack told Louis about a theatre up for rent in Haverhill, thirty miles north of Boston. They made the trip together, but Mayer was disenchanted, to say the least.

'This theatre is a dump!' he cringed.

'But it has possibilities,' Mack said.

'I can see *that*, but rebuilding it will take money and I only have fifty dollars on me.'

'If you're willing to gamble that fifty dollars on a binder [a form of insurance], I can help you raise the money.'

Mayer took the chance, much to Margaret's dismay, but she had faith in her husband, the junkman. Mack helped him come up with the necessary

$650, and Louis was in business. The only problem was the reputation of the Gem theatre. Nicknamed the 'Germ', it was nothing more than a burlesque house with tobacco-stained floors and broken-down seats. Mayer did most of the redecorating with the help of Margaret and a burly handyman. Word got around that the new proprietor was dedicated to films of good taste. He renamed the theatre the Orpheum, and it opened on Thanksgiving Day, 28 November 1907. The Haverhill *Evening Gazette* wrote about the event:

> The new Orpheum theater on Essex Street was opened yesterday as a moving picture theater, many changes having been made in the house which has been especially fitted up for the new programme. The theater is well-situated for its purpose with a good stage as well as auditorium so that the change from vaudeville to moving pictures did not entail more than the work on interior decorating. The programme will be frequently changed as the new reels are received and it is planned to conduct the theater along the same lines as those practiced in the best houses of that kind in the country.

Mayer's competition in Haverhill consisted of two nickelodeons, known as 'dens of iniquity'. But he was dedicated to the decent people of the community, and he proved it by showing *Passion Play*, which depicted the life of Christ from the Annunciation to the Ascension. Though a commercial film criticised by many preachers, it was a fascinating religious tableau picture. Mayer was now a well-known and upstanding citizen in the community. His art of making money attracted businessmen who would back him in other ventures. The opening of the new Colonial Theater in 1921 was a big event. Even the mayor made a speech to applaud Mayer and his latest project.

Louis was crushed that his mother was not alive to share his success. She had died from a botched gall bladder operation in 1913. For weeks he wailed over her grave, mourning the greatest loss of his life. Her portrait hung over his bed for a long time. Mayer's daughter, Irene, wrote in her memoirs, 'In emotional moments my father would tell my sister and me how his sainted mother had knelt on the floor and kissed the hem of my mother's garment . . . she held extraordinary power over him.'

Louis recognised the profits to be made in film distribution and set out to meet the people who could make this possible for him. He put his brother in charge of the New Orpheum, while his brother-in-law operated the Colonial. Mayer let it be known he was looking for film properties to distribute in the New England region. He acquired the franchise to release *The Birth of a Nation* in 1915, and the money rolled in.

With his backers, Louis took over the Alco Company, a near-bankrupt film distributor. The new company, with Mayer as its secretary, was named the Metro Pictures Corporation. The lawyer handling Alco's bankruptcy was J. Robert Rubin, a Wall Street attorney who would also work for Metro and later for Louis. It was Rubin who suggested that Irving Thalberg contact Mayer when the young man wanted to leave Universal.

Daughter Irene recalled her surprise and delight when her father began inviting movie stars like Francis X. Bushman home for dinner. It was on the evening actress Anita Stewart was a guest, Irene said, that 'We found out she was going to make pictures for our father. We began to realise he was adding this activity to his business.'

Virtuous Wives, the film Mayer made with Stewart, was so successful that he formed the Mayer Production Company. In 1918 the Mayers went to California for the filming of *In Old Kentucky*. He set up studio operations in a eucalyptus grove adjoining the Selig Zoo at 3800 Mission Road. Until his headquarters was built, Louis used a cubbyhole at the zoo office where the cowboys kept their gear. Colonel Selig, who was himself planning to make animal films, kept up to a thousand assorted beasts; it's possible Mayer chose this location because he needed horses for *In Old Kentucky*.

Mayer's secretary, Florence Browning, described him as a strange and dramatic man. When he was expecting an important client, Louis would begin to cry and gasp for air until she calmed him down with comforting words and a glass of water. He feigned fainting spells and seizures if he was 'up against it' at meetings, or stuck with someone he didn't like. Florence would again come to the rescue and lead him to a couch where he lay 'dying' until the person left. Mayer would use similar tactics in later years with his MGM players – he could cry and faint on cue.

In 1920 Mayer hired Mildred Harris Chaplin, who was going through a nasty divorce from Charlie. Though she had little experience as an actress, he said she was famous for being married to the famous comedian and that would make the public curious enough to come and see *Polly of the Storm Country*. He was to make several more films with Mildred, but moviegoers lost interest after she was forced to drop 'Chaplin' from her name.

But in April 1920, Mayer was attending a party at the Alexander Hotel in Los Angeles when Charlie Chaplin came in and sat at a nearby table. After ugly words were exchanged, Mayer got up and went to the lobby.

Chaplin followed him and challenged him: 'Take off your glasses!' he shouted. Louis removed his spectacles with his left hand and, with his right, hit Chaplin on the jaw. Chaplin fell backwards into a potted palm. Mayer put on his glasses again and was greeted with cheers and applause from his friends. 'I only did what any man would have done,' he remarked.

Until now, Mayer's films had been distributed by First National, but when Metro was sold to Marcus Loew, president of the company that owned Loew's theatre chain, Robert Rubin suggested Mayer take over distribution, and so for a short time Mayer was distributing for himself, First National and Metro. Louis became increasingly busy and needed an assistant to take over production of his films while he handled business matters. Irving Thalberg was the man everyone in Hollywood was talking about. Hired as a secretary to the head of Universal Pictures, Carl Laemmle, Irving had proved his worth and was soon in charge of operations in California. Just 22 years of age, he was known about town as the Boy Wonder. Mayer had met the young man once socially and had taken a liking to him.

When Thalberg failed in his efforts to get a raise in pay at Universal, he told Robert Rubin he was available to work elsewhere. Rubin thought Mayer might be interested and arranged a meeting, which took place in November 1922 at the home of another attorney, Edwin Loeb. Thalberg and Loeb were talking together when they heard Mayer call out, 'I can't find the doorbell!' He barged in and glared at Loeb. 'Don't you have a doorbell, Edwin?'

'I do,' Loeb replied, 'but since when do you use them? Louie, this is Irving Thalberg.'

The two men shook hands and Mayer offered him a cigar. 'Thank you, but I don't smoke,' the young man said.

'You're a smart fellow,' Mayer commented, cutting off the top of his cigar with a gold gadget and lighting it with grand puffs of authority. Ignoring Thalberg, he conversed with Loeb. 'I'm making a film called *Pleasure Mad* and I'm having a problem with the director. It's been advertised and sold to theatres, but it's too risqué. I don't make that kind of picture. I'm so upset I might throw the whole thing in the garbage.'

'That would cost you, Louie.'

'I'm more interested in clean films. I won't put my name on a picture I'd be ashamed for my own daughters to see! What would you do, Thalberg? I have Mrs. Mayer and two daughters to think about. And you have your mother.'

'And father,' Irving mentioned. 'As to your problem, the director takes orders from you. The producer has the final say and you should make that clear.'

Mayer said he had another appointment and had to leave. 'I like the young man,' he told Loeb. 'Tell him I'll be in touch.'

Daughter Irene remembers Irving coming to the house for dinner, 'He was so handsome and bright,' she said. 'Edie and I were mesmerised by him. But our father made it clear that we were not to go out with him. When we socialised, one dance with Irving was the limit. He had a bad heart and wasn't expected to live past his thirtieth birthday. My father did not want a young widow in the family.'

Thalberg had indeed been born with a weak heart. He survived rheumatic fever as a young man, and his mother, Henrietta, had nursed him night and day even after giving birth to a daughter. Mayer often commented on how impressive was Irving's love for his mother. 'My father wore Irving proudly,' Irene said, 'like a decoration on his lapel.' Thalberg, in return, told his parents, 'I never met anyone like Mayer.'

Marcus Loew, meanwhile, was unhappy with the output of films from Metro. The company was floundering after the loss of Rudolph Valentino. He met with Frank Joseph Godsol, head of the Goldwyn Company, who had been put in charge of the studio when Samuel Goldwyn was ousted. Godsel explained that his film company was in debt and, with the exception of its facilities in Culver City, California, had little of value to offer. Loew suggested that the two companies should merge into the Metro-Goldwyn Corporation.

Once again, Robert Rubin saw a golden opportunity for his friend Louis B. Mayer, who rushed to New York. Loew was reluctant to work with Mayer, but was impressed with his executive staff, which would include Thalberg, production supervisor Harry Rapf, and a small but talented roster of directors and stars. Mayer, it was decided, would become first vice-president of the new corporation, while Thalberg would be the second. Mayer's salary would be $1500 and Thalberg's $650, while both would receive a percentage of the profits. The corporate offices of the new company, to be known as Metro-Goldwyn-Mayer, would remain in New York at Loew's, Inc. Loew would be president and Nicholas Schenck his vice-president.

Mayer liked Goldwyn's idea of using a roaring lion for the company's logo, and *Ars Gratia Artis*, 'Art for Art's Sake', as its slogan. Several lions were screen tested to find their best angles, and the chosen beast was shown facing forward with confidence and defiance. Mayer decided it should give two fast roars, with a pause before a third. To this day, Leo the Lion introduces each MGM film with the same authority.

The merger was ratified in March 1924. MGM would take over Goldwyn's studio location in Culver City, six miles south of Hollywood. On these 172 acres were thirty sound stages, a fire department, police force, executive offices, dressing rooms, recording studios, a wardrobe building, carpentry facilities, and a back lot of 128 acres for location filming, along with a magnificent colonnaded administration building on Washington Avenue. At the studio's zenith, it had over 4000 employees.

Much to Mayer's frustration, he was unable to buy the cemetery that overlooked the property. To be sure, it was an eyesore. Many stars who visited MGM for the first time were depressed by the sight of graves on the grassy hillside looming over the studio site. Actor Billy Haines joked, 'Mayer controls the newspapers, the fan magazines and the police department, but he can't convince the undertaker to sell his property.'

Today, though, the list of celebrities buried at the Holy Cross Cemetery is too long to mention. Among them are Bing Crosby, Rita Hayworth, Loretta Young, John Candy, Jimmy Durante, John Ford, Bela Lugosi, Audrey Meadows and feared Hollywood columnist Louella Parsons.

On 26 April 1924, Mayer officiated at the ceremony to celebrate the great merger that gave birth to Metro-Goldwyn-Mayer. Presented with a huge key engraved in gold with the word 'SUCCESS', Mayer told the crowd, 'I hope it is given to me to live up to this great trust. It has been my argument and practice that each picture should teach a lesson, should have a reason for existence. With seventeen of the greatest directors in the industry calling this great institution their home, I feel that this aim will be carried out . . . This is a great moment for me. I accept this solemn trust and pledge the best that I have to give . . . you can count on it that Metro-Goldwyn-Mayer will reach a point of perfection never approached by any other company. If there is one thing I insist upon it is quality . . .'

Rustic cowboy comedian Will Rogers arrived at the celebration on horseback. 'Sorry I'm late, folks! I forgot my chewing gum and had to go back home to get it. I know why this show was a half hour late in starting. Marcus Loew's cheque wasn't certified.'

Planes flew overhead dropping rose petals on the guests, who included a collection of stars. From Goldwyn had come Billy Haines, Conrad

Nagel, Mae Murray, John Gilbert, Eleanor Boardman and Blanche Sweet; from Metro, Buster Keaton, Ramon Novarro and Jackie Coogan. Mayer provided Renee Adoree, Lon Chaney, Barbara La Marr, Marie Provost and Norma Shearer.

The Navy band played patriotic songs; three hundred Navy personnel in smart white uniforms were led by the commander of the Pacific Fleet. Meanwhile, the stars from Metro, Mayer and Goldwyn looked each other over. During the festivities, actor Billy Haines remarked, 'While Mayer was speaking the gospel, all the stars were making up their minds who they wanted to take to bed.'

Haines later commented, 'It's so sad Rudolph Valentino wasn't there with us. He left Metro when they quarrelled over money. That's why the studio failed. I looked over at Ramon Novarro while the little man Mayer was babbling and we were both thinking the same thing. Why couldn't we gay guys be at the same studio? We three were very close but not jealous of each other. Valentino would not have clashed with Mayer because he was married, Ramon behaved himself. Me? Well, that's another story.'

One of the first films MGM inherited from Goldwyn was *Ben Hur*. It was being filmed in Italy and there were serious production problems. As Ben Hur, George Walsh was replaced by Ramon Novarro, and Fred Niblo took over from Charles Brabin as director. Mayer and his family sailed for Rome on the *Majestic* to inspect the mess that had been reported to Irving Thalberg. As would become typical of MGM, a lavish farewell party was thrown at the Ambassadors for the Mayers, who were also given a warm send-off at the railway station.

Seventeen-year-old daughter Irene said her excitement soared, but was soon subdued by her father who forbade her to make friends with boys her own age. She and Edie had been raised as young ladies who did not wear nail polish or elaborate dresses. They were, after all, part of the MGM image and should act accordingly. In Paris each girl was allowed to buy one gown. 'I don't want any embarrassment going through customs,' Mayer stressed. 'Can you imagine the headlines?'

It was decided that production of *Ben Hur* should cease in Italy and begin again in Hollywood with Thalberg in charge. Mayer had worked hard in Rome and was eager to get home, but he wanted to discuss business with Swedish director Mauritz Stiller, who was shooting a picture in Germany. When Mayer viewed the film, he was in awe of the leading lady, Greta Garbo. He told his daughter, 'I want Stiller all right, but I'm more interested in the girl.' After Irene caught a glimpse of her leaving an elevator and thought she was drab and overweight, Mayer told Garbo, 'You know, Americans don't like fat women.'

But, since Stiller said he would not sign a contract with MGM unless he could take along his protégée, Mayer put on an effective act. He'd have to think about that, he said, but he signed her up for $100 a week. The legend of Garbo's discovery has been recounted, disputed, retold and disputed again. Was Mayer more interested in her or in Stiller? The answer to that is both. He went after the director but discovered a star. Mayer was, after all, a maker of stars, and the plump Garbo, even in dowdy dress and taffeta hat, possessed star material underneath it all.

Under the supervision of Irving Thalberg, *Ben Hur* went into production. Ignoring doctor's orders, Thalberg overtaxed his strength. He paced back and forth in the middle of the Circus Maximus, shouting orders as he strove for perfection. *Ben Hur* was MGM's first major success thanks to Thalberg – even though he suffered a heart attack during production. Devastated, Mayer broke down in tears. He went into his office to wait, with the door closed, for that fateful phone call. Doctors were not optimistic, but Thalberg rallied. When his mother Henrietta called Mayer, he wept. 'Thank God,' he told her. 'Tell him to forget about work. He should get a lot of rest.'

'Louie,' she responded, 'Irving wants to view the *Ben Hur* rushes.'

'He's not strong enough to do that. I won't permit it.'

'He can see them on the ceiling of his bedroom, Louie. Please send them over. If it weren't for work, he'd die.'

Mayer told his daughters how amazing Thalberg was, but how he worried about his health and how much he admired Henrietta. 'She is a godsend,' he said. 'When he was so ill as a teenager, she got him out of bed because she refused to believe he would be an invalid. She is better than all the doctors in the world.'

Irving was involved with Rosabelle Laemmle at this time, but when he met the flighty actress Constance Talmadge he fell deeply in love. Henrietta told Mayer her son would die before his thirtieth birthday if he continued the affair. 'I don't want him to get married,' she said.

'He's been dating several girls,' Mayer explained. 'One of them is under contract to us.'

'Norma Shearer.'

'Yes. She's a hard worker. A very nice girl. She's dating others, but I think she's set her sights on Irving.'

'That's the problem, Louie. They want him because he has power.'

'Constance doesn't need him, Henrietta. She's a star in her own right.'

'I'm very concerned about her hold on Irving. He parked in front of her house all night until she came home with Billy Haines and his boyfriend.'

Mayer laughed. 'They're homosexuals, Henrietta.'

'That's why I'm worried, Louie. Irving was relieved . . . in fact, happy that she had spent the evening with them.'

'I'll keep an eye on him, my dear. I have spies everywhere.'

Norma Shearer was a determined woman. Thalberg put her down and continued to do so after she signed a contract. She complained to him constantly. Annoyed and too busy for such nonsense, he referred her to Mayer.

'*Pleasure Mad* is a fine film,' he told her. 'And we gave you one of our best directors.'

'Reginald Barker is a beast!' Norma exclaimed.

'He tells me you're not a professional.'

'How can I be? He yells at me. You have no idea how frightening that can be.'

He turned on her and yelled, 'You're a fool! And you're a coward. How can you allow a director to ruin your career? Maybe Barker is right. You're not a professional and probably don't deserve to be in the film!'

Nobody had told Norma that Mayer was a remarkable actor. She began to cry, but suddenly jumped out of her chair and exclaimed, 'I'll show you!'

And she did. Thalberg told his secretary, 'I think Miss Shearer can take care of herself.'

Eventually he asked her to a premiere or two, followed by dinner and dancing at the Coconut Grove. And, when Irving finally realised he could never have Constance Talmadge, he proposed to Norma, much to Mayer's delight. The mogul rushed home that night to tell his family, 'Irving's going to marry her! Henrietta's accepted the situation.'

In 1926 Mayer built a Mediterranean-Spanish house with a red tiled roof on the beach in Santa Monica. It cost $28,000, and there were four bedrooms and, incredibly, thirteen marble bathrooms. The house and pool were built on thirty-foot pilings to protect the property from harsh weather. Mayer's household staff consisted of three servants, a chauffeur and a handyman. His neighbours included Samuel Goldwyn, Jesse Lansky and eventually Irving Thalberg and Norma Shearer, who were married on 29 September 1928. Mayer was best man and his daughters were bridesmaids.

By now Greta Garbo had arrived in Hollywood, becoming an instant star in *The Temptress*. Stiller, however, failed as a director at MGM, and would eventually return to Sweden. When Garbo and John Gilbert appeared in *Flesh and the Devil* they became lovers, on and off the screen. Garbo soon moved in with Gilbert, and though Mayer was usually opposed to his stars having love affairs, he allowed the studio to publicise this highly charged romance. As a result, *Flesh and the Devil* was a box-office smash. According to writer Anita Loos, Garbo was using Gilbert: 'She was no different from any other actress who spread her legs to get ahead.' Over the years Greta would change her story about the affair with Gilbert. He was her greatest love, she said. He was only a friend, she insisted. Garbo was bisexual so her personal life was a tangle of both men and women.

Gilbert's movie career came to a halt after his first sound picture, *His Glorious Night*. His high-pitched voice did not match his tall, dark, virile, handsome image. Moviegoers laughed and Gilbert was finished. It was suggested that the bass on the sound equipment had not been turned up. Was Mayer behind this? Gilbert had, after all, gone over his head to Nicholas Schenck who signed him to a million-dollar contract. Thalberg tried to help Gilbert by putting him in a gangster film, *Gentleman's Fate*. Reviews were mixed, but Gilbert's fans had turned away from him by now, his image tarnished.

And the way that his second marriage to actress Leatrice Joy ended after their daughter was born outraged Mayer. How could a man leave his wife and baby? Thalberg insisted that, on the contrary, Leatrice had left Gilbert in the ninth month of her pregnancy and had afterwards refused to allow him to see the baby. West coast publicity chief Howard Strickling said,

> Mayer and Gilbert clashed from the start. They hated each other. Jack was one of the nicest guys in Hollywood. Everyone liked him. But he made mistakes and each time he did, Mayer pounced and made it worse. Garbo requested him for *Queen Christina* and Mayer refused. When she threatened to quit, he changed his mind. Jack was wonderful in the film, but, once again, reviews criticised him. Garbo got all the attention because she'd been off the screen for a year. When Jack was ignored he realised he was through at MGM. But he was under contract and couldn't make a film for any other studio. He put an ad in the *Hollywood Reporter* about MGM refusing to release him so they did, but there were no offers. After his third marriage to Virginia Bruce ended he turned to the bottle and drank himself to death.

Thalberg and Mayer's daughter Irene attended the funeral. Mayer himself did not.

MGM was not the first studio to release a talkie. Warner Brothers had beaten them with *The Jazz Singer*, in which Al Jolson had a few lines of dialogue and sang two songs. After Nicholas Schenck demanded Mayer convert the studio to sound, moviegoers heard Leo the Lion roar for the first time introducing *The Broadway Melody* with Bessie Love and Anita Page.

Mayer was one of the founders of the Academy of Motion Picture Arts and Sciences. The first award ceremony was held on 17 May 1929, in the Blossom Room of the Hollywood Roosevelt Hotel, built by a syndicate that included Mayer, Douglas Fairbanks, Mary Pickford, Joseph Schenck, and Marcus Loew. *The Broadway Melody* won an Oscar for Best Picture, and Mayer accepted the award on 30 April 1930 at the Coconut Grove. It would be the first of many Oscars earned by MGM.

Mayer was on hand for the award the night after his daughter Irene married producer David O. Selznick. It had been a hectic few months for Mayer: his other daughter, Edie, had married producer William Goetz in a lavish affair at the Biltmore Hotel on 19 March. The groom was head of production at 20th Century-Fox and later at Universal Studios. As an independent producer he was the first to pay film stars a percentage of profits in lieu of salary.

Now Irene, engaged to Selznick, was anxious to get married. They decided to have a meeting with her father at MGM.

'I think you should wait,' Mayer said.

'How much can a man take?' Selznick asked.

'Referring to the fact that my daughter is a virgin and you're a cocksman?'

Irene defended her fiancé. 'After all, Dad, David has been a gentleman through it all. We've been going out for a few years.'

'He hasn't waited for you.'

'I don't want to hear it,' Irene exclaimed. 'I don't believe it.'

'Your sister just got married. I can't expect the same guests to go out and spend lavishly on gifts. It's not fair. Also, take into consideration that your grandfather Mayer died on the eighteenth of this month. Have some respect.'

Selznick was losing his temper. 'I've arranged with Paramount for a vacation on the twenty-ninth. Do you want to disrupt their schedule?'

'You've made travel plans?' Mayer hissed. 'Without consulting me?'

'We thought you'd have no objection,' Irene said.

'Your mother and I were married on June fourteenth. I think it would be a sentimental idea for us to share our anniversaries.'

'I want my own anniversary!' Selznick barked with a reddened face.

'And I'd like some time with my daughter before she leaves home. I'd also like to know you better.'

'You've had plenty of time for that, Mr. Mayer. I see no reason to wait.'

'You should learn to control your sexual urges, David. Have some dignity. Prove you're a gentleman who loves a woman for what she is, not for what you can get from her in the bedroom.'

'I've had enough of you, Mr. Mayer!' David yelled, pounding his fist on the desk. 'Are you coming, Irene?'

'I'll stay for a bit,' she said.

Selznick stormed out of the office and slammed the door. Mayer ignored it and told Irene she should teach him better manners. 'If you can't handle him now, you never will.'

'You have brought me up to be honest and loyal. I've promised to be his wife and I'll belong to him. I can't fly two flags.'

Mayer felt the sting of Irene's remark. She was his favourite. They had been closer than most daughters and fathers. He confided in her, talked business with her, turned to her for consolation. Now he felt betrayed. Irene turned to her mother, who settled the matter. She would be married at the beach house on 29 April. Mayer let it be known that the wedding would be a smaller event due to the fact that her grandfather had died recently. It was a white-tie affair, nonetheless, that began at 8:30 p.m. Irene wore a magnificent white satin empire gown. She was so upset over the disturbing argument with her father that she pleaded with him to forgive her as they walked arm in arm to the altar of white roses. When they approached the rabbi, Mayer told her to 'hush.' Irene was not a blushing bride.

David Selznick was born in Pittsburgh on 10 December 1902. His father, Lewis, was a successful film distributor and producer whose beginnings had been similar to Mayer's. David worked for his father and was hired by MGM in 1926 as a script reader, working his way up to become head of the scenario department. During production of *White Shadows in the South Seas*, he argued with Thalberg over who would direct the film and was dismissed.

Irene was already seeing Selznick at the time, but was in New York on vacation. Mayer asked if she'd heard from her beau. When she said, 'No,' he smiled and exclaimed, 'That's right. He's left the studio. We kicked him out. I don't think you'll be hearing from him.' Irene read in *Variety* that David had moved to Paramount as a production supervisor.

He was involved with other women, including actress Jean Arthur (whom he referred to as 'lost ecstasy'), Joan Crawford, Carole Lombard and assorted hookers. Selznick had an enormous sexual appetite which he sought to satisfy before and after marriage. Aware of his dalliances, Irene confronted him more than once. On one occasion he had actress Loretta Young pinned up against the wall in his office when Irene walked in and told her, 'Oh, honey, give him a kiss. It's not going to hurt you.'

Mayer had been faithful to his wife Margaret since their marriage, but now she was in ill health and behaving irrationally. Always the righteous one, he had to be careful not to betray either his daughters or his MGM family, who believed he was above adultery. Mayer had a brief affair with P.B. Schulberg's wife, Adeline, who was in her late thirties. The romance faded out on its own.

Then he met former Ziegfeld girl, Jean Howard, who was younger than his daughters. He fell hopelessly in love. He signed her to an MGM contract and wooed her with expensive jewellery. She was unaware of his feelings, but enjoyed his company on their nights out. In public, they made sure they were seen in the company of friends to avoid rumours, but rumours were rife anyway. Planning a trip to Europe with Margaret, he bought Jean and a female friend steamship tickets to Paris and was at the pier to meet them. On the ride to the hotel he told Jean that Margaret had agreed to a divorce so they could be married. Jean was shocked. He offered her $5 million if she would accept his proposal.

At the George V hotel in Paris, though, Mayer received a detective's report that Jean was involved with Hollywood agent Charles Feldman. As Jean recalled, 'I was in love with Charles Feldman and planned to marry him. Before I could tell Mayer, he found out from a detective agency. When I went to his room he was white and shaking. He drank down a glass of scotch and stormed around the room. Then he started to jump out the window. We all held him down on the floor. He moaned and wept. It was terrible.' Howard Strickling and Jean managed to grab Mayer just in time, and he was sedated. Jean Howard returned to Hollywood and later married Charles Feldman.

Margaret had a hysterectomy, after which she was never the same. Traumatised from the operation and under doctor's orders not to have sex, she had a nervous collapse and was put in a sanitarium. Though theirs had been a marriage in name only for several years, Mayer was lonely without her. Margaret would come home now and then, but she was delirious and unpredictable.

Louis concentrated on running Metro-Goldwyn-Mayer, now the biggest and most prestigious movie studio in the world thanks to such films as Garbo's first talkie, *Anna Christie*, Harry Carey's *Trader Horn*, Gable and Shearer in *A Free Soul* and *Grand Hotel* with Joan Crawford, Greta Garbo, John and Lionel Barrymore, and Wallace Beery.

When Irving Thalberg suffered his second heart attack at the end of 1932, after the studio's Christmas party, Mayer called David Selznick to head up his own production unit at MGM. Irene was adamant that he should not accept her father's offer, but David reminded her they had only $6000 in the bank and Mayer was willing to pay him $4000 a week. Irene thought he should not – and she emphasised *not*, absolutely.

Despite the birth of a son, Jeffery, on 4 August 1932, they separated often. David's gambling debts were outrageous and his silly affairs with women were well known. Irene knew that her husband was not thinking clearly. His father's death in January had nearly destroyed him, which was apparent when David collapsed at the funeral. But the couple were reconciled, living in the Beverly Wilshire Hotel until they could afford to build a house.

On 14 February 1933, Selznick signed a contract with MGM that called for a minimum of six films in two years. Mayer claimed, 'I hired David to spare Irving,' but it didn't appear that way to Hollywood insiders – nor to Irving, who was in Europe when it happened. Unfortunately, he had to read it in *Variety*, which made it appear that he had been replaced. It was an embarrassment, heartbreaking to the 'Boy Genius'. Yet, in truth, Mayer was indeed sparing Irving, not replacing him.

On 10 March, Los Angeles was hit by an earthquake. Buildings shook, some collapsed and 54 people were killed. Irene wrapped her baby in a blanket and walked down ten flights to the street. Trying to gather her thoughts, she saw a limousine approaching. Mayer opened the door. 'Hurry up and get in,' he said.

For Irene, the earthquake was only one more nerve-racking incident in her life. David was unhappy at MGM. She was right, he confessed. He was surrounded by Thalberg supporters who resented David's intrusion. Irene said, 'It was your decision, so get on with it!' Moving into her own home eased the stress for Irene. She tried to separate herself from Mayer who, like David, insisted on confiding in her about business. As she had said previously, 'I cannot fly two flags.'

Thalberg returned from Europe in August and met, in New York, with Nicholas Schenck, who informed him that Selznick was not his replacement. The two men would have separate production units, relieving Irving of a heavy workload so that he might concentrate on Norma's films. He would now report to Schenck, not to Mayer.

There was no animosity between Thalberg and Selznick – each admired the other's achievements – but David wanted to prove he was as good as Irving, or better. He produced *Dinner at Eight* with Jean Harlow, Wallace Beery and the Barrymore brothers, *Viva Villa!*, *David Copperfield* and *Dancing Lady*. Schenck was full of praise for David and told him, 'I hope you can take over Mayer's job.' But in 1935 he began to criticise Selznick's work. His films were over budget and were not making money.

In the spring of 1935, David resigned from MGM. 'I'm forming my own production company,' he told Thalberg.

'I'm planning to do the same in a few years,' Irving said. 'Do you have enough money?'

'No.'

'I'd be willing to invest $200,000 for stock in your company. I'll put it in Norma's name so no one will know.'

Mayer was furious with David and swore to get even. Yet in the end he gave in to sentiment. After all, Selznick was his son-in-law, and that was family. So Louis eventually agreed to invest in Selznick International Pictures. Mayer had a habit of blowing his stack at someone, then cooling off and showing sincere warmth to his victim.

On 18 May 1936 Irene gave birth to another son, Daniel. Mayer was an unusual Jewish father because he had always wanted daughters. Often he moaned about not having a son, but in truth he was more than satisfied. His daughter Edie was not close to him; they eventually quarrelled bitterly over a trivial matter that nonetheless caused him to omit her from his will. He and Irene, though, were very much alike. She thought like a man, he said. She had his spunk and determination and was not interested in 'going Hollywood'. Edie, in contrast, wanted only the best.

In May 1936, Margaret Mitchell's novel, *Gone With the Wind*, was a best seller. Everyone in Hollywood had a copy, so it was just a matter of time before it was made into a movie. When Mayer spoke to Thalberg about the book, he supposedly replied, 'Forget it. No Civil War movie ever made a cent.' Selznick, however, was interested. He approached Warner Brothers about distribution of the film, but his financial backers wanted the best of the best – MGM.

Mayer, of course, held all the aces. He had Clark Gable under contract and moviegoers would accept no one else as Rhett Butler. Selznick was willing to sign Ronald Colman at Warner Brothers in the role, but Schenck stepped in and convinced Selznick's backers to sign with Mayer instead. MGM had secured both the distribution rights and ownership of *Gone With the Wind*.

In fact, Clark Gable did not want to play Rhett Butler. In all his previous films the girl had been in love with him, while, Scarlett, the heroine of Mitchell's book, wasn't, and he felt this might tarnish his macho image. And Gable was anti-Semitic. He detested Mayer and resented having to work for another Jewish producer, David O. Selznick. But he had no choice.

Mayer had suffered a blow when Irving Thalberg died suddenly on 14 September 1936. The young producer had caught cold and was too ill to attend MGM's annual picnic, so Louis left the picnic early in order to pay a visit to Irving. Before leaving, he talked with Norma and expressed his deep concern. He loved Irving, despite their differences and the frequent violent quarrels they had had of late. Louis confessed his deep hurt over Irving's desire to leave MGM and set up his own production company. The studio would not be the same, Mayer told Norma, but he would accept Irving's decision. He went home in a deep state of depression.

Mayer kept in close touch with Norma but was not at Thalberg's bedside when he died. He helped Norma with the funeral arrangements, closing down MGM on the day of the funeral. He attended the services, but was not invited to the interment at Forest Lawn in Glendale, an indication of Norma's feelings for him. And, when she attempted to obtain Irving's MGM stock, Mayer balked. While their lawyers were negotiating, Norma had begun *Marie Antoinette*. Halfway through she called in sick and was not available to work. Only when Mayer agreed to give her the MGM stock did she resume filming.

One of Louis's favourite contract players was soprano Jeanette MacDonald. He had been obsessed with her when she was at Paramount Studios, trying but failing to lure her to MGM. So he promised her the moon and the stars and, when she signed her contract, Jeanette sat on his lap. Precisely when the affair began isn't known, but she did not resist his first advances. He held the key to the vault of spectacular MGM musicals, made possible by the finest directors, technicians and musicians in the world. He promised to make her a star. When he succeeded, their intimacy ended, though he would still take control of her personal life.

Jeanette was one of the few women he seduced. Mayer was above such behaviour in his personal relationships. With very few exceptions he fell in love with madonnas, not whores. Mayer's ideal woman was actress Greer Garson, whom he discovered on the London stage. When he invited her for dinner, she brought her mother and stole Louis's heart.

There were rumours that he had forced Jean Harlow to submit, but they were untrue. In fact Thalberg put her under contract despite Mayer's objections, after which she made millions for MGM.

Harlow's untimely death at the age of 26 was a shock to everyone. Here again, over the years much has been written about the subject. It has been claimed that her mother, a Christian Scientist, refused to allow doctors to see Jean. This is not true – a doctor and nurse were in attendance. But, while her mother thought Harlow was 'drying out' from a severe case of alcoholism and did not want it made public, in fact Harlow was afflicted with kidney disease secondary to the scarlet fever she'd had as a teenager.

Jean's mother did decline Mayer's offer of his personal physician, refusing to let him see her. He told publicity chief Howard Strickling, 'The next time one of our stars gets sick, the studio's got to find out what's the matter.' Mayer attended the funeral, having sent a heart of red roses five feet tall and pierced by a golden arrow.

Jean had died leaving her last movie, *Saratoga*, unfinished. Many thought Mayer's idea of completing the film for release using a double was ghoulish. But fans did not agree. They wanted to see Harlow one last time.

In the late thirties, Mayer met Hedy Lamarr in England. She had gained a name for herself running about nude in *Ecstasy*, a film made in Germany. Her rich husband had tried to buy up all the copies, but failed. She escaped Austria by posing as her maid and used her jewels to obtain a divorce.

'We don't make movies like *Ecstasy*,' Mayer told her. 'Our ladies take off their clothes only for their husbands. They don't have orgasms on the screen.'

'Mr. Mayer, I had no idea the cameras were rolling.'

'They usually do if you're making a movie.'

'You think I'm vulgar?' she asked.

'We make family pictures. Clean and wholesome. If you're interested, I can sign you to a contract for $125 a week.'

'No, thank you.'

The next day Hedy changed her mind and boarded the *Normandie* for New York. Knowing Mayer was on the ship, she paraded around in beautiful gowns with every handsome man on board.

'Five hundred dollars a week,' he said.

'For now,' Hedy responded.

She was breathtaking in *Ziegfeld Girl* but she goes down in Hollywood history with her performance of 'I Am Tondelayo' in *White Cargo*. After a series of bad films she asked Mayer to be released from her contract. Though Hedy appeared not to have a brain in her head, it became known that she and a friend had invented 'spread spectrum', the basis for the cellular phone and other wireless communications, including the internet. Hedy was acclaimed only late in life, and she died a very wealthy woman after years of struggling. Was that really our beautiful Hedy who was once arrested for stuffing Ex-Lax and make-up into her purse without paying? Yes, it was, but she had the last laugh. Hedy was worth $3 million when she died.

David Selznick now began the search for his Scarlett O'Hara. Every actress in Hollywood began speaking with a Southern accent and pressed their agents for a screen test. Among those who tried out for the role were Tallulah Bankhead, Susan Hayward, and Lana Turner. Katharine Hepburn wanted the part of Scarlett very much but would not lower herself to do a screen test.

Religious groups were known to picket theatres and even shut them down, so Selznick had to make sure there was no scandal connected with *Gone With the Wind*. Paulette Goddard was originally the forerunner in the race to get the part, but was unable to prove she was married to Charles Chaplin.

The night Selznick began filming with the burning of Atlanta on MGM's back lot, his agent brother, Myron, showed up with a British actress. 'David, meet Scarlett,' he said. Selznick took one look at Vivien Leigh and knew his search was over. But Selznick was still mindful of the need to avoid scandal. She was given the part, but was not to be seen publicly in the company of the married Olivier.

Clark Gable, meanwhile, was desperately trying to divorce his second wife so he could marry the zany actress Carole Lombard. Mayer negotiated with Ria Gable, loaned Clark the divorce settlement, and got his wife to Reno, while Gable and Lombard eloped during a break in filming.

Gable might have been more cooperative playing Rhett – but he found fault with his wardrobe, the shooting schedule, speaking with a Southern accent, and with director George Cukor. In the end Gable got everything he wanted – Cukor was out and Clark's buddy, director Victor Fleming, was in. Selznick, on the other hand, claimed Gable had not complained – that it was Cukor's adaptation of the script that caused friction. In any case, David paid $5000 to use the word 'damn' in the famous final scene when Rhett leaves Scarlett.

During production Selznick relied heavily on Benzedrine to keep him awake for the long hours necessary. According to Irene, the drug gave him feelings of superiority. David thought he was indestructible, she said. *Gone With the Wind* premiered in Atlanta on 15 December 1939. The rest is history.

Almost as exciting were the Academy Awards. The Selznicks entertained the leading players at their home before leaving for the Coconut Grove. There was only one problem – David forgot to take Irene. He jumped into a car with Clark and Vivien and sped away. Arriving at different times, they sat at separate tables while puzzled Hollywood insiders tried not to notice. David accepted his Oscar for Best Picture and also won the Irving Thalberg Award for 'most consistent high quality of production'. When they arrived home she asked tearfully, 'How could you?' Selznick responded that he'd never forgive himself. In later years, Irene said she had only pity for him. It's interesting, however, that no one else commented on this 'separation' at the Oscars. Surely it was bait for gossip columnists. Some sources even claim that Irene and David arrived at the Coconut Grove together, but Irene writes in her memoirs about David's abandoning her and how unhappy she was that they did not celebrate his victories together.

When Irene became pregnant, David suggested an abortion and she obliged. Did Mayer know? Though Irene usually told him everything, it seems unlikely that she admitted to depriving him of a third grandchild. But Mayer was all too aware that his daughter's marriage was in trouble. He knew that David was chasing after several actresses, including Joan Fontaine, though she denied any intimacy with him. Louis and Irene discussed Selznick's indiscretions, and schemed to take *Gone With the Wind* away from him if he went to Warner Brothers with it. But that battle was won before it began.

Ironically, Louis and Irene went through their divorces at the same time, and his remarriage coincided with David's.

Mayer had little time for an active social life. He was an excellent dancer, however, and enjoyed nightclubbing with or without a date. At his home he often entertained his teenage contract players at pool parties on Sundays. He enjoyed these 'command performances', though they did not. This is only one example of how Mayer tried to keep his MGM family together.

But, like most families, he had to deal with black sheep. Spencer Tracy, for example, was an alcoholic, who disappeared for weeks and often destroyed movie sets in a drunken rage. But he also won Oscars; when told Tracy was a bastard Mayer replied, 'Yes, but he's our bastard.' In 1942 Katharine Hepburn sold *Woman of the Year* to Mayer. Requesting Spencer Tracy to co-star, she proceeded to fall in love with him. Since he was married, their affair, well known in Hollywood, was never revealed by the press. But Mayer sanctioned it because he knew Hepburn could tame Tracy. And she did, often going from bar to bar to find him and sober him up.

Louis did not have such good luck with Judy Garland, who had become a major star in *The Wizard of Oz*. Overweight, she was allowed only Mama Mayer's chicken soup in the commissary while the other teenagers feasted on hamburgers and hot dogs at a nearby table. In show business since she was a child, Judy was given uppers and downers by her mother to help her keep up with a gruelling schedule, and MGM doctors were given permission to do the same. Judy was teamed with Mickey Rooney in the *Andy Hardy* movies and together they made musicals that were smash hits.

In an attempt to get away from her domineering mother, Judy eloped with composer David Rose, recently divorced from comedienne Martha Raye, and a decade older than Judy. She called Mayer for permission to go on a honeymoon. He refused, telling her to get back on the set of her current film, *Babes on Broadway*. She became pregnant, but Mayer felt motherhood would be bad for her youthful image so she had an abortion and was divorced. When she fell in love with the handsome actor Tyrone Power, Mayer stepped in once again. MGM often assigned studio publicists to 'look after' their stars and report back to Mayer. So it was with Betty Asher, who became Judy's confidante. Among other things, Asher apparently filled Garland's head with lies about Power sharing one of her love letters with his friends.

Though Judy was one of the most talented stars in Hollywood, she felt inferior to luscious Lana Turner and Hedy Lamarr. Wanting to be cast in more adult roles, she was upset over *Meet Me in St Louis* and challenged director Vincente Minnelli. But she changed her mind when she saw the rushes; he had succeeded in making her look beautiful on screen. Judy decided he was her saviour and, within a few months, they were living together. Mayer soon sanctioned their marriage. Minnelli was a homosexual, but that didn't make any difference in a town as bisexual as Hollywood. Mayer's wedding present to the Minnellis was a three-month honeymoon in New York. But when Judy found Vincente in bed with a man, she attempted suicide.

From then on it was downhill all the way. Addicted to a variety of drugs, she reported late for work if she showed up at all. After MGM suspended her in 1949 Judy admitted, 'I've been a bad girl.' But Mayer still sympathised with her and tried to convince the studio to loan her the money to pay for her stay at a Boston hospital. The request was rejected at first, so Mayer promised to pay Judy's hospital bills out of his own pocket. By the following year her tardiness was costing too much money and MGM fired her. She again attempted suicide. Her career was a seesaw from then on: the highs were very high, and the lows were the lowest. She died of an accidental overdose of sleeping pills in June 1969. In the course of Garland's decline at MGM Mayer commented, 'It's a shame Judy had to grow up.'

Elizabeth Taylor also had a stage mother, Sara. According to actor Peter Lawford, Sara was attracted to Mayer. When she complained about a film scheduled for her daughter, Mayer informed her that he made the decisions at MGM and his stars did what they were told. But Elizabeth stood up to her boss. 'Don't you ever talk to my mother like that!' she cried. 'You and your studio can go to hell!' She ran out of his office and never set foot in it again during her eighteen years at MGM.

There were rumours that Mayer was having an affair with Sara, but MGM press agent George Nichols doubted it. 'That would have given her power and that was something Mayer did not want.'

When Elizabeth married hotel heir Nicky Hilton in 1950, MGM orchestrated and paid for the wedding, but the marriage ended after less than a year. She fought to get out of making her last film for MGM, *Butterfield Eight*, and threatened to cause trouble. Elizabeth did manage to get her husband Eddie Fisher a role in the movie, and after she had suffered a near-fatal bout of pneumonia during the making of the film, in the end it earned her an Oscar.

*

To his dismay, Mayer lost three of his top box-office actresses in the early forties. Greta Garbo left after making the awful *Two Faced Woman* in 1941, and Norma Shearer did likewise following the forgettable *Cardboard Lover* in 1942. Then Joan Crawford asked to be released from her MGM contract in 1943 because her films were so poor. Mayer had tears in his eyes when he let Joan go; she had been the first star 'manufactured' by Metro-Goldwyn-Mayer. Mayer saw in Crawford a workhorse, a go-getter, a hustler and a beautiful tramp. 'As long as she doesn't get laid on Sunset I don't care,' he told one of his spies.

The minion jotted down 'sunset' and the word got around. Joan wanted to know, 'Did he mean on Sunset or at sunset?'

Mayer did not want his Andy Hardy, as portrayed by Mickey Rooney, to marry his new starlet, Ava Gardner. He suspected she was a virgin and intended to stay that way until she became a bride. 'Mickey just wants to get into her pants,' Mayer told Howard Strickling. 'He doesn't have to marry her to do that.'

'She wouldn't go to bed with Mickey if you threatened to cancel her contract.'

So Mayer suggested a quiet wedding. He did not want to flaunt the fact that Andy Hardy was old enough to get married. Mickey's MGM publicity agent went along on the couple's honeymoon to keep reporters away and control any fans who might mob Mickey. Ava commented, 'I saw more of Les than I did of my husband.'

When Ava and Mickey were divorced, Mayer promised her that if she did not ask for the half of Rooney's earnings that she was entitled to, he would in return put her in better films. He also sided with Ava during her affair with Frank Sinatra, who was unable to get a divorce from Nancy Barbato. Mayer might have called her a whore, but he cancelled Sinatra's MGM contract. 'With L.B., I always knew where I stood,' Ava said.

In 1943 Louis B. Mayer was the highest-paid executive in the United States at $900,000 a year. Even his enemies admitted he earned it. Indeed, he was a clever businessman and a manipulator. What he never understood was women. When Margaret suffered a nervous breakdown she was put into Riggs Sanitarium in Stockbridge, Massachusetts. Only Irene knew that her parents were separated.

Louis thought that if money could buy a star, it could also buy a wife. He fell in love with Ginny Simms, who had become famous as a singer with Kay Kyser's band in 1938. Born in San Antonio, Texas, on 13 May 1913, Ginny was a tall, beautiful brunette. She and Kyser had fallen in love but never married, and in 1941, Ginny broke her ties with him and got her own radio show, also appearing in minor films. Mayer made an effort to make her an MGM star in *Broadway Rhythm*, in 1944, with George Murphy and Gloria De Haven. Mayer promised Ginny $1 million if she'd marry him. Wealthy in her own right and insulted by his offer of money, she turned him down.

Mayer mourned his break-up with Ginny until he was introduced to dancer Ann Miller. Born Lucille Ann Collier on 12 April 1923 in Houston, Texas, her father was a criminal lawyer who defended Baby Face Nelson and Bonnie and Clyde. Fed up with her husband's infidelities, Ann's mother obtained a divorce and moved to California where Ann began her career as a dancer in nightclubs. In 1937 she was discovered by Lucille Ball and an RKO casting director. Only fourteen years old, she was tall for her age at five feet seven with long, shapely legs. Ann lied about her age and got away with it. An accomplished tap dancer, she was not only very talented, but beautiful as well. Mayer took her dining and dancing with her mother and fell in love again.

Ann found him most attractive and fascinating. Her mother, Clara, enjoyed his company, too, and often cooked dinner for him. Living in a rented house now, Louis found these invitations a blessing. Ann fell in love with him and might have considered his marriage proposal if she could have continued with her promising career, but the old-fashioned Mayer wanted a housewife and hostess. Hollywood insiders, however, thought they would work out their problems and marry eventually. Mayer had yet to file for divorce due to Margaret's precarious mental state, though it wasn't a question of if, rather when he would be a free man.

Mayer tried to buy out Ann's contract from Harry Cohn, head of Columbia Pictures. His repeated begging and pleading convinced Cohn to make Ann a big star in a lavish musical so that Mayer would have to pay a hefty price for her contract. Buying and trading stars was routine in Hollywood, but Ann felt her worth was based on her relationship with Mayer and not her talent. Fed up, she decided to marry a former boyfriend, Reese Llewellen Milner, the heir to an iron works fortune. When Ann told Mayer of her decision, he took an overdose of sleeping pills and was close to death when a servant found him. Ann rushed to his side and saw him through the crisis.

On 6 February 1946 she married Milner, but he turned out to be a wife beater. When she became pregnant, one of their fights was so violent that she fell down a flight of stairs. Her spine was severely injured and she lost her baby. Ann filed for divorce from her hospital bed. Once she recovered Harry Cohn refused to take her back so Ann humbled herself, approached Mayer and was signed to an MGM contract.

Who can forget Ann Miller dancing five hundred taps a minute in *Easter Parade, On the Town,* and *Kiss Me, Kate?* After several failed marriages, Ann appeared with Mickey Rooney on Broadway in the smash musical *Sugar Babies.* She said, 'At last I am a star and not second banana.' Ann died of cancer in January 2004 at the age of 81.

In 1948 Margaret divorced Louis and received a $3 million settlement. As did Irene Mayer Selznick – David's longtime affair with actress Jennifer Jones was the last straw for Irene. Yet Selznick would continue to consult her and lean on her until his death in 1965. He and Mayer also remained close.

Louis was involved with a perky brunette, forty-year-old Lorena Danker. A former Busby Berkeley showgirl who had appeared in several films, she was now a widow with a young daughter, Suzanne. Irene thought Lorena was a life saver. 'She was always fun to be with. At times she treated my father like a little boy, tickling him and joking. When he was upset, she knew how to calm him down – make him feel better. Lorena was a very good dancer as was my father. It was fun watching them together.'

And she came along at the right time for Mayer, who was having difficulty at the studio. MGM's profits were down and they were no longer winning Oscars. Nicholas Schenck persuaded 43-year-old Dore Schary away from RKO, making him associate vice-president in charge of production at MGM on 1 July 1948. Mayer, a conservative Republican, and Schary, a liberal Democrat, were at odds from the beginning, but not only politically. In the post-war years, the public wanted realism and Schary was the man to satisfy them with pictures like *Battleground, The Red Badge of Courage* and *The Asphalt Jungle.* Mayer preferred make-believe – the fairy-tale world of escapism where people could forget their problems. Forget the war. Enjoy peace and love and family traditions. He tried to turn back the clock.

But the golden years of the powerful moguls were coming to an end. Soon the government would force the studios to divest themselves of their lucrative theatre chains. Movie stars were making too much money and their contracts were not being renewed. Schary hated stars. He thought they were spoiled and overpaid, and favoured character actors who were not known simply for their looks. He was also opposed to the studio contract system, preferring to sign an actor to make only one or two pictures.

Louis married Lorena Danker on 3 December 1948, in Yuma, Arizona, five months after Selznick wed Jennifer Jones. He bought a luxurious house at 332 St. Cloud Street. Lorena hired none other than Billy Haines to decorate their home. It must have been amusing to Billy. After all, Mayer had refused to renew his contract because he was a homosexual.

On 29 March 1950, the Academy of Motion Picture Arts and Sciences gave Mayer an award for 'distinguished service to the motion picture industry'. In a brief speech he said he was most proud to receive this honour from his peers. Perhaps Hollywood insiders knew Mayer was on his way out. There were rumours he might announce his retirement that night.

In 1950 MGM's profits rose and Schary got the credit. The consensus was that Mayer had spent the past four or five years paying more attention to his race horses than to affairs at the studio. He sold his thoroughbreds, cringeing at the auction when Jack Warner bought the best of them.

It was just a matter of time before Mayer had had enough. He knew Schenck was trying to get rid of him and had hired Schary to take over the helm. After 27 years at MGM he resigned in June 1951. His contract players were shocked. Unlike the Thalberg days, there was no Schary camp. Few liked him and most feared that Mayer would take the tradition of MGM with him. It was true – he could not adjust to a new era. Andy Hardy had grown up. He didn't kiss and blush any longer, and his jalopy was long ago rusted in a junk yard. The orange blossoms that had fallen on Jeanette MacDonald and Nelson Eddy were being trampled by bobbysoxers and rock 'n' rollers. The sophistication of *The Thin Man*'s Nick and Nora Charles was passé, and Mrs. Miniver's bomb shelter was a playhouse for her grandchildren.

Mayer's own ideal family was crumbling, as well. To his horror, Edie and William Goetz hosted a fundraiser for Adlai Stevenson, who was campaigning for the Democratic presidential nomination. For Mayer this was bad enough but when the party was held at Dore Schary's house, he blew his stack. Louis screamed at Edie over the phone. She made it clear she was behind her husband's choice. Mayer threatened that whenever he saw Goetz on the street he'd turn his head away. Then he bellowed, 'On second thoughts, if I see either one of you, I'll turn my head away!' That was the last time father and daughter spoke. Without hesitation, Mayer disinherited Edie and her children.

On 19 November 1952, the Screen Producers' Guild presented its Milestone Award to Mayer in the ballroom of the Biltmore Hotel. Norma Shearer sat next to him at the speaker's table, frequently squeezing his hand as the evening progressed. Most of the MGM stars were present among the 700 guests. When Norma stood up to speak her eyes filled with tears. She referred to Mayer as 'the man who more than anyone else helped create the job of producer as he is known today'. She went on to thank him for 'the happiest days of my life, the days which brought me the very most of life'. Norma was criticised for saying that it was Mayer who gave her the most happiness without mentioning her husband, Irving Thalberg, although she did say that she met 'my Prince Charming' through Mayer. Hurt by the criticism, Norma did not attend a Hollywood function again.

On 24 May 1954, Margaret Mayer died of a heart attack. She left $2 million, her jewellery and the beach house, which was sold to actor Peter Lawford and his bride Patricia, John F. Kennedy's sister. Edie and Irene hated each other these days and fought bitterly over their mother's estate.

In 1955, Schary and Nicholas Schenck clashed over *Bad Day at Black Rock*, which was to star Spencer Tracy. Schenck was opposed to making a film that turned out to be an overwhelming success. Schary felt his days were numbered, but it was Schenck who resigned. When Joseph Vogel took over the reins, he fired Schary, and Mayer began scheming to get his studio back.

The struggle and power play that followed took its toll on him. He was 72 and tired. He yearned for Leo the Lion and reportedly said, 'I will move my bed into the studio in Culver City.' But his sentiment was considered corny by those who could have put him back in power. He was too old, they said. Defeated and exhausted, Mayer checked into the UCLA Medical Center in September 1957. His personal physician told Irene that Louis had leukaemia. It was terminal. She did not tell her father the truth, and nor did anyone else if we are to believe what she wrote in her memoirs. Lorena was with him, of course, trying to deal with the situation in her own way because Mayer relied so heavily on Irene.

Howard Strickling was one of the few allowed to see Louis, who listened to news of MGM's rapid decline. He was greatly uplifted by visits from David Selznick and Katharine Hepburn. Edie did not come, perhaps of her own accord or maybe because she was told not to. His last words were to Strickling: 'Don't let them get you down. Nothing matters . . . nothing matters.'

Louis B. Mayer went into a coma and died at 12:35 a.m. on 29 October 1957. The following day Irene received orchids and a warm letter from David:

How strange, this vacuum he has left. It is not love that has been lost, nor tenderness, nor even paternal protection. Rather it is as though we had all lived fearfully in the shadow of a magnificent forbidding Vesuvius, which has suddenly been removed . . . Yet I could stand in awe. And I can feel that the world this day is different than all the days of our lives before . . . Because I have been so shaken by your father's death. I have sought its meaning. I think I have found it. The strange finish of your father's bizarre life can have meaning if, and only if, our own life is the fulfillment of what his might and could have been, if only he had had your character.

The funeral was held at the Wilshire Boulevard Temple on 31 October. Jeanette MacDonald sang, 'Ah, Sweet Mystery of Life', and Spencer Tracy read the eulogy written by David Selznick. He was laid to rest at the Home of Peace Cemetery.

Mayer's estate was worth about $7.5 million. Most of this money was left to the Louis B. Mayer Foundation, a fund for charitable organisations. Lorena received $750,000 and their home. Irene was left $500,000, but Louis disinherited Edie and her family, because 'I have given them extremely substantial assistance during my lifetime through gifts and financial aid to William Goetz, and to the advancement of his career (as distinguished from that of my former son-in-law, David O. Selznick, who never requested nor accepted assistance from me) in the motion picture industry.' Mayer did, however, leave his stepdaughter Suzanne $500,000.

The great studio that boasted it 'had more stars than there are in the heavens' could brag no longer. By the time Mayer died, the major players had departed MGM. The only stars to last out their deferred contracts and receive pensions were Cyd Charisse and Robert Taylor. Esther Williams, the Million Dollar Mermaid, chose to leave the studio and forfeit $3 million. Ann Miller commented, 'They don't make stars like us anymore. I have the name because of the wonderful years at MGM. That was Mr. Mayer's bag, the family thing. The studio was the family and he was the daddy.'

Jimmy Stewart said, 'I don't want to sound like "give-me-the-good-old-days". But to be realistic, the big studios were an ideal way to make pictures because they were home base for people. When you were under contract, you had a chance to work at your craft all the time. But the whole thing became too expensive.' Ricardo Montalban said, 'MGM spoiled me for eight years. They didn't renew my contract, and I felt completely alone and afraid.'

Walter Pidgeon returned to MGM to make a film in 1972. 'Believe me, my homecoming was no sentimental affair,' he said. 'Everybody's gone except for a few technicians. The difference from the old days is fantastic and very sad. In the good old days each star had his own suite of rooms. After work we'd go to someone's suite – Lionel Barrymore's, Gable's, Fred Astaire's, mine – have a couple of belts, and hash over how things had gone. It was like a club.'

Van Johnson said he was so happy at MGM he didn't want to go home at night. Groucho Marx said, 'After Thalberg's death I lost interest in making movies. The fun had gone out of picture making.' Gene Kelly recalled, 'At MGM everyone was simpatico, one with another. Everyone was pitching in. It was fun. We didn't think it was work.' Robert Taylor said, 'My memories of L.B. will always be pleasant, and my days at MGM are my happiest period professionally.' June Allyson confessed, 'MGM had been mother, father, mentor and guide, my all-powerful and benevolent crutch. When I left it was like walking into space.' Howard Keel said, 'Actors are not personalities any longer.'

David O. Selznick died in 1965, William Goetz in 1969, Dore Schary in 1980, Edie Goetz in 1988, and Irene in 1990. Lorena Danker Mayer remarried, as did Jennifer Jones. In 1976 Selznick's daughter, Mary Jennifer, threw herself from the 22nd floor of a building on Wilshire Boulevard. She was 22 years old.

After MGM had gone through a series of presidents, Las Vegas financier Kirk Kerkorian gained control in 1969 by buying up 48 per cent of the stock. He auctioned off the studio's prize possessions and sold the back lot to housing developers. Kerkorian invested the profits into the MGM Grand Hotel in Las Vegas. In 1979 he described MGM as primarily a hotel company and, in 1986, the famous MGM sign and Leo the Lion were removed from the Culver City studio. Many in Hollywood blame Kerkorian for ruining Metro-Goldwyn-Mayer. Lorimar Pictures took over the lot and removed Robert Taylor's name from the main building. Finally, Sony Entertainment of Japan bought the property.

MGM was a beautiful lady who was raped repeatedly, beaten up and left to die, but her memory on film will be with us forever, thanks to a junkman from Russia.

'Of course we shall have sex. As long as we have men and women in the world, we will have sex. And I approve of it. We'll have sex in moving pictures, and I want it there. But it will be normal, real and beautiful sex – the sex that is common to the people in the audience, to me and to you. A man and woman are in love with one another. That's sex and it is beautiful. In the movies and in life.'

– Louis B. Mayer

3

John Gilbert

In August 1926 he began filming *Flesh and the Devil* with a beautiful Swedish actress making her third film in America. After a brief meeting in her dressing room they began shooting a love scene so torrid that the cameramen blushed. Director Clarence Brown remembered, 'They were doing a love scene as though no one else existed. It seemed like an intrusion to say, "Cut!"'

Their open-mouth kisses, the likes of which had never been seen before in films, barely passed the censors. The acting was superb, as was the chemistry between the leading players, who proceeded to complete their lovemaking at home. They became the most celebrated and publicised couple in the world when *Flesh and the Devil* premiered on 9 January 1927. The *Herald Tribune* wrote, 'Frankly we have never seen a seduction scene so perfectly done.'

The handsome leading man was making $10,000 a week, lived in a 'castle' on top of a hill and was the most popular male star in the world. After the death in 1926 of Rudolph Valentino, who had previously shared the Hollywood throne with him, the heir apparent had no equal.

John Gilbert was a vital heartbeat in the silent era and one of the brightest stars shining in MGM's galaxy. But we will never know the real reason he did not make the transition from silent films to talkies. Hollywood historians disagree. Was his voice too shrill? Did Louis B. Mayer hate Gilbert so much that he tampered with the sound? Or did his voice simply not match his image? What we do know is that Gilbert fell from grace and died a broken-hearted man.

His story becomes sadder and more intriguing because he and Greta Garbo were lovers, on and off the screen. She admitted that Gilbert was the love of her life, even though she jilted him at the altar more than once. But Garbo never married, because she had no desire to be tied down, either to a man or a woman. That she was bisexual is one reason Greta kept a low profile when she became famous.

One of Garbo's few public appearances was with Gilbert at a Hollywood premiere in 1926. In a rare photograph they are seen in the company of the MGM's boy genius, Irving Thalberg, and his future wife, actress Norma Shearer. Garbo used Gilbert as any other woman would use a man – to get what she wanted.

John Gilbert was born John Cecil Pringle on the morning of 10 July 1899 in Logan, Utah, about seventy miles north of Salt Lake City. His mother, Ida Adair, had a burning desire to be an actress and she studied elocution and singing. When a travelling repertory company came to Logan she joined the troupe and married the producer, John Pringle. To her dismay she became pregnant, so she went home to her father's house in Logan to give birth. Ida was so disgusted by motherhood she refused to look at her son, John, for the first 24 hours of his life. Two weeks later she took John to relatives in Wasatch Valley, hoping to leave him there, but no one was willing to take him in. So she joined her husband in Montreal, but they were divorced soon after. John, nicknamed 'Jack', would not see his father again for 26 years.

Ida Adair lived a hit-and-run life on the road, working whenever and wherever she could. Jack grew up familiar with the smell of dingy boarding houses and greasy eateries. Spending most of his time backstage, he had few friends his own age and little education. He taught himself how to read by following scripts when the players were on stage. Ida had many boyfriends, but the lack of privacy when she brought them home played on her nerves and she grew tired of her responsibilities as a mother. 'I think she hated me,' Gilbert said. 'She would hug me and then push me aside.' When he was six years old Ida left him with a seamstress and her prostitute daughter in a one-room apartment on Amsterdam Avenue in New York City. Jack slept on a mat in a corner of the room and was told to leave if a paying customer complained of his presence. 'I was only seven but I knew more about the world than many people ever discover . . . I learned the bitter lessons of life from chambermaids, drunkards, livery-stable hustlers, street women.'

Jack was reunited with his mother shortly after her marriage to a comedian named Walter Gilbert, who adopted him and paid for his education at Hitchcock Military Academy in San Rafael, California. When he found out his mother was working in San Francisco, he wrote for permission to visit her. Ida agreed and arrangements were made, but when he opened the door to her dressing room he found her drunk and dishevelled. She demanded to know what the hell he was doing there. That night he cried himself to sleep. Ida's health declined and she died of tuberculosis on 29 September 1913. 'Poor mother,' Jack recalled. 'All she ever wanted was to gloriously play New York. Nothing and no one else in her life was ever as important. She had auditioned for powerful producers such as David Belasco, but nothing ever came of it. Life condemned her to wander from one filthy dressing room to another, harried by debt and with something tearing at her . . . the desire to do great things, and the bitter knowledge that she could not do them.'

Walter Gilbert could no longer afford to send his stepson to school. He gave fourteen-year-old Jack ten dollars and put him on a train for San Francisco where the boy scrubbed floors and washed dishes in a saloon for two dollars a week and sold tyres for seven dollars a week. He moved on to Spokane, Washington, where he worked as stage manager for the Baker Stock Company.

When Jack went to see the movie *On the Night Stage* starring William S. Hart one afternoon, he was shocked to see his mother's old friend Herschel Mayall in the film. Jack figured that if Mayall could make it in the movies, he could too. He went to see his stepfather, who was working as a director in Portland, about getting into the movie business. Gilbert referred him to a friend, Walter Edwards, a director for Thomas Ince of the New York Motion Picture Corporation in Los Angeles. Jack got a job as an extra, and his first assignment involved putting on war paint and playing an Indian.

Gilbert's first real break came in William S. Hart's western classic, *Hell's Hinges*. Hart wrote about Jack in his autobiography, *My Life – East and West*: 'He [Gilbert] was one of the fifteen-dollar-a-week extras, "actor boys" we used to call them. I noticed his eagerness to please and I could see he had training. I asked who he was and recognised the name of a well-known stock actress.' Hurt was, of course, referring to Ida Adair.

Hart described Jack as being thin to the point of emaciation, but willing to do anything he was asked to do. Making *The Apostle of Vengeance*, Hart suggested Gilbert for the part of his dangerous younger brother who gets killed in the end. Jack was so nervous that his teeth rattled. 'I put my arm around the boy,' Hart said. 'I told him, "Look laddie, we've got to go through this and we're going to do it. So just lock your teeth and let's go. And just remember you're making good, that no one is going to hurt you or take the part away from you."' Thomas Ince liked Jack, though he was too skinny to be thought of as a romantic leading man. With six films behind him, however, Gilbert was listed in the credits and earning eighteen dollars a week.

Jack had his first sexual encounter with a small blonde actress, Effie Stewart. They fell in love and lived together for three months. Unfortunately Effie soon became too demanding and Jack broke up with her on the bus ride to the studio where they were making *Civilization*. Because they worked together, Effie had hopes of winning him back. But a balcony collapsed that day while she was standing on it and she was pronounced dead at Santa Monica Hospital. Jack was devastated. He hated himself for having hurt Effie just before she was killed and buried himself in hard work to forget.

In those days actors were expected to wear their own clothes except when playing costume parts. Offered the lead in *Hater of Men*, Jack was able to borrow money for a proper wardrobe and the part was his. When he reported for work on the first day, no one recognised him in a suit and tie. Almost six feet tall though weighing only 115 pounds, he was no longer the skinny, frightened, gawky kid. In a snappy suit he was a gentleman. He never forgot the effect that the right clothes could have on a man.

Gilbert made eleven films in 1917 and nine the following year, but with little success. With the First World War in progress, it was just a matter of months before Jack would be drafted, so producers did not want to take a chance on him. Financially, he was in a bad way and was forced to move from his ocean-front rooming house to cheaper accommodation. In August 1918 Gilbert received his draft notice. He was to leave for Kelly Field in Texas within ten days. Down on his luck, he assumed that death awaited him on the battlefield and prepared for the end. He told this to Olivia Burwell, a young Southern girl he was dating.

'I don't think it matters to anyone if I live or die,' he said.

'I care,' she whispered in return.

Three days later, on 26 August, they were married. If nothing else, Jack had someone to love and to wait for him. A week later he received word that all troop movements had been cancelled due to the Spanish influenza that would eventually kill twenty million people – in fact it would kill more Americans than the Germans. All inductions came to a halt until 11 November, the day the Armistice was signed. When Gilbert reported for duty he was given a uniform and his discharge papers at the same time. But, because of the influenza epidemic, the studios had shut down as well. Jack found himself married to a woman with whom he had nothing in common. Without money, he cursed the situation. On his own, he could survive, but having a wife was a burden.

Gilbert was elated to receive a call from the famous French director Maurice Tourneur, who wanted him for *The White Heather* opposite the stunning actress Mabel Ballin. As soon as Tourneur signed him to a contract, Jack and Olivia moved into a hotel and he put a down payment on a Buick roadster. But Tourneur had no more work for Gilbert, who was soon back where he started. Jack borrowed money to send Olivia back to her family in Mississippi, promising to send for her when his financial situation improved.

Eventually Tourneur apologised to Jack and pleaded with him to come back, and Gilbert was able to make *Heart o' the Hills* with Mary Pickford. Tourneur was more reliable this time. Jack was given the male lead in *The White Circle* and *Deep Waters*, both released in 1920.

Gilbert was doing well now. He sent money to Olivia but made no mention of when he wanted her to return to Hollywood. Working for Tourneur eighteen hours a day left him little time for socialising – until he met actress Leatrice Joy, whom he had worked with in *One Dollar Bid* in 1918. She was one of the original screen vamps, along with Theda Bara, Valeska Stratt and Virginia Pearson.

Beautiful and talented, Leatrice was born in New Orleans in 1893. She attended the New Orleans Convent of the Sacred Heart until her father became ill with tuberculosis. In 1915 Leatrice auditioned for the NOLA Film Company and was hired. Her strict mother, Mary Zeidler, did not think much of the acting profession, but they needed money so badly that she accompanied her daughter to California where Leatrice began appearing in plays and films. When Leatrice met Gilbert again, they became inseparable, despite the objections of Mrs. Zeidler. She had every reason to dislike Jack. That he was an actor was bad enough, but he was also a married man. Worse, he was on his way to becoming a divorced man. He drank hard liquor, which was against her Christian Science beliefs, and his outspoken manner was too crass for her. Jack bought Leatrice flowers and candy and took her for Sunday drives, but Mrs. Zeidler always had something to complain about.

Leatrice signed a four-year contract with Samuel Goldwyn for $700 a week, three times Jack's salary. They couple wanted to get married, but Olivia Burwell decided to hold out until Gilbert was making good money and could afford a hefty settlement before divorcing him. Leatrice wanted them to get married right away in Mexico. Jack finally agreed and they moved into a stucco cottage with a sloping red roof in Laurel Canyon. Mrs. Zeidler hoped Jack would be charged with bigamy – then Leatrice would have to forget about him.

As well as acting, Gilbert had tried scriptwriting and directing. Though he was adept at both, there was always something or someone who blocked his advancement in both fields. He signed with William Fox to make *Shame* in 1921. Jack played a man who finds out his mother was Chinese. When he looks in the mirror he sees reflected almond eyes, long nails and, behind him, a Chinese laundry. The Toledo *Blade* nonetheless wrote, 'Intimate views of Chinatown, John Gilbert's bare-handed fight with a wolf, and some of the best screen acting we've ever seen are a few of the high spots in William Fox's production of *Shame* . . . With a poor cast it would have been the rawest kind of melodrama . . . John Gilbert, in the role of the young millionaire, easily carries off honors in his very heavy part.'

Fox was so delighted that he offered Jack a three-year contract for a $1000 a week.

William Fox, born in Tulchva, Hungary in 1879, dominated the movie industry of the 1920s. He had set up a leading production company and owned various movie theatres both in America and abroad. Fox's empire had begun when he bought a single nickelodeon which he expanded into a chain of theatres. This did not prove a sufficiently lucrative enterprise, however, so he formed a production company. By 1915 Fox had a monopoly and was strong-arming the movie industry. It was a beautiful monopoly: Fox Pictures made the films, and they were viewed in Fox-owned theatres. Fox Film Corporation was the progenitor of 20th Century-Fox Studios.

Leatrice was furthering her career as well. She received an offer from Cecil B. De Mille, whom Jack disliked intensely. 'How can you work for that silly son-of-a-bitch?' he complained. 'He treats people like cattle and acts like he's doing them a favour by paying them nothing at all for the privilege of working for him.' But Leatrice didn't take his advice. Though she was earning $750 a week with Goldwyn by the time her contract expired, she accepted De Mille's offer of $150. It wasn't the money that bothered Jack. It was Leatrice's independence, her lack of trust in his judgement and her loyalty to De Mille – who, Jack suspected, was trying to seduce Leatrice. The Gilberts now fought over absolutely everything, both at home and in public.

De Mille, concerned this would have an adverse effect on Leatrice, took control when she came to work one day with eyes swollen from crying. He said her work should come first and if this continued he would have to replace her. Leatrice packed her bags and left Jack that night. He tried to win her back, but she remained loyal to De Mille.

Gilbert grew tired of sitting home alone and began dating actress Barbara La Marr, who was labelled 'The Girl Who Was Too Beautiful'. Born in 1896, she died not long before her thirtieth birthday in 1926. Barbara ran away from home when she was fourteen and hit the screen in 1920. During her brief lifetime she married five times and, getting by on only two or three hours' sleep a night, became a cocaine addict and alcoholic. At the time Gilbert dated Barbara she was living life a mile a minute. She had many lovers and was as carefree as Jack would have liked to be.

Barbara wasn't the only girl in his life. He was also seen in the company of actress Lila Lee, the apple-cheeked WAMPAS Baby of 1922 (selected by the Western Association of Motion Picture Advertisers). She co-starred with Rudolph Valentino in *Blood and Sand*. Jack also courted actress Bebe Daniels, who was more sensible than his other lovers. In 1930 she married actor Ben Lyon, who later became a producer and was the man responsible for changing Norma Jean Baker's name to Marilyn Monroe.

Leatrice was reconciled with Jack and the couple were married, but after Cecil B. De Mille stepped in again she went to stay with her mother. Gilbert, meanwhile, moved out of their Laurel Canyon home and into a Spanish hacienda with screenwriter Carey Wilson and Paul Bern, a writer, director and intellectual. These were classy gents, witty, bright and funny. No one turned down their party invitations and the séances they held intrigued their neighbour, Charlie Chaplin.

But Jack's life was always interrupted just as he was finding his feet. When he ran into Leatrice again at a party and danced with her, that was it. She moved in with him and his room-mates until they bought a house on the corner of Sweetzer and Fountain Avenues in Hollywood. Once again De Mille interfered, loaning Leatrice out to Paramount Studios in New York for two films. She was gone for three months. Because De Mille then offered her a part in his extravaganza *The Ten Commandments*, Leatrice moved in again with her mother. 'Jack thought it was a terrible thing for me to do,' she said, 'but it wasn't quite as heartless as it sounds. De Mille would insist that Jack and I separate anyway. I didn't think I could stand another drag-out fight between Jack and De Mille.' Leatrice only went out on platonic dates, but her social life was written up in the newspapers much to Jack's embarrassment.

In 1923 Dorothy Herzog interviewed Gilbert for *Photoplay*. She wrote that he was reasonably well known but not famous, and had a reputation as a very difficult man to get along with: 'a temperamental, bombastic, broadside slinger of ye President's English'. But she found Jack to be very charming. The next time Dorothy visited Gilbert, though, he was a mess. 'Leatrice has left me again,' he groaned, lighting one cigarette after another. 'De Mille refuses to put her in a film if she stays with me. I won't get her back until she finishes the picture.' When Leatrice returned to Jack, he expressed his desire to have children, but she argued it would ruin her career if she had a baby. He responded, 'I'm going to have a child. If you won't have a child by me, I'm going to go out and find a prostitute who will.' Leatrice knew he was serious. By Christmas 1923 she was pregnant.

Jack was excellent as a Southern gambler in *Cameo Kirby*, directed by John Ford. Irving Thalberg was so impressed that he signed Gilbert to a contract for $1500 a week on 10 April 1924. This was the year in which Metro-Goldwyn-Mayer was formed and Thalberg became vice-president in charge of production. Because he had a weak heart and was not expected to live past the age of thirty, he was carefully watched by his mother Henrietta. Very upset that Irving was carousing with Gilbert until all hours of the night, she complained to Louis B. Mayer who, in turn, talked to Gilbert about it. 'You have a beautiful wife,' he said. 'Why don't you stay home with her and leave Irving alone. You're going to be a big star, so keep your nose clean.' Jack nodded – and went on with his life exactly the way he saw fit. Leatrice, who did not want to be seen in public while she was pregnant, chose to stay at home. However, she was happy for Jack to be seen with the right people at the right places and no one was more respected than Irving Thalberg.

Author Elinor Glyn had taken Hollywood by storm. Her naughty novels were all the rage, while she was considered an authority on manners and etiquette. Elinor came with plenty of flair. She wore flowing dresses with veils and boas, long false eyelashes and outrageous make-up. Her air of British sophistication mesmerised the elite, who felt inferior in her company. And she was well ahead of her time where sex was concerned. A passage from her 1907 novel, *Three Weeks*, runs: 'They were on the tiger [rug] by now and she undulated round and all over him, feeling his coat, and his face, and his hair, as a blind person might, till at last it seemed as if she were twined around him like a serpent.' Though it reads quaintly today, the depiction of an unmarried couple undulating on a carpet was sensational at the time, and Elinor was branded as sinful as her heroine. Sixty years old when she arrived in Hollywood, her once youthful beauty was still apparent. Thalberg loved her and her racy books. He told Jack, 'I'm going to buy Glyn's novel *His Hour* and I want you to play Prince Gritzko.'

Gilbert, who was a connoisseur of great literature, stooped to read the novel because it was the main topic of conversation in Hollywood. 'It's trash,' he told Irving.

'Of course it's trash,' Thalberg laughed, 'but it's what the public wants and it'll make you a star. But first I have to persuade Elinor you're right for the part because she supervises her films. I'll take you to a reception in her honour at the Ambassador Hotel.'

Elinor turned to meet Jack, extended her hand for him to kiss and said, 'Ahhh, behold the black stallion!' She was taken with Gilbert but unimpressed that he was about to be a father. 'You can't do that,' she harped, waving her hankie in the air. 'The Great Lover doesn't change diapers. Don't be ridiculous!'

Jack was so amused and flattered that he began taking her to nightclubs, premieres and parties. At the Venice amusement pier, he made sure Elinor walked over every air jet, her veils and layers of silk flying all around her. Oh, yes, he would be perfect in the role of the prince in *His Hour*.

He and his leading lady, Aileen Pringle, received rave reviews for the film, but afterwards Jack told Thalberg for the first time, 'I don't want to play the great lover anymore.'

'It made you a star.'

'Yes, but I hated doing it. Aileen and I played the parts of utter fools.'

Aileen, who was intimate with Gilbert off and on over the years, was invited by newspaper tycoon William Randolph Hearst and his mistress, Marion Davies, to producer-director Thomas Ince's 43rd birthday party. The celebration would take place on board Hearst's 280-foot yacht the *Oneida*, during a jaunt to San Diego. At the time, Hearst was negotiating with Ince to use his Culver Studios as a base for Cosmopolitan Pictures, formed to boost the movie career of his beloved Marion. Among the guests were Elinor Glyn, Louella Parsons – and Charlie Chaplin, whom Hearst suspected was having secret trysts with Davies.

The party ended tragically. The official version of what happened is that Ince, after indulging in too much alcohol and rich food, suffered a serious attack of indigestion. Unconscious, he was carried off the yacht and taken home to his wife and children, who were at his bedside when he died. There was no autopsy. Ince was cremated immediately after the funeral.

The unofficial version was murder. Hearst thought he saw Chaplin with Davies in a secluded spot, took his diamond-studded pistol and shot him. But it was Ince who had been with Marion, and he got a bullet in the head. Witnesses to the incident were sworn to secrecy. Louella Parsons, who supposedly saw the bullet hole in Ince's head, was given a lifetime contract to write a gossip column for Hearst's newspaper, and Ince's widow received a lucrative trust fund.

Gilbert was devastated by the death of the man who had been willing to take a chance on him in 1915. If it hadn't been for Thomas Ince, who knows what path Jack might have taken. Would life have dealt him a better hand?

Gilbert began spending Sundays at director King Vidor's house for tennis and refreshments. This was how he met actress Laurette Taylor, who fell in love with him. It isn't known exactly how Jack felt, but he certainly didn't run too fast when Laurette chased him. Already the toast of Broadway, she had come to Hollywood to make a movie of *Peg o' My Heart*, a successful Broadway play she had starred in. She was beautiful, bouncy, talented, greatly admired – and married.

When Laurette took the train back to New York she sent Jack a telegram, which was opened by Leatrice. It read: *Darling, Thank you for the roses. It was equally hard to leave you. Always, Laurette.* It was the last straw for Leatrice, who left without telling Jack where she was going. He was frantic until someone told him where she was. Immediately he sent her a basket of roses with a note of apology. In return she sent him a wire: *Darling, Thank you for the roses. It was equally hard to leave you. Always, Leatrice.*

Jack's attempt at reconciliation failed, so he asked his friend Paul Bern to intercede. Bern, who later married Jean Harlow, was short, bald and pot-bellied, but very charming and intelligent. Known as the Father Confessor, his was a good shoulder to cry on, and he convinced Leatrice to return home to be with Jack when she had their baby. She drove back to the house, only to find the front door wide open, music blasting and several drunken men passed out on the floor. The next day, 19 August 1924, Leatrice filed for divorce. In her complaint she stated that 'Gilbert and a number of his men friends were enjoying a wild carousal, wearing dressing gowns and pajamas. In the last year Gilbert continued to bring large quantities of liquor into their home. As a result her nerves became affected and on account of her delicate condition she is unable to work.' On 6 September 1924, she gave birth to a daughter, Leatrice Joy II, leaving word that Gilbert should not be allowed to see the baby. He did at least manage to get into the hospital and hold his daughter. But at Leatrice's request he moved out of their house and into the Athletic Club

The Gilbert separation was big news and Jack was strongly criticised. In an attempt to win his wife back and maintain his Great Lover image, he gave several interviews in which he admitted getting caught up in his new career, but claimed that this was the first time in his marriage that he had not felt inferior to his wife. 'Leatrice was a star first,' he said. 'She didn't care to be Mrs. John Gilbert, but Miss Leatrice Joy – De Mille star.'

The righteous Louis B. Mayer was shocked at Jack's behaviour. 'Leatrice Joy is a sweet young lady who was forced to return to her mother to give her baby a home,' he told Thalberg. 'It's a good thing I'm leaving for Europe or I'd take care of Gilbert personally. Straighten him out while I'm gone or I don't want to set my eyes on him.'

L.B. Mayer disliked Jack intensely, though it isn't known precisely why. He had hated him from the start, and for no apparent reason. But Gilbert's apparent abandonment of Leatrice when she was about to give birth appalled Mayer. A defender of motherhood, he was given extra cause to detest Gilbert when Leatrice charged him with alcoholism. The accusation was unfounded, of course. Apart from the occasional binge, Jack drank no more than anyone else.

Gilbert's *He Who Gets Slapped* premiered in November, receiving excellent reviews. He and Norma Shearer played bareback riders in love, while Lon Chaney as the heroic circus clown stole the picture, as he always did. The *New York Times* said the picture should be held up as a model by all producers. *Photoplay* wrote, 'The acting is remarkably fine. Norma Shearer and John Gilbert as the lovers are delightful.' Jack followed up with *The Snob*, again with Norma. This time he played a schoolteacher who uses every means to get what he wants. The man is a liar, an adulterer, a hypocrite and a scoundrel. Critics loved *The Snob* and said this was Gilbert at his best. The role of a cad had certainly appealed to Jack, who was still keen to avoid being typecast as a screen lover.

Mayer, in the meantime, had gone to Italy to sort out the difficulties in the filming of *Ben Hur*, and he went on to Germany to sign up Swedish director Mauritz Stiller and his protégée – Greta Garbo.

Gilbert, against Thalberg's wishes, next made *Wife of the Centaur*, starring Eleanor Boardman and directed by King Vidor. Jack played an adulterer who leaves his sweet wife for an older woman but then returns home. The *New York Review* said of him, 'Gilbert adds to his growing laurels', while the *Evening Graphic* claimed, 'There was not a single flaw in his performance.'

Thalberg was delighted. He had tried to talk Gilbert out of doing *The Snob* and *Wife of the Centaur* because of Leatrice's divorce action. Though she had not charged Jack with adultery, the theme of both movies might have put him in a bad light. But he survived and came out ahead, so Thalberg decided to put him in his first major production at MGM – *The Merry Widow* with Mae Murray. And the film would become a classic, though not before difficulties with the director, Erich von Stroheim. Thalberg had fired him twice before, for spending too much and shooting excessive film footage. Thalberg never let his personal feelings interfere with talent, and von Stroheim was a brilliant director, but he put his foot down when von Stroheim opposed using Gilbert in *The Merry Widow*. Von Stroheim also wanted to eliminate the classic ballroom waltz (in which Clark Gable was an extra), while Mae Murray, who had done the play on Broadway, insisted it stay in. Though Gilbert wasn't anxious to do the dance number, he agreed with Murray and walked off the set. Mae went to L.B. Mayer, who demanded that the great waltz scene remain.

According to Murray, Jack was very nervous doing the waltz. 'I wish I were in South America,' he mumbled.

Von Stroheim, who could be heard cursing on the sidelines, eventually shouted, 'Cut! It was lousy. I knew it would be. The showgirl and the amateur!'

Murray went after von Stroheim with both fists, screaming, 'Dirty hun! Ya dirty hun!' She stormed off to her dressing room and took off her gown in a rage. Then she received a phone call from the MGM gateman with a message. 'Mr. Gilbert says to tell you he has left for South America. He says to forgive him and goodbye.'

Mae, wearing only her feathery headdress and undergarments, ran out to the parking lot and stopped Jack. The guard asked him to go along with Mae, whose half-naked state was hardly appropriate for an MGM star. She took Jack to her dressing room and closed the door. Sometime later, Jack agreed to continue working on the film. Murray informed Mayer, who responded, 'I'd be happy to fire that sex degenerate!' But Thalberg came to the movie set and, after a talk with von Stroheim, a compromise was found. The great waltz was retained, but in a shortened version.

The Merry Widow was very well received. Critic and playwright Robert Sherwood wrote, 'The main things are von Stroheim's direction, von Stroheim's profound knowledge of composition and scenic effects, and John Gilbert's magnificent performance as Prince Danilo. Gilbert gives an eloquent, vibrant, keenly tempered interpretation of what might have been a trite romantic character. At every point he sparkles with brilliance and at times he bursts into flames.'

Photoplay said the film would make Gilbert 'the greatest of them all'.

Jack, who was now making $2000 a week, said this was the happiest time of his life. It was surely the luckiest. Thalberg, who believed in following one success with another, put Gilbert in the war epic *The Big Parade* alongside the adorable Renee Adoree. There are many good scenes in the picture, but the film clip most often shown is of Jack going off to war in a truck full of soldiers while Renee runs after him, her arms outstretched.

Gilbert went to New York for the premiere of *The Big Parade* on 20 November 1925 at the Astor Theater. He had visited Leatrice several times to see the baby and the couple were close once again. Since she was on vacation in New York herself, he invited her to attend the opening with him. Inside the theatre Jack was riveted to his seat. 'The house lights dimmed,' he said, 'and I ceased to exist for the world as if dead for two hours. Then the audience applauded and cheered. The picture was over but I couldn't get up. Not until everyone had left the theatre was I able to stand.'

When he read the reviews the next day Gilbert said that no such adjectives had been used to describe a movie before. Critic Robert Sherwood claimed that *The Big Parade* could be ranked among the few genuinely great achievements of the screen, while the *New York Times* described it as a 'superlative war picture. The acting is flawless throughout.' Gilbert cried, and then staggered to bed and slept around the clock.

Sadly there were no Academy Awards in 1925. If there had been, Gilbert would surely have deserved to win Best Actor for the skills he displayed in both *The Merry Widow* and *The Big Parade*.

Jack and Leatrice talked of remarrying and began house hunting, but, as usual, there was a snag. She wanted him to see a lawyer about signing a paper to guarantee that he would provide for the baby. Jack was highly insulted. Didn't she know he would do that anyway, without making it legal and embarrassing him? Their reconciliation ended almost before it began.

Though his personal life was a mess, John Gilbert was the topic of the day. Men copied his long collars and French cuffs. Until Jack Gilbert wore a blue shirt it was incorrect for men to wear anything but white during the day. Fan magazines wrote about his favourite foods, his hobbies, his pets, the thickness of his black hair and his navy blue necktie with polka dots. Everything he did was the right thing to do and everything he wore became the new trend.

Jack next made *La Bohème* alongside Lillian Gish, with whom he fell in love briefly. But she kept her distance, even during filming. When Irving Thalberg asked, 'Where are the love scenes?', director King Vidor shrugged and answered that Miss Gish was opposed to doing anything like that. Thalberg made them reshoot, whereupon Miss Gish sighed, 'Oh, dear, I have to go through another day kissing John Gilbert . . .'

In February 1926 Jack attended the premiere with Norma Shearer. She was patiently waiting for Thalberg to propose marriage, which he did the following year.

Greta Garbo and her mentor, Mauritz Stiller, arrived in Hollywood on 10 September 1925 and were met by MGM publicity people, reporters and photographers. Photos of her taken that day show a frizzy-haired, frightened twenty-year-old shrouded in flowers and flanked by little Swedish girls in delicate costume bonnets. One reporter wrote that Garbo had a run in her stocking and her shoes needed new heels. When asked where she was staying in Hollywood, Greta replied, 'I will look for something not too expensive, a room with a private family.' She did not make a good impression that day.

Born Greta Lovisa Gustafsson on 18 September 1905 in Stockholm, Sweden, Greta had yearned to be an actress from an early age, even though she was overweight and too tall at five feet seven inches. She worked as a soap lather girl in a barber shop and sold hats in a department store, where she was discovered by producer-director Erik Petchler in 1922. He suggested that Greta audition for the state-sponsored Royal Dramatic Theatre Academy and she was accepted. The following year Greta met director Mauritz Stiller and was cast in *The Saga of Gösta Berling*, about a defrocked minister who falls in love with a virginal countess.

Stiller was the first to recognise the beauty of her brown-black hair, grey-blue eyes and long lashes. He changed her name to Garbo, insisted she lose twenty pounds and set out to make her a star. She put herself in his hands, though they were not intimate because forty-year-old Stiller was a homosexual. Greta was enthralled by his wisdom, even when he criticised her unmercifully during rehearsals. She played a prostitute in *The Joyless Street*, but it was *The Saga of Gösta Berling* that caught the attention of Louis B. Mayer. He offered Stiller $1000 a week and Garbo $400 to join MGM. The last thing Mayer said to her before he left for home was, 'Lose some weight. American men don't like fat women.'

But when Greta arrived, she hated California. In a letter home she wrote, 'Oh, you lovely little Sweden. I promise when I return to you my sad face will smile as never before.' She complained of having nothing to do and going to bed early. 'I don't care if I act like a little old woman,' she said.

Thalberg first put Garbo in *Torrent* with popular actor Ricardo Cortez, but the picture was not directed by Stiller. *Variety* said she had everything – looks, acting ability and personality. She was not impressed. 'Americans have spoiled their beautiful country with tall buildings, too many cars and too much noise.' The studio, she said, was hideous.

Thalberg was so pleased with *Torrent* that he rushed Garbo into *The Temptress* with Antonio Moreno, and this time Stiller was to direct. In her role as a married woman who follows her lover to Argentina and disaster, Garbo is stunning. But Stiller's slow method of directing and his bitter disputes with Moreno were holding up production, so Thalberg replaced him. '*The Temptress* is terrible and so am I,' she said. 'Everything went wrong. I am not a good actress.'

Gilbert, meanwhile, was riding high. He was making $10,000 a week and had built his dream house, a Spanish hacienda on top of a mountain on Tower Road. The master bedroom had French doors overlooking the garden, there was a guest room, a pool, tennis courts and servants' quarters. It wasn't the typical Hollywood house built by a famous movie star, but it was elegant and comfortable.

He was seeing Leatrice, hoping they would eventually settle their differences. One has to wonder: if she had chosen Jack over a career would it have made a difference in his life? Could she have saved him from the unhappiness that lurked around the corner?

On a visit to Mayer's office to discuss his next project, Jack brought up the idea of adapting John Masefield's *The Widow in the Bye Street*, in which a young boy has an affair with the mistress of a drayman who is serving time in prison. Mayer didn't like the idea. 'You can't make a movie about a whore!' he bellowed. 'A nice boy falling in love with a whore? What kind of movie would that make?'

Gilbert answered, 'You're making other pictures with the same theme.'

'Only someone like you would bring a whore into a story about a mother and her son.'

'What's wrong with that?' Jack asked. 'My own mother was a whore.'

Mayer lunged at Gilbert, threatening to cut off his balls. Jack said, 'If you did, I'd be more of a man than you!'

This is one version. In the others, Mayer punches Jack in the face. But it doesn't really matter who did what to whom. Gilbert would suffer for calling his mother a whore. Mayer's daughter, Irene, said her father was very bitter. Regarding his feelings toward Jack, she said, 'I never saw such hatred in my life.'

Jack played a swashbuckler in *Bardelys the Magnificent* with Eleanor Boardman. Directed by King Vidor, the film was well received, but Gilbert was trapped by his enormous success in *The Big Parade*. 'No film will ever excite me as much,' he said.

With the exception of Mayer – and Henrietta Thalberg – everyone liked Jack. He was kind, he was fun and he was well read. But he also suffered from a lack of confidence. During every minute of his fame, he was plagued by fear and depression. Eager to please and cooperate, at the same time he was wary of those who would take advantage of him. He trusted Irving Thalberg, but did not agree with him about the roles he was given. Being typecast as the great lover had become a bore and an insult to his talent.

Yet Thalberg had a way with his stars, even if they did not agree with him. He always looked out for their welfare, taking into account what the public wanted, and always tried to find a balance. Women were attracted to Gilbert and men wanted to be like him – that was the balance, plain and simple. Jack would have to live with that to maintain his status at the box office. This was how Thalberg approached *Flesh and the Devil*. Gilbert agreed to appear in the film because he was curious about his new leading lady. When he'd seen her on the MGM lot one day, he'd smiled and said, 'Hello, Greta.' Barely acknowledging him, she had responded curtly, 'It is Miss Garbo.'

The first day on the set of *Flesh and the Devil*, Greta met director Clarence Brown who noticed how nervous she was. He went to Jack's dressing room and asked him to come out and meet Garbo. 'To hell with her,' Gilbert said. 'She can come to me!'

So Brown brought her to Jack's dressing room and she relaxed. 'She was mad about him before they met,' Brown said. 'She raved about Gilbert to everyone.'

Director Clarence Brown said, 'It was the damnedest thing you ever saw. When they got into their first love scene nobody else was there. These two were alone in a world of their own. It seemed like an intrusion to yell, "Cut!". I motioned the crew over to another part of the set and let them finish what they were doing. It was embarrassing.'

And so it was, that first day on the set of *Flesh and the Devil*, that the couple fell in love. The film is a story of love and adultery with a tragic ending. Garbo hated these roles as much as Gilbert did. 'I am tired of playing the adulteress who dies in the end,' she complained to Mayer. But, he explained, 'At MGM, the bad ones always pay the price.'

Until Garbo entered his life, Jack had been hoping Leatrice would share his new house with him. But she complained about his guest room, which was decorated like a monk's cell. In Hollywood famous married couples always had their own rooms and she also refused to sleep in his drab second bedroom. So when Garbo came to live with him, Jack had the room transformed into a miniature Louis XVI boudoir, all blue and ivory and gold, with a black marble bathroom. Jack built a small cabin for Greta at the back of his property, planting a pine grove because she missed the scent of pine that reminded her of Sweden. Since she suffered from insomnia, he built an artificial waterfall to lull her to sleep. Whatever she wanted, he was willing to give, and more.

Unlike Leatrice, Greta listened to Gilbert and took his advice. He secured her a new manager and a new contract. Her salary jumped from $750 to $3000. Although Mayer knew she was worth the money he hated Gilbert for being the one responsible, and the hatred between the two men grew more intense.

Flesh and the Devil broke all box-office records. The acting was brilliant and the lighting unsurpassed. In one scene Jack lights Greta's cigarette and the reflection on her face is stunning. The love scenes, too, were unsurpassed, not only in the clinches but when they share a glass of wine, her lips touching the rim where his have been. It was also the first film to show a man and woman lying horizontally, but this hardly mattered. Regardless of how they positioned themselves, Gilbert and Garbo were the greatest lovers to grace the screen. The *Herald Tribune* said, 'Frankly, we have never in our career seen a seduction scene so perfectly done.'

During this stage of her life, Garbo was very sociable and enjoyed entertaining with Jack on Sunday afternoons. They played tennis and had pool parties, when Greta often went swimming topless without blinking one of her long eyelashes. She was a free spirit without a conscience. But she had sympathy for Mauritz Stiller; although he was directing pictures at Paramount, he was not faring well. Garbo often slipped away to visit him in Santa Monica. But she was not truthful with Jack, who assumed she and Stiller were intimate.

Gilbert had proposed marriage many times. Once they got as far as City Hall. As they were climbing the stairs she turned around and ran away. But the worst occasion was the wedding of King Vidor and Eleanor Boardman at Marion Davies's house in Beverly Hills. Jack and Greta had had dinner with the couple and Jack proposed a double wedding. Greta agreed, surprisingly, so they took out a marriage licence, using their real names in order to keep it a secret. King Vidor, however, thought Mayer should know that his two most valuable stars were getting married. When Greta found out, she began having doubts. On the day of the wedding Jack saw her drive away in her car. He called Marion Davies, but Marion hadn't seen Greta. Jack still hoped for the best — maybe she was holding to the tradition that the bride should not be seen before the wedding . . .

As the hour of the Vidor–Boardman wedding approached, Jack became very nervous. Louis B. Mayer emerged from the guest bathroom and patted Gilbert on the back. 'What's the matter with you?' he asked. 'What do you have to marry her for? Why don't you just fuck her and forget about it?'

Jack grabbed Mayer by the throat, pushing him through the bathroom door to the floor where he repeatedly banged Mayer's head on the tiles. Mayer's aide Eddie Mannix pulled them apart. Eleanor Boardman watched as Mannix picked up Mayer's eyeglasses and wiped his face, but Mayer pushed him away and took a step toward Jack. 'You're finished, Gilbert!' he shouted. 'I'll destroy you if it costs me a million dollars!'

Jack left shortly after the ceremony and got drunk. The next day he broke out in a sweat, realising what he had done and fearing he would suffer the consequences. He called Thalberg, who told him, 'Mayer is Mayer, but a contract is a contract. Keep your nose clean, Jack, and he can't touch you.'

Thalberg, whom Garbo cherished, later asked her why she wouldn't marry Jack. 'Don't you see him as a husband?'

'No,' she replied, 'and I don't see myself as a wife.'

After being stood up and humiliated, Gilbert told Greta that if she continued to live in his house she would have to pay rent. She stayed – but he never saw a cent. He had a brief affair with Renee Adoree on the set of his next film, *The Show*. Renee knew he was on the rebound and did not expect anything more than a close friendship.

Shortly after he finished filming *The Show*, Gilbert went to New York to receive *Photoplay*'s award for Best Actor in *The Big Parade*. While he was there, Jack went to see Nicholas Schenck, President of Loews, Inc., the parent company of MGM. Schenck, who admired Louis B. Mayer professionally but detested him personally, told Jack not to worry because he could handle Mayer. 'Jack, stay in New York and have some fun,' he said. Feeling much better, Gilbert went to the Algonquin Hotel where he met the members of the famous Round Table – Robert Benchley, Robert Sherwood, James Thurber, George Kaufman, and the very talented and funny Dorothy Parker, the only female in the group. Jack spent a week with them, mostly in the company of Dorothy Parker whose rare humour brought him back to life. He forgot about Louis B. Mayer and the elusive Garbo.

When Jack returned home, Greta was there to greet him with words of love and apologies. But she soon went to see Mauritz Stiller. Jack, having had a few drinks too many, followed her. When Greta refused to let him in, he climbed the wall to the balcony and Stiller knocked him to the ground. Gilbert went to the police station to complain about Stiller, but was arrested for drunk and disorderly conduct and sentenced to ten days in jail, though he only served a day and a half.

Writer Anita Loos commented, 'There is enough dyke in me to know that Garbo must have detested him [Gilbert] . . . She did what every actress has done since the word whore has been changed to the word actress. She went out with him and gave him a casual lay from time to time for the sake of her career. On safe ground she gave him a fast broom.'

Eleanor Boardman liked Greta but thought she was the most selfish person she had ever known. 'She had no real love for Jack. She used him. She was a taker not a giver.'

Jack's leading lady in his next film, *Twelve Miles Out*, was Joan Crawford. Known for her many love affairs, she would have had a fling with Jack if he had not been so much in love with Garbo. 'He was very moody,' Joan said. 'I could always tell how the romance was going by his mood. Clearly he was suffering.'

Garbo and Gilbert next co-starred in *Love* (originally titled *Anna Karenina*), about a married woman who leaves her husband and child for another man. Realising her fate, she finally throws herself in front of a moving train. Theatre marquees reading 'Garbo and Gilbert in *Love*' drew huge crowds. MGM usually discouraged their contract players from having affairs, but in this case even Louis B. Mayer looked the other way. *Variety* raved about Jack and Greta in *Love*: 'They are in a fair way of becoming the biggest box office team this country has yet known. Both are strong away from each other and have proved it. But combine that double strength with a reasonable story and who or what can stop it?'

In 1927 Gilbert finally got his chance to make a movie based on John Masefield's *The Widow in the Bye Street*. In the film, renamed *Man, Woman and Sin*, his co-star was the tragic Jeanne Eagels, who would take a deliberate overdose of heroin at the age of 35. One critic thought it was Gilbert's best work since *The Big Parade*.

Jack and Greta made another attempt at marriage and again she backed out. She continued to live with him off and on. They fought and they made love and they broke up. Garbo often said she hated Hollywood and wanted to move to Utah or Montana and settle down. Jack thought she was crazy.

'You're in love with Garbo the actress,' she often said.

'You're damn right!' he replied every time.

It appears as if neither knew the true meaning of love. He would always speak of her fondly, but in later years Garbo continued to confuse everyone about her true feelings for Gilbert: 'I loved him and don't know why we never married' . . . 'We were just friends' . . . 'He was the love of my life' . . . 'I don't know what I ever saw in him' . . . 'I was in love with him but I froze. I was afraid he would tell me what to do. I always wanted to be the boss.'

Mauritz Stiller died in Sweden on 8 November 1928 at the age of 45. Greta collapsed on the set of *A Woman of Affairs* with Gilbert when she heard the news. She went to Sweden for three months when the film was finished. Jack received several letters from her, and a phone call on New Year's Eve.

Gilbert still carried a torch for Garbo, but he was elated with a new three-year MGM contract sanctioned by Nicholas Schenck The studio would pay $250,000 a picture with a limit of two films a year. Gilbert's last silent film, *Desert Nights*, was released on 9 March 1929.

Irving Thalberg's intuition about films did not fail him often, but he was wrong to believe that talking pictures were just a fad. Even after Warner

Brothers' *The Jazz Singer* with Al Jolson was released in October 1917, Thalberg called it a gimmick. The film, which was only 25 per cent sound, cost Warners half a million dollars to produce. Jolson's first words on the screen would go down in film history. He tells his audience: 'Wait a minute! Wait a minute! You ain't heard nothin' yet. Wait a minute, I tell ya, you ain't heard nothin'! Do you wanna hear "Toot Toot Tootsie?" Alright, hold on, hold on.' Then, to the bandleader: 'Louis, play "Toot Toot Tootsie!" Three choruses, you understand. In the third chorus I whistle. Now give it to 'em hard and heavy. Go right ahead!'

Then came Warners' all-talkie *Lights of New York*, a cheap gangster melodrama that cost only $23,000 to make. In one long sequence, a telephone prop is rather conveniently placed near the actors. Why Warners chose to make this pedestrian movie remains a mystery. They did, however, make a million dollars just testing the water.

But MGM was above all that. They would preview a film with a small audience, but never in theatres across the country. They were interested in quality films, not in making history.

The introduction of sound to motion pictures wiped the slate of studio power clean. All the successes and failures of the past were rendered inconsequential. Everyone returned to ground zero, back to the drawing board, as all of Hollywood began learning a new and complicated method of film making.

Actor Billy Haines commented, 'It was the night of the *Titanic* all over again, with women grabbing the wrong children and Louis B. Mayer singing "Nearer My God to Thee".'

The important thing, in the eyes of studio executives, was not so much to make a great sound picture, but to make one post haste. But there was a huge expense both in building soundproof studios and in converting movie theatres for sound. The star system would be thrown into disarray, while the overseas market would be decimated.

When the movies started to talk, they ceased to move. Film making regressed to the era of Méliès – cameras were stuffed into soundproof booths, while editing became purely transitional and cross-cutting, montage and fluid camera movement were eliminated.

William Fox soon developed Movietone, which recorded sound straight to celluloid. The technology was in low supply and high demand, and MGM lingered in complete silence. In fact it was Nicholas Schenck who demanded that MGM get prepared for sound. Thalberg remained unconvinced, his main concern being how audiences would react to hearing their stars talk for the first time. 'Audiences have formed their own idea of how each star sounds,' he said. 'They've heard the voices in their head in picture after picture, and what they hear coming from the screen may be disappointing. It's very risky.'

The medium was still unsure of its method, and the musical genre seemed the most adaptable to the sound stage. Music is what Americans thought of when they thought of sound as performance and so sound came to film in the form of song. Soon every studio had at least one musical in the works.

But it was MGM and Thalberg who walked away with the first Oscar by taking their time to produce a first-class film for their sound debut. Jack Warner, being the genius behind the Vitaphone and producer of *The Jazz Singer*, had the obvious advantage, but MGM, the last studio to introduce sound, ironically struck first with *The Broadway Melody* in 1929. Not only was the picture the first sound musical, it was MGM's first sound feature. *The Broadway Melody*, with engaging numbers such as 'The Wedding of the Painted Doll', 'Broadway Melody', and 'You Were Meant for Me', cost only $280,000 to produce but grossed over $4 million.

It was the simplicity of the movie that allowed MGM to get it out there first, despite the fact that virtually every studio had a head start. Although *The Jazz Singer* was ruled ineligible in the Best Picture category (it was thought unfair for a sound film to compete with silents), Warner Brothers production head Darryl F. Zanuck was presented with a special Oscar at the very first Academy Awards ceremony in May 1929, for producing the pioneer outstanding talking picture. But *The Broadway Melody* was the first talkie to win the Best Picture award. And in the end it had been Irving Thalberg who was responsible.

Musicals were one thing, but no one knew how the public would react to sound in melodrama. Art directors began designing sets in such a way that microphones could be hidden in lamps, ashtrays, vases, behind chairs and tables. Actors were warned to remain within range of the bulky camera crates and mobile sound catchers. The movies stopped moving. It was in this manner that speech began to erase silence and dialogue to replace subtitles. Thalberg experimented with audible effects, adding street noises, ringing telephones, slamming doors and the applause of theatregoers. Meanwhile, through his windows he looked out at the boxlike tombs being readied for future pictures. He believed the decision to abandon silent movies was unwise. It seemed as if shutting out the sunlight from the stages symbolised the coming of darker days for all of them.

Joan Crawford, who made the transition very well, recalled that Hollywood was in a panic. 'My voice was all right,' she said, 'but pronunciation became very important. MGM brought in the best diction teachers in the country. I was told to read the newspaper out loud in front of the mirror every morning. When I see my old films my voice was a bit shrill, but that was the norm. We learned to lower our tones and practised this over and over to get comfortable with it.

'We were all scared shitless. We watched the beautiful flowers being dug up and trees cut down to make room for cement alleyways and foundations for more sound stages. I remember our gardener crying and trying to save his beautiful roses as the bulldozers approached.'

Thalberg brought in Norma Shearer's brother, Douglas, to be in charge of sound. He was sent to Bell Laboratories in New Jersey, where the latest equipment was being developed, before he put a crew together. Doug was Irving's brother-in-law, which caused many people to shake their heads, but Shearer proved his value. During *The Broadway Melody* Thalberg thought one of the dance numbers was too static. Douglas suggested, 'The cast could mime for the cameras to the already recorded music played back to them over loudspeakers.'

'Can that be done?' Thalberg asked.

'It should work,' Douglas replied, unsure as yet of a procedure that was to become the standard in Hollywood.

It was not talent that made an actor successful in talkies. Purely and simply, it was whether or not the public felt that the tone of their voices was in tune with their image. Nothing could be done to perfect that.

When Garbo returned from Sweden in March 1929, Jack picked her up in San Bernadino to avoid the crowds and the press. He proposed to her one last time and she refused one last time. He told her how much he suffered whenever she was away, especially at night. Both insomniacs, they kept each other company – she with a warm glass of milk, he with a stiff scotch. He hated being alone, he said. They were meant for each other.

Though Garbo wanted to go her own way, she did not want to break off the relationship.

'Not this time,' he said. 'It's all or nothing.'

A few days later, while Greta was whisked off to Catalina Island to make a film, Jack began seeing blonde actress Ina Claire. She was older than Gilbert by seven years, ambitious, sophisticated, slim, poised, and intelligent. Six weeks after meeting her at a party, Jack proposed marriage. On 9 May 1929 Harry Edington, agent of both Gilbert and Garbo, received a frantic call from Greta begging him to stop the wedding. 'He belongs to me,' she sobbed. 'We never should have parted.' Edington said he couldn't do that; the wedding in Las Vegas was only hours away. 'The only person who can do that is you,' he said, knowing Garbo wasn't the type to make a public display of herself.

So Jack and Ina were married in Las Vegas on the morning of 10 May, returning immediately to Hollywood so Jack could resume filming his first sound film, *Redemption*. Ina, an accomplished stage actress, tried to help him with his speech and dialogue. 'This was something new to him,' she explained. 'But his masculine pride, his professional pride . . . I was the last person he wanted to tell him anything about acting.' When Ina was asked how it felt to be married to a great star she replied, 'Why don't you ask Mr. Gilbert?'

Redemption was directed by, of all people, Lionel Barrymore. Though L.B. Mayer's feelings about Jack hadn't changed, he managed to put his hatred aside for the sake of his beloved MGM. After all, Gilbert's name on the theatre marquee guaranteed money in the bank. Mayer assigned Barrymore, with Thalberg's sanction, to direct and guide Jack in his sound debut. But the picture was so bad it was shelved for the time being. Gilbert then performed a spoof of *Romeo and Juliet*, in colour, with Norma Shearer in *Hollywood Revue of 1929*, which featured all the MGM stars except Garbo. Jack did well in what was his first speaking part to be seen by the public. It was a small skit but long enough to judge him by, and there were no complaints. MGM, anxious for him to make a feature talkie, rushed *His Glorious Night* into production. Again directed by Lionel Barrymore, the film was finished in thirteen days. Jack played a cavalry officer in love with a princess. Because he is a commoner she cannot marry him, but she agrees to spend 'one glorious night' with him and stays forever.

As soon as *His Glorious Night* was finished, Jack and Ina sailed to Europe on their honeymoon. They argued constantly; Ina, who didn't think he was sophisticated enough for her elite friends, told him what to say and how to behave. Jack was not a country bumpkin, but Ina made him feel like one. However, he was far better known in Europe than Ina and fans flocked around him, leaving her in the background. In the late twenties stage performers considered movie actors beneath them, in much the same way that film stars would later feel about television performers, and Ina Claire was more proud of her Broadway successes than her movies.

Unfortunately, she met Jack when he was going through the transition from silent films to talkies, and like every other motion picture star, he was not himself. Gilbert had every reason to worry. No less than 90 per cent of the popular stars of the twenties would be ruined.

When Jack arrived in New York after his honeymoon he was informed that *His Glorious Night* was a failure. Yet the reviews had generally been good. In the New York *American*, Regina Carew wrote, 'Any doubt as to Jack Gilbert's success in talkies is dispelled by his appearance in *His Glorious Night*. John makes the grade with ease and, if anything, speech adds to his charm. The picture leaves no doubt as to his continued popularity as a star of the talking screen.'

The New York *Review* wrote, 'A sophisticated continental romance was robbed of its full entertainment value by bad photography and poor recording . . . with Gilbert not quite sure of himself as in his silent past. His voice is neither remarkable nor displeasing but it is not that which one would associate with the Great Lover of the screen.'

The *Hollywood Reporter* said, 'Gilbert has not yet hit quite the perfect note of intonation for the microphone but, barring a certain over-resonant delivery of lines his enunciation is crisp and fine . . . He will make great headway in the talking medium in light comedy. The intelligence of his work is even more marked in sound than in silents.'

Variety criticised the story, the dialogue and the director: 'Barrymore apparently had a nervous reaction in the cutting room. This is borne out in the way the sequences literally grasshopper into one another. Conversation barely starts in one room when it cuts lightning-like to veranda steps and back to the bedroom or the dinner table.'

However, the *New York Times* reported, 'It is evident that the producers intend to keep Mr. Gilbert before the public as a screen lover, for in this current narrative, he constantly repeats "I love you" to the princess as he kisses her. In fact, his many protestations while embracing her caused a large female contingent to giggle and laugh. But Mr. Gilbert's responsibility does not lie with his lines and therefore he is to be congratulated on the manner in which he handles his speaking role. His voice is pleasant, but not one which is rich in nuance. His performance is good . . .'

It's true that there was giggling when Gilbert romanced his leading lady, Catherine Dale Owen, with the famous line, 'Oh, beauteous maiden, my arms are waiting to enfold you. I love you, I love you, I love you.' In fact, in the 1952 movie *Singin' in the Rain* Gene Kelly uses this dialogue in his character's first flop talking film as an illustration of the amusing production flaws which occurred in the early days of the talkies. But what exactly caused Gilbert's voice to sound so incongruously high-pitched is still debated – including the suggestion that Louis B. Mayer was ultimately responsible, in an attempt to ruin Jack's career.

Hedda Hopper, who had a part in *His Glorious Night*, explained, 'I watched John Gilbert being destroyed on the sound stage by one man, Lionel Barrymore. Whether by diabolical intent or accident, I'll never know, but Jack's first speech was, "I love you, I love you, I love you." In forming these words his mouth and nose came together almost like a parrot's beak. I used to see glee on Lionel's face as he watched Gilbert.' According to writer Anita Loos, Barrymore was suffering from disabling arthritis and taking heavy doses of morphine. 'Anyone could have manipulated him and did. It was common talk at the studio. Everyone knew but Jack.'

In her 1985 biography of her father, entitled *Dark Star*, Leatrice Joy Fountain wrote that she had talked to director Clarence Brown, who said the bass on the recording was not turned up for Gilbert. 'All you heard was treble. Of course, it was a mistake.' When Leatrice asked him if Mayer might have been responsible, Brown replied, 'Louis B. Mayer was my best friend in pictures. I was there from the early days until 1952 and we never had a cross word. I'm not going to say anything about anyone who is not here to defend himself.'

And Mayer's daughter, Irene, claimed that her father had come home with reviews of *His Glorious Night* saying proudly, 'That should take care of Mr. Gilbert.'

Still, one has to wonder whether Mayer was truly responsible for the sound not having enough bass. After all, it was he who, together with Thalberg, had chosen two talkies for Gilbert based on successful plays by famous playwrights and adapted by top scenarists.

Another problem for Jack was money. The stock market crash rendered him practically broke. Though he had given Ina permission to redecorate the house on Tower Road, he decided to wait. Ina moved out and rented a house of her own. With his life closing in on him, Gilbert began to drink in earnest. He reported to the studio every day hoping for another chance – and it seemed to have come when *Redemption* was released. Thalberg thought he could correct the adverse reaction to Gilbert by finally giving him heavier roles. But the critics panned the film. Many unfavourable magazine articles about Jack appeared, predicting his doom. Half drunk and angry one day, he approached Jim Tully who wrote for *Vanity Fair*. 'Get up!' Jack hissed. Tully obliged, knocking Gilbert on the floor with a straight right to the jaw.

Gilbert was given a role in *Way for a Sailor*, about three seamen left adrift when their ocean liner goes down. But MGM, in violation of Jack's contract, gave Wallace Beery top billing. Gilbert's pride was hurt. But he did not let on to Thalberg who was sure his career would be saved. 'What about a movie with Garbo?' Jack asked.

'I'm working on that,' Thalberg replied. 'She's slated for *Susan Lenox*, the perfect vehicle for you. Then *Red Dust* with Jean Harlow.'

But in the end, a new actor on the MGM lot made both pictures. His name was Clark Gable, and he had been discovered in the stage play *The Last Mile*. Hollywood offered big salaries to actors trained in the theatre and they were usually willing to 'lower' themselves for the money. Gable was one of these. He didn't want to be in films, but he had proven himself on Broadway and was tempted by the lucrative contract offered him. So Gable was in and Gilbert was out.

Garbo was more successful in her sound debut, *Anna Christie*. The theatre marquees read, 'Garbo Talks!'. And her opening dialogue was memorable – 'Gimme a visky, ginger ale on the side, and don't be stingy, babee . . .'

Gilbert became somewhat of a recluse after his divorce from Ina Claire in 1931. He made a gangster picture called *Gentleman's Fate* that did little for him. The *New York Times* said of it, 'Mr. Gilbert has a bad time from the start.' *The Phantom of Paris* was Jack's best talkie to date, but the public wasn't interested in him any more. He had let them down too often. It was the time of the Great Depression and money was tight. His fans made a choice at the box office, and they chose not too see him.

It was no secret that Jack, despite suffering from bleeding ulcers, was now drinking heavily. His few remaining friends came to visit him on Tower Road only if he invited them. King Vidor remained faithful, as did writer Adela Rogers St. Johns with whom he was intimate. And Irving Thalberg was still in Jack's corner. In 1932 he came across a story Gilbert had written four years previously entitled *Downstairs*, about servants in the home of an aristocratic Viennese household. Thalberg asked Lenore Coffee to write the screenplay and Monta Bell to direct. 'We'll do it right this time,' he told Jack, who threw his arms around Irving in gratitude.

Time magazine loved *Downstairs* and predicted that Gilbert would soon be on top again. Kenneth Anger reported in his 1975 book *Hollywood*

Babylon that Jack was excellent in the film, but the harm had already been done. Fan magazines and gossip columnists between them had convinced the public that Gilbert was finished. One critic wrote about *Downstairs*, 'Why did the studio permit it to be made?'

You can't take the ring back once the bell tolls.

During production of *Downstairs*, Jack and his 21-year-old co-star Virginia Bruce fell in love. They were married on 10 August 1932 on the MGM lot with Irving Thalberg and Norma Shearer as their witnesses. Virginia's father asked for a marriage contract – in which, much to Jack's amusement, he guaranteed his daughter was a virgin. Jack agreed to change his will, leaving everything to Virginia, and he took her parents along on their European honeymoon. But the trip was overshadowed by the suicide of Jack's friend Paul Bern only two months after his marriage to Jean Harlow. It was revealed after his death that his genitals were underdeveloped and there were rumours that he was impotent and perhaps bisexual. Jack believed Louis B. Mayer was behind these shocking revelations.

His contract expired, Gilbert returned to pick up his belongings at MGM and was further humiliated to find out his dressing room was being remodelled to accommodate Mayer's son-in-law, David O. Selznick.

Jack waited by the phone for a film offer but he hardly expected to hear from MGM producer Walter Wagner. Yet Garbo, who was making *Queen Christina* and wanted to replace her original co-star, Laurence Olivier, requested Gilbert – and Mayer gave his approval. On 23 August 1933, filming began. Jack said that Garbo was wonderful to him. Their love scenes were so steamy that she asked director Rouben Mamoulian to tone them down. Jack was a married man, she explained. He and his wife had a new baby girl, Susan Ann, and it would be inappropriate for her to make torrid love with him in the movie. Jack's reaction to this was, 'Backward, turn backward, O Time, in your flight.' One wonders if Garbo was actually concerned that Gilbert might get carried away if they were too passionate in their lovemaking. Being predominantly lesbian, she was not afraid for herself.

Jack was concentrating completely on *Queen Christina*, for his survival depended on its success, and ignored his wife and daughter. Virginia, taking this as an affront, filed for divorce. After all, how could she compete with the Great Garbo?

In their settlement Virginia received two insurance policies, $42,000 worth of property and $150 a month in child support. Jack blamed himself for the divorce. Afraid of giving a bad performance, and working in an unfriendly environment at MGM, he had made *Queen Christina* under tremendous pressure. 'The whole thing kept twisting in me like a knife,' he said. 'Through it all I forgot how young Virginia was. I won't marry again. I can't imagine any girl taking me seriously.'

Queen Christina was not one of Garbo's better offerings. It received mild reviews and is probably more revered today than it was in 1933. Most disappointing, it was not Gilbert's comeback movie. Even a picture with Garbo couldn't revive the magic that had withered away when he recited, 'I love you, I love you, I love you' in *His Glorious Night.*

Jack had signed a seven-year contract with MGM in order to make *Queen Christina* and now the studio had him in chains. They had no more roles for him and he could not work for another studio. On 29 March 1934 he published a message on the back page of the *Hollywood Reporter*:

Metro-Goldwyn-Mayer will neither offer me work nor release me from my contract

Jack Gilbert

As a result, to save face and unfavourable publicity MGM released him. In a June 1934 interview for *Movie Classic* Jack said, 'I have been on the screen for twenty years and I have managed to squeeze out of it complete unhappiness. Today I can't get a job. Four years ago I had a contract calling for $250,000 a picture. Today I can't get a job for $25.00 a week or for nothing at all . . . I want the simple right of every creature that walks the earth, the right to earn my own living.'

Harry Cohn, head of Columbia Pictures, eventually offered Jack a part in *The Captain Hates the Sea*, about a newspaperman who's trying to stop drinking and write a book. Much of the movie was shot on an old tug, which made everyone sick. To compensate the cast and crew, including Jack, drank plenty of liquor. During filming Cohn wired director Lewis Milestone: 'Hurry up. The costs are staggering.' The reply was: 'So is the cast.'

At the end of *The Captain Hates the Sea*, the wife asks, 'Did you stop drinking?'

'No,' Jack replies. And that was the last word delivered by John Gilbert on a movie set.

The *New York Times* called the film a meaningless production: 'John Gilbert who clutters up the ship's bar has no bearing on the story . . . something must have gone agley.'

*

When actress Marlene Dietrich heard about Gilbert's declining heath, she decided to do something about it. She wrote to her daughter Maria, 'Gilbert has emerged out of his "trunk" and enjoys life again like a child. Everything was really easy until he fell in love with me – then it got difficult, because he has a force that one secretly yearns for and when one finds it – one gets frightened. He is out of his mind that I don't want to and I really don't know why I don't – because he would really be worth it and it would make him so happy, but I'm not so sure it would be so easy to get out of it again – the passion is so hot.'

Marlene, an expert cook, fussed over Jack's meals and tried to wean him off the bottle by keeping him busy socially. Though a very sexy and promiscuous woman, she was more concerned about restoring Jack's health than satisfying his needs in bed. 'But he thought that I didn't love him if I didn't so I did. He wasn't very good. Those that "look" it so much never are.'

Dietrich made arrangements for Jack to appear with her in *Desire*, but he suffered a mild heart attack while they were in his pool and was replaced by Gary Cooper. Marlene stayed by Jack's side day and night, until one day Garbo drove up in front of his house in her battered Packard. Most likely she had come by simply to inquire about his health since she was going on vacation to Sweden, but Marlene was very jealous. It seemed to her that Jack was much too excited by the visit and spent too long chatting and laughing with Greta. So she left by the back door.

Because he was ill, Marlene did not stay away from Jack for long. She decided to arrange Christmas at the Tower House for him and his daughter, Leatrice. There was a beautifully decorated tree with many gifts under it and she prepared a delicious dinner. But she left so he could spend the day alone with his little girl.

Jack's health worsened. He had promised to see Leatrice on New Year's Day but cancelled, explaining that he wasn't feeling well. During the predawn hours of 9 January 1936, Jack had a convulsion that woke Marlene. Knowing he was dying, she called a doctor who would keep his mouth shut. She hastily packed her bag, removing any traces that might indicate she had been living there, then called her maid who managed to pick Marlene up without being noticed. The last thing she remembered was the sight of Jack's back, arched high in agony, while the doctor injected him with a powerful stimulant. Dietrich's daughter later heard on the radio that Gilbert had died alone and she wondered why. She found her mother in the bedroom wearing a monk's black robe, lighting candles next to a picture of Jack. Marlene stayed in her room alone for several days . . .

John Gilbert was declared dead at 9:05 a.m. on 9 January 1936 at the age of 37. The cause of death was given as a heart attack, but according to his daughter, he choked to death on his own tongue.

Garbo was attending the theatre in Stockholm when she heard the news. She went to her seat, leaving after the curtain went up to avoid the press.. Eventually, she had to face reporters. When asked about Jack's death she supposedly said, 'What is that to me?' She was so distressed at such reports that she broke her code of silence and stated that it was 'vicious misquoting' about a man for whom she felt deeply.

Though Marlene said Jack had made out a new will, it was never found. His entire estate, with the exception of $10,000 for his daughter, was left to Virginia Bruce.

Marlene attended Jack's funeral with Gary Cooper. She collapsed in his arms walking down the aisle to her chapel seat and wept during the entire service. Irving Thalberg was appalled at her behaviour.

Afterwards Thalberg caught up with Gilbert's former wife Leatrice and informed her, 'You know, Jack was on the verge of a real comeback. He had a contract waiting to be signed, but I honestly believe he didn't want it anymore.' This wasn't true, of course; it was only an attempt on Irving's part to make John Gilbert seem alive again. Thalberg himself died eight months later.

Jack was buried at Forest Lawn Cemetery in Glendale. His simple gravestone read 'In Memoriam', with his signature below.

According to producer David O. Selznick, John Gilbert should have played Rhett Butler in *Gone With the Wind*. That's a nice way to be remembered . . .

'You know what started all this, my so-called decline, was the terribly unfortunate role in which I broke into talkies, *His Glorious Night*. I played a passionate love scene à la silent-film stuff. You know, all gushing . . . blahh . . . My God, the people just laughed. I couldn't blame them.'

– John Gilbert

The Films of John Gilbert

Matrimony (Ince-Triangle, 1915)
Aloha Oe (Ince-Triangle, 1915)
The Aryan (Ince-Triangle, 1916)
The Corner (Ince-Triangle, 1916)
Civilization (Ince-Triangle, 1916)
The Last Act (Ince-Triangle, 1916)
Hell's Hinges (Ince Triangle, 1916)
Bullets and Brown Eyes (Ince-Triangle, 1916)
The Apostle of Vengeance (Ince-Triangle, 1916)
The Phantom (Ince-Triangle, 1916)
The Eye of (the) Night (Ince-Triangle, 1916)
Shell 43! (Ince-Triangle, 1916)
The Sin Ye Do (Ince-Triangle, 1916)
The Weaker Sex (Ince-Triangle, 1917)
Princess of the Dark (Ince-Triangle, 1917)
The Dark Road, (Ince-Triangle, 1917)
Happiness (Ince Triangle, 1917)
The Millionaire Vagrant (Ince-Triangle, 1917)
Hater of Men (Ince-Triangle, 1917)
The Mother Instinct (Ince-Triangle, 1917)
Golden Rule Kate (Ince-Triangle, 1917)
The Devil Dodger (Ince-Triangle, 1917)
Doing Her Bit (Triangle, 1917)
Up or Down (Triangle, 1917)
The Dollar Bid (Paralta, 1918)
Nancy Comes Home (Paralta, 1918)
Shackled (Paralta-Hodkinson, 1918)

Wedlock (Paralta-Hodkinson, 1918)
More Trouble (Pathe, 1918)
The Mask of Riches (Triangle, 1918)
Three X Gordon (Paralta-Hodkinson, 1918)
Sons of Men (Paralta-Hodkinson, 1918)
The Dawn of Understanding (Viagraph, 1918)
The Busher (Paramount-Ince, 1919)
The Man Beneath (Haworth for Robertson-Cole, 1919)
The White Heather (Tourmeur-Hiller and Wilk, 1919)
The Red Viper (Tyrad Pictures, 1919)
Widow By Proxy (Famous Players-Lasky, 1919)
Heart o' the Hills (First National, 1919)
Should a Woman Tell (Metro, 1919)
The White Circle (Famous Players-Lasky, 1920)
The Great Redeemer (Metro, 1920)
Deep Waters (Famous Players-Lasky, 1920)
The Bait (Paramount-Artcraft, Hope Hampton, 1921)
The Servant in the House (Walgreen Film, 1921)
Love's Penalty (Hope-Hampton, 1921)
Shame (Fox, 1921)
Ladies Must Live (Mayflower Photoplay, 1921)
Gleam o' Dawn (Fox, 1922)
Arabian Love (Fox, 1922)
The Yellow Stain (Fox, 1922)
Honor First (Honor Bright, 1922)
Monte Cristo (Fox, 1922)
Calvert's Valley (Fox, 1922)
The Love Gambler (Fox, 1922)
A California Romance (Fox, 1922)
While Paris Sleeps (Hodkinson, 1923)
Truxton King (Fox, 1923)
The Mothers of Youth (Fox, 1923)
St. Elmo (Fox, 1923)
The Exiles (Fox, 1923)
Cameo Kirby (Fox, 1923)
Just Off Broadway (Fox, 1924)
The Wolf Man (Fox, 1924)
The Lone Chance (Fox, 1924)
His Hour (MGM, 1924)

Married Flirts (MGM, 1924)
He Who Gets Slapped (MGM, 1924)
The Snob (MGM, 1924)
The Wife of the Centaur (MGM, 1924)
The Merry Widow (MGM, 1925)
The Big Parade (MGM, 1925)
La Boheme (MGM, 1926)
Bardelys the Magnificent (MGM, 1926)
Flesh and the Devil (MGM, 1926)
The Show (MGM, 1927)
Twelve Miles Out (MGM, 1927)
Man, Woman and Sin (MGM, 1927)
Love (MGM, 1927)
The Cossacks (MGM, 1928)
Four Walls (MGM, 1928)
Show People (MGM, 1928)
The Masks of the Devil (MGM, 1928)
A Woman of Affairs (MGM, 1928)
Desert Nights (MGM, 1929)
The Hollywood Revue of 1929 (MGM, 1929)
His Glorious Night (MGM, 1929)
Redemption (MGM, 1930)
Way For a Sailor (MGM, 1930)
Gentleman's Fate (MGM, 1931)
The Phantom of Paris (MGM, 1931)
West of Broadway (MGM, 1931)
Downstairs (MGM, 1932)
Fast Workers (MGM, 1933)
Queen Christina (MGM, 1933)
The Captain Hates the Sea (MGM, 1934)

4

Clark Gable

He was an unlikely candidate for 'King of Hollywood'. His big ears made his head look like a sugar bowl, he had hands like an ape and false teeth. His leading ladies complained about his bad breath. But he didn't care: they could take him or leave him. They took him. His lovemaking left a lot to be desired but as one woman put it, 'I couldn't get excited until I looked up and saw it was Clark Gable who was making love to me. Then I climaxed.'

He was one of a kind and there will never be another like him. Somehow his facial flaws merged into rugged handsomeness. Because he had played a convict on Death Row in the play *The Last Mile*, MGM cast him as the bad guy who pushed dames around and waited for them to light his cigarettes before he ungallantly blew smoke in their faces. Women found this exciting, while henpecked men stood up for their rights and gave their wives a boot in the backside.

The older, wealthy women he married made it possible for him to pursue an acting career. When he had accomplished his goal, he dumped them. But fate stepped in, taking away the one woman he loved in a fatal plane crash. After a period of mourning, he joined the Air Force. He had a death wish, but he survived and returned to MGM.

There was no love lost between MGM mogul Louis B. Mayer and Gable. He fought the system all the way and became a legend. Yet if he were alive he'd dispute this because, in his own way, the man was humble. Perhaps it was part of his charm. A tall, well-built guy, he looked as if he could kill with one swift blow, and Howard Strickling feared he would. But Gable behaved himself – with the exception of booze and women, his two great passions.

He had never thought of winning an Oscar, and when he got one for a film he hated he gave it away. *Gone With the Wind* didn't appeal to him because his leading lady in the story was in love with another man and that didn't fit his image. He was forced to play Rhett Butler and this time he expected an Oscar for his efforts; he was not a good sport when he lost out to an Englishman. So he got drunk, cursing both Louis B. Mayer and producer David O. Selznick.

Clark Gable had his faults, but his attributes outweighed them. He was a man's man, and as American as apple pie. He was a skilled fisherman and an avid hunter. He could take a car apart and put it back together. He lived on a ranch and would often be seen driving his own tractor, and loving it. He was as neat as a pin – with the exception of his hats, which he refused to have cleaned. There's a puzzle for a psychiatrist, but let's not try to analyse too far. It might destroy our illusions about a man who stood out among all the others. We adored him for all the things he wasn't, because we love rogues. Besides, who looks under a man's hat?

Clark Gable was born in Cadiz, Ohio, at 5:30 a.m. on 1 February 1901, weighing in at almost eleven pounds. The doctor's fee was ten dollars. Giving birth to such a big baby was difficult for the frail and sickly Adeline Gable, who had been warned not to have children. She died seven months later. Her husband William was a wildcatter, a speculative prospector after oil, but he never discovered black gold. He did, however, find another woman, Jennie Dunlap. 'She was the best thing that ever happened to me when I was a kid,' Clark said. 'She treated me like her own.'

When Clark was five years old, the Gables settled in Hopedale. The well-bred Jennie wanted only the best for her 'Clarkie'. She dressed him like a little gentleman, helping him with his homework and dedicating herself to his well-being. 'She wanted me to be somebody,' Clark said in later years. 'This wasn't easy because my father was the kind of guy who believed in being born, working hard and dying. Jennie encouraged me to play the piano, to sing and to read. My father thought this was a waste of time. He wanted me to work with my hands, to be a man.'

At fourteen Clark was six feet tall and weighed 155 pounds. Thelma Lewis, a pretty redhead, was his first date, 'He wasn't good-looking,' she confessed. 'His ears were too big and he had bad teeth. He couldn't dance because he was all feet. He wasn't interested in school, except for playing the alto horn in our band. His one bad habit was chain smoking, and he'd never give it up.'

The turning point in Clark's life was his father's decision to buy a farm. 'I had to get up at four in the morning and feed the livestock and ploughed until it was time to take the bus to school,' he said. 'I just didn't have what it takes to be a farmer. When I was sixteen I went back to Hopedale and hauled water for the miners for five dollars a day. A buddy of mine, Andy Means, said he was going to Akron because there were good paying jobs in the rubber industry. I bought a Model T and decided to go with him.'

William demanded that Clark stay home and work on the farm. It was Jennie who convinced him to let his son go in peace, her only regret that he had quit school. Clark found a job as a timekeeper at the Miller Rubber Company for $25 a week. 'I'd never been to a movie,' he recalled. 'We didn't have theatres where I came from. I loved westerns, but it never entered my mind about becoming a movie star. It was the stage that thrilled me. The Music Hall on Exchange Street was featuring a play called *Bird of Paradise*, about the South Sea Islands. I'd never seen anything so exciting in my life.' Clark found a job at the Music Hall as callboy; paid nothing except tips, he slept in the theatre, showered at the YMCA and did odd jobs. He was hungry and broke, but when he got a walk-on part he was the happiest guy in the world. It called for three words, 'Good evening, sir.' Only the receipt of a telegram dampened his excitement. Jennie was seriously ill. Clark arrived home just in time to be with her when she died. 'I lost my best friend,' he said.

While he waited to receive a $300 inheritance from his grandfather, Clark worked with William in the Oklahoma oil fields, but on his 21st birthday he went home to collect his money. William was angry when his son did not return. 'I told the stubborn mule if he left me this time, he needn't come back. I was through with the sissy.'

Clark headed for Kansas City where, he heard, a new repertory company was being organised. Instead he ended up working with a tent show for ten dollars a week. 'I hawked plays dressed as a clown on street corners and played the French horn in the orchestra,' Gable said. 'I was a big guy so they had me putting up the tent and doing heavy work.' He mentioned an affair with an older woman, a member of the tent show who he claimed had only one eye. Was he kidding? With the sense of humour he displayed in later years, it's possible. Even when he was every woman's passion on the screen, however, he often bedded down the ugliest. Why? 'She was there,' he would say.

When the tent show closed he hopped a refrigerator train and got off in Bend, Oregon, working there for a lumber company. Then he hopped a freight car for Portland, hoping to find a theatre there. To avoid starving, Clark sold ties in a department store. It was there he met Earle Larrimore, who was directing an amateur acting group, the Red Lantern Players. On 23 July 1922, he played the part of Eliza, a Negro cook, in *When Women Rule*. In *The Villain Still Pursued Her*, he dressed as a baby and appeared on stage in a huge crib. It didn't matter how much the audience laughed, as long as they reacted.

It was when Clark auditioned for the Astoria Stock Company that he met 22-year-old Franz Dorfler, who had given up school teaching to become an actress. Five feet two inches tall, with light brown hair and soft dreamy eyes, she was spunky and bright. The company hired her that night, but not Gable. So as not to lose out altogether, he offered to walk her home. She refused, but he followed her and by the time they arrived at her house, he almost had her convinced that he couldn't live without her. 'I found it difficult to ignore him,' Franz said:

> He wasn't good looking or mature, but he was lonely, under-nourished and sad. Clark was very jealous of any man who talked to me. Though he was annoying, there was something about him that I can't explain. He had a way with people. I was going on tour with the stock company and he offered to work for nothing, to fill in for the other actors, because he knew all the parts. He helped with the scenery and carried the trunks. I think it was his determination that convinced me he could succeed at anything. He was my first beau and I was his first girlfriend. We had been looking for each other and sealed it with a kiss.

When the stock company closed down, Franz and Clark went to her parents' farm in the Willamette Valley, near Portland. He earned money picking hops and spent his spare time trying to impress the Dorflers, but they considered Clark a drifter and convinced Franz to live with her brother in Portland to think over his marriage proposal. In an effort to become a model citizen, Gable took a job as a lineman at the telephone company. Having thus been persuaded to change their minds about Clark, the Dorflers gave Franz permission to marry him, and a Christmas wedding was planned. Convinced that they could be Lunt and Fontaine one day, she told Clark about a new drama teacher who had just arrived in Portland.

Josephine Dillon was born in Denver, Colorado, in 1888 and graduated from Stanford University in 1908, completing her education in New York and Paris. Having chosen the theatre, she earned a starring role on Broadway, but according to her, she did not have the personality for performing and preferred teaching others how to act.

Gable enrolled in Dillon's evening classes, where she remembered him showing up with a different girl every night. After several readings, and watching him entice females into his grasp, Dillon decided he was a student of life. Though he was pale and tired looking, he had a winning smile along with the eagerness so necessary for the theatre. Desire often compensates for lack of talent, she said.

Whatever it was, Josephine saw something in Gable. It's doubtful if she was attracted to him at this point: she was too professional for that. He said he'd work hard, do whatever she wanted him to do. Surprisingly, Dillon decided to concentrate on him and was rather taken aback when he told her, 'You're a fine-looking girl!' She was hardly that. Josephine had short dark hair, a low forehead, a broad nose with exaggerated nostrils and thin lips, but she was small and carried herself well. Clark was taken with her, though she was thirteen years older. Perhaps it was his mother complex, or maybe she simply represented the world of theatre – touching her was touching Broadway. For fun, he also touched the younger women who pursued him; as Josephine thought, they were not the type of girls a guy would consider marrying.

Franz came home to find her boyfriend transformed. He raved about acting and the stage, avoiding any talk of their forthcoming marriage until she confronted him.

'Well,' he stammered, 'a doctor once told me I should never get married.'

'Why?' she asked.

'I'd rather not discuss it,' he replied.

Clark's excuse was so far-fetched, she was speechless.

Considering Franz a threat, Josephine decided to close her school in Portland, and told Gable she was going to Hollywood because there were thousands of actors registered there. When she was settled she'd send for him. When her competition left, Franz expected to resume her relationship with Clark. But he avoided her – though not out of any loyalty to Josephine. He was seeing other women. Several months later he told Franz he was going to Hollywood. 'I threw his love letters into the fireplace,' she said, 'and cried every night for years because I never heard from him.'

In August 1924, with fifty dollars in his pocket, Gable arrived in Hollywood, where he found Josephine reading and typing scripts for Paramount Studios until her drama school was established. The relationship between Dillon and Gable has always been a mystery. Those who knew him in later years found it hard to accept that he was not intimate with her as payment for her tutoring him. 'One woman is just like another,' he said. But she insisted their relationship was strictly professional.

After four months in Hollywood, Josephine wanted Clark to quit his job as a mechanic and begin making the rounds of theatrical producers. But it took him less than a month to miss his weekly income and to feel the sting of rejection. Though Josephine thought he was lowering himself, he sought work as an extra in the movies. He would never forget the thousands of actors waiting at the studios, many of whom slept on the street to be first in line. Clark's dream was crumbling – Josephine controlled the money, and without a few bucks in his pocket, he was caged. As strange as it seems, he decided that marriage was the only way to gain his freedom. He told Josephine, 'If I didn't have to live in a hotel, that would help out the finances.'

So the couple were married by the Reverend Meadows in his rectory on 18 December 1924. Clark gave his age as 24, she hers as 34, though she was two years older. He moved into her tiny bungalow. There was no honeymoon and, according to Dillon, no wedding night. Yet there was only one bedroom . . .

Josephine emphasised their togetherness as student and teacher, at work every day and every night – reading, practising how to breathe correctly, memorising lines, working on diction and social graces. She chose their friends carefully, surrounding Clark with struggling artists, painters, and composers who were talented and cultured. Sometimes the upper crust would slum at these parties for their own amusement, and Clark was attracted to wealth. When he walked into a roomful of people, his eyes roamed for women wearing expensive jewellery. The first time Josephine found him whispering into a diamond-studded ear she was crushed. How long would it be before a younger and wealthier woman took Clark away from her? How long could he hold out in a city of lavish mansions and rich movie stars who flaunted themselves in polished McFarlans, Rolls-Royces, Packards, and Lancias?

Though he hated the thought of acting in films, Gable was thrilled to get a bit part in the silent film *White Man*. He was paid fifteen dollars a day, but it's doubtful Josephine saw any of this money. He came home with a set of secondhand golf clubs. One can only imagine how she felt, knowing he was playing on the links while she read and typed all day. The only way she could keep him at home was to work him unmercifully. Often he felt pressured going over the same recitations again and again, listening to her criticisms until he was compelled to run out and slam the door behind him.

Many years later each of them complained about the other's compulsion to act. 'I don't know what he thought about other than the theatre,' she said. 'He never discussed anything else with me.'

Gable, in turn, grumbled, 'I'd come home and she'd start teaching. I wasn't walking right. I entered the room all wrong. My voice was too high. She never did anything but teach, teach, teach.'

He managed to get work as an extra for five dollars a day in several movies, including *The Merry Widow* with Mae Murray and John Gilbert. How did Gable do it? He wasn't handsome or talented in 1925 and yet he managed to appear in a spectacular MGM film. How? The truth is that he was desperate enough to allow himself to be seduced by the popular movie idol, Billy Haines. According to William J. Mann in his biography of Haines, *Wisecracker*, the two men met at MGM and were intimate at the Beverly Wilshire Hotel. 'It wasn't a blow job,' a friend insisted. 'Billy fucked him in the men's room. Billy was the fucker, never the fuckee.'

Ironically, Haines was the best friend of Gable's love, Joan Crawford. Surely he told her about his folly, for she confirmed it after Clark's death. Apparently Gable played the gigolo during these lean years, although not with men. If he smelled money, he would stalk his prey with a smooth line and plenty of humility.

Meanwhile, Josephine was working on his behalf. Jane Cowl was about to open in the L.A. stage production of *Romeo and Juliet*. Clark auditioned and got the part of a spear carrier for thirty dollars a week. During rehearsals he was Cowl's obedient servant. She offered to teach him how to effectively carry a spear on stage, the lessons being conducted in her dressing room. Where else? Then she raised his salary to forty dollars a week.

Having money in his pocket made him more tolerant toward his wife. He bought her two gifts – a pair of shoes and an alarm clock. She said, 'He wanted to make sure I was able to walk to work on time.' Poor Josephine! In the stage production of *What Price Glory*, Dillon took over direction of the play, disrupting the cast and making Clark nervous. Within days she was banned from the theatre.

Lullaby took Clark to San Francisco, but he did not send money to Josephine. He did, however, send his laundry home, expecting it to be ready when he arrived. Instead of complaining, she paid to have his front teeth capped, carrying the debt long after Clark was out of her life.

In 1926 he seduced another leading lady, Pauline Frederick, during his fourth play, *Madame X*. She was 44 years old, famous, rich and divorced three times, a femme fatale in and out of costume. Pauline simply went from one phase of youth to another. On opening night she received more than thirty curtain calls while Gable drooled in the wings.

In *Chicago* he next played a loudmouthed newspaperman, coat collar up, with a cocky grin and a lumberman's stride. It was his first chance to use Josephine's upstaging trick. When he wasn't stage centre, Clark managed to get attention by standing still with a smirk on his face and the devil in his eyes. He was such a hit that MGM talent scouts expressed an interest. But he turned them down. He wanted the Broadway stage.

Again Josephine came to the rescue, though Clark wasn't keen on joining a repertory company in Houston as she suggested. When he balked, she tried to impress upon him the importance of doing a different play every week. 'I don't learn that fast,' he said. She insisted that the experience would be invaluable, not to mention the salary of $200 a week and the chance to play leading roles.

Just as Franz Dorfler had been responsible for Gable's meeting Dillon, Josephine was responsible for his meeting his second wife. She was from Houston, but met him in New York when he was playing in *Machinal*, which opened at the Plymouth Theatre on 7 September 1928.

Ria Langham had auburn hair worn in a fashionable wavy bob, ivory skin, and soft dark eyes. She was a tiny five foot two and resembled Franz Dorfler. Ria, however, wore expensive matching hats, gloves and shoes, tweed or wool suits, and an heirloom pin that held a silk scarf in place. She was stately, proper, and plain.

Born Maria Franklin on 17 January 1884 in Kentucky, she was married at the age of seventeen. Four years and one son later, Ria moved in with her aunt in Houston, got a divorce, and married millionaire contractor Alfred Thomas Lucas, 22 years her senior. She had two children and lived in a palatial home, becoming the belle of Houston society. Ten years later Lucas died, leaving her a fortune. A marriage to Denzil Langham lasted only two years. It was her daughter, Jana, who saw Clark in Houston and took her mother backstage to meet him. He was anxious to fit into Ria's gracious way of life, and she was equally anxious to show him how it was done. When *Machinal* closed he found himself broke again but she offered to support him, suggesting he have it out with Josephine. But Josephine refused to give him a Mexican divorce. 'I filed in California,' Dillon said. 'I asked for nothing, no settlement and no alimony. But he would have to wait a year before the divorce was final.'

In April 1930, assuming that he was now a free man, he married Ria. There is no record of where or when they exchanged their vows, but in biographical sketches Gable gives 1930 as the year of his marriage to Ria.

With the exception of his Broadway credits, no information was given as to where or how Gable lived in New York. This is unusual since MGM's publicity staff took great pride in retracing the lives of their stars. Carefully, Gable's two years in New York were barely mentioned. If anyone had told Clark at this time that he would become an MGM star he might have punched him in the mouth. No sir, he was staying on Broadway. One producer remembers Gable making the rounds, looking for another play. 'My memory of him is vivid,' the man said, 'because he used white paint on his gold teeth and sometimes the paint streaked.'

A turning point in his life came when he received a phone call from Lillian Albertson Macloon, who had chosen him for rep plays in California. She thought he'd be perfect for the part of Killer Mears in *The Last Mile*. 'Spencer Tracy is playing the part on Broadway,' she told Gable on the phone. 'I suggest you take in the performance and let me know if you'd be interested in doing it out here in Los Angeles.'

Clark saw the play and was in awe of Tracy – which was one reason he decided not to accept the offer. 'How can I follow a guy like that?' he told Lillian.

She laughed. 'You won't have to be that good out here.'

He fought Lillian – and Ria – all the way. He couldn't possibly take a role that Tracy had perfected, and, besides, he hated California. But the two women were persistent and so he headed west. There were only four weeks to rehearse *The Last Mile*, a powerful story about prisoners on Death Row and their desperate attempt to escape, but Gable was in command of his audience at the Majestic Theater in Los Angeles on 7 June 1930 – his greatest triumph to date. He continued to ignore the talent scouts, though, and wanted nothing to do with agents – until he met Minna Wallis, sister of producer Hal Wallis. She didn't try to fill his head with big ideas and never mentioned a screen test, admitting that she too was just starting out. Gable liked her refreshing approach. In fact Minna took him to Pathe, which was proof enough that Clark liked her very much. William Boyd was being filmed in *Painted Desert* and the casting director thought Gable would fit in very well, adding, 'I assume you can ride a horse.' Clark's mouth dropped open, but Minna said, 'He certainly can!'

The deal was for $750 a week. Whether it was the money or the thought of riding a horse, Gable felt faint. 'I can't ride,' he said.

'You'll learn,' she smiled.

He went to Griffith Park Riding Academy and told the instructor his problem. The instructor took Gable and a small horse to the top of a hill and said, 'Get on and meet me at the bottom.' By the end of the week Clark could ride fairly well. But Pathe was heading for bankruptcy, so Minna went to Warner Brothers hoping to get Clark a part in *Little Caesar*. Jack Warner took one look at the screen test and said, 'What the hell am I going to do with a guy who has ears like that!'

Gable told Minna, 'I hate this racket and I hate Hollywood.'

'But your wife and her kids just arrived. Besides, RKO and MGM are interested in you. Buck up!'

It was Irving Thalberg at MGM who finally signed Gable to a one-year contract for $650 a week on 4 December 1930. Publicity chief Howard Stricking liked him at first handshake. 'He was a big guy, but a gentle one, We became lifelong friends.'

'If it hadn't been for Howard,' Clark said, 'I never would have lasted.'

Gable's first film was *The Easiest Way* with Constance Bennett, in which he played Anita Page's laundryman husband. He looked much younger on the screen, almost pretty, while portraying the type of guy who would not be pushed around. Meanwhile, MGM set out to make a man out of Clark. He worked out in a gym and learned how to use a gun, control an expensive fishing rod, and perfect his stance on a horse. Howard Strickling commented, 'He was a natural. He wanted to learn. He wanted to be a star. He cooperated with us all the way. Our only problem was Ria, who looked like his mother so we avoided mentioning her. They were seldom photographed together.'

MGM preferred their male stars to remain single and available for the millions of women who dreamed that they might have a chance – reason enough at least to buy a ticket at the box office.

Clark's next movie was *Dance, Fools, Dance* with Joan Crawford. She recalled, 'I was terrified the first time we met because he was a stage actor and that gave him an edge.' But actually Gable was the one who was terrified. 'My God, she's a star. She'll make me look like a jerk.'

Crawford was MGM's first manufactured star, moulded to fit the image of what they wanted her to be. They got rid of her name, Lucille Le Sueur; a fan magazine used her for their 'Pick-a-Name' contest and Joan Crawford was born. 'Sounds like crawfish,' she moaned to her friend Billy Haines, who helped her learn the ropes of how to behave in Hollywood and how to handle the MGM brass.

Joan was 24 when she married Douglas Fairbanks Jr. But the elder Fairbanks and his wife, Mary Pickford, did not approve of Crawford so an invitation to their royal residence, Pickfair, was not likely. MGM cleverly co-starred Joan and Doug in *Our Modern Maidens*, released in 1929, thus sending an indirect message to the residents of Pickfair: 'If we've accepted your son, why can't you accept our daughter?' It worked – the doors of Pickfair were soon opened to Joan. Just in time, too, because her legion of loyal fans were ready to burn down the mansion.

Joan and Clark could identify with each other. They both had unhappy childhoods and left home at an early age, struggling to stay afloat. Hard-working and determined, they never took their success for granted. In later years she claimed they were too much alike to have a successful marriage. 'We were attracted to each other instantly,' Joan said. 'I had what he wanted and he had what I wanted. The electricity between us smouldered on the screen, too. We meant every kiss and embrace. God, we had balls in those days!' It wasn't easy for Clark to go home to Ria after being with Joan, but MGM kept him so busy he had little time to think. He was Jean Harlow's leading man in *The Secret Six*. In due time, they, too, would have a sizzling affair.

Ria was anxious to have Joan and husband Doug for dinner. Gable said, 'I don't think so.'

'But, darling, I should love to meet the family.'

'No you wouldn't,' he snapped. 'They're not Park Avenue society, my dear. Hey, I'm tryin' to learn my lines.'

'For what?'

'*Finger Points* with Richard Barthelmess, and then *A Free Soul* with Norma Shearer.'

'Oh, she's married to your boss, Irving Thalberg! Why don't we have them over for dinner?'

'Because I haven't got the goddamn time for socialising,' he exclaimed. 'And I don't kiss asses.'

In *A Free Soul*, Clark played a tough racketeer and Norma a spoiled rich girl who likes rough sex and gets it from him. Eventually, she begins making fun of his shabby manners and flashy clothes. He knows what he is, but she says it once too often. So Gable sweeps her up in his arms. Norma coos, and Clark throws her back on the couch, making sure she stays there. When Norma stands up to protest, she is pushed back 'where you belong!' Audiences loved it. After all, here was a poor guy trying to make a crooked buck during the Depression, and here was a rich dame who changed her furs as often as she changed her stockings.

Gable had balanced the scale of the sexes. Audiences were bored with romantic Valentino types, and here was a man who could carry women off to a cave. If a girl played coy, he either booted her in the backside or threw her over his shoulder.

In fact many people believed they had seen him actually strike Norma in the course of the scuffle, and MGM received thousands of letters about 'the guy who slapped Norma Shearer'. It is a snippet of misinformation that follows him to this day. His abuse of Norma was so popular with fans that he socked Barbara Stanwyck for real in *Night Nurse*. Joan Blondell, who was also in the film, said, 'When Gable walked up on the set the first day, Barbara and I had to sit down. He was overpowering.'

Irving Thalberg described Clark best: 'He was the man every woman wanted and every man wanted to be.'

Though Gable was now making $850 a week, Minna Wallis wasn't satisfied. Knowing that every studio in Hollywood wanted him, MGM offered $500 more a week, which would be put in trust. Minna went along with it, because she knew Ria was paying the bills.

At the beginning of *Sporting Blood*, the name flashed across the screen: 'Starring Clark Gable'. No more 'with' or 'and' – he would share top billing from now on. But a problem emerged that almost ruined his career. After MGM found out that Gable's New York marriage to Ria was not valid in California, the couple were rushed into a second ceremony, which took place on 19 June 1931. As they were leaving the courthouse, the 'newlyweds' were attacked by the press. Ria broke down completely. 'Please don't print this,' she pleaded. 'I have three children.' Later she was mortified over losing control and she rarely permitted an interview after that. Clark remained expressionless and composed as he led Ria to a limousine.

If MGM was concerned about such publicity, they soon had something else to offset it. Greta Garbo wanted Gable for her next film, *Susan Lenox – Her Rise and Fall*. In this one, he went after the girl and, though it wasn't one of his best films, he held his own beside Garbo. Then a call came from the big boss, Louis B. Mayer. He sat Clark down, saying he had received a letter from Josephine Dillon Gable. Though she was polite and dignified, she did not paint a pretty picture of Clark. He owed her money and had made no effort to repay it. She needed money desperately. Now the press was knocking on her door. What should she do? Clark offered $200 a month provided she did not talk about him to the press, and she signed the agreement. Clark, who was very close with a dollar, quietly fumed. Would he ever be rid of her? Would she never stop using his name, which linked them together? It didn't matter that she was no longer allowed to speak to reporters, because the damage was done.

When Josephine took credit for her ex-husband's acting skills, respected writer Adela Rogers St. Johns wrote to the contrary. She defended Clark, and made Josephine appear to be an opportunist. Adela had more than one reason for taking his part – she had been intimate with him. Minna Wallis remained a loyal agent for the same reason. Though both women knew his worth as an actor, they were equally taken with him as a lover. Adela said in later years, 'He wasn't a satisfying lover until I looked up at his face and realised it was Clark Gable who was making love to me. Then I climaxed.' There were rumours that she gave birth to his baby, but she denied this, saying, 'Don't you think if I had Gable's baby I'd shout it to the world!'

However, it was Joan Crawford who stole his heart. Their passion was evident in *Possessed*. She played a shop girl who goes to New York and becomes the mistress of a rich lawyer, played by Gable. After hours, they often met at the beach, but their dressing-room encounters were indiscreet and rumours about the affair reached Ria. Rather than confront him, she took her children to New York, asking MGM to make the arrangements because she was travelling as Mrs. Clark Gable. At every stop along the way, Ria spoke to the press. By the time she arrived in New York, the whole country knew who Mrs. Clark Gable was.

L.B. Mayer decided it was time to put out the fire on the set of *Possessed*. Summoning Clark to his office, Mayer asked him angrily, 'Do you have any idea what I went through with your first wife to shut her up?'

'I'm paying for it.'

'If you think two hundred dollars is payment due, my friend, you're wrong. You're getting away with murder. If Josephine had gotten a lawyer, she'd be living in a decent neighbourhood with a decent income. However, I don't think the present Mrs. Gable is that stupid.'

'I'm in love with Joan,' Clark spoke up.

'There's no such thing as love in this town. Now listen to me carefully. The affair with Joan is over. You will call your wife and ask her to come home. You love and miss her. In the future you'll take Ria out dining and dancing. Let the world see what a happy couple you are.'

Clark made the call and Ria came running back to Hollywood.

Mayer confronted Joan, threatening to cancel their contracts if they continued the affair. 'If I do that,' he added, 'no other studio in town will hire you. I'll see to that.' Such was the power wielded by Louis B. Mayer.

Gable hated every minute of *Hell Divers* with Wallace Beery, about naval aviators. His nerves were frayed, his moods were black and his outlook was depressing. 'I can't take it anymore,' he told Minna. 'Now they want me to play a minister with Marion Davies in *Polly of the Circus*. Well, damn it, I won't do it. I'm going to hide out in Palm Springs while you do some negotiating, honey.'

Marion Davies was so upset she begged her lover, William Randolph Hearst, to do something about it. Hearst told Mayer to give Clark what he wanted. So on 22 January 1932, Gable signed a two-year contract for $2000 a week and made the film. It was terrible, but his affair with Marion made it all worthwhile. Clark needed his freedom. Since Ria had attached herself to MGM, he was surrounded on all sides. Mayer controlled his working days and Ria controlled his weekends.

Gable's next film, *Red Dust*, was a box-office smash. His leading lady was Jean Harlow, known affectionately at MGM as 'The Baby'. But during production her husband, MGM executive Paul Bern, committed suicide. It was one of the major scandals of 1932 when word got out that Bern was impotent. When she married, Jean had told close friends she was tired of being mauled by men and that Paul loved her for her mind, which was a blessing for the busty, sexy actress. Gable was there for her when she resumed filming after a brief period of mourning. They were together constantly, clinging together on the movie set and making love at the Chateau Marmont hotel on Sunset Boulevard. Mayer was aware of this but did not want to upset Jean, who was teetering on the edge after her husband's suicide. Maybe Gable could see her through the pain. So, as long as they were discreet, he did nothing about it. Joan Crawford knew Clark was bedding Jean, whom she disliked intensely. She casually mentioned it to Gable, but he denied it.

Red Dust was labelled the epitome of sexual daring. When *Time* magazine criticised the movie's brazen moral values, the lines at the box office just grew longer. Gable dumps Harlow for a married woman (Mary Astor) in the film, but that wasn't what the fuss was about – adultery was widely accepted in films. It was a nude Jean taking a bath in a rain barrel and telling a bare-chested Clark to 'scrub my back' that created the sensation.

He wasn't happy about shaving his chest for the scene, but hairy ones were considered obscene at that time.

In his first interview, Gable talked about being a star. 'It isn't looks and it isn't experience,' he said. 'It isn't ability because everyone knows there are stars who can't act worth a damn. The public makes the stars. But they don't know what they want . . . You want to be a movie star? Maybe you'll like it and maybe you wouldn't like it. You might not be happy at all.'

And that was also his last interview. He was told to keep his mouth shut. There were times, however, when he was quoted: 'It's my business to work, not to think.' And, when asked about his new house, 'It's a hell of a lot better than the dump I lived in before out here.'

Mayer tried to reason with him. 'Your fans don't want to hear those things. You've got to give them the impression you love working for MGM where there are more stars than there are in heaven. The public would give anything to be in your shoes. Why do you think they pay to see you?'

'Damned if I know,' Gable replied.

Though he had countless affairs, Clark was careful not to talk about those. When actress Lupe Velez made it known she wanted him he said, 'She has a big mouth and will blab it all over town what a lousy lover I am.'

The only significance about *Strange Interlude* with Norma Shearer is the moustache Gable had to grow – it became his trade mark, because he never shaved it off. He went to Paramount to make *No Man of Her Own* with Carole Lombard, who gave him a ham with his name on it. She had him pegged from the start. 'I'm one leading lady he didn't seduce,' she announced.

When Joan Crawford returned from Europe, she decided to become friendly with Ria, both to make things easier on Clark and to pacify Mayer. The Gables attended dinner parties at her home and moved into a house in Brentwood, around the corner from Joan. She and Ria actually got along very well. Joan liked rubbing elbows with society women, and Ria enjoyed Hollywood gossip. She was especially thrilled when Clark made a movie with Helen Hayes.

Ria was the only one. *The White Sister* was terrible, and Clark blamed Mayer's son-in-law, David Selznick. 'I don't make movies with madonnas,' he told Ria. 'Irving Thalberg's in Europe recovering from a heart attack. And if he dies, I'm sunk.'

'L.B.'s in your corner, darling.'

'Or backing me into one,' he scowled.

Gable's problems intensified when his father showed up on his doorstep, thanks to Ria, who was hoping for a reconciliation. Clark had no choice but to offer William a home with all the fringe benefits – cook, maid, butler, flashy car, and expensive clothes discarded by his famous son. Mayer expected no less. His family of stars were expected to take care of their families. It was the American way.

The following year, 1933, was to be another difficult one for Gable. He had no way of knowing he was just around the corner from glory, and it would be uphill all the way. Missing Thalberg's keen perception and understanding ways, Mayer took over, dealing with Gable ruthlessly. His only saving grace was making *Hold Your Man* with Jean Harlow. When Mayer decided to put him in *Dancing Lady* with Crawford, he had mixed emotions. Joan, in the middle of divorce proceedings, was putting the pressure on Gable. He responded that Ria would clean him out financially if he left her, though in reality he was having his cake and eating it, too, and he liked it that way. Crawford saw him whenever possible, but she was becoming interested in actor Franchot Tone, whom she would later marry.

Gable took time off to have his rotten teeth removed. While he was waiting for his gums to settle before being fitted for false teeth, he joined the Masons. Several of his close friends swear that his loyalty to the organisation was such that he would not go to bed with a girl if anyone in her family was a Mason.

When he returned to work in September 1933 he had it out with Mayer. 'Do you hate Thalberg so much you'd blackball his projects? If he were here taking charge of production, I'd get a decent film!'

Mayer smiled with glee. 'If you're so faithful to Thalberg, maybe you'd like to work on one of his projects.'

'It has to be better than the shit I've been shovelling.'

Mayer had to punish Gable and he knew how to do it. He owed Columbia Pictures a favour. They were working on a silly caper called *It Happened One Night*. Thalberg liked it, but it had been rejected by Mayer, who had instead agreed to loan Robert Montgomery to Columbia to make the picture. But now he changed his mind. Calling Harry Cohn, head of Columbia, he told him, 'Gable's been a bad boy. I'd like to show him who's boss around here. You can have him.'

Clark, who knew every actor in town had turned down the part, threatened to walk out on his contract until Ria talked him out of it. Claudette Colbert agreed to make the film for the money, and for the chance to work with Gable. But Clark, who had switched to bourbon for this flop, was drunk when he met director Frank Capra. Frank offered to go over the script with him. 'Or would you rather read it yourself?'

Gable replied, 'I don't give a fuck what you do with it!'

Mayer gloated. He had got rid of a rotten script and saved his precious Robert Montgomery. Best of all, Gable was suffering.

The story of a runaway heiress and a newspaper man travelling together from Miami to New York was mundane and boring, but the brilliant Capra forged ahead. His tools were weak – one bourbon-slugging leading man and a prissy leading lady who did not want to show her leg in the hitch-hiking scene or remove any of her clothes before the 'walls of Jericho', the blanket Gable used to divide the motel room for the lady's privacy. There was plenty of ad-libbing and many last-minute changes were made. They all came about spontaneously – and came right.

Clark was seen undressing for bed in the film, and it was revealed that he was not wearing an undershirt – for the simple reason that it wasted time after taking off his sweater and shirt. When men followed Gable's example, the sale of undershirts dropped drastically.

Before the release of *It Happened One Night*, Clark portrayed a dedicated intern in *Men in White* with Myrna Loy. MGM sent him on tour to promote the film, and it was an experience never to be forgotten. His public had never seen him in the flesh and they went wild. He was touched and kissed and grabbed and poked, stripped of buttons, cuff links, sleeves, shoes and hair. One cannot possibly imagine the terrible reality of what one has become during the long months locked up in a studio. Suddenly the doors of the outside world are flung open, and a billion eyes stare and two million hands reach out. It is hard to believe this is love and not war. Gable was completely bewildered and confused. His only consolation was women – women, women everywhere, and they were all his! Ria had no choice but to accept it. More than once she walked into their hotel room to find her husband kissing and fondling a girl. She accepted the fact that he was 'getting his feet wet'. Of greater concern to her was the possibility of a serious romance, like that with Joan Crawford.

It Happened One Night opened at Radio City Music Hall on 23 February 1934, with no fanfare. After one week, the film was distributed around the country – and it took off. People needed to laugh during the Depression and this movie was hilarious in a down-to-earth way, with no pretences or boring gags. The critics changed their minds, but still no one expected big things.

Gable meanwhile was making *Manhattan Melodrama* with Myrna Loy, and *Chained* with Joan Crawford. Then the unthinkable occurred. *It Happened One Night* was nominated for Academy Awards in five categories – Best Actor, Best Actress, Director, Writer and Best Picture. The consensus was that it didn't have a chance of winning anything, but MGM were not taking any chances, and raised Clark's salary to $3000 a week.

He should have been happy, but he wasn't. 'Every time I get more money,' he told Joan, 'something comes along to take the gravy.' This time it was William Gable's marriage and a new house. And Ria decided it was time to use his money instead of hers. Though he was generous when he had to be, Clark was always very close with a buck.

After Office Hours with Constance Bennett was Gable's last movie in 1934. While everyone in Hollywood buzzed about the Oscars, he decided not to go: 'Who wants to sit around and smile watching someone else win?' he asked Ria. Somehow she convinced him to attend. He hated every minute of putting on the dog for those who would destroy him. He fortified himself with plenty of bourbon at the Biltmore Hotel on 27 February 1935.

To everyone's amazement, *It Happened One Night* walked off with awards for all nominated categories. Claudette Colbert had boarded a train for New York and was rushed to the Biltmore to receive her Oscar. Clark was up against Frank Morgan in *Affairs of Cellini*, and Carole Lombard's ex-husband, William Powell, in *The Thin Man*. In a drunken daze he heard his name and managed to reach the podium without stumbling. He thanked the Academy and, during his exit, mumbled to himself, '. . . I'm still going to wear the same size hat . . . the same size hat . . .'

Gable seemed to have beaten the system – Metro-Goldwyn-Mayer, one of the biggest in the world – and its almighty dictator, L.B. Mayer. Clutching his Oscar, he glanced over at the mogul with a 'fuck you' expression on his face. But Mayer's attitude was merely that one of his contract players had won an Academy Award and that was good enough for him. Clark had to chuckle to himself. He had defied all the principles of acting – he had lived on bourbon, worn one outfit, worked only four weeks, and didn't make a pass at his leading lady. Figure it.

Did success go to his head? In one aspect, yes. He fired Minna Wallis and signed with the biggest and the best agency, Berg/Allenberg. They claimed they paid Minna $25,000, but she denied it. Was she angry with Gable? Hurt, maybe, but still willing to share his bed when he wanted her.

*

Clark's next movie, *Call of the Wild*, was filmed in Mount Baker, Washington. He was glad to get away from the studio, and from Ria. His leading lady was 22-year-old Loretta Young, who had eloped with actor Grant Withers when she was nineteen. A devout Catholic, she had the marriage annulled a few months later. In 1933, she had an affair with Spencer Tracy who left his wife for her, but Loretta had second thoughts and broke off the relationship. A year later, during a snowstorm that shut down production of *Call of the Wild*, she became involved with Gable.

Director William Wellman recalled, 'We had big trouble. Gable was tending to business, and not the business of making pictures. He was paying a lot of attention to monkey business, and I called him on it. He was a big man, I am not, but there was a big something in my favour, his face. He made his living with it. He might have beaten my brains out. I don't know, but I do know that I could have made a character man out of him in the process.'

Clark and Loretta were enjoying each other during the long cold days and nights. Without identifying the stars, Hollywood gossip columnists hinted that their hot combination in the state of Washington should have melted the snow and ice by now. Ria was prepared to admit that her gravest fear had come true. But Clark returned to Hollywood in one of his darkest moods. Loretta had told him she was pregnant, though she would deal with it alone. He looked at her mother and said, 'She was married before. I thought she knew how to take care of herself.' A few months later Loretta announced she was retiring from films for a year due to 'health problems'. She went to Europe before returning secretly to Hollywood, settling in a house outside Los Angeles where she had a baby girl.

After completing *Mutiny on the Bounty* and *China Seas*, Gable left for a few weeks in South America. He stopped off in New York where he received a telegram, 'Beautiful, blue-eyed, blonde baby girl.' Clark tore the wire into small pieces and flushed it down the toilet. When he returned to Hollywood, he confirmed his separation from Ria: his new address was the Beverly Wilshire Hotel.

On 23 January 1936, Gable attended Jock Whitney's gag party. Carole Lombard, whom he hadn't seen in a few years, arrived in a screaming ambulance, wearing a hospital gown, and entered on a stretcher. Dazzled by her prank, Clark danced with her most of the evening. Loretta attended the party, too, and managed a few private minutes with him. Would he like to see the baby? Of course he would. Late one night, they arrived in separate cars at the tiny house in Venice where little Judy was asleep in a dresser drawer. He handed Loretta $400 and said, 'Buy her a decent bed.'

She recalled angrily, 'That was the only time he ever gave me anything for the baby.' She set up a trust fund for Judy, and had her attorney inform Clark so he could contribute without being detected. But he never did.

Judy was placed in a Catholic facility, St. Elizabeth's Infant Hospital, in San Francisco. In June 1937, Loretta announced she was adopting a baby girl. Clark called her persistently, but she put him off. Hollywood insiders were meanwhile waiting for her to make one false move that would confirm Gable was the father of her 'adopted' child. He was in love with Loretta and she with him, but he was an impatient man and soon grew tired of her rejections. Loretta almost changed her mind when Gable began seeing Carole Lombard on a steady basis. But Loretta decided that their child would always be a link between them and no one could take that away from her. It was odd, though: Clark was baptised a Catholic and neither he nor Loretta had ever married in the Church, so they could have been married and blessed by the Catholic Church. He was willing, but she felt it would be an admission that she had given birth out of wedlock. Though he would not be identified as Judy's father, her reputation would be tarnished. So she watched, in despair, as her man was swept away by the screwy Carole Lombard.

Carole was born Jane Alice Peters on 6 October 1908, in Fort Wayne, Indiana. When she was six years old, her mother, Bessie, took Jane and her two brothers to Los Angeles on vacation and never returned home. At sixteen, Jane was doing cartwheels on her front lawn when she was discovered by a movie director. She signed a five-year contract with 20th Century-Fox for $75 a week. The studio changed her name to Carole Lombard and she was on her way, making *Marriage in Transit* with Edmund Lowe and *Hearts and Spurs* alongside Buck Jones. But at the age of eighteen, Carole was in a serious automobile accident. A sharp piece of glass cut into the right side of her face from nose to ear. She endured four hours of pain without anaesthesia while her face was being stitched. After the healing process was complete, she underwent plastic surgery. The procedure was a long one, and 20th Century-Fox terminated her contract. When she recovered, Carole found a job with Mack Sennett, the famous comedy producer whose Keystone Kops were all the rage. In 1930 she signed with Paramount for seven years at $350 a week. After making two films with William Powell, she married him on 26 June 1931.

Carole was raunchy, tough, romantic, strong-willed, sexy, sophisticated, and hell on wheels. She enjoyed profanity, but carried her four-letter words with dignity. The first time Carole rode a horse she exclaimed to a group of observers, 'I don't know why the hell everybody thinks this is so great. It's like a dry fuck.'

Carole was known for her loyalty to friends, especially those in trouble. When her pal, actor Billy Haines, was let go by MGM because he was gay, she hired him to decorate her house. Once the work was done, he refused her cheque. 'She had given me a chance when no one else would,' Haines said. 'I was in great demand after that. Carole's mother was a great gal, too. She always had a numerologist and astrologer on retainer. They lived by the stars and by adding up pertinent numbers. They loved to play poker on Saturday night, when odd-looking metaphysical folks would gather around the table and cut the cards. Sometimes it looked like a Gypsy camp, but I found them fascinating.

'Carole was unpredictable. After I finished decorating her house she arranged a party, but when the guests arrived all the contents has been removed. I was miffed, but she followed up with another party so everyone could see my work.'

Carole's marriage to the very distinguished and proper William Powell was an odd one, considering how different they were. After their divorce, everyone wondered who would be nuts enough to marry Lombard. Maybe it would be singer Russ Columbo – the pair were inseparable. But in 1933 he was admiring an old gun with a friend when it went off. The bullet ricocheted off the table, striking Columbo just above the eye. Two hours later he was dead. Carole was devastated. 'His love for me was the kind that rarely comes to any woman,' she said.

Lombard was just five foot one and weighed 112 pounds. Blonde and slim, she looked like a chic New Yorker and talked with a Boston accent, of sorts. She never wore a bra or panties under her slinky satin evening gowns. She also had money – her grandfather had established one of the first electric companies in California, and helped finance the laying of the Atlantic cable. He was supposedly a director of the first board of New York National City Bank.

As for Gable, she said, 'Here's one gal who isn't chasing him!' He laughed it off and continued to see other women. He was a great guy but selfish, so she adjusted to his way of life, learning to hunt and fish so as to be with him, and giving up her life as the girl-about-town in slinky evening gowns. Without realising it, Clark fell in love with Carole. When she moved out of her mother's home and into a house in secluded Bel Air, he rented a house close by.

*

Life was good for Gable – until Irving Thalberg died of pneumonia in September 1936. Clark was a visibly shaken usher at the funeral. Though L.B. Mayer had taken credit for discovering him, it was Thalberg who recognised that indefinable 'it' in the actor. It was Irving who Clark thought of when he imprinted his big feet and huge hands in cement outside Sid Grauman's Chinese Theater.

In April 1937 Gable appeared at Los Angeles Federal Court as a witness for the prosecution in the United States Government's case against Violet Norton, an Englishwoman who claimed he had fathered her fifteen-year-old daughter. Gable stated he'd never been in England, and proved it when Franz Dorfler testified that Clark had been staying with her parents in September 1922, the month Violet Norton said she had conceived. Norton was deported to Canada. All smiles, Clark remarked, 'As affairs go, the one she described was a long-distance project. It would have set a world's record.'

With a straight face, Carole agreed: 'That's right. You have all you can do to make it at close range.'

Clark wanted to play an Irish statesman in *Parnell*, a part he thought would prove his ability as a dramatic actor. But it was a terrible film – one he tried to forget. Carole had stickers of *Parnell* made, and stuck them everywhere as a reminder that he wasn't God. Gable blamed Joan Crawford, who had refused to be in *Parnell*. Refusing to speak to him nowadays, she also turned down the lead in *Saratoga*, and Jean Harlow stepped in. Harlow showed up on the set with her fiancé William Powell. Jean and Clark, happy at last – she with Carole's ex-husband and he with Powell's ex-wife. But Harlow was taken ill during *Saratoga* and the world was shocked when she subsequently died from kidney disease. Grief-stricken, Clark leaned on Carole. She was strong in supporting him, but she had realised how short life can be.

In the autumn of 1938, columnist Ed Sullivan ran a 'King and Queen of the Movies' contest. Clark Gable and Myrna Loy were the winners, and they were crowned at a formal ceremony held at MGM. Gable's title stuck for the rest of his life. Carole attended the coronation and whispered to a friend, 'If Clark had an inch less, he'd be Queen of Hollywood!'

Gable was teamed with Myrna Loy in *Test Pilot* and *Too Hot to Handle*, but she claimed there was never anything between them – despite his best efforts. 'He and his wife Ria offered me a ride home from a party,' Loy recalled. 'He insisted on walking me to my door and tried to kiss me – right there in front of his wife! I pushed him off the porch into the shrubs.'

Idiot's Delight, Gable's next project, was one of his best. He teamed up with Irving Thalberg's widow, Norma Shearer. Single and on the look-out, she had already seduced Mickey Rooney and Jimmy Stewart, though she couldn't catch the handsome Tyrone Power. Clark thought she was hungry for sex. 'She kisses like a frustrated whore,' he said. 'She doesn't wear any underwear and flaunts it.' Laughing, director Clarence Brown whispered, 'Irving couldn't satisfy her. For a long time she's had no passion. Why don't you try your luck?'

'Because,' Clark replied, 'She owns a big hunk of MGM stock that Irving left her so she has a lotta power around here. I'm not gonna fool with that! Besides, if Carole found out I'd never live to see my fortieth birthday. She had one of the chorus girls fired so I'm not taking any chances.' But it was Clark's respect for Thalberg that ultimately held him back from an affair with Norma.

In *Idiot's Delight*, Gable is a song-and-dance man who travels the theatre circuit along with six blondes. At the end of the 'Puttin' on the Ritz' number, the girls carry him off stage. Though he made a hilarious Harry Van, Clark appeared tired and drawn. He was drowning his sorrows over Ria with the bottle. He wanted to marry Carole, but a divorce would cost him a fortune. To add to his miseries, the big chatter around Hollywood was David O. Selznick's *Gone With the Wind*. There were rumours that author Margaret Mitchell had patterned Rhett Butler after Clark – not to mention the fact that the public wanted him to play the part. But he didn't want to be Rhett Butler, because his leading lady, Scarlett O'Hara, loves another man. 'In all my films the girl is nuts about me. It's an image thing,' he explained.

In late 1938 *Photoplay* magazine published an article that shocked not only its readers but Hollywood as well. Entitled 'Hollywood's Unmarried Husbands and Wives', it cited various couples who had been dating for several years but had no marriage plans. The article caused a number one scandal. Since the studios controlled what the fan magazines printed, it rocked the likes of Louis B. Mayer and his son-in-law, producer David Selznick. Any actor connected with *Gone With the Wind* had to be free of scandal, for fear that church groups would picket the theatres and thus reduce the profits. Ria Gable came forward to say, 'I've always told Clark he could have a divorce any day he asked for it.' In defence of Gable, it should be said that while he did not want to give Ria half of the money that MGM were putting in trust for him, MGM didn't want him to either; it was their security should Clark try to walk out on his contract.

Gable finally made an announcement that he was going to divorce Ria, and lawyers on both sides began negotiations. He and Carole began house hunting and fell in love with a white brick Connecticut 'farmhouse'. In 1938 the Encino property was in the wilderness, filled with fruit trees and surrounded by mountains. It was Carole who laid out the $50,000 for the house and property. This was a well-guarded secret, of course. Who would believe that Clark Gable was unable to raise the money?

Clark's problems with Ria mounted when she issued a statement that he had no reason to 'presume' anything regarding the divorce. She was insulted that he was about to make the first move. Within days, Clark apologised: 'After years of separation it is only natural that Mrs. Gable should institute proceedings that will assure her freedom.'

The pressure was on. Not only was Mayer going to deal with Ria, he had to deal with Selznick's request to borrow Gable to play Rhett Butler. 'I'll be tied up for a year!' Clark grumbled.

'Six months at the most,' Mayer said.

'Who's playing Scarlett?'

'Ask my son-in-law.'

'I don't like Selznick.'

'Neither do I.'

'I'm being bounced around like a tennis ball and I don't like it. It's all over Hollywood that Selznick wants Gary Cooper to play Rhett.'

'That's because my son-in-law's an ass.'

'So I'm second choice?' Gable fumed.

'Third. He couldn't get Errol Flynn. You think you're the only actor in Hollywood?' Mayer smirked.

'No, but you do.'

'As for Scarlett, I think Paulette Goddard is the favourite to play her. Problem is she can't prove her marriage to Charlie Chaplin. She says the mayor of Catalina performed the ceremony, but Catalina doesn't have a mayor. If she was an MGM contract player, this could have been avoided.'

Gable had no idea how his divorce was related to his role in *Gone With the Wind*. Once Mayer had made up his mind to deal with Ria, he began negotiations with Selznick. Behind closed doors, Clark became Rhett. While he fumed, Ria would collect $300,000, and his contract and trust would be dealt with accordingly.

Gable had barely managed to get through Margaret Mitchell's best-selling novel about the Civil War and wasn't sure how to play Rhett, but he had read enough to know that whoever played Scarlett O'Hara would be a threat to him. Meanwhile a green-eyed, 26-year-old beauty was three thousand miles away in England, pining away for her married lover, Laurence Olivier, who was filming in Hollywood. Carrying a copy of *Gone With the Wind*, she boarded a plane for Los Angeles.

David Selznick's brother, Myron, was an agent and agreed to meet with her. 'My God, you're Scarlett!' he yelped, and David was equally stunned when he saw her during the first night of filming, the burning of Atlanta on MGM's back lot. Vivien Leigh would become Scarlett – on one condition. Vivien was having an affair with actor Laurence Olivier. Although the couple were both in the process of obtaining divorces, they were forbidden to stay in the same hotel room or to be seen together in public.

The cast of *Gone With the Wind* had to learn to speak with a Southern accent. Gable flatly refused – and got away with it. But could he tame the energetic and beautiful Miss Leigh? On the first day of filming, he ranted because she was late. She approached him fearlessly and said, 'I quite agree, Mr. Gable. If I were a man, I'd tell Vivien Leigh to go right back to merry old England!' He turned around and gazed into her green eyes and between her breasts, taped together to increase her cleavage. Without saying a word, he smiled, took her arm and strolled with her around the set. It was magic, everyone said. Unfortunately, it was actually more like lightning that struck before the storm.

Vivien attached herself to director George Cukor, studying her lines with him in the evenings. Gable complained about him to Selznick and Mayer. 'That fag is giving her an advantage,' he said. 'And I don't appreciate his calling me "dear" in front of everybody.' So, on 12 February 1939, less than a month into production, Cukor was fired. Rumours persist to this day that Gable did this because Cukor was gay and a friend of Billy Haines. Did he know about Clark's involvement with Haines? Clark thought so. And he resented the fact that Cukor favoured Vivien Leigh. Clark said she should not have been cast as Scarlett; the part should have been given to an American actress.

Cukor, on the other hand, denies he was fired because of his connection to Haines, and believes he was unfairly labelled a 'woman's director'. Whatever the reason, Gable's good friend, director Victor Fleming reported for work the next day.

Gable, who made sure there was a 'no overtime' clause in all his contracts, left the studio every night at six. Vivien called his behaviour 'common': factory workers might punch time clocks, but not dedicated actors. No one suspected he was having an affair with Vivien, but he did sneak off with one of the supporting actresses. Carole was suspicious, and not very quiet about it at home. Gable was amused at this, but when Cukor was fired, she teased him about the Billy Haines affair. 'Do you think George would say anything?' she asked, swallowing a smile.

'I don't like gays.'

'Or Jews or Negroes.'

'But Mayer is Jewish.'

'That's what I mean.'

'If it hadn't been for gays and Jews there would be no Hollywood,' she retorted.

Ria Gable left for Las Vegas in January 1939 to begin divorce proceedings. Six weeks later Clark was a free man. He proposed to Carole and they eloped to Kingman, Arizona on 29 March. She told friends in private, 'Clark hasn't had a very happy life. He needs someone to look after him, but don't tell him that.'

He was still having innocent flings. One of the best Gable stories, one which friends swear is true, took place in a hotel room when a dowdy maid walked in and found him still in bed. He grinned sheepishly. 'Why don't you join me?'

'How much?' she asked.

'I would think, my dear, just being with me is payment enough.'

She didn't think so and left the room.

Carole kept up with him when he bragged about his conquests. 'I even did it in the swimming pool. You know it's hard to do under water.'

'Yes, it is,' she said.

His mouth dropped open. 'What kind of girl are you?' he exclaimed. 'Doing a thing like that and having the nerve to tell me about it!'

They kidded around, but they were very serious about having a baby. She gave up horse riding because the doctor thought that might be the cause of her failure to conceive. 'We've tried every position there is,' she said. 'We'd fuck in a pile of manure if we thought it would work.' Carole also told friends not to visit them on Sundays. 'That's the day we concentrate on having a baby,' she winked.

The spectacular premiere of *Gone With the Wind* was held in Atlanta, Georgia, on 15 December 1939. Gable stepped up to the microphone and announced, 'This is Margaret Mitchell's night and your night. Just let me be a spectator going in to see *Gone With the Wind*.' In fact, instead of watching the movie he chose to have a long talk with the author. After everyone was seated, they ducked into the ladies' room for privacy, where Mitchell told Clark she had modelled Rhett Butler on her first husband.

At the Hollywood premiere, mobs of fans prevented him from viewing the film. He remained in the manager's office until everyone had left the theatre. And he did not attend the New York premiere.

Carole concentrated on making her husband happy in his new home. She told the household staff Clark hated the colour pink, 'and for God's sake never have his hats cleaned.' She laughed every time she saw his hats lined up like museum pieces. 'Pa's funny,' she said. 'He wants his shoes shined before he feeds the chickens, and then puts on a dirty hat!'

Strange Cargo with Joan Crawford was an excellent film. The pair still had that special something together on the screen – and probably after hours, He did, however, believe she thought of herself as a prima donna.

'You're across the street from the photographer,' he scowled, 'so why did you take a limousine?'

'It's in my contract.'

'Howard Strickling told me you refused to go in until Norma did, so you both went round and round. He had to play traffic cop. And what about feeding her lines and knitting with walrus tucks? That was not professional.'

'Norma annoys the hell out of me. She got all the good roles 'cause she slept with the boss.'

'And I suppose you got the star on your dressing room door 'cause you were the Virgin Mary.'

'How did you get into films, honey?'

'That's what I always said, Joanie. You and I came from the same slums and had to play dirty.'

'Which reminds me, I'm sorry you didn't get the Oscar for *Gone With the Wind*. I thought you deserved it.'

'I had an English girl for a leading lady and lost out to the Englishman Robert Donat. I didn't think he was so hot as Mr. Chips. I'm tellin' ya, Joanie, the foreigners are taking over Hollywood.'

Clark and Joan remained friends for a lifetime. According to her, lovers, as well.

Rosalind Russell, Gable's co-star in *They Met in Bombay*, was no threat to Carole, but Lana Turner was. Gable went against Mayer's wishes to make *Honky Tonk* with Lana, but the film was a smash. The romantic Gable–Turner combination was so hot their pictures landed on magazine covers. Carole heard rumours and began showing up on the set, until Lana got so flustered that she burst into tears and ran to her dressing room. The Gables fought bitterly over his new leading lady. Carole threatened to confront the 'lovers' on the set and 'kick them both in the ass'.

'I'll have her fired!' she said.

'You can't do that.'

'Then I'll have you fired!'

The MGM stars were to be protected from all dangers – and that included their spouses. So a quiet alert was called on the set of *Honky Tonk* whenever Carole drove through the studio gate. Finally Mayer closed the set to all visitors, including Mrs. Gable. Lana Turner has consistently denied an affair with Clark over the years, yet he claimed to have been intimate with all his leading ladies. Looking at a photo of the MGM actresses he once commented, 'Aren't they beautiful, and I've had them all.' During production of *Boom Town* Clark had had a fling with Hedy Lamarr. The film was such a hit they were cast again in *Comrade X*. According to Hedy they had quickies in their dressing rooms because Lombard could usually sense his infidelities. But for some reason she did not suspect Hedy.

Carole blew her top again when she found out MGM were going to co-star Clark and Lana in *Somewhere I'll Find You*, but she would have to live with it. The dictates of MGM came first.

The lives of all Americans were changed on 7 December 1941, and Hollywood was no exception. The Gables became involved with the Hollywood Victory Committee, and Clark was appointed chairman of the Screen Actors Division. It was logical that he should ask Carole to make a war-bond tour of her home state, Indiana. She wanted Clark to go along but he had to begin work on *Somewhere I'll Find You*. Before she left, Carole placed a blonde dummy in Clark's bed with a note: 'So you won't be lonely', and gave her secretary five notes for Gable – one for each day she would be gone. On 12 January 1942 Carole boarded a train with her mother, Bessie, and Clark's personal public-relations man, Otto Winkler.

After selling $2 million in war bonds, Carole was anxious to get home and suggested, 'I think we should fly back.' Winkler didn't like the idea, so they flipped a coin and Carole won. But when Bessie, a proficient numerologist, jotted down the flight data she came up with a fatal number. She showed it to Carole, who was a believer but laughed it off. So, on 16 January, they boarded a TWA plane.

What was Clark doing while his wife was away for five days? He was in Washington, D.C., pulling strings, trying to get into the Air Force. He returned to Hollywood the day after Carole's departure. The press and his friends give different accounts of what he did and where he was, although they agree that he was filming with Lana Turner. He planned a welcome-back party for Carole at the ranch with a few close friends. To get even with her little prank, Clark put a male dummy with an erect penis in Carole's bed.

It was Howard Strickling who received the call that Carole's plane had come down near Las Vegas. He chartered a plane and called Clark. Search parties were being organised to climb the snow-covered Table Rock Mountain; a Western Airlines pilot had seen Carole's plane hit the mountain and burst into flames.

Clark insisted on joining the rescue party, but halfway to the crash site, an MGM official said to him, 'Carole wouldn't want you to see her in that plane wreckage, Clark.' He thought for a moment and then turned back. It was a blessing that he did. He was spared the agony of seeing Carole's charred, decapitated body, and nearby it a script, a remnant of her ruby clip which had been a gift from Clark, and strands of her blonde hair. On the way down the mountain with the bodies, the rescue party stopped at a way station and sent a telegram to Clark: 'No survivors. All killed instantly.' The next day he was driven a few hundred feet from the crash site by a pilot, who explained, 'There's no chance that Carole suffered for even a second. All 22 passengers didn't know what happened.'

Clark accompanied the bodies of his wife, her mother and close friend Otto Winkler back to California. He wore Carole's burned ruby clip around his neck in a gold locket and kept the strands of her hair. Carole had requested to be clothed in white and placed in a modestly priced crypt in Forest Lawn Memorial Park, Glendale, California. On 22 January 1942, services were held at the Church of the Recessional in Forest Lawn. There were no prayers or hymns, only the Twenty-third Psalm and a favourite poem of Carole's. When it was over he returned to the ranch. Later that evening his secretary gave him the fifth and last note Carole had left behind. His sobs echoed through the house and into the valley . . .

Joan Crawford said Gable had come to her the night Carole was killed. 'He was so drunk and he cried. A stranger walked through my door that night and never returned. He was never the same. He was in another world and never came back to us.'

Carole left her estate to Clark. Her brothers, deliberately eliminated from the will, never spoke to Gable again. He had invited them to Carole's homecoming dinner, but after the funeral the friendship ended. Friends said they resented the serious quarrel over Lana Turner, the obvious reason Carole had rushed back home to her death. Then there was the persistent rumour that Clark was with another woman on the night his wife was killed. After all, he had sent someone else to the airport when the plane was en route. For Gable, having a last quickie before his wife came home was typical. He had often said to her, 'If my flings mean nothing to me, why should they mean anything to you?'

Now, though, Carole was gone, and he became obsessed with her bedroom. He left everything as it had been when she departed. Somehow she was alive there, her presence evoked by the smell of Chanel No. 5 and the powder puff that touched her vibrant face, with some powder that had spilled on her dressing table. For a while it was his private shrine.

On 23 February 1942, he reported back to work on *Someday I'll Find You*. L.B. Mayer told everyone on the set to pretend nothing had happened. Joan Crawford invited him to her home for dinner almost every night until he finished filming. 'Clark could drink a quart of booze before dinner,' she said. 'We made love occasionally but I tried to lure him from the bedroom because there was little satisfaction in it for me anymore. When he joined the service he said he wasn't coming back, but wouldn't explain it. That meant Clark had a death wish and I was very concerned.'

On 23 August 1942, Gable was sworn into the Air Corps as a $66-a-month 41-year-old buck private. He could have had a commission, but instead chose to earn it at the Officer Candidate School in Miami Beach, Florida. He graduated on 9 October, volunteered for aerial gunnery duty and was sent to Tyndall Field in Panama City, Florida. As a first lieutenant he grew a moustache again, had his uniforms custom made and sent home for his English shoes. In January Clark received his gunnery officer wings and was sent to Polebrook, England, eighty miles from London.

Hitler put a $5000 price tag on Captain Gable – dead or alive. 'I'll never bail out,' Clark responded, 'Hitler can have me dead or not at all.' He didn't give a damn. If Carole could brave a seventeen-hour flight in bad weather to save her marriage, he'd make it up to her by facing death head on.

Defying all odds he looked for trouble, volunteering for the most dangerous missions over Germany and wondering why he was spared. But what his fellow officers really wondered was why he chose ugly women for sex. Clark replied, 'Because they really appreciate it and aren't a bother. They go away when it's over.' Meanwhile his commanding officer was trying to get rid of him: 'The guy gives me the willies. He's trying to get himself killed. Yeah! So he can join his wife.' Gable was discharged on 12 June 1944 with the rank of major.

On a New York vacation he was introduced to society hostess Dolly O'Brien, a blue-eyed blonde who had been a Powers and Conover model, her pictures appearing in no fewer than seventy magazines. Her second husband, Julius Fleischman, had given Dolly a $5 million divorce settlement. Dolly was a bouncy society darling who liked the company of young men. Six years older than Clark, Dolly never showed her age. He relished her socially prominent friends, whose pleasures were catered to at nightclubs, yacht clubs and country clubs.

Then there was Anita Colby, fashion consultant and coordinator for David Selznick Studios. She was thirty years old, blonde and another former Conover model. Another frequent date was Kay Williams, who put Gable in his place on their first evening together.

'Why don't you get undressed?' he suggested.

'Why don't you shit in your hat?' Kay replied.

MGM, meanwhile, was looking for a good movie with which to welcome Clark back from the service. Their choice of *Adventure*, though, couldn't have been worse. Greer Garson, who had won an Oscar for *Mrs. Miniver*, was his leading lady, but there was absolutely no chemistry between the stars. The promotional slogan was 'Gable's Back and Garson's Got Him.' One critic added, '. . . and they deserve each other!' Clark was hurt and embarrassed; nonetheless, the film was a blockbuster. Still, he refused to walk past a theatre that was showing *Adventure*. His growing hatred for MGM was fuelled by their choice of homecoming movie for him. Fortunately, his fans did not let him down.

Loyal to the memory of Carole Lombard, he did not rendezvous with women at the ranch. Instead he maintained a suite with its own private entrance at the Bel Air Hotel. Though four years had passed since her death, Carole's bedroom remained as she had left it. Her toiletries, atomisers, and towels were displayed as she would have liked. It was as if she were about to return at any minute. He bought every film she had made and viewed them whenever the mood struck him.

Joan Crawford, divorced from her third husband, Philip Terry, in 1946, won an Oscar for *Mildred Pierce*, a Warner Brothers picture. She asked Mayer to let her out of her contract since they had no films for her and he did not try to convince her otherwise. The fact that MGM did not fight to keep her after eighteen years was a hurt she never forgot.

'I hate heels, and this character is a heel! The book is filthy rotten!'

'That's why it's perfect for you, Clark.'

'Take your script and shove it.'

Mayer smirked. 'I had no idea you were so proper. What is it you don't like about *The Hucksters*?'

'I won't tolerate acting an affair with a married woman. The guy I play is oversexed. He's a satyr.'

'You should be able to play the part without looking at the script. Do you know what Sam Goldwyn said about you? He said, "When Robert Montgomery walks on the screen you know he has balls. When Clark Gable comes on, you can hear them clacking together." That's why you're right for *The Hucksters*.'

'Make the dame single and give my guy some character, I might do it.'

'As I see it, you want to be a kinda bastard who kinda likes to fuck and kinda wants to get even with the boss. Is that it?'

'Kinda.'

'I don't know why I play games with you,' Mayer said, leaning back in his chair. 'I could ruin you tomorrow if I wanted to. If you push me too far, I will.'

'Referring to?'

'You ran down and killed a woman when you were drunk at the wheel, remember? It was 1933. I got a guy here at MGM to take the rap. He spent a year in prison.'

Gable stiffened. 'That was your decision, not mine.'

'That's right. I make the decisions around here and don't you forget it!'

'You'd threaten me for a shit movie like *The Hucksters*?'

'That's right, big shot, so think it over. Meantime I'll have the writers clean up the script to *my* liking.'

Gable knew Mayer would be jeopardising MGM by opening up an old can of worms. He barely remembered hitting that woman, but he did remember going the wrong way up a one-way street. Or was it on that dangerous curve in the road? That was almost fifteen years ago and Mayer had never mentioned it until now. Gable waited it out and read the revised script. He tested with a new English actress, Deborah Kerr, who would play the female lead, and a fairly new MGM starlet, Ava Gardner, who balked at being typecast again as the good-natured girl who's never good enough for the hero. Clark called her, asking her to reconsider.

'I'm fed up!' she said.

'Honey, when you've been around as long as I have, then you can say that.'

'The only reason I'd do the film is because of you.'

'Then do it,' he said. 'We'll have fun. You'll see.'

Gable and Gardner were attracted to each other from the start. She had been married to Mickey Rooney and bandleader Artie Shaw, and had an affair with billionaire Howard Hughes. By the time Ava met Clark, she was ready for him. They were both passionate, good drinkers who did not take their affairs seriously. She used profanity like Lombard, much to Clark's amusement. Were they intimate? The consensus is that they were; Ava was a nymphomaniac who was not about to let Gable get away. They both denied any involvement with each other, claiming they were the best of friends until his death. They adored each other, regardless.

Gable was reunited with Lana Turner in *Homecoming*. She was in love with Tyrone Power at the time, but Power would break her heart when he married Linda Christian. Clark was dating actress Paulette Goddard who said, 'If I don't get the man, I get a car or diamond ring.' Clark gave her nothing. When she asked him to kiss her for the press, he refused. Paulette laughed it off. 'Well, that's that, sugar!' According to Gable, she came on too strong.

Gable proposed marriage to both Dolly O'Brien and Anita Colby, and both turned him down. Dolly wanted to live on the east coast, he didn't. Anita said he drank too much, but he was not about to cut down. 'You're lonely, Clark. Please don't rush off and do something you'll regret,' she said.

By 1948 television was taking its toll on the movie industry. MGM was forced to face deficits of $6.5 million. Their contract players were not winning Oscars or making the prestigious 'ten best' lists. Mayer, who had begun searching for another Thalberg, hoped it would be Dore Schary, who had just resigned as production head of RKO. Though Schary put MGM in the black again, he was not popular with the contract players, including Gable. Clark refused to play in *Quo Vadis*. 'I'm not going to be seen in Roman garb with my bloody knees sticking out,' he barked.

'You'll go on suspension,' Schary threatened.

'That's fine with me.'

Schary knew he meant it and put him in *Any Number Can Play* with Alexis Smith, a forgettable film that few even of Gable's keenest fans remember. *Key to the City* with Loretta Young, in contrast, was a fun movie. Loretta had married producer Tom Lewis, who adopted her 'adopted' daughter Judy. Loretta, who had given birth to a son by Lewis a few years before, had a miscarriage during production. When the movie was completed, Loretta and Tom held a party to celebrate. Gable came alone. He was interested in seeing Judy, but at the same time reluctant to meet her. Loretta finally invited him to the house when Lewis wasn't there, for Tom did not know the truth about his stepdaughter. In fact Judy, now fifteen years old, was still in the dark herself. Why did the famous Clark Gable want to chat with her? Why was her mother so adamant about her not going upstairs to wash her hair? Even when he said goodbye he merely thanked her for a nice afternoon.

Judy Lewis found out only in 1958 that Gable was her father. Her fiancé, Joe Tinney, eventually told her the truth when she expressed concern about her 'unknown' father. How could she marry and have children not knowing her background? Some years later Judy confronted Loretta, who admitted the truth but referred to her daughter as a 'mortal sin'. Mother and daughter had their ups and downs, but at least they were reconciled before Loretta's death in August 2000.

In the summer of 1949, Clark attended a dinner party given by Minna Wallis. One of the guests was Lady Sylvia Ashley, whom Clark had known casually as Mrs. Douglas Fairbanks Sr. Like most of his female companions, Sylvia was a Lombard lookalike. Ten years younger than Clark, she had been divorced twice and widowed once. She was born Sylvia Hawkes in England and had married Lord Anthony Ashley, heir to the ninth Duke of Shaftesbury, thus becoming Lady Sylvia Ashley. When she had an affair with Fairbanks, Lord Ashley accused her of adultery, and three years of disgrace followed. She married Fairbanks in 1937 but he had a fatal heart attack two years later. In 1944 Sylvia married Edward John, Lord Stanley of Alderley. Within months, however, he charged her with adultery and began divorce proceedings that lasted four years. In 1948 Sylvia settled down in the $50,000 Malibu beach house left to her by Fairbanks. Less than a year later she set her sights on Clark Gable.

On 17 December 1949, Gable's biggest alcoholic binge to date began at a party given by agent Charles Feldman. Sylvia's behaviour was shocking. She was 'all over' Clark according to guests. The next day he called Howard Strickling. 'I'm going to marry Lady Ashley,' he slurred.

'Who?' Howard asked.

'Lady Sylvia Ashley! I want you to make all the arrangements and tomorrow won't be too soon.'

Three days later Clark married Sylvia at the home of a friend. They spent their honeymoon in Hawaii, accompanied by Howard Strickling who knew Gable was on a binge and feared he might have regrets. He did. Joan Crawford had little to say except, 'If I were still married to Douglas junior, Gable would be my father-in-law!' Sylvia's biggest mistake was redecorating the ranch. She put all of Carole's belongings in storage and painted her bedroom pink!

After Clark played a racing driver in *To Please a Lady* alongside Barbara Stanwyck, Sylvia accompanied him to Durango Colorado for *Across the Wide Missouri*. But she was not about to rough it with the cast and crew. They were both glad to get back to the ranch, but her society friends were constantly around, as well as frequent house guests. Clark, who was becoming fed up with Sylvia's formal lifestyle, told Ava Gardner during the making of *Lone Star* that he was going to get a divorce, and in April 1951 he came home one night and told Sylvia to pack up her things and get out. She went to Nassau hoping he would change his mind. When she returned all the locks had been changed.

On 31 May 1951, Sylvia filed for divorce. Clark restored his beloved ranch to its original décor; Carole's possessions were put back where they belonged and the hideous pink bedroom painted white again. And on 21 April 1952, Clark faced Sylvia in Santa Monica Court, where she received an uncontested interlocutory decree and a $150,000 settlement to be paid over a five-year period. She could have obtained much more, but she hoped they would be reconciled. It didn't happen and the amazing Sylvia soon married Prince Dimitri Djorjadze. Always more satisfied with a title, this time she scored big.

On his way to Africa to film *Mogambo*, the remake of *Red Dust*, Gable checked into the Dorchester in London to prepare for *Let Me Go* with Gene Tierney. They did not have an affair, though he romanced her over cosy dinners. 'I knew he was lonely and vulnerable,' Gene said. 'He was seeing a girl in Paris who managed to get a large topaz ring from him. He was upset when she talked to the press about marrying him, and ended the relationship. His biggest thrill was the delivery of a custom Jaguar. With the camera still rolling, Clark ran out in the rain to take a ride in his new car. He told me if he couldn't be an actor he'd like to be a mechanic – that he could take a car apart and put it back together.'

Gable's leading ladies in *Mogambo* were Ava Gardner, who was now married to Frank Sinatra, and a newcomer, Grace Kelly, who resembled Lombard. There was a mutual attraction almost immediately though the age difference bothered him; she was 23, he was 51. But Grace did the chasing, going on safari with him and becoming quite adept with a gun. Gable liked her spunk, the way she would go without make-up and be a good sport in such rustic surroundings. He was flattered that she was in love with him. It was taken for granted they were 'practically living together'. When an assistant director delivered a revised script to Gable's tent one night, he found him in bed with Grace. Clark was embarrassed, but she took it in her stride. She had been around and took sex for granted.

She had loosened up further by the time they returned to England to shoot interiors. Grace's mother had heard rumours about her romance and was waiting in London. Clark took them out for dinner once before leaving for Holland to make *Betrayal* with Lana Turner. Like Gable, Lana was concerned about the future since MGM were no longer renewing the contracts of their major stars. Mayer had been forced out by now, and Dore Schary, who did not believe in pampering contract players, was in charge. 'They couldn't afford us,' Lana said. 'We were all frightened.'

Gable's own negotiations for a new contract did not work out so he left MGM of his own accord. He left the studio without fanfare after having lunch with some technicians. 'I never should have gotten this far,' he told them. 'Here I am, though, *Mogambo*'s a hit and I don't have a job.' He released a statement to the press, ending with: 'I wish to pay tribute to my friends and associates who are no longer alive, whose help and guidance over the years meant so much to me.' By paying tribute to those who were 'no longer alive', he was going for the jugular – referring, most likely, to Irving Thalberg and director Victor Fleming. Mayer, of course, was still around; maybe Gable had second thoughts about the mogul after Dore Schary took over, but he would never admit it. When MGM wanted Clark back for a film, he told his agent, 'Rub it in and see how high we can get those sons-of-bitches. And when you get their very best offer, tell them to shove it up their ass.'

He made *Soldier of Fortune* alongside Susan Hayward for 20th Century-Fox. Filmed in exotic Hong Kong, the movie had everything the critics and the public wanted. Before leaving for the Orient he had begun seeing Kay Williams, an old flame. She had recently divorced her third husband, sugar heir Adolph Sprechels II, with whom she had two children, Joanie and Bunker. In Hong Kong Clark was asked about his relationship with Kay. 'She's just a friend,' he commented. She called him long distance and gave him some of his own medicine. 'Listen to me, you son-of-a-bitch. Don't do me any favours. It will be a long time before I'll marry you!' Just like old times with Carole, he chuckled.

Kay was 39 when she came back into Gable's life. They settled their differences and she was waiting for him at the airport when he returned from Hong Kong. He next began preparations for the western, *The Tall Men*, with Jane Russell. When he arrived in Durango Mexico with Kay, they were greeted by a company seventy-five strong, three thousand head of cattle and three hundred horses. Released in 1955, *The Tall Men* was one of Gable's best. There was plenty of action, cowboys and Indians and, of course, a bumpy love affair.

On 11 July 1955, Clark and Kay drove across the California line to Minden, Nevada, and were married by a justice of the peace. He called her Kathleen and occasionally 'Ma', his nickname for Carole, while she called him 'Pa'. Kay was untroubled by the ever-present ghost of Lombard and concentrated on Clark's happiness. Three months after they were married Kay became pregnant, but she lost the baby. Clark was disappointed, but finding out he could still father a child was a revelation, while doctors said that Kay, despite a minor heart ailment, would still be able to give birth again.

In the spring of 1956, Gable made *A King and Four Queens* with Eleanor Parker, and the following year, *Band of Angels* with Yvonne DeCarlo, who said, 'Clark didn't warm up to me until I lost my composure and blurted out some four-letter words. He liked that and we became pals. Kay was fun, too. She'd be very quiet and then tell Clark to get off his ass. He'd grin and do it. He loved dirty jokes.'

The Teacher's Pet with Doris Day was only moderate. Clark, who looked his age in the film, was incompatible with Doris. They got along just fine, but on the screen they lacked chemistry. In 1957 Gable co-starred with Burt Lancaster in a submarine epic, *Run Silent, Run Deep*. *But Not For Me* with Lilli Palmer was mediocre, yet critics were unanimous about anything Gable did these days. 'He still has it,' they said. 'Even if the story's bad, Gable's everlasting charm will keep you in your seat.'

In 1959 the Gables sailed for Europe. After a holiday in Austria, he began filming *It Started in Naples* with Sophia Loren. This romantic comedy did very well. With Gable and Loren on the marquee, who cared what the picture was like?

Eating pasta every day put weight on Clark. At 230 pounds he had become too heavy, but he had no intention of working in the near future. He ignored every script sent to him until he received a call from his agent about *The Misfits*. 'It's a screenplay by Arthur Miller. He wrote it for his wife.'

'Who's she?'

'Marilyn Monroe.'

'I'm not doing any picture written for a dame. Besides, she's too young.'

'Will you do me a favour and just read it?'

Gable did not like *The Misfits*. He failed to understand what Miller was trying to get across. He liked the part of the drifting cowboy, but Gay Langland was a complex man whose character had depth and meaning underneath a rugged exterior. Howard Strickling advised him against taking the part for other reasons: director John Huston was too complicated, claimed Strickling, Montgomery Clift was a moody method actor on booze and pills, and surely no one needed to remind him of the unpredictability of Marilyn Monroe. In fact she wanted nothing to do with *The Misfits*, either, until Miller said Gable would be her leading man. 'My mother gave me a picture of him when I was a kid,' Marilyn said. 'She told me to pretend he was my father and I did. I became very close to that face. Gable became my fantasy.'

Clark asked for the impossible, and got it – ten per cent of the gross, a guarantee of three-quarters of a million dollars, $48,000 a week for overtime, and complete control over the script. He accepted it, went on a crash diet and got his weight down to 195 pounds. But he couldn't pass the insurance physical for *The Misfits*. He had to remain in bed for a week before the doctor would sign the necessary papers.

He was patient with Marilyn, who threw up when she met him on the first day of filming. From then on she was either late or didn't show at all. Gable, meanwhile, was on time, knew his lines and just wanted to get the shoot over with. Filming in Reno in July, temperatures reached over 115 degrees. Becoming restless, he began doing his own stunts, which most young actors would have refused to do. He balanced himself on the hood of a car, rolled across it, and fell to the pavement. In another scene, he was dragged by a truck travelling at 25 miles per hour. Wrestling with a wild stallion, he became snarled in a lariat and was dragged face down until a wrangler could stop the horse.

But whatever pain he suffered was soon forgotten when Kay told him she was pregnant. She tried to stay calm, but she was upset over two things: the way Marilyn was chasing after her husband – she deliberately let the bed sheet fall off her breasts when they did one of their most sexy scenes – and Clark's insistence on doing his own dangerous stunts. Though he loved Kay with all his heart, Gable was frustrated that he couldn't have a fling with Monroe. He was a man, after all.

On 18 October 1960, the entire cast of *The Misfits* flew back to Los Angeles. When Gable viewed the film, he told producer Frank Taylor, 'I want to shake your hand. I now have two things to be proud of in my career – *Gone With the Wind* and this.' On 4 November he said goodbye to the cast but, feeling unwell, did not stay for the farewell party. The next day he suffered pains in his chest so severe he had to lie down. The following morning he collapsed after trying to get dressed. Gable had suffered a coronary thrombosis and was in critical condition at Presbyterian Hospital. In 48 hours he was sitting up in bed, and the pacemaker was removed from his room. On 16 November, he was reading when Kay kissed him goodnight. The doctor reported, 'Around eleven, Clark turned the page of a magazine he was looking at, put his head back, took a deep sigh, and died.'

Kay held her husband in her arms for two hours.

The King of Hollywood was buried with full military honours by the United States Air Force. Services were held at the Church of the Recessional at Forest Lawn Memorial Park in Glendale, California. Among the pallbearers were Spencer Tracy, Jimmy Stewart, and Robert Taylor. Clark Gable was laid to rest in a crypt next to Carole Lombard.

Blaming herself for Gable's death, Marilyn Monroe tried to commit suicide. She remained in her bedroom with the shades drawn for days until she could no longer live with the guilt. In mid-December her maid found Marilyn about to jump out of her bedroom window and pulled her back. A few weeks later she was admitted to Payne Whitney Clinic by her psychiatrists.

Gable's reviews in *The Misfits* were overwhelming, the best of his career. The *New York Times* said, 'Clark Gable was as certain as the sunrise. He was consistently and stubbornly all man.'

John Clark Gable was born on 20 March 1961.

'What do you do for a living, Mr. Faulkner?'
'I'm a writer. What do you do for a living, Mr. Gable?'

The Films of Clark Gable

Forbidden Paradise (Paramount, 1924)
The Merry Widow (MGM, 1925)
The Plastic Age (FBO, 1925)
North Star (Associated Exhibitors, 1926)
The Painted Desert (Pathe, 1931)
The Easiest Way (MGM, 1931)
Dance, Fools, Dance (MGM, 1931)
The Secret Six (MGM, 1931)
The Finger Points (FN, 1931)
Laughing Sinners (MGM, 1931)
A Free Soul (MGM, 1931)
Night Nurse (Warner Brothers, 1931)
Sporting Blood (MGM, 1931)
Susan Lennox: Her Fall and Rise (MGM, 1931)
Possessed (MGM, 1931)
Hell Divers (MGM, 1931)
Polly of the Circus (MGM, 1932)
Strange Interlude (MGM, 1932)
Red Dust (MGM, 1932)
No Man of Her Own (Paramount, 1932)
The White Sister (MGM, 1933)
Hold Your Man (MGM, 1933)
Night Flight (MGM, 1933)
Dancing Lady (MGM, 1933)
It Happened One Night (Columbia, 1934)
Men in White (MGM, 1934)
Manhattan Melodrama (MGM, 1934)

Chained (MGM, 1934)
Forsaking All Others (MGM, 1934)
After Office Hours (MGM, 1935)
Call of the Wild (United Artists, 1935)
China Seas (MGM, 1935)
Mutiny on the Bounty (MGM, 1935)
Wife vs. Secretary (MGM, 1936)
San Francisco (MGM, 1936)
Cain and Mabel (Warner Brothers, 1936)
Love on the Run (MGM, 1936)
Parnell (MGM, 1937)
Saratoga (MGM, 1937)
Test Pilot (MGM, 1938)
Too Hot to Handle (MGM, 1938)
Idiot's Delight (MGM, 1939)
Gone With the Wind (MGM, 1939)
Strange Cargo (MGM, 1940)
Boom Town (MGM, 1940)
Comrade X (MGM, 1940)
They Met in Bombay (MGM, 1941)
Honky Tonk (MGM, 1941)
Somewhere I'll Find You (MGM, 1942)
Adventure (MGM, 1945)
The Hucksters (MGM, 1947)
Homecoming (MGM, 1948)
Command Decision (MGM, 1948)
Any Number Can Play (MGM, 1949)
Key to the City (MGM, 1950)
To Please a Lady (MGM, 1950)
Across the Wide Missouri (MGM, 1951)
Callaway Went Thataway (MGM, 1951)
Lone Star (MGM, 1952)
Never Let Me Go (MGM, 1953)
Mogambo (MGM, 1953)
Betrayed (MGM, 1954)
Soldier of Fortune (20th Century-Fox, 1955)
The Tall Men (20th Century-Fox, 1955)
The King and Four Queens (US, 1956)
Band of Angels (Warner Brothers, 1957)

Run Silent, Run Deep (US, 1958)
Teacher's Pet (Paramount, 1958)
But Not for Me (Paramount, 1959)
It Started in Naples (Paramount, 1960)
The Misfits (US, 1961)

5

Robert Taylor

He was so handsome they said he was beautiful, and called him 'Pretty Boy'. He was the man with the perfect face. Make-up experts who measured his facial features said it was impossible to improve on perfection. Much to his embarrassment, rumour had it that he was gay. Was he or wasn't he? Mogul Louis B. Mayer decided for him – the young man was heterosexual. He was a nice kid from Nebraska; how could he be anything but a nice guy who dated girls? He was confused, however. Arriving in Hollywood, he joined a theatre group and was seen in the company of homosexuals. What did he know? He'd never met one before. Then MGM discovered him. Mayer liked the 22-year-old, changed his name and created a legend. The past was forgotten, except for his homey roots in Nebraska, the publicity department's delight. He did what he was told without complaining, but was harassed by the press. In an early movie, he was shown naked from the waist up. Newspaper headlines heralded the hair on his chest. My God, he was a man after all!

Like Gable, his name was mentioned in a scandalous fan magazine about his relationship with a famous actress. Were they living together? In 1938? God forbid! MGM rushed him to the altar. Again, he took it in his stride and made the best of it. Still he was taunted. It was an arranged marriage, they said. Isn't that what MGM did for homosexuals to spare their image?

His early years in Hollywood were heralded. He was so popular that L.B. Mayer chose him to star in the first film MGM made abroad. But he was haunted by his good looks. His acting was secondary, much to his distress. He tried to cover his face with hats and beards, feeling more comfortable that way. A big moneymaker for MGM, no one bothered to counsel him on how to overcome his handsomeness, and act out his roles despite such a blessing.

The longest-lasting contract player in Hollywood history, he managed to survive the loss of Louis B. Mayer, his mentor and, unlike his peers at the studio, was still given roles that elevated his image. He said shortly before his death in 1969, 'I wish today's young actors had a studio and boss like I had. It groomed us carefully, kept us busy in picture after picture, thus giving us exposure, and made us stars.'

Robert Taylor was born Spangler Arlington Brugh on 4 August 1911 in Filley, Nebraska. His father, Andrew, a farmer, took up medicine to better care for his frail wife, Ruth, who became pregnant in his second year of medical school. It was a shock to both of them. After eight years of marriage, they had to accept the fact that Ruth's health would be tested to the full. At 7:00 a.m. on a hot August day their son was born, and Ruth almost died.

During the long days in bed throughout her pregnancy, she had thought about names for her child. If it were a boy, she'd call him Arlington. 'I was very romantic and sensitive,' she explained. 'The hero's name in a book I was reading was Arlington. I decided that would be his middle name.' Spangler was traditional in the Brugh family, handed down through generations of Pennsylvania Dutchmen. But he would be known by his middle name, Arlington or 'Arly'.

Though Ruth was improving physically, she had become totally immersed in her affliction, a weak heart, employing it finally as her identity before the world. She enjoyed being pampered and took great satisfaction in receiving pity. She ruled over everyone – her tactic being, 'If you won't let me have my way, I'll get even for always. I'll die.'

To ease his mother's burden, Arly was sent to the country where he learned to fish, hunt and ride a horse. When he was five years old he returned home. His father was now in private practice and his mother much improved, but she wanted Arly with her. She tutored him until he was seven and cried the day she took him to school. 'I've lost my son,' she sobbed. He was dressed in Little Lord Fauntleroy velvet outfits, with the result that the other boys made fun of him and chased him home.

In grammar school, Arly took up the cello, a hobby that would determine his destiny. Now living in Beatrice, Nebraska, he became a member of the Boy Scouts of America and attended church every Sunday with his family. In junior high, Arly was the first 'elected' president of the student body. In the holidays he stocked wheat and mowed lawns. He owned a horse, Gypsy, which he kept at a nearby farm. Though his life appeared to be typical for a young man, Arly was dominated by his mother. With this upbringing he learned to be gentle with women, treating each as if she were his mother. He would also, in his adult years, be attracted to older women. Though he defied Ruth very seldom, he did appear in school plays despite her disapproval.

After graduating from high school, Arly attended Doane College in Crete, Nebraska, playing the cello in a string quartet to help pay his college expenses. The group performed over the radio, earning fifty dollars for each performance. He took cello lessons from Professor E. Gray, a man whom he idolised. In Arly's sophomore year, Gray announced that he was accepting a better position at Pomona College in Claremont, California. This was a blow to young Arly and at the age of twenty he made the most important decision of his life – to follow the professor. Ruth was so anxious for him to become a concert celloist that she let him go.

At Pomona, the professor begrudged his protégé all outside activities. Arly's public speaking became so polished, however, that he was asked to join the Drama Club. He continued to play in the college orchestra, but gave up his cello lessons. When he played the part of the disillusioned Captain Stanhope in *Journey's End*, it was such a success that he decided to pursue acting.

In 1933, his parents attended his graduation. Four months later, Dr. Brugh died, and Ruth moved with Arly into a three-room apartment. He told his mother about a screen test at MGM arranged by actor Joel McCrea, and another screen test at Goldwyn Studios. He was optimistic but decided to improve his acting skills at the Pasadena Playhouse. Its director, Gilmore Brown, was a homosexual and took a liking to Arly. He began attending parties given by lesbians and homosexuals; hence the later rumours that Robert Taylor was gay.

MGM publicity chief Howard Strickling, although biased perhaps, said Taylor had found himself in strange company. He might have been converted to Gilmore's way of thinking – if MGM hadn't made him an offer. And why wouldn't they? With his black hair, widow's peak and blue eyes, he was a natural for the screen. He signed an MGM contract on 6 February 1934, for $35 dollars a week. This made him the lowest-paid contract player in history. 'He had the looks, but not the training,' Strickling claimed. Joel McCrea, an alumnus of Pomona, recalled, 'I got a letter of introduction about Taylor – Arly then – and I took him over to MGM. He made a test for a crime short with Virginia Bruce and he was made.'

It was L.B. Mayer's secretary, Ida Koverman, who thought up the name Robert Taylor. 'I couldn't support my mother on thirty-five dollars a week,' Bob said, 'so I went to see Mr. Mayer. He sat down with me and explained how to budget. Then he went on about having two daughters and not being blessed with a son, but if he had a son who worked for a nice man and a wonderful studio, he'd tell him not to ask for a raise.' He left Mayer's office and ran into his agent. 'Did you get the raise, Bob?'

'No,' he replied. 'but I got a father.'

Within a few months Taylor was earning fifty dollars a week. He was loaned out to 20th Century-Fox to make *Handy Andy* with Jean Parker, and to Universal for *There's Always Tomorrow* with Binnie Barnes, before finally making *West Point of the Air* for MGM. But it was the first in a series of featurettes called *Crime Does Not Pay* that the public noticed. In the next, *Buried Loot*, he played an embezzler with a scar across his face. Despite this disfigurement, MGM began receiving letters about Taylor, and he was cast in *Society Doctor* with Chester Morris, Virginia Bruce and Billie Burke. Though Morris was the established star, it was Taylor who received the attention in his first major role. *Times Square Lady* and *Murder in the Fleet* followed. In *Broadway Melody of 1946* Taylor sang 'I've Got a Feelin' You're Foolin'. In the film he played a theatrical producer in conflict with newspaper columnist Jack Benny, while his love interest in the film was Eleanor Powell.

Actress Irene Dunne had been slated to make *Magnificent Obsession* and was looking for a leading man. Director John Stahl suggested Robert Taylor. 'Neither of us knew much about Bob,' Dunne said, 'but he seemed right for the part of Robert Merrick.' Taylor portrayed a playboy whose drunken antics on his yacht cause the death of a famous physician. Eventually he takes up the medical profession and with the film's humanitarian depiction of the great doctor, Taylor's performance in *Magnificent Obsession* lifted him to instant stardom.

Women nevertheless said they were too busy admiring his looks to appreciate his acting, while men studied his face looking for an imperfection. He was the biggest thing since Rudolph Valentino died in 1926. But Robert Taylor was different. Valentino's appeal was to the lower side of woman's nature – slick and dangerous. Taylor was the all-American boy. Women's dreams of him were pure and romantic. He was Norman Rockwell, *Reader's Digest*, a church picnic, white slacks and blazer; while women wanted him, they knew he was above sex and they liked him that way.

By 1935 Taylor was making $750 a week. MGM began their usual publicity campaign, which began with a visit to their star's hometown. Bob's visit to Beatrice was sincere, and, in his humble, almost naïve way, he thought everything would be just the same. Instead the town turned out to celebrate his rise to stardom. He made a brief speech: 'I know this thing might just be a flash in the pan. Don't know, but for some reason my looks caught on, but that can't carry you far. I don't know much about acting – I realise that better than anyone – but I'm going to work hard at it, and before the bloom wears off, maybe I can learn something and make a career out of it. If I don't, so what? I'll go back to school and get my medical degree, just like I had planned to do in the first place.'

According to friends, Ruth Brugh was very glamorous and raved about the delightful weather in California. While she bragged and boasted, Bob was asking a friend to send him the Beatrice *Sun*. 'I really miss it,' he said. He continued to receive his hometown newspaper for the rest of his life.

Like Clark Gable, Bob's first interview with the Hollywood press was a disaster.

'What do you think was your driving force in *Magnificent Obsession?*' a reporter asked.

'A screen metamorphosis is more psychology than histrionics,' Taylor replied. 'The thing is to analyse the character you are playing and then the various stages of self-development become a logical outgrowth of that individual finding himself.'

L.B. Mayer called Bob to his office. 'Did you actually say that?' he asked.

'Yes sir, I did. Anything wrong?'

'Yes, you sounded like your jockstrap was on too tight. For the time being, keep your mouth shut.'

Taylor was beginning to feel the heat. He needed some fresh air and freedom. So, when he found a house on the outskirts of town, he told Ruth it was time for him to be on his own. 'I'll arrange for a nurse to stay with you,' he told her, 'and I'll visit during the week.'

Ruth put her hand over her heart and sat down, trying to catch her breath. 'I want you to be a good boy,' she said soberly. 'I don't want you running around with women and drinking. Sex is the devil and girls are little devils in disguise.'

Bob knew his mother had become a religious fanatic; it was one reason why he needed a place of his own. After his affair with Virginia Bruce, he would frequent the 'cat houses' near the MGM lot, as did many of the other male stars. 'I think L.B. Mayer hand-picked each one of the girls and made sure they were clean,' he said. 'They were studio rejects and probably making more money than I did.'

On Taylor's first publicity trip to New York he felt the personal sting of the press. They had begun a private war with him, calling him their 'popular headache' at the office and at home. One newspaper wrote:

> In case you care, Robert Taylor of the movies regards himself as a red-blooded man, and resents people calling him beautiful! As he came into Grand Central Station where hundreds of screaming women were waiting, the curly-haired screen star was asked point blank, 'Do you have hair on your chest?' He smiled and said he thinks people are belittling him when they refer to him as beautiful. Pressed for an answer, he said, 'I'm a red-blooded man and I resent people calling me pretty – and for your information, I'VE GOT HAIR ON MY CHEST!'

Later he said that he thought his innocence was showing and he found it almost impossible to control his temper. When he stopped for a light on Sunset Boulevard in his car, a man in the next vehicle said, 'Hey, Bob, what's your definition of love?'

'. . . I guess admiration and respect.'

'No sex?'

'The light's changing.'

'What about the physical side of love?'

'Oh, that's different,' Taylor said, stepping on the gas.

The next day this conversation was in the morning paper. L.B. Mayer reminded Bob to keep his mouth shut. He was also reminded that the studio had the right to drop a contract player at the termination of certain intervals. The actor, on the other hand, had no privileges: he had to stay with the studio until the end of his seven-year contract. Mayer felt obliged to discipline Bob as he did his other stars. 'Remember we are a family at MGM,' he said proudly. 'Your actions reflect on everyone here. We stick together to uphold our high standards.'

Irene Hervey was a contract player at MGM when she met Taylor. It was love at first sight, but their romance was doomed from the beginning. They became officially engaged, but MGM intervened. They made it clear to Bob that, single and available, he was a good investment; married, he would lose his female admirers. Taylor was crushed. Irene thought he should stand up to Mayer, but Bob thought they should wait. Irene did just that for two years and then began dating singer Allan Jones. 'By the time the studio gave us permission to marry,' Hervey said, 'I had decided Allan had more potential than Bob so I became Mrs. Allan Jones.'

Bob carried a torch for Irene – until he met 'The Queen'.

It was at the old Trocadero in Hollywood late in 1936 when Marion and Zeppo Marx invited Barbara Stanwyck and Robert Taylor to dinner. When he asked her to dance she turned him down: 'No, Zeppo wants me to meet a Mr. Artique.'

'Never heard of him,' Bob replied. 'Artique, Artique . . . wait a minute, Artique is R.T. That's me!'

Though Barbara was disheartened over her impending divorce from Broadway star Frank Fay, and Taylor was hurting over the loss of Irene Hervey, one would never have known watching them on the dance floor that night.He sent her a dozen long-stemmed roses the next day and so their affair began.

Soon afterwards, his film *Private Number* with Loretta Young opened at Grauman's Chinese Theater on Hollywood Boulevard. It was the first time Bob had seen his name in lights. 'I was terribly impressed,' he said.

Barbara reminded him quietly but firmly, 'Don't let it go to your head, buster. Loretta has been working for years to get her name up there. You've only been at it a short time. The trick is to keep it up there!'

Taylor later said that was the best advice he ever had.

This time MGM reversed its outlook and took advantage of Taylor's relationship with a woman. He co-starred with Barbara in *His Brother's Wife*. One critic wrote that he was 'just not the type to be exposed to heat and fever-bearing ticks and Metro's special effects'. Mayer laughed. 'It seems to me, Bob, you're too pretty to be a doctor and too delicate to trudge through the jungle and certainly too sweet to be bitten by bugs. Keep up the good work!'

In *The Gorgeous Hussy* with Joan Crawford, Taylor is killed at the beginning of a film that was mediocre at best. Barbara and Bob socialised with her good friend Joan and her husband Franchot Tone. Having been New York hoofers, both girls spoke the same language.

Columnist Ed Sullivan interviewed Bob, asking, 'You're from Nebraska?'

'Yes, and someday when I get my hands on some money, I want to go back to the farm.'

'And take Barbara with you?'

'We're not planning marriage, Ed. That's all I can say, but I can tell you she's the greatest person I've ever met. She has helped me an awful lot. I've always liked the girls, but I wish some of them wouldn't make saps of themselves over me.'

'Getting back to Barbara . . . do you think she'd like Nebraska?'

'Don't know.'

Taylor never did take Barbara Stanwyck to Nebraska. He had enough instinct even then to know she would not have fitted in. Her vocabulary was explicit, laced with raunchy adjectives. She and Ruth clashed from the beginning. Both were domineering and possessive, and Bob was in the middle. Yet, despite the influence they had on Taylor, L.B. Mayer was still the ultimate force in his life. He promised Bob great things and kept his promise when he put him opposite Greta Garbo in *Camille*. In fact it was production chief Irving Thalberg who thought Taylor would be perfect as Garbo's young lover, and director George Cukor agreed. 'Bob Taylor was the most handsome actor in Hollywood,' he said. 'He was scared to death to play opposite Garbo, of course, I recall all she said to him was "How do you do?" and then kept her distance until she falls in love with him in the film. I explained to Bob that off camera Greta lived her part as intently as she did when the cameras were rolling. She caught him off guard in one scene when she was supposed to kiss him, but cupped his face in her hands and kissed him all over his face. It was very erotic.'

Did Bob learn anything from working with Garbo? Only confidence, he said, because what she had was inborn. Having made silent films, she spoke with her eyes, a technique lost in talkies. When the picture was finished, he and Greta did not speak to each other again. He never approached her on the back lot or in the commissary: he respected her that much. But when he died, she called a friend in tears. 'Robert Taylor is gone,' she wept.

Camille was a smash hit. Critics expressed surprise that Taylor had played his part so skilfully.

Barbara Stanwyck was born Ruby Stevens on 16 July 1907, in Brooklyn, New York. Her mother was killed getting off a streetcar when Ruby was four years old. Her father, a bricklayer, could not face taking care of three children and disappeared. The last anyone heard of him was that he had been working on the Panama Canal and had died at sea. Ruby's sister Mildred, a chorus girl, became head of the family. But she was unable to care for her brother and sister, so they were put in foster homes. If Ruby had anything to look forward to it was spending summers on the road with her sister. She admired the dancers and picked up whatever steps she could. School meant nothing to her. All she could think about was being on her own and getting a job as a hoofer. Ruby quit school and took odd jobs until she found a job at the Strand Theater in Times Square as a dancer, paying $35 a week. This led to other jobs in the chorus, but often she was out of work. Billy LaHiff, owner of the Tavern on Forty-eighth Street, fed young hopefuls and tried to help them find jobs. He introduced Ruby to producer, director and playwright Willard Mack, who was casting *The Noose* and hired her as a chorus girl. The show went on the road but it bombed. Mack revised the script, shuffling the cast into different roles. Ruby handled herself so well with the few lines she was originally given that he gave her a juicy part in the third act.

Before Ruby signed the contract, however, Mack decided to change her name. In an old English theatre programme he noted that a Jane Stanwyck was listed as a player in *Barbara Frietchi*. Thus Barbara Stanwyck was born. As she was about to sign her name, she got as far as 'Bar', looked up at Mack and asked, 'How do you spell Barbara?' From then on she always used two capital Bs in her name – BarBara.

Barbara was a big hit in *The Noose*. Though she showed promise as an actress, it was her close relationship to Willard Mack that boosted her career. When *The Noose* closed, she appeared in another Broadway show, *Burlesque*, and it was Oscar Levant who introduced Barbara to 'Broadway's Favourite Son', Frank Fay. The pair got on well: they had brassy exteriors, and both knew the language of the street. He was the kind of guy Barbara might have met in Brooklyn and, despite his fame, she was comfortable in his company. She married Fay on 25 August 1928. When Warner Brothers offered him a movie contract, Barbara accompanied him to Hollywood. While he hosted *Show of Shows*, Barbara made the rounds, but no one wanted her. Finally, though, director Frank Capra signed her to make *Ladies of Leisure*. He told her bluntly she was not beautiful; if she was going to be a success, he said, it would be for her acting, not her looks.

Critics said, 'Miss Stanwyck triumphs in *Ladies of Leisure*.' After a second success with her next effort, *Illicit*, she was offered contracts with several studios. She declined. Frank Fay, meanwhile, had failed in Hollywood, and their regular marital disagreements turned violent. Hoping to salvage their marriage, they adopted a ten-month-old baby whom they christened Dion Anthony Fay. Barbara was so in love with Frank that she could not admit to herself that being a mother was not part of her nature. Having a baby in the house only increased the tension in the Fay household. He drank heavily and became physically abusive. In August 1935 Barbara filed for divorce and moved into a ranch in the San Fernando Valley, outside Los Angeles. In the fall of 1936 she was introduced to the love of her life.

The five-foot-five-inch, auburn-haired Stanwyck had blue eyes, weighed 115 pounds, and was four years older than Robert Taylor. When they met, he was just a kid, while Barbara had never been a child. He was well-educated, she was not. He liked the country, she was a city girl. He liked women in frilly clothes, she chose tailored outfits. He loved to hunt, she was terrified of guns. What, if anything, did they see in each other? Taylor needed to be mothered, and she told him what to do and how to do it. They were both chain smokers and drank gallons of coffee. Neither 'went Hollywood', they preferred staying home rather than attending stuffy parties.

Mayer arranged for Taylor to appear with Barbara in *This is My Affair* at 20th Century-Fox, and this was followed by *Broadway Melody of 1938*. Now it was time for Mayer to change Bob's image from virgin lover to he-man. He put him in *A Yank at Oxford*, the first MGM film made outside the United States. On his way to England, Taylor stopped off in New York and he was mobbed wherever he went. Women tore off his clothes, frequently managing to run off with his shoes. It was the same in London. Seen on the balcony of Claridge's Hotel, he casually flipped a cigarette to the ground below. There was a mad scramble for the butt and several people were injured in the scuffle.

Taylor knew he would be in England for six months and missed Barbara so much he proposed marriage to her on the phone. She said they'd talk about it when he got back. Barbara might have flown to London, but she was terrified of aeroplanes and preferred the security of Los Angeles. Taylor soon forgot he was lonely. His role of Lee Sheridan in *A Yank at Oxford* was an athletic one. He showed off in front of his British classmates at track meets and rowing in the bump races. Most important, though, was the publication of a picture of Taylor in athletics trunks and undershirt. Paris was the first to announce the 'hairy news'. Underneath his photo, dated 28 August 1937, appeared the caption, '*Mon Dieu, Quel Homme!*' – 'My God, what a man!' The American press announced, 'Robert Taylor Bares Chest To Prove He-Ness!'

Suddenly, after making fun of Taylor for so long, American males felt obliged to prove their own virility. In Hollywood a 'chest toupee' shop opened for those men who would otherwise be embarrassed, especially since men's bathing suits were passé and trunks alone were acceptable on the beaches.

Barbara had great compassion for Bob at this time – she knew how hurt he was about all the silly publicity – but still she refused to visit him in England. She told the press, 'Can you imagine what would happen if I went? It's bad enough for him alone. We wouldn't have a moment's peace.' In any case, she knew L.B. Mayer would not approve if Bob married.

On the early morning of 14 December 1937, Taylor returned to New York on the *Queen Mary*. He granted a brief interview in his stateroom and was asked how the British press had treated him. 'Polite,' he emphasised. 'They don't grab you on the street or bother you while you're eating dinner.'

When he disembarked, swarms of reporters surrounded him, throwing questions left and right. Who was the hairdresser who created his widow's peak? When did he plan to get married? Did he have hair on his legs? 'God DAMN!' he blurted out, and rushed for a limousine. On the train to Los Angeles he told an MGM publicity man, 'I was able to relax in England. In less than ten minutes back here I lost it.'

'We offered to meet the press, Bob, but you said they'd call you a spoiled snob if you didn't face them yourself. There's an interesting article in the newspaper that might interest you. Here, read it.'

THE PRESS AND MR. TAYLOR

Our sympathies go out to Mr. Robert Taylor, the young personable motion picture actor, for being forced again to submit to the severe questions, not to say heckling on whether he regards himself as beautiful. One of the reporters said that apparently men did not like Mr. Taylor and ascribed this unfortunate state of affairs to the fact that Mr. Taylor is so handsome.

This is so much bosh! New York has some of the handsomest reporters in the world so there is no reason why they should be jealous of Mr. Taylor. Perhaps the reason is to be found in the shifting news in this country. It used to be big news when Stanley found Livingstone, when a crown prince was born or when a great economic upheaval shook the world. Today's news is whether Mr. Taylor thinks he is beautiful and how he feels, if at all, about Barbara Stanwyck.

Mayer was pleased with *A Yank at Oxford*. He told Bob to be patient, the film would change his image. The reviews were excellent and, surprisingly, only a few critics mentioned his good looks. They admired his virility and considered him an actor with promise.

But he would face another problem that was out of his control – Barbara's custody hearing in court. She wanted to bar Frank Fay from seeing their son while Frank, in turn, accused her of trying to replace him with Robert Taylor in Dion's life. Stanwyck lost the battle and Fay was granted visitation rights. While Bob was in England, his new ranch, within walking distance of Barbara's house, was finished. Fifteen miles from Los Angeles in the San Fernando Valley, the couple hoped to be left alone, but fan magazines featured articles about his walking to her place to use the pool and her visiting him in the evenings.

MGM followed *A Yank at Oxford* with a series of rugged roles. After *Three Comrades*, Taylor played a boxer in *The Crowd Roars*, and next came the bloody *Stand Up and Fight* alongside Wallace Beery. In February 1939, Barbara and Bob announced their engagement, but MGM had yet to give him permission to marry. As a matter of fact he wasn't sure he wanted to. During his six months in England he'd grown up, he wasn't afraid any more. He had great respect for Barbara but doubted he was in love with her. Then *Photoplay* magazine published a scandalous article about Hollywood couples who had been practically living together for years 'without the benefit of marriage'. Clark Gable and Carole Lombard eloped as soon as Gable's divorce was final. Bob was stunned when Mayer stopped production of *Lady of the Tropics* for 24 hours. Taylor walked out of Hedy Lamarr's arms into Barbara's in front of a San Diego judge a few minutes after midnight on 14 May 1939, so as to avoid the unlucky thirteenth. A reception was held at the Hugo Victor Café in Beverly Hills at two o'clock that afternoon. In later years Bob confessed that MGM had masterminded the whole affair: 'The only thing I was allowed to say was "I do". I wasn't even sure if I was in love.'

Barbara returned to her ranch and Bob went to see Ruth, who was hysterical. She felt ill and weak. 'Will you check my heartbeat every so often during the night . . . just to make sure?' she asked weakly. So Bob spent his wedding night with his mother. Once again Taylor was criticised but he told a friend, 'Hell, Barbara and I have had many wedding nights in the past three years. What's the big deal?'

After a brief honeymoon with Barbara at the Bucks County, Pennsylvania, home of playwright Moss Hart, Taylor started his next movie, *Flight Command*. He took the part of a cocky Navy ensign, becoming so involved with his role as a flier that he decided to take flying lessons. He spent all his spare time in the air with an instructor while Barbara cringed on the ground. This new hobby was the beginning of many disagreements. She felt he was already spending too much time on hunting and fishing trips with his buddies. When Barbara made arrangements for them to move back to Los Angeles, Bob was not happy. He enjoyed going home to the country at night and riding his horse. That his career was in a slump after *Remember?* with Greer Garson didn't help matters.

Then, he recalled, 'When I was just about convinced I had been forgotten, Mayer handed me the script of *Waterloo Bridge*. It was an actor's dream.' The film was a cinematisation of Robert Sherwood's play, the bittersweet story of a British soldier in love with a ballerina. When he is reported killed in action, she turns to prostitution. Her lover returns, but she feels unfit to marry him and throws herself in front of a truck on Waterloo Bridge where they met for the first time. Since it was the custom of English officers during the First World War to wear a moustache, Taylor was required to grow one – the moustache he would shave off and grow again with monotonous regularity over the years. His leading lady was Vivien Leigh, who had also appeared in *A Yank at Oxford* before she became famous in *Gone With the Wind*.

Taylor's popularity having been restored with the release of *Waterloo Bridge*, director Mervyn LeRoy thought he would be perfect in *Escape* with Norma Shearer. It was a good follow-up. Then, in 1941, *Billy The Kid* was reborn on film. For Taylor, it was first of many westerns and his first colour film. He had to learn a fast draw with his left hand, but he had no problem riding like the wind on a horse. In *When Ladies Meet* he was reunited with both Joan Crawford and Greer Garson. Though he said comedy was not his forte, here he was very much at ease being amusing.

In 1940 and 1941, both Barbara and Bob were busy – she in Hollywood, and he frequently on location. Because they were separated most of the time, there were the inevitable divorce rumours. Taylor sent a letter to Jim Reid of *Motion Picture* magazine: ' . . . The rumor, though unfortunate, did not come as a surprise. Actually we have been expecting it. It seems inevitable that when picture people have been married over a year, rumors of this sort arise . . . all such rumors are entirely unfounded and untrue.'

Their fans bought it, but Hollywood insiders knew better. Barbara, her maternal instincts undimmed, called Bob 'Junior', telling him what to do. In fact, the separations caused by their career commitments held the marriage together. If they had been forced to live under the same roof seven days a week, neither could have tolerated the other.

In 1941 Taylor's leading lady in *Johnny Eager* was Lana Turner, and he commented, 'When she says "Good morning" I melt.' She claimed in her memoirs that there was a strong mutual attraction but that they were not intimate – but then Lana always portrayed herself as the perennial virgin.

She was involved with Bob, but did not want to break up his marriage. Meanwhile he went ahead and asked Barbara for a divorce. She cut her wrists in a feeble suicide attempt. Lana, who could sense a scandal brewing, soon broke her ties with Bob.

In Norma's Shearer's last movie *Cardboard Lover*, Taylor is handicapped with a silly role that wasn't worth the time. But he was thrilled with *Bataan*, a war movie starring Lloyd Nolan, Robert Walker, Thomas Mitchell and Desi Arnaz. George Murphy, also in the film, said, 'Bob was relieved to walk around with a five o'clock shadow and shabby uniform. He hated primping for the camera.'

In February 1943, after the release of *Song of Russia*, a film he hated, Taylor was sworn into the United States Navy. He applied for active duty but was turned down because he was 31 and too old for combat. After basic training he was sent to the Naval Instructors' school in New Orleans. There he got along well with another instructor, Tom Purvis, who was the same age, and the two men remained friends for life. 'We were in the air one day,' Purvis said, 'and did a right slow roll. It was perfect, but Taylor looked as if he were going to throw up, and he moaned, "I just lost my cigarette lighter. It's down there in the Mississippi River!"'

'So what?'

'So what?' Taylor yelped. 'Barbara will flip her lid. It cost her three hundred dollars!'

'Explain what happened. She'll understand.'

'You don't know Barbara,' was Taylor's reply.

On 5 November 1945, Bob was discharged from the Navy as a senior grade lieutenant. He did not want to go back to Hollywood. 'I've been the happiest in the service,' he told Purvis.

In 1943, Taylor had been given a new MGM contract for $4000 a week. It was the first Hollywood contract to carry a protective clause in the event of dollar inflation. When he returned to the studio in 1945, so as to avoid taxes he did not ask for a raise; instead, the studio gave him a new twin-engine Beechcraft worth $75,000. One of his navy buddies, Ralph Couser, was hired by MGM as Bob's co-pilot.

His homecoming film was *Undercurrent* with Katharine Hepburn, an unlikely leading lady for Taylor. But the critics were kind, and so was Miss Hepburn who told this author, 'I think Bob was one of the most underrated actors in the business.'

At Mayer's house for dinner one evening, Taylor confessed he lacked confidence as an actor these days. 'You were great in *Waterloo Bridge*,' Mayer exclaimed.

'Don't know. I never saw it,' Bob answered.

Mayer arranged to have the movie shown immediately after dinner. Bob told his boss, 'I never thought I could act until I saw that screening. There it was in black and white. I was good!' After that, Taylor always said *Waterloo Bridge* was his favourite film.

If he lacked confidence in himself as an actor, he felt worse when he began losing confidence in his virility. Since his return from the Navy, he had been unable to make love to Barbara. He told her he had a prostate problem, but she questioned this excuse. Since he was so close to his Navy buddies, she suspected he was gay. Whenever Ralph Couser called, she would holler, 'Hey, Bob, your wife's on the phone!'

However, it was Barbara who was bisexual. During the Roaring Twenties no one cared who was straight and who was gay, and she had given herself to lesbian hoofer Marjorie Main in the early days. Even during her marriages it was always oral sex she craved, as she made explicitly clear at a party Bob held for his buddies. John Wayne recalled, 'We were having a great time, but it was getting late, I guess. All of a sudden we heard Barbara, who was standing at the top of the stairs, shout at Bob, "Get up here and get down on it!" How embarrassing it was for everyone. I felt sorry for Bob, who motioned for us to leave.'

It was well known that Stanwyck treated her husband like a son. She bought him a motorcycle and proceeded to show him how to use it. When she bought him a new car, she did the same thing. But Barbara was no mother. She sent her adopted son Dion to military school soon after she met Bob, rarely seeing the boy. On the few occasions they did meet, she shook his hand. Eventually, he got into trouble. She used it as a good excuse to disinherit him.

There is no doubt Barbara had heard the rumours that Bob was gay, but with her lesbian background, she thought nothing about it because they had great sex. Indirectly, there were witnesses to their shared passion. Barbara once arranged a surprise birthday party for Bob. While he was getting out of his car, the guests hid in the darkened rooms. Bob burst through the front door, took off his clothes and headed for the stairs, telling Barbara he was ready. There he was in the raw in front of a host of friends and peers. It was a funny scene – and for Barbara it was proof of their love and bedroom compatibility – but Bob never got over it.

Eventually the years of being dominated caught up with him. As had been the case when he spent six months in England making *A Yank at Oxford*, he grew up. Without his mother and Louis B. Mayer hovering over him, he discovered his own strength. While he was in the Navy, he became independent of Barbara and began to resent her interference. As his discharge loomed, he dreaded going home to her, though he would never spell it out even to Tom Purvis, to whom he confided almost everything. Barbara was a major factor in Bob's reluctance to return to Hollywood, and Tom knew it. 'He was scared of her,' Purvis said. 'She could make life miserable for him at home, nagging him about everything. This drove him away, of course. Either he took off to hunt and fish with his buddies or he took his plane for a spin. Since Barbara hated both hobbies, she was unlikely to follow him. The wrath came when he went home. She would make him suffer for choosing his buddies over her.'

Eventually Barbara accused Bob of being homosexual and that hit him hard. He, too, started to wonder if he was gay. The years of being heckled and labelled a homosexual came back to haunt him. Now he couldn't perform with his wife, and he wanted his marriage to work out. Convinced there was something wrong, Taylor went to a psychologist. The doctor had known Bob socially, and was well acquainted with Barbara and Ruth.

'He was extremely upset. There was no doubt in my mind he needed help. I asked him directly if he had the urge to be with a man. He said the idea appalled him. Homosexuals had chased him for years and he disliked them intensely. Then I asked if he got excited by other women. He said seeing a sexy girl excited him. Since this was not a professional visit, I was able to advise him as a friend to see another woman – to find out if he could perform.'

That woman was Ava Gardner, his co-star in *The Bribe*. She wrote in her memoirs that they had a beautiful affair, with no thought of anything beyond that. 'He wasn't happy,' Ava said. 'He was plagued by memories of the "Pretty Boy" era. It was demeaning. He would never get over it. He wasn't happy with Barbara, either, but he didn't want to be just another divorced man in Hollywood.'

Bob made headlines when he testified before the Un-American Activities Committee, set up to inquire into Communism in Hollywood. He mentioned the names of those who disrupted meetings of the Screen Actors' Guild. He said he had agreed to make *Song of Russia* only after the government had put pressure on him; the film, he had been told, would influence the American people in favour of Russia. 'I don't think the picture should have been made,' he said, adding that he would never work in any capacity with a Communist, even if it meant the end of his career.

Taylor was criticised for his testimony by the Russians and by his left-wing peers in Hollywood. He said he didn't care and would testify the same way all over again. Regarding Communists, he said, 'They should all be sent back to Russia or some other unpleasant place.'

In this respect, Barbara was in total agreement with her husband, but by now this was the only positive aspect of their marriage. They went to Europe, but their vacation was a boring failure. Barbara was anxious to go back to work, Bob to get in his Beechcraft for some peace and quiet. He begged Barbara to fly with him to Palm Springs, but she declined to go anywhere near his plane. After her friends suggested she should share one of his hobbies, however, she agreed to fly with him – and was terribly ill from sheer fright.

Bob called Tom Purvis and said he was going to England. 'I'm making a film called *Conspirator* with a little girl I think might be something one day. I think her first name is Elizabeth but I know we have Taylor in common. She's only seventeen.'

As filming progressed, he took notice that the 'little girl' was not so little after all. 'She was stacked,' he said. 'We were doing a bedroom scene and I got aroused. It was embarrassing. I took the cameraman aside and told him to shoot me from the waist up. Go figure it. I'd worked with the most beautiful women in Hollywood so I should have been seasoned. I was attracted to Elizabeth but she was only seventeen so I left it alone. Ironically, I introduced her to Michael Wilding and she fell in love with him.'

Taylor's next movies, *Ambush* and *Devil's Doorway*, were rated 'good', but he considered himself in a professional slump that had begun when he returned from the service. Nevertheless, though he had not made a good film since *Waterloo Bridge* and *Johnny Eager* in the early forties, he was given a new MGM contract and more money. Bob's leading lady in his next project, *Quo Vadis?*, was Deborah Kerr, who later agreed with Katharine Hepburn that Taylor was a much better actor than he was ever given credit for. The studio had been working on *Quo Vadis?* for two years; though L.B. Mayer disapproved of the script, his new production chief Dore Schary had gone ahead with it. Clark Gable had flatly refused to play the Roman officer, Marcus Vinicius, in this $7 million production – at the time the most expensive in movie history.

Bob lived like a king in Rome. He occupied the entire upper floor of a new apartment house – he had eight rooms, five servants and a chef who was the former cook for the king of Italy. Bob also had a girlfriend, an attractive extra, Lia DiLeo. Though he was very discreet, word got back to Barbara, who called her agent and good friend, Helen Ferguson. 'I'm flying to Rome and you're going with me!'

MGM photographed the happy couple sightseeing. Bob pointed out places of interest while Barbara looked fascinated. She couldn't have been more bored, however. Her purpose for being in Rome was to confront Bob about another woman. She badgered and nagged him until he blurted out, 'At least I can get it up with her!'

A stunned Barbara threatened him with divorce. 'I'll bleed you for the rest of your life!' she said, before returning to Los Angeles sick at heart.

The day Bob departed, Lia DiLeo was waiting for him in the lobby of his apartment building. He was taken by surprise when she flung herself into his arms and covered his face with kisses. The press cameras clicked and flashed. Taylor had been neatly framed. He smiled, pushed her gently aside and rushed to his limousine. Lia told reporters, 'Bob is tired of Barbara and he told me so.'

Taylor refused to comment, and when he did it was MGM publicity chief Howard Strickling who made a statement on behalf of both Bob and Barbara:

> In the past few years, because of professional requirements, we have been separated just too often and too long. Our sincere and continued efforts to maintain our marriage have failed.
>
> We are deeply disappointed that we could not solve our problems . . . There will be a California divorce. Neither of us has another romantic interest whatsoever.

Columnist Louella Parsons wrote, 'It is almost certain that the Italian girl had nothing to do with the Taylors' decision to divorce. Trouble started long before Bob went to Rome. I spoke to Barbara and I am inclined to think when they decided to end their marriage it came suddenly. It was Bob who asked for his freedom.'

On 21 February 1951, Barbara appeared in court. She told the judge that her husband wanted to be a bachelor again, that he 'enjoyed his freedom in Italy and wanted to continue his life without restrictions'. The judge granted the divorce. Barbara was awarded their $100,000 mansion and 15 per cent of Taylor's earnings until she remarried or either party died.

Three months after Barbara's appearance in court, she made another – this time with Bob, at Ciro's in Hollywood. She told reporters, 'The divorce won't be final for a year and there's no use trying to keep it a secret that I'm carrying a torch for Bob, but it is too early to say whether or not we will be reconciled.' Barbara said it was her second date with Bob since the divorce was granted. 'There will be no other man in my life,' she stated.

Bob was, of course, seeing other women. Virginia Grey had been one of Clark Gable's favourites until he got drunk and eloped with Lady Sylvia Ashley. Bob now began seeing Virginia, but they spent the evenings at her place rather than going out in public. 'When it was time to say good night, I left the room for a minute and he disappeared,' Virginia said. 'I guess he didn't want to commit himself to another date. I don't know how Barbara knew about us, but she did. A few years later we appeared in a film together and she let me have it. Words I cannot quote. I had done the unthinkable. I had gone out with Robert Taylor.'

Another actress remembers Bob as a frustrating man to date. 'Called you Saturday night but guess you had a date.' She didn't. 'It's lonely here on location. Don't know why you didn't come along.' He didn't ask.

Barbara might have been pining for Bob, but she had her good times too. Robert Wagner, her 21-year-old co-star in *Titanic*, claimed he had an affair with her. She had helped him during the filming, and perhaps he reminded her of another Bob – young and innocent. She took up where she left off with girls, as well. During *Clash by Night*, Barbara was patient with the new starlet, Marilyn Monroe. Ever the professional, Stanwyck would not stand for an actor not knowing his lines or reporting late for work. Marilyn did both and ordinarily Barbara would have spoken up on the set – 'Get with it or get out.' Not so with Marilyn, whose lack of confidence in herself led her into many beds. She was not a lesbian but could be accommodating to both sexes for fear of rejection. Barbara was unusually kind to her, especially when the news broke that Monroe had posed for a nude calendar. She told the press she had been broke and needed money to repair her car. After her sob story was accepted by the public, her career blossomed. Marilyn also admitted she had slept her way to the top: the casting couch was always readily available. 'If I didn't take advantage of it, there were plenty of girls waiting in line.'

Marilyn could only benefit from intimacy with Stanwyck, who remembered her own years of struggling and giving into those who could help her up the steep ladder to fame. Actor Clifton Webb, a talented homosexual, referred to Barbara as 'my favourite American lesbian'.

But she was willing to give up everything if she could have Taylor back in her arms.

*

It was a difficult time for Bob. Not only was he adjusting to his divorce, but L.B. Mayer resigned on 31 August 1951, stepping aside for Dore Schary. Bob's career did not suffer during the transition, but without his mentor he did not get the lump in his throat that he had always felt when he signed a new contract with Mayer standing behind him. And he watched helplessly as, one by one, his MGM pals departed. Gable left in a huff and Lana Turner in tears. They were making too much money, so Schary did not renew their contracts.

Schary disliked stars – but he took a liking to Taylor. Perhaps it was Bob's humility and his eagerness to please, so unlike his co-workers. MGM was not the same, but Taylor would wait it out and collect his pension. He'd earned it.

Westward the Women was regarded with particular esteem, not so much because of Taylor but because of the story itself – one of women going west to find husbands, enduring hardships along the way. Then Bob was given the script for *Ivanhoe*. 'I'd rather do a western,' he said. Schary refused to give in: '*Ivanhoe* is my pride and joy, Bob.' So Taylor went to England and co-starred with Joan Fontaine and Elizabeth Taylor. The film became a classic and Bob became MGM's knight in shining armour.

One of Taylor's favourite leading ladies – on and off the screen – was Eleanor Parker. They were to make three movies together. The first was *Above and Beyond*, the story of Colonel Paul Tibbets, who pressed the trigger that fired the atom bomb over Hiroshima in 1945. Miss Parker, who portrayed Tibbets' wife, was an established actress who had been nominated for an Oscar for *Detective Story*. She met Taylor in 1952 and they almost married, but according to Bob she was very much like Barbara, independent and domineering. He was, of course, still seeing his ex-wife. One reporter mentioned that they were seeing more of each other than they did when they were married.

Bob's appearance on Ed Sullivan's television show *Toast of the Town* was an unprecedented move. It was the first time a major Hollywood studio had allowed one of its contracted stars to appear on television. Taylor was promoting *Above and Beyond* for MGM, but the press ignored the film and concentrated on the growing cooperation between Hollywood and television.

Soon after, Ava Gardner appeared with Bob in *Ride Vaquero!*. What one critic had to say, however, summed up the film: 'Nothing could have been as static as the dusty shenanigans of the clattering of such urban buckaroos as Robert Taylor, Ava Gardner and Howard Keel, and mercifully some fine Technicolor backgrounds.'

Taylor next reluctantly accepted *Knights of the Round Table*, in which he played a trim, military Lancelot: 'I'm getting mighty tired of wearing iron jock straps,' he said. But his knight-in-shining-armour epics always received good reviews – and they made millions for MGM, helping keep the studio going during the 1950s when moviegoers increasingly stayed home to watch television.

On 23 May 1951, 27-year-old Ursula Thiess arrived in the United States from Germany. During the Second World War she had been forced into farm labour and lived in unheated barracks, worked long hours and too often faced starvation. Her marriage to actor-producer George Thiess was an unfortunate wartime union, but she bore him two children – first a daughter, Manuela, and then a son, Michael. Eventually she divorced Thiess and took up modelling. She was living with her children in one furnished room when Howard Hughes spotted her picture in a magazine. He offered her a contract at RKO and, two weeks after she arrived in the United States, Ursula's picture was on the cover of *Life* magazine. Before long she had appeared in *Monsoon*, *Kiss and the Sword* with Robert Stack, and *Bengal* with Rock Hudson.

On 24 April 1952, her agent invited her to accompany him and his wife to dinner at the Coconut Grove, along with a blind date – Robert Taylor. Bob called her the next day and many dates followed. They were often seen at nightclubs, mainly for Ursula's benefit as an up-and-coming Hollywood actress. Taylor told reporters Ursula was truly lovely: 'She has the most beautiful eyes I've ever seen. They're brown with specks of gold. And her lashes are at least a half an inch long – I'm not exaggerating!' When asked about marriage, however, he only said, 'Sure, I want to get married again, but I don't know when or to whom.'

Then, suddenly, Ursula and Bob were no longer part of the social scene. She surprised him one night by preparing German pancakes for dinner. She was an amazing cook, he said – amazing not least because she hadn't struck him as the domestic type. From then on they spent evenings at home.

This cosy arrangement would have to change, however. Having left her children with her mother in Hamburg, Ursula decided it was time for Manuela to come to the United States. Since Bob was staying with his mother, he was now practically living with Ursula. But, after eighteen months of dating him, she felt the relationship was going nowhere. Obviously Bob was avoiding marriage after his disastrous union with Barbara, whom he was nonetheless still dating. So Ursula broke up with Taylor, just as he was leaving for Egypt to make *Valley Of The Kings* with Eleanor Parker.

Having heard that Eleanor was anxious to resume her affair with Bob, Ursula began playing the same game, and made sure she was linked with other men in gossip columns. Bob wrote to her several times a week, but his letters went unanswered. When he returned home Ursula refused to see him – until one night he wouldn't take no for an answer. He had, he explained, something he wanted to show her. She responded that she had dinner guests and he was welcome to join them. Bob arrived at her apartment but refused to eat. Instead he sat in a corner, drank a gallon of coffee and smoked a pack of cigarettes. Embarrassed, the dinner guests departed, whereupon Bob presented Ursula with an engagement ring. 'Will you marry me?' he asked.

And on 24 May 1954, two years to the day after they met, Ursula and Bob were married in the middle of a lake on a cabin cruiser in Jackson Hole, Wyoming. Their good friends Ivy Mooring and Ralph Couser were the witnesses. After the brief ceremony, Bob called his press agent with the news. He and Ursula left immediately for Cloverdale, California, where Bob was scheduled to make *Many Rivers to Cross*. The MGM press agents had one problem to face – Eleanor Parker, Bob's leading lady, had not heard about his marriage. When she was told, Eleanor broke down in tears. Bob told a friend in later years that she came close to breaking up his marriage, which was only a few days old. Exactly what he meant, though, is not known.

Eleanor pulled herself together, of course. She and Bob gave fine performances in *Many Rivers to Cross*. Regrettably it was their last film together – regrettably because, of all Bob's leading ladies, it was Eleanor who complemented him best.

Stanwyck, shocked by Bob's elopement, swallowed her pride and repeated, 'It's true I'm still carrying a torch for him. There will be no other man in my life.'

Ursula was obliged to make one more movie for RKO. She co-starred with Robert Mitchum in *Bandido*, filmed in Mexico. A few months later the Mitchums hosted a formal party at Romanoff's in Los Angeles, at which Bob and Ursula shared a table with Lana Turner and her husband, Lex Barker. Suddenly, Barbara Stanwyck barged through the door, drunk and demanding to see 'Taylor and his German broad'. Lex managed to get rid of her, while Bob was so stunned he was unable to react. Nothing more was said about it.

After Taylor filmed *Quentin Durwood*, he was scheduled to make *The Last Hunt* in South Dakota. He wanted Ursula to go with him but she announced she was pregnant. He called Purvis, exclaiming, 'God damn, I never knew a guy like me could get so excited over something that happens all the time! You know, Tom, the best thing I ever did was marry Ursula.'

Terrance, known as Terry, was born on 18 June 1955, whereupon Manuela ran away from home because she resented the intrusion of a new child in the house. She was found, but was never truly happy in the Taylor household afterwards.

Someone else was unhappy too. Barbara Stanwyck was making a film on the day Terry was born. When the news that Robert Taylor had become the father of a baby boy was announced over the loudspeaker, Barbara burst into tears and fled to her dressing room.

In 1954 Taylor had been voted the most popular male star in the world by the Hollywood Press Association, representing 500 million moviegoers. In the same year Winchester voted him Outdoorsman of the Year for 'good marksmanship and sportsmanship in the field'. When the Taylors moved into their new home in Pacific Palisades, Ursula wanted Bob to display his trophies, but instead he hid them. In contrast, in 1951 he had been given Harvard's Lampoon Award for the worst acting that year in *Quo Vadis?* He showed up to accept this award and said, 'By golly, I finally won an award and I never worked harder in my life!'

Taylor made two more good films, *D-Day the Sixth of June* and *The Power and the Prize*, for release in 1956. During an interview that year he said, 'There are two types of stars in Hollywood – actors and personalities. Well, I'm a personality.'

'What do you consider Clark Gable, Mr. Taylor? '

'A friend who likes to hunt as much as I do.'

'Is there any reason you consider yourself a personality rather than an actor?'

'Hell, if you've seen any of my movies you'd know the answer to that. People come to the theatre to see Robert Taylor, not a good piece of acting. I learned a long time ago to accept myself for what I am. That doesn't mean I'm not trying to do better.'

The reporter followed Bob from the commissary to the set of *Tip on a Dead Jockey*, whereupon Taylor sat down and fell asleep. When the director woke him up, the reporter asked, 'Do you always go out like a light?'

'Yep. All I have to do is close my eyes.'

Tom Purvis read the interview in the newspaper and reminded Bob how he had once ended up in a ditch after falling asleep behind the wheel of a car. 'My eyes were tired, that's all,' Taylor said. 'Funny thing, I'm never really tired . . . bored, maybe, but not tired.'

Bob's mother, sinking deeper into her religion, still reminded him constantly about the evils of Hollywood. She did, however, get along with Ursula; she babysat occasionally and was a regular guest on holidays. But Bob never invited her to live with him.

On 29 October 1957, Louis B. Mayer died. Bob spoke well of his mentor. 'The only time I couldn't get in to see him it was when he changed my name. I wanted Ramsey Taylor and he knew it. After waiting around, I finally got the message.'

In 1958 Taylor made *The Law and Jake Wade* and *Saddle the Wind*, two good westerns that he had reason to be proud of. But that was the year he and MGM parted company, and *Party Girl* with Cyd Charisse was his last film as a contract player. He goes down in Hollywood history as having the longest-running movie contract ever – 24 years. 'I should have left them six years ago,' he said at the time, 'but it's hard when you've been with a studio for so many years. I couldn't save any money on salary. Now I hope to make enough to retire. I've established a price – $200,000 per picture and a percentage of the gross. Maybe I'll have something to show for my life.'

In 1959 Taylor bought a 113-acre ranch in Mandeville Canyon, just twenty minutes from Los Angeles, for $940,000. The 'Ursulor Rancho' was Bob's first real home. He referred to it as 'the farm', and it came complete with a kidney-shaped swimming pool, corrals, a guest house and sixteen miles of bridal path. Manuela and Michael were living there as well, but were not happy with Bob as a stepfather, claiming he was too strict. Both children were arrested for various offences. He nevertheless paid their fines, bail, school tuition and living expenses. But when they got into trouble, he let Ursula handle the situation.

Bob's first film on his own was *The Hangman* with Tina Louise. He admitted it was dreadful, but critics gave him the benefit, as they did in *The House of the Seven Hawks*: 'The picture's one distinction is that Robert Taylor, with a minimum of material, is still showing his successors how a dull job can be well done.'

Tessa Taylor was born on 16 August 1959. It was a good year for her famous father. His TV show *The Detectives* debuted a month later on

ABC-TV, but Robert Taylor didn't see it. He didn't own a TV set. Why had he succumbed to television? 'M-O-N-E-Y,' he told columnist Hy Gardner. Two years later the show, now on NBC-TV, was expanded from a half hour to an hour and was renamed *Robert Taylor's Detectives*, but after the 1961–62 season it was cancelled. Bob wrote to Tom Purvis that everything was going wrong. Manuela and Michael, both on drugs, were forbidden from coming to the ranch. Taylor felt they were a bad influence over Tessa and Terry, and though Ursula was the one who always appeared in court, the press used Robert Taylor's name in connection with their problems.

In 1963 Bob found time to have a long overdue physical examination at Scripps Clinic. X-rays showed a spot on his lung, but it turned out to be the same one he'd had since he was two years old. Those few days waiting for the results were sheer hell and he said, 'I'll never go through that again.'

He was surrounded by death now. Taylor had already been a pallbearer at Clark Gable's funeral. Gary Cooper died a few months later, and his very close friend Dick Powell was dying of throat cancer.

Critics liked Bob in *The Miracle of the White Stallions*: 'Robert Taylor, weathering prettily with the years, seems more and more able to portray hard bitten men. This, for an actor who used to be too beautiful for words, is high praise.' He was a bit young for grey hair, he said, and had not put on weight. 'But the sands have shifted,' he laughed. *Cattle King* was a fine western. One critic pointed out, 'There is no actor in Hollywood who sits a horse as well as Robert Taylor.'

Bob's marriage to Ursula was a romantic one. They loved each other more as time progressed. Actress Rhonda Fleming said they often attended her parties and frequently made eye contact. 'They could be in a crowded room and find each other just for a glance,' she said. 'This is so rare in Hollywood. I envied them and so did everyone else.'

According to Tom Purvis, Bob considered himself a very lucky guy, but he was a worrier.

> If he didn't have anything to worry about, he'd go out and find something. Bob always worried about money. He said he was always a dollar short or a day late. I had good luck investing money and brought Bob into some of my ventures, but they failed and I could never figure out why. He had a business manager who made millions for such clients as Bing Crosby, but not for Bob. He had to put his mother in a nursing home and that cost $1000 a month. Then there was his

alimony. He had to pay Barbara fifteen per cent of his salary. She was a very rich woman. Not many people in Hollywood knew about this. One time Bob ran into Barbara on location. They barely spoke, but he told his buddies about the alimony. They were shocked. This was her way of maintaining a link to Bob. Maybe to punish him, too. Hell, she didn't need the money and he did.

In 1964 Taylor got a call from producer-director William Castle about appearing in a thriller entitled *The Night Walker*. His agents, it seems, had committed him to the film with none other than Barbara Stanwyck. 'I'll have to give this some thought,' he said, gritting his teeth. 'Send over the script.' He told Ursula it was a good one, but he would have turned it down. It was too late now. When asked how he felt about co-starring with his ex-wife, Taylor replied, 'Who could pass up the opportunity of working with such a wonderful, talented woman?' Ursula was on the set of *The Night Walker* often and hoped to make friends with Barbara. 'Why don't we have her over for dinner one night, Bob?'

Without further explanation he said, 'You don't know Barbara like I do.'

The movie was filmed without incident. 'It was as if we were never married,' Bob commented. Reviews were excellent. 'William Castle has two old pros enriching this new eerie suspense thriller, *The Night Walker*. Barbara Stanwyck and Robert Taylor, coming out of semi-retirement from films, are the invaluable assets in the Universal release.' Bob remarked that he didn't know he was in semi-retirement.

It was a very depressing day when Taylor went to see Ruth in the nursing home. Doctors said she was hanging on bravely for an eighty-year-old woman, but she would be a vegetable for the rest of her life. She didn't recognise Bob. After he left, Ruth turned to the nurse and said, 'Wasn't he a nice man?' Driving home, Taylor recalled a conversation he'd had with Ruth a few years ago. She talked about her weak heart, how she never felt well and knew she would die soon. Bob laughed. 'Mother, you'll probably outlive me.'

She did.

In January 1966, Bob's close friend Ronald Reagan announced his candidacy for Governor of California. He had been host of the television series *Death Valley Days*, and his contract ran until September of that year. The Democratic party claimed it was unfair for him to have exposure on television so several stars, including John Wayne, Clint Walker, Rory Calhoun and Taylor, volunteered to fill in for Reagan until the end of his contract. In September Bob signed on as host and occasional star of *Death Valley Days*. Producer Bob Stapler said he would send Taylor scripts to look over, so he could choose the ones he wanted to star in. 'He kept turning everything down,' Stapler said. 'I couldn't figure it because Bob was an easy guy to work with. I knew he was anxious to play in several episodes and I picked out the best scripts. Finally I asked him what was wrong. Taylor said he was not going to play a younger man and that was that. I outsmarted him. I told my secretary when I found a good story for Taylor to change the age of the leading man to forty-five and from then on Taylor never turned anything down.'

Appearing on weekly television brought Bob's face before the younger generation, who categorised him as a well-built, rather handsome middle-aged actor who must have been something special once. Their mothers and grandmothers, of course, remembered him as a beautiful screen lover, and now here he was doing a dirty old western TV series. 'The public's never satisfied,' he said, 'but I'm used to that.'

With the exception of the made-for-TV western *Return of the Gunfighter*, Taylor's movies were now forgettable. Bob was weary of filming on location even if Ursula went with him. He was satisfied with the TV series and would try to get by financially without making movies. As 1968 progressed, Ursula noticed a change in Bob. He was cranky and tired. Often he was impatient with her, almost insulting. Bob Stapler made the same observations. Though Taylor never took a day off, he was tired and annoyed by little things. He went to bed at eight every night because, he said, he had to get up early. Ursula said, 'Bob was always an early riser. Now he was making a point of it.' He began drinking heavily to 'ease the pain of life'. 'Bob had a persistent cough,' Ursula said. 'At night he'd get violent attacks that were forgotten the next day.'

He finished his work on *Death Valley Days* in September 1968 and was scheduled to do a spaghetti western in Italy, but it was cancelled. After a party one evening, Bob came home and coughed so violently that he doubled over and fell to his knees. Ursula pleaded with him to go to the doctor, but he reminded her what he had been through in 1963 waiting for the doctors to make up their minds what was wrong with him. What he didn't tell her was that X-rays two years previously had shown a growth on his lungs which was getting bigger. Only Tom Purvis knew the truth.

Doctors, suspecting Rocky Mountain spotted fever, wanted to operate.

Taylor said he'd think about it. 'Would you let them cut you open?' he asked Purvis. 'No,' was the reply. Bob had made up his mind to take his chances, but Ursula pleaded with him to have the operation for the sake of his family. Finally he agreed and on 8 October 1968, a portion of his right lung was removed. It was announced to the press that Taylor indeed had Rocky Mountain spotted fever. Bob believed it too; only Ursula knew he had cancer. The doctors were sure they had taken all of it out, though to be on the safe side they recommended radiation treatment. Bob received bags of fan mail and messages from ex-president Eisenhower, John Wayne and many other colleagues.

Taylor was not improving and he maintained a high temperature. An infection was suspected and in November he was back in surgery. Bob wrote to Purvis, 'They found an abscess, a pretty big one. It was sealed off so no antibiotic could reach it. They inserted a draining tube from my throat to my lung. We hope that does the trick. The doc wanted to give me morphine, but I don't want any drug dependency.'

Getting Bob to and from St. John's Hospital was a difficult task, since the press were staked out on Mandeville Canyon Road. Fortunately they couldn't see the ranch from there, so Taylor lay down in the back seat of the car on his trips to the hospital for radiation treatment. Having lost a lot of weight, he did not want to be photographed. Reporters also hung out at the hospital, talking to his doctors – who refused to give away any information – and waiting for a glimpse of Taylor. Finally, on 3 December 1968, the newspapers printed the truth:

ROBERT TAYLOR CONFIRMS HE HAS LUNG CANCER

Robert Taylor, one of Hollywood's most enduring stars, confirmed rumors today. He is undergoing treatment for lung cancer. He has been appearing in the television series *Death Valley Days*, but his working schedule will be sharply curtailed now. Taylor said he was in no pain but that he was very weak and had lost about thirty pounds.

Some movie colony friends had feared the worst when the fifty-seven-year-old actor's right lung was removed eight weeks ago. But doctors said a number of small tumors found in the removed lung were not malignant. Taylor said his wife knew differently. 'I didn't say anything then because it's a very private matter, isn't it? . . . I'm putting myself and all my faith in the hands of my doctors.'

On Christmas Day, Ursula was told that Bob had terminal cancer. There was no hope. She regretted forcing him to have an operation. Maybe if he had taken his chances without surgery, he might have avoided long months of suffering.

On 25 February 1969, Bob wrote to Purvis: 'I'm losin' this one and as lousy as I feel and as fast as I'm goin' broke, I'd just as soon it would hurry up and come to an end fast. It would be better for Ursula and the children and everybody.' He ended the letter with 'Good fishin'.' According to Tom, this was Bob's way of saying goodbye.

Barbara Stanwyck dropped by for a brief visit and said she would not be collecting her alimony any longer. But, as Bob often said, no one knew her the way he did.

Fearing the end would come while she was absent, Ursula spent most of her time with Bob in the hospital. On 26 May 1969, she collapsed on finding her son Michael dead from a drug overdose. Bob insisted on returning home after Michael's funeral. Doctors protested, but he said he wanted to go home one last time. He went back to the hospital on Thursday, 5 June 1969. Before he lapsed into a coma, he asked Ronald Reagan to 'Tell Ursula, be happy . . .'

On the morning of Sunday, 8 June, Bob died in Ursula's arms.

The funeral was held on 11 June at the Church of the Recessional at Forest Lawn Cemetery, Glendale, California. Ursula told Barbara she could sit with the family in private, but Stanwyck preferred making a grief-stricken entrance to the chapel. Wearing yellow, heavily sedated and sobbing, she gave a fine portrayal of the widow – to the annoyance of everyone else in the church.

Ronald Reagan gave the eulogy, pausing occasionally to choke back his tears:

How to say farewell to a friend named Bob? He'd probably say, 'Don't make a fuss. I wouldn't want to cause any trouble.' How to speak of Robert Taylor – one of the truly great and most enduring stars of the golden era of Hollywood? What can we say about a boy named – well, a boy from Nebraska with an un-Nebraskan-like name of Spangler Arlington Brugh? . . .

Now there were those in our midst who worked very hard to bring him down with the label 'Pretty Boy'. And, of course, there's that standard Hollywood rule that true talent must never be admitted as playing a part in success if the individual is too handsome or too beautiful.

It's only in the recent years of our friendship that I've been able to understand how painful all of this must have been to him – to a truly modest man, because he was modest to the point of being painfully shy. In all the years of stardom, he never got quite over being genuinely embarrassed at the furore that his appearance created. He went a long way to avoid putting himself in a position where he could become the center of attention. . .

It takes a rare and unique actor to be believable, as he was believable, in costume epics like *Ivanhoe, Knights of the Round Table,* and at the same time as a fighter in *The Crowd Roars,* and the almost psychopathic *Billy the Kid.* Some of his pictures live on as true classics . . .

Today I am sure there is sorrow among the rugged men in the northwest who run the swift water of the Rogue River and who knew him as one of them. There are cowpokes in a valley in Wyoming who remember him and mourn – mourn a man who rode and hunted with them. And millions and millions of people who only knew him by way of the silver screen, and they remember with gratitude that in the darkened theatre he never embarrassed them in front of their children . . . I'll remember how a fellow named Bob really preferred blue jeans and boots. And I'll see him squinting through the smoke of a barbecue as I have seen him a hundred times.

He loved his home and everything it meant. Above all, he loved his family and his beautiful Ursula – the lovely Manuela, all grown up; little Tessa, and Terry, his son, a young man in whom he had great pride.

In a little while the hurt will be gone. Time will do that for you. Then you will find you can bring out your memories . . . You are going to be proud of simple things . . . Simple things he had like honour and honesty . . . standing up for what he believed and, yes, even a simple old-fashioned love for his country . . .

I think, too, that he'd want me to tell you how very much he loved your mother. What happiness she brought him and how wonderful she is. The papers say he was in the hospital seven times, actually he was out of the hospital seven times. He needed the strength that he could only get from being in that home so filled with her presence.

He spoke to me of this just a few days ago. It was uppermost in his mind, and I am sure he meant for me to tell you something that he wanted above all else. Ursula, there is just one last thing that only you can do for him – be happy. This was his last thought to me.

I don't pretend to know God's plan for each of us, but I have faith in his infinite mercy. Bob had great success in the work he loved, and he returned each day from that work with the knowledge there were those who waited affectionately for the sound of his footsteps.

As was the custom in Hollywood, Bob's friends were invited to the ranch after the funeral to 'have a drink on him'. Ursula included Barbara, much to the distress of Tom Purvis and others, who were very uncomfortable to have her at the ranch. She proceeded to get drunk and invited Ursula to take a walk before she left. Barbara wanted Bob's widow to know, 'If there is anything I can do for you, Ursula, anything, just let me know.'

Bob's warning that 'You don't know Barbara as I do' appeared all too accurate, however, when she billed the Taylor estate for 'back alimony'. It couldn't have come at a worse time; there were many financial obligations facing Ursula. When she found out what Barbara had done, she became violently ill. Her psychologist friend Ivy Mooring explained that this was Barbara's way of clinging to Bob to the very end. It was not revenge, it was love. Yet one has to wonder why she changed her mind. Was it being in Ursula's company, seeing the ranch that Bob loved so much? Seeing his beautiful blonde children, who so enraged her when they were born? Or did alcohol change her mind?

We will never know.

Ursula finally sold the ranch in 1971 and moved to Bel Air. She remarried happily, but lost her third husband, ironically, to lung cancer.

This author met Bob's widow in December 1969. I was writing a book about Taylor and she was helpful although, she said, it was not what Bob would have wanted since he was such a private person. I told her Taylor deserved to have his life's story in libraries all over the world. Ursula was most gracious to me and even called friends who could give me further help. Bob had been gone for only six months so I felt rather odd imposing on her, but she agreed to all my requests even while trying to guard her late husband's privacy.

There were Christmas presents placed on bookshelves and on the mantel over the hearthstone fireplace. I also noticed a coffee table that I had heard about; it had been the only item Bob took when he divorced

Barbara. Made from an offering table that he had cut down, he had found it in a church on location somewhere. His friend, the actor George Montgomery, had sanded and finished it into a splendid piece of furniture.

My six-year-old daughter, Elizabeth, played with Tessa while I talked to Ursula. Later I asked Liz what she used to do with Robert Taylor's daughter. 'We took a hike, had peanut butter and jelly sandwiches and listened to Beatle records.' When Tessa and Terry were youngsters at school they were unaware that their father was famous, until they found out one day on the school bus. Bob and Ursula made sure their life was as normal as possible. At Christmas, the children received over a hundred presents. Yet Ursula, following the German tradition, gave them a gift each day for two weeks before Christmas, while any remaining gifts were given away to needy children. Bob played Santa Claus over the intercom and the kids believed it, at least until Terry became aware it was ol' Dad and not Saint Nick.

Ursula explained, 'We did everything possible to keep the children from being spoiled. It wasn't easy because they mingled with the children of celebrities who were pampered. Bob stuck to his guns. When Terry wanted a new bike, Bob said his old one was good enough until it was about to fall apart.'

Rather than bother Ursula in the following months, I spent a good deal of time with his handyman, Art Reeves. Art knew the Taylors better than anyone else and was most informative.

At first, Barbara Stanwyck refused to see me, though she later changed her mind. A hour or so before our appointment, she cancelled. Her lame excuse was that her marriage to Bob had been so long ago. I found out later that, among other items, she had kept every letter he wrote to her. Barbara remembered every little detail of her relationship with Bob. The consensus was that she was drunk – either when she agreed to see me or when she bowed out. One of her acquaintances said, however, that she would not like me to see how she had surrounded herself with Bob's pictures and other mementos of their life together.

In 1985, Barbara's $3 million mansion in the exclusive Trousdale Estates neighbourhood caught fire. She begged the firemen to let her go back in the house for some 'priceless articles'. Friends tried to calm her down, but she was sobbing and trying to break away from them. 'You don't understand,' she exclaimed. 'There are letters and pictures of Bob that I can't replace.' A few years previously she had been robbed of her jewellery. Here again, it wasn't the money value that mattered, rather the fact that the pieces had been gifts from Taylor. And when Barbara was dying in 1990, she said Bob had come for her – that they would renew their love in the afterlife.

I rather doubt that.

At NBC, my employer for many years, I had seen celebrities come and go, but never went out of my way to meet them. Then in 1963 I got word that Robert Taylor was in the building to do an afternoon talk show. I arrived at the studio early to get a front seat. The producer of the show spotted me and wondered what I was doing at a TV show, it was a first for me. When I told him the reason, he literally dragged me down to the main floor where Taylor was talking to a small group. Well, I said to myself, enjoy the introduction and get the hell back to your seat in the studio. We shook hands. Then, to my horror, everyone else left and I was alone with Robert Taylor.

The first thing I noticed was his widow's peak. It was like a magnet. In fact he was everything I expected, and that doesn't happen often. Usually, movie stars are disappointing, which was one reason I didn't want to meet him. Maintain that image, was my motto. I was totally unprepared for a conversation with Taylor. Fortunately, however, I had read enough about him to know he hated to talk about himself and his film career, so I asked about the ranch. He liked that. While he was giving me a vivid description of 'the farm', and how his chickens weren't laying eggs, I studied his face. He was 52, but his face was flawless. His forehead, cheekbone structure, nose, chin and lips were perfectly proportioned. Then there was his striking black hair, blue eyes and deep resonant voice. Like his enemies in the thirties, I looked for an imperfection. There was none, of course, except for a few lines around the eyes.

Finally I told him how happy I was that he was acting in *Robert Taylor's Detectives* on NBC, but why did he avoid publicity tours, for goodness sake? We had been expecting him for a long time.

'I like to do a day's work and get home to my family,' he replied. 'But my TV show is a good one and worth publicising.'

'I'm told you don't like to travel on business.'

'I'd rather not. Doing a weekly TV show is tough. I work outdoors in the heat and I'm usually bushed at the end of the day.'

'One hundred degrees and over . . .'

He sighed. 'Yes. We did a show recently in the railroad yard. I'm sure it was 120 there.'

'Your wife appeared with you in one episode. Will she do it again?'

He smiled. 'No, I don't think so. We got letters complaining that I didn't kiss her. Why?'

'Why?' I laughed.

'Because that's not my character. I'm a tough detective. The idea is solving a crime, not romance, but you can't satisfy everyone.'

'What about movies?'

'Finding a good script these days is almost impossible. I just finished *The Miracle of the White Stallions*. Filmed in Austria. The Lipizzaner stallions are amazing.'

'But you ride a horse well.'

'Yes, quarter horses, but the Lipizzaners are trained to perform in perfect unison. I had to learn how to handle them. It was a wonderful experience.'

I extended my hand and he shook it. 'Well, it's been a sincere pleasure meeting you, Mr. Taylor.'

'Thank you. I enjoyed it.'

The producer said a few words to Bob and then walked with me back to my seat in the studio. 'You know,' he remarked, 'celebrities like Robert Taylor demand respect by their very presence. One doesn't tap him on the shoulder or yell out his name from across the room. One waits until he acknowledges you. Bob is a very humble guy and wouldn't care, but he carries himself like a star and it creates an aura of pride and – yes, royalty.'

'Well, he was voted second to Clark Gable for the title of King of Hollywood.'

'My secretary shook hands with Bob and said she was never going to wash her hands again.'

I looked down at my right palm. 'You've given me food for thought,' I said.

Robert Taylor was posthumously inducted into the Cowboy Hall of Fame in 1970. It was an honour he would have accepted with great pride. He was heralded in his hometown of Beatrice, Nebraska on 2 October 1994, when a stretch of highway between Filley, his birthplace, and Beatrice was named the Robert Taylor Memorial Highway. Terry Taylor took a fast spin on the road and was given the first speeding ticket issued on the highway named after his father.

Ursula and I were given the key to the city of Beatrice by the mayor, who asked me later, 'Are you satisfied now?'

'I came down pretty hard on you, didn't I?'

'You did.'

'Not once did you honour Taylor so I spoke up, that's all. Look what happened. A weekend celebration of his films and the highway dedication. The idea is that he's not forgotten. Good guys usually are.'

For Bob Taylor it was a long journey from Beatrice to his resting place at Forest Lawn Cemetery in Glendale, California. I went to Forest Lawn to put flowers on Taylor's crypt. He'd been cremated and his ashes entombed in the Garden of Freedom, where an inscription on a gold plaque reads, 'And a lifetime to go.'

'Barbara taught me everything I know. I never would have met anyone like her in Nebraska.'

           – Robert Taylor

The Films of Robert Taylor

Handy Andy (Fox, 1934)
There's Always Tomorrow (Universal, 1934)
A Wicked Woman (MGM, 1934)
Society Doctor (MGM, 1935)
West Point of the Air (MGM, 1935)
Times Square Lady (MGM, 1935)
Murder in the Fleet (MGM, 1935)
Broadway Melody of 1936 (MGM, 1935)
Magnificent Obsession (Universal, 1935)
Small Town Girl (MGM, 1936)
Private Number (Fox, 1936)
His Brother's Wife (MGM, 1936)
The Gorgeous Hussy (MGM, 1936)
Camille (MGM, 1937)
Personal Property (MGM, 1937)
This is My Affair (Fox, 1937)
Broadway Melody of 1938 (MGM, 1937)
A Yank at Oxford (MGM, 1938)
Three Comrades (MGM, 1938)
The Crowd Roars (MGM, 1938)
Stand Up and Fight (MGM, 1939)
Lucky Night (MGM, 1939)
Lady of the Tropics (MGM, 1939)
Remember? (MGM, 1939)
Waterloo Bridge (MGM, 1940)
Escape (MGM, 1940)
Flight Command (MGM, 1940)

Billy the Kid (MGM, 1941)
When Ladies Meet (MGM, 1941)
Johnny Eager (MGM, 1942)
Her Cardboard Lover (MGM, 1942)
Stand By For Action (MGM, 1943)
The Youngest Profession (MGM, 1943)
Bataan (MGM, 1943)
Song of Russia (MGM, 1943)
Undercurrent (MGM, 1946)
The High Wall (MGM, 1947)
The Secret Land (Narrator: MGM, 1948)
The Bribe (MGM, 1949)
Ambush (MGM, 1949)
Devil's Doorway (MGM, 1950)
Conspirator (MGM, 1950)
Quo Vadis? (MGM, 1951)
Westward the Women (MGM, 1951)
Ivanhoe (MGM, 1952)
Above and Beyond (MGM, 1952)
I Love Melvin (MGM, 1953)
Ride, Vaquero! (MGM, 1953)
All the Brothers Were Valiant (MGM, 1953)
Knights of the Round Table (MGM, 1953)
Valley of the Kings (MGM, 1954)
Rogue Cop (MGM, 1954)
Many Rivers to Cross (MGM, 1955)
Quentin Durwood (MGM, 1955)
The Last Hunt (MGM, 1956)
D-Day, the Sixth of June (Fox, 1956)
The Power and the Prize (MGM, 1956)
Tip on a Dead Jockey (MGM, 1957)
Saddle the Wind (MGM, 1958)
The Law and Jake Wade (MGM, 1958)
Party Girl (MGM, 1958)
The Hangman (Paramount, 1959)
The House of Seven Hawks (MGM, 1959)
The Killers of Kilimanjaro (Columbia, 1960)
The Miracle of the White Stallions (BV, 1963)
Cattle King (MGM, 1963)

A House is not a Home (Embassy, 1964)
The Night Walker (Universal, 1965)
Savage Pampas (Daca, 1966)
Johnny Tiger (Universal, 1966)
Where Angels Go . . . Trouble Follows (Columbia, 1968)
The Day the Hot Line Got Hot (AIP, 1968)
Devil May Care (Feature Film Corp of Amer., 1968)
The Glass Sphinx (AIP, 1968)

6

Spencer Tracy

Considered by his peers to be the best actor in Hollywood during the golden era, Spencer Tracy remains in that league. The American Film Institute voted him ninth on their list of greatest screen legends in 1999. His advice to young thespians was, 'Know your lines and don't bump into the furniture.' He was a born actor and a notorious scene-stealer, an accomplishment not so easy to achieve when you're sharing the screen with the likes of Clark Gable. He was a master at being someone else, but not at being himself. Life was a chore for him so he eased his pain with alcohol and became MGM's bad boy. As Joan Crawford once told the mighty mogul Louis B. Mayer, 'He's a bastard!'

'That's true, but he's *our* bastard,' Mayer replied with pride.

He had affairs with actresses Myrna Loy, Jean Tierney, Joan Crawford, Loretta Young, Grace Kelly and Ingrid Bergman during his 27-year romance with Katharine Hepburn. A devout Catholic, he chose neither to divorce nor to live with his wife and children. Inconsiderate of others, he once paid a visit to his family unannounced and turned on the lawn sprinklers while his wife was having a garden party. Ladies in beautiful picture hats screamed and scattered but it was too late. He got a big kick out of that.

He admitted to being drunk for 25 years, while the studio always paid off the police and bartenders carefully covered up his drunken escapades. MGM might not have renewed his contract had it not been for Katharine Hepburn, who signed on with the studio and wanted him to co-star with her. Louis B. Mayer had faith that she could keep Tracy in line and he was right. In fact she did more than that: she kept this bad boy alive despite his deteriorating health. When he went off on binges, she would go from bar to bar until she found him and sobered him up for work the next day. He treated her shabbily, yet she sat at his feet in awe of the man and always gave him top billing in the films they made together.

He blamed himself when his son was born deaf. One reason he did not get a divorce was the guilt. It haunted him until the day he died.

Spencer Bonaventure Tracy, born on 5 April 1900 in Milwaukee, Wisconsin, was the son of a devoutly Irish Catholic family. His mother was a saint and his father a drunkard. He was as rebellious in his youth as he was to be as an adult. Spencer was known for school truancy, preferring at the age of seven to hang out underneath the bar at a friend's saloon and sample leftover drinks. To please his mother, he became a Boy Scout and an altar boy, but he hated school and said the only reason he attended was to learn how to read the subtitles in silent movies.

Spencer did, however, graduate from the eighth grade. He enrolled at the Marquette Academy to be with his friend Bill O'Brien, who went on to become the famous actor Pat O'Brien. It came as quite a surprise to Spencer's family when he began to take an interest in Catholic theology and consider the priesthood. When the First World War broke out, however, he joined the Navy and changed his mind about becoming a priest. In January 1921 he decided on Ripon, a small college near Fond du Lac, Wisconsin. Spencer tried out for a school play, *The Truth*, and got the lead part. His drama coach was so impressed he wrote to the Academy of Dramatic Arts in New York about an audition for Tracy, who was admitted in 1922 with flying colours along with his pal, Pat O'Brien. They graduated a year later, but acting jobs were not forthcoming. O'Brien moved on but Tracy, who was not so lucky, decided to go back to Milwaukee. Before he had a chance to pack his bags, though, he received a telegram from the Leonard Wood Stock Company to go on tour for forty dollars a week. Spencer had little money left, but that's all he needed to get drunk.

On the thirty-minute trip from New York City to White Plains, Spencer noticed a striking brunette on the train and struck up a conversation. Louise Treadwell was joining the Leonard Wood Stock Company, too. Four years older than Tracy, she had more acting experience and got the lead roles while he took bit parts; nonetheless, when she was offered a job with the Repertory Theater of Cincinnati, Louise told them she wanted

Tracy as her leading man. Though she was a Protestant, Spencer proposed to her and they were married on 12 September 1923.

When Tracy accepted a secondary role in *A Royal Fandango*, a play headed for Broadway, he and Louise moved to an apartment in Brooklyn. But the play closed within weeks, which was a devastating blow to Tracy – because his wife was now pregnant. He sent her home to live with his parents while he moved from one repertory company to another. Louise gave birth to a son, John, on 26 June 1924. While Spencer was back on the road, she realised the baby was deaf. When Tracy took a job at the Montauk Theater on Long Island, he sent for his wife and baby, and soon found out for himself about John. 'What's the matter with him?' he asked. 'He doesn't seem to hear me.'

'He never will,' she explained. 'John is totally deaf.'

Tracy went on the first drunken binge of his life, disappearing for days until he was found at the St. George Hotel in Brooklyn.

In 1926 actress Selena Royle, who had worked with Tracy, recommended him to George M. Cohan, producer of forthcoming Broadway plays *Yellow*, *The Baby Cyclone*, and *Whispering Friends*. Tracy was now an established Broadway actor, but insomnia, feelings of remorse over John's deafness, bouts of depression and heavy drinking made him look much older than he was. This turned out to be a blessing in disguise – he was perfect for the role of Killer Mears in *The Last Mile*, a play about prisoners on Death Row and their desperate escape attempt. The play opened on 13 February 1930 and was a hit. When Clark Gable was asked to do the play in Los Angeles, he almost turned it down after seeing Tracy's performance. 'How can I follow a guy like that?' he asked. Fortunately he took the part, and was discovered by a Hollywood talent scout. Tracy had the same luck; having seen him in the play, director John Ford signed Spencer for 20th Century-Fox to make *Up the River*, a prison farce with Humphrey Bogart. The studio put him under contract for $1200 a week after the run of *The Last Mile* ended in November 1930.

While Louise concentrated on helping John to learn sign language, Spencer focused on booze and women. He was arrested trying to recklessly back his car out of a parking lot next to a whorehouse. Police took a drunken Tracy to the county jail where he remained until Fox bailed him out.

Spencer considered the films he was making to be frivolous and boring. He made eight forgettable movies in 1932 before getting his big break in

20,000 *Years In Sing Sing* alongside Bette Davis. *The Power and the Glory*, the life of a railway tycoon, was a plum role, but Tracy was almost fired when he disappeared for a week, holed up somewhere with his liquor bottles. Jean Harlow, who co-starred with him in *Goldie*, said Spencer would show up in the morning wearing his evening clothes and still drunk or hungover.

In 1932 Louise gave birth to a daughter, Susie, who was perfect in every way. It had been nine months of agonising waiting for Spencer. The Tracys moved to a twelve-acre ranch in the San Fernando Valley and raised chickens, but Spencer refused to have them killed. His friend James Cagney said, 'It was like an animal shelter instead of a farm.'

Though Tracy lived in California, he frequently took the train east and checked into the St. George Hotel in Brooklyn with a suitcase full of liquor. There he would strip naked and get into the bathtub, remaining there for a week without once using the flushing facility. He would then clean up, put the empty bottles in a suitcase and return to California.

In 1933, Tracy was loaned to Columbia Pictures to make *A Man's Castle* with twenty-year-old Loretta Young. Though he denied any romantic entanglement, Spencer set up residence at the Beverly Hills Hotel, after which Louise announced their separation on grounds of incompatibility. Tracy got into regular fist fights with reporters and photographers during his trysts with Young. The affair came to a heartbreaking end on 24 October 1934 when Loretta told the press she could not marry Tracy because they were both devout Catholics. A few months afterwards she was in Clark Gable's arms, giving birth to his daughter in secret nine months later. Spencer finally went back to Louise, but not before a good deal of pleading on his part.

On 11 March 1935, Tracy was making *Dante's Inferno* in Yuma, Arizona, when he was taken into custody for destroying his hotel room and resisting arrest. For a month he was out of control. He reported back to work and fell asleep on the movie set while it was closed down for the night. When Spencer woke, he trashed the set to the tune of $100,000. He had to be put in a straitjacket and driven home. A statement was issued by 20th Century-Fox to the effect that Tracy had asked to be released from his contract – a dignified way of saying he had been fired.

Irving Thalberg, vice-president of production at MGM, signed Tracy as a contract player on 2 April 1935 – to the dismay of Louis B. Mayer, who complained, 'We already have one drunken son-of-a-bitch, Wallace Beery. We don't need another.' But Thalberg got his way.

*

Following *Murder Man* and *Riffraff*, Tracy made *Whipsaw* with Myrna Loy, who had portrayed Mrs. Nick Charles in the very popular *Thin Man* films. She and Spencer had an affair that ended when the movie was finished, though it resumed a year later when they co-starred in *Libeled Lady*. At the same time Tracy still carried a torch for Loretta Young, defending her honour when director William Wellman made a disparaging remark about her at the Trocadero nightclub. Wellman had been directing Young and Clark Gable in *Call of the Wild* when the two stars bedded down together and held up production. Tracy took a swing at Wellman, missed his mark and was knocked to the floor.

Louis B. Mayer, upset with the bad publicity that followed the incident, wondered if Spencer would be acceptable in the role of a priest in *San Francisco*. Tracy was sceptical as well, but he nevertheless delivered a superb performance opposite Jeanette MacDonald and Clark Gable, and was nominated for an Academy Award as Best Actor. He lost to Paul Muni (*The Story of Louis Pasteur*), but his nomination afforded him a raise in salary from $1000 a week to $5000.

Irving Thalberg next chose Spencer to play the Portuguese fisherman in *Captains Courageous*. Tracy balked for several reasons. He was not keen on having his hair curled and did not want to compete with child star Freddie Bartholomew, because kids usually stole the picture. 'I had to sing,' Tracy said. 'I'm tone deaf, but I got through the damn thing. It was a song about little fish, pronounced "Leetle Feesh" I guess. I never heard a Portuguese accent like mine. It wasn't good, but it was Freddie's picture and should be.' Spencer behaved during production: he admired director Victor Fleming, a hard-drinking man's man who knew how to get along with the likes of Tracy and Gable.

Spencer was now seen in nightclubs with fifteen-year-old Judy Garland. When the studio brass at MGM warned him not to get involved with her it was his pleasure to disobey. Though it's implausible to assume they were intimate, some reliable sources claim they were. During the production of *Mannequin*, Tracy had a wild affair with Joan Crawford, who was just as famous as he was when it came to having sex with co-stars. At first she was anxious to work with Spencer because of his honest and uncomplicated approach to acting. Her style was just the opposite, and she always needed several takes to get a scene right. 'Don't be so serious,' he laughed. 'Take it slow and easy.'

'My part calls for a serious approach,' she argued.

'OK,' he shrugged, 'but don't be so uptight about it.'

Maybe Joan was uptight on the movie set but she wasn't on their first date. When Tracy took her home, she slammed the front door and seduced him in the entranceway, a habit of hers that many men experienced. When she came down with pneumonia, Tracy helped her recuperate by taking her to the Riviera Club for polo lessons. 'Spencer – I called him "Slug" – was so different off the set,' she said.

> We got to know each other much better, and he helped me overcome my fear of horses. I was wound up too tight, but nothing seemed to bother him. He made me laugh even though I was going through a bitter divorce from Franchot Tone. I didn't know which way to turn. What I didn't know is that Spencer was a very disturbed man. They were going to do *Mannequin* on Lux Radio Theater and he accepted for both of us. I was terrified of doing radio. During rehearsals I stuttered, I was shaking, and I flubbed my lines. He yelled at me, 'Jesus, Joan, I thought you were a pro!' I burst into tears and went home. Spencer was a bastard . . . an unmitigated son of a bitch!

In 1938, Tracy was nominated for Best Actor in *Captains Courageous*, along with Charles Boyer for *Conquest*, Fredric March for *A Star is Born*, Robert Montgomery for *Night Must Fall*, and Paul Muni for *The Life of Emile Zola*. On the night of the Academy Awards ceremony at the Biltmore Hotel, he was in hospital recuperating from a hernia operation. When C. Aubrey Smith read out Spencer's name, Louise Tracy walked to the podium. Most of the Hollywood community had never seen the attractive lady whose husband was carousing around town with other women. She grasped the Oscar firmly and said, 'I accept this award on behalf of Spencer, Susie, Johnny and myself.' Louise was given a generous ovation. L.B. Mayer took the opportunity to say, 'Tracy is a fine actor, but he is most important because he understands why it is necessary to take orders from the front office, because he understands why it is important to obey directors, because he understands that when the publicity department asks him to cater to certain values, it is a necessary inconvenience.'

The mighty Mayer had said it in front of Hollywood, God and on the radio for all to hear, and he hoped Tracy would take the hint. And he did. The next day, when Louise handed him the Oscar in the hospital garden, he gave her credit for his success, not Louis B. Mayer.

Tracy teamed up with Gable again in *Test Pilot*, which also co-starred his former lover, Myrna Loy. In their three films together, Gable always got the girl, but Spencer at least managed to do some scene stealing. Clark recalled, 'Myrna and I are sitting in the front seat of a convertible, Spence is sitting in the middle of the back seat. Myrna and I are having a "hot" conversation, and Spence has a line or two, but the bastard was chewing gum. That did it. Nobody paid any attention to my trying to seduce Myrna, because all eyes were on Spence chewin' gum.'

For the death scene at the end of the film, Tracy lay in Gable's arms for what was meant to be a brief farewell. As he stretched it out, Gable shook him and cursed, 'Die, goddamn it, Spence! I wish to Christ you would!'

Maybe Gable got the girl in the films, but he wasn't as lucky as Tracy in regard to Myrna Loy. She pushed Clark off her porch into the shrubs when he tried to kiss her goodnight.

In 1938 *Boys' Town* was released. Spencer played Father Flanagan, founder of the Nebraska home for wayward boys. Once again, Tracy didn't think he deserved to play a priest. And, once again, he was afraid Mickey Rooney would walk away with the movie, as he had feared Freddie Bartholomew would do in *Captains Courageous*.

In fact, for the second year in a row Tracy was nominated for an Oscar, this time along with Charles Boyer in *Algiers*, James Cagney in *Angels with Dirty Faces*, Robert Donat in *The Citadel*, and Leslie Howard in *Pygmalion*. Spencer was present, and sober, at the Biltmore Hotel on 23 February 1939 to accept the award. He was the first actor to win two years running.

Spencer was now living at the Beverly Wilshire Hotel, married in name only. Louise would eventually agree to a divorce, but Spencer was too guilt-ridden over John's deafness to go through with it.

Tracy was superb in *Northwest Passage* with Robert Young, but resented being cast opposite Hedy Lamarr in *I Take this Woman*. He supposed L.B. Mayer was using him to boost Miss Lamarr's movie career in 1940, a common practice under the studio system but one Spencer thought was beneath him. He didn't balk, however, when MGM traded him to Darryl Zanuck for *Stanley and Livingstone* in exchange for Tyrone Power's services in *Marie Antoinette*. As journalist Henry Stanley, Tracy recited the famous line, 'Dr. Livingstone, I presume?' Filming on location in Oregon was too isolated for Spencer and he showed signs of going off the deep end again, so director King Vidor arranged for a beautiful woman to visit the movie set. Spencer did not know that she was a prostitute – as if that would make a difference to him. At least he didn't have to pay for her services as he usually did.

In 1941, Tracy fell in love again. Actress Ingrid Bergman was having an affair with director Victor Fleming when filming of *Dr. Jekyll and Mr Hyde* began. She was married to Swedish physician Peter Lindstrom and had a daughter, Pia, but Fleming was irresistible and a masterful lover, according to past conquests Clara Bow and Norma Shearer. However, 25-year-old Bergman soon turned from Fleming to Tracy, causing tension on set.

Ingrid said Spencer was not happy doing two characterisations, the sane doctor and the monster Mr. Hyde. 'He wanted to play himself, his own personality, which of course was the warm and marvellous personality that had made him a great movie star.'

Spencer was not known for his discretion and Ingrid's husband found out about their affair. After their break-up, she resumed her romance with Fleming, who died of a heart attack shortly after directing her in *Joan of Arc*. When Bergman died 33 years later, she still kept his picture on her night table.

MGM chief of publicity Howard Strickling was disappointed in Tracy. 'He went after Bergman to compete with Victor,' he said. 'But he fell in love with her like he did with Loretta Young. It wasn't worth losing his friendship with Fleming, believe me. A good friend doesn't do that. Tracy was a difficult man.'

As Spencer predicted, *Dr. Jekyll and Mr. Hyde* received bad reviews. He was more than anxious to follow up with *The Yearling*, but production in the Florida Everglades was cancelled due to bad working conditions.

When Tracy returned to Los Angeles scratching the mosquito bites he had suffered on location in Florida, Katharine Hepburn was waiting for him. She had sold the rights to *Woman of the Year* to Louis B. Mayer for $211,000, signed a contract with MGM, and made it known she wanted Spencer Tracy to co-star in the film. They had never met, but she had seen all his films and was an ardent fan.

The story of their introduction has been told many times, but it's worth relating again. It was in front of the Irving Thalberg Building on the MGM lot. Katharine was five feet seven inches tall without the spiked heels she usually wore. Tracy was only five feet nine. She realised this as he and producer Joe Mankiewicz approached. 'Oh, dear,' she said, 'I fear I might be a bit too tall for you, Mr. Tracy.'

Mankiewicz smiled coyly and responded, 'Don't worry, Kate, he'll cut you down to size.'

Hepburn deliberately wore four-inch heels to intimidate men. 'The idea,' she said, 'is to put a man in his place.' Though she got along very well with L.B. Mayer, Katharine would stand over him like an amazon, one hand on her hip and the other pointing at his face as if to scold him. 'Works every time,' she said.

But not with Tracy, who told Mankiewicz after his introduction to her, 'I don't want to get mixed up in anything like this.' Hepburn had a feeling he was disenchanted. 'I don't think he liked the mannish suit I was wearing,' she said. 'I'm quite certain he thought I was a lesbian. It was not long before he was disabused of that notion, however.'

Katharine Houghton Hepburn was unique in every respect. She was born on 12 May 1907 in Hartford, Connecticut. Her father was a doctor and her mother the president of the Connecticut Women's Suffrage Association. The Hepburns were not prudish about nudity and they discussed sex as openly as they did politics. Kate had adored her older brother, Tom, who hung himself in 1921. She was only thirteen when she found his body in the attic. Kate was convinced that her brother had been trying to re-enact the hanging scene in *A Connecticut Yankee in King Arthur's Court*, a trick he had tried once before. She refused to believe he had committed suicide and grieved so deeply that she adopted his birthday, 8 November, as her own, a fact she did not reveal until she was well into her eighties.

In 1928 Kate graduated from Bryn Mawr and set her sights on the theatre. After several failed attempts on the stage she married Ludlow Ogden Smith on 12 December 1928. 'Luddy', who came from a wealthy, prominent family, was prepared to give Kate whatever she wanted, but all she asked for was that he change his name to Ludlow Ogden so she would not be known as Kate Smith, like the popular singer. Two weeks after the wedding, Kate returned to the theatre. She and Luddy obtained a Mexican divorce in 1934. Eight years later he filed in Hartford, telling the court he doubted the legality of the Mexican decree. One week later he remarried.

Hepburn was discovered by RKO Studios in Hollywood when she appeared on Broadway in *The Warrior's Husband* in 1932. She accepted their offer of $1500 a week and headed west. Director George Cukor was shocked when he met the skinny, freckled Kate in a grey suit, her hair swept up primly under a pancake hat. He showed her sketches of the costumes she would be wearing in *Bill of Divorcement*. 'What do you think of these?' he asked.

'I don't think a well-bred English girl would wear anything like that,' she replied.

'What do you think of what you have on?'

'I think it's very smart,' she exclaimed.

'Well, I think it stinks!' Cukor said bluntly.

Kate's screen test was no better than her outfit. Cukor said she looked like a gargoyle and barked through her nose, but he noticed something that others overlooked. With the camera to her back she picked up a highball glass, moving with enormous feeling; Cukor described it as a 'sad lyric moment'.

In 1933 Kate won an Oscar for Best Actress for her delicate performance in *Morning Glory*, and had a serious affair with director Leland Hayward, who jilted her and married actress Maureen Sullivan in November 1936. The brokenhearted Kate did not mope for long. While she was playing golf at the Bel Air Country Club, millionaire Howard Hughes landed his plane on the fairway and joined in the game. He and Kate began living together in 1937. Though they talked about marriage, however, she knew she would have no privacy as Mrs. Howard Hughes – not to mention his various infidelities.

In 1939 Hepburn appeared on Broadway in *The Philadelphia Story*. Howard Hughes financed the play and bought the movie rights for her. At the same time Kate was hounding producer David O. Selznick for the part of Scarlett O'Hara in *Gone With the Wind*. 'The part was written for me,' she told him.

'I can't imagine Clark Gable chasing you for ten years,' he replied.

After this let-down, Hepburn sold *The Philadelphia Story* to Metro-Goldwyn-Mayer for $175,000. She considered Louis B. Mayer one of the most honest and trustworthy people she had ever met, and signed a contract with MGM, the studio she had admired for a long time.

Tracy proved his genius as an actor when they began filming *Woman of the Year*. During a scene set in a cocktail lounge, Katharine accidentally tipped over a glass of water. She expected Tracy to stop filming but he went right on with his lines and handed her a handkerchief. She thought, 'You son-of-a-bitch,' as she started cleaning up the water which was now dripping on to the floor, saying 'Excuse me' as she got under the table and continued with her lines. 'We kept it in the film,' she said.

Tracy was annoyed that Hepburn was always around on the set to find out what was going on, interrupting conversations and sticking her nose into everyone's business. 'How the hell did I let myself get involved in this?'

he complained. Every chance he got, Spencer insulted her. When she pronounced his name 'Spensuh', he responded with, 'Why do you always have to sound like you've got a broomstick up your ass?'

She liked to rehearse. He did not. When she asked for a retake he moaned, 'What a bore.' She analysed her roles. He learned his lines, recited them and then wanted to go home. She believed in studying. He believed in instinct. When method actors emerged, looking for motivation, Tracy said simply, 'You come in the fucking door because it's the only way to get in the fucking room. That's your motivation!'

Hepburn said she knew right from the start that she would fall in love with Tracy. From his initial reactions, he had resented her pushy masculine ways. He needed to be the dominant one and was surprised when she let him. In the beginning Kate was just another woman who was annoying but yielding in private. The fact that he was married didn't bother her in the least. She was married too, but had been separated from her husband for a long time. Kate was first and foremost a career woman who had no desire to have children. So Spencer was perfect for her. The fact that she loved him more than he loved her made no difference to Hepburn, who accepted his heavy drinking as part of the package. Tracy cut down on alcohol when he became involved with Kate, but he went on one bender during the making of *Woman of the Year*. She canvassed his favourite bars, found him and sobered him up with tender loving care. Kate never scolded or criticised Spencer on such occasions. Her concern was keeping their close relationship a secret. They were not seen in nightclubs or restaurants together, and snuck out of hotels by separate entrances.

The press knew about the affair but didn't write about it, while Louise was busy with the John Tracy Clinic for the Deaf, which provided free services to preschool children with hearing loss.

After making the forgettable *Tortilla Flat* with Hedy Lamarr and John Garfield, Tracy teamed up with Kate again in *Keeper of the Flame*. He plays a journalist who is writing about the death of a national hero while Hepburn, as the widow, tries to hide the truth that her husband was an undercover fascist.

Spencer, playing the part of a dead pilot whose ghost returns to bring together his girlfriend and a rookie, now made *A Guy Named Joe* with a young actor called Van Johnson. Johnson had a serious car accident during filming, and suffered a fractured skull and facial injuries. Tracy and his leading lady Irene Dunne visited Johnson several times a week when he was in hospital. MGM wanted to replace Johnson, but after Tracy refused to go ahead without him the production was postponed for two months. Johnson's car accident was not the only problem during production. Spencer teased Dunne so unmercifully that she spoke to L.B. Mayer about the abuse. Ironically, director Victor Fleming defended Tracy, but the bickering was halted only by Johnson's near-fatal accident. With Hepburn away visiting her parents in the east, Spencer had too much time on his hands before filming resumed. Though he was drinking heavily, Tracy had behaved himself in public since he knocked a fan unconscious at the Rainbow Room in New York City, an incident MGM managed to keep quiet. Kate soon realised her presence in Spencer's life made a difference, and she began looking for movies they could make together so she could keep an eye on him.

Hepburn now approached Mayer about *Mourning Becomes Electra*, but he called it a filthy tale of incest and refused to make the film. She told the *Los Angeles Times*, 'We simply cannot confine ourselves to typical musicals and light comedies and expect in all ways to satisfy the people in foreign countries . . . If censorship stands in the way then perhaps there is some need for modification and change.'

Mayer did not relent, despite his great respect for Hepburn, but he did give the go-ahead for *Without Love* in 1944, about a couple who marry for convenience rather than love. Tracy's buddies were saying that he would do whatever Kate wanted him to. She convinced him to do a Broadway play, *The Rugged Path*, in November 1945. He stayed sober, but the show closed in January 1946. Spencer's visit to Kate's family made more impact than the play – he referred to the Hepburns as 'fruitcakes'. They didn't like him very much either.

While Kate was filming *Undercurrent* in Hollywood, Spencer went on a binge in New York. He was taken, in a straitjacket, to Doctors Hospital, and assigned to a room on a floor otherwise reserved for women, where he remained for a week suffering from delirium tremens. Kate was now more determined than ever to take care of Spencer. She turned down good offers, such as *The Ghost and Mrs Muir*, until she could find a vehicle in which to co-star with Tracy. She chose *The Sea of Grass*, a story about a nineteenth-century cattle baron and a sensitive city girl, but it proved to be a miserable picture.

Spencer made *Cass Timberlane* with the beautiful Lana Turner and though the pair did not light up the screen, the film did well at the box office. He was then slated to play a presidential candidate in *State of the Union*, with Claudette Colbert as his estranged wife, but when her demands were not met, Tracy suggested Hepburn. 'My God,' director Frank Capra exclaimed. 'Do you think she'd do it?'

'I dunno. But the Bag of Bones has been helping me rehearse. She might do it for the hell of it.'

'When do we start?' Kate wanted to know.

Angela Lansbury, who was also in *State of the Union*, said she was terrified to work with Tracy and Hepburn. 'What was exciting about working with them,' she said, 'was their presence. I mean collectively. Their personalities as well as their talents were orchestrated so marvellously. It was almost as if they had a secret language all their own. I began to think of them as one person, really. I suppose most people did.'

Tracy made *Edward, My Son* in London in the autumn of 1948 with Deborah Kerr. Katharine accompanied him to England and stayed at Claridge's, while he was the house guest of Laurence Olivier and his wife Vivien Leigh at their estate, Notley Abbey. But Spencer hated the fog and rain, complained about being cold all the time and made it known that he couldn't wait to get back to California. In any case, he and Kate were looking forward to starting work on *Adam's Rib*, a movie about married lawyers who are on opposite sides in a murder case. And the film turned out to be one of their best.

After finishing the wartime drama *Malaya* with Jimmy Stewart, Tracy resumed his heavy drinking when he found out Kate wanted to return to the Broadway stage in Shakespeare's *As You Like It*. Before the New York opening, the play was to go on tour for nine months. The pair's relationship was seriously strained and they argued bitterly. On one occasion, he struck her. Spencer did not remember the incident and Kate did not bring it up. But she told a close friend about it, saying she was afraid of him after that. He called her several times a day during her tour with promises to give up drinking. Always hopeful, she asked him to join her in Cleveland, but after he arrived his presence was kept secret even from the cast. On 22 January 1950, the play opened on Broadway to moderate reviews. Hepburn stayed in her New York townhouse, and Spencer was seen stumbling in and out at all hours, stoned out of his mind. He managed to pull himself together, however, for *Father of the Bride* with Elizabeth Taylor, and the sequel, *Father's Little Dividend*. And he was splendid in both films.

When Louis B. Mayer left MGM and Dore Schary took over, it was a confusing time for Metro's contract players. Tracy didn't seem to care one way or the other but Kate did not like the trend towards realism that Hollywood was taking. Though she fought against censorship regarding sex, she wasn't interested in Schary's leaning towards violent films. When she was offered *The African Queen* with Humphrey Bogart, Kate jumped at the chance to work opposite him and to go on location in Africa. Tracy tried to talk her out of it, but to no avail, and he began drinking again. She spoke to their good friend, director George Cukor, who was building a guest house on his estate. Could Spencer live there while she was in Africa? Cukor was delighted: he had a great admiration for Tracy and was deeply concerned about the star's alcoholism.

Another thorn in Spencer's side was the making of *The People Against O'Hara*, a dreadful film about a drunken ex-district attorney. His salvation was a secret rendezvous with Kate in Italy. 'Spencer loved Rome,' she said. 'We had a glorious time. Picnics, sightseeing, and walks in the country. The press never caught on to us. We drove all over the place, but they never got a picture of us together.'

In July 1951 Kate finished location filming in Africa and flew to London for more filming at Shepperton Studios. Tracy, anxious to see her after a three-month separation, arrived in England ahead of her and went out for dinner with producer Willian Goetz and his wife Edie, L.B. Mayer's daughter. Another guest was actress Joan Fontaine, who was filming *Ivanhoe*. During the evening Spencer was every inch the gentleman, but he called Joan later on and invited her for dinner the following night – 'Just the two of us.'

Fontaine said it took a minute for it to sink in that he was flirting. 'What about Kate?' she asked.

'What about her?'

'Well, Spence, out of respect for Kate's feelings I really don't think it's a good idea for us to go out alone, I'm afraid I just can't . . .'

'What? You just don't understand, Joan. You see, Kate and I are just good friends. Friends, nothing more.'

'Oh, boy,' Joan laughed. 'That's what they all say.'

Wouldn't she reconsider?

'I'm afraid not,' she responded. 'Not only is there Kate to consider, but you are a married man.'

Tracy said she had the situation all wrong. 'I can get a divorce any time I want to,' he insisted, 'but my wife and Kate like things just as they are.'

Fontaine, stunned by Spencer's overtures, was relieved to go on location and get away from him. Did Joan know Kate was bisexual and enjoyed the likes of Claudette Colbert, Greta Garbo, Judy Garland and Irene Selznick?

On the bright side, Tracy's son John had overcome his hearing impairment. He was now speaking, lip-reading and working as an artist for Walt Disney Studios. He married and in 1952 made Spencer a grandfather when his wife gave birth to a healthy baby boy, who was named Joseph Spencer Tracy.

Humphrey Bogart won an Oscar for his performance in *The African Queen*, and Kate was nominated for Best Actress, but lost to Vivien Leigh in *A Streetcar Named Desire*. Hepburn ended her MGM contract with *Pat and Mike*, another good movie she made with Tracy about an athlete and her manager. It was in this movie that he described Kate: 'Not much meat on her, but what's there is choice.'

In private she mothered him day and night, making sure there was plenty of coffee to keep him going without booze, and he was making progress in his battle with the bottle. But then Hepburn spun him around with her plan to perform in *The Millionaires* on the London stage. Tracy considered this a betrayal on her part, as if she were distancing herself from him entirely. As a result, he had an affair with Gene Tierney, his leading lady in *The Plymouth Adventure*. Gene had become famous for her portrayal of *Laura*, but her personal life was racked by tragedy. During her marriage to fashion designer Oleg Cassino, she gave birth to a retarded daughter, and a series of nervous breakdowns and attempted suicide followed. She had affairs with Joseph Fitzgerald Kennedy – who told her bluntly he could never marry her because she wasn't a Catholic – and with Kirk Douglas. She broke off with Douglas by saying, 'I'm going to marry Spencer Tracy.'

Douglas was incredulous: 'He was a married man and deeply involved with Katharine Hepburn. I couldn't believe it when Jean claimed Spencer wanted to run off with her.'

When the cast and crew of *The Plymouth Adventure* moved to London, Spencer continued his affair with Gene, forever looking over his shoulder for fear Kate would find out. She did, but she never mentioned it, because the affair ended when filming did.

Tracy was winding down, however. Years of alcohol abuse had begun to affect his heart, kidneys and liver. He was also impotent on occasion, which bothered him more than any other medical problem. Kate forged ahead as she always did, consulting specialists about Spencer's problem.

She apparently succeeded, because he was just as flirtatious with other women. Hepburn worried about this but her enormous energy and adventurous nature always gave her the incentive to move on to other projects. She urged Spencer to make *Broken Lance* with Robert Wagner and Richard Widmark in Arizona.

No longer afraid to fly, Tracy was able to meet Kate when she was on location in Europe, but he remained concerned that his romance with her would become public. In London, they took up separate residences, he at Claridge's and she at the Connaught. After one of her visits to Spencer, the hotel manager asked to speak with him in private. Suspecting the worst and prepared for a fight, Tracy went to see to the manager. What he actually wanted to do was explain the hotel's dress code. Would Miss Hepburn please wear a dress when she walked through the lobby. Kate thought that was idiotic, so from then on she took the freight elevator.

In *Bad Day at Black Rock* Tracy played a one-armed veteran looking for the Japanese-American father of a war hero. He was nominated for an Academy Award, but lost to Ernest Borgnine's portrayal of *Marty*. While Kate was in Venice filming *Summertime*, Tracy was set to make *Tribute to a Dead Man* with the gorgeous Grace Kelly, whom he had personally requested as his co-star. Grace was well-known for her many love affairs with older, married men; well aware of this, Spencer soon began his courtship of the future Princess of Monaco. They were photographed having dinner and the picture made all the newspapers. Kate had already heard rumours about the couple and the publicity confirmed they were true. The only consolation was that Spencer's affair with Grace was a brief encounter. When she changed her mind about co-starring with him in the film, she was suspended by MGM.

Tracy wasn't pleased with his new leading lady. Greek actress Irene Papas was taller than Kate. He was scheduled to report for work on location in Montrose, Colorado in June but did not show up. According to MGM press agent Jim Merrick,

> Spencer finally emerged five days late. We were able to shoot around him, but it was very unprofessional. He looked around the sets and the beautiful Colorado scenery and said he was going to the motel for a nap. I went to see him later that day and was told he had checked out.
>
> Howard Strickling, our head of publicity, arrived to see if there was anything he could do. We wrote articles about Spencer every day as if he was on the job. The delays were costing MGM around thirty

thousand dollars a day. Eight days later he showed up and said, 'Let's get to work.' Then he complained about every little thing. Every little thing was wrong, the location and the hours and the food. Then he refused to work after lunch. Then he told us he didn't think he could finish the picture.

We called Kate, who was on tour in Australia doing Shakespeare. She did her best. She talked to Strickling and she talked to Spence. If she had been nearby I think he would have been OK.

Dore Schary was consulted and that was it for Tracy. He was through. I was there when they told him. He sat down and cried like a baby. It was terrible. He said his career was ruined. He was through, and all the time he's sobbing. Strickling and I were all for giving him another chance, but the studio had had enough of Tracy over the years. They overlooked a lot of things, but not this time.

Spencer was desperate when he found out Kate would be gone for four months, but she had her goals and one of them was going Shakespeare, and that's what she was doing in Australia with the Old Vic. I'm not so sure Spence understood that. If he did, he still thought that he came first. That was Spence.

James Cagney replaced Tracy in *Tribute to a Bad Man*, which was a very popular film at the box office.

The news that the greatest actor in Hollywood had been fired was a shock, but also a sign of the times. Movies were now in competition with television and many big stars were not asked to renew their contracts. Now that Kate had fulfilled her dream to act in Shakespeare she was able to be with Tracy. She would have to do just that if he was going to survive with his declining health.

He made *The Mountain* with Robert Wagner, the story of a plane crash in the Alps. The film was shot in France with Kate looking on. She then flew with Tracy to Cuba for the filming of Ernest Hemingway's *The Old Man and the Sea*. Spencer got drunk on the flight, but Kate sobered him up in time to face the cameras. The problem during filming was not his ability to work, but his ability to deal with fellow boozer Hemingway, who would ask him, 'Can't you take a goddamn drink without getting drunk?' Egged on, Tracy had a drink and at once turned into Mr. Hyde. He and Hemingway destroyed a Havana bar to the tune of $150,000. Warner Brothers mogul Jack Warner wanted to fire Tracy and replace him with Ernest Borgnine but changed his mind, moving production back to Hollywood instead.

While the set for the film was being built, Kate rushed Spencer into *Desk Set*, an amusing movie about a computer inventor and the brainy head of a network's research department. In one of the pair's better scenes, he invites her to lunch, but instead of a swanky New York restaurant, he takes her to the roof in the dead of winter with sandwiches from a deli. While she shivers from the cold, he tests her intelligence with questions that make him out to be the fool. About her role in *Desk Set*, Kate said, 'The woman is always pretty sharp. She needles a man, a little like a mosquito. Then he slowly puts out his big paw and slaps the lady down, and the American public likes to see that. In the end he's always the boss of the situation, but she challenges him. That in simple terms is what we do.' Referring to her real-life relationship with Tracy she said, 'To most men I'm a nuisance because I'm so busy I'm a pest, but Spencer is so masculine that once in a while he rather smashes me down, and there's something nice about me when I'm smashed down.'

After *Desk Set*, Tracy returned to filming *The Old Man and the Sea*, which was now being shot in a tank filled with 750,000 gallons of water on the Warner Brothers back lot. It was not a good picture. Playing a Mexican fisherman, he refused to speak with an accent and gave the impression that he had no interest in acting. The film was way too long, dragging on and on with no feeling or suspense. Tracy was, however, nominated for an Oscar in 1958, but he lost to David Niven in *Separate Tables*.

In fact 1957 was altogether a difficult year for Spencer. His good pal Humphrey Bogart died of cancer in January. Bogart's widow, Lauren Bacall, wanted Spencer to deliver the eulogy at the funeral, but he explained, 'I couldn't do it – I just couldn't – I wouldn't be able to get through it. I loved old Bogie. I could do it for someone I wasn't that emotional about, but not for dear Bogie. Please understand.'

Grieving over the passing of his friend, Tracy was confronted with his son John's bitter divorce from his wife Nadine, who testified that 'John repulsed me after the birth of Joey. If I put my arm around him he would say, "Leave me alone".' She got custody of Joey and Spencer got drunk.

In October Hepburn received word that L.B. Mayer was dying of leukaemia and wanted to see her. She obliged, of course, and was saddened to find that he was effectively dying of a broken heart after being ousted from MGM. He said he wanted Spencer to deliver the eulogy at his funeral and Kate assured him he would. Mayer afterwards told his daughter Irene, 'I'm so glad Kate and I are such good friends.'

Tracy gave the eulogy written by his son-in-law David O. Selznick at the Wilshire Temple on 31 October. The rabbi offered him a drink

The Boy Genius Irving Thalberg with his wife, actress Norma Shearer *(top left).*

Louis B. Mayer with Judy Garland *(top right)* in a rare pose of friendship. She hated him intensely.

The handsome but tragic John Gilbert *(left)* – and *(below)* in rehearsal with Ralph Bellamy and director Harry Beaumont on the set of *West of Broadway,* 1931.

Clark Gable, with Billie Burke *(left)* and Constance Bennett in *After Office Hours*, 1935 *(above)*. Gable did not win an Oscar as Rhett Butler in *Gone With the Wind*, 1939 *(right)*.

Robert Taylor and Katharine Hepburn had no chemistry on the screen in *Undercurrent*, 1946.

Taylor with Eleanor Parker, who wept when he married someone else not long after filming *Valley of the Kings*, 1954.

Spencer Tracy, seen here with a young Mickey Rooney, won an Oscar for his portrayal of Father Flannigan in *Boys' Town*, 1938 *(left)*.
Below, Tracy with Rita Johnson in *Edison, the Man*, 1940.

The very talented Mickey Rooney, with Kathryn Grayson and Lewis Stone in *Andy Hardy's Private Secretary*, 1941 *(top)*, and with Buddy Hackett in the hilarious *It's a Mad, Mad, Mad, Mad World*, 1963 *(above)*.

Peter Lawford was beginning to show
signs of self-destruction in the 1970s
(right).

Frank Sinatra, with Jill St. John in
Come Blow Your Horn, 1963 *(below)*.

Elvis Presley, greeting his fans at the musical gates of Gracelands *(inset)*, and in his favourite movie, *King Creole*, 1958.

Ramon Novarro with Myrna Loy in *The Barbarian*, 1933 *(left)*.

Van Johnson, MGM's boy-next-door, with Gloria DeHaven *(left)* and Arlene Dahl in *Scene of the Crime*, 1949 *(below)*.

beforehand but Spencer said, 'If I did, Rabbi, I might bury you instead of Mr. Mayer.'

Tracy's relationship with Louise was a friendly one. He supported her in grand style and called her regularly. When he made out a new will in 1957 he told Kate he was leaving everything to his wife. Hepburn came from a wealthy family and her father had always handled her finances cleverly. 'Dear God,' she laughed. 'Don't you think I have enough money?'

After *The Last Hurrah*, a movie about a dying politician's last campaign, Tracy, tired, ill, and lacking the desire to act, decided to retire. But when producer-director Stanley Kramer approached him about playing the famous lawyer Clarence Darrow in *Inherit the Wind*, Spencer could not turn him down, and Kate was in agreement. The movie was based on the famous trial between Darrow who defended evolution and William Jennings Bryan, played by Fredric March, acting in defence of the Bible. Kramer knew he was taking a big chance with Tracy even though he had been on the wagon for some time. But, despite the serious theme, Tracy told Kramer, 'I think we can have some fun with this one.'

Joe Mankiewicz, who had introduced Hepburn to Tracy, now directed her in *Suddenly, Last Summer* with Elizabeth Taylor and Montgomery Clift. Kate plays Clift's evil mother. But it was a turbulent shoot. Mankiewicz overdid her ugliness in the picture, emphasising her wrinkles and liver spots, and as a result she was grotesque on screen. Though she had never been considered beautiful in the classic sense, Kate felt this time her ugliness was overdone. She was also angry that Elizabeth Taylor was frequently late, although Joe explained that she was suffering from an impacted wisdom tooth. Mankiewicz himself was impatient with Clift who had been on drugs and alcohol since a near-fatal auto accident. But when there was talk of his being replaced, Kate jumped to his defence.

All in all, she locked horns with Mankiewicz many times. When Elizabeth was late, Hepburn began directing some scenes to get the ball rolling, whereupon Mankiewicz threatened to close down production. 'We will resume shooting, Miss Hepburn, when the Directors' Guild card which I ordered for you arrives.' Kate was furious and walked off the set.

On the last day of filming Hepburn asked Mankiewicz in front of the cast and crew whether he was finished with her.

'Absolutely,' he said.

'You're quite sure you don't need me for retakes or dubbing or additional close-ups?'

'I've got it all, Kate, and you were great.'

'You're absolutely certain I'm through with this picture?' she asked.
'Absolutely.'

'Then,' she hissed, 'I want to leave you with this!' And she spat in his face.

Hepburn nonetheless received her eighth Academy Award nomination for the film, but lost to Simone Signoret in *Room at the Top*.

In 1960, Tracy's good friend Clark Gable died of a heart attack. They had co-starred in several very good films together and were drinking buddies. On one occasion they went to Tucson with MGM boss Eddie Mannix, checked into a hotel and went on a booze fest. Out of boredom they apparently began playing jacks and the game was hot. The phone rang and it was L.B. Mayer, who wanted to talk to Mannix.

Spencer said, 'He can't come to the phone right now.'

Why, Mayer demanded to know.

'Because he's on his threesies,' Spence replied and hung up.

Tracy, the same age as Gable, now believed his own time was running out. Columnist James Bacon described the scene on the set of *Inherit the Wind*: 'Kate wasn't there and Spence was kinda drunk. All through the movie he had liquor stashed where no one would look. What surprised me was that he was drinking but in control because he wasn't like that. Then he showed me the empty bottles hidden behind a wall. There must have been a hundred and fifty of them.'

In late 1960 Tracy played a priest in *The Devil at Four O'Clock* in Hawaii with Frank Sinatra, who plays one of three convicts trying to evacuate a children's hospital before a volcano erupts. Tracy liked Frank, but considered him unprofessional; Sinatra frequently failed to show up and when he did he often left early. Tracy complained that he had to play the scenes in which Sinatra was supposed to feature looking over his shoulder at a coat hanger. It wasn't worth the effort – *The Devil at Four O'Clock* was not a good picture. Spencer probably did it for something to do before making *Judgment at Nuremberg* in Germany with an all-star cast of players – Burt Lancaster, Maximilian Schell, Marlene Dietrich, Montgomery Clift, Richard Widmark and Judy Garland. Tracy plays the American judge in the film and his thirteen-minute speech at the end was shot in one take. Once again he was nominated for an Oscar, but it was Schell who took home the statuette.

In January 1962 *Look* magazine published an interview with Spencer Tracy about his life and his close relationship with Hepburn. Veteran journalist Bill Davidson put it all down on paper. Tracy talked candidly about his alcoholism, waking up somewhere not knowing how he got there, his blackouts, his temper, his separation from Louise and about 'my Kate'. Although the public took it for granted that Tracy and Hepburn were more than just friends, to finally see it in print was staggering. Author Davidson said, 'I was immediately exonerated by writers in Hollywood.' Kate, though, was heartbroken. Over the years she had gone out of her way to hide her personal ties to Tracy and now he had voluntarily exposed them. He denied giving the interview and blamed the press, but only he could have known about the private moments between them that were revealed in the *Look* article.

Stanley Kramer now told Kate that he wanted Tracy for his very funny *It's a Mad, Mad, Mad, Mad World*. She consulted with Spencer's doctors, who said the dry desert air outside Los Angeles would be healthful for his emphysema. Tracy got top billing although he was only in twenty per cent of the movie. The dry air was good for Spencer's breathing problems and the cast of comedians was good for his soul. His co-stars were, among many, Sid Caesar, Mickey Rooney, Phil Silvers, Jonathan Winters, Buddy Hackett, Milton Berle, Jimmy Durante and Carl Reiner. In the film, everyone is after buried treasure which they are desperate to keep for themselves. Tracy is the police captain who tracks them down, but wants the money as well.

According to Kramer, Spencer was in poor health. 'He had bad colour and no stamina whatsoever. But even though his lack of energy showed, I think he had the best time ever during the making of the film. The comedians worshipped him, but they also made him laugh. Jonathan Winters' impersonation of Kate and Spence in *Woman of the Year* was hilarious. He had the lines and the voices down pat. '

For Tracy, laughter was the best medicine. Kate was by his side, of course, making sure he did not work more than six hours a day. A double was used in the more active scenes, but this was barely apparent to the layman.

It's a Mad, Mad, Mad, Mad World was a smash hit. Bosley Crowther at the *New York Times* wrote:

Mr. Tracy seems the guardian of a sane morality in this wild and extravagant exposition of clumsiness and cupidity. While the mad seekers are tearing toward the money in their various ways – in automobiles that race each other in breathtaking sweeps of hairpin turns in the wide-open California desert, in airplanes that wobble overhead, Mr. Tracy sits there in wise complacence, the rigidity of the law. And then, by a ruse I dare not tell you, he shows how treacherous his morality is.

Spencer stayed close to home after he finished *Mad World*. In June 1963 Jim Bacon was surprised to find him at the bar in Romanoff's in Beverly Hills. They had a few drinks and were having lunch when Tracy passed out, his face in the mashed potatoes. Bacon, who had heard that Spencer and Kate were renting a house at Trancas Beach a few miles from Malibu, put the unconscious Tracy in the car and took him there. Bacon was trying to drag him to the door when Kate appeared in a rage. 'Goddamn you, Bacon! You and Gable were always trying to get him drunk. You've always been an evil companion for Spence!' With that she reached for something to throw at Bacon, who dropped Tracy like a ton of bricks in the driveway, got into his car and sped away.

A month later Kate thought Spencer was well enough to leave home for a few hours to go on a picnic, but they never reached Malibu. Tracy found himself gasping for breath in the car, so Kate called the fire department and went to the hospital with him. Doctors diagnosed the attack as pulmonary oedema and kept Tracy in the hospital for two weeks. He nevertheless reported to work for *Cheyenne Autumn*, a John Ford western, as well as *The Cincinnati Kid* with Steve McQueen, but was advised by doctors he was not well enough to do either picture.

In the spring of 1965 the *Virginia Law Weekly* asked Hepburn to compose an article about privacy. Her theme was 'The Predicament of the Public Figure':

In the beginning of my career in 1932 I had the right to consider privacy my right – and so I fought for it – a wild and vigorous battle – Quite successful – I thought – I went to a great deal of trouble – I went way, way out of my way – the few people I knew could keep their mouths shut.

Today it is extremely difficult to control one's privacy – even if one is not a public figure . . . Both the public and the press feel that they have an absolute right of access to the most intimate details of your life – and by this you must read largely sex life – I used to go through the most elaborate schemes to avoid the press – I felt that nothing of my private life was any of their business.

Kate went on about sex and pills: 'Don't hide it – Talk – tell it – It is never your fault.' The strain on her was beginning to show as she vented her anger in this article. She was right, of course, but Katharine Hepburn was also a celebrity, a star, a woman in love with the greatest actor in Hollywood, and everyone knew it. She had won more Oscars than anyone else and she was a rebel who wore slacks when no woman, other than Marlene Dietrich and Greta Garbo, dared. Dietrich flaunted it only in her films, and Garbo was rarely seen in public – so it was Hepburn who got the publicity because she didn't own a dress. And the stress of trying to keep the man she loved alive unnerved her as she watched him grow older and weaker.

In September 1965 Tracy underwent successful surgery to remove his prostate but complications set in when his kidneys shut down. He was attached to a kidney dialysis machine, a relatively new procedure, and given the last rites of the Catholic Church. Kate and Louise took turns to visit the hospital so that one of them was at his bedside at all times. After six weeks in hospital, Tracy went home to his little cottage on George Cukor's property. There were no film offers because Spencer was no longer insurable. He spent his days with Kate listening to classical music, painting, sculpting and when he was up to it, flying kites.

Because they rarely went out socially, they pounced on visitors for the latest Hollywood gossip. 'Who's going to bed with whom?' Tracy asked. 'Who's getting a divorce?' When they heard that his friend Frank Sinatra was going to marry Mia Farrow, who was 28 years his junior, he laughed uproariously. Kate moaned, 'Oh, God!' They received an invitation to the wedding reception in July 1966, and Tracy said, 'I wouldn't miss this show for anything!' So Kate went along with his wishes – but they arrived separately.

Though Spencer avoided the subject of death, he told his friend, writer Garson Kanin, 'I watched my father die of cancer. Right then and there I made plans. Anything like that ever happened to me, I'd check out. And I will too . . .'

Kate said, 'If you have a hopeless disease, no matter how many people are trying to keep you alive, you have a perfect right to do whatever you want to do . . . I've had friends in the last stretches of cancer who've killed themselves, and I really don't blame them. I thought they were very sensible. But of course it's different for everyone. If you have someone who just adores taking care of you, it's terrible to disappoint her . . .' Translated, she meant, 'Please don't do it, Spence. I want you to live and I want to take care of you.'

Not working wasn't easy for Tracy, so he sometimes visited the sets to watch the action. When asked why he didn't take up directing, he replied, 'I don't have the patience. Hell, I'd probably kill the actors.'

Being cooped up with Tracy had its effect on Kate too. She was forced to put up with his insults and putdowns in front of guests. 'Who asked your opinion?' he would bark at her. 'For Christ's sake, don't you understand English?' Or his favourite, 'You sound like you've got a broomstick up your ass.' When she threw a log in the fire, he blurted, 'Don't ever – and I mean ever – do that again in front of company.' Kate just smiled and curled up at his feet like a naughty puppy.

Stanley Kramer finally came up with a movie for Tracy. It was about a wealthy liberal couple whose daughter wants to marry a handsome and accomplished black man. Sidney Poitier agreed to make the picture before Kramer approached Kate and Tracy. 'I think it's great for Spence,' she cheered.

'I want you to play the wife,' Kramer replied.

'Me?' she asked. 'I'm surprised.'

Hepburn put up her salary of $250,000 and Kramer his $750,000 as security in case something happened to Tracy during the filming of *Guess Who's Coming to Dinner*. Kate did not hesitate for one minute, but Kramer knew he was putting in jeopardy all the money he had, along with his reputation. It was Spencer, though, who was truly frightened. He had problems breathing and tired easily. Could he get through another movie? Kramer asked, 'Are you just going to sit here waiting for oblivion?'

A week before starting the movie, Tracy had a severe emphysema attack. Kate called the fire department and rescue workers administered oxygen. He did not have to be hospitalised, but it scared him enough to change his mind about working. Kramer understood. It was not too late to call the whole thing off, but he told Tracy he would not do the movie without him. Spencer looked at Kate and said positively, 'OK. I'll do it!'

On 15 February 1967, Tracy and Hepburn appeared at a press conference to introduce her 23-year-old niece Katharine Houghton, who was going to play her daughter in *Guess Who's Coming to Dinner*.

It was a heartwarming film. In the end one forgets the interracial problem and concentrates on Tracy who gives his blessings to the couple and tells his wife, 'If what they feel for each other is even half what we felt then that is everything.' Kate's eyes filled with tears. He was paying tribute to her with someone else's lines – words he was too proud to say on his own.

Hepburn had been a pest during filming, annoying Stanley Kramer over camera angles, the movie set and other directorial functions. She harped at Kramer until Spencer told her, 'Don't bug him! Don't bother him! Jesus, he's worked it out, for Christ's sake!' He knew Kate so very well that he knew what she was doing when his back was turned. Sneaking on to the set, she sat down and put her feet up on a table. 'Put your feet down!' he shouted, but she ignored him. 'We'll start working when she learns to sit like a lady.' She stuck her tongue out at him and put her feet down.

Her age now apparent in her scrawny neck, wrinkled and with protruding bones, Kate tried to approach her scenes from an angle or kneeling on the floor.

'Why the hell are you kneeling?' Tracy asked.

'Spencer, I thought it would be more effective if . . .'

'Spensuh! Christ, you talk like you've got a feather up your ass all the time. Get out of here, will ya?'

'I just thought that . . .'

'Why don't you read the lines, do what he says and get on with it?'

Production ended on 26 May. Tracy did not stay for the wind-up party. He went home and called his close friends about how thrilled he was to have finished the movie.

Kate had moved into the little cottage on the Cukor estate to be with Spencer when his social activity came to a halt. One of his favourite nights had always been getting together with his Irish buddies, James Cagney, Pat O'Brien, Frank Morgan and Frank McHugh. He called it Irish Night. They met at Chasen's or Romanoff's and finally at Kate's place. When Spencer had to bow out, it was clear the end was near.

He had a buzzer near his bed so Kate could respond if he needed anything, and he usually did during his sleepless nights. On 10 June he did not ring and she wondered why. At 3:00 a.m. she heard him shuffling into the kitchen. Kate got out of bed and was about to open the door when she heard a cup smashing on the floor. Then there was a thump. She found Spencer dead on the floor and held him in her arms.

Cukor's gardener helped her put Tracy in bed where he lay in peace for the first time in many years. Kate lit candles and tried to gather her thoughts – one of the few times the always clear-headed Hepburn did not know how to proceed.

Who was qualified to handle the situation? Howard Strickling was the best person to proceed with the details and handle reporters. After all, Tracy had been a married man living with a famous actress and now he was dead. Dignified arrangements had to be made and a cover story put up to protect Spencer and his family. Strickling would tell the press that Spencer's housekeeper had found his body at 6:00 a.m. and called his brother Carroll, who arrived with the doctor. The truth would not come out until Kate's book *Me* was published in 1991.

Louise arrived with Susie and John. Kate had already laid out the clothes for Spencer to wear in his coffin. When she pointed this out to the undertakers, Cunningham and Walsh, Louise said, 'But I'm his wife, I should . . .'

'Oh, what difference does it make,' Kate sighed.

Then Mrs. Tracy stunned Hepburn, saying, 'I thought you were just a rumour.'

Kate later wrote, 'For almost thirty years Spence and I had known each other. Some rumour.'

Tracy was wearing pyjamas and a red flannel robe when he died. Hepburn retrieved the nightclothes and kept them for many years. She went to the funeral parlour after hours to sit with Spencer – to be with him for as long as she could.

The *New York Times* commented that Tracy's death 'breaks one more strong and vibrant cable in the slowly crumbling bridge between motion pictures of this generation and the great one of the past.'

On the morning of the funeral Kate and a friend decided to 'see the old boy off'. They went to Cunningham and Walsh and helped the undertakers put Tracy's coffin in the hearse. They followed in their car, before turning round a few blocks from the church and going home.

A requiem Low Mass was said at the Immaculate Heart of Mary Roman Catholic Church in Hollywood. The mass was given by Monsignor John O'Donnell, Tracy's advisor on *Boys' Town*. Louise arrived with Howard Strickling and her children. Among the six hundred invited were Frank Sinatra, James Stewart, George Cukor and director John Ford. Hepburn paid her respects to Louise before going home to Connecticut.

Tracy, whose estate was estimated to be more than $500,000, was buried at Forest Lawn Cemetery in Glendale in the Garden of Everlasting Peace.

Katharine and Spencer were nominated for Oscars for *Guess Who's Coming to Dinner*. Kate was in Europe when she received the news that she had won. When told that Spencer had lost to Rod Steiger's *In the Heat of the Night*, Hepburn paused. 'Well,' she said, 'that's OK. I'm sure mine is for the two of us.'

*

Kate, walking her dog one afternoon, ran into Susie Tracy who asked if it was Lobo, her father's dog. Kate nodded and said the pooch was doing fine, and then extended her friendship to Susie who began seeing and getting to know the love of her father's life.

Louise Tracy died in 1983, clearing the way for Hepburn to honour Spencer in her own way. In a documentary, *The Spencer Tracy Legacy*, Kate shared a letter she had written to him eighteen years after his death:

Dear Spence:

Whoever thought I'd be writing you a letter? You died on the tenth of June in 1967. My golly, Spence, that's fifteen, no eighteen years ago. That's a long time. Are you happy, finally? It is a nice long rest you're having . . . making up for all your tossing and turning in life?

You know, I never believed you when you said you just couldn't get to sleep. I said, 'C'mon you, sleep.' If you didn't sleep, you'd be dead, you'd be so worn out.

Then, remember that night when, I don't know, you felt so disturbed? And I said, 'Well, go on in, go to bed, and I'll talk you to sleep. I'll just talk and talk, and you'll be so bored you're bound to drift off.'

Well, I went in and got an old pillow, Lobo the dog, and I lay there watching you and stroking the old dog. I was talking about you and the movie we just finished, *Guess Who's Coming to Dinner*, and my studio, and your new tweed coat, and the garden, and all the nice sleep-making topics, new cooking and dull gossip. But you never stopped tossing. To the right . . . to the left . . . shove the pillows, pull the covers – and on and on and on. Finally, and really finally now, just then you quieted down. I waited a while. Then I crept out.

You told me the truth, didn't you, Spence? You really could not sleep. And I used to wonder then, 'Why, why, Spence?' I still wonder. You took the pills: they were quite strong. I suppose you'd have to say that without them, you never would have slept at all.

Living wasn't easy for you, was it? What did you like to do? You loved sailing, especially in stormy weather. You loved polo, but then Will Rogers was killed in that airplane accident, and the fun went out of it for you, didn't it? Tennis, golf, swimming? No, not really. Walking? No, it didn't suit you. That was one of those things where you could think at the same time – of this, of that.

Of what, Spence? What was it? Was it some specific life-thing, like being a Catholic – and you felt a bad Catholic? No comfort, no comfort. I remember Father Sitwik telling you that you concentrated on all the bad, none of the good which your religion offered . . .

But why the escape hatch? Why was it always opened to get away from the remarkable you?

What was it, Spence? What was it? I meant to ask you, 'Did you know what it was?'

Spencer Tracy had an extraordinary life, but one that was filled with pain and guilt. Facing the truth was not one of his attributes. He never told Hepburn he loved her. She assumed he did because they were together for such a long time. He never broke his tie with Louise, blaming his loyalty on a deep Catholic faith that did not exist. He imposed his own paralysis to punish himself. He was caught between the devil and the deep blue sea. Whatever decision he made was the wrong one. Hepburn eased his torment by not holding out for marriage, but she wondered whether this helped or hindered a possible solution to Tracy's remorse. She said he took the easy road instead of facing the situation and straightening it out. It would have been the honest thing to do for both Spencer and Louise. He should have been more direct, faced it and made life easier for both of them and for her. Hepburn died of natural causes in June 2003 at the age of 96.

Yet we remember the Dr. Jekyll in Spencer Tracy and this is what he would want. Acting was his life and he was the master.

'The way the studios operated was good for a young actor. Hell, you were always working, and that's the way to master a profession. Actors today, they play one part in a television series for years. How can they grow? They can't. That's why actors today are not as good as they were. Acting in stock was no big deal, but it trained people for the acting profession, and now, that's all gone.'

– Spencer Tracy, 1960

The Films of Spencer Tracy

Up the River (Fox, 1930)
Quick Millions (Fox, 1931)
Six Cylinder Love (Fox, 1931)
She Wanted a Millionaire (Fox, 1932)
Sky Devils (United Artists, 1932)
Disorderly Conduct (Fox, 1932)
Young America (Fox, 1932)
Society Girl (Fox, 1932)
Painted Woman (Fox, 1932)
Me and My Gal (Fox, 1932)
20,000 Years in Sing Sing (Warner Brothers, 1932)
Face in the Sky (Fox, 1933)
Shanghai Madness (Fox, 1933)
The Power and the Glory (Fox, 1933)
The Mad Game (Fox, 1933)
A Man's Castle (Columbia, 1933)
Looking For Trouble (United Artists, 1934)
The Show-Off (MGM, 1934)
Bottoms Up (Fox, 1934)
Now I'll Tell You (Fox, 1934)
Marie Galanie (Fox, 1934)
It's a Small World (Fox, 1935)
Murder Man (MGM, 1935)
Dante's Inferno (MGM, 1935)
Whipsaw (MGM, 1935)
Riffraff (MGM, 1936)
Fury (MGM, 1936)

San Francisco (MGM, 1936)
Libeled Lady (MGM, 1936)
They Gave Him a Gun (MGM, 1937)
Captains Courageous (MGM, 1937)
Big City (MGM, 1937)
Mannequin (MGM, 1938)
Test Pilot (MGM, 1938)
Boys' Town (MGM, 1938)
Stanley and Livingston (Fox, 1939)
I Take This Woman (MGM, 1940)
Northwest Passage (MGM, 1940)
Edison, the Man (MGM, 1940)
Boom Town (MGM, 1940)
Men of Boys Town (MGM, 1941)
Dr. Jekyll and Mr. Hyde (MGM, 1941)
Woman of the Year (MGM, 1942)
Tortilla Flat (MGM, 1942)
Keeper of the Flame (MGM, 1942)
A Guy Named Joe (MGM, 1943)
The Seventh Cross (MGM, 1944)
Thirty Seconds Over Tokyo (MGM, 1944)
Without Love (MGM, 1945)
The Sea of Grass (MGM, 1947)
Cass Timberlane (MGM, 1947)
State of the Union (MGM, 1948)
Edward, My Son (MGM, 1949)
Adam's Rib (MGM, 1949)
Malaya (MGM, 1950)
Father of the Bride (MGM, 1950)
Father's Little Dividend (MGM, 1951)
The People Against O'Hara (MGM, 1951)
Pat and Mike (MGM, 1952)
Plymouth Adventure (MGM, 1952)
The Actress (MGM, 1953)
Broken Lance (20th Century-Fox, 1954)
Bad Day at Black Rock (MGM, 1955)
The Mountain (Paramount, 1956)
Desk Set (20th Century-Fox, 1957)
The Old Man and the Sea (Warner Brothers, 1958)

The Last Hurrah (Columbia, 1958)
Inherit the Wind (US, 1960)
The Devil at Four O'Clock (Columbia, 1961)
Judgment at Nuremberg (United Artists, 1961)
How the West Was Won (MGM, 1962)
It's a Mad, Mad, Mad, Mad World (United Artists, 1963)
Guess Who's Coming to Dinner (Columbia, 1967)

7

Mickey Rooney

Spencer Tracy might have been considered the best actor in Hollywood, but he himself had another opinion. He thought the young man who played Andy Hardy was the most talented. He could sing and dance, act, and play just about every musical instrument. He was mogul Louis B. Mayer's ideal of the all-American boy and his pet contract player.

He was only five feet three inches tall, but all man, according to his eight wives. He was cute, energetic, talkative, and always in love.

Actor Nathan Lane said, 'He's a total psychotic. He's very adorable, but there isn't enough Ritalin in the world for him.'

When he left MGM and had to face life without a lucrative and guaranteed weekly salary, he hit bottom and was ostracised by his peers in Hollywood. As he was getting dressed for the 1951 Academy Awards to present an Oscar, the Board of Governors withdrew their invitation. A decade earlier he had been the most popular star in the world.

He tried alcohol and pills, attempted suicide, and declared himself bankrupt. It took many years, but finally he proved his worth when Hollywood presented him with a Lifetime Achievement Award. He is a true survivor, unlike his frequent co-star Judy Garland whom he considered his sister. They were both 'born in a trunk', their talents abused by others and, eventually, by themselves. But he had the will and the energy to see it through . . .

Mickey Rooney was born Joe Yule Jr on a dining-room table in Brooklyn, New York on 23 September 1920. His parents, Joe and Nellie Yule, were vaudeville performers, and two weeks after his arrival the newborn baby was on the road with them. Joe was a hard-drinking Scotsman who met his chorus-girl wife backstage. When his son was born, he was found drunk at the bottom of a laundry chute singing Scottish songs. Joe considered his son a burden and referred to him as 'that kid'.

At seventeen months little Joe was discovered hiding on stage with his mouth organ. When an actor found him he asked him to play it – and Joe did just that, to the delight of the audience. The manager was so impressed that he offered the Yules three dollars a week for their son to perform 'because he looks like a midget'.

The 'kid' made his debut in a tuxedo singing 'Sweet Rosie O'Grady' and he brought the house down. One of his other jobs was hawking the show in front of the theatre: 'Step right up! Only a few seats left!'

Young Joe loved performing on and off stage, travelling and living in hotels, but this life came to an end the day Nellie found her husband with another woman. She left him and moved in with her sister in Kansas City, and at last her son was able to find out what life as a normal kid was all about. Nellie, however, was eager to get back on the stage and accepted an offer from a theatre group headed for Hollywood. When she arrived there, the job fell through, so Nellie decided to make Joe the star in the family. She found another job as manager of a bungalow court that afforded her free room and board, and finally succeeded in getting her son into a musical revue at the Orange Grove Theater in downtown Los Angeles.

He was spotted by a talent scout from Fox Studios who cast him as a midget in *Not To Be Trusted*, and this was followed by *Orchids and Ermine* at Vitaphone, a division of Warner Brothers, with the beautiful Colleen Moore. These films led to Joe's big break in a series of films based on the popular cartoon figure, Mickey McGuire. Nellie dyed her son's blond hair black for the audition and he got the part for five dollars a day. Joe was ten years old when Nellie put him in Ma Lawlor's Professional School for show-business children, where he met Frances Gumm (Judy Garland) for the first time. Ma Lawlor didn't provide much of an education to her 'students', but she was certified by the L.A. Board of Education.

By the end of the series Joe was using the name Mickey McGuire, but when Universal Studios wanted to cast him in *The Information Kid*, they did not want him identified with the cartoon character. The publicity department considered calling him Mickey Yule, but Nellie remembered an actor named Pat Rooney. 'How about Mickey Rooney?' she asked.

On a lunch break during the McGuire series, Mickey peeped into an open office at Warner Brothers and introduced himself.

'Who are you?' he asked the man working there.

'My name is Walt Disney. Come over here and sit on my lap.'

Mickey looked at the drawing on Disney's desk and said, 'My gosh, that's a good-looking mouse.'

'It sure is, Mickey. Say, Mickey, Mickey. How would you like me to name a mouse after you?'

'I would sure like that, but right now I gotta go and get a tuna sandwich.'

Rooney swears this is a true story.

Mickey made a series of pictures under his new name before producer David O. Selznick discovered him in 1933. He told his father-in-law, Louis B. Mayer, that he should hire Mickey, but the MGM mogul dismissed the idea. So Selznick took him on himself to play in *Manhattan Melodrama* with Clark Gable, Myrna Loy and William Powell. Mickey, who played Gable as a youth, was seen only briefly. The film did well at the box office, but its main claim to fame is that it was the movie that gangster John Dillinger was watching before he was gunned down by the FBI as he left the theatre.

Louis B. Mayer finally took notice of Rooney and put him under contact in 1933 for $150 a week, but his salary quickly escalated as he became more important to the studio. Mickey made eleven films at MGM in 1934, six in 1935 and three in 1936. He also appeared on the stage as the mischievous fairy Puck in Shakespeare's *A Midsummer Night's Dream*, performing at the Hollywood Bowl for a month before touring the country.

In 1935 Warner Brothers turned the production into a movie starring James Cagney, Dick Powell, Hugh Herbert, Arthur Treacher, Victor Jory and Anita Louise alongside Rooney. The *New York Times* wrote: 'Mickey

Rooney's remarkable performance as Puck is one of the major delights of the work . . . He is a mischievous and joyous sprite, a snub-nosed elf who laughs with a shrill delight as the foolish mortals blunder through Oberon's fuzzy domain.'

Though Mickey wanted to attend high school like other teenagers, his filming schedule prevented it. So Nellie put him in MGM's Little Red Schoolhouse on the studio lot. His classmates, including Jackie Cooper, Deanna Durbin, Bonita Granville and Gloria DeHaven, were under the supervision of Mary McDonald.

The one-storey schoolhouse was in fact white, not red, and was located in the centre of MGM's many sound stages. The children were supposed by law to have five hours of education each day, whether in school or with a tutor on the movie set. Miss McDonald was a prim lady with her hair in a bun and a watch pinned on her blouse. She was strict about homework assignments and rapped her students' hands with a ruler if they were not paying attention. Rooney said she looked like something out of central casting. The tutors did the best they could to teach reading, writing and arithmetic on the set in between takes, when the children were more interested in learning their lines.

When Mickey was sixteen he bought a blue 1937 two-door Ford convertible with leather seats. It was perfect for picking up girls and necking with them, parked in the hills above Los Angeles.

In *Captains Courageous* Mickey played the captain's son trying to cope with a spoiled brat (Freddy Bartholomew) who falls off a luxury liner and is taken aboard a fishing vessel. Spencer Tracy won an Oscar for his portrayal of Manuel, the Portuguese fisherman who rescues the boy. This was Rooney's third film alongside Bartholomew who, with his English accent, played the good little boy to Mickey's bad little boy – the impish kid with blond hair and turned-up nose who was the personification of American youth.

Nobody expected much from an MGM programmer entitled *A Family Affair*. Based on the wholesome Broadway play *Skidding*, it featured Mickey as an awkward adolescent named Andy Hardy and depicted his trials and tribulations in small-town America. Lionel Barrymore played his father, Judge Hardy, and Spring Byington Andy's mother. Yet the film was such a huge success when it was released in 1937 that L.B. Mayer decided to make a series of movies starring Andy Hardy. The first, *You're Only Young Once*, featured a new and permanent cast of players – Lewis Stone as the judge, Fay Holden as Mrs. Hardy, Cecilia Parker as Andy's sister, and Ann Rutherford as his girlfriend, Polly Benedict.

Mickey Rooney did not lose his identity to Andy Hardy because they were one and the same. The series made millions for MGM and boosted Rooney to number one at the box office. In 1937 he signed a new contract with Metro for $750 a week, escalating to $1250, $2500 and $5000 with bonuses. By way of celebration, Mickey, Nellie and her new accountant husband Fred Pankey bought a new house with a swimming pool on five acres within commuting distance of MGM in the San Fernando Valley. It wasn't luxurious, but it was Mickey's first home and that made it very special.

The patriotic Louis B. Mayer believed in clean entertainment, apple pie, virginity and the American flag. He considered MGM's cast of contract players as his family and urged them to feel the same way. To many of them it was a blessing because they came, like Mickey, from broken homes.

The name of Mayer's game and fame was a four-letter word: love. Little kisses would lead to bigger kisses and they in turn led to one lasting kiss at the church altar. Andy Hardy's huge crescendo was an innocent kiss that sent him reeling, though old jalopies had the same effect on him. He was usually subject to temptations, gave into them, but was rescued by his father after one of their famous man-to-man talks. Andy quarrelled with his sister as all brothers do and he had crushes on older women as all boys do. He never had enough money and his car was always breaking down, so his nose was often dirty from working underneath his jalopy. Though he was closer to his father, there was always and forever deep respect for his mother. One of the *Andy Hardy* scripts was changed to reflect this. When he doesn't eat his dinner one day Andy is supposed to say, 'It wasn't very good, Mom.' God forbid, though, that Mother should have provided a bad meal, so the line was changed to read, 'It was a fine dinner, Mom. A lovely dinner. But I just wasn't hungry.' And Mr. Mayer smiled again . . .

The idea was that American moviegoers should feel at home with the Hardy family, relax and watch themselves on the silver screen. Everyone knew an Andy Hardy or had one in the family. More important, everyone wanted a mother and father like Andy's – parents who were concerned, loving, and understanding.

Because Mickey had a youthful face he was able to play a teenager well into his twenties. From 1937 until 1946, the 26 *Andy Hardy* films grossed $111 million, over half a billion in today's dollars.

The *Andy Hardy* movies were also a stepping stone for MGM starlets like Lana Turner, Donna Reed, Kathryn Grayson and Esther Williams. Judy Garland played Betsy Booth, who is secretly in love with Andy. He, however, turns to her for advice about his problems with other girls. Judy made three Hardy films and was so in tune with Mickey that MGM later put them in several spectacular musicals.

Off the movie set, Garland was in love with Rooney who, like Andy, had his eye on glamorous girls such as Lana Turner. This had a profound effect on Judy, who looked in the mirror and saw a chubby, unattractive brunette. According to MGM press agent George Nichols, 'Garland never thought of herself as pretty because she wanted to be beautiful, and that just wasn't Judy. Her looks and her voice were unique. She was one of a kind and there will never be anyone like her. I understand why she felt the way she did. There she was at MGM surrounded by the most beautiful girls in the world, and Judy felt she couldn't compete. It all started with her big crush on Mickey who thought of her as a sister.' Rooney admitted in later years that he would have pursued Judy if he had not been swayed by Hollywood's overblown conception of beauty.

Lana Turner attended the Little Red Schoolhouse in 1938. Her presence did not help raise Mickey's grades as he spent the time daydreaming about her. Miss McDonald's ruler tapped his knuckles more than once but this did little to take his mind off the auburn-haired beauty with 'the nicest knockers I have ever seen'. Mickey, who had known Lana before she came to MGM, was brassy enough to ask her out – and she accepted. According to him they had a great time, both on the dance floor and in the front seat of his convertible, parked on Mulholland Drive. She was oversexed, he wrote in his delightful autobiography, *Life is Too Short*.

But when she came to the studio, Lana stopped seeing him. Mickey thought she had outgrown him, but he found out later that it was because she had aborted his baby. Lana nonetheless denied it in public. Even from semi-retirement, she emerged on television in 1991 to deny absolutely and definitely that she had been pregnant with Rooney's baby. Mickey replied, 'If it didn't happen it was the most beautiful dream I ever had.' Lana, of course, had been trained by MGM to maintain a clean image and she was still doing that many years after the end of her contract with the studio. Mickey wasn't sure how he felt about Lana's confession. Her supposed pregnancy had come at a time when they were both up-and-coming stars, not to mention the fact that they were both very young.

Mickey had no problem getting girls. He was as famous as Clark Gable, and as cute as Robert Taylor was handsome. He was fun to be around and made people laugh. He had a sporty car and a royal entrée to every nightclub and restaurant in Hollywood. He was the 'It' boy.

Louis B. Mayer invited his young contract players to his home every Sunday. They swam in his pool, ate hot dogs and paid homage to their 'father', who kept an eye on them to make sure they were having a good time. His invitation was more like a command: no one dared *not* show up when asked.

Mickey was very flexible and fun loving, so he made the most of these occasions and tried to convince Judy Garland to do the same. She was eager to be accepted. Like Mickey, she came from a broken home and was devastated when her father died. She said he was the only person who understood her at that time, in contrast to her pushy stage mother.

Following *Judge Hardy's Children*, Mickey made *Love Finds Andy Hardy*, in which Judy plays sweet Betsy Booth, and Lana the new girl in town. Andy asks two girls to the Christmas Eve dance, but when he finds himself without a date he goes with Betsy.

Mickey was having a ball, both on and off the movie set. He was the reporter's delight and the press was his delight. But the type of publicity he was getting did not reflect the innocence of Andy Hardy, whose father always told him to kiss wisely.

'I love you, Mickey.'

'Thank you very much, Mr. Mayer.'

'However, I'm not happy about your reputation.'

'Sir?'

'Girls.'

'I date a lot, I guess.'

'I'm not talking about dating, Mickey. I'm talking about fucking.'

'Sir?'

'You heard me. Andy Hardy doesn't fuck around.'

'But I'm not Andy Hardy. I'm Mickey Rooney and I like girls.'

'And booze.'

'No, sir. I'm too young to drink.'

'I have here a picture of you with a glass of champagne in your hand.'

'That was ginger ale, sir.'

'But your fans don't know that. A champagne glass holds champagne.'

'Everyone knows how old I am so who would serve me liquor?'

'If you enjoy being Andy Hardy then you'll be Andy Hardy and stand for what Andy Hardy stands for.'

'Are you saying you want me to be Andy Hardy off camera?'

'That's what I'm saying.'

'I won't do it. You're asking the impossible,' Mickey barked and left the office with Mayer on his heels. Grabbing Rooney's lapels, he said, 'Listen to me! I don't care what you do in private. Just don't do it in public. In public, behave. Your fans expect it. You're Andy Hardy! You're the United States! You're the Stars and Stripes. Behave yourself. You're a symbol!'

Mickey nodded. 'I'll be good, Mr. Mayer. I promise you that.'

'All right,' said Mayer, letting go of Rooney's lapels.

But if Mickey thought he had won the battle he was wrong. Mayer knew better. Maybe his precious Andy Hardy would try to do his best but that wasn't enough. He needed someone to look after him, and that someone was from Howard Strickling's publicity team – Les Peterson, who from now on would be with Mickey at all times to keep him out of trouble. He was at Rooney's side during interviews, drove him to nightclubs, made bets for him at the race track and composed articles for fan magazines supposedly written by Mickey. It was a successful MGM campaign and Andy Hardy became more popular than ever.

As did Mickey Rooney after *Boys' Town* with Spencer Tracy. The story of Father Edward J. Flanagan, who founded a home for wayward and homeless boys in Nebraska, was a factual one and brilliantly filmed, in part on location in Omaha. One of the most famous scenes is the one in which Rooney is playing poker, a cigarette in his mouth, his hat cocked and his feet up on the table. Tracy grabs him by the lapels, throws the cigarette away and pushes him into a chair. 'That's better,' he tells Mickey in a soft voice. Tracy won the Oscar for Best Actor, and Mickey received a miniature statuette for 'bringing to the screen the spirit and personification of youth'. *Boys' Town* was a favourite when it was released in 1938 and it remains so today.

In *Stablemates* Mickey co-starred with Wallace Beery, who invited him to dinner at Errol Flynn's house. When Mickey arrived, two lovely nude girls answered the door. Mickey was dumbfounded, his eyes bulging with delight. Flynn laughed and told him, 'You can take another look. Take two!'

Also at the dinner party were Spencer Tracy, Robert Taylor and Clark Gable. They were enjoying themselves away from the prying eyes of Louis B. Mayer, whose spies nonetheless told him all about the stag party.

When Mickey turned eighteen on 23 September 1938, he received a $15,000 bonus from Louis B. Mayer. After *Out West With the Hardys*, Rooney made Mark Twain's *The Adventures of Huckleberry Finn*; according to the *New York Times*, the main character was more Mickey than Huck, and the movie painted Finn as an advance member of the civil rights movement. But Rooney's name on the marquee guaranteed success and, like so many films released in the 1930s, *The Adventures of Huckleberry Finn* became a film classic.

Babes in Arms, Mickey's first musical together with Judy Garland, was a smash hit. It was directed by Busby Berkeley, who was equally known for his genius and his alcoholism. A relentless perfectionist who did not work by the clock, Busby's approach to filming was the same as his direction of Broadway plays. He did not shoot a musical number in short takes; instead he insisted on doing the entire number from beginning to end. This did not allow for stand-ins so Mickey and Judy had to work twice as hard, often into the small hours of the morning. But their combined efforts in *Babes in Arms* turned out a spectacular musical, as described by Frank Nugent in the *New York Times*:

> On the Broadway stage *Babes in Arms* is said to have provided a tolerable evening of music and comedy; we wouldn't know about that. All we know is that on the Broadway screen under the direction of Busby Berkeley, and with more so-called 'credits' than you would dare shake a stick at, *Babes in Arms* – to express it in two words – is Mickey Rooney. Now, it probably isn't Mickey Rooney's fault if he dominates the picture he is in . . . To us who have watched Mickey Rooney grow from a cloud no bigger than a man's hand on the horizon into a juvenile institution on whom Metro-Goldwyn-Mayer leans as the Ibsen drama used to lean on Mrs. Fiske, the screen version of *Babes in Arms* will come as no surprise . . . Not that Master Rooney does not personally justify himself; on the contrary. His adenoidal imitation of Clark Gable and his super-sibilant, explosive portrait of Lional Barrymore may well be among the more cherished impersonations of the modern screen.

In other words, Mickey stole the movie. But one has to remember that Judy Garland was a beginner trying to get her balance, and she did just that as Dorothy in *The Wizard of Oz*, also released in 1939. Mickey admitted he did not know how good Judy was until they did *Babes in Arms*. 'We were magical on the screen,' he said. For his outstanding performance in *Babes*, MGM gave him a $18,000 bonus, while Judy received a special Oscar for *The Wizard of Oz*. It was presented to her by Mickey, who also lent her support when she sang 'Over the Rainbow' for her peers at the Academy Awards.

One of the responsibilities of MGM contract players was going on tour to promote their films. In those days American theatres featured stage shows along with their movies and the most popular attraction was having a movie star appear in person. Mickey and Judy went on a blitz to Washington, New Haven, Hartford and New York City to publicise *Babes in Arms* and *The Wizard of Oz*. They were mobbed by thousands of cheering fans wherever they appeared, but it was an exhausting tour and Judy fainted backstage at the Capitol Theater in New York. Rooney had to cover for her, but he had more than enough ammunition and enjoyed himself immensely. Wherever there was an audience, Mickey was energised.

Rooney was nominated for an Oscar for *Babes in Arms*, although in 1939 the competition was very keen: Clark Gable in *Gone With the Wind*, James Stewart in *Mr. Smith Goes to Washington*, Laurence Olivier in *Wuthering Heights*. But for *Goodbye, Mr. Chips*, it was Robert Donat who won the award for Best Actor.

The public assumed (and hoped) that nineteen-year-old Mickey and Judy, seventeen, were an item. He asked Les Peterson how to respond. 'If that's what the public wants, let them,' he told Mickey. 'You and Judy are good friends so take her rollerskating or to an amusement park like other teenagers do. It's good for your images.' And they did spend a lot of time together, confiding in each other and sharing the problems that were plentiful at their age, especially for Judy.

Mickey frequently went to the race track – a hobby that would become a dangerous habit. His favourite pastime, though, was girls. One evening he and two other friends were at the apartment of Phil Silvers, who thought a prostitute was appropriate for the occasion and decided to have a contest. Who could stay with her the longest? Mickey was with the girl for twenty minutes, was proclaimed the winner and went home. Silvers asked the call girl, 'Did Rooney really last twenty minutes?'

'Yeah,' she laughed. 'Four minutes of fucking and sixteen minutes of imitations.'

Mickey, though, denied it, claiming the numbers were in reverse.

In 1939 Rooney made five movies, including *The Adventures of Huckleberry Finn*, *The Hardys Ride High*, *Judge Hardy and Son* and *Babes in Arms*. In *Andy Hardy Gets Spring Fever*, he has a crush on his drama teacher and thinks she feels the same way about him. Though Andy is always in the throes of love, this time he falls very hard and one cannot help having sympathy for him; Mickey was just as adept at garnering tears as he was at getting laughs.

In 1939 Mickey was reunited with his father Joe Yule, who was working in burlesque in Los Angeles. When his name appeared on the marquee as 'Mickey Rooney's Father', Louis B. Mayer had a fit. Andy

Hardy's daddy in a girlie show? He demanded that MGM's legal department contact the Follies management to protest, but the marquee remained the same and Mickey refused to intervene. But when all else fails, money talks – so Mayer offered Yule a three-year contract for a $100 a week 'because father and son wanted to work on the same lot'. When asked how it came about that he was now working at Metro, Yule replied, 'Mickey might have had something to do with it.' But there was little for Yule to do at MGM. He had, after all, been hired simply to get him out of burlesque, so as to avoid embarrassment.

Strike Up the Band was another exceptional musical featuring Mickey and Judy, and the tough critic at the *New York Times* came through again for Mickey:

> Roll out the red carpet, folks, and stand by. That boy is here again, the Pied Piper of the box office. The eighth or ninth wonder of the world. The kid himself – in short, Mickey Rooney. With the capable assistance of Judy Garland he strutted into the Capitol [Theater] at the head of *Strike Up the Band* and it should surprise no one that the show is his from beginning to end . . . Call him cocky and brash but he has the sort of exuberant talent that keeps your eye on the screen whether he's banging the drums, prancing through the conga, or hamming the old ham actors.

While Judy and Mickey were promoting *Strike Up the Band* in New York, Mickey ran into actress Norma Shearer, queen of the MGM lot and widow of the Boy Genius, Irving Thalberg. After dinner together she invited Mickey to her suite at the Waldorf Astoria Hotel for a nightcap. At 38, Norma was still very attractive – and somewhat frustrated, because Thalberg, with his weak heart, had been unable to satisfy her sexually.

Norma had recently devoured Jimmy Stewart. The MGM Boys, though, stayed away from her: they were loyal to Thalberg's memory and she held a huge amount of MGM stock. Don't tangle with the Queen of the Lot, was their motto. Clark Gable, who co-starred with Norma in several films, knew she was trying to seduce him too, but would have no part of it. 'Why does she prance around the set with tight dresses and no panties?' he asked.

Chasing after Gable was expected, but trying to seduce a nineteen-year-old Huckleberry was something else. In his amusing autobiography, *Life is Too Short*, Mickey wrote, 'We had a drink, sitting on the couch together. She edged over to me, getting very kittenish, very languid. When she turned her face toward mine and closed her eyes, I finally realized what was up.' Reluctant to make a move, Mickey kissed her and said goodnight.

Back in Hollywood, Norma pursued Mickey and was blunt about wanting to go to bed with him. If that was all there was to be to it, he saw no reason not to oblige and began visiting Norma during the filming of *Marie Antoinette* in the elaborate trailer built for her on the MGM lot. 'Her French boudoir,' commented Mickey, 'was appropriate for our liaison – lovemaking French style – with me sitting on the couch, my pants at my ankles and her on her knees. Here was the grand lady herself copulating with Andy Hardy.'

L.B. Mayer, who knew about the affair, hoped it would be short-lived, but it wasn't. He already had his hands full with *Photoplay*'s article about 'Hollywood's Unmarried Husbands and Wives', which cited Robert Taylor and Barbara Stanwyck and Clark Gable and Carole Lombard as living together without benefit of marriage. Having rushed both couples to the altar, Mayer did not need further scandal concerning America's favourite son, Andy Hardy, in bed with Irving Thalberg's widow. Mickey didn't care. He was enjoying himself with the passionate Norma. But soon enough, wealthy as she was, she became afraid that by offending Mayer she would no longer get the films she wanted. So she ended the affair and instead hopped into bed with gangster movie star George Raft.

Rooney was busy with his *Andy Hardy* movies in 1940, also teaming up once again with Garland in another musical, *Babes on Broadway*. Judy was having problems with her love life. She was crushed when bandleader Artie Shaw eloped with Lana Turner even though she had not been involved with Shaw – in fact he had no idea she felt anything for him. On the rebound and anxious to get away from her stage mother, Judy decided to marry composer David Rose, ten years older and a rather boring fellow. Mickey wanted to talk to her about it. It was common knowledge that Judy was in love with him but he didn't know how to approach the subject without getting himself in too deep, so he wished Judy well and left her house. In his autobiography he writes about what might have happened if he had married Judy and came to no conclusion. So she eloped with David Rose and was back on the set of *Babes on Broadway* 24 hours later.

In *Babes*, Mickey performed a production number, 'Bombshell from Brazil', dressed up like the bouncy Carmen Miranda in a long slit skirt, bolero blouse with falsies, a fruity headdress and platform shoes, wearing false eyelashes, heavy rouge and lipstick. While he was filming in this get-up, he was introduced to a new MGM player from North Carolina. It was her first day on the lot and she was taking a tour of the sound stages. Mickey introduced himself to her. She said hello. He couldn't take his eyes off this girl with the green eyes, chestnut-coloured hair, high firm breasts, tiny waist and long beautiful legs. He had seen many lovely starlets at MGM but none like her. He asked her out for dinner. She said she was busy. He was dumbfounded. Did she know he was Hollywood's biggest male star in drag?

While Mickey was having lunch in the commissary, the girl came in with press agent Milt Weiss. Les Peterson invited her to join Rooney and his friends. She declined. At that point he stood up and waved to her. 'Jesus,' she thought. 'He must have shrunk! Then I remembered the platform shoes he was wearing when I met him.'

Mickey called her every night to invite her to dinner and every night she politely turned him down. He pursued her at the studio with gifts and flowers, and dispatched emissaries with messages. Milt Weiss told her she should reconsider. 'No one is more famous than Mickey Rooney. Being seen with him would be a big boost to your career.'

When he called her again, she was friendlier, but again turned him down for dinner because she didn't want to leave her sister Bappie by herself.

'Bring her along!' he exclaimed.

That night they had dinner at Chasen's and danced at Ciro's. 'He's too short for me,' she thought. 'My God, the top of his head just reaches my shoulders.' When Mickey proposed marriage, her reply was, 'You must be crazy.'

Ava Lavinia Gardner was born near Smithfield, in Grabtown, North Carolina on 24 December 1922. The youngest of seven children born to a hard-drinking sharecropper and his religious wife, she lived in a white clapboard four-bedroom house on three hundred acres of tobacco land where Ava walked barefoot through the tobacco fields picking bugs off the plants, and rolled her first cigarette at the age of five. She was a lazy free spirit with no ambition, while her mother allowed her to date only occasionally and constantly preached the evils of sex.

When the Great Depression hit in 1929, tobacco prices tumbled and her father Jonas was forced to sell the Gardner home and property. They rented a boarding house in Newport, Virginia and, with Ava's help, her mother Molly cleaned the rooms and cooked meals. When Jonas died of a streptococcus infection, they moved back to North Carolina. 'Mama was so busy working,' Ava said, 'she didn't notice I was growing up.

Suddenly I had breasts and Mama didn't know what to do about it except to keep me away from boys. I wasn't allowed to wear make-up like the other girls. If I did have a date, Mama was waiting for me and chased him off if he tried to kiss me.'

Ava soon blossomed into a beautiful young woman with an exquisite figure. Her only glimmer of hope was sister Bappie who had married Larry Tarr, a photographer from New York City. In 1940 Bappie decided it was time for her little sister to get away from home for a few days. Tarr, impressed with Ava's beauty, took photographs of her and put one in his Fifth Avenue studio window. Barney Duhan, an errand boy for Metro-Goldwyn-Mayer, saw the photo and wanted to ask the beautiful girl for a date. Pretending to be a big shot from the studio, he called Tarr who said Ava had gone back to North Carolina, but he would send for her. A flustered Duhan said that would not be necessary, but to send some pictures of her to Marvin Schenck at MGM.

On Ava's next visit to New York, Tarr called the studio and spoke to talent scout Ben Jacobson who knew nothing about her but wanted to see the pictures anyway. He was so impressed that he asked Tarr to bring Ava to Metro's New York offices. He, in turn, called Ava's mother about bringing her back to New York for a screen test.

When Jacobson sent her 'silent' screen test to California, mogul Louis B. Mayer was intrigued, so she went to Hollywood and was tested again. 'Ahuhm Arvuh Gahdnah,' she said with a thick Southern accent. MGM producer George Sidney remarked, 'She can't act, she can't talk, but she's a terrific piece of merchandise.'

Ava's mother agreed to allow her eighteen-year-old daughter to go to California provided she was chaperoned by her older sister, Bappie. Hollywood was not as glamorous as Ava expected but she nevertheless signed a seven-year contract with MGM for fifty dollars a week, and began elocution lessons with Metro's renowned voice coach, Lillian Burns.

A few days later she met Mickey. He took control of her personal life, driving her to and from the studio every day. These short trips were vaudeville shows. He entertained her with gossip and funny stories, and Ava began to find him rather amusing. Mickey took her to premieres and gave her the spotlight, but she gave him neither her heart nor her body. Surprisingly, he didn't date anyone else at the same time, but this treatment left him very frustrated. On one occasion he decided that being chauffeured in his Lincoln would free both his hands, but Ava held him off and slammed the car door in his face.

L.B. Mayer was growing uneasy. He told publicity chief Howard Strickling, 'I know Rooney all too well. All he wants to do is get into her pants.'

'He'll marry her to do it.'

'That kid's got me by the balls. His teenage fans won't like it if he gets married. Andy Hardy is worth millions. If Gardner would give him what he wants, we'd have no worries. Suppose . . .'

'Forget it,' Strickling interrupted. 'Ava wouldn't go to bed with him if you threatened to cancel her contract.'

'That's what I said. They *both* have me by the balls.'

By November 1941 Ava was no longer avoiding Mickey's marriage proposals, because he had won over Bappie. Finally she said yes, but he had to get permission from L.B. Mayer, the greatest actor at the studio. 'You're breaking my heart, Mickey,' he sobbed.

'I'm in love,' Rooney choked, tears running down his face.

Mayer cried and Mickey cried. Their sobs could be heard in the outer office where Ava was waiting.

'I can't prevent you from getting married,' Mayer said calmly, 'but you'll do it my way, Mickey – quietly and without fanfare. Les Peterson will handle everything. He'll get the marriage licence, find a church and accompany you on your honeymoon sometime in January. I'll let you know when.'

Ava wanted to wear a white gown and walk down the church aisle. 'That's for everybody else,' Mickey said. 'It can't be that way for us, honey. You wouldn't want a circus of fans and reporters spoiling our wedding day, would you?'

Mayer hosted a bachelor party for Rooney, a luncheon at MGM, with Clark Gable, Robert Taylor, Spencer Tracy, Lewis Stone, Lionel Barrymore and Jackie Cooper among the guests. Taylor's advice was to go easy and not sprain his back. Gable suggested nibbling on the ear. Spencer Tracy told the story about the sink and the marbles. 'You'll never have a year like the first,' he said. 'Every time you make love to her then, you put a marble in the sink. After that, every time you make love to her, take a marble out. You'll never empty the sink, Mickey.'

Ava didn't have the money for a trousseau so MGM gave her a small bonus to buy a sheer long white nightgown, matching slippers, a simple dark blue tailored suit and shoes. Very early on Sunday, 10 January 1942, Ava, Mickey and Les Peterson drove north towards Santa Barbara. Squeezed into a second car were Mickey's parents, Bappie and an MGM photographer. At 11:00 a.m. they were married at a little Presbyterian church tucked under the foothills of the Santa Ynez Mountains.

After the ceremony, Peterson rushed to a phone and called Howard Strickling before accompanying the newlyweds to the Del Monte Hotel in Carmel. Ava was terrified – she was about to engage in the act that her mother had scorned and ridiculed. Mickey was so nervous he put his pyjamas on backwards. But their wedding night was mutually satisfying. The groom was thrilled that his bride was a virgin and she found sex exhilarating. The next morning she was warm and receptive. 'Beautiful morning, darling,' she cooed.

'Yeah,' he said, hopping out of bed. 'Perfect for golf.'

A new set of irons was part of Mickey's trousseau. In a daze, Ava tagged along with him and the MGM photographer to the golf course. 'On my honeymoon I saw more of Les Peterson than I did of my husband,' Ava said. 'He was in the dining room for breakfast, lunch and dinner. Everywhere but the bedroom.'

The Rooneys moved into an apartment in Wilshire Palms near Westwood and Ava settled down. When she came home after a day at the studio, she would kick off her shoes and prepare dinner. When Mickey arrived, he would change his shoes and prepare for a night on the town. If Ava wasn't in the mood to go out, he went alone. When she agreed to party with him, he was jealous of any man who danced with her. Why didn't he make up his mind, she wanted to know. When she sat on the sidelines he complained and when she didn't he still complained.

Two months into the marriage, Ava was rushed to hospital with an inflamed appendix. 'Mickey rushed in and out bearing gifts and books and spraying kisses,' she wrote in her memoirs. 'Then I came home, happy and contented and, God almighty, it was clear to me he'd been entertaining girls in my bathroom and bed. My bathroom! My bed!' One year and five days after their marriage began, it was finished. 'It didn't work,' Ava said, 'and the main reason was Mickey's inevitable philandering.' Though she was entitled to half of everything he owned, Mayer convinced Ava to ask for only $25,000. In return, they would advance her career. He kept his promise: Ava became a star in *Whistle Stop* with George Raft and *The Killers* with Burt Lancaster.

The divorce decree was granted on 21 May 1943, but they dated occasionally, ending up in bed where they got along very well. So well, in fact, that Mickey began stalking Ava and eventually tried to break down her door. She called MGM, and Mayer rushed Mickey into *A Yank at Eton*, to be filmed in Connecticut.

*

Despite the Second World War, Mickey's marriage and divorce, the *Andy Hardy* series continued: *Andy Hardy Meets Debutante* with Judy Garland, *Andy Hardy's Private Secretary* with Kathryn Grayson, *Life Begins for Andy Hardy* again with Judy, and *The Courtship of Andy Hardy* with Donna Reed.

Andy Hardy's Double Life with Esther Williams was the beginning of the end for Andy. The *New York Times* critic said, 'The quality of the Hardy films seems to be on an obvious decline. Mickey Rooney seems bored with Andy, as well as he might be, and Lewis Stone acts weary of playing his patient, long-suffering dad . . . The ageless juvenility of Mr. Rooney as Andy is beginning to wear.'

During his marriage, critics did not refer to Mickey's personal life, but said he was a 'strutting Andy Hardy and hoped he would get his comeuppance'.

The Human Comedy, though, was an excellent film in which Mickey played a small-town messenger boy whose brother is killed in action. He is the first to see the telegram informing the family and doesn't want to go home with the news. Based on a story by William Saroyan, the movie touched the hearts of audiences in 1943 when Americans needed strength and courage. That servicemen must pay the ultimate price for peace in the world is a subject hard to deal with if your brother is part of that sacrifice, and Rooney is superb as the confused young man trying to cope with his loss. He was nominated for an Oscar for the film but lost to Paul Lucas in *Watch on the Rhine*.

Mickey was now 23 but still youthful enough to make *Andy Hardy's Blonde Trouble*. The *New York Times* liked the film but concluded, '. . . it's safe to say we'll have Mickey Rooney in college now for the next eight years.' But he was philosophical about it, because he was slated to co-star again with Judy in the musical smash *Girl Crazy*, featuring such songs as 'Embraceable You', 'Rockabye Baby', 'Fascinating Rhythm', 'But Not for Me', 'Girl Crazy', 'I've Got a Crush on You', and 'Biding my Time'.

This time the *New York Times* raved, 'Hold your hats, folks! Mickey Rooney and Judy Garland are back in town. And if at this late date there are still a few die-hards who deny they are the most incorrigibly talented pair of youngsters in' movies then "Girl Crazy" should serve as the final rebuttal . . . If that Rooney boy isn't careful he may possibly find himself President someday.' Critics thought Judy had outgrown her adolescence graciously and sang with an appealing sincerity that was irresistible. But actually Judy was going through difficult times. Her marriage to David Rose ended when she was forced to abort their baby. Then she began a love affair with the handsome, bisexual and married Tyrone Power. His reluctance to ask for a divorce took its toll on Judy, who began drinking and taking pills during *Girl Crazy*.

Mickey tried to help her with encouraging words and they finished the picture, but Rooney was under pressure himself because he had received his draft notice. L.B. Mayer was equally concerned and set about keeping Andy Hardy out of uniform by claiming that Mickey could do more for the war effort in films. He was irreplaceable, Mayer said, and quoted Lt. General Dwight D. Eisenhower's statement that 'Motion picture entertainment is as important to the people on the home front as butter and meat.' Mayer refused to give up until his appeals to the draft board made the newspapers. His attempt at Mickey's deferment was bad publicity at a time when American men were either being drafted or volunteering for duty. Rooney was allowed to make one last film, *National Velvet* with Elizabeth Taylor, before going into the Army. The night before reporting for duty, he went out with Ava and she promised to wait for him.

On 25 June 1943 Rooney reported to Fort Riley, Texas as a buck private. Whenever he phoned Ava, her sister said she wasn't available and his daily letters went unanswered. Tired of his phone calls at all hours of the night, Ava finally called him. When he heard her voice, he was in heaven – until she told him to stop writing and calling. It was over between them. Mickey cracked when he read in the newspaper that Ava was dating billionaire Howard Hughes. According to author Roland Flamini in his book *Ava*, Mickey wept, and for the first time in his life began to drink heavily. Desperate, he went AWOL to fly to Los Angeles where the military police were waiting at the airport to take him back to Texas. MGM's Howard Strickling managed to keep the incident out of the newspapers. Even in Mickey's autobiography he mentions flying to Los Angeles to see his mother but says nothing about going AWOL.

Because of his star status, Rooney was assigned to Special Services to entertain American servicemen overseas. Now stationed at Camp Sibert, Alabama, he was invited to attend the premiere of *National Velvet* in Birmingham. At a party afterwards, Mickey had more than a few drinks and was inebriated when he was introduced to seventeen-year-old Betty Jane Rase, Miss Birmingham for 1944. He proposed marriage that night and on 30 September, they tied the knot. Mickey had known his bride only a week before he sailed for Europe to entertain the troops. In July 1945 Betty Jane gave birth to Mickey Rooney Jr, who weighed six pounds and seven ounces.

On 15 February 1946, General Eisenhower gave Mickey the Bronze Star for 'exceptional courage in the performance of his duties as an entertainer

. . . His superb personal contribution to the morale of the Armed Forces in the European Theater of Operations cannot be measured.' Three days later Rooney was on his way to Fort Dix in New Jersey, where he was processed for discharge. On 9 March he stepped off the plane in Los Angeles where his mother and wife were waiting. 'Good God,' he thought, 'is that Betty Jane? Jesus, she's a few inches taller!' His advice to short men was not to marry a teenager until she was full grown.

Mickey was 26 now, but MGM still put him in *Love Laughs at Andy Hardy*. Moviegoers were happy to have the Hardy family back, but with the changing cultural climate of postwar America, it was time for Andy and the gang to call it quits. *Summer Holiday*, a remake of *Ah, Wilderness*, was Rooney's first flop, though he got good reviews as a boxer in *Killer McCoy*. The *New York Times* wrote, '. . . whatever one may think of him [Rooney] as a prizefighter, he is a wonderful little actor, whether doing a dance routine, fighting, displaying anguish upon hearing of the death of his dear mother, consoling the wife of the opponent his blows killed or passing wisecracks at a lunch counter waitress.'

But Rooney was miscast as composer Lorenz Hart in *Words and Music*. Bosley Crowther of the *New York Times* was brutal:

> As played by Mr. Rooney, this deterioration of Mr. Hart deserves some sort of recognition as the year's prize grotesquery. From a bouncing, explosive little fellow who seems to drive everyone a little nuts, Mr. Rooney suddenly slips into a grim, melancholic vein, for no other apparent reason than that he has been jilted by a girl whose only objection seems to be that he is a runt. And his florid flings at gay abandon, his puff-eyed pleas for sympathy and his final groping trek from the hospital to the theater are among the most horribly inadequate and embarrassing this reviewer has ever watched.

Judy Garland performed several songs with Mickey in *Words and Music*, but they failed to register. The pair weren't kids any longer. Judy, now married to director Vincente Minnelli and mother of Liza, was going through postnatal depression and abusing amphetamines. Mickey was drinking too much and was frequently late for work. He took out his unhappiness on pregnant Betty Jane, who went home to her mother in Birmingham for the birth of Timmy in January 1947. A year and a half later they were divorced.

Rooney and MGM got a divorce, too. When Louis B. Mayer turned down his request to do an *Andy Hardy* radio series with his own production company, Mickey almost got into a fistfight with his boss, though he admitted later that his ego had got the best of him. He was, after all, giving up a salary of $5000 a week and his pension for $49,000 a year. Tension filled the air at MGM when Dore Schary became head of production, easing Mayer out. According to Mickey he told Schary to go fuck himself.

In January 1949 Rooney was introduced to 24-year-old actress Martha Vickers, who had made a name for herself in *The Big Sleep* with Humphrey Bogart and Lauren Bacall. Martha, who was in the process of getting a divorce from Hollywood press agent A.C. Lyles Jr, was level headed, bright, a good listener, beautiful – and the same height as Mickey. She told a friend, 'I had always been a fan of the Andy Hardy series, and was impressed that Mickey was actually modest and not noisy and all over the place as some people said. He was very intelligent and quiet . . .'

Mickey called her the next day for a date and she invited him to dinner with her family at their house in the Valley. In return, he asked them to a homemade duck dinner at his apartment in Laurel Canyon. After that, he and Martha went everywhere together, except to bed right away. In April, Mickey gave her an engagement ring. He wanted to elope to Las Vegas. But Martha preferred a church wedding, so they were married at the Christ Memorial Unity Church in North Hollywood on 3 June. During the champagne reception held at the church Mickey said, 'If I don't make this one last, there's something wrong with me.'

The newlyweds moved into a small bungalow in Encino – Mickey was short of cash these days due to gambling losses and lack of work. The movies he did make, such as *Quicksand* and *The Big Wheel*, were forgettable. In *The Fireball*, he played an orphan who becomes a professional roller skater. The *New York Times* commented, 'Never let it be said that Mickey Rooney doesn't try . . . Mr. Rooney is the whole show, seems completely aware of it, and does everything but chew the camera to prove it.'

Mickey tried hard at everything but marriage. Soon up to his old tricks again, he was rarely home with Martha who was pregnant and drinking too much. Fed up with making movies, he told her, 'Maybe I'll get out of the business.'

'Why don't you?' she smiled. 'You could always get a job as a milkman or something like that.'

Mickey walked out in a huff and was nowhere to be found when Martha gave birth to Teddy on 13 April 1950. When he finally showed up at Valley Hospital he vowed to make his marriage work. Besides, he had nothing else to do these days. The fans, reporters and photographers who used to chase him everywhere were now ignoring him.

Then came a ray of hope. He was asked by the Academy of Arts and Sciences to present an Oscar at the 1951 awards. He was already putting on his tuxedo when he got a call from Johnny Green, the Academy musical conductor, telling him not to attend because he had been married too often and had a bad reputation. Andy Hardy sat down and cried.

Mickey was never out of work, but he spent more than he earned. Like so many MGM players, he had no conception of money: it was always there, and more was always coming in.

On 31 August 1951 Martha filed for divorce. On the stand she said, 'Mickey had a bad temper. He seemed to look for reasons all the time to pick a fight – simply for an excuse to leave the house. He spent most of our married life away from home. And it was the worst when I was expecting a child. Many times he would get in an argument and say he wanted a divorce or wanted me to leave him, and would storm out of the house – and I'd not see him for three or four or five days. Then he'd just wander into the house like nothing happened at all and ask for his dinner or something . . . He was extremely abusive and sometimes drinking.'

Martha threw away the high heels that Mickey insisted she wear in order to look taller than he was. Strange that he didn't want her in the flats she preferred.

Already behind in his alimony payments to Betty Jane, he had a difficult time paying Martha. Then the IRS knocked on his door, claiming he owed $35,000 in back taxes. Plagued by insomnia and depression, he called his actor friend Sig Frolich. 'I gotta get out of town,' Mickey exclaimed. 'We're going to Houston. We can hide out at the Shamrock Hotel.' Ironically, the year before, Ava Gardner's affair with the married Frank Sinatra had been exposed when she went with him to the opening at the Shamrock. On 7 November 1951 she and Frank were married.

Mickey arrived in Houston with his friend and a cache of barbiturates. He gulped them down, but never enough at one time to kill him – just enough to sleep, then wake up and take another dose. Two weeks later he told Sig, 'I've had enough sleep. Let's go home.'

Mickey tried a comeback at MGM in 1951, earning a meagre $25,000 in *The Strip*, a terrible B movie. Since Dore Schary was not enthusiastic about Rooney, he then signed a three-picture deal with Columbia for $75,000 a picture.

Mickey swore off marriage and a string of affairs followed, including one with stripper Tempest Storm in 1952. He made a down payment on a full-length mink coat, which was more than Elvis Presley gave her five years later for hours of bliss. Only Tempest knows whether Mickey kept up the payments on the coat or if it was repossessed.

He claimed he would have married her if he hadn't met tall 23-year-old redhead Elaine Mahnken, a nude model, at the Woodland Hills driving range. He made his approach by offering to teach her how to hit the ball. Elaine was working as a carhop at a drive-in restaurant until she could get an acting job. According to her, Mickey knew far more about her than she did about him. 'I certainly didn't know he was in any kind of financial trouble. While we were dating, he used to drive me down Tarzana Boulevard and say to me as he pointed out the window, "I own this side of the street and I own that side of the street." It sounded as if he owned half of the San Fernando Valley. Not that that had anything to do with my feelings about him, but he did act the big shot for my benefit.'

True to form, Mickey proposed to her every day for a month until she said yes. Before Elaine could change her mind, he chartered a plane for Las Vegas and they were married at the Wee Kirk of the Heather Wedding Chapel on 15 November 1952 at 1:00 a.m. It happened so fast Mickey didn't have time to buy Elaine a wedding ring, so they borrowed one. When the couple settled down at Rooney's house in Woodland Hills he bought her diamond wedding and engagement rings. The jeweller came to repossess the rings when Mickey failed to make a down payment, but he managed to convince the debt collector that they would be paid for over time, and he kept his word.

Elaine, her ex-husband Dan Ducich already deeply in debt to the Vegas mob, was concerned about Mickey's gambling. In 1954 Dan called her for money in desperation, but Mickey refused to help. A few months later Ducich was found on the street in downtown Las Vegas with a bullet in his head. According to Rooney, the devastated Elaine blamed him for her former husband's death, but she denied this to Arthur Marx, author of *The Nine Lives of Mickey Rooney*: 'If Mickey was unhappy with me that early in the marriage, he'd have to have been a fool to stay with me for the next seven years . . . Personally, I think Mickey should have considered himself lucky to have somebody like me who was interested in making a nice home for him, who cared about him, who cared about his animals, who cared about the family, and tried to pay the bills.'

In 1952 Rooney made *A Slight Case of Larceny* with Eddie Bracken for MGM. It was a humorous film about two old army buddies who buy a gas station and do very well until a large oil company opens up across the street. This prompts the boys to siphon gas from the pipeline leading to their competitor's hoses.

Mickey's career got back on track when Maurice Duke offered to manage him. A professional harmonica player, Duke had known Mickey for several years and considered him one of the best actors in Hollywood. James Michener's *The Bridges of Toko-Ri* was the turning point for Rooney. In the film he plays a helicopter pilot who rescues downed fliers during the Korean War. The part of the cocky Irishman who always wears a green derby hat seemed made for Mickey, and the critics agreed. The film had a big budget and an all-star cast including William Holden, Grace Kelly and Fredric March. Many of his scenes are with Holden, whose plane goes down at the end. Mickey attempts to save him but they are both gunned down and die in a Korean ditch. This was the adult Rooney, the funny Rooney, the talented Rooney emerging at last. Rumour had it that Mickey narrowly missed out on an Academy Award nomination for *Bridges*.

Rooney had already tried to get his own show on television, but two pilots failed. In a third attempt, he played a network pageboy trying to work his way upstairs. His weekly salary was $3500. *Hey, Mulligan* made its debut on Saturday, 4 September 1954 at 8:00 p.m. on NBC, opposite the very popular Jackie Gleason in *The Honeymooners* on CBS, which got a 49 rating to Mickey's seven. But Gleason liked Rooney and watched his show when he wasn't on the air himself. On his 38th birthday Mickey was staying at the Essex House in New York. At about 7:30 p.m., two beautiful girls knocked on his door and announced, 'We're your birthday presents, Mr. Rooney. Jackie Gleason sent us.'

Even though the ratings for *Hey, Mulligan* were low, it might have stayed on the air if Mickey had used his head. But when he was successful he got too cocky and one doesn't do that with a sponsor. He was invited to a golf tournament by the Pillsbury Flour Company in Le Sueur, Minnesota. Peter Jurow, president of the company, pointed out the cities where its sales needed help. 'You can stay with us forever, Mickey, if you can pick up the sales where we're weak.' But Rooney answered, 'Hey, that's not my job. You hired me as an actor!'

Then, on the golf course, he left the Pillsbury president because he was playing too slowly. 'I have a stomach ache,' Mickey lied, walking off the course. He might still have saved himself that night at a gala celebration at the Pillsbury mansion if Jurow hadn't approached Mickey with, 'Hey, Charlie, it's time to go into your act.'

'What act? And my name's not Charlie. It's Mickey Rooney!'

'We want you to sing and dance for us.'

'I don't feel up to it right now.'

'What do you mean you don't feel up to it? We own you.'

'You don't own anybody, pal.' Then he turned to Maurice Duke and said, 'Let's get out of here. I can't stand this bunch of crows for another minute!'

Pillsbury soon dropped its sponsorship of *Hey, Mulligan*, and the show ended its TV run on 7 June 1955.

Mickey's inborn temper escalated while he was being weaned off barbiturates. Elaine stayed with him during his battle with drugs and his womanising, which she knew all about. On one occasion, when he openly flirted with a girl at a party and slipped her a piece of paper with his phone number on it, Elaine slapped him hard across the mouth. Unlike his other wives, she saved her allowance, putting a down payment on a cabin at Lake Arrowhead. But Mickey didn't like the country life. He stayed in Hollywood and fell in love with Barbara Ann Thomason, a 21-year-old blonde starlet.

Elaine didn't care. She was seeing someone else, too, and asked Mickey for a divorce. He wanted to have an open marriage and gave her a fur coat worth $4500, the same one he had given Barbara. But Elaine was too sensible for such an arrangement. On 15 June 1958 they separated officially and he moved into a rented house with Barbara in Sherman Oaks. On 12 August, she took an overdose of sleeping pills and accused Mickey of throwing her into the pool to bring her around, but she had to recant her story when Mickey proved he had been at a party when the incident happened. They continued to live together despite numerous quarrels and misunderstandings.

He tried to reconcile with Elaine, but she went ahead and obtained an interlocutory decree of divorce on 21 May 1959. She was awarded the houses, $50,000 in cash and $1750 monthly for ten years. Rooney kept up with this financial arrangement for a year because he now had a wife and baby to support. On 1 December 1958 he married Barbara Thomason in Mexico, claiming he had divorced Elaine there in May. On 13 September 1959 Barbara gave birth to a six pound ten ounce baby girl, Kelly Ann.

*

Mickey's career had become a seesaw. In 1956 the Academy nominated him for Best Supporting Actor in *The Bold and the Brave*, the story of three GIs in Italy during the Second World War. He was especially good in the dice game scene where he bets $30,000 under a blanket during an air raid. However, Anthony Quinn won the award for *Lust for Life*. Two years later Mickey made the awful *Andy Hardy Comes Home*, in which Andy's grown up now and visits his hometown of Carvel with his wife and kids. But no one cared very much about Andy any more. He also acted in *The Comedian* on the TV drama series *Playhouse 90*, receiving an Emmy nomination. He didn't win, but Mickey said that suddenly everybody had decided he could act. He played Las Vegas too, and made good money, but gambled it away.

On 1 December 1959 Mickey, after having too many martinis, made a fool of himself on the *Tonight Show*. The host, Jack Paar, became bored with Mickey's endless promotion of his tyre business and to relieve the tedium asked, 'What kind of a woman was Ava?'

'Ava,' replied Mickey, leaning over close to Paar, 'Ava's more of a woman than you'll ever know.'

'Have you ever watched the *Tonight Show*?'

'No,' Rooney hissed.

'Are you enjoying my show tonight?'

'Not necessarily.'

'Then would you care to leave?'

When the audience applauded, Mickey got up from the guest chair and left. Paar later said, 'That was the only time I ever got a hangover from just listening. It's a shame. He was a great talent.'

The next day Rooney met with Paar and apologised. 'I'm sorry I was drunk,' he said.

Mickey then played a Japanese photographer in Truman Capote's *Breakfast at Tiffany's* with Audrey Hepburn. The *New York Times* said, 'Mickey Rooney's buck-toothed Myopic Japanese is broadly exotic.' But who else could have played the part of Mr. Yunioshi with such sincerity and humour? One wonders why Mickey was ashamed of doing it, unless, like Spencer Tracy, he felt it was beneath him to wear heavy make-up and false teeth.

In *Requiem for a Heavyweight* with Jackie Gleason and Anthony Quinn, Rooney was superb as the prizefight trainer. This time the *New York Times* wrote, 'Mickey Rooney's delineation of the trainer is equally restrained, and while he does not have Mr. Gleason's opportunities, he too is sad, defeated and sentimental without being lachrymose.' Mickey was proud of this movie, but complained about *It's a Mad, Mad, Mad, Mad World*, which started production in Palm Springs on 26 April 1962. Again one has to wonder why he was unhappy – unless it had to do with the fact that he was only one of 29 comedians in the film. But he accepted the meagre $125,000 fee because he needed the money. With so much competition, it was hard for Mickey to steal the show, but he was very funny with his sidekick Buddy Hackett, trying to find the buried loot that everyone in the story is looking for with such hilarious zeal. *It's a Mad, Mad, Mad, Mad World* stands up today as one of the funniest movies ever made.

Shortly after finishing *Mad World*, Mickey declared bankruptcy, with debts amounting to approximately $500,000. Newspapers had a field day, asking, 'How did Mickey blow $12 million?' He explained that alimony alone had cost him $5 million.

By now Mickey had three children with Barbara – Kelly Ann, Kerry Yule and Michael Joseph – one baby a year. But he continued to have flings. What did women see in him? 'What is an orgasm, after all, except laughter of the loins?' he wrote in his memoirs. Barbara, like all of his wives, knew he had affairs with other woman when he was away from home so she insisted on going with him to Yugoslavia for *The Secret Invasion*, even though she was eight months pregnant. On 13 September 1963, Barbara gave birth to their fourth child, Kimmy Sue.

Rooney tried his luck on television with a new show, *Mickey*, which made its debut on 24 September 1964 and ended on 13 January 1965. Mickey claimed the show was not renewed because one of the public's favourite actors in the series, Sammee Tong, committed suicide in October 1964; his character, Sammee Ling, had been so popular that ABC cancelled the show. But Mickey was confident about his future on television and bought a new house in the exclusive area of Brentwood for $135,000 a few days before he declared bankruptcy. The house had been reduced from $200,000; the previous occupants had died in freak accidents and it was now considered bad luck.

Among Rooney's friends was handsome French star Alain Delon, who now introduced him to his frequent stand-in, Milos Milocevic. Mickey offered to help Milos get into films, hiring him as chauffeur and flunky until he could find work. Milos was of great help around the house when Mickey performed in a revival of *A Funny Thing Happened on the Way to the*

Forum at the Valley Music Theater in Woodland Hills. With standing ovations and top reviews, Mickey felt like his old self again.

In October 1965 Rooney flew to the Philippines to make a war movie, *Ambush Bay* with Hugh O'Brian. Before leaving for the airport he shook Milos's hand and said, 'Take good care of my wife while I'm gone.' When Mickey was playing a marine trying to escape the Japanese in the Philippines, Milos was given a small part in *The Russians are Coming, the Russians are Coming* which was being filmed in Fort Bragg, California. Barbara went with him and a torrid love affair between them began. When Mickey came home he suspected something and confronted Barbara, who admitted she was in love with Milos. On 11 December the Rooneys separated officially, and Milos moved in with Barbara and her four children in Mickey's Brentwood house.

Rooney opened with a one-man show at the Latin Quarter in New York on 28 December. He sang, danced and told jokes. When he returned to Los Angeles on 20 January, he checked into St. John's Hospital in Santa Monica where he was diagnosed with a rare blood disease he had picked up in the Philippines. From his hospital bed he filed for divorce on 29 January, asking for custody of his four children. Barbara went into a panic over losing her kids and considered going back to Mickey. Milos meanwhile told her best friend Margie Lane, 'If Barbara even looks at another man, I'll shoot her and myself.'

Unaware of this threat, Barbara made plans to visit Mickey in hospital to discuss the fate of their children. Afraid that she would be reconciled with Mickey, Milos attached a microphone to her bra and arranged for a private detective to record the conversation in the next room. Mickey talked with Barbara for an hour. In tears, and forgetting she was wearing a microphone, she blurted out her desire to save their marriage and promised never to see Milos again. Margie Lane had dinner with Barbara and Milos that evening. 'I had been with her the night before. At this point she had asked Milos to leave, otherwise she would lose her children. He refused and she didn't know what to do about it.' They finished dinner and returned home around 8:30. Margie and Barbara were to meet the next day and try to find a way to work things out.

The following morning, 31 January 1966, Wilma Catania, who was staying in the guesthouse, became suspicious when she knocked on Barbara's bedroom door and got no answer. She and the maid prised open the locked door and found the dead bodies of Barbara and Milos. She lay face up with a bullet hole in her jaw; he was on his stomach, dead from a bullet wound in his temple. Next to his body was Mickey's chrome-plated .38 calibre revolver. The police determined that it was a simple case of murder–suicide.

Mickey was getting ready to check out of the hospital when he heard the news. 'No, no. God, no. My poor four babies . . . my poor little girl Barbara,' he sobbed before collapsing. The children were taken to their grandmother's house and Mickey stayed in hospital overnight. Weighing less than a hundred pounds, he was a shell of a man at Barbara's funeral on 5 February at Forest Lawn Cemetery in Glendale.

Mickey gathered his children together and rented a house in Beverly Hills. Still haunted by thoughts of Barbara's murder, wondering how to sell the Brentwood house that seemed plagued with bad luck and trying to pay his bills, Mickey now had to cope with his mother's death, ten days after Barbara's. Drugged out and needing help with a household of kids, he became dependent on 45-year-old Margie, who was willing to come to his assistance. On 10 September she and Mickey were married in Las Vegas. 'Aunt Margie' took care of the children, hired and fired the household help, and did the shopping, managing all this despite moving three times before December when she came down with the flu. 'I didn't want Mickey to catch it,' she said, 'so I moved to my girlfriend's house to recuperate.' He didn't want her back so she filed for divorce on Christmas Eve. Lawyers on both sides argued for a long time before they agreed on a settlement of $350 weekly alimony for Margie. The divorce would not become final until December 1969.

Whatever Mickey was offered in the way of work, he now accepted. He did stage shows and appeared as a guest on television. And he made some bad investments.

How To Stuff A Wild Bikini, released in January 1966 and starring Frankie Avalon and Annette Funicello, was one of the worst 'beach' pictures ever made. The *Times* said, 'Never mind how to stuff a bikini. Get yourself a pelican, stay home with it, and watch TV.' Mickey made the film for only $5000. His new agent, Bullets Durgom, told him he couldn't work for him if he appeared in such bad pictures.

'I needed the money,' Mickey said.

'I'd rather loan it to you!' Durgom exclaimed.

Mickey stayed in touch with Judy Garland, who was struggling to survive mentally, physically and financially. Both were on drugs, but Mickey was doing his best to come off them. It would take ten years. As for the talented Judy, she took one too many sleeping pills by mistake while she was in London and died on 22 June 1969, her husband finding her slumped over on the toilet. Mickey heard about it when he was playing golf and dropped to his knees crying, 'Why, Judy, why?' When he went to the funeral at Campbell's Funeral Home in New York City, he slipped in the back entrance, but decided not to view the casket and left again quietly.

While Mickey was waiting for his divorce decree from Margie, he met 25-year-old Carolyn Hackett, a tall, attractive blonde secretary from Beverly Hills. She was divorced with a three-year-old son, James. Mickey married Carolyn in Mexico on 12 April 1969 and again in Las Vegas on 28 May. Because his divorce wasn't to be finalised until December, neither marriage was legal in California. One joke that went around was, 'Mickey Rooney's been married so many times he has rice marks on his face.' He could take the heckling, but being an actor out of work in a town called Hollywood was finally getting to him. He and Carolyn moved to Ft. Lauderdale, Florida, with her son.

Actor Eddie Bracken, who had played in *A Slight Case of Larceny* with Mickey in 1953, asked Mickey if he'd like to play the lead in a play called *Three Goats and a Blanket* at the Coconut Grove Theater. The part might have been written with Rooney in mind. It was a comedy about alimony, a modern spin on the ancient legal custom of awarding 'three goats and a blanket' to a wife who was no longer wanted. Mickey played a TV producer who can't afford to pay alimony, so his ex-wife allows him to sleep on a cot in her living room until he finds a job. Rooney and Bracken toured all over the country with the play.

Mickey went to court to get custody of his and Barbara's four children, who were now living with her parents. But the judge decided this arrangement should remain and, in the end, Mickey agreed that it had been for the best, because the four turned out very well. In any case, Carolyn gave birth to a daughter, Jonell on 11 January 1970.

Mickey continued to make movies, all of them bad until he appeared in Jack Haley Jr's *That's Entertainment*, hosted by a series of movie stars who introduced film clips of the great MGM musicals. The movie was very successful but it gave Mickey work for just one day, for which he earned the minimum wage of $385.

What kept Rooney going through these difficult years? How did he live through it all? He found Jesus Christ, that's how. He was sitting in the coffee shop at Harrah's in Lake Tahoe one day when a busboy came up behind him. 'Mr. Rooney?'

'Yes?' Mickey responded.

The busboy leaned over and whispered in his ear, 'Mr. Rooney, Jesus Christ loves you very much.'

Mickey described the busboy as having blond curly hair and a rosy complexion, and wearing a white jacket. He smiled and disappeared into the kitchen. Mickey tried to find him but was told no one fitting that description worked at the coffee shop. 'God,' he asked, 'who am I that you should send an angel to me? I, who have been paying so little attention?' He became a member of the Science of Mind Church and proclaimed, 'I live a Christian life.'

Mickey turned to agent Ruth Webb in 1971 when he discovered that it was she who had thought he'd be perfect for *Three Goats and a Blanket*. She displayed great faith in Mickey, setting out to improve his image and find him acting jobs worthy of his talent. 'We started with the dinner theaters,' she said. 'We were doing very well until he went home to Florida.' Carolyn had left him and filed for divorce in 1974. Mickey turned to Quaaludes, a popular new drug known for giving users both highs and lows. The effects hit Rooney on stage in Houston and he collapsed. Ruth Webb rushed to Texas, staying by his side while he suffered from hallucinations: 'I heard weird music and the cries of ghosts and banshees. I walked right up the walls that surrounded me,' he recalled. Felled again, Mickey did not know which way to turn, but Ruth was there for him. 'My house is your house,' she said.

Mickey left Houston and moved into Ruth's house in Hollywood Hills, where he slept on the couch. Everybody in Hollywood knew and loved Ruth, who shared her home with a live-in lover, her son, and her elderly mother, along with assorted animals and actors when in need. She introduced Mickey to a Christian Science healer who helped him through another difficult time. He appeared on *Hollywood Squares* and was a popular guest on TV talk shows, but he was now best known in show business as 'King of the Dinner Theater Circuit'.

Mickey continued to make one or two movies a year, none of them successful until Francis Ford Coppola asked him to play a former jockey who takes in a young runaway and his horse and teaches the boy to ride. The film was *The Black Stallion*, released in 1979, and Mickey was nominated for Best Supporting Actor. He lost the Oscar to Melvyn Douglas in *Being There*, but it didn't matter. He was back in the game.

While Rooney was living at Ruth Webb's house, his son Mickey Jr introduced him to 38-year-old country and western singer Jan Chamberlain. He described her as very blonde and very warm – in other words, Mickey was charmed by the lady. He moved in with Jan and her two children. A year later, on 28 July 1978, they were married in the Conejo Valley Church of Religious Science. They settled in a development called Red Sail, an island home in Westlake Village, thirty miles northwest of Hollywood.

In 1978 Mickey was offered a Broadway musical, *Sugar Babies*, an old-fashioned burlesque show. He called it a 'bullshit idea' and turned it down. Producer Harry Rigby was willing to guarantee him $5000 a week for 26 weeks, whether the show was a success or bombed. So, in March 1979, Mickey agreed to do the show, performing alongside dancer-actress and former MGM contract player, the still talented 56-year-old Ann Miller. They toured in five cities: San Francisco, Los Angeles, Chicago, Detroit and Philadelphia.

Sugar Babies was so popular that by the time it was set to open in New York City, advance ticket sales amounted to over $1 million. When the curtain went up at the Mark Hellinger Theater on 8 October 1979, the audience saw the back of a little man in an old brown coat and beaten-up top hat. He slowly turned around, whereupon the crowd stood up cheering and gave Mickey Rooney a 24-minute ovation. At the end, he and the cast took eight curtain calls. After the show, celebrities filled his dressing room and fans were at the stage door begging for autographs. But, like all opening nights on Broadway, there was the usual agonising wait for the reviews to come out early the next morning.

Walter Kerr at the *New York Times* said:

> The occasion is essentially a Rooney occasion (it seems to me extremely unlikely that anyone would have shaken the mothballs off sixty-year-old routines, and done them, throttle open and with all flags flying, without him) and the indefatigable Rooney is exactly as energetic, exactly as talented as he was when at the age of three or four, he rammed a cigar into his mouth, raked a derby over his brow, and made a star of himself. Which is very, very energetic, and even more talented.
>
> Liked Miss Miller, too, in stunning shape at whatever age she must be, ready to leap from a baggage cart, whip off gloves and overskirt, and tap as though there'd been no yesterday. And I had a grand time, thank you.

Clive Barnes at the *New York Post* raved, 'The show is solidly on the shoulders of Broadway's most promising newcomer, yes, oddly enough, it is a first for Mr. Rooney . . . He is the epitome of the clown. With his lopsided grin, his geriatrically boyish air, his warmth and total naturalness, Rooney is something to experience. Rooney is the true icing on *Sugar Babies*, a top banana if we ever had one.'

Time magazine wrote, 'Mickey Rooney has the grease paint in his blood and the house in his pocket.'

The *New Yorker* said about Mickey, 'His skills as a performer are greater than ever. I would have been content if the opening night at the Mark Hellinger had lasted until morning: when that prospect dimmed I resolved to make do with repeated visits to the production just as it stands.'

Newsweek wrote, 'Mickey is the heart, soul and body of the enterprise: not even eight tall wives have exhausted that heart, which for 57 years and 8 months has belonged to show business. As for the soul, only a boundless and rebounding one could have kept Mickey going through the professional and personal ups and downs that life and Louis B. Mayer devised for him. And it's all writ large in the small body: at five feet three inches, Mickey isn't short, he's just transcendentally truncated.'

Rex Reed said in the *Daily News*, 'Mickey Rooney and Ann Miller . . . knocked me senseless with their dazzle, turned their new home at the Mark Hellinger into New Year's Eve on Times Square, and sent show business soaring into orbit . . . if burlesque or even vaudeville were ever this good, then we were dumb losers to let it go.'

What a comeback, and deservedly so, for Mickey Rooney! He was already making $10,000 a week and when *Sugar Babies* proved successful, he signed for a percentage deal which made him about $30,000 a week. He was worth it. When he took time off for a vacation, the theatre was half-empty, proof that the show would not have been a hit without him.

In 1981, Mickey made *Bill*, a TV movie about a retarded old man who faces life after 46 years in an insane asylum. For this performance he received a Golden Globe Award, an Emmy and the Peabody Award for outstanding achievement on television.

On 30 August 1982, *Sugar Babies* closed after a three-year run, going on the road for another five years. 'I could hardly afford not to go,' Mickey said. 'In some cities like Chicago, I was knocking down fifty thousand dollars a week.'

*

In April 1983, the Academy of Arts and Sciences awarded Rooney a special Oscar for Lifelong Career Achievement. Bob Hope, the MC, referred to Mickey as 'the kid who illuminated all our yesterdays and the man who brightens all our todays'.

When *Sugar Babies* played London in 1989, Mickey called Ava and she invited him for dinner. He accepted, but stood her up because he was afraid to see her again. He was happy with Jan but even so had fantasised about Ava from time to time. 'I'd heard she was just as beautiful as she'd ever been,' he said, 'and I know she was twice as salty.' Ava had suffered a minor stroke in 1986; she had been in ill health ever since, and she died of pneumonia on 25 January 1990.

Mickey discovered there were problems with his health after he became a spokesman for Inside Track, an imaging technique that reveals problems with the heart. On 18 December 2000 Mickey tried out the device, and it showed he had a blocked artery. He chose to undergo multiple bypass surgery two days later at the Los Robles Regional Medical Center in Ventura County. Still spunky at eighty, he was released from hospital on Christmas Day. He told reporters he would return to work with Jan in their variety show *One Man – One Wife* in six weeks. 'We're booked solid,' he said. About his wife Mickey said, 'I love everything about her. She keeps me together.'

On 24 March 2003, Mickey Rooney attended the Academy Awards. MC Steve Martin told the audience, 'He was the biggest box-office star in all thirty-eight states.' Seated at the back, Mickey stood up and waved, and Martin told him, 'I'm sorry we couldn't get you a better seat but Vin Diesel is here.' Later Mickey and other past Oscar winners gathered together on stage and were introduced to a crowd that responded with a standing ovation.

Recently, Mickey was interviewed by Robert Osborne on the Turner Classic Movie channel. He spoke with great affection about Louis B. Mayer and showed a photo of them sitting together in a theatre. Mayer was listening, Mickey talking. Some things never change.

'Hollywood itself was once a fair lady under a pink parasol who blushed when a suitor approached. Now she's a painted old whore who can't wait for the gang bang to begin.'

– Mickey Rooney

The Films of Mickey Rooney

Orchids and Ermine (First National, 1927)
Emma (MGM, 1932)
The Beast of the City (MGM, 1932)
Sin's Pay Day (Mayfair, 1932)
High Speed (Columbia, 1932)
Officer Thirteen (Allied, 1932)
Fast Companions (Universal, 1932)
My Pal, the King (Universal, 1932)
The Big Cage (Universal, 1933)
The Life of Jimmy Dolan (Warner Brothers, 1933)
The Big Chance (Eagle Pictures, 1933)
Broadway to Hollywood (MGM, 1933)
The World Changes (Warner Brothers, 1933)
The Chief (MGM, 1933)
Beloved (Universal, 1934)
I Like It That Way(Universal, 1934)
Love Birds (Universal, 1934)
Half A Sinner(Universal, 1934)
The Lost Jungle (Mascot, 1934)
Manhattan Melodrama (MGM, 1934)
Upperworld (Warner Brothers, 1934)
Hide-Out (MGM, 1934)
Chained (MGM, 1934)
Blind Date (Columbia, 1934)
Death On The Diamond (MGM, 1934)
The County Chairman (Fox, 1935)
Reckless (MGM, 1935)

The Healer (Monogram,1935)
A Midsummer Night's Dream (Warner Brothers, 1935)
Ah, Wilderness (MGM, 1935)
Riffraff (MGM, 1935)
Little Lord Fauntleroy (Selznick/United Artists, 1936)
The Devil Is a Sissy (MGM, 1936)
Down the Stretch (Warner's, 1936)
Captains Courageous (MGM, 1937)
Slave Ship (20th Century-Fox, 1937)
A Family Affair (MGM, 1937)
Hoosier Schoolboy (Monogram, 1937)
Live, Love and Learn (MGM, 1937)
Thoroughbreds Don't Cry (MGM, 1937)
You're Only Young Once (MGM, 1938)
Love Is a Headache (MGM, 1938)
Judge Hardy's Children (MGM, 1938)
Hold That Kiss (MGM, 1938)
Lord Jeff (MGM, 1938)
Love Finds Andy Hardy (MGM, 1938)
Boys' Town (MGM, 1938)
Stablemates (MGM, 1938)
Out West With the Hardys (MGM, 1938)
The Adventures of Huckleberry Finn (MGM, 1939)
The Hardys Ride High (MGM, 1939)
Andy Hardy Gets Spring Fever (MGM, 1939)
Babes in Arms (MGM, 1939)
Judge Hardy and Son (MGM, 1939)
Young Tom Edison (MGM, 1940)
Andy Hardy Meets Debutante (MGM, 1940)
Strike Up the Band (MGM, 1940)
Andy Hardy's Private Secretary (MGM, 1941)
Men of Boys Town (MGM, 1941)
Life Begins For Andy Hardy (MGM 1941)
Babes On Broadway (MGM, 1941)
The Courtship of Andy Hardy (MGM, 1942)
A Yank at Eton (MGM, 1942)
Andy Hardy's Double Life (MGM, 1942)
The Human Comedy (MGM, 1943)
Girl Crazy (MGM, 1943)

Thousands Cheer (MGM, 1943)
Andy Hardy's Double Trouble (MGM, 1944)
National Velvet (MGM, 1944)
Ziegfeld Follies (MGM, 1946)
Love Laughs at Andy Hardy (MGM, 1946)
Killer McCoy (MGM, 1947)
Summer Holiday (MGM, 1948)
Words and Music (MGM, 1948)
The Big Wheel (United Artists, 1949)
Quicksand (United Artists, 1950)
He's A Cockeyed Wonder (Columbia, 1950)
The Fireball (20th Century-Fox, 1950)
My Outlaw Brother (United Artists, 1951)
The Strip (MGM, 1951)
Sound Off (Columbia, 1952)
All Ashore (Columbia, 1953)
Off Limits (Paramount, 1953)
A Slight Case of Larceny (MGM, 1953)
Drive a Crooked Road (Columbia, 1954)
The Atomic Kid (Republic, 1954)
The Bridges of Toko-Ri (Paramount, 1955)
The Twinkle in God's Eye (Republic, 1955)
Francis in the Haunted House (Universal-International, 1956)
The Bold and the Brave (RKO, 1956)
Magnificent Roughnecks (Allied Artists, 1956)
Operation Mad Ball (Columbia, 1957)
Baby Face Nelson (UA, 1957)
Andy Hardy Comes Home (MGM, 1958)
A Nice Little Bank that Should be Robbed (20th Century-Fox, 1958)
The Last Mile (United Artists, 1959)
The Big Operator (Zugsmith/MGM, 1959)
Platinum High School (Zugsmith/MGM, 1960)
The Private Lives of Adam and Eve (Zugsmith/Universal-International, 1960)
Breakfast at Tiffany's (Paramount, 1961)
King of the Roaring Twenties (Allied Artists, 1961)
Requiem For a Heavyweight (Columbia, 1961)
Everything Ducky (Columbia, 1962)
It's a Mad, Mad, Mad, Mad World (United Artists, 1963)
Secret Invasion (United Artists, 1964)

Twenty-Four Hours to Kill (Assoc. British, 1965)
The Devil in Love (Fair, 1966)
Ambush Bay (United Artists, 1966)
How to Stuff a Wild Bikini (American-International, 1966)
The Extraordinary Seaman (MGM, 1968)
Skidoo (Paramount, 1968)
The Comic (Columbia, 1969)
80 Steps To Jonah (MPI-Warners, 1969)
The Cockeyed Cowboys of Calico County (Universal, 1970)
Hollywood Blue (Sherpix, 1970)
B.J. Lang Presents (Coburt/Maron Films, 1971)
Evil Roy Slade (Universal, 1972)
Richard (Bertrand Castelli/Aurora City Group, 1972)
Pulp (United Artists, 1972)
The Godmothers (Mickael Viola, 1973)
Ace of Hearts (Mundial Films, S.A., 1974)
Thunder County (Trans-International, 1974)
That's Entertainment (MGM, 1974)
Journey Back to Oz (Filmation, 1974)
From Hong Kong With Love (Christian Fechner-Renn, 1975)
Rachel's Man (Afton Films/Hemdale, 1975)
Find the Lady (Quadrant, 1976)
The Domino Principle (Avco-Embassy, 1977)
Pete's Dragon (Buena Vista, 1977)
The Magic of Lassie (International Picture Show, 1978)
Donovan's Kid (Buena Vista, 1979)
The Black Stallion (Zoetrope/United Artists, 1979)
Arabian Adventure (Columbia/EMI, 1979)
My Kidnapper, My Love (Roger Gimbel Prod/EMI, 1980)
Leave 'Em Laughing (Chas. Fries Prod., 1981)
The Fox and The Hound (Buena Vista, 1981)
The Emperor of Peru (CinePacific/Babylone, 1981)
Bill (Alan Landsburg, 1981)
Senior Trip (QM/K. Johnson Prod., 1981)
The Black Stallion Returns (United Artists, 1982)
Bill: On His Own (Alan Landsburg, 1983)
The Care Bears Movie (Goldwyn, 1985)
It Came Upon A Midnight Clear (Columbia, 1984)
Bluegrass (Alan Landsburg, 1988)

Eric The Viking (UIP, 1989)
My Heroes Have Always Been Cowboys (Martin Poll, 1991)
Sweet Justice (Triboro, 1992)
Silent Night, Deadly Night 5:The Toy Maker (Still Silent, 1992)
Maximum Force (PM Entertainment, 1992)
The Legend of Wolf Mountain (Hemdale, 1992)
Revenge of The Red Baron (New Concorde, 1994)
Boys Will Be Boys (Uniplex, 1997)
The Face on the Barroom Floor (Begum, 1998)
Babe: Pig in the City (Universal, 1998)
Phantom of the Megaplex (Walt Disney, 2000)

8

Peter Lawford

His was a bizarre life. His father, who was knighted by the Queen of England, impregnated his mother while both were still officially married to other people. She wanted a girl and dressed her son like one. Living in luxury, he was pampered – but not loved until his nanny seduced him when he was ten years old. She and her girlfriend taught him what sex was all about.

When his parents lost their money during the Second World War, he became a movie star and married the sister of the President of the United States. He flew on Air Force One, was a regular guest at the White House and arranged orgies at his Los Angeles beach house for the President. He was caught in the middle of the mysterious death of a movie goddess and covered up for the White House, taking his secret to the grave. But the good life ended with the President's assassination. For solace he turned to booze, Quaaludes and cocaine. Shortly after his third marriage he lapsed into a coma, suddenly sat up in bed as blood poured out of his pores, and died. But that wasn't the end. Unable to pay the funeral expenses, his wife was forced to remove his ashes from a Hollywood crypt and scatter them across the Pacific Ocean. Even in death he was humiliated.

Peter Lawford was the teenager's delight. He was handsome, debonair and talented. He also had an English accent that gave him an aura of aristocracy. Admittedly he couldn't sing or dance, but he did both in the classic 1947 musical *Good News*. He was quite good as an RAF flyer in *Son of Lassie* and charmed Judy Garland in *Easter Parade*. But Dore Schary, who replaced mogul Louis B. Mayer at MGM, wasn't interested in Lawford and he left the studio in the early 1950s. As a member of the famous Rat Pack, he became more popular than ever.

Peter's mother, May, who was born in England, was an outrageous flirt as a young girl, but was unprepared for marriage in 1902. She was stunned on her wedding night with her first husband, Major Harry Cooper. 'Sex was too messy,' she complained, fleeing from the honeymoon bed in tears. Harry should have known she was not promiscuous, but he believed the rumours about his wife's dalliances and blew his brains out.

May didn't mourn for long. Now a beautiful 22-year-old widow, she loved to drink champagne and dance till dawn. In 1906 she married Captain Ernest Vaughn Aylen. May tried to avoid being intimate with him as well, but he was madly in love with her and the marriage lasted seventeen years. He wanted children very much, but she did not become pregnant until 1922. Aylen was not the father, however; May had been having an affair with his commanding officer, Sir Sydney Lawford. Discovering she was pregnant May moaned, 'Peter was an awful accident!' After his birth on 7 September 1923, she confessed the truth to Aylen, who sued her for divorce naming Lawford as co-respondent. Sir Sydney and May were married in September 1924. Aggressive and naughty, she was rewarded with a title and addressed as Lady Lawford.

Having travelled around the world three times before he was fifteen, Peter was sophisticated and spoke three languages, but he was lonely without the companionship of boys his own age. Dominated by the unstable Lady May, he was ill-equipped for normal life. At the age of ten

Peter was seduced by his governess and had his first climax. He had no idea what was happening. At fourteen, he injured his right arm when it went through a glass door. Pulling it out caused serious damage. Doctors wanted to amputate, but May wouldn't have it. According to Peter, she demanded that they save his arm – and they did. But he never regained full use of his right hand, which remained disfigured. In films he learned to hide it, usually tucked in a pocket.

May's concern was not so much the pain her son had suffered, but that his deformity would make him unsuitable to appear in films. She was determined he would be an actor and, despite Sir Sydney's objections, she pursued her dream. In 1937, May convinced him to relocate to Los Angeles because the warm weather would benefit Peter, who was pale and thin following the operation on his arm and a long rehabilitation. She wasted no time calling agents who could get her son into the movies. Peter took a small role in *Lord Jeff* with Mickey Rooney at MGM, but there were few parts for him after that. In need of money, the Lawfords accepted the offer of a villa in Palm Beach, where Peter took odd jobs.

When the Second World War broke out, Hollywood's handsome leading men either volunteered for military service or were drafted. Peter, however, was assessed as 4-F due to his arm injury and grabbed this opportunity to break into motion pictures. He borrowed money, drove to Los Angeles and signed up with Sue Carol's talent agency. Sue had been an actress and was married to actor Alan Ladd. Unable to find work for Peter at first, she suggested he apply for a job as an usher at the Village Theater in Westwood. A few weeks later Sue told him that MGM was looking for a young British boy for *Mrs. Miniver*. Peter got the part and the film won the Oscar for Best Picture in 1943, while leading lady Greer Garson gained the Best Actress award and Teresa Wright was Best Supporting Actress.

In June 1943 Peter signed a one-year contract with MGM for $100 a week. Studio head Louis B. Mayer was very impressed, not only with Peter but with Sir Sydney and Lady Lawford as well After all, royalty was what MGM represented. Howard Strickling, head of the studio's publicity on the west coast, was thrilled because he didn't have to fictionalise Peter's background. The fact that the Lawfords were flat broke was all right, Howard said. Most royals of low rank had a title but no money. In 1944, Peter signed another one-year contract with MGM for $200, and the Lawfords were able to buy furniture for their bare house.

Peter wasted no time in taking advantage of the beautiful girls at MGM. He dated Judy Garland, but fell in love with Lana Turner. To Mayer's distress Lana was known as the 'Night Club Queen'. She could party until dawn and still report for work looking radiant. After Mayer warned her about her conduct, she complied for a while but soon returned to her old habits. And anyway, the MGM Guys were not expected to behave themselves. It was a man's world, after all.

Peter wanted to marry Lana. They had exciting sex, he said. He was also intimate with Judy, but they were closer as friends than lovers. Engaged to Lana, Peter was in his glory – until she disappeared. He feared that she had been kidnapped, but it was worse. She was hiding out with the sexy Turkish actor Turhan Bey. Peter was devastated, even though he had been seeing other women during his affair with Lana. Meanwhile, Lady Lawford was upset over her son's running around every night. She became suspicious when he became chummy with actors Van Johnson and Keenan Wynn, who were rumoured to be gay. When May came home one evening and found Van, Keenan and his wife Evie sitting in the living room with her son, she threw them out and refused to allow them back in the house. Then she went to see Louis B. Mayer.

'I think my son is a homosexual,' May exclaimed.

'What makes you think so?' he asked.

'By the company he keeps.'

'Have you mentioned this to anyone else?'

'Never!'

'I'll handle it, Lady Lawford.'

'Can't you put him in a sanitarium?'

'We'll see.'

Mayer summoned Peter and, without mentioning May, said he'd heard rumours about his sexual preference. Peter was shocked when Mayer suggested psychiatry and hormone shots. 'I am not gay, sir. I can't imagine who would say such a thing.'

'We can help you.'

Peter suggested to Mayer that he ask Lana Turner about their affair. 'She'll tell you the truth,' he said. Mayer did just that and soon apologised to Peter, who found out only much later that it was his mother who had approached Mayer about the possibility that her son was homosexual. She could have destroyed Peter's career – though Mayer would, most likely, have demanded that Peter get married, as he did with other actors. After all, he arranged for Evie and Keenan Wynn to divorce so that she could marry their good friend Van Johnson, in order to dispel rumours that he was gay.

*

Peter's career was in high gear during this period. *Son of Lassie* was one of his more popular films, but working with America's favorite collie was no picnic. 'They took better care of the dog than they did of me,' he said. 'If there were any stunts, Lassie was protected at all costs and I was on my own. He was affectionate with me because I had raw meat concealed in my clothes.' Peter filmed *Son of Lassie* in British Columbia. 'I had a hotel room and the dog had a suite of rooms,' he recalled. 'But I got top billing for the first time so it was worth it.'

Indeed it was. Lawford received excellent reviews for his portrayal of a man who loves his dog, loses his dog, and – for a happy ending – finds his dog again. Peter's popularity soared when the movie was released, despite keen competition from Lassie. 'If you do a film with an animal,' he said, 'it will upstage you every time. All he has to do is wag his tail and no one pays attention to anyone else.'

MGM apparently paid attention to Peter, however. In 1945 they signed him to a seven-year contract for $500 a week with options. He was living with his parents in a dingy apartment that was unsuitable for a star of his magnitude, so he obtained a mortgage through MGM like most contract players. The mortgage was deducted from his salary. Unable to afford a place of his own, Peter bought a house with a connecting apartment for himself. The Lawfords were now among the smart set living on Sunset Boulevard.

After filming the classic *The Picture of Dorian Gray*, Peter made *Two Sisters from Boston* with June Allyson. June was married to actor-producer Dick Powell, but she and Peter were instantly attracted to each other and a discreet romance followed. But Mayer's spies reported back to him about the affair and he put an end to it. The strict mogul was opposed to his players getting involved with one another. When he said they were a family, some Hollywood insiders chuckled, 'L.B. considers it incest.' Actually he did not want dissension in the ranks, and broken romances within the family were a disaster. June and Peter clicked on screen in *Two Sisters from Boston* and their chemistry was again apparent in *Good News*.

Peter first met Elizabeth Taylor when they made *The White Cliffs of Dover* together in 1944. Only twelve years old at the time, she had blossomed into a beautiful and sexually alluring young lady at sixteen, when she made *Julia Misbehaves* with Peter. Elizabeth was mad about him, but unfortunately for her they would often meet accidentally at the beach, and Peter said he was turned off by her heavy thighs. Peter was, at that time, very particular about women. This would change, of course, but in 1948 he preferred the perfection of Ava Gardner, with whom he did have an affair.

Meanwhile Elizabeth confided in her mother about Peter, and he received a call from Mrs. Taylor. Would he ask Elizabeth for a date? He said she was too young, but agreed to talk to her daughter who had taken to her bed in tears over him. They had a long talk that seemed to satisfy her. Peter was as sensitive as Elizabeth and tried his best not to hurt her – and he wanted to make sure there were no rumours about them, because MGM had made it known that she was their 'untouchable'. During the filming of *Julia Misbehaves*, Elizabeth was supposed to say in one scene, 'Oh, Richie, what are we going to do?' Instead she blurted out, 'Oh, Peter, what am I going to do?' Everyone on the set howled with laughter. Elizabeth and Peter would remain friends to his dying day.

MGM decided to co-star June Allyson with Peter again in *Little Women*, which was also to feature Elizabeth Taylor and Janet Leigh. In the film he loves Jo, played by Allyson, but she pursues a career and he marries Elizabeth instead. The tomboy scenes between June and Peter are adorable. Nervous in his company, she leans too close to the fireplace and her petticoats catch fire. Not knowing what to do, he tries to put out the fire, but it proves an embarrassment for both of them. And they romp in the country, sit on the grass and discuss their hopes for the future. Off the set, however, Peter and June were no longer on friendly terms. It's not known why he looked upon her unfavourably, but he told friends that he disliked June intensely.

He wasn't too keen about Rita Hayworth, either. They had a brief affair but it was boring, according to him. 'She was the worst lay I ever had,' Lawford said, while Rita commented about herself, 'Men go to bed with Gilda and wake up with Rita Hayworth.' Her sensuous dance in the movie *Gilda* had not gone unnoticed – Prince Aly Khan courted her, but she became an unhappy princess. He had many women to compare her with and sexually she wasn't at the top of his list.

Princess Margaret of Great Britain was another who found Peter irresistible, but he chose not to pursue her. He had all he could handle in Hollywood. From many accounts Lawford was bisexual. Actor Sal Mineo, for one, claimed to have had an affair with him. And rumours lingered about his involvement with Keenan Wynn. It is unlikely they were true, though Peter did have a fling with Wynn's wife Evie. Then there were the beach boys that were often seen with him in a compromising fashion that might have been misunderstood. Peter was excellent on a surfboard and spent a lot of time at the beach. Possibly he was a latent homosexual, but his closest friends had no doubt he was heterosexual. Peter was the pursued, not the pursuer. Men and women alike followed him and swooned over him. He nonetheless mentioned to the MGM make-up people that he thought his nose was too big. They told him, 'Forget about it.'

Esther Williams, the Million Dollar Mermaid, was Peter's leading lady in *On an Island with You*. He knew Esther's swimming sequences would be the centre of attention just as the wagging of Lassie's tail had been. But Peter was so good-looking and earnest in his roles that it was difficult *not* to notice him. The film was colourful and entertaining and it boosted Peter's popularity. He was, by now, a household name and as big a draw at the box office as Van Johnson.

Easter Parade followed, mainly featuring Fred Astaire and Judy Garland. But Ann Miller's dancing, too, was spectacular – and then there was Peter, who chased Garland and was in turn chased by Miller. The film was a huge success and remains popular on TV today. There was a humility in Lawford on screen. Though he was a leading man at times, he was frequently second banana. But whichever he played, he remained the same patient, under-standing gentleman. Like other contract players, he did what he was told and made whatever films he was assigned to do. Peter was given roles suitable to his image and capabilities. MGM was noted for its good casting, and made few errors in judgement.

But the grand studio that Mayer built was about to change hands. He resigned from MGM in 1951, and Dore Schary took over. It was a dismal time for the contract players at Metro. Mayer was one of a kind, an old-fashioned moviemaker who was dedicated to his family of stars – as he was to Leo the Lion, who introduced his magnificent motion pictures. Perhaps, though, the time had come for a different approach to film making. If the public had made it through the Great Depression and the Second World War, Schary thought they were ready for realism on the screen. He refused to glamorise life or pamper Mayer's spoiled stable of stars. Just as Mayer had refused to compromise, so did Schary.

Peter made the delightful *Royal Wedding* with Fred Astaire and Jane Powell, but he had little to do in the film other than listen to Jane serenade him with love songs. In 1952 his contract with MGM expired and it was not renewed. Peter, however, was one of the few at the studio not frightened to be on their own. He looked forward to freelancing and getting some solid roles.

*

Peter's good friend, actor Robert Walker, had meanwhile died in 1951 after doctors gave him a shot of sodium amytol during an alcoholic stupor. Peter had enjoyed Walker's company and that of his girlfriend Nancy Davis, who would later marry Ronald Reagan and become First Lady. According to Peter's third wife, Patricia Seaton, Nancy was a passionate young starlet who engaged in oral sex with both Bob and Peter. 'I can remember when Peter and I were watching the news after [Ronald] Reagan was elected . . . He laughed and said that when she was single, Nancy Davis was known for giving the best head in Hollywood.'

Two years after Walker died, Sir Sydney Lawford passed away at the age of 87. Peter did not want to attend his father's funeral, fearing he couldn't handle it. He did, however, and had to face the fact that he was now stuck with his detested mother.

Peter went to Columbia Pictures to make *It Could Happen to You* with Judy Holliday, who had won an Oscar in 1950 for Best Actress in *Born Yesterday*. She fell in love with Peter and he took full advantage, but he was soon bored with the affair.

Shortly after Ava Gardner announced her intention to divorce Frank Sinatra, Peter met her, quite by accident, on the street. They had a drink together and went their separate ways. But Sinatra suspected more was going on between Ava and her former lover. He threatened Peter and spent the next five years refusing to talk to him.

In 1952 John F. Kennedy from Massachusetts was elected senator. Peter had met his sister, Patricia, several years before at a party and their paths crossed again in late 1953 in New York City. The pair had dinner several times and flew to Palm Beach together for Christmas. She was spending the holidays with her family at their mansion, while Peter was the house guest of Henry Ford. He and Pat saw each other every day and night, so it was only natural that Peter meet her father, Joe Sr. He remarked later, 'I don't like the British and I don't like actors.' But he told Pat, 'He's a pleasant guy,' and left it at that.

Joseph Kennedy Sr knew Hollywood very well. He had been involved in making movies in the twenties, when he became infatuated with actress Gloria Swanson. His wife, Rose, knew about the affair and had to endure Gloria's visits to their home in Massachusetts. Joe Sr thought nothing of introducing his mistress to the family. But the Kennedy children accepted the situation; like their mother, they understood that even if Catholic men were promiscuous, they always came home to roost.

Peter had predicted he would not marry until he was thirty, but even then he was reluctant. In early 1954 he told Pat over dinner that he'd like to marry her someday. She asked, 'How about April?' He pulled back and stammered, 'I don't think we should make that decision at this time.' But Pat wasn't put off at all. She was flying to Tokyo to see her boyfriend, Frank Conniff, a correspondent with the International News Service. Peter soon realised, however, that he didn't want to lose Pat. He phoned her long distance and she flew home immediately.

Following protocol, he had to ask her father for her hand in marriage. Peter recalled that the first thing Joe Sr said was, 'If there's anything I'd hate more for a son-in-law than an actor, it's a British actor!' He gave his approval, however, and proceeded to check Peter out thoroughly. 'He had already made sure I had money in the bank,' Lawford said. 'That was the first thing he wanted to know, but I had saved a good sum of money so that was no problem.' Kennedy went through the F.B.I. for information and contacted Louis B. Mayer about Peter's rumoured homosexuality. Mayer related his own investigation, and Joe Sr was satisfied. Kennedy was also impressed with Lawford's womanising, having had his share of affairs. That Peter liked prostitutes merely confirmed his manliness as far as Joe Sr was concerned. Rose Kennedy was not thrilled with Peter, but she recognised Pat's love for him and gave her consent also.

Lady May Lawford, on the other hand, despised the Kennedys, considering them nothing but shanty Irish, and she clashed with Joe Sr. It was well known to the Kennedys that she thought they were beneath the Lawfords – but no one cared.

Pat and Peter were married on 21 April 1954 at a church on East 89th Street in New York City. The reception was held at the posh Plaza Hotel. The *New York Daily News* reported:

> The bride's father, ex-Ambassador to the Court of St. James Joseph P. Kennedy, the bride-to-be Patricia Kennedy, her mother and her sister Jean, who was to serve as maid of honor, were waiting at the back of the church, beside the baptismal font – when there was a sudden great roar from the street.
>
> Joe Kennedy grinned down at his lovely daughter.
>
> 'He's here, Pat.'
>
> The bridegroom, handsome Hollywood actor Peter Lawford, son of an honored British soldier and knight, had arrived at the Church of St. Thomas More in E. 89th Street, where he was to claim yesterday

as his bride one of the seven (living) children of the fabulous clan of Boston, London, New York, Chicago, and Palm Beach, Fla.

In a few minutes the vows were made and the multimillionaire's daughter and her actor-bridegroom, who had heard the Rev. John J. Cavanaugh, former president of Notre Dame University, say that they must . . . 'have faith in each other' and learn to 'surrender individuality,' were coming down the aisle together radiant and touchingly proud to belong to each other.

For all its simplicity, there was magnificence in the dress the bride wore. It was made by Hattie Carnegie of pearl-white satin in the new style of fullness drawn to the back and falling into a long train. With it, she wore a voluminous tulle veil attached to a cap of satin, and carried a bouquet of white orchids. Her only attendant, her sister Jean, wore a Dior creation of taffeta in a pink and blue hydrangea print, with a large blue hat. She carried an old-fashioned bouquet.

Waiting outside in 89th St. the crowd of 3000 persons broke through police barriers and surrounded Peter and Patricia when they emerged at 4:15 p.m. from the church. Even after the couple managed to enter their automobile at the curb, the vehicle was unable to move for five minutes. Finally 23 policemen cleared the path.

Patricia is the third of the Kennedys to marry in less than a year. Eunice was married to Robert Sargent Shriver of New York last May, and in September, Senator John Kennedy was married in Newport, R.I., to Jacqueline Bouvier.

Although yesterday's ceremony and reception did not attempt to rival in size or splendor the other two Kennedy nuptial events, it was strikingly beautiful. Pink snapdragons with white lilies decorated the church and pink flowers and candles glowed at the reception in the Plaza's ballroom.

There the elegance of the bride's attire was observed again when she rose from her table for the first dance with her dashing bridegroom. For their memorable whirl, Emil Coleman played 'No Other Love Have I.' . . .

The bride was given in marriage by her father, with three of her brothers serving among the ushers: Senator Kennedy and Robert Kennedy, both of Washington, D.C., and Edward M. Kennedy of Boston.

It'll be a honeymoon in Hawaii. *New York Sunday News*, April 25, 1954.

There was no intimacy between the bride and groom until their wedding night. Pat had been brought up to believe that a woman had intercourse to have children. Her knowledge of lovemaking was nil and she crossed herself before engaging in sex. Peter would seek out other women shortly after the wedding . . .

Pat was not beautiful: it was her spunk, honesty and sense of humour that was appealing. From the beginning she was in awe of Peter and worshipped him as an avid fan. Becoming his wife was a dream come true, but he felt trapped from the beginning. News coverage of his marriage was less than flattering – Patricia Kennedy marries actor. He cared not at all that she was wealthy in her own right and came from a distinguished family, but he cared very much that he had second billing. His consolation was her brother, Senator John Kennedy, who, like himself, was a ladies' man. They hit it off right away. Jack was interested in meeting Hollywood starlets and envied Peter his many affairs with them. They would become very close in the years to come and share secrets that would have destroyed Jack's future in politics.

For their first two years of marriage, the newlyweds lived in rented houses in Malibu, California. Joe Sr offered to buy them a house but Peter wanted to be responsible for that. Already he felt like a gigolo, though it wasn't true. Pat paid for vacations and parties and her more frivolous desires while Peter did what most husbands did, providing for the household expenses. If he were going to take on these responsibilities, however, he had to work and the film industry was not as lucrative as it had been in the 1940s. Lawford's type was outmoded. He turned to agent Milton Ebbins who became a mentor and friend, guiding Peter's career and seeing him through the rest of his most unusual life.

Ebbins' advice in 1953 was to get into television. Peter balked at this, saying that Hollywood looked down on the boob tube and felt that any actor who lowered himself to it was a traitor. It was the $5000 a week that changed his mind. After reading over many scripts Peter chose *Dear Phoebe*. In the show he was to play Bill Hastings, a college professor who gives up teaching to write an advice-to-the-lovelorn column in the *Los Angeles Times* under the name Phoebe Goodheart. The NBC show made its debut on 10 September 1954. It did very well, but Peter called it quits at the end of the first season after a dispute with the writer-producer.

Four months into the marriage Pat became pregnant, much to Peter's distress. He wasn't particularly fond of children and did not look forward to the obligations entailed in being a parent. Because he was so particular about a woman's appearance, Peter was offended by Pat's protruding belly, though she never put on much weight and in fact fooled many people who found out she was pregnant only a week or so before she gave birth to a son, Christopher, on 29 March 1955. Peter had no patience when the baby cried, and he often went to a friend's house to sleep. To make matters worse he had to put up with his mother-in-law Rose, who took care of Christopher for the time being.

Though he adored his son, Peter wasn't capable of love. His relationship with his mother had voided any capability to form close attachments for any length of time. At MGM he had been surrounded by beautiful actresses and he found it difficult to accept the Kennedy women, who were known for their intellect and ambition rather than their attractiveness. Pat was fun to be with but was not an exciting bed partner. She knew one position and participated only when she had to perform. Peter wanted the type of sex that he would never get from his wife. At the age of ten he had enjoyed his first orgasm orally and this is how he wanted to be aroused. Pat, like her mother, pretended not to know her husband was finding pleasure elsewhere. However, Joe Sr knew about Peter's dalliances and even his platonic friendships with women. Jean Carmen, a friend of Marilyn Monroe's, was warned to stay away from Peter, who was shocked and angry to find that his private life was being monitored.

He was both overwhelmed and appalled by the Kennedy clan on visits to the family home in Hyannis Port. They ate informally at a big table, where dishes were passed around and arms grabbed for bread. His only salvation on such occasions was Jackie Kennedy, who preferred not to participate in touch football or the rowdy family meals if she could avoid them. He much preferred eating Jackie's cucumber sandwiches while they sat together quietly on the porch facing the ocean.

But Peter wasn't so loyal to Jackie when her husband wanted to play around in Hollywood. Lawford introduced Kennedy to Marilyn Monroe at a party. She was with her husband, Joe DiMaggio, and Jack was with Jackie, but what Kennedy saw, Kennedy wanted. After Marilyn's divorce in 1955, she began seeing Jack in New York until he had an operation on his back. After his hospitalisation he recuperated at the family home in Palm Beach.

Pat gave birth to a daughter, Sydney, on 25 August 1956. She and Peter had been looking for a house on the beach and had often admired the beachfront home in Santa Monica that Louis B. Mayer had built and given to his wife when he divorced her. When Margaret Mayer died she left the place to her quarrelling daughters, Edie Goetz and Irene Selznick, who were anxious to sell it. Peter bought his ex-boss's legendary house for $95,000. When the news came that Lawford was living in the house that Mayer built, it was a prestigious coup for him. While most people assumed Pat had paid for it, she in fact footed the bill only for much-needed repairs to the tune of $20,000.

Peter was linked again to Metro-Goldwyn-Mayer, portraying Nick Charles in the TV series *The Thin Man* on NBC. The show, which debuted on 20 September 1957, was based on MGM's famous series of popular films starring William Powell and Myrna Loy. In the TV version Phyllis Kirk played Nora, while the third important member of the cast was the couple's terrier, Asta. With bitter memories of Lassie, Peter avoided doing scenes with the dog, but there was more chemistry between him and Asta than he had with Phyllis. Then there was the problem of living up to the comedic high standards of the movies, in which Nick is constantly tipsy from his famous martinis. Peter, who refused to copy William Powell, realised he nonetheless had to portray Nick as an imbiber, but TV audiences didn't see it that way and sent in letters of complaint. Though Lawford was a good choice to play the debonair Nick Charles, he failed to capture the subtlety of a sophisticated boozer. Viewers' feelings were mixed. Some wanted to see Nick high as a kite, while others considered it improper.

The show ended after two seasons, though NBC aired reruns for a third. Peter, who had worked seven days a week making *The Thin Man*, was glad to be free of it to concentrate on John Kennedy's 1960 presidential nomination. Both Pat and Peter were so busy campaigning that they ignored their crumbling marriage.

Jack wanted Peter's opinion on speeches and advice on how to look good on camera during the debates with his opponent, Richard Nixon. Maybe Nixon should have consulted Peter instead; his make-up was terrible, while the good-looking Kennedy didn't need much make-up to impress voters. But the consensus was it would be a very close election.

Frank Sinatra, keen to climb on the Kennedy bandwagon, was reconciled with Peter after five years of silence. Peter was in heaven now – he looked up to Frank as if he were God. Having no faith in himself, he basked in Sinatra's shadow, while Frank basked in the shadow of John F. Kennedy. Although he barely beat Nixon, Jack became president of the United States in 1960.

Sinatra celebrated by asking Peter to join the Rat Pack, which at that point comprised Dean Martin, Sammy Davis, Jr. and Joey Bishop.

Lawford said he wasn't sure why the group was called the Rat Pack – it was also known as 'The Clan' – but they were a cool group with their own vocabulary. Women were 'broads', a penis was a 'bird', God was 'the big G', death was 'the big casino' and a good time was 'a little hey-hey'. The group travelled the world together, stayed at the best hotels and entertained in Las Vegas. Their 'show' was never rehearsed, which made them unpredictable and very funny.

Dean Martin, who knew Frank had a violent temper, kept their friendship as impersonal as possible, while Sammy Davis once made the mistake of criticising Sinatra in an interview. 'I love Frank,' he said, 'and he was the kindest guy in the world to me when I lost my eye in an auto accident and wanted to kill myself. But there are many things he does that there are no excuses for. Talent is not an excuse for bad manners . . . I don't care if you are the most talented person in the world. It does not give you the right to step on people and treat them rotten. This is what he does occasionally.'

Sammy's quote made the newspapers in Chicago where Frank's good friend, gangster Sam Giancana lived. Lawford told author Kitty Kelley,

That was it for Sammy. Frank called him a 'dirty nigger bastard' and wrote him out of *Never So Few*, a film we were starting at the time. Sammy embarrassed Frank in front of the Big Boys. Those Mafia guys mean more to him than anything. So Sammy was quite lucky that Frank let him grovel for a while and then allowed him to apologise in public a couple of months later . . . He can get so mad that he's driven to violence, especially if he's been drinking, and I'm not kidding. I know. I've seen it. Look what happened with Ava. He threatened to kill me. When we got back together, Pat and I named our daughter Victoria Francis after him. We set up corporations to produce each other's movies, and we went into the restaurant business together, but even Pat, who adored Frank, was still scared of his temper.

Victoria Francis Lawford was born on 4 November 1958, and another daughter, Robin Elizabeth, on 2 July 1961. But Peter wasn't home long enough to complain about their crying during the night. He had a busy life, both with the Rat Pack and with his brother-in-law, John Kennedy.

Sinatra was responsible for Peter's being cast in *Never So Few*, a Second World War story set in Burma and filmed on the MGM back lot that Lawford knew so well. It wasn't like old times, however: Louis B. Mayer was dead and Dore Schary had been fired. Sinatra was in charge now, regardless of which studio made his movies. No one would argue that he yielded great power in Hollywood. He could write his own ticket and include the Rat Pack in his projects without interference from studio executives, who were not keen on having Lawford in their films. During negotiations, Peter's agent Milt Ebbins had to fight for good money. But if it didn't go well, all he had to say was, 'I'll have to tell Frank.' That clinched it. Peter was hired.

One of Peter's contributions was *Ocean's 11*. Sinatra was anxious to play the part of Danny Ocean, a safecracker who, with ten of his ex-army buddies, robs five Las Vegas casinos on New Year's Eve. It was a dull movie with a great ending – the 'eleven' pull off the heist and put the money in a friend's coffin being shipped to California. Only at the funeral do they realise the body is being cremated. But it made money and that was what mattered.

The Rat Pack filmed in Las Vegas during the day and performed at the Sands Hotel at night. Frank, Sammy and Dean stole the show, of course, with Joey Bishop getting a joke in from time to time. In truth, Peter was out of place and had little to do but stand there to be admired. If he didn't show up he wasn't missed. But he was Jack Kennedy's brother-in-law, and that made him important. He tried to drink like Frank but he couldn't. Sinatra and Martin pretended to get drunk for laughs. Lawford didn't know that – he got drunk for real.

He could keep up with the others as far as women were concerned, though. He liked prostitutes and didn't mind sharing them, according to one hooker. We'll call her Jill to protect her identity. 'I think I was a favourite,' she said.

I was with the Rat Pack several times, but never participated in an orgy. When they wanted a girl, they separated with the one they wanted. I never saw Dean Martin leave with a girl. I think he preferred watching television in his room alone. I recall asking Sammy about him and he said Dean had women, but not as often as the others. Frank was very sexy and well endowed. So was Peter, who was my favourite even though he liked threesomes. I didn't mind. That was part of my job. He liked to chat in between sex. We talked about his movies at MGM and the leading ladies he slept with. He was very open about that. Seems he bored easily because they got serious. When the affairs were over he ignored them, he said. I thought that was a cold thing to do, but he said if he was friendly, they'd get the wrong idea.

He was wonderful in bed, but he liked foreplay best. He liked to be spanked. I'm told he got into bondage later on and was too rough. I could see that coming. Men who like to be spanked usually don't stop there. God, he was handsome! I also was at his beach house when Kennedy was there. Pat Lawford was out of town. There were orgies, nude bodies everywhere. Kennedy liked to watch. He was terrible in bed. It was the opposite with Peter. I only had one session with Sinatra who barely looked at me. I was there to serve him and that's all. I met Marilyn Monroe, too. She was very sweet but uncomfortable with hookers around. She'd stay for a drink or two and leave unless Kennedy insisted she hang around.

My memories are of Peter, mostly. I felt at ease with him, and he tipped well.

According to Jill, the Rat Pack were a silly bunch, childish and immature. Most of their jokes were corny, but they laughed anyway. 'They thought they ruled the world,' she commented. 'Especially Sinatra. Peter was humble but, let's face it, he never had it so good. Because of Frank he had Hollywood in his pocket and because of Kennedy he was part of Camelot.'

Jill did very well as a prostitute. She saved her money, had several facelifts and kept herself in shape. She worked until she was 45 and then opened up her own beauty parlour in Las Vegas. She hired beauticians who were very attractive. Did she pimp for them? She said no, but I think she did. Otherwise how could she retire ten years later? She has a mansion in Beverly Hills and mingles with the elite. Jill completely hid her real identity. The last thing she told me was how upset she was that Peter's life ended in shambles, but he was a victim, according to her. No one could have survived living with such horrible memories.

Peter began drinking more than he should and so did Pat, who knew about the other women in his life. She performed in bed as a wife should. He initiated it, of course, to prove that he was faithful and that he needed her for his sexual relief. Though he was away from home most of the time, Peter tried to be a good father, but he didn't know how to go about it, or how to love. He had lived a life of privilege and fame without love and now he was too old and too uninterested to find out what it entailed. The only love Peter knew was described in a speech by Jack Kennedy at his inaugural celebration: 'A great deal of our praise and applause should also go to my brother-in-law Peter Lawford. He has been a citizen of this country less than a year, but already he has learned a citizen's delight in paying off a political debt . . . I want Frank and Peter to know that we're all indebted to them and we're proud to have them with us.'

Sinatra had a great deal to do with Kennedy's winning the presidency. He asked his good pal Sam Giancana 'to do everything possible' to help Jack beat Nixon in some key states. The mob paid off election officials and the dirty deal was done. In return Giancana expected Kennedy to reciprocate by easing up on organised crime. But his brother, Bobby, didn't see it that way . . .

Though Peter's marriage was falling apart, as Kennedy's brother-in-law there was nothing he could do about it. So he and Pat took advantage of the many invitations they received from wealthy society folk in New York City and the elite in Hollywood, and attended dinners at the White House. In a *Cosmopolitan* article Stephen Birmingham wrote about the couple: 'Everything they do seems almost irritatingly easy for the Lawfords. They seem to have reached top positions in all sorts of heady areas with no more effort than the sun expends when it rises in the morning.'

Everyone was impressed with Peter and Pat as they basked in the good fortune that he said was 'just an accident'. The parties at his beach house were no accident, however. Neighbours complained to each other, but not to Peter. After all, the President of the United States and his secret service agents had landed on the beach in a helicopter in a flurry of excitement and sand. It was an honour to have Kennedy as a guest in the neighbourhood.

But when the parties started, it was impossible to sleep. Prostitutes overflowed, propositioning men who strolled on the beach. They could be seen in compromising positions through the windows of the Lawfords' house and scampered in the nude on the porch. According to one of Peter's neighbours, he was discreet himself, but had put on a great deal of weight and was out of shape. He looked much older than his 37 years.

He had an unimportant part in the Academy Award-winning film *Exodus* and appeared with the Rat Pack in *Sergeants 3*, a spoof of *Gunga Din*. Critics said the film was tedious and unfunny. The London *Sunday Express* wrote: '*Sergeants 3* gives the impression of having been made for the private amusement of the Rat Pack – which has the motto: "If you're in, you're very, very in, and if you're out you're dead, Daddyo." The Clan may find it all quite hilarious. But to an audience that is not "in", the joke looks as thin as Mr. Sinatra . . . The film works neither as a straight Western, nor as a spoof of the genre . . . This time the Rat Pack is very, very out, not to say dead, Daddyo.'

In *The Longest Day*, Lawford was lost in a cast that included John Wayne, Henry Fonda, Robert Mitchum, Rod Steiger, and many others. One critic said the film was unaffecting precisely because every part was played by a star. Yet, despite his competition, Peter received good reviews, and the movie is regarded as a classic for its bloody depiction of D-Day.

Lawford portrayed a playboy senator in *Advise and Consent*, a film about personal shenanigans in Washington. Was he playing his brother-in-law, his fellow actors asked? How would the president accept his role? Peter said Kennedy had read the book and loved it. In fact, he was going to allow filming in the White House. That's nice, everyone said, but is that why you got the part to begin with? Director Otto Preminger, by no means a fool, already had Henry Fonda, Charles Laughton, Walter Pidgeon and Franchot Tone. Who needed Peter other than as an entrée to the president? Kennedy, who loved to be in the company of Hollywood stars, invited the cast to lunch at the White House. What a thrill it was. Lawford was almost as important as the President on this occasion.

Then Jackie Kennedy had her say: there would be no filming in the White House, and that was that! An outraged Preminger took it out on Peter, whose good scenes were cut. From now on he would be the fall guy – the one who was used and abused. Though women still chased after him, they said, 'There's what's his name, the president's brother-in-law!'

During the Christmas holidays in Palm Beach, Joe Sr suffered a stroke. He would live for eight more years, half-paralysed, in a wheelchair and in a world of his own.

Sinatra had included Peter in the Rat Pack and in his films because he was close to the president. Giancana had used Sinatra for the same reasons, and had got Kennedy elected. But now Bobby Kennedy, as attorney-general, was out to get the mob and the heat was on. Because Sinatra was an occasional guest at the Kennedys' Hyannis Port compound, he felt sure he could convince Jack to overrule Bobby's relentless attack on organised crime. The attempt backfired. An impatient Giancana considered killing Frank, and possibly Peter too. There was still time, however, because Kennedy was going on a political jaunt to California and planned to stay at Sinatra's house in March 1962. Peter had made all the arrangements. Frank was so thrilled that he built a concrete heliport in the grounds, and put up a solid gold plaque that read 'John F. Kennedy Slept Here.'

But Bobby thought better of it. 'How will it look if you stay there?' he asked his brother. 'Giancana was Frank's guest in that same house. Everyone knows about their connection. Don't risk it.'

The fun-loving Jack laughed it off at first. He was looking for some action and he thought Bobby was a party pooper. After all, Frank and Peter had arranged for Marilyn Monroe to join him at Frank's. But then, realising Bobby was right, he called Peter to tell Sinatra his plans had been changed. Peter called Bobby and pleaded with him, but to no avail. 'I called Frank,' Lawford explained, 'and he was livid. He took a sledge-hammer and tore up the concrete landing pad. Then he found out Jack was going to stay at Bing Crosby's house – another singer and a Republican! He blamed me for setting this up when I knew nothing about it. He took me out of his next movie, *4 for Texas* and *Robin and the 7 Hoods* and put Bing Crosby in. I asked Jack to invite Frank to the White House for dinner and he did. All were forgiven except for me. He refused to have anything more to do with me.'

And when Sinatra wrote someone off, so did Hollywood.

John Kennedy and Marilyn Monroe had their rendezvous, not so discreetly, at Crosby's house in Palm Springs. The press, however, never exposed the president's trysts. His only worry was that Jackie would find out. Peter picked up Marilyn who, posing as JFK's new secretary, wore a black wig and carried a shorthand pad for her flight on Air Force One. She stayed in a secluded cottage on the grounds. Jack had an informal gathering there and left no doubt whatsoever what was going on between the two. Marilyn, dishevelled and wearing only a robe, appeared rather drunk. It was obvious to the other guests that they were spending the night together.

Although Peter was close to Marilyn, he was never intimate with her. When he picked her up for their only date, he was disgusted that she hadn't cleaned up after her dog. He had to do it and he was turned off. He was protective of her, however, and otherwise enjoyed her company. Pat was fond of her, too, so she was a welcome guest at the beach house. Marilyn told Peter how she felt about Kennedy – maybe, she said, she would be First Lady someday. 'I couldn't believe it,' he said. 'She really thought Jack was going to divorce Jackie and marry her. I told her not to get her hopes up. He was Catholic and the President of the United States. He had to be careful, but Marilyn had made up her mind. I was worried about her. She was smart but mentally unstable. She was very sensitive and had attempted suicide more than once. To Jack she was just another fuck.'

If Kennedy spent time at Peter's beach house, Marilyn moved in. Jack liked to have sex in the bathtub with her and told Peter to take pictures of them in the act. What they didn't know was that the house was bugged. Many people were out to get Kennedy – what better way than to have him on tape making love to Marilyn Monroe, whose house would also be bugged and her phone tapped?

Marilyn began filming *Something's Got to Give* in April 1962. Peter arranged for her to sing 'Happy Birthday' to Kennedy at Madison Square Garden on 19 May. Director George Cukor gave her permission to take a few days off from filming at that time, but Marilyn's tardiness and illnesses were holding up production, so Cukor changed his mind. But Marilyn was determined. She had a sensational $12,000 gown made that was nothing more than mesh and rhinestones fitted on to her nude curves. Peter picked up Marilyn in a helicopter, which landed on the heliport at 20th Century-Fox where she was filming. He whisked her on board during the lunch break and headed for the airport.

Peter was the MC at Kennedy's birthday bash. Marilyn did not appear on schedule. Scared to death, she hesitated for a long time before Peter was finally able to announce, 'Mr. President, the late Marilyn Monroe!' She slithered on stage, removed her fur coat and revealed herself in the 'nude' dress. In a breathless, sexy tone she sang 'Happy Birthday'. When she left the stage Kennedy took the microphone and said, 'Thank you. I can now retire from politics after having had, ah, "Happy Birthday" sung to me in such a sweet, wholesome way.'

Later that evening Marilyn attended a party. Bobby Kennedy, who had danced with her five times, seemed a touch envious when Jack left with her. The couple retired to the Carlyle Hotel for what was to be their last night together. After Marilyn returned to Los Angeles, she was unable to reach Jack on his private line, a privilege she had treasured. On Saturday, 27 May, Peter called her from Hyannis Port. He told Marilyn she would not be allowed to see or talk to Jack Kennedy again. She would never be First Lady. In fact she was nothing but another fuck to Jack.

Harsh words, indeed. Why didn't Peter tell her the whole truth – that FBI chief J. Edgar Hoover had warned Kennedy that his careless affairs were dangerous at a time of crisis with Cuba? That Marilyn's bold appearance at his birthday party was evidence of their intimacy, so much so that Jackie Kennedy did not attend? Marilyn broke down after Peter's telephone call. Her publicist and friend Pat Newcomb stayed with her that weekend and kept her sedated. Somehow Marilyn reported to work the following Tuesday. On her 36th birthday, 1 June, the cast of *Something's Got to Give* gave her a small birthday party. It was the last day she would spend on a movie set.

Ill with a serious sinus infection, Marilyn did not return to work and was fired by Fox. Her leading man, Dean Martin, refused to continue making the picture without Monroe. His contract stated he had the right to choose his co-stars and production was shut down completely. Suffering from blinding sinus headaches, Marilyn composed letters to Jack Kennedy. Peter referred to them as pathetic; Bobby Kennedy considered them dangerous and decided to intervene personally. On 23 June Peter invited Marilyn to a dinner party at his house to meet Bobby.

Though she was not attracted to him, Marilyn was thrilled to be in Bobby's company and, maybe, she could talk him into a reconciliation with his brother. But it seems that he became smitten with Marilyn and decided to have a fling with her. He was at her house on Sunday, the day after the party, and on Monday, called Fox to renegotiate Marilyn's contract. She was asked to return to finish *Something's Got to Give* and was signed to do another movie, *What a Way to Go*, for a total of $1 million. In early July, Bobby returned to Los Angeles and attended a barbecue at Lawford's house. Marilyn was there as well and, later in the evening, she strolled with Bobby along the beach. He spoke to her of many things: politics, Fidel Castro and the atomic bomb. In an effort to converse with him intelligently, Marilyn made notes of their conversations. She showed her notes to friends who warned her it was dangerous. The F.B.I. found out, and concluded that Marilyn was a 'security risk'.

Bobby returned to Washington to find J. Edgar Hoover waiting for him with the same warning he had given his brother. When Marilyn dialled Bobby's private number and couldn't reach him, she called his home. Bobby was furious.

Did Marilyn tell him she was pregnant? Most likely it was Jack's baby, but her close friends differ on this. Nonetheless, she had an abortion, the last of many in her lifetime. If she had failed with the president, she wasn't giving up on Bobby. He had led her to believe they would marry, she said. Marilyn appealed to Pat Lawford, who said Bobby was still a little boy and that marriage was out of the question. Just as important, Pat said, her mother Rose was adamant that her sons behave themselves now that their younger brother Ted was losing the race to become senator from Massachusetts.

On instructions from Bobby, Pat invited Marilyn to join her and Peter for a weekend at Cal-Neva Lodge in Lake Tahoe, owned by Frank Sinatra and Sam Giancana. Bobby, who planned to be in Los Angeles, had told Pat to get Marilyn out of town. She wasn't keen on going to Cal-Neva, but once Peter hinted that Bobby might be there, she flew with the Lawfords to Tahoe in Sinatra's private plane. Apparently Frank was in on the game as well. Though he and Peter hadn't spoken in a long time, they were both anxious to stop Marilyn from exposing her Kennedy affairs to the press.

This was exactly what she threatened to do, hoping it would get back to Bobby. And it did. In fact, it became a well-known fact that she was so upset at the way he and Jack had used and abused her, that she was anxious for the world to know.

What happened and why at Cal-Neva is a mystery. Marilyn was rarely seen at the lodge even by room service waiters, who were greeted at her door by Peter. He claimed she had tried to commit suicide, but after her death her psychiatrist, Ralph Greenson, said this was not the case. Photographer Billy Woodfield, who worked for both Marilyn and Sinatra, said Frank had dropped off some film when he returned from Cal-Neva. He was shocked to see pictures of a doped-up Monroe having sex with Giancana. F.B.I. agent Bill Roemer verified this, claiming he had recorded a conversation between gangster Johnny Roselli and Giancana. 'From the conversation I overheard, it appeared she may have had sex with Giancana. Roselli said to Giancana, "You sure get your rocks off fucking the same broad as the brothers, don't you?"'

Those who caught a glimpse of Marilyn said she was heavily drugged that weekend and was in a fog when she left abruptly on Sunday with Peter. He had little patience with her by this time. Even in her drugged state, though, she was determined to get even with Bobby. 'I'm going to blow the lid off this whole damn thing!' she told friends.

On Friday night, 3 August, Pat Newcomb and Peter took Marilyn for dinner at La Scala. They were expecting Bobby, but he didn't show up. Once again, witnesses said Marilyn was either intoxicated or drugged. When she arrived home she called Pat Lawford, who said Bobby was spending the weekend at the St. Francis Hotel in San Francisco with his family. Marilyn called there repeatedly and left messages. Unable to sleep, she was a mess the next day – the last day of her life. Marilyn's house-keeper, Eunice Murray, arrived around 8:00 a.m. with her nephew, Norman Jefferies, who was installing a new kitchen floor.

When Pat Newcomb got up around noon, she and Marilyn argued over Pat's loyalty to the Kennedys. Their disagreement had begun the night before when Bobby failed to arrive for dinner. Marilyn told Pat to leave, but she apparently hung around until Bobby did turn up. He arrived at Marilyn's around three or four with Peter, who told the others to leave. By the time Murray and Jefferies returned, Marilyn was in a rage. Murray called Dr. Greenson to come over right away, saying Marilyn was out of control. Upset and in tears, she called hairdresser Sidney Guilaroff and informed him Bobby had threatened her, telling her, 'There's more than one way to keep you quiet.' When she lunged at Bobby he threw her on the floor before offering to pay her off. Still present, Peter tried to calm things down. Much of this fight was caught on audiotape placed in the house, either by the Mafia or the F.B.I.

Bobby, who had left Marilyn's house without resolving the situation, apparently went to his room at the Beverly Hilton Hotel. Peter was having a small dinner party that night. At 7:30 he answered the phone, saying nonchalantly that it was 'only Marilyn'. Around nine Pat Newcomb showed up at the beach house and announced that Marilyn could not come because she was ill. At about the same time Bobby Kennedy was seen going into Marilyn's house with two men, later identified as detectives assigned to Kennedy as security officers. One of them was carrying what looked like a medical bag. Bobby told Mrs. Murray and Jefferies to leave. They went to a neighbour's house, but returned when Kennedy was seen leaving. Eunice Murray explained:

We heard Marilyn's dog Maf barking in the guest cottage and noticed the door was wide open. We found Marilyn nude, lying face down on the day bed clutching the telephone. I thought she was dead, but she wasn't. While I was waiting for the ambulance, Peter Lawford and Pat Newcomb showed up. When she saw Marilyn she screamed hysterically. Paramedics put Marilyn on the floor and dropped her in the process. They placed her on her back and gave her CPR. She was coming around when Dr. Greenson came in, pushed her left breast aside and gave Marilyn a shot of adrenalin in the heart, but he hit a rib. I heard a pop and she was dead. Her body was moved to the bedroom and the phone placed in her hand.

Around midnight, Beverly Hills police officer Lynn Franklin pulled over a black Mercedes for speeding on Olympic Boulevard. Lawford was driving. In the back seat were Robert Kennedy and Dr. Ralph Greenson. Peter explained he was in a rush to get Attorney-General Kennedy back to the Beverly Hilton Hotel on urgent business. Officer Franklin waved them on, with a warning to slow down.

Peter was told to collect any evidence connecting the Kennedys to Marilyn. Drunk and frantic, at around 3:00 a.m. he went to see private investigator Fred Otash, an old friend. Peter explained that Marilyn was dead and that he had tried to remove everything that would link her to the Kennedys, but he wanted Otash to finish the job. The deed was done.

The police weren't called until Bobby was safely out of town and back in San Francisco. Dr. Greenson and Mrs. Murray had their cover-up story down pat: she had got up at 3:00 and was alarmed when she saw a light in Marilyn's room. Having knocked on the locked door and got no response, she went around the house, looked in the window of Marilyn's bedroom and saw her motionless body clutching the phone. She called Dr. Greenson, who broke the window and got into Marilyn's bedroom. He pronounced her dead and told police she had committed suicide. On her night table various sleeping pills and tranquillisers were scattered about.

Peter called Jack Kennedy early on 5 August. Was he reporting in to tell the president everything had worked out just fine? Pat Lawford, who was in Hyannis Port, fainted when she heard about Marilyn. She packed her bags and left for Los Angeles to attend the funeral. Peter told the police he had been the last one to talk to Marilyn; she had said goodbye to everyone and then fallen silent. That supposedly explained the phone in her hand. 'I should have gone to her,' Peter said, 'but my agent said I should think twice since I was married to the president's sister. So I called Marilyn's attorney to check on her. He called and Mrs. Murray answered the phone. She said Marilyn was fine. I'll never forgive myself for not going to her right away.' Peter stated that she had attempted suicide a week earlier at Cal-Neva. 'This time she succeeded,' he added.

When asked if Marilyn and Bobby Kennedy were involved, Lawford replied, 'Nonsense!' Yet his neighbours had seen a helicopter leaving from the beach in front of his house in the early hours of 5 August and complained about the noise. Peter didn't care. He was determined to get

Bobby to Los Angeles airport and back to San Francisco, where he attended church that day.

Marilyn's former husband Joe DiMaggio arranged her funeral and banned the Kennedys and her Hollywood 'friends', including Sinatra, from attending. Pat and Peter Lawford were astonished and embarrassed to be barred from the service. They and Pat Newcomb immediately closed the beach house and hid out at Hyannis Port. Peter gave a brief phone statement to the press. 'I can't believe her death was anything but an accident,' he said. 'I just can't believe she's not around.'

Pat Newcomb went to Europe, as did Mrs. Murray. It appears as if the Kennedys had rewarded them for helping out with the cover-up. One wonders, on the other hand, what Peter got out of it, except grief and unhappiness. His marriage was over, but Jack Kennedy told him not to divorce until after the 1964 election. He and Pat got through the time in a haze of alcohol. They put on an impressive act in public, but barely spoke when they were alone. She threw him out more than once but, again, she had to take him back to avoid bad publicity.

Peter turned down any movie roles that would put him in a bad light and embarrass the Kennedys. In early 1963 he made *Dead Ringer* with Bette Davis, who described Peter as 'out of it' and 'on his way out'. She felt sorry for him. 'It's unfortunate,' Davis remarked.

On Wednesday, 20 November, Jack Kennedy called Peter. 'Jackie's agreed to go on a political jaunt with me to Texas. You know how much she hates these trips, but she's going. We leave tomorrow. Isn't that great?'

Peter was appearing with Jimmy Durante at Harrah's in Tahoe when he took the call that Jack Kennedy had been shot in Dallas. He scurried to pack before hearing that the president was dead and at the news, he threw up and collapsed. With a friend's help, he flew to Los Angeles, to find crowds of people and reporters surrounding the beach house. Pat was in such a state of shock that she couldn't cry. She and Peter flew to Washington, D.C. that night. They stood beside Bobby and behind Jackie as the president's coffin passed by and John F. Kennedy Jr saluted his father.

After the funeral, Peter returned to Tahoe and somehow managed to perform with Durante. The Kennedys were displeased, but this was the only way Lawford could cope with the loss of Jack. When asked whether it was Lee Harvey Oswald who had killed Kennedy, Peter replied, 'It was higher up.'

While most Americans hugged and clung to each other following the loss of their president, Peter and Pat were further apart than ever. They were set to divorce when Bobby announced his plans to run for the Senate. When Pat found an apartment on Fifth Avenue in New York City, Peter explained that they wanted their children educated in New York, while he worked in Los Angeles – hence the two residences. Pat took all reminders of Jack Kennedy with her. To get even, he shipped a truckload of five-gallon plastic containers of water to her with a note: 'Dear Pat: You forgot to drain the pool.'

In the 1965 film *Harlow*, Peter played Jean's husband, Paul Bern, the MGM executive who had committed suicide. Carroll Baker was cast as the blonde bombshell who died at the age of 26 of uraemic poisoning.

The movie was based on a book by Irving Shulman that was highly criticised at the time and has since been proven to be more fiction than fact. For Lawford though, the story of Harlow struck too close to home. Bern had suffered from impotence and so now did Peter. Harlow had been a favourite of Marilyn's and the two blondes were often compared to one another – both died at an early age and under mysterious circumstances. There were rumours that Jean's mother, a Christian Scientist, had refused to admit a doctor to see her daughter, although it wasn't true. There were also rumours that Jean had died of a botched abortion – that wasn't true, either. Her marriage to the short, balding, pot-bellied Paul Bern had been a surprise, both to her fans and to Hollywood insiders. Jean said she was relieved to be with a man who wasn't 'all over her'. When he shot himself in the head, there was speculation that Harlow had done it. She had been in the same house and found the body, but MGM rushed her to her mother's house where, supposedly, she had spent the night. The note that Louis B. Mayer found was not a suicide note at all, but an apology for 'last night'; it fitted perfectly.

Peter was drunk throughout the filming of *Harlow*. He had to use cue cards and looked terrible. Carroll Baker thought his acting was brilliant in the scene where he begged forgiveness for his inadequacies. 'Please, Jean, don't expose me to people for what I am.'

When Bobby won the election in 1965, Peter hoped to mend his marriage. Desperately lonely, he did not want to sever his ties with the Kennedys. He had nothing else after Sinatra had put out the word in Hollywood not to hire him. Though he wasn't fond of Bobby, Peter had been the one who saved him from disaster when Marilyn was murdered. Ironically, it was Bobby who refused to allow Peter to talk to Pat and told him he was not to contact or see her again.

The day after their 1965 divorce became final, however, Peter and Pat had dinner in New York. She wanted to discuss his health. He had been suffering with stomach pains and Pat thought he should have a complete physical examination. He checked into Lahey Clinic in Boston. Doctors said his liver was twice its normal size and if he continued to drink, he'd be dead within six months. Peter did not heed the doctor's advice.

He was only 42, but appeared much older. Young women continued to chase him, he still had magnetism and a charming manner, but neither of these could get him a role in a good film. Instead he took unimportant ones in *A Man Called Adam* and *The Oscar*. In the latter he plays a has-been. When actor Stephen Boyd sees his old friend waiting on tables, he offers him a small part in one of his movies. 'Look, I made the money and blew it,' Lawford answers. 'New kids were arriving on every bus. So I died. I don't want to be dug up like some corpse and have to die all over again.'

It must have torn Peter apart to say those lines. He was running out of money but still spent it freely. His passion was the helicopters that would land on the beach and take him to the airport, or wherever he wanted to go. Suddenly, though, the Santa Monica police decided to enforce a city ordinance forbidding helicopters to land in residential areas. Who did he think he was? John F. Kennedy?

Sammy Davis was one who stood by Peter. They co-starred in *Salt and Pepper*, a James Bond take-off. They had a ball in London while they were filming. It was like the old days – plenty of booze and girls and, something new to Peter, marijuana. He had once opposed any type of drug, but now relied on grass to cut down on his alcohol intake. Though panned by the critics, *Salt and Pepper* was very popular at the box office.

Lawford got a good break when he was cast in *Buona Sera, Mrs. Campbell* with Gina Lollobrigida, Shelley Winters, Phil Silvers and Telly Savalas. It was about three American soldiers during the Second World War who have an affair with an Italian girl. She becomes pregnant and contacts each one for child support. They oblige her for twenty years and finally meet during a reunion in Rome. It was an amusing and colourful film that was good for Peter. Though he was attracted to Gina Lollobrigida and she to him, he was afraid to take a chance with her in the bedroom because of his impotence. In order to achieve orgasm he was into weird excitement these days, in the form of bondage or threesomes.

Jill said she had heard Peter was kooky in bed. 'He wanted to be tied up and whipped,' she said. 'He was into all kinds of things and he was able to get young girls to play his sex games. Sometimes he paid prostitutes, but the amazing thing is how many girls just waited for a chance to be with him. Maybe Hollywood turned their back on him, but Peter still had the Rat Pack image and was famous for being part of the Kennedy mystique. His MGM days were long forgotten. His popularity was a result of his life off the screen.'

Bobby Kennedy, who had ignored Lawford after Marilyn's death and tried to keep him apart from Pat, needed him in 1968. He was going to run for president. Bobby needed Hollywood supporters and Peter found them, but he stayed out of the political spotlight himself. Kennedy's backers thought he was too 'hippy' to represent Bobby. Peter was now into the swing of the sixties. He had long hair and wore beads around his neck.

He was also responsible for the only divorce in the Kennedy family. Peter was understanding about not mingling with the Kennedys – it would have been uncomfortable with Pat around, anyway. But deep in his heart, he hoped to be invited to dinner at the White House, to be a part once more of what had once been Camelot. Jackie felt the same way. When Bobby announced his candidacy she said, 'Won't it be wonderful when we get back in the White House?' Bobby's wife Ethel glared at her and asked, 'What do you mean, "we"?'

Then, in June 1968, Bobby was shot in the head at the Ambassador Hotel in Los Angeles by Sirhan Sirhan. He lingered for two days before dying on 6 June. Peter should have been grateful that he was invited to the funeral but instead he displayed appalling judgement, showing up with a girl who wore a mini-skirt that left nothing to the imagination. After this outrage the Kennedys were finished with him forever.

Though Jill had fond memories of Peter, she was privy to all kinds of information and was losing interest in what he was doing. She said,

I could not believe that his nose was in the air when he was close to JFK, though I heard this from reliable sources. It wasn't like the Peter I knew. He used to send women to my beauty salon in Vegas. I thought that was very thoughtful. There he was dining at the White House and yet he hadn't forgotten to send business my way. You can't imagine what I heard about Peter from people who were there to see and hear what was going on. There's no doubt he was used by the Kennedys. No doubt whatsoever. He was their servant, their whipping boy, their flunky. They were responsible not only for his split with Sinatra, but for the Marilyn Monroe tragedy. Peter has been offered big bucks to tell the truth and he won't do it. By God, I would and I'm a Democrat!

Even when Peter didn't have a dime he refused offers to talk about Marilyn's death. It wasn't until 1983 that Anthony Summers, author of *Goddess*, located Eunice Murray's nephew Norman Jefferies, who finally revealed the truth. He told Summers, 'I guess they can't electrocute me in a wheelchair.' Jefferies, who was never interviewed by the police, had hidden out for 21 years, afraid to reveal what he had witnessed.

Peter didn't live to read *Goddess*, which was published in 1985. It's a shame, because he might have come forward. Or would he?

The April Fools in 1968 was one of Lawford's better films. He was well cast as a handsome, unhappily married tycoon. *Variety* claimed he was excellent. So why couldn't he find work in Hollywood? One reason was his reputation; during the Sinatra and Kennedy years he had snubbed producers and directors because he didn't need them. Now he did, but they never forgot his arrogance. Peter was seen on TV, however, appearing regularly on the popular talk shows hosted by Johnny Carson and Mike Douglas.

In 1969 Lawford was devastated when his pal Judy Garland died of an accidental overdose of barbiturates. She had been going through bad times as well, but really she was too frail to endure the agonies of performing. Judy died $2 million in debt.

The same year Peter was faced with getting rid of his Santa Monica beach house. Like Judy, he needed money to pay long overdue bills. Now that Pat and the children had moved out, he found the Western White House an empty shell of memories and little else. Several girls moved in with him, but they never stayed for any length of time because he was drunk, morbid and impotent. If they didn't leave on their own, he soon grew bored and got rid of them.

Beach houses in Santa Monica were not in demand in 1969 as they are today. Peter asked $207,500, but settled for $142,000. Today it would be worth $10 million. After he settled his debts he was left with very little money. In 1971 he rented a penthouse in the Sierra Towers at Doheny and Sunset.

In 1972 Peter was a guest on the popular TV show *Laugh-in* with Dan Rowan and Dick Martin. It was a very, very funny show and the big stars in Hollywood were eager to be on it. Peter, at 47, began dating Rowan's twenty-year-old daughter, Mary. She said he was the most gorgeous man she had ever seen. Like the other young girls who were fascinated with Peter, Mary Rowan was in awe of the famous movie star who was President Kennedy's former brother-in-law. Dan Rowan, though, was opposed to the relationship. He thought Lawford was too old for his daughter.

But she soon moved in with Peter, who had relocated to a cheaper apartment building on Cory Avenue. Mary thought older men were so much more understanding. She explained, 'Peter has gotten me interested in economics and sociology, what this country is all about, things I never really thought about before. This is an intellectual man and he's tremendously involved with what's happening today. That's good for me.'

Dan Rowan was shocked when Mary said she was marrying Peter, who was just a year younger than his future father-in-law. He tried without success to talk her out of it, but after she announced her marriage plans, he told the press, 'I've known Peter Lawford for a number of years and I've always found him to be a gentleman. He and Mary have been going steady for a year now and seem to know each other very well. I'd rather see her marry a man closer to her age than mine. But they are in love.' Peter joked, 'I was hoping for a younger father-in-law.' The marriage took place on 30 October 1971, in Puerto Vallarta, Mexico. Peter's son Chris was best man.

May Lawford died of heart disease on 23 January 1972. She was cremated and her ashes were scattered over the Pacific Ocean.

They Only Kill their Masters, which Peter made the same year, was one of the last movies filmed on the MGM back lot. The plot revolved around a woman found dead on the beach; she has apparently been killed by her Dobermann pinscher, but it turns out that she was murdered. In spite of the cast, which included James Garner, Katharine Ross, Harry Guardino and June Allyson, the film was a dud.

Despite Lawford's appearances on television he wasn't making enough money to pay for his glamorous lifestyle. He began to rely heavily on cocaine, Quaaludes and marijuana. Mary was able to adjust to Peter's financial plight, but not to his drug abuse. She was planning to leave him when he became seriously ill and was rushed to Scripps Clinic, fifty miles south of Los Angeles, in November 1972. Doctors removed a large cyst from his pancreas. He lost fifty pounds during his illness, but made a remarkable recovery. Several months later, still in bad health, Peter began drinking and popping pills again. Mary filed for divorce.

Eighteen-year-old Christopher Lawford was also now a drug addict. After he was expelled from school, Pat sent him to live with Peter. Father and son were closer than ever now that they had something in common. They got along very well sharing drugs while bills piled up in Lawford's mail box.

In 1973 Elizabeth Taylor returned to Los Angeles after her separation from Richard Burton. She took a liking to Christopher and they began seeing each other. When reporters asked Peter if his son was having an affair with Elizabeth, he denied it. But he was worried that Chris might in fact be involved with the 41-year-old actress, and he introduced her to used-car dealer Henry Wynberg with whom she was to have a torrid romance.

Jill claimed that Peter was dealing drugs. 'I heard this from more than one good source,' she explained. 'One of my clients who lived and socialised in Los Angeles told me she was at a party and actually saw him selling stuff. She was shocked and so was I. But I know he was in hock. Everyone knew that. They tried to attach his salary but his business agent avoided that by having his cheques made out to Peter's production company, Chrislaw, which he had formed in the sixties. I know that marijuana leads to hard drugs and that's what happened to Peter. He was into heroin, as well. Few addicts escape that.'

In 1973 Lawford was one of a host of MGM's greatest stars who narrated *That's Entertainment*, a selection from the best of the studio's musical films. This nostalgia movie was a box-office smash. With the help of make-up and casual attire, Peter looked rather good. His salt-and-pepper hair gave him an air of distinction and of course the familiar English accent brought back fond memories.

When Jill saw the film she thought the rumours of his drug abuse must have been exaggerated. 'Peter was able to pull himself together when he was on camera,' she was told. 'Afterwards he was confused and lost touch with reality. In this sense he was true to his art – the show-must-go-on nonsense – but he handled it somehow.'

In June 1976 Peter met 25-year-old Deborah Gould, an aspiring actress. She fell in love with him – just like that. 'I had never met anyone like him before,' she said. Ten days later he proposed marriage. 'We never did have sexual relations before the wedding,' she confessed. 'I don't know why. It wasn't that I was opposed to it. I know he found me very attractive, but I've never been able to figure out why he didn't want to have sexual relations before the marriage.'

Though Deborah had taken drugs, she thought Peter's habit was dangerous and he agreed to quit. 'He really seemed to mean it,' she said. 'He'd beg me to stay with him and help him. He wanted me to promise I'd never leave him. I had every reason to think he'd quit.'

They were married at a friend's house in Arlington, Virginia, on 25 June. Deborah wore a simple wedding gown and Christopher a tuxedo. Peter, high on Quaaludes and vodka, wore a leisure suit with his shirt open at the neck. At the reception he flirted with other women. This led to an argument with Deborah, which escalated into a shouting match in front of guests who were glad to go home. The next morning Peter couldn't remember getting married. He told friends his reason was that Deborah was supplying him with drugs, although she denied it.

Lawford, who feared being alone again, managed to behave himself in the early days of the marriage. But he and Deborah were intimate only for a short time, until he began relying on drugs again and became impotent. He wanted to engage in three-way sex, which didn't appeal to her.

'You don't think you're bisexual, but you are,' he said. 'You love women.'

'What are you saying? That you like men? That you're gay?'

'I like anybody who's beautiful,' Peter replied.

Lady May Lawford wrote in her book, *Mother Bitch*:

Homosexual Peter tried hard to be thought one – by being persistently with Van Johnson – even after he met trouble and was bailed out. Louis B. Mayer sent for me and asked if Peter was one. I mentioned their friendship (?). Instead of giving him the standard treatment of hysterics, I said, 'You spent thousands on Judy Garland to find out if she is a dope addict! Send Peter to Menninger's and in one day they'll test his glands and you've got your "yes" or "no" – a medical fact.' I never said he was one, nor do I think so.

Lady Lawford was a nut, most likely. One only has to read the book to come to that conclusion. It's her word against everyone else's. She damns Mickey Rooney for teaching Peter how to lie in his early days at MGM, but she harps on continually about Van Johnson. She knew MGM had forced Johnson into marriage when he was allegedly in the habit of exposing himself in the men's room – there are no secrets in Hollywood.

While Johnson, however, was a likeable guy who wasn't sure if he was straight, bi or gay, Lady Lawford was opposed to sex in any form. Her first husband told her, 'You're like sleeping with a wet umbrella! You become so stiff and cold. All you know how to say are two phrases – don't and hurry up. It's a good thing you don't have to make a living off of sex, you'd starve to death!' She writes about rubbing red meat on her nightgowns to feign menstruation. Peter was a mistake, she emphasises, a dreadful mistake. While she was giving birth to him, the labour pains were so bad that she put a gun in her mouth. A nurse came into the room just in time. 'I hate babies,' Lady Lawford said. 'They run at both ends; the smell of sour milk and urine. I never saw Peter until he was washed and perfumed. Ugh! Peter was such a mistake!' May said Peter didn't know how she felt about him, but even if she didn't tell him to his face she must have shown it in many ways.

Deborah finally left Peter after another of many quarrels and fled to Henry Wynberg's house. Hoping for another chance, she invited Peter to a big dinner party. He arrived in a sulk and made remarks about her relationship with Wynberg, who was staying at Elizabeth Taylor's house while she was out of town. As usual Peter looked around the room for pretty girls, and his eye fell on seventeen-year-old Patricia Seaton, who lived with Wynberg off and on. She noticed Peter too, and asked Henry who he was. She'd never heard of him or his movies. Within minutes Lawford made his move with the old line, 'There's something about you I like.' They chatted for a few minutes until Patty said she was going home. 'I'll take you,' he said.

As they were leaving Deborah asked her, 'What are you doing?'

'I'm leaving,' Patty said as Peter took her arm.

'With my husband?' Deborah barked.

Patty had no idea what she was talking about and Peter said nothing. When he kissed her in the car he noticed there was something askew with her face. 'I just had surgery on my jaw and it's wired shut,' Patty explained.

'Oh, great!' Lawford said sarcastically. He took her to Hugh Hefner's Playboy mansion anyway, though nothing happened in a mirrored room designed for wild sex. Patty went home with him, and stayed until his lawyer advised him it was dangerous to be living with a woman during his divorce proceedings. Peter abided by the rules for a week before asking Patty to move back in with him. By now she was a smitten teenager. Going to dinner with Peter Lawford was an experience. When they left the restaurant, there would be reporters everywhere, photographers would be taking pictures and fans jumping on the limousine. She was impressed when their picture appeared in the papers the following day.

She was not, however, impressed by Peter's lovemaking. The wires had now been removed from her jaw and she expected the well-known stud of the 1940s to perform. He didn't. They had oral sex and nothing more. He was very romantic, however. He left notes for her every day and usually a small gift – a token of his love. Patty adored him so much she agreed to have sex with another woman while Peter watched. It was enthralling to be introduced as 'Mrs. Peter Lawford'.

Author James Spada relates in his revealing book, *Peter Lawford: The Man who Kept the Secrets*, how Peter was into very weird sex. In New York City, while visiting his children on one occasion, he met a pretty model in her twenties. They discussed their mutual interest in sexual experimentation. He said he derived pleasure from having his nipples lacerated with a razor by a woman. He could achieve orgasm, he explained, if his nipples were pinched hard. Then, when she excused herself to go to the bathroom, Peter asked, 'Can I watch?' He followed her on his hands and knees, then slumped against the wall and wanted her to slap him. She tried, but couldn't bring herself to do it. 'But I enjoy it!' he cried. He later proposed marriage, but she couldn't handle it. The whole incident was too much to fathom.

Patty soon began seeing other men for 'normal' sex. Peter knew about it and didn't care – except for one incident after he had taken too many drugs, when he put a gun to her head when she came home. Though she was indulging in cocaine and prescription drugs with Peter, Patty wasn't sure what else he was taking until she found needles that he used to inject Talwin, an intramuscular painkiller which she had begun taking herself for menstrual cramps. Peter went to a number of doctors and pharmacies so he could get the prescriptions he wanted without question.

Peter shared all kinds of drugs with Christopher. For his birthday he gave him a container of cocaine. And they shared the same girls – Peter delighted in watching his son have sex with them. Patty remembers coming home from a holiday with Peter to find Christopher standing on the ledge of the apartment building, about to jump. The police managed to grab him and Peter went with his son to the hospital, where Christopher almost died from an overdose of heroin and depressants.

The relationship between father and son was altogether a dangerous one. Peter wanted to be a friend to him, as he did to all his children. He insisted they call him by his first name, not 'Dad'. Christopher was crying out for discipline, but he didn't get it from his father. In fact, Peter in many ways took after his own father – a quiet, laid-back man who preferred to remain in the background.

In the late seventies and early eighties, Peter made several forgettable films – *Rosebud, Won Ton Ton, The Dog who Saved Hollywood, Angels Brigade*, and *Body and Soul*. He appeared on TV game shows and in episodes of *Fantasy Island, The Love Boat*, and *Matt Houston*. Any money he made went on drugs. He borrowed money from friends who had stuck by him, like Elizabeth Taylor. He had always been able to rise to the occasion when working but he was slowly losing even that ability. He was now considered by most producers in Hollywood to be unreliable.

On 17 September 1983, Peter flew to Hyannis Port for his daughter Sydney's wedding. The Kennedys would have preferred him not to be there but Sydney insisted. He stumbled and fell during the rehearsal but got through the wedding ceremony itself without another accident. He brought a black girl to the reception and proceeded to get very drunk Apart from Sydney, he was shunned by everyone except Jackie Kennedy Onassis, who made it her business to sit and talk with him.

Patty, having left Peter for several months, returned to find him living in filth. He hadn't cut his nails or his hair, or changed the sheets on his bed. She managed to get him off booze for a while, but when he went on another binge, Patty knew he would die unless he got professional help. Elizabeth Taylor had entered the Betty Ford Clinic in Rancho, Mirage, California, to get off pills and alcohol. Patty urged Peter to do the same, and got him there by telling him they were having dinner with Betty Ford. Reluctantly he entered the clinic on 12 December 1983. He rebelled at first. Washing his own clothes was beneath him, so his gave his dirty laundry to Patty. But he soon adjusted and became a model patient, attending Alcoholics Anonymous meetings and cleaning his room. In fact, Peter enjoyed vacuuming so much he almost wore out his carpet when he arrived home. All was going well. Peter was a different man. He was gaining weight, his usual tanned complexion had returned and he was acting almost human again.

Patty took over their finances, trying to pay some bills and balancing their bank account. When she received a statement from American Express she questioned several charges for a helicopter, but found they were legitimate. During his six weeks at the Betty Ford Clinic, Lawford had arranged for his drug dealer to take a helicopter to a hidden desert area where he could be supplied with cocaine without anyone noticing.

Patty said Peter looked wonderful when he left the clinic, but three days later she received a call from a bartender that he had passed out from consuming too much liquor. She had to bring him home.

In *The Peter Lawford Story*, Patty said she now left Peter again and settled in Hawaii. On one of her return trips she went to Las Vegas. Frank Sinatra had refused to perform when Peter and Patty came to see his show, but she was able to contact him and he urged her to call Peter, 'because I hear he's in a very bad way'. By this time Lawford was, according to Patty, a walking corpse who had no will to live. He began experiencing extreme stomach pains, so she took him to hospital where he was rushed into surgery with a bleeding ulcer. The doctors didn't expect Lawford to live, but he did. The following day he and Patty were married. She wore a white dress and he a hospital gown. The groom weighed a mere 120 pounds.

Back home Peter was fed through a tube every ninety minutes. He seemed to be making a slow improvement until doctors removed the tube. Then he began bleeding profusely, and he never recovered. His kidneys and liver barely functioning, he was allowed to go home, but he collapsed and was rushed to Cedars-Sinai Medical Center. At 8:50 a.m. on 24 December 1984, he sat up in bed struggling, blood gushing from his nose, ears and pores. Lady May Lawford's unwanted son was dead.

Peter was cremated on Christmas Day. On 26 December Patty, his four children and a few close friends gathered at the Westwood Memorial Park where his ashes were interred near the burial place of Marilyn Monroe.

In 1988, Patty was told by the new owners of Westwood that Peter's ashes would have to be removed since the funeral expenses had not been paid. Patty claimed that the Kennedys refused to help out financially, but according to James Spada, she had received $50,000 pension money from the Screen Actors Guild and could easily have paid for the funeral, which cost less than $10,000. The Kennedy children finally agreed to pay if Patty relinquished Peter's ashes, but she refused. On 25 May 1988, she arrived at Westwood with 'friends' from the *National Enquirer*, and had the urn removed. A limousine took her to Marina del Rey; there she boarded a boat while tabloid photographers took pictures. Peter Lawford's ashes were scattered over the Pacific Ocean.

'My dear Jack,

How are Marilyn and Bobby? Give them my love. If you should run into Steve McQueen or Vic Morrow, give them my best. Take care of you.

Love,

Peter'

– Portion of a letter written by Peter Lawford to John F. Kennedy
when he was in the Betty Ford Clinic

The Films of Peter Lawford

Poor Old Bill (BIP/Wardour, 1931)
A Gentleman of Paris (Stoll/Gaumont, 1931)
Lord Jeff (MGM, 1938)
Random Harvest (MGM, 1942)
A Yank at Eton (MGM, 1942)
Mrs. Miniver (MGM, 1942)
Junior Army (MGM, 1942)
Eagle Squadron (Universal, 1942)
Thunder Birds (20th Century-Fox, 1942)
London Blackout Murders (Republic, 1942)
Random Harvest (MGM, 1962)
Girl Crazy (MGN, 1943)
Sherlock Holmes Faces Death (Universal, 1943)
The Purple V (Republic, 1943)
The Immortal Sergeant (20th Century-Fox 1943)
Pilot No. 5 (MGM, 1943)
Above Suspicion (MGM, 1943)
Someone to Remember (Republic, 1943)
The Man from Down Under (MGM, 1943)
The Sky's the Limit (RKO, 1943)
Paris After Dark (20th Century-Fox, 1943)
Flesh and Fantasy (Universal, 1943)
Assignment in Brittany (MGM, 1943)
Sahara (Columbia, 1943)
West Side Kid (Republic, 1943)
Corvette K-225 (Universal, 1943)
Mrs. Parkington (MGM, 1944)

The White Cliffs of Dover (MGM, 1944)
The Canterbury Ghost (MGM, 1944)
Son of Lassie (MGM, 1945)
The Picture of Dorian Grey (MGM, 1945)
My Brother Talks to Horses (MGM, 1946)
Two Sisters From Boston (MGM, 1946)
Cluny Brown (20th Century-Fox, 1946)
Good News (MGM, 1947)
It Happened in Brooklyn (MGM, 1947)
On an Island With You (MGM, 1948)
Easter Parade (MGM, 1948)
Julia Misbehaves (MGM, 1948)
Little Women (MGM, 1949)
The Red Danube (MGM, 1949)
Please Believe Me (MGM, 1950)
Royal Wedding (MGM, 1951)
Just This Once (MGM, 1952)
Kangaroo (20th Century-Fox, 1952)
You For Me (MGM, 1952)
The Hour of 13 (MGM, 1952)
Rogue's March (MGM, 1952)
It Should Happen to You (Columbia, 1954)
Never So Few (Canterbury/MGM, 1959)
Ocean's 11 (Warner Brothers, 1960)
Exodus (Preminger/UA, 1960)
Pepe (Columbia, 1960)
The Longest Day (20th Century-Fox, 1962)
Sergeants 3 (Essex-Claude/UA, 1962)
Advise and Consent (Columbia, 1962)
Dead Ringer (Warner Brothers, 1964)
Harlow (Paramount, 1965)
Sylvia (Paramount, 1965)
A Man Called Adam (Embassy, 1966)
The Oscar (Greene-Rouse/EM, 1966)
Salt and Pepper (United Artists, 1968)
Buona Sera, Mrs. Campbell (Columbia, 1968)
Hook, Line and Sinker (Columbia, 1969)
The April Fools (National General, 1969)
One More Time (United Artists, 1970)

They Only Kill their Masters (MGM, 1972)
That's Entertainment (MGM, 1974)
Rosebud (Universal, 1975)
Won Ton Ton, The Dog Who Saved Hollywood (Paramount, 1976)
Angels Brigade (Arista, 1980)
Body and Soul (Cannon, 1981)

9

Frank Sinatra

He went to the 'big casino in the sky' accompanied by a bottle of Jack Daniels and a pack of Camel cigarettes: no wonder his tombstone reads, 'The best is yet to come'. Why didn't somebody slip copies of *Playboy* and *Hustler* magazines in his coffin? After all, his idea of heaven before his death was broads and booze. What else is there in life? Well, there's love, but he blew that and then tried to kill himself.

When 'the most beautiful animal in the world' walked out of his life he learned how to sing from the heart, and thus he became a legend.

His friends were gangsters and he relished their company. He asked for their help in getting John F. Kennedy elected in 1960. He, along with his Rat Pack buddies, put Las Vegas on the map. He brought class to Sin City by putting the casino bosses in tuxedos, and made it possible for black celebrities to walk into hotels through the front door. When he was good, he was good. When he was bad, he was better.

I was a bobbysoxer in the era when women fainted at his feet. I thought he was too skinny and lacked appeal – then I met him in an elevator and changed my mind. He had charisma, all right. He didn't have to sing to prove that.

On his deathbed he muttered, 'I'm losin'.' But he would never admit that at the blackjack table, or to his nemesis, the press. One reporter said it took him twenty minutes of cursing to say 'No' to being interviewed. Refused credit at a hotel in Las Vegas, he got into a fist fight with the boss and was knocked on his backside. Even his friends cheered at that. Maybe he'd find some humility. But he never did. He got revenge – his way . . .

Frank Sinatra had good reason for trying to stop publication of Kitty Kelley's *His Way* in 1986. In the end, the sensational biography sent Frank fleeing to Europe until things cooled off. Readers found out a great deal about Ol' Blue Eyes from Ms. Kelly. The first shocking revelation was that his mother had made money by performing abortions when he was growing up. Then we learned that Frankie could get any girl he wanted even before he became famous. The voice helped – and also the fact that he was so well-endowed. His mother married him off to a sweet Italian girl, Nancy Barbato, who suffered for over a decade. He left her $250,000 when he died. He was worth millions but, hey, it's the thought that counts. Frankie took care of his second ex-wife, Ava Gardner, when she was seriously ill. But he didn't do anything for third wife Mia Farrow, except offer to break Woody Allen's legs when he left Mia for their adopted daughter. His widow, Barbara, the only family member with him when he died, inherited the bulk of his estate. She deserved it.

Francis Albert Sinatra was born in Hoboken, New Jersey, on 12 December 1915. He weighed over thirteen pounds, and the doctor's forceps punctured one of his eardrums and scarred the left side of his face. He was to be the only child of Italian immigrants Dolly and Anthony Martin Sinatra; she was from Genoa and he from Sicily. Anthony, who couldn't read or write, took up boxing, while Dolly was a midwife and used her knowledge to perform abortions for $25. When husband Marty broke his wrists and had to give up fighting, Dolly found him a job at the fire department. She had a mouth like a sewer and enough ambition for both of them. So, eager for money and a home of her own, she borrowed the cash to buy a tavern for Marty to run. With the guts and determination of a successful politician, Dolly ruled the roost.

Frank entered high school in 1931 but was expelled a month later for bad behaviour. Dolly was furious. They had moved to a better neighbour-hood by now and she had big plans for her son, even though he wasn't the brightest kid on the block. Dolly was arrested after one of her abortion patients almost died. On probation, she continued her business in the basement of her house.

Frank was on his own most of the time and hung out with musicians. He couldn't play an instrument but he could sing a little and he began performing at school dances. He wanted to join a local trio, The Three Flashes, but they didn't want him until Dolly convinced them otherwise, and so The Three Flashes became The Hoboken Four. They appeared on *Major Bowes Amateur Hour* and went on tour. Frank regularly stole the spotlight, which the other three singers resented, and fist fights ensued every time they performed.

Unable to take the beatings, Frank returned to Hoboken. He began seeing eighteen-year-old Nancy Barbato, whose father was a plasterer from Jersey City. Dolly approved. She had seen the girls her son was going out with and was afraid he would get into trouble. Nancy, she assumed, would remain a virgin until her wedding night.

Dolly, once again, used her clout and found Frank a job as a singing waiter at the Rustic Cabin above the Jersey Palisades, where he earned fifteen dollars a week. While working there he met the attractive 25-year-old Toni Francke and got her pregnant, as Dolly predicted. In November 1938, Toni took out a warrant for Frank's arrest on morals charges. Marty's gentleness with Toni's family got Frank out of jail, but Toni still didn't hear from him. So she went to see Dolly, who locked her in the cellar and had her arrested for disturbing the peace. After Toni was released on probation, she took out another warrant for Frank's arrest. Her family, however, wanted nothing to do with a young man whose mother performed abortions, so charges against Frank were dropped.

Dolly had had enough of Frank's running around with women; she wanted him to settle down and get married to a nice Italian girl like Nancy Barbato. Frank wanted his freedom, but Dolly said that was dangerous. Nancy nevertheless swore that she would not pin him down, and the wedding was held at Our Lady of Sorrows Church in Jersey City on 4 February 1939. After a brief honeymoon in North Carolina, the couple moved into a three-room apartment in Jersey City. Frank continued working as a singing waiter at the Rustic Cabin and Nancy took a job as a secretary for $25 a week.

Harry James, who had just formed his band, soon signed Frank to a two-year contract for $75 a week. After the band appeared at the Hippodrome Theatre in Baltimore and the Roseland Ballroom in New York City, a reporter approached James about the skinny, unknown singer who acted like a celebrity. 'Not so loud,' James said. 'The kid's name is Sinatra. He considers himself the greatest vocalist in the business. Get that! No one ever heard of him. He's never had a hit record. He looks like a wet rag. But he says he's the greatest. If he hears you compliment him, he'll demand a raise.' In fact, Frank demanded more than that. Tommy Dorsey was better known than Harry James at the time so when he offered Sinatra a job, Frank told Harry the truth. James tore up his contract and wished him well.

It was a smart move on Frank's part. Within months his recording of 'I'll Never Smile Again' was number one in the hit parade. Sinatra was in awe of Dorsey, and asked the bandleader to become godfather to his daughter Nancy, born on 7 June 1940. It was a family affair. Dorsey loved Dolly, who often invited the entire band for a delicious old-fashioned Italian dinner at her home. The only disharmony was Frank's continued unfaithfulness. When Nancy found out she called Dolly, who laced into her son. She called him a bum and damned him for his recklessness. Frank didn't talk back to his mother. He just continued on his merry way.

When the Dorsey band went to Hollywood to appear at the Palladium, they drew such a crowd that Paramount Studios signed them to film *Las Vegas Nights*. This was Frank's first movie, but he went unbilled. He did, however, fall in love with a blonde starlet and move in with her. But it didn't last long after he met a young debutante from a prominent New York family. She was what Sinatra referred to as 'class'. He told a friend she was 'too far above him' to do anything wrong. She admired his talent and introduced him to some of her society friends. He wasn't exactly a nobody these days; *Billboard* had named him the top band vocalist. After his recordings with Dorsey, which included 'Night and Day', Sinatra decided to go it alone. Thirteen thousand dollars a year was no longer enough money to pay for his talent. 'I'm going to be real big,' he told friends, 'bigger than Bing Crosby.'

The MCA talent agency bought Sinatra's contract from Tommy Dorsey for $60,000. Rumour had it that Frank's mobster friends threatened Dorsey with a gun to ensure his agreement. Dorsey denied it at the time, but years later admitted that he had been forced into the deal by three thugs. Sinatra never forgave him for that. When Tommy died in 1956, Frank did not offer his condolences. 'When I wanted out of my contract it cost me $7 million!' Then he stamped his foot on the stage and hollered, 'Do you hear me, Tommy? You hear me? I'm talking to you!'

How did Dorsey feel about Frank after their split? 'He's the most fascinating man in the world, but don't stick your hand in the cage.'

On 30 December 1942 Sinatra made his debut at New York City's Paramount Theatre with Benny Goodman's band. Press agent George Evans was asked to see the show. Impressed with a few teenagers who swooned over the skinny singer, he decided to fill the theatre with bobbysoxers who would be paid five dollars to scream, yell and faint when Frankie was on stage. Evans also placed an ambulance outside the theatre in case a passed-out teenager had to be rushed to hospital. It was all a gimmick – a million-dollar gimmick. Outside the Paramount long lines of young girls stretched for blocks. The gossip columnists took notice and started writing about 'The Voice', a nickname thought up by Evans. Frankie, caught up in the frenzy, began caressing the microphone as if making love to it, whereupon cute girls in sweaters and skirts collapsed in the aisles and were carried out of the theatre.

Evans did not try to hide the fact that Sinatra was a married man and insisted he wear his wedding ring. It didn't matter to his fans, they wanted him anyway. But Evans knew these devoted teenagers would not tolerate adultery from their idol and he discouraged Frank's extramarital affairs. He also became friends with Nancy, a homebody who made her own clothes and did her own hair to save money. He insisted that she be fitted for a new wardrobe, have regular appointments at the hairdresser and get her teeth capped. According to Kitty Kelley, he even recommended that she have cosmetic surgery to correct her prominent nose. Evans emphasised Nancy's place in Frank's public life and how important it was that she should look the part in his career activities.

Frank, a regular on *Your Hit Parade*, appeared on radio programmes such as *The Jack Benny Show* and was now being courted by Hollywood. 'I'm flying high,' he cheered. Then the Second World War broke out. Evans feared the worst. Would it look good if Frankie avoided the draft by claiming he had a child and a wife expecting her second baby? There was no need to worry. Sinatra's shattered eardrum classified him as 4-F.

So Frank went to Hollywood to film *Higher and Higher* and *Step Lively* at RKO. He wasn't with Nancy when she gave birth to Frank Jr on 10 January 1944. Frank sang to his wife and baby on his CBS radio show, but he later claimed that they thought another child would save their marriage, which was essentially over after the first year. He would do anything for his career, and salvaging his marriage was important to his image. When he signed a contract with RKO, he bought an estate in the Toluca Lake area of the San Fernando Valley.

Nancy found her husband's success difficult to believe. 'He's going to make a million dollars this year,' she said. 'Six years ago I couldn't afford meat sauce for spaghetti because it was too expensive.'

Sinatra's invitation to the White House came as a surprise. He was speechless in the company of Franklin D. Roosevelt, though in an interview he was casual about it. The president, meanwhile, was criticised for welcoming a man who wasn't fighting for his country. And Sinatra saw the dark side of fame when teenage boys threw eggs and rotten tomatoes at him in Times Square. Bobbysoxers piled on top of the boys until the police removed the culprits, while Frank made a hasty retreat.

MGM mogul Louis B. Mayer, recognising Sinatra's popularity, signed him to a contract in 1944. The studio quickly found an excellent vehicle for Frank, *Anchors Aweigh* with Gene Kelly and Kathryn Grayson. In the film he and Kelly play two sailors on leave in Los Angeles. They both fall in love with Grayson, who chooses Kelly in the end. Frank's dancing numbers were above par. Although no threat to Kelly, he held his own and that wasn't easy. Kelly was a perfectionist who insisted on endless rehearsals; this annoyed Frank, who liked to go home after the first take. Kelly and Grayson said he was easy to work with, however, despite an unfortunate remark he supposedly made to a reporter: 'Pictures stink and most of the people in them do too. I don't want any more movie acting. Hollywood won't believe I'm through, but they'll find out I mean it.'

Sinatra denied saying it. 'Now, wouldn't I be a sucker to shoot off like that? Hollywood and the picture people have been good to me. Sure, I'm going to stay in pictures. That is, as long as they want me. But as for those things the paper quoted me as saying, I was downright amazed when they showed me the clipping. I couldn't believe that such a story could be made of some reporter's imagination.'

But reporter Hal Swisher went on the record in *Daily Variety*, saying Frank had definitely made the nasty statement, on 8 October at the Hollywood Bowl during filming of *Anchors Aweigh*, and demanding a retraction of Sinatra's denial. MGM's publicity department responded quickly with a statement from Sinatra:

> It's easy for a guy to get hot under the collar. Literally and figuratively, when he's dressed in a hot suit of Navy blue and the temperature is 104 and he's getting over a cold to boot. I think I might have spoken too broadly about quitting pictures and about my feeling toward Hollywood. I'm still under a contract to RKO, which has six years to run. I have one more commitment at Metro following *Anchors Aweigh* and believe me I intend to live up to my obligations.

But Frank's impulsiveness got the better of him again when he called the U.S.O. 'shoemakers in uniform' during a brief tour of army bases in Europe. In response, the Army newspaper wrote, 'Mice make women faint too'. Lee Mortimer, columnist for the Hearst newspapers, claimed that while most celebrities volunteered their services, Sinatra was being paid $30,000 a week to entertain the troops.

Sinatras's battles with the press were just starting. Despite some bad publicity, however, he had no problems with the ladies. In his MGM dressing room he made up a list of desirable women and crossed them off after making conquest of each.

Lana Turner was just one. Frank seemed to care not at all that he was a married man when he was seen dining with Lana in Palm Springs. The affair was noted by Hollywood columnists, but Frank made no attempt to explain away his cosy dates with the 'Sweater Girl'. Nancy announced her separation from Frank, but Lana told columnist Louella Parsons there was nothing to the rumours. 'I'm not in love with Frank and he's not in love with me,' she stressed. 'I would never break up a marriage.'

There was, though, more to the relationship, as Lana would admit in later years. There was talk of marriage and she took it to heart. Sinatra was to learn the hard way that Louis B. Mayer would not tolerate his married stars having blatant extramarital affairs. What they did in private was their business but in public they were properties of MGM. Frank, bearing gifts, returned to Nancy and all was forgiven. If the public gained the impression that Sinatra was a good-for-nothing husband and a braggart, they still bought his records. 'Saturday Night (The Loneliest Night in the Week)', 'Dream', 'Nancy', 'They Say It's Wonderful' and 'Day by Day' were great hits.

But Frank was caught up in too many webs. He began running with the Mafia, spending time with them in Havana, carefree and oblivious. His friendship with the likes of Lucky Luciano was discovered by a newspaper reporter, who damned Frank in his column: 'Mr Sinatra, the self-confessed savior of the country's small fry, by virtue of his lectures on clean-living and love-thy-neighbor, his movie shorts on tolerance, and his frequent babblings into the do-good department of politics, seems to be setting a most peculiar example for his hordes of pimply, shrieking slaves, who are alleged to regard him with the same awe as a practicing Mohammedan for the Prophet.'

Columnist Lee Mortimer never had a kind word to write about Frank. When he was leaving Ciro's nightclub on 8 April 1947, Mortimer was jumped by four men and held on the ground while Sinatra punched and kicked him. Frank was arrested the following day; once again the MGM attorneys stepped in, demanding he pay Mortimer $9,000 in damages.

Sinatra now made *On the Town*, another musical with Gene Kelly. The pair played two sailors on leave in New York City, where the movie was filmed. Frank, who was very self-conscious about his looks, had to wear toupees, while his ears were taped back and his backside was padded. According to Kelly, Frank's rear end was actually concave. The film was given very good reviews and it remains a classic to this day. Critics did not single out Frank, however. He blended in well with an all-star cast including Ann Miller, Vera-Ellen and Betty Garrett, as well as Gene Kelly.

Take Me Out to the Ball Game, on the other hand, was a forgettable movie. This time Frank and Gene Kelly played vaudevillians and baseball players. Esther Williams did not seem to fit the theme, although she does manage a casual swimming pool sequence while Frank and Gene ogle from their balcony. Judy Garland had originally been slated to play the manager of the baseball team, but was admitted to hospital for detoxification. June Allyson, who was to take Judy's place, then discovered she was pregnant. So Esther was assigned the role. She was excited about working with Sinatra. In her memoirs she wrote, 'I not only adored the way he sang, but admired his underrated natural approach to acting.' But she did not get along with Gene Kelly, who didn't want her in the movie. She was too tall and she couldn't dance. He shot barbs at her about every little thing. He was rough on Sinatra as well, but Frank was in awe of Kelly who got along well with anyone in awe of him.

Frank bought a new house in Holmby Hills for $250,000 and was planning to build another one in Palm Springs for $150,000. Nancy gave birth to their third child, Christina, on 20 June 1948. While she and the children stayed in their new Los Angeles home, Frank was partying in Palm Springs with Ava Gardner, whom he met when she was married to Mickey Rooney.

When they were introduced Sinatra commented, 'Hey, why didn't I meet you before Mickey? Then I could have married you myself.' And after a few dates they became intimate. 'My God, it was magic,' she said. 'We became lovers forever – eternally. I truly felt that no matter what happened we would always be in love.'

One night they 'shot up' the desert town of Indio, California, with Frank's .38s, smashing streetlights and store windows and almost killing a man. When they were arrested and put in jail, Frank called his press agent who paid off the police and everyone else concerned. Even the man who was grazed by a bullet accepted an offer of $10,000. Fortunately, the press were unaware of the incident, but Hollywood insiders knew all about it.

Knowing that Ava was getting involved with Sinatra, Lana Turner warned her. She and Frank had been very serious, she said. He had been planning to divorce Nancy and marry her. Lana had been making arrangements for the wedding when, one morning, she read in the newspaper that Frank had gone back to Nancy. Ava liked Lana and appreciated her concern, but replied that she and Frank were deeply in love and would be married eventually. They tried to be discreet and yet they didn't care who found out. Frank's Catholicism was one reason he was reluctant to get a divorce. Though he and Nancy had been apart most of the time and there was little left of his marriage, he was afraid to make a decision.

After all, Ava's marriages to Mickey Rooney and bandleader Artie Shaw had failed. Divorced from Rooney, Ava had settled for only $25,000, though she was entitled to half of everything Mickey owned. According to Howard Strickling, Mayer had promised that if she were to go easy on Rooney, he'd get her good parts in films.

On 17 October 1945 she had married Shaw, who later explained that the constant interference of MGM had led to the break-up of their marriage in less than a year. According to Ava, on the other hand, 'He told me to leave so I left.' Ava then had a series of sexually charged affairs with billionaire Howard Hughes, and actors Robert Walker, Howard Duff, Robert Mitchum, Peter Lawford and Robert Taylor. But they soon bored her. She was a beautiful nymphomaniac who drove men crazy.

When she met Frank Sinatra, though, the world began to spin a little faster. Ava had been out with married men before but this was dangerously different and she knew it. Otherwise, she would not have gone off with him to the opening of the Shamrock Hotel in Houston, Texas. Frank flew into a rage when a photographer tried to take their picture in a restaurant. There was no fight, but the widespread publicity hurt Ava's reputation. 'We were so in love we didn't think,' she said. On 14 February 1950 Nancy Sinatra again announced her separation from Frank, whereupon Louis B. Mayer warned Ava and Frank that their affair would bring about adverse publicity. It did. Her fan mail was very critical of her behaviour, many letters referring to her as a slut and a whore. The Catholic Church, too, was in an uproar.

In March 1950 Ava, who was on her way to Spain to make *Pandora and the Flying Dutchman*, stopped off in New York to attend Frank's opening night at the Copacabana. It was a big night for him and he wanted to succeed, but he was upset and nervous about Ava's trip to Europe. Maybe she was a successful actress but she had never been out of the country and that worried him. How long would she be away and would she be taken in by smooth Spanish men who had only hit-and-run romance in mind?

His relationship with Ava was unstable, despite their love for each other. Ava was at the Copa to cheer Frank on and show her confidence in him, but his rendition of 'Nancy with the Laughing Face' infuriated her. She wanted to know why he sang 'that fucking song', so he dropped it from his repertoire. Their constant bickering gave the gossip columnists plenty of good copy and often made the headlines. Frank's pal, mobster Mickey Cohen, told him to go back to his wife and kids, but Sinatra ignored the advice. Cohen's bodyguard was Johnny Stompanato, the handsome hood who later became involved with Lana Turner and was accidentally stabbed by her daughter Cheryl in April 1958. When Sinatra asked Cohen to keep Stompanato away from Ava, Mickey refused; he never got involved in his men's relationship with 'broads', he said, and besides, Frank should go home to Nancy.

Frank was suffering from a case of the jitters at the Copa. He had problems with his throat and feared he might lose his voice. It hardly helped matters when Artie Shaw invited Frank and Ava to see him perform at the opening of the jazz club, Bop City, with a dinner party after the show. 'I think Frank hated me,' Artie remarked. 'He wanted to sing for me, but I told him I didn't use boy singers.' Sinatra warned Artie never to speak to Ava – or else. Shaw pointed to Frank's bodyguard and made a crack, 'If you're so tough, why do you need him?' Ava decided to go to Bop City without Frank. She was bored with mothering him and listening to him talk on the phone to his ten-year-old daughter Nancy, who constantly pleaded with him to come home. Ava was having doubts about Frank's ability to give up his family.

When she ran off to see Artie perform, Sinatra was infuriated. He had gone back to the Hampshire House expecting to find Ava there. Incensed, he called Shaw's apartment, got her on the phone, and exclaimed, 'I just wanted to say goodbye!'

'Where are you going, Frank?' she asked. 'Can't I come, too?'

'Not where I'm going, baby.'

Ava heard a pistol shot and then another. She screamed, dropped the phone and rushed to the hotel, accompanied by Artie and friends.

The gunshots caused a commotion on the eighth floor of the Hampshire House. Columbia Records chief Manie Sachs scurried from his room. Producer David O. Selznick told him, 'I think the son of a bitch shot himself!'

They ran into Frank's suite. Finding the bullet holes in his mattress, they switched it with the mattress in Sachs' room before police arrived. Ava hysterically pushed her way through the jammed hallway, only to see Sinatra sitting up in bed reading a book. Needless to say, the incident made the front pages.

MGM demanded that Ava immediately report for work on *Pandora and the Flying Dutchman* in Spain. Getting her out of the country and away from

Frank was the studio's solution. She was reminded of the morals clause in her contract and that they could suspend her without pay if she did not oblige. The studio, keen to get rid of Sinatra since his blatant affair with Ava, bought out his contract for $85,000. But before he received the cheque Nancy's lawyers took various monies due her, and he was left with only the crumbs. MCA, the agency that handled Frank, also dropped him, announcing that he wanted to be a freelance artist. So, with no money and no agent, Sinatra was left out in the cold.

In April 1950, Frank saw Ava off at the airport. For her it was a sad and tender goodbye, but he promised to visit her in Spain as soon as he had finished his engagement at the Copa. He called her every day, but Ava found salvation in the role of Pandora – and in the Costa Brava, eighty miles north of Barcelona, where much of the filming took place. She was impressed with the lazy spirit of the people, dancing the flamenco and drinking in dark corners of unpretentious nightclubs. She was equally inspired by Mario Cabre, who played the matador in *Pandora*. He was not Spain's greatest bullfighter, but had a showy style in the ring which appealed to spectators. He also dated socialite beauties and wrote romantic poetry. To Ava, he was the ideal Latin type – tall, handsome, broad-shouldered, and narrow-hipped. Strumming a guitar, he serenaded her with verses of love and devotion. MGM took advantage of this by ensuring that his love odes to Ava were printed in the newspapers alongside cosy pictures of the couple. L.B. Mayer hoped this would precipitate the break-up of her relationship with Frank, who retaliated by making threatening phone calls to her. Fed up with his childishness, she took off with Cabre, even though the Spaniard meant nothing more to her than a sexual fling.

Frank was not performing well at the Copa. He complained about everything and everyone. His nemesis, columnist Lee Mortimer, bet $100 that Sinatra would not finish his Copa booking. To spite him, Frank forced himself to show up for every show – until one night he opened his mouth and nothing came out. Bandleader Skitch Henderson said it was terrifying. 'I saw the panic in his eyes,' he recalled. 'It became so quiet in the club. Frank gasped and said "Goodnight," and raced off the stage.'

Sinatra's physician reported that he had suffered a submucosal haemorrhage of the throat and suggested he take a two-week vacation. Billy Eckstein replaced him at the Copa.

Against doctor's orders, Frank flew to Spain. Rumours came through customs that he was carrying an expensive package, which turned out to be a $10,000 diamond and emerald necklace. He joined Ava at the Sea

Gull Inn, where she was staying. Mario Cabre, who was in Genoa, spoke freely to reporters: 'Ava Gardner is the woman I love with all the strength in my soul.' Ava in turn told the press how she felt about Mario: 'We all adore Mario. He's a wonderful guy, but there is no question of love. The whole story is absurd.' As for Sinatra, she said, 'Frank's a wonderful guy, too. The press and everybody is talking about marriage. It's too soon. Frankie hasn't even got a divorce.'

Sinatra, looking pale and thin, explained, 'Ava and I have been chaperoned every minute we've been together. She's a terrific girl. All I can say is there is no change in the matrimonial situation.'

Though they stayed in separate villas and were accompanied by Frank's friend, songwriter Jimmy Van Heusen, it was a mistake for the ailing Sinatra to rush off to Spain with a $10,000 necklace that was obviously for Ava, while Nancy celebrated Mother's Day without a gift. Frank admitted it was bad judgement on his part.

Talking too loud in public was bad judgement as well. At a crowded dinner table Frank told Ava, 'If I hear that Spanish runt has been hanging around you again, I'll kill him and you!'

'We're making a fucking movie together,' she snapped. 'He's supposed to be my lover – how can he avoid being near me? Besides, I haven't raised hell about Marilyn Maxwell, have I?'

'That's different. We're old friends.'

'Well, Mario and I are new friends,' Ava spoke up.

At this stage in his life Frank was to be pitied, but he was still a married man flaunting an affair, and a sick performer who was more concerned about Ava than his vocal cords. His records weren't selling and few club dates were forthcoming. Yet he had bought Ava an expensive necklace far beyond his means. Newspapers in the United States were roasting Sinatra, who decided to fly home earlier than expected after days and days of damp weather in Spain. When he arrived in New York he told the press, 'The only present I gave Ava was six bottles of Coke. Ask the Barcelona customs people.' Frank arrived in Los Angeles just in time to read about Ava's triumphant reunion with her bullfighter. Mario had engulfed her in his arms with 'Hello, baby.' Sinatra brushed it off as a publicity stunt, but he was worried and signed a property settlement with Nancy. She was to keep their Holmby Hills home and was given custody of the children, along with one-third of his gross income up to $150,000 and ten per cent of the gross above that figure until her death or remarriage. Frank kept the house in Palm Springs and a 1949 Cadillac convertible.

In June 1950 Ava flew to London with the cast and crew of *Pandora and the Flying Dutchman* for studio work. Frank later flew in for an appearance at the London Palladium. His reviews were excellent. The *Sunday Chronicle* wrote, 'Bless me, he's good!', while *The Times* said, 'To a people whose idea of manhood is husky, full-blooded, and self-reliant, he has dared to suggest that under the crashing self-assertion, man is still a child, frightened and whimpering in the dark.'

For Frank and Ava, their brief stay in London was a chance for happiness at last. The English reporters were considerate and scarce, offering the famous couple peace and a good deal of freedom. One English clergyman, citing the blatant affair, labelled back-street women as 'painted trollops who worship at the shrine of Saint Ava Gardner'. Nonetheless, Ava and Frank were presented to Princess Elizabeth and Prince Philip. It was a very special occasion for the skinny singer from Hoboken.

Ava went back to Hollywood to play Julie, a tragic half-caste, in *Show Boat*. Frank went back to nothing. When his TV and radio shows were cancelled Ava called her friend Howard Hughes for help. Frank sang two songs in RKO's forgettable *Double Dynamite* before Universal offered him *Meet Danny Wilson*, a musical with Shelley Winters. But she claimed that the picture began in chaos and ended in disaster. 'Mr. Sinatra was in the process of divorcing Nancy to marry Ava Gardner. I think he thought that's what he wanted. His children were quite young and there were always psychiatrists and priests and his kids visiting him on the set. Everyone in Hollywood knew his struggle to divorce or not to divorce.'

Shelley, who had a tendency to gain weight, joked that Frank was losing a pound a week, making her look heavier. They worked well together – but he was ready to crack. No one remembers what sparked the vicious argument between Winters and Sinatra, during which he called her a 'bowlegged bitch of a Brooklyn blonde' and she called him a 'skinny no-talent, stupid Hoboken bastard'. But with tension mounting, production was shut down. A studio executive spoke to Shelley about her co-star. 'Mr. Sinatra is going through a terrible and troubled period of his life and career. He's going against his religion and he has periods when he loses his voice. Perhaps you could examine his own humanity and realise the terrible trouble that young man is in and understand the reasons that are making him behave the way he did.'

Winters agreed to go back to work and began preparing for the final scene, in which Frank's last line was supposed to be, 'I'll have a cup of coffee and leave you two lovebirds alone.' Fade out. But instead he came out with, 'I'll go have a cup of Jack Daniels, or I'm gonna pull that blonde broad's hair out by its black roots.'

Shelley threw a bedpan at Frank and hit her mark. She went home, refusing all calls until Nancy Sinatra succeeded in getting through. In tears she asked a favour of her friend. 'Shelley, Frank doesn't get the $25,000 until the picture's finished. The bank might foreclose the mortgage on the house. My children are going to be out on the street. Please finish the picture.'

So Winters went back to work again, telling Sinatra he could say any damn thing he wanted. *Meet Danny Wilson* was finished in five minutes. *Time* magazine commented, 'The movie cribs so freely from the career and personality of Frank Sinatra that fans expect Ava Gardner to pop up in the last reel.' Other critics considered *Meet Danny Wilson* good entertainment. Unfortunately Sinatra fans did not flock to the Paramount to see him, either on the screen or in person.

Always restless, Ava thought Frank was still spending too much time with his family. She considered these get-togethers hypocritical and unnecessary. She also resented his visiting her on the set of *Lone Star*, where he found her enjoying laughs with her co-star Clark Gable. Spencer Tracy hung around as well, telling jokes and having a few drinks in her dressing room. Frank, in contrast, sat in a corner moping, unhappy because Ava was enjoying herself. He noticed her I-don't-give-a-damn attitude and fell apart when she announced her plans to visit Mexico when the film was finished. She was going her own way. Sinatra went to Nancy and begged for his freedom. 'If I can't get a divorce,' he moaned, 'where is there for me to go and what is there for me to do?'

On 29 May columnist Hedda Hopper hinted that Nancy was losing public sympathy and support from Hollywood insiders. After a year and a half of sizzling publicity and bitter arguments, maybe it was time she considered the children.

Having made a stopover at El Paso, Texas, during a flight to Mexico, Ava dashed for the plane while Frank snarled at reporters, 'You miserable crumbs! You S.O.B.s!' *Newsweek* wrote that Sinatra was losing control. MGM publicity chief Howard Strickling had already spoken to Ava about Frank's unpleasant outbursts, which were hurting her image. After all, she was on her way up the ladder of success and he was on his way down. She had been trained by MGM always to smile and have a kind word with the press.

Sinatra's influence on her was not good, but Ava seemed oblivious – until Frank's bodyguard threatened to kill a photographer at the Beachcomber Club in Acapulco. During the fracas, Ava wept while Sinatra continued cursing the press. The episode was written up in U.S. newspapers. Three days later their private plane landed in a quiet area of Los Angeles airport where Sinatra's Cadillac was waiting. He stepped on the gas pedal, pinning reporters against a fence, just missing them by a hair. Frank leaned out the of the window and yelled, 'Next time I'll kill you!!'

William Eccles, an airport photographer, described what happened next. 'Sinatra turned the car into me to scare me away. I figured he'd swerve from me so I shot the picture and didn't move. He slammed on the brake, and at the last minute I jumped. I went up over the fender and rolled off on my stomach, dropping my camera. It was a hit-and-run case. I could have sued.' Eccles did file a criminal complaint, but he withdrew it when Frank apologised. Once again, Howard Strickling pleaded with Ava to end her affair with Sinatra. 'The Legion of Decency might ban your films,' he explained. 'You're on the brink of international stardom. The premiere of *Show Boat* is coming up. Think about it.'

The *Hollywood Citizen News* wrote, 'It takes a big man to fill the shoes of a big position. It takes a man of depth to keep his balance when constantly in the spotlight. On both counts, Sinatra doesn't measure up.' Hedda Hopper said, 'A year from now when their romance is over, Frank will be thin as your backbone and Ava will be more beautiful than ever.'

In mid-August 1951 Sinatra flew to Reno for a singing engagement at the Riverside Hotel and established residency for a Nevada divorce. Sporting a moustache and a broad smile, he shocked reporters by greeting them with, 'I hope I'm gonna get along with you fellows.' When Ava arrived he again met the press, telling them that he and Ava would be married, but Nancy hadn't followed through with her divorce plans.

On the Labor Day weekend they went to Lake Tahoe, staying at the Cal-Neva Lodge owned by mobster Sam Giancana. When, during a heated argument, Ava admitted having a one-night tryst with Mario Cabre, Frank went crazy. He insulted her so severely that she drove back to Los Angeles. As she walked into her house the phone rang. It was Frank's buddy, Hank Sanicola. 'Ava, hurry back. Frank's taken an overdose!' She and her sister Bappie raced back to Lake Tahoe, only to find that Frank hadn't taken enough phenobarbital tablets even to have his stomach pumped.

Ava wrote in her memoirs that she could have killed him. 'I know now that Frank's mock suicide dramas – his desperate love signals to get me back to his side – were, at root, calls for help.' She went on to say their love was deep and true, even though the fact was that they couldn't live with each other any more than they couldn't live without each other. And she admitted, 'All I know is if Frank had lost me or I'd lost him during those months, our worlds would have been shattered.'

But Sinatra denied that he had attempted suicide, while Ava herself, holding his hand, said at the time that the whole thing was ridiculous. It was the last straw as far as MGM was concerned. The studio took matters into their own hands and decided their wedding would take place on 19 September, the day after Sinatra's six-week residency in Nevada ended. Two days before the proposed date, Frank and Ava 'went public' in Hollywood at the premiere of *Show Boat* at the Egyptian Theater and the public cheered, calling out 'Ava!' and 'Frankie!'

But while the audience was applauding Ava's portrayal of Julie, Nancy Sinatra was contesting the Nevada divorce, revisions of the property settlement and back alimony of $40,000. She sued Frank for legal fees and secured a lien on his Palm Springs home for security. On 31 October 1951, Nancy was granted an interlocutory decree of divorce in Santa Monica, charging her husband with mental cruelty. The next day Ava and Frank flew to Las Vegas for a four-minute private hearing before Judge A.S. Henderson. They checked into the Sands Hotel, posed for photographers and had a champagne dinner to celebrate.

Frank did not want MGM involved in the wedding. Ava wanted to work with Howard Strickling, although Sinatra did not, and she promised to call Howard first so MGM could make the announcement. Arrangements were made for the couple to be married in Philadelphia at the Germantown mansion owned by Isaac Levy, founder of CBS. They picked up their marriage licence on Friday, 2 November. Since Pennsylvania law required a three-day waiting period, they then went to the Hampshire House in New York. On Saturday night they partied at the Sugar Hill Nightclub in Harlem, getting into a heated argument after Frank had supposedly been flirting with another woman. 'Let's call off this fucking wedding,' Ava hissed, and she threw her six-carat engagement ring across the room. 'I can't even trust him on the eve of our wedding!' she screamed.

On Sunday the wedding was still off. Dolly Sinatra intervened with an invitation to a homemade Italian dinner in Hoboken. Dolly loved Ava's casual, unpretentious manner and considered it an omen of friendship that her birthday was Christmas Day and Ava's Christmas Eve. While Ava was having fun with the Sinatra clan, the newsmen were busy in

Philadelphia trying to find out the date, time and place of the wedding. When Frank was alerted, he decided that the ceremony should be held at the home of Lester Sachs, brother of Columbia Records mogul Manie. On Wednesday, 7 November, Frank and Ava were finally married. 'Well,' he beamed, 'we made it!'

The honeymooners flew to Miami – forgetting Ava's suitcase. The press respected their privacy but one photographer got a poignant photo of the couple strolling barefoot on the beach, hand in hand. Frank's trousers were rolled up and Ava wore his jacket over a casual blouse and skirt. When the trousseau arrived they flew to Havana for a few days.

The Sinatras were planning to live in Frank's Palm Springs house, and the fan magazines were full of articles about Ava's plans to redecorate and how she loved following Dolly's Italian recipes. But, just two weeks after the wedding, Ava called Artie Shaw. 'I can't handle it. It's fucking impossible!'

'We all know that,' Shaw responded. 'Give it two more months and it'll get worse.'

'It can't get worse.'

She replied that divorce would ruin them both.

But the truth is that the Sinatras thrived on their stormy marriage. Their domestic tornados were actually thrilling – especially for Ava, who quickly became bored in paradise. One of their mating calls was her perfume. After a fight he would go downstairs or to another room, sulking in a deep state of depression. Then, a little while later, he would catch the scent of sweet passion and run back to her.

The year 1952 was Frank's worst. Proof of this was his eagerness to make peace with the press. He arrived in New York prepared for interviews and pictures. But the newsmen ignored him completely and not one flash bulb popped in his face. He even sent a note to the Press Photographers Association: 'I'll always be made up and ready in case you ever want to shoot any pictures of me.'

Variety carried the headline: 'Sinatra Croons Sweetly to the Press – "So Sorry Now."' Meanwhile the *New York World-Telegram* wrote: 'Gone On Frankie '42; Gone In '52' and 'What a Difference a Decade Makes – Empty Balcony.'

Sinatra jokes were going around. When a bobbysoxer at the Paramount was asked how she liked Frankie, the teenager sighed, 'I think Frankie Laine's wonderful!'

At the Chez Paree nightclub in Chicago, which seated 1200, only 120 people showed up for Frank's performance. 'We need a vacation in Hawaii,' he told Ava.

'I can't,' she said. 'I'm scheduled to do a film.'

'And I said we're going to Hawaii!'

As a result, MGM suspended Ava without pay. So, she hired super-agent Charles Feldman, who informed Metro he would not negotiate Ava's contract while she was on suspension. The studio conceded. In May 1952 she planted her hands and feet in wet cement in a special ceremony in front of Grauman's Chinese Theater on Hollywood Boulevard. It would take Frank thirteen more years to achieve this honour.

Sinatra's career was now limited to nightclubs, but he was having recurrent problems with his throat. Friends referred to these infections as 'guilt germs'. Despite his divorce, Frank was still torn between his family and Ava; she still thought he was spending too much time with his children, with whom she had no relationship. Nor did she like the cronies who were always around him, but she put up with it until one night when he ignored her for two hours over dinner while carrying on lengthy conversations with his buddies. Ava left abruptly and wasn't missed until Frank was ready to leave. Two days later she called him from Italy. She had gone to the airport directly from the restaurant and boarded the first plane to Rome.

In September 1950 Frank played the Riviera in Fort Lee, New Jersey. *Variety* wrote, 'Whatever Sinatra had for the bobbysoxers he now has for the café mob. It adds up to showmanship rather than any basic singing appeal. His performance is notable for self-assurance and a knowing crowd, whatever the misadventures of his personal life and career.'

When Ava attended the New York premiere of her film, *The Snows of Kilimanjaro*, she was alone. In between shows Frank raced from New Jersey to Manhattan, and he brought his wife back to the Riviera for the last show. But when Ava saw his former girlfriend, Marilyn Maxwell, sitting in the front row, she froze. Sinatra then sang 'All of Me' in Maxwell's direction – or so Ava assumed – and she stormed out of the club, flew back to Hollywood, and mailed her wedding band to Frank at the Riviera with a bitter letter. Sinatra told Sammy Davis Jr, 'That's what happens when you get hung up on a chick.' To reporters he said, 'It's only a mild rift.' Ava refused to answer his phone calls – but when Frank showed up in person, she ran into his arms. It was the calm before the storm.

Soon afterwards, according to Ava, Frank wanted to go away for a few days, but she had plans with Bappie. Becoming testy, he teased,

'Since Lana is staying at the house in Palm Springs, if you want me I'll be there fucking her.'

Ava laughed it off, but could not forget that Frank and Lana had once been deeply involved. She and Bappie drove to Palm Springs, where they spotted Frank driving back and forth in front of the house. As soon as he left, Ava went in the front door and joined Lana, who was with her business manager, Ben Cole. Ten minutes later Frank burst through the door and shouted, 'Get the hell out of my house!' Ava responded that it was her house too, and he yelled, 'I bet you two broads have been really cutting me up!' He called Lana a whore and she ran out of the house in tears. Ava began packing up her belongings, all the time arguing loudly and bitterly with Frank who threw her clothes in the driveway. Neighbours eventually called the police. Lana and Cole, returning for their suitcases, took Ava with them to a rented house. 'We never referred to that night again,' Lana said.

But vile rumours persisted, among them that Frank had found her and Ava in bed together. The headline of the *Los Angeles Mirror* was, 'Boudoir Fight Heads Frankie and Ava to Courts', while the *Los Angeles Times* wrote, 'Sinatra-Ava Boudoir Now Buzzes. Too Much Left to the Imagination.' Louella Parsons reported that Frank had discovered Ava with Lana, unintentionally implying that the girls had been in bed together.

Turner's former secretary Taylor Pero explained that Lana had fled to Palm Springs to get away from her abusive boyfriend, Fernando Lamas. She and Ava had been comparing notes on Artie Shaw and Frank when he burst in during the conversation. Pero said that after the big fight in Palm Springs, Ava and Lana had gone to Mexico for a vacation. The late Jackie Gleason stated that 'Frank could not forget what he heard. He'd call me in the middle of the night for a long time to talk about what happened because he was so hurt.'

This break-up was more serious than the others. It was their commitment to appear at a rally for Democratic presidential candidate Adlai Stevenson that finally brought them back together – again. Ava walked out on stage and said, 'Ladies and gentlemen, I can't do anything myself, but I can introduce a wonderful, wonderful man. I'm a great fan of his myself. My husband, Frank Sinatra!'

Years later Ava said, 'Frank and I might have had the most on again, off again marriage of the century, but it always struck me as fascinating the way our lives seemed to double back and reconnect.'

*

When Frank read *From Here to Eternity* by James Jones he immediately identified with Private Angelo Maggio, a tough Italian-American G.I. 'Columbia Pictures was doing the film,' he said, 'and I wanted to play Maggio. I just knew I had to do it. I knew Maggio. I went to school with him in Hoboken. I was beaten up with him. I might have been Maggio.'

Sinatra went to see the blunt, hard-bitten head of Columbia, Harry Cohn, who told him, 'You're a singer, not an actor, Frank.'

'About the money . . .'

'Who's talking money?'

'I used to get $150,000 a picture.'

'Used to,' Cohn grunted.

'Yeah, but I'll do it for a thousand a week.'

'I'll think about it.'

Frank sensed Cohn wasn't buying, so he told his agents he'd do the picture for nothing. Cohn relished telling the story about Sinatra's pleading. 'He owes $110,000 in back taxes but he offered to pay me if he could play Maggio.'

Ava spoke to Cohn's wife, Joan, to explain the seriousness of the situation. 'I'm afraid Frank might kill himself,' she said. 'All I'm asking is that Harry give him a screen test. That's all.' Ava had done this on her own without Frank's knowledge. Cohn realised he might want Ava for a picture someday and she would flatly refuse if Frank wasn't given a chance. Sinatra tried to get in touch with Cohn who was unavailable, but news leaked out that Eli Wallach was being tested for the part of Maggio.

Ava was scheduled to film *Mogambo* with Clark Gable in Africa and would be there for at least five months. She paid Frank's travelling expenses so they could be together. On 7 November 1952, they celebrated their first wedding anniversary on a Stratocruiser bound for Nairobi. Ava and director John Ford did not get along so, in typical Ava style, she was waiting to get even with him. On introducing her to the British governor and his wife, Ford asked her, 'What the hell do you see in that 120-pound runt?'

'Well,' she replied, 'There's only ten pounds of Frank but 110 pounds of cock.'

Ford, who could curse better than anyone, was shocked, but the governor roared with laughter.

Five days after arriving in Africa, Frank received a cable to report for a screen test at Columbia as soon as possible. Thirty-six hours later he was in Hollywood. Producer Buddy Adler and director Fred Zinnemann were impressed, but Harry Cohn had the final say and he was out of town. Frank flew back to Africa to spend the holidays with his wife.

Several days after Frank's departure, Ava collapsed on the set. She told John Ford she was pregnant and wanted to have an abortion in London. Ford tried to talk her out of it but she said, 'This is not the time.'

'This is going to hurt Frank when he finds out.'

'He's not going to find out,' Ava replied.

MGM arranged the abortion. Twelve pounds thinner, discouraged and weary, she returned to Nairobi. Just before Christmas Frank returned, laden with gifts he had paid for with her money. He also brought pasta, along with all the ingredients required to make Dolly's spaghetti sauce. 'Frank was very thoughtful,' Ava recalled. 'He put up a Christmas tree and decorated it. He also installed a shower in a little wooden hut behind my tent and pumped water from the river.'

But Sinatra's humility did not last. Eventually he received word that the part of Maggio was his at $8000. 'I'll show those mothers!' he exclaimed over and over again, pacing back and forth in front of the tent waving the cable. 'I'll show them!'

Ava liked him better down and out. 'When Frank was on top he was a sacred monster, convinced there was no one else in the world except himself,' she said.

Sinatra lived, dreamt and ate the part of Maggio. Co-star Montgomery Clift idolised Frank. One major disturbance occurred when Frank wanted to play a scene with Monty sitting down, regardless of the script. Director Zinnemann didn't like the idea; nor did Clift, but Sinatra persisted. The pair argued, and Frank slapped Monty out of his drunken stupor. They were such good friends, though, that Sinatra knew he could get away with it. After all, he had slapped Clift more than once before to sober him up.

Produced at a cost of $2.5 million, *From Here to Eternity* grossed $20 million within a year. And the critics were unanimous about Sinatra – he was superb. The picture was nominated for an Academy Award, as were all five leading players – Sinatra, Clift, Burt Lancaster, Deborah Kerr and Donna Reed. Because Clift and Lancaster were both nominated in the Best Actor category, Sinatra was classified as a Supporting Actor. This was to be an advantage, since William Holden won the Oscar for Best Actor in *Stalag 17*.

In May 1953 Frank was booked on a three-month singing tour through Europe and he asked Ava to accompany him. And because he asked rather than insisted, she went. Columnist Louella Parsons now wrote, 'The nervous unhappy Frank Sinatra, who declared war on newspaper people and let his hot Italian temper get him in trouble, is a character of the past. The new Frankie has put on weight. His eyes are clear and better still, he's happy. This is the new Frankie.'

The 'Battling Sinatras', as the press referred to the couple, had not seen each other for four months and their reunion was more romantic than either had expected. According to Frank, the tour would be their second honeymoon, and he added, 'I feel great and my voice is better than ever.'

However, the trip got off to a bad start when their car broke down and they missed the flight to Milan. They were forced to fly to Rome where, ironically, several of Ava's films were playing. Her fans and the press alike ignored Frank, and he was booed midway through his concert in Naples because the crowd wanted 'Ava! Ava!' After the police were summoned, it was agreed that she should make an appearance to appease the angry crowd. She walked on stage, waved and walked off, and the audience went wild. They booed Frank with renewed vigour, repeating Ava's name over and over again. She boarded the plane for Milan alone.

After Sinatra played to half-filled theatres in Denmark and Sweden, he cancelled the rest of the European leg of the tour and returned to meet Ava in London. One evening they invited Stewart Granger and his wife, Jean Simmons, to the Ambassadors nightclub where Frank was appearing. The Grangers arrived at the Sinatras' apartment during a violent argument that ended in total silence. Frank said he was going ahead and asked the Grangers to drive Ava to the club. 'He's impossible to live with,' she hissed. At the club, however, Sinatra sang his love songs to her and Ava cried, 'Look at the goddamn son-of-a-bitch! How can you resist him?'

Ava had almost completed *Knights of the Round Table* and planned to attend both the New York premiere of *From Here to Eternity* and Frank's opening at the 500 Club in Atlantic City. But he told her, 'I have to rehearse. I have a career too, you know!' Their ensuing fight was so violent that the other tenants called the landlord, who threatened to evict the couple. Frank arrived at the Waldorf Astoria in New York on 12 August. Meanwhile Ava went to Madrid for a rest and there met Spain's most famous bullfighter, Luis Miguel Dominguin, whom Ernest Hemingway described as a combination of Don Juan and Hamlet. There was an instant attraction between Ava and Luis, who was suffering from a bad goring to the stomach.

Upon Ava's return from Spain, she checked into the Hampshire House without getting in touch with Frank. He read of her arrival in

New York in the newspapers just like everyone else. Frank told reporters he couldn't understand her actions, while Ava's public statement was, 'It's my marriage and my life!'

Again it was Dolly Sinatra who got them back together, by means of inviting them separately to dinner. Neither knew the other was coming. But the minute they saw each other, they were instantly reconciled. Frank moved into the Hampshire House with Ava. But when he began coming in at four in the morning, she complained bitterly. 'Don't cut the corners too close on me, baby,' he warned.

On 2 October they attended the premiere of *Mogambo* at Radio City Music Hall, and they flew to Hollywood the next day. Almost immediately Frank went to Las Vegas for an appearance at the Sands Hotel, and Ava attended the Los Angeles premiere of *Mogambo* without him. When a picture of Sinatra in the company of two Las Vegas showgirls appeared in the newspaper, Ava's attorney set up an appointment with Frank, but he failed to show up. On 29 October 1953, MGM officially announced that the Sinatras had reluctantly exhausted every effort at reconciliation. Frank could not eat or sleep. He told columnist Earl Wilson, 'If it took 75 years to get a divorce, there wouldn't be any other woman.'

Ava laughed. 'Frank doesn't love me. He would rather go out with some other girl, almost any other girl.' Sinatra insisted Ava's place was with him, but Ava wanted to get as far away from Frank as possible. She flew to Rome to film *The Barefoot Contessa*. Frank attempted suicide by cutting his wrists and was hospitalised with a nervous breakdown. His subsequent recordings of 'My One and Only Love' and 'There Will Never Be Another You' were poignant enough to touch the hearts of all those who had loved and lost. According to conductor Nelson Riddle, 'It was Ava who did that, who taught him how to sing a torch song. That's how he learned. She was the greatest love of his life and he lost her.'

Ava had been planning to spend the Christmas holidays in Madrid with Luis Dominguin until Frank showed up with a bad head cold. The Sinatras went into seclusion for a few days before he quietly boarded a plane for New York. When the beautiful Greek statue of Ava in the title role of *The Barefoot Contessa* caught Frank's eye, he had it installed in his backyard as a shrine. There were pictures of Ava all over his house, including the bathrooms. He tore up a photo of her and then tried to put it back together, but found he was missing a piece. The doorbell rang and when Frank answered it, a draught blew the missing piece into the air. He was so happy he gave his gold watch to the delivery boy. His nights were spent sitting in the dark with a bottle of brandy, while Ava's pictures alone were illuminated. 'I know we could have worked it out,' he told friends.

But Dominguin was a strong competitor. The splendidly built Spaniard was all that Sinatra was not. Luis had thick black hair while Frank wore a toupee. Luis was fearless in and out of the bullring, while Frank's strength lay in his bodyguard. Luis was a romantic, attentive companion, whereas Frank wanted his cronies around all the time. Dominguin's close friends were Picasso and Stravinsky and Hemingway. Sinatra's pals were hoodlums and gangsters.

But on 25 March 1954, Sinatra claimed his Oscar for Best Supporting Actor at the Pantages Theatre in Hollywood. He kissed Nancy Jr and shook his son's hand before running up on stage. Ava, nominated for Best Supporting Actress in *Mogambo*, lost to Audrey Hepburn in *Roman Holiday*. She sent a congratulatory telegram to her husband. Sinatra said, 'The greatest change in my life began the night they gave me the Oscar.'

Frank dated Judy Garland, but dumped her because she wanted to get married. He then had an affair with Elizabeth Taylor who became pregnant. Instead of proposing to her, he arranged for an abortion. But no woman could make him forget Ava. She had bought a house in Madrid in March 1954, while Frank spent much of his time in Las Vegas. He owned nine per cent of the Sands Hotel, where he performed at the Copa Room for $100,000 a week. Even then Sinatra drew large crowds to the small town in the desert with only four hotels. He was the guy who made Las Vegas famous – classy, too, when he suggested that the casino bosses wear tuxedos. Voted the most popular male vocalist, Frank now had clout and he used it. The Mafia ruled Vegas and they recognised Sinatra's worth.

So did Hollywood, after his Oscar win. He played an assassin in *Suddenly*, a down-and-out singer in *Young at Heart* with Doris Day, a doctor in *Not as a Stranger* with Robert Mitchum, a gambler in *Guys and Dolls* with Marlon Brando, and a drug addict in *The Man with the Golden Arm*.

Debbie Reynolds was engaged to Eddie Fisher when she made *The Tender Trap* with Frank. She was very surprised when one day he said, 'I want to talk to you.' Over lunch he wanted to know if she really loved Fisher. Debbie said she did. 'Very difficult life to be married to a singer,' he said shaking his head. 'Very hard. You should think twice about this. You're too young. You'll never be able to make it work. I know.'

During the 1955 holiday season, the Holmby Hills Rat Pack held their first meeting. According to their leader, Humphrey Bogart, it was all a joke – the group's only function was 'the relief of boredom and independence'. Judy Garland was First VP, Bogart's fourth wife Lauren Bacall was Mother, Judy's third husband Sid Luft was Cage Manager, agent Irving 'Swifty' Lazar was Recording Secretary and Treasurer, Nathaniel Benchley was Historian, and Sinatra was Pack Master or Chairman. Actor David Niven, Mike Romanoff, Jimmy Van Heusen, and singer Kay Thompson were also members, while Bogart was Rat-in-Charge of Public Relations.

Frank was in awe of Bogart, a well-educated and polished man not at all like the characters he played in films. He was all that Frank wanted to be. Lauren Bacall attracted Frank, too. There were rumours that they were involved in a relationship that has not been clearly identified. Bacall enjoyed Sinatra's company and Bogart became irritated if they lingered too long together. 'It's too bad if he's lonely,' he told his wife, 'but that's his choice. We have our own road to travel, never forget that – we can't live his life.' In February 1956, Bogie was diagnosed with throat cancer. During his fatal illness it was apparent to close friends that Frank and Lauren were having an affair. As usual, he hesitated before getting involved. Bogart died on 14 January 1957.

Following *High Society* with Bing Crosby and Grace Kelly, Sinatra filmed *The Pride and the Passion* with Cary Grant and Sophia Loren in Spain. His role as a Spanish peasant boy was a good one but he fought about everything – his lines, his accommodation and the length of his stay in Spain. When Ava didn't hear from him, she made the first move, but they were together for only one night, and this only aggravated his mood more on the movie set. Producer-director Stanley Kramer said, 'When Sinatra walks into a room, tension walks in behind him . . . He was impatient . . . He wanted to break loose so we shot all of his scenes together and he left early.'

Frank was always destined for trouble, although he managed to lie his way out of most difficulties. He attempted to help Joe DiMaggio catch wife Marilyn Monroe in a compromising position. In what was referred to as the 'wrong door raid', they mistakenly barged into the apartment of an elderly woman who sued. Sinatra, under oath, testified that he had nothing to do with it but he was proven wrong. Marilyn soon divorced DiMaggio, who changed his mind about his friend Frank when Sinatra began not only dating Monroe but sharing her with other men. Sinatra even considered marriage to Marilyn a few months before her death in 1962, when she was being treated shabbily by the Kennedy brothers. 'If she's Mrs. Frank Sinatra, no one will mess with her,' he said.

Columnist James Bacon believes Frank deliberately broke into someone else's apartment during the 'wrong door raid' in order to protect Marilyn. But it's doubtful whether Sinatra would have married her. Though he was into kinky sex and prostitutes, he had a thing about 'class' when it came to women. When Monroe was staying at his house for a while, she was in the habit of walking around nude in front of his friends until he reprimanded her. This was typical of the delightful Marilyn, but not Frank's idea of the proper wife.

Frank, however, considered Lauren Bacall a classy dame and the couple finally had an open relationship in 1957. She described the affair as 'erratic', blaming the difficulties on Frank's problems with Ava. It took him a year to propose marriage but when he did, she accepted. He left for Miami the following day, but read in the newspaper that Bacall had told reporters about their engagement. She called him to explain, but Sinatra was angry and suggested they should not see each other for a while. They didn't speak again for a long time. Ava then called Frank from Spain. 'I hear you called off the wedding,' she said.

'What wedding?'

'To Betty Bacall.'

'Jesus, I was never going to marry that pushy female!'

Ava was amused.

But Bacall wrote in her memoirs that Frank had acted like a shit. He was too cowardly to tell the truth, she wrote.

Sinatra's television show, which aired from October 1957 to June 1958, was a flop for one simple reason – he did not want to rehearse. Frank had the impression all he had to do to be a hit was just show up. He denounced Elvis Presley and rock 'n' roll, describing Presley's kind of music as 'deplorable, a rancid-smelling aphrodisiac'. Frank was jealous, naturally. Elvis was a revolution as he sang and wiggled his hips and vibrated his legs. A sensation in 1957, he was untouchable by the great Sinatra, who finally recognised Presley's popularity by welcoming him home in a 1960 TV special after his stint in the army. Elvis sang 'Witch Craft' and Frank performed 'Love Me Tender' in a fine duet that brought the house down. Thanks to Presley, the show achieved the highest TV rating in five years.

Maybe Sinatra didn't make the grade on television, but his films, such as *A Hole in the Head* with Edward G. Robinson, and *Some Came Running* co-starring Shirley MacLaine, were successful at the box office. MacLaine was Frank's very close friend but wished he would work harder at acting. 'He won't polish,' she said. 'He feels polishing would make him stagnant.'

Sinatra's performances with the Rat Pack showed that at least some of the time, he was right about that. The group – which now consisted of Sammy Davis Jr, Dean Martin, Peter Lawford, who was married to Pat Kennedy, and comedian Joey Bishop – performed unrehearsed with great success. They took up where Frank left off at the Sands Hotel, and their efforts helped consolidate the position of Las Vegas as the boom town that it is today.

On 14 July 1957, Sinatra's marriage to Ava was officially over. It had taken her four years to go through with the divorce. She charged him with desertion and absence for more than six months. Frank, accepting the fact that Ava would always be the love of his life, now moved on. The majority of his subsequent romances were 'friendly' ones with women who enjoyed intimacy without a marriage licence – Marlene Dietrich, Anita Ekberg, Jill St. John, Grace Kelly, Shirley MacLaine, Kim Novak and Natalie Wood, to name only a few.

And after Jack Kennedy's death, Frank dated Jacqueline Kennedy, who was not immune to his charms. He wanted to be a major part of her life, but she thought better of it and suddenly made herself unavailable when he called.

Frank and his best pal Sam Giancana had been instrumental in getting Jack Kennedy elected president in 1960, buying votes in the key states of Illinois and West Virginia. Frank introduced beautiful Judith Campbell, with whom he he'd had an affair, to Kennedy. When they became lovers, Sinatra handed her over to Giancana. 'You've got the world in the palm of your hand,' he told Campbell.

So did Frank. He was connected with both crime boss Giancana and President John F. Kennedy. How much better could it get? Shortly after the election Sinatra had a heliport constructed in the spacious grounds of his Palm Springs house, built a guest cottage for the Secret Service, installed extra telephone lines, and erected a separate flagpole for the presidential flag. He told friends his residence would be the Western White House. Frank went all out for his friend Kennedy. He planned entertainment for the inaugural festivities at the National Guard Armory in Washington, but Rat Packer Sammy Davis Jr wasn't included because he had married a white girl, Swedish actress Mai Britt. This angered Dean Martin, who now claimed he was too busy making a movie to attend the gala.

But to Sinatra, everything was Kennedy, Kennedy, Kennedy. He gold-framed every note from Jack and put up a plaque in his house which read, 'John. F. Kennedy Slept Here'. Should there also have been a plaque for Sam Giancana, a far more frequent guest?

Frank was invited to the Kennedy compound in Hyannis Port and revelled in it. But all the publicity about his friendship with the Mafia bothered Bobby Kennedy who, as attorney-general, was out to nail Sam Giancana. Peter Lawford tried to reason with Bobby about the Sinatra matter. They couldn't dump him after all he had done for them, right? No, Bobby declared, and told Lawford to mind his own business. Poor Peter tried his best to pacify Bobby, who had more control over his brother than anyone else. Jack Kennedy told Lawford it would be improper for him to stay at Frank's place again since Giancana had been a guest there: 'Bobby's investigating him, so find another house for me to stay in Palm Springs.'

When Lawford told Frank, he took a sledgehammer to the heliport and never spoke to Peter again. They had recently made the very successful *Ocean's 11* together – it was Lawford who thought Sinatra would be perfect in the role of Danny Ocean – but afterwards Frank no longer asked Peter to appear in his movies. Frank was so mortified that he left town the weekend Kennedy stayed at Bing Crosby's estate.

Frank now surprised everyone by announcing he was going to marry dancer Juliet Prowse. But their 1962 engagement lasted just six weeks because, according to Sinatra, she refused to give up her career. During production of *G.I. Blues*, Juliet had an affair with Elvis Presley who said, 'She has a body that would make a bishop stamp his foot through a stained glass window.' Supposedly Frank broke up the affair after surprising them on the movie set, though in fact he actually only caught them playing cards in her trailer. The Prowse–Sinatra engagement has always been in question but the pair remained friends.

Juliet performed for him with other celebrity friends in Nevada at the Cal-Neva Lodge. The property had been bought by Sam Giancana in 1960, though the owners were recorded as Sinatra himself, his old friend Hank Sanicola and Dean Martin. In a few years Frank would own a half interest. In 1962 the F.B.I. investigated a prostitution ring operating openly via the registration desk. That same summer Frank had a fight with Deputy Sheriff Richard Anderson, who then died in a mysterious car accident. F.B.I. director J. Edgar Hoover suspected Sinatra of foul play, although nothing was proven. Then, when a brawl broke out in Giancana's bungalow, the F.B.I. began their investigation in earnest. Frank's gambling licence was revoked in 1963, and he voluntarily gave up his interest in Nevada casinos, which included the Sands and the Desert Inn. It was not until 1981 that he was able to get a new gaming licence.

It was altogether a bad year for Frank. President Kennedy was assassinated in November 1963, and Frank Sinatra Jr was kidnapped on 8 December. He was taken at gunpoint at Harrah's Lodge in Lake Tahoe. The kidnappers asked for $240,000 in small bills which Frank, according to complicated instructions, delivered in a paper bag, after which his son was released. The three culprits were caught and most of the ransom money retrieved. There were rumours that the kidnapping was a hoax perpetrated to boost young Sinatra's singing career, but in fact it was all too real.

In 1964 Frank was filming *Von Ryan's Express* at 20th Century-Fox in Hollywood when he met nineteen-year-old Mia Farrow, the daughter of director John Farrow and Maureen O'Sullivan, who played Jane in the Tarzan movies.

'I liked Frank right away,' Mia said. 'He rings true. He is what he is. I prefer older men. I feel more comfortable with them . . . I don't have boyfriends or girlfriends my age. They frighten me.' If Mia liked older men, she certainly found one in Sinatra, who was thirty years her senior. The day they met she invited herself along on a trip to Palm Springs, spending her first weekend with Frank there. At the time she was playing Allison MacKenzie in the TV series *Peyton Place*.

Mia, bone thin with long blonde hair, was completely different from the busty brunettes Sinatra seemed to prefer. At the difficult age of fifty he was reliving his youth with Mia, who was wise for her age and determined to marry him. When Frank gave her a mink coat and a nine-carat diamond ring, Dean Martin commented, 'I've got scotch older than Mia.'

Recalling the Lauren Bacall fiasco, Maureen O'Sullivan asked Frank if she should announce his engagement to Mia. 'Sure,' he said. But there was no rush to the altar and in the meantime Mia cut off her blonde hair. When Frank asked her why she had done this she replied, 'I was too vain about it.' On 19 July 1966 they were married at the Sands, but before the secret wedding took place he called Ava, 'because she's the love of my life.' 'Ha!' she laughed at reporters, 'I always knew Frank would end up in bed with a little boy!' (Did Sinatra know Ava had had an affair with Mia's father in 1953?)

Frank Jr gasped, 'I don't believe it!' Dolly said it wouldn't last.

When comedian Jackie Mason appeared at the Aladdin in Las Vegas, he poked fun at Sinatra's hair transplants and elevator shoes. 'Frank soaks his dentures and Mia brushes her braces . . . then she takes off her roller skates and puts them next to his cane . . . he peels off his toupee and she unbraids her hair . . .'

Mason received threatening phone calls but refused to change his act. Six days later three bullets were fired through the glass door of his hotel room in Las Vegas. A few weeks after that, at an appearance in Miami, Mason quipped, 'I don't know who it was that tried to shoot me . . . After the shots were fired all I heard was someone singing: Doobie, doobie, do.' Then, on 13 February 1967, while Jackie was sitting in a car in front of an apartment building in Miami, a man wearing brass knuckles yanked open the door and smashed him in the face, breaking his nose and cheekbones. 'We warned you to stop using the Sinatra material in your act,' the attacker said. Jackie got the message this time. Years later, though, he said Sinatra was a vicious bastard. 'Yet people act like fawning idiots around him . . . Cowering to Sinatra makes him feel important, I guess. It just makes me sick.'

There was always violence around Frank. He could be the kindest of men, and the meanest. When a little old man asked for his autograph, he was beaten up. Yet the next day, when he read about some poor sailor who had been robbed and beaten in New Orleans, Frank paid his hospital bills and gave him the money to get back on his feet.

Sinatra's brawny bodyguards were always around to seek vengeance, if necessary. On his own in a showdown, he was a loser. After his nemesis, Howard Hughes, bought the Sands, Frank was refused credit in the casino because he was borrowing too much money. With a stunned Mia by his side, he drove a golf cart through a glass window. In a drunken rage he confronted the Sands' executive vice-president, Carl Cohen, who knocked Frank down with one punch, splitting his lip open and knocking out a few teeth. Cohen was so popular that Las Vegas wanted him to run for mayor. Frank meanwhile signed a contract with Caesar's Palace.

In 1967 Mia was given the lead in *Johnny Belinda*, which was to be aired on network TV. It was a role she desperately wanted, but prior to filming she had to be sent to hospital. According to producer David Susskind, her body was covered with welts and bruises. But Mia begged him not to replace her, telling him, 'I'm an actress first and a wife second.' In some scenes her bruises are evident, even with heavy make-up. Mia then began filming *Rosemary's Baby* despite protests from Frank, who wanted her to co-star with him in *The Detective*. She said there was no problem, but filming of *Rosemary's Baby* took longer than expected. Frank began calling her every day on the movie set, screaming so loudly that others several feet away could hear what he said. Frank harassed Mia in much the same way he had Ava when she was making *The Snows of Kilimanjaro*. In November Sinatra's lawyer appeared on the movie set of *Rosemary's Baby* with divorce papers. Mia sobbed her heart out, but she did not ask for alimony. On 16 August 1968 their Mexican divorce was final.

Early that year Frank had been making *Lady in Cement* in Miami Beach during the day and appearing at the Fontainebleau at night. One of the prostitutes who served him complained that he had ordered ham and eggs for breakfast and eaten them off her chest with a knife and fork. She sued, but settled out of court. Then Frank came down with pneumonia and called for Ava, who came with thirty pieces of luggage. She was sincere about playing Florence Nightingale, but Sinatra, with a temperature of 104 degrees, partied anyway. 'A piano got pushed out the upstairs window,' she said. 'That was too much for me so I left.'

Marty Sinatra suffered a cardiac arrest and died on 24 January 1969. Because Frank would be arrested if he returned to New Jersey after he refused to testify before the State Commission on Investigation into Organised Crime, Dolly agreed to move to Palm Springs. Sinatra blamed Mario Puzo, author of *The Godfather* in 1963, for his link to the mob. (Was he the model for fictional singer Johnny Fontane, who regains his career thanks to godfather Marlon Brando in Coppola's movie?) Frank confronted Puzo in a restaurant, calling him filthy names and threatening to kill him.

Sinatra now performed regularly at Caesar's Palace in Las Vegas, and it was just a matter of time before he took advantage of his star status there. In 1970 the I.R.S. discovered that Frank was scamming cash from the casino by cashing in chips that he was given for free. When casino manager Waterman confronted Sinatra inside the casino, Frank reacted violently and Waterman pulled a gun. That ended the fight, but there were visible marks on Waterman's throat where Sinatra had been holding him. Frank vowed never to perform in Las Vegas again – but he returned two years later when Caesar's Palace offered him $400,000 a week, a record at that time.

Sinatra continued making movies. He was very good in crime films such as *Tony Rome* with Jill St. John in 1967, and *The Detective* co-starring Lee Remick in 1968. But *Dirty Dingus Magee* in 1970 was a flop, despite the comedic flair Frank displayed in the film. Then, in 1971, Frank announced his retirement. He gave his farewell performance at a benefit for the Motion Picture and Television Relief fund in Los Angeles at which he set his life to music, starting with 'All or Nothing at All' and concluding with the song that reflected his lifestyle, 'My Way'.

But he soon resumed his career, in a 1973 television special that received reviews ranging from mediocre to bad. He was older and fatter, and little of his voice was left, the critics said. He went on to tour five countries but cancelled his shows in Germany after the press greeted him with insults. In London, audiences gave him standing ovations but Prince Charles commented, 'He's a very strange person. He could be terribly nice one minute and . . . well, not so nice the next.'

Sinatra ended the tour in Australia, where he refused to talk to the press and on stage referred to the Fourth Estate as a group of bums and fags. Female reporters were hookers, he said, 'But I'm not particular, I'll give them a dollar fifty.'

In response the Labor Party in New South Wales asked, 'Who the hell does that man Sinatra think he is?' They demanded an apology, but Frank refused to lower himself. As a result, he was blackballed in Australia. His shows were cancelled, the Waiters' Union cut off room service at his hotel, and the Transport Union refused to refuel his Gulfstream jet. Frank's lawyer finally issued a statement that his client 'accepts that working members of the Australian media would be doing less than their professional duty if they did not make every effort to keep the public informed about the visit of an international celebrity.' Without actually expressing an apology, Frank was allowed to continue his tour.

Back in the U.S., Sinatra did a live television special from Madison Square Gardens. But the ratings were low, and the critics hit lower. Rex Reed wrote that Frank's manners were appalling. 'All of this might be tolerable if he could still sing. But the saddest part, the hardest part to face about this once-great idol now living on former glory, is that Frank Sinatra has had it. His voice has been manhandled beyond recognition, bringing with its parched croak only a painful memory of burned-out yesterdays. Frank Sinatra has become a bore.'

*

To the surprise of everyone, including his family, Frank became a Republican, supporting President Richard Nixon and then California Governor Ronald Reagan. Through his connections at the White House, he had the type of power he enjoyed referring to as 'class'. He was also linked to such beauties as Victoria Principal, Jacqueline Bisset, Angie Dickinson, Hope Lange, Sophia Loren, Gloria Vanderbilt, and Tuesday Weld. Zsa Zsa Gabor claimed he refused to leave her house after a date because he had 'a terrible headache'. Her maid put him to bed and the next morning he was after Gabor again. With her young daughter in the next room, she avoided a scene by giving in. 'I hated Frank and he knew it,' she said. Zsa Zsa wrote in her memoirs that she was sure Sinatra wanted to prove to her that he was a better lover than Rubi Rubirosa, the renowned playboy who was a master in the bedroom.

Frank also enjoyed the company of Louis B. Mayer's widowed daughter, Edie Goetz, but when he proposed marriage she replied, 'Well, Frank, I can't marry you. You're nothing but a hoodlum!'

It was during his 'retirement' that Sinatra began taking an interest in his neighbour, Barbara Marx, who was married to Zeppo, the youngest of the Marx brothers. She frequently played tennis with Frank's house guest and good friend, Vice-President Spiro Agnew. At the time there were rumours that Barbara and Agnew were interested in each other but that was not the case. Barbara began spending more time with Frank and sued Zeppo for divorce in 1973.

Barbara Jane Blakeley Marx, a beautiful blonde with soft blue eyes and a splendid figure, was a former showgirl at the Riviera Hotel in Las Vegas. Born on 16 October 1930 in Glendale, California, she married Robert Harrison Oliver, an executive with the Miss Universe pageant, and had a son, Bobby. After their divorce, Barbara moved to Las Vegas and met Zeppo Marx, whom she married in 1959.

From the start Barbara allowed Frank his temper tantrums and insults. Whatever he wanted to do and wherever he wanted to go, it was fine with her. On one occasion he slapped her in public because she laughed at him, but she was in love and determined to marry him. The only problem was Dolly, who despised Barbara and voiced her contempt in front of everyone, including Frank. He just shrugged it off, even when his mother called Barbara a whore. Unsure whether he wanted to get married again, he called off the relationship in 1974.

Frank began seeing Jacqueline Kennedy Onassis again and even considered marrying her, but she, like Edie Goetz, felt he was beneath her.

He was too close to the mob and had, after all, arranged dates for her late husband Jack. When Barbara saw their pictures in the newspapers, she flew to New York City to be with him, and in May 1976 Frank gave her a seventeen-carat engagement ring worth $360,000.

Ava Gardner told the press she was glad that Frank had found happiness with Barbara. 'Even though we were divorced long ago,' she said, 'I've always counted on Frank to advise me in business affairs. He's always been generous with his time and interest. I'm sure his new wife won't object if I continue to call on him in the future.' Sinatra would not let her down. Financially, he was always there for Ava in sickness and in health.

Frank and Barbara were married on 11 July 1976 at the home of a friend in Beverly Hills. He gave her a Rolls-Royce, and she gave him a Jaguar. She redecorated his Palm Beach house to her liking, but in Frank's favourite colours. She travelled with him on singing engagements and he lavished her with furs, jewels and designer clothes. Their life would have been ideal, except that Frank's family weren't keen on Barbara. He wanted to adopt her son, Robert, but his children objected and he abided by their wishes.

Then there was the stubborn Dolly. Frank's mother still refused to accept her daughter-in-law. On Thursday, 6 January 1977, she chose to take a private plane to Las Vegas for Frank's opening at Caesar's Palace rather than fly with Barbara and her party. Shortly before the curtain went up Sinatra was told his mother's plane was missing, but he went on with the show anyway. The search parties did not find the wreckage until Saturday; there were body pieces scattered in the snow and one of Dolly's dresses was found hanging from a tree.

Frank was devastated. He often said that men do not cry in public, but he did at Dolly's funeral. In his grief, he turned to religion, embracing the faith of his birth, Catholicism – as did Barbara, who was Protestant. In the eyes of the Church his marriages to Ava and Mia were invalid, but the revised Code of the Canon Law made it possible for him to annul his marriage to Nancy despite their three children. The *Los Angeles Herald Examiner* wanted to know whether Frank had made the Vatican an offer they could not refuse. Close friends said Frank's sudden devotion to the Catholic Church was due to his mother's death. A devout Catholic, she had always worried about Frank's soul. Would they be reunited in the hereafter? When Barbara completed her instruction, she and Frank were married by a Catholic priest in 1978.

Sinatra's impossible dream had been to become a member of the prestigious Knights of Malta. The Maltese Cross is given for service to humanity and outstanding accomplishments, and among the sanctified members are Alexander Haig, Conrad Hilton, J. Edgar Hoover and Joseph Kennedy. To receive this award would have impressed Dolly more than anything else – not to mention the honour of being among just a few hundred to be exalted in a thousand years. Mobster Jimmy Fratianno, knowing how much the award meant to Frank, claimed he could get him in for $10,000. Sinatra bought the scam and was inducted into the Knights of Malta.

After going all out to get Ronald Reagan elected president of the United States in 1980, Frank was named chairman of the inaugural gala. The newly elected president was criticised for his friendship with Sinatra, but Reagan was steadfast. 'We've heard those things about Frank,' he said. 'We hope none of them are true.' He also stressed that there was a side to Sinatra that no one knew about – his generous contributions to charity and the way he would give up his valuable time to sing at benefits and for other worthwhile causes. Reagan emphasised that Frank would be very upset if his charitable side were publicised.

At the inaugural festivities Sinatra sang 'Nancy with the Reagan Face' for the First Lady. He wasn't invited to stand on the platform for the swearing-in ceremonies, but he showed up anyway and no one stopped him. Kitty Kelley hinted in her book *His Way* that Frank had an affair with Nancy Reagan. He flew to Washington without Barbara for private lunches with the First Lady and danced with her exclusively at parties, but it's doubtful that there was anything intimate to their relationship. Though Barbara once walked out on him when his attention was focused on Nancy during a dinner party, it was due to his rudeness rather than her jealousy. Sinatra was still, in essence, just a kid from Hoboken. He championed every chance to be with the elite, and one can't get any higher in society than the White House. Inspired, perhaps, by the exhilaration of the Reagan era, Frank released *Trilogy*, his first album in five years. It went gold within weeks.

On 6 October 1986, Ava Gardner was flown from her home in London to St John's Hospital in Santa Monica, California, suffering from a persistent virus that developed into pneumonia. During her recuperation she suffered a minor stroke. At the same time Frank was admitted to the Eisenhower Medical Center in Rancho Mirage, a suburb of Palm Springs, after an acute attack of diverticulitis. On 9 November, doctors removed an abscess from his large intestine during a two-hour operation. He was in a great deal of pain, but no cancer was found in the twelve inches of large intestine removed.

Ava was still confined at St John's when Frank was discharged from hospital on 17 November. He made sure she did not want for anything. Money was no object. In March Ava was back in London, but her respiratory problems persisted and she returned to St John's in January 1988. Frank spent $50,000 to have her flown from London to Los Angeles in an air ambulance. He called her every day and sent her huge floral arrangement with a note signed 'Chi-Chi', her old nickname for him. On 25 January 1990, Ava, at the age of 67, died of pneumonia in London. Her body was flown to Smithfield, North Carolina, where the funeral took place on the 29th. She was buried in the Gardner family plot. Frank sent a beautiful spray of flowers with a message, 'With my love, Francis'. Ava's sister Bappie said Sinatra sent her flowers every year on her birthday, 24 December. The bouquets would wilt and die, but Ava never threw them out until the next one arrived.

Sinatra had looked after Ava through the years. How many times they tried to reconcile isn't known, but it's more often than has been publicised. When Ava's lover, actor George C. Scott, beat her up, Frank hired two bodyguards. He told *Photoplay* in 1965, 'If there's one guy I can't tolerate it's a guy who mistreats women. They are real bullies and what they need is a real working over by a man of their own size.' Scott wasn't cut down to size, but his clothes were. When he returned to his hotel one night he found that all his shirts and sweaters and suits had been cut off at the shoulders.

Frank felt the same about Mia Farrow. After a twelve-year relationship with Woody Allen, she found out he was having an affair with her adopted seventeen-year-old daughter, Soon-Yi. Frank offered to break Woody's legs.

His loyalty extended to Elvis Presley, whose pals Red and Sonny West published *Elvis, What Happened?* in 1977. In a blow to the singer's image, the book revealed Presley's dependency on drugs. Elvis tried to talk them out of it, to no avail. Sinatra offered to 'do something serious' to stop publication of the book, but received no feedback from Presley. Frank, who more than anyone else understood the heartbreaks of show business, called Elvis when he was in hospital. 'Don't let the bastards kill you,' he said, referring to the pressures put on performers of their magnitude. Presley died a few months later.

*

Sinatra made his last movie in 1980 after a ten-year hiatus. *The First Deadly Sin* revolved around an ageing detective on the track of a psychotic murderer while his wife, played by Faye Dunaway, wastes away in hospital. His character is reminiscent of Dirty Harry, a role Frank turned down. Though Clint Eastwood was perfect as Harry Callahan, Sinatra might have given an equally effective rendition of 'Go ahead, make my day.' He certainly proved himself capable as a detective on the screen. He appeared as a guest star on the *Magnum* TV series with Tom Selleck, and might have made more episodes if the producers hadn't insisted on getting receipts for his expenses.

In September 1989 Sammy Davis Jr was diagnosed with throat cancer. His last performance was at Harrah's in Lake Tahoe, the night before his first radiation treatment. He thought the cancer was under control until February the following year. On 13 March Sammy was released from Cedar Sinai Hospital to spend his last days at home. Frank paid him a visit, which must have been painful since Davis's weight had dropped to eighty pounds. He died on 16 May 1990 at the age of 64. Frank and Dean Martin were honorary pallbearers. Sammy was heavily in debt to the I.R.S. when he died, and it was rumoured that Frank helped out his widow financially.

It was Dean Martin's turn next. After his 35-year-old son, Dino Jr, was killed in a plane crash in March 1987, Martin was never the same. In September, Frank had suggested an extended concert tour, telling Sammy Davis Jr that it would be good for Dean, who had been grieving in seclusion. The tour opened at the Oakland Coliseum on 13 March 1988, but before going on stage Dean asked, 'Will someone tell me why we're here?' A week later, in Chicago, Frank made a comment that Dean's singing was not up to par. It was not meant as an insult, but it was all Martin needed to fly back to Los Angeles and check into hospital, claiming kidney problems in order to cover himself for bowing out of his contract. That Frank was angry is no surprise. Dean sometimes tried to perform after that but he lacked the spirit. All he wanted to do was watch westerns on television – and die. On Christmas morning, 1995, Martin, at the age of 78, died in his sleep.

Barbara attended the funeral without Frank, who was not in good health himself. On 6 March 1994, he had been singing 'My Way' during a concert in Richmond, Virginia, when he fell off his stool and hit his head on a speaker, landing on the floor. Hospital tests revealed nothing medically wrong with him. On 1 November 1996, however, he was hospitalised for pneumonia and hooked up to a heart monitor. Three months later Frank had what doctors described as an 'uncomplicated' heart attack, but he was not seen again in public. On Thanksgiving Day 1997 Nancy Jr put the following posting on Sinatra's official website: 'We realize he [Frank] has been through a lot in his 81 years and that God may have a schedule other than what we would like, but he is tough and who is to say that he won't get back in the race?' Frank turned 82 on 12 December, but he wasn't himself. He had given his family specific instructions not to take 'heroic measures' to keep him alive. On 23 January, once again he was admitted to hospital with high blood pressure, and on 1 February he was back in Cedars for 'tests'.

On the night of 14 May Frank summoned one of his two nurses, complaining of chest pains and dizziness. Minutes later he had a severe heart attack and was rushed to the Cedars emergency room at 9:30 p.m. Barbara, who was having dinner at Morton's with friends, was notified and rushed to the hospital. She told Frank, 'Fight, fight, fight.' He replied in a whisper, 'I'm losing,' then closed his eyes and went to 'the big casino in the sky'. It was 10:35 p.m., but Sinatra could not be pronounced dead until a doctor was summoned to make it official at 10:50. Nancy Jr wasn't there because she was watching the last episode of *Seinfeld*, and Frank Jr was returning a video.

The Empire State Building in New York City bathed itself in blue lights for Ol' Blue Eyes, while in Las Vegas the lights were turned off for one minute. The city that Frank built was silent; cars stopped on green lights, and thousands held candles in tribute. When the lights came on again they could see a large picture of Sinatra in lights at Caesar's Palace. The crowd cheered and drivers honked their horns.

Frank's body was taken to the McCormick mortuary in Inglewood. Dressed in a blue suit, he remained there for five days. Mia Farrow visited the open casket for a final farewell. Supposedly she slipped a ring that said 'Dream' in the casket, while Nancy Jr put some Tootsie Rolls, Blackjack gum and Cherry Life Savers in Frank's pockets.

Catholics who live in Beverly Hills attend the Good Shepherd Catholic Church on Bedford Avenue. Elizabeth Taylor married her first husband, Nicky Hilton, there in 1950. The oldest church in Beverly Hills, it has seen some spectacular funerals. The biggest was for Rudolph Valentino, who died at the age of 31 in 1926. There were also final farewells for Gary Cooper, Alfred Hitchcock, Eva Gabor and Peter Fitch at the Good Shepherd, but one of the most famous funerals held at the church was that of Norman Maine in the 1954 movie *A Star is Born* with Judy Garland.

But the most famous farewell was to Frank Sinatra. At a rosary service on the night of 19 May, Mass cards bearing a picture of Frank holding a puppy were handed out. The following day, the elite of Hollywood attended the funeral: Liza Minelli, Jack Lemmon, Mia Farrow, Tom Selleck, Jerry Lewis, Debbie Reynolds, Larry King, Tony Curtis, Gregory Peck, Wayne Newton, Sophia Loren and Nancy Reagan, to name but a few.

In his speech, Kirk Douglas told Barbara, 'Frank loved you very much. We all know that, so don't cry too much. Think of Frank up there with Dean Martin and Sammy Davis Jr. Boy, heaven will never be the same!' Gregory Peck described Sinatra as a 'reckless rogue, a sentimental fella'. Frank Sinatra Jr described his father as having the mystic romance of Rudolph Valentino, the aloofness of James Dean, the sexiness of Marilyn Monroe and the appeal of Elvis Presley. He said his dad had 'lived to a ripe old age, and it wasn't because he took care of himself.' One of the more sentimental segments of the service came midway through the service when Frank's song, 'Put Your Dreams Away' was played.

His casket was flown to Palm Springs and buried in Desert Memorial Park, next to his mother and father. His tombstone reads, 'The Best is Yet to Come, Francis Albert Sinatra, Beloved Husband and Father'. Ironically, his last encore, on 25 February 1995 at Marriott's Desert Springs Resort and Spa, had been 'The Best is Yet to Come'.

Sinatra left the majority of his estimated estate of $200 million to Barbara, who got the houses and up to $3.8 million. Frank's children, Nancy, Frank and Tina, received $200,000 each plus undivided interests in a Beverly Hills office building. They had already been given rights to much of Sinatra's music catalogue and also received undisclosed amounts in living trusts. Each of his grandchildren received $1 million, his stepson, Bobby, $100,000 and, thoughtfully, he left $250,000 to his first wife, Nancy. He included a 'no contest clause' in his 1991 will, disinheriting anyone who contested the will.

There is no love lost between Barbara and Frank's children, who claim she held their father 'hostage'. Perhaps, though, there was some guilt on their part that they were not with Frank when he died.

'You only live once,' Sinatra said, 'and the way I live, once is enough.'

Despite his questionable lifestyle, 'The Chairman of the Board' is remembered for his music, which will endure regardless of trends. His style is ageless. Guys, sitting at the bar after too many drinks, can still identify with

Sinatra wailing, 'Set 'em up, Joe' and 'There'll never be another you'. Listening to the words, they believed Ol' Blue Eyes wasn't immune to heartbreak. He carried a song from start to finish with ease, and if he was off key, that was only to be expected, because lonely lovers are likely to choke with remorse. He made you forget your troubles with 'I've Got the World on a String' and 'Fly Me To the Moon'. His cocky tone in these songs reminded you that you could be a little cocky too.

His anger and neuroses were not expressed in his music, and that's why his voice will go on and on, while his nastiness is forgotten. Even though Ava Gardner had no desire to be with Frank in later years, she played his records constantly. It was his music that she adored, not the bastard Mr. Hyde he could become. My bobbysoxer girlfriends changed with Sinatra as they grew older and fell in love, while our boyfriends hated him in the forties and cried with him a decade later. We rocked with the sounds of Elvis but made love to the sounds of Sinatra. And we still do.

Author Pete Hamill wrote in his book, *Why Sinatra Matters*, 'It was mandatory to chronicle his wins and losses, his four marriages, his battles, verbal and physical, with reporters and photographers. His romances required many inches of type. There were accounts of his fierce temper, his brutalities, his drunken cruelties. Some described him as a thug or a monster, whose behavior was redeemed only by his talent . . . He was clearly a complicated man.'

But his music will always matter.

'Being an eighteen-carat manic depressive and having lived a life of violent emotional contradictions, I have perhaps an overactive capacity for sadness and elation.'

– Frank Sinatra

The Films of Frank Sinatra

Las Vegas Nights (Paramount, 1941)
Ship Ahoy (MGM, 1942)
Reveille with Beverly (Columbia, 1943)
Step Lively (RKO, 1944)
Higher and Higher (RKO, 1944)
Anchors Aweigh (MGM, 1945)
It Happened in Brooklyn (MGM, 1947)
Miracle of the Bells (RKO, 1948)
Kissing Bandit (MGM, 1948)
Take Me Out to the Ball Game (MGM, 1949)
On the Town (MGM, 1949)
Double Dynamite (RKO, 1951)
Meet Danny Wilson (Universal-International, 1952)
From Here to Eternity (Columbia, 1953)
Suddenly (Libra/Warner Brothers, 1954)
Young at Heart (Arkin Productions/Warner Brothers, 1955)
Tender Trap (MGM, 1955)
Man With the Golden Arm (Otto Preminger, 1955)
High Society (MGM, 1956)
Not as a Stranger (Stanley Kramer/United Artists, 1955)
Guys and Dolls (Samuel Goldwyn, 1955)
Johnny Concho (United Artists/Kent, Frank Sinatra, 1956)
Around the World in Eighty Days (US, Michael Todd, 1956)
Joker is Wild (Paramount, 1956)
Pal Joey (Columbia, 1957)
Pride and the Passion (United Artists/Stanley Kramer, 1957)
Some Came Running (MGM, 1958)

Kings Go Forth (US/Ross-Eton, 1958)
Never So Few (MGM/Canterbury, 1959)
Hole in the Head (US/Sincap, 1959)
Pepe (Columbia, 1960)
Can-Can (TCF/Suffock-Cummings, 1960)
Oceans 11 (Warner/Dorchester, 1960)
Devil at 4 O'Clock (Columbia, 1961)
Sergeants 3 (US. Essex -Claude, 1962)
Road to Hong Kong (United Artists/Melnor, 1962)
Advise and Consent (Columbia/Alpha-Alpine/Otto Preminger, 1962)
Manchurian Candidate (United Artists/MC, 1962)
Come Blow Your Horn (Paramount/Lear and Yorkin, 1963)
List of Adrian Messenger (Joel/Universal, 1963)
4 For Texas (Warner/Sam Company, 1964)
Robin and the 7 Hoods (Warner-PC, 1964)
Marriage on the Rocks (Warner/A-C/Sinatra, 1965)
None But the Brave (Warner/Eiga/toho/Artanis, 1965)
Von Ryan's Express (TCF, Saul David, 1965)
Cast a Giant Shadow (Mirisch/UA, 1966)
Assault on a Queen (Paramount/Seven Arts/Sinatra Enterprises, 1966)
Tony Rome (TCF/Arcole/Millfield, 1967)
Naked Runner (Warner/Artanis, 1967)
Detective (TCF/Arcola/Milfield, 1968)
Lady in Cement (TCF/Arcola/Milfield. 1968)
Dirty Dingus Magee (MGM, 1970)
That's Entertainment (MGM, 1974)
First Deadly Sin (Filmways/Artanis, 1980)
Cannonball Run II (Golden Harvest/Warner, 1984)

Frank Sinatra's Awards

1954 Golden Globe for Best Supporting Actor in *From Here to Eternity*
1958 Golden Globe for Best Motion Picture Actor in *Pal Joey*
1971 Cecil B. De Mille Award
1971 Jean Hersholt Humanitarian Award
1973 Life Achievement Award from the Screen Actors' Guild
1985 Presidential Medal of Freedom
1994 Grammy Legend Award
1997 Congressional Gold Medal

10

Elvis Presley

With a sexy, fiery energy and a crazy vulnerability, he oozed danger and lust and made it acceptable to the masses. Blending rhythm and blues, country and gospel music, he helped break down the barrier between black and white. His 1954 recording of 'That's Alright (Mama)' was the birth of rock 'n' roll, paving the way for musicians like the Beatles.

He came along at the right time in the fifties to show America what TV could do and, though unaware of it, used the medium to shock and revolutionise. He had no idea why he was damned and criticised for being himself. Naturally sultry with a vibrant innocence, he crossed the line to become the greatest cultural icon of the twentieth century.

Twenty-six years after his death in 1977, he was still going strong. For the third year in a row, he made more money than any other dead celebrity – $40 million. Even in death he is still the King.

Elvis Presley came from very humble beginnings. Graceland, his home in Memphis, is, by contrast, an estate. It looms from a distance, on a hillside, like a southern mansion in *Gone With the Wind*. Some visitors are disappointed while others, like myself, see the warmth of a man who was torn between his roots and his fame. His glittering costumes are on display, as is his mama's simple house dress, similar to those our mothers might have worn. Elvis bought Graceland for Gladys Presley, but she was never comfortable there. To her the house was too big and too fancy — and, frighteningly, a symbol of what life had in store for her.

Born Gladys Love Smith in Saltillo, Mississippi, to a sharecropper father and an invalid mother in 1912, she worked in the cotton fields with little time for school. At seventeen she ran away with a married man, but stayed with him for only a few days. When her father died two years later, she suffered what is described as a 'brief hysterical paralysis'. Now the breadwinner, Gladys moved her family to Tupelo and found a job as a seamstress. Although a religious girl, she also enjoyed an occasional night out drinking and dancing.

Then she met Vernon Presley, a handsome, lazy boy three years younger, and married him on 17 June 1933 after a brief courtship. For less than $200 he built a two-room house (bedroom and kitchen) next door to his father's home. What tourists see today at Graceland is a far cry from the shack where the Presleys lived.

When Gladys became pregnant, she had a premonition that she was carrying twins. On 8 January 1935, at 4:00 a.m., she gave birth to a stillborn son, Jesse Garon. At 4:35 a.m., a twin, Elvis Aaron, was born. The doctor's fifteen-dollar fee was paid by welfare.

Elvis was named after his father, Vernon Elvis Presley, and Mr. Presley's good friend, Aaron Kennedy. 'Aron' was the spelling the Presleys actually chose, apparently to make it rhyme with 'Garon', the middle name of his twin. But when, towards the end of his life, Elvis sought to change the spelling of his middle name to the biblical 'Aaron', he learned that state records already listed it that way. The official spelling of his middle name is 'Aaron', as inscribed on his tombstone.

On 10 January 1933, Jesse Garon Presley was buried at Princeville Cemetery; the grave was unmarked because Vernon could not afford a headstone. Since Gladys was unable to have more children, the loss of her child was a tragedy that would haunt Elvis – he was the twin who survived.

Gladys lost her mother to tuberculosis in 1937 and was faced with another devastating blow a year later when Vernon was sent to prison on a forgery charge. He had added a zero to a four-dollar cheque, for which he spent sixteen months behind bars. During his absence, Gladys and Elvis formed a bond that would grow stronger over the years. They were very protective of each other until her death – and, for Elvis, forever after. Emotionally, Vernon was an outsider.

Elvis and Gladys communicated in a language all their own that was a combination of hillbilly and baby talk. He called her 'my little baby' and nicknamed her 'Satnin', the brand name of a lard product – soft, round and cosy. Elvis massaged her 'itsy-bitsy sooties' when she came home from a long day at work in the laundry during Vernon's absence. Even at the age of five, Elvis was aware of his father's lack of warmth and attentiveness to Gladys, whose hopes and dreams were focused on her son. Vernon, like his father Jesse, was a womaniser. When he began to cheat on Gladys isn't known, but when Elvis found out that his mother was also being physically abused, he tore into Vernon and threatened to kill him.

The music at the First Assembly of God Church, which he attended regularly with his parents, had a deep effect on Elvis. He loved to sing gospel. He grew up listening to the black blues singers in the neighbourhood and country music on the radio. In 1945, Elvis entered a youth talent show at the Mississippi-Alabama Fair and Dairy Show held in Tupelo. Singing 'Old Shep', he won the second prize of five dollars and free admission to all the fair's rides. Unable to afford a bicycle, his parents bought him a guitar for $7.95 at the Tupelo Hardware Store. Elvis took lessons from anyone in the neighbourhood who could strum. He also learned from Tupelo's Mississippi Slim, who had his own local radio show.

In September 1948 the Presleys packed their belongings in a trunk which was then strapped to the roof of their 1939 Plymouth, and drove to Memphis. Rumour had it that Vernon was bootlegging and had to leave Tupelo or face another jail sentence. Regardless, they were searching for a better life financially.

They lived in one-room federal housing equipped with only a hot plate, and shared a bathroom with other families. Nine months later they moved to Lauderdale Courts public housing project, which was at least a move in the right direction. Vernon got a job stacking cans at the United Paint Company while Gladys worked from time to time as a seamstress and waitress. She kept a close eye on Elvis, walking him to Humes High School and checking on him if he did not come straight home after classes. She was determined he would not lack an education like the others in their family. He maintained a C average, but had no interest in any particular subject.

Although a shy teenager he had the nerve to wear sideburns, let his dirty-blond hair grow, and used greasy pomade to make the colour darker and shiny so as to look like actor Tony Curtis. Elvis blackened his hair with shoe polish, before deciding to dye it permanently black. Gladys encouraged him, especially in his eagerness to look like Curtis whose black hair and contrasting blue eyes had made him a screen idol.

Elvis was no idol in 1949, however. His classmates mocked and teased him. According to Red West, who was a senior at that time, a gang of boys once cornered Elvis and tried to cut his hair. West, a football player, intervened, saying, 'If you cut his hair, you'll have to cut mine.' The bullies backed down. Elvis refused to conform. Six feet tall, weighing 150 pounds and with occasional bouts of acne, he wore striped trousers and a pink jacket when pink was a colour for girls only. In other words, Elvis was nothing special, but he made sure he stood out from all the others in school because that's what he wanted. As 'poor white trash', what did he have to lose?

In his senior year Elvis won the school's annual talent show. He sang 'Keep Those Cold Icy Fingers Off Me' and received more applause than any of the other contestants. Most of his classmates didn't know he could sing; nor did his teachers, who pushed him back on stage for an encore. 'Gee,' he said, 'I think they liked me!'

Elvis graduated from Humes High School on 3 June 1953 and went to work as a delivery truck driver for Crown Electric Company, attending electricians' school at night. As a belated birthday present for Gladys, who had turned 41 on 25 April, he recorded a four-dollar demo record of 'My Happiness' and 'When Your Heartaches Begin' at Sun Records. Producer Sam Phillips wasn't there so his assistant, Marion Keisker, helped Elvis make the recording. On 5 July, Presley went back to Sun with Scotty Moore on lead guitar and Bill Black on bass to record 'That's Alright (Mama)', with 'Blue Moon of Kentucky' on the flip side. Phillips took the recording to WHBQ disc jockey Dewey Phillips (no relation to Sam) who, after playing it on the air, was besieged by listeners who wanted to hear it again. Elvis, scared out of his wits and in total shock, managed an interview with Dewey on the radio and became an overnight celebrity in Memphis.

Sun Records signed Elvis to his first recording contract, but he continued to work for Crown Electric, playing small club dates and local gigs with Scotty and Bill. Presley, whose five singles with Sun had been regional hits, was invited to perform on *The Grand Ole Opry*, the most prestigious country music show in the country, on 25 September 1954. The conservative audience were not enthusiastic about Elvis, who wore a gaudy country shirt, red satin pants and eye shadow. 'I Don't Care if the Sun Don't Shine' and 'Good Rockin' Tonight' got applause, but the Opry bigwigs were put off by his 'nigger' interpretation and the eye shadow that made people wonder if he was gay. It was a painful disappointment to Elvis, who was not invited back.

On 16 October, however, Presley was a big hit on *Louisiana Hayride*, the live Saturday night radio programme which was the Opry's big competitor. Frank Page introduced Elvis: 'Just a few weeks ago, a young man from Memphis, Tennessee recorded a song on the Sun label . . . in just a matter of weeks that song has skyrocketed right up the charts. It's really doing well all over the country. He's only nineteen years old. And he's a singer who's forging a new style.' Elvis brought the house down with 'That's Alright (Mama)' and was signed to a one-year contract with the *Hayride*.

The only problem for Elvis, Scotty and Bill was that they had to drive from Memphis to Shrevesport, Louisiana, every week; because of this they were limited to performing only in the South. For each *Hayride* stint Elvis earned eighteen dollars, Bill and Scottie twelve dollars. But they managed to perform throughout Texas, Louisiana, and Ohio, sleeping in their car and gaining a reputation. Elvis was described in one article as the new rage, who sang hillbilly in R&B time. 'Can you figure it? He wears pink pants and a black coat. *If* he doesn't suffer too much popularity, he'll be all right.'

In Kilgore, Texas, future country singer Bob Luman recalled, 'This cat comes out in red pants, a green coat, pink shirt and socks, and he had a sneer on his face. He stood before the mike for five minutes before he made a move. Then he hit his guitar and two strings break. So there he was and he hadn't done anything. These high school girls are swooning and fainting. Then he starts to move his hips like he has a thing for his guitar.'

*

Presley's phenomenal showmanship soon came to the attention of Colonel Tom Parker. The Colonel had managed famous cowboy star Gene Autry, Opry star Hank Snow and country singer Eddy Arnold, who fired him in 1953 for unknown reasons. Born Andreas von Kujik on 28 June 1909 in Breda, Holland, Parker came to America illegally at the age of seventeen, joined the army and took the name of his commanding officer, Tom Parker. After his discharge from the service he promoted a carnival, the Johnny J. Jones Exposition. In 1940, he became the director of the Humane Society in Tampa, Florida, and was elected dogcatcher. It was a bizarre move but a clever one: Parker got a free apartment and free transport in order to hustle donations for homeless animals. For the first time, the Humane Society showed a profit. He opened up the first pet cemetery of its kind in the country, and promoted his Dancing Chickens which performed on a hot plate covered with straw. Parker's ambition wasn't fulfilled by animal acts, however. He now went after bigger game, making a star out of singer Eddy Arnold and negotiating a movie contract for him with the help of the William Morris Agency.

It was the Colonel's associate, Oscar Davis, who brought Presley and Parker together at a diner in Memphis in February 1955. A big cigar in his mouth, the Colonel was blunt with Elvis. 'How long are you gonna sing in honkytonks?' he asked. 'And how long are you gonna record for Sun Records? You're not gettin' anywhere.' Elvis, thinking Parker wasn't interested, was devastated. The Colonel knew that Presley had great potential, but played it cool and didn't sign him right away. Instead he sent him, with great success, on tour with Hank Snow. Elvis failed to get on *Arthur Godfrey's Talent Scouts*, a network television show, but he was making big strides with audiences on the road. Young girls broke through barricades in a near-riot to see the singer whose vibrating legs and sleepy eyes were driving them crazy.

The Colonel remained patient and took his time, dangling fame and fortune in Presley's face. In August 1955 Elvis signed a management contract with Hank Snow Attractions, which was jointly owned by Snow and Parker. But it was the latter who took control of Elvis. On 20 November 1955, RCA bought Presley's contract from Sun Records for $40,000, with a $5,000 bonus for Elvis. With this money he moved his family into a four-room apartment, as well as buying himself a new $175 guitar and a 1951 Cosmopolitan Lincoln.

On 10 January 1956, two days after his 21st birthday, Elvis recorded 'Heartbreak Hotel' for RCA. The gospel quartet, the Jordanaires, backed him up on the record, and it sold 300,000 in the first three weeks. Presley's first single to sell a million copies, it earned him a gold record award. In March his first album, *Elvis Presley*, also went gold after selling a million.

But his rise to stardom was keeping him away from home most of the time. His absence took a toll on Gladys who was being abused by Vernon. Though Elvis had once pounced on his father and threatened to kill him, he wasn't around to keep an eye on the situation. Since Gladys and Vernon were both heavy drinkers, the arguments and abuse were alcohol-related, but Elvis knew nothing about this. He had no idea how his new celebrity was affecting his mother, who felt ill-equipped to cope with his absence, his fame, and her suspicions that Vernon was seeing other women. She was bloated from the booze and putting on weight, which led to an excessive consumption of diet pills. She had inherited the family trait of depression, but it would go untreated due to the lack of medical and psychological knowledge at that time. He faithfully called her every day on the phone and this was of some consolation to her. How sad it was, though, that Gladys had to suffer as her son rose to heights of stardom beyond anyone's comprehension.

On 3 April 1956, Elvis appeared on an edition of the *Milton Berle Show* broadcast from the aircraft carrier, the USS *Hancock*. Three days later he signed a seven-year contract with Hal Wallis and Paramount Pictures. Between 23 April and 9 May, Elvis appeared at the New Frontier Hotel in Las Vegas to only lukewarm reviews, but his single 'Heartbreak Hotel' and his first album, *Elvis Presley*, hit number one in the music charts. The number of enthusiastic Presley fans was increasing dramatically and they caused havoc wherever he appeared in person. On the road, he was occasionally forced to end his shows early when overzealous teens stormed the stage – but the greatest impact to date came with his second appearance on the *Milton Berle Show*. His sexy rendition of 'Hound Dog' caused such a sensation that he was publicly ridiculed the next day by the 'morally concerned' establishment and the religious community. The kids just said, 'Who cares?' But the Colonel did, apparently, because a month later Elvis wore a tuxedo when he sang a toned-down 'Hound Dog' on the *Steve Allen Show*.

Ed Sullivan, whose programme was one of the most popular on television, had said he would never allow Elvis to appear on his show. But he soon changed his mind, signing Presley to three appearances for $50,000, the highest amount ever paid to a performer up to that time.

Columnist Hy Gardner, on his late-night television show, *Hy Gardner Calling*, broadcast a split-screen interview with Elvis, who was staying at the Warwick Hotel in New York City.

'Are you getting enough sleep?' Gardner asked.

'No, not really, but I'm used to it,' Elvis replied, 'and I can't sleep any longer.'

'What goes through your mind to keep you awake?'

'Well, everything has happened to me so fast during the last year and a half – I'm all mixed up, you know? I can't keep up with everything that's happened.'

Gardner mentioned the criticism he'd had to endure. Did he have any animosity?

'Well, not really,' Elvis said. 'Those people have a job to do and they do it.'

'Have you learned anything from them, Elvis?'

'No, I haven't.'

'You haven't, huh?'

'Because I don't feel like I'm doing anything wrong.'

Gardner tried to elicit some kind of confession of wrongdoing but instead Elvis surprised him by saying, 'I don't see how any type of music could have a bad influence on people when it's only music. I mean, how would rock and roll music make anyone rebel against their parents?'

Gardner confessed that the bad publicity might have helped Elvis and, after all, he had been enabled to help his parents, '. . . so I think I'd look at it that way, Elvis.'

'Well, sir, I tell you, you have to accept the bad along with the good. I've been getting some very good publicity, the press has been wonderful to me, and I've been getting some bad publicity – but you got to expect that. I know that I'm doing the best that I can, and I have never turned a reporter down, and I've never turned a disc jockey down, because they're the people that can help make you in this business . . . as long as I know I'm doing the best that I can.'

'You can't expect to do any more,' Gardner said kindly. 'I want to tell you it's been just swell talking to you, and you make a lot of sense.'

On 9 September 1956, Elvis appeared on the *Ed Sullivan Show*, opening with a high-tempo 'Don't Be Cruel'. The most startling aspect of the performance was that the back-and-forth movements of his penis appeared to be visible, though in fact Elvis had padded his crotch to make it look that way. Sullivan was in hospital at the time, but his producer quickly changed camera angles, so television viewers saw Elvis only from a distance and to the side.

Jack Gould wrote in the *New York Times*, 'When Presley executes his bumps and grinds, it must be remembered by the Columbia Broadcasting Company System that even a twelve-year-old's curiosity may be over-stimulated. Over the long run, however, maybe Presley is doing everybody a great favor by pointing up the need for early sex education.'

Eighty per cent of TV viewers watched the show, and 85 per cent tuned in for Presley's second appearance. On a third performance for Sullivan, however, Elvis was shown only from the waist up.

Gladys worried that her son was being overworked and should slow down, but this was not the time, Elvis said. Besides his road shows and television appearances, he was embarking on a movie career. Gladys prayed that he would meet a nice Southern girl and settle down. Whenever he brought a girl home, Gladys went out of her way to encourage marriage, but she had to contend with the Colonel's decisions and one of them was that his golden boy should remain unattached. If he was single and available, girls would think they had a chance with him, an important element in maintaining his 'come and get me' image. This was also MGM's theory about their male stars: until they were firmly established as screen idols, marriage was out of the question. As opposed to the MGM contract players, however, who resented being told what to do, Elvis obeyed Parker. The Colonel, he believed, was his saviour.

On 15 December 1956, Elvis gave his last performance on *Louisiana Hayride*. After his final song, 10,000 teenagers headed for the exit. Horace Lee Hogan, founder and producer of the show, ran to the microphone and said, 'Please, young people, *Elvis has left the building*. He's in his car and driving away. Please take your seats.'

Elvis had plenty of girls, girls, girls. On stage, he would sing to the prettiest one and arrange to meet her after the show. Sometimes he had two girls in the back seat of his car; plenty of petting occurred, but he did not go all the way with most of them. Nor did he have intercourse with his 'steady' girlfriends, Dixie Locke, June Juanico, Dottie Harmony and Anita Wood. Elvis said he was a virgin until he was eighteen, but did not mention with whom he had his first experience. His close attachment to Gladys might have been the reason he was never intimate with women who had children. To him it was too closely related to actually going to bed with his own mother.

Elvis had a foot fetish, as well, and was turned off by girls who did not have delicate feet like Gladys's. He loved to fondle and suck women's toes and, in baby talk, whispered how much he loved their 'itty-bitty' feet. He also disliked black lingerie, which he said only bad girls wore.

In his first film, *Love Me Tender*, Presley fell in love with his leading lady, twenty-year-old Debra Paget, but she turned down his marriage proposal. Not having been rejected very often, he hid in the bushes outside her house and discovered, to his dismay, that she was dating billionaire Howard Hughes. Outclassed, he gave up on Debra, but he never got over her completely.

Love Me Tender, co-starring Richard Egan, was the story of two brothers, during the Civil War, who love the same girl. Presley's recording of the title song sold almost a million copies even before it was released. Above the Paramount Theater in New York City a fifty-foot cardboard cut-out of Elvis was unveiled before the movie's premiere on 15 November 1956.

A month later the *Wall Street Journal* reported that Elvis merchandise had grossed $22 million. He was the new symbol of American youth, an image that changed the world, its style of dressing, its music and its attitude toward sex. Ed Sullivan, who had been critical of Presley, now said that Elvis was a decent and fine boy, and he was delighted to work with him. Coming from Sullivan, the most influential celebrity on television, this was high praise.

Before Elvis made his next film in January 1957, he had plastic surgery on his nose to alter it slightly, and work was done on his face to clear up the acne scars that had plagued him since he was a youth. He looked better than ever.

The story of *Loving You*, with Lizabeth Scott, Wendell Corey and Dolores Hart, was based on Presley's life – it was about a young rock singer who attains stardom with the help of an aggressive press agent. In the film Gladys can be seen sitting in an aisle seat of a theatre applauding Elvis as he performs. Poor Gladys. She must have wanted to be with her son so much that she was willing to go on camera. It was time to ease up, she told Elvis. They had plenty of money, but they were rarely together as a family. He had plans to rectify that. He purchased Graceland Mansion in March 1957 for $100,000. Situated on thirteen acres in Whitehaven, a suburb of Memphis, the house had been built in the thirties and named after the original owner's mother, Grace.

Gladys was overwhelmed and lonely there. 'They don't let me do nothin',' she told a friend. 'I want to do my own cookin' and raise my chickens like I used to.' Elvis complied by turning the backyard into a miniature farm, complete with a chicken coop, donkeys and pigs. But

Gladys wanted her son to come home. 'You got it all, son, so why can't you spend more time in Memphis? I guess 'cause you don't want to.'

'Mama, you don't know how it is,' he said.

Gladys might have countered with, 'You don't know how it is here,' but she didn't tell him about being abused by Vernon, who luxuriated in Graceland and all the frills that went with it, including other women. Gladys took Benzedrine and consumed vodka to excess to ease the pain of loneliness, which only worsened when Elvis decided to make Hollywood his second home.

One of his biggest thrills was filming *Jailhouse Rock* in May 1957 at MGM, the centre of the Hollywood galaxy – the studio that bragged it had more stars than there are in heaven. Elvis was very impressed. The day he arrived with his entourage, assistant director Bob Relyea received a call from the front gate. The guards needed help immediately. Fans were rushing the cars and the secretaries were out of control. Stars, directors, technicians and other MGM personnel were hanging out of the windows, desperate to get a glimpse of Elvis.

It was a big day for the studio that Louis B. Mayer built – a shot in the arm for the few movie legends still under contract. Two years earlier Clark Gable had walked out in a huff and now his dressing room was being taken over by Elvis Presley, who couldn't believe it. 'Is that Van Johnson?' he gasped. 'My God!' Johnson stared in disbelief, too, and bowed. He later remembered, 'It was like royalty!' Presley would be associated with MGM for fourteen years.

One of the reasons Elvis wanted to rent or buy a house in Hollywood was that he had been thrown out of the Knickerbocker Hotel for rowdy behaviour and causing damage. He moved on to the Beverly Wilshire, but needed his privacy. He became involved with actress Natalie Wood, who wanted to marry him. When Elvis hesitated, she threatened to jump from his hotel window. As for marriage itself, he said, 'Why buy a cow when you can steal the milk through a fence?'

In *Jailhouse Rock*, Elvis had difficulty with the big dance number because he couldn't learn the steps. So he suggested using his own routines, and it worked. The film premiered in Memphis on 17 October 1957, and quickly went into the top five at the box office. The title song was a smash hit, too.

That year the Presleys enjoyed their first Christmas at Graceland, before Elvis received the draft notice that he had been expecting. Because of his celebrity, he was given the privilege of going into Special Services, which would entail entertaining the troops and eating at the officers' mess. Elvis discussed this at great length with the Colonel, who thought Presley should go into the Army like any other draftee with no special privileges. Gladys burst into tears when she found out that her son would not, after all, be under the protection of Special Services.

The Colonel, determined that Presley fans should not forget him while he was away, made plans for Elvis to record several songs to be released during the two years he was in the Army. He was also rushed into *King Creole*, the picture that many critics, and Elvis himself, considered his best. It was filmed in New Orleans and Elvis shared a room there with actor Nick Adams, who claimed the pair had a brief affair. A scandal magazine ran an article with the headline 'Presley's Powder-Puff Pals', showing a picture of Elvis and gay Liberace above the caption 'Two prominent bachelors'.

In fact the only influence the famous pianist had on Presley was showing him how to dress with flair. Elvis, who hadn't found his image as yet, can be seen in a film clip trying on Liberace's gold lame jacket. As for Nick Adams, we'll never know the truth, since he died under mysterious circumstances on 7 February 1968. According to David Bret in his book, *Elvis: The Hollywood Years*, Colonel Parker held secret information about a homosexual affair between Elvis and Adams. Toe the line or else. 'That's why Parker had so much control over him.'

That control was to be maintained. As late as 1967 the Colonel persuaded Elvis to raise his management fee from 25 per cent to 50 per cent. Presley could have toured internationally for millions of fans, but Parker, an illegal alien, could not obtain a passport, and Elvis went nowhere without the Colonel. In fact Parker took more and more from Presley near the end.

On 24 March 1958 Presley was inducted into the U.S. Army and assigned serial number 53310761. The following day he was given his famous G.I. haircut at Fort Chaffee, Arkansas, with reporters on hand. On 29 March he arrived at Fort Hood, Texas for basic training, while his parents moved to a temporary residence nearby. Elvis thrived in the army. He lost fifteen pounds, came out third in tank gunnery and scored well in marksmanship.

Gladys was impressed – except that her son had grown up. The army had made a man out of him. She had lost what she cherished most, his innocence and his little-boy attitude toward her. Soon he would be shipped to Germany, a place so foreign to her she had no idea where to find it on the map. In August 1958, after a violent quarrel with Vernon, she collapsed. Doctors in Texas suspected hepatitis and suggested she see her doctor in Memphis. Unable to get a weekend pass, Elvis watched his parents board a train for home on Friday, 8 August and waited for news about Gladys's condition, blaming himself over and over again for not recognising the symptoms of her declining health.

Gladys was admitted to hospital on Saturday. The following Monday she was barely conscious and Elvis rushed to her bedside the following night. Unable at first to get a pass, he had threatened to go AWOL before finally being granted permission to fly to Memphis. When Gladys saw him she exclaimed, 'Oh my son, oh my son.' She seemed to rally, but Elvis refused to leave her until she insisted he get some rest on Wednesday night.

Early the next morning, 14 August, at the age of 46, Gladys Presley died of liver disease before Elvis could reach her. His wailing cries of grief echoed through the hospital corridors. Alan Fortas, a member of Elvis's entourage, said, 'Repeatedly Elvis cried out, "I lived my whole life for you." But, of course, a good case could be made that it was precisely the other way around – and that Gladys lived her whole life for her son. Rarely have two people wounded each other so deeply out of love.'

The press and public were told Gladys Presley had died of a heart attack, but the real cause was cirrhosis of the liver.

The next day the hearse carrying the body of Gladys Presley arrived at Graceland. Barely able to stand up, Elvis cried, 'Look, Daddy. Mama's comin' home. She's back!'

Visitors were both touched and appalled to see Elvis hug and kiss Gladys in her silver coffin, begging her to come back. 'Look at those tiny little hands,' he said. 'And look at her little sooties, she's so precious . . .' Finally Elvis was given a sedative to help him sleep, so he would not see his mother's body being removed to the Memphis Funeral Home. The funeral was almost too much for Elvis to bear and it was worse at Forest Hill Cemetery, where Elvis threw himself over his mother's glass-covered coffin. 'Goodbye, darling. Goodbye, darling. We'll keep the house, darling. Everything that you loved. We won't change a thing.' When the casket was being lowered into the ground, Elvis jumped on it, crying out her name and begging his mama not to leave him until he was gently restrained. The inscription on Gladys Presley's tombstone read, 'She was the sunshine of our home.'

Before returning to Fort Hood, Elvis gave strict orders not to change anything at Graceland; his mother's room, he insisted, should remain as she left it. Peter Brown and Pat Broeske in their book, *Down at the End of Lonely Street: The Life and Death of Elvis Presley*, claim that he went on a sex spree like never before, as if he was now free from the guilt and psychological frigidity imposed by Gladys, who had wanted him to seek chaste candidates for marriage rather than the 'beautiful itty-bitty' things Elvis lusted after. He wanted a blonde, a redhead and a dark brunette all in the same evening. His buddies, however, surmised that he did not go beyond foreplay with these girls.

On 19 September 1958, Elvis boarded the USS *General Randall* for Germany. Reporters were there in force and the Colonel gave them what they wanted. Elvis had to borrow a duffel bag because his own was already on board. He walked up the gangplank numerous times so that photographers could get good pictures of Presley 'going off to war'.

Arriving at Bremerhaven, West Germany, on 1 October, he then boarded a train for Friedberg, twenty miles from Frankfurt. Since Vernon and his mother Minnie Mae planned to join him, Elvis rented a three-storey, four-bedroom house and continued his sexual conquests, which included young girls under sixteen.

He also discovered prostitutes for the first time, but his terror of sexually transmitted diseases led to a fear of sexual penetration. Possibly Presley was shy, as well, because he was not well-endowed and referred to his penis as 'little Elvis'. But there were no complaints from the women with whom he had intimate relations. Stripper Tempest Storm described him as an 'impatient lover', who enjoyed 'a marathon' session of lovemaking. Elvis climbed an eight-foot fence to get to her room and entered panting, 'I'm as horny as a billy goat in a pepper patch! I'll race ya to the bed.' Elvis loved women, although as producer-writer Joe Mankiewicz said, 'Everyone in Hollywood is bisexual.' When I questioned him further, he laughed and said, 'Well, once, anyway.'

It was in Germany that Elvis began to take pills. Someone tipped him off about amphetamines, which gave him the ability to stay up all night on army assignments. He claimed the pills were safe for anyone to take because a doctor prescribed them.

Priscilla Beaulieu was fourteen years old when her mother and stepfather, a captain in the army, moved from Texas to Germany. She was a beautiful young lady with dark hair and deep-set eyes and, like Elvis, was lonely and confused. Only recently she had found out that her real father, a navy pilot, had been killed in a plane crash when she was six months old. She had been told all along that Paul Beaulieu was her father when actually he had adopted her after marrying her mother, Ann, when Priscilla was three. She felt out of place beside her sister and two brothers, who were born after Ann's marriage to Beaulieu.

Priscilla began hanging out at a community centre in Wiesbaden called the Eagle Club and it was there she met Currie Grant, the entertainment director of the club. 'Are you a fan of Elvis Presley's?' he asked.

'Who isn't?' she laughed.

'I'm a friend of his. My wife and I go to his house quite often. How would you like to come along some evening?'

Of course she would, as long as her father gave his consent. After checking out Currie Grant with his commanding officer, Beaulieu gave his permission, providing that Priscilla was home by eleven o'clock. That evening she wore a navy blue sailor dress with white socks and shoes. When Elvis was introduced to her, he was struck by her amazing resemblance to Gladys. 'What have we here?' he said. They sat down together, his eyes boring into her. 'So, do you go to school?'

'Yes,' she replied.

'. . . junior or senior in high school?'

'Ninth.'

'Ninth *what*?'

'Grade.'

'Ninth grade? Why, you're just a baby!'

He played the piano and sang for her until it was time for her to leave. A few days later Currie said Elvis wanted to see her again. After a few minutes together he told her, 'I want to be alone with you, Priscilla.'

'We are alone,' she said nervously.

'I mean *really* alone,' he whispered. 'Will you come upstairs to my room?' *His* room?

'There's nothing to be afraid of, honey. I swear I'd never do anything to harm you. Please?'

She followed him upstairs and he talked to her about his fears. Would his fans forget about him? Would he still have a career when he returned home? He was afraid. And he could tell by instinct that she was afraid too. When Elvis kissed her goodnight on the forehead, she held on to him. It was he who eased her away. The fourth time Presley called Priscilla, her parents said they wanted to meet him. He showed up accompanied by Vernon. Paul Beaulieu was blunt. What did he want with his daughter? Vernon looked down at the floor, but Elvis spoke up. 'I'm lonely, sir, and I happen to be very fond of her. She's very mature for her age and I need someone to talk to. You don't have to worry about her, Captain. I'll take good care of her.'

After that, Priscilla and Elvis saw each other every night. She admitted begging him to go all the way, but he refused. They did everything but have intercourse, she said. He would never do that with a girl he was seeing on a steady basis, according to what he told other women. Priscilla didn't know that Elvis was sleeping with his nineteen-year-old secretary; this did not necessarily involve sex, however. He would have his fun for an hour or so and then call her to come to bed. From his childhood until his death he was afraid to sleep alone.

In Suzanne Finstad's 1997 book *Child Bride: The Untold Story of Priscilla Beaulieu Presley*, the facts about Elvis's adorable virgin are disputed by those who knew her in Germany. Currie Grant, for example, claimed it was Priscilla who approached him about meeting Presley and that she had intercourse with him for the chance to meet her idol.

Elvis was angry and hurt when Vernon said he was going to marry Dee Stanley, a 35-year-old blonde with three children. Reluctantly Elvis gave his blessings, while telling close friend Joe Esposito, 'I think she's marryin' him because he's my daddy. I'll never call her Mom.' On 3 January 1960, Vernon Presley married Dee Stanley. They lived at Graceland briefly before moving to a house nearby. He did not attend the wedding. And it was Dee who, after her divorce from Vernon, wrote a book about Elvis, claiming his relationship with Gladys had been incestuous.

On 20 January Elvis was promoted to sergeant. By now, however, he was making plans for his discharge from the army in two months. Colonel Parker sent a camera crew to film background footage in Germany for Presley's next movie, *G.I. Blues*. 'I've been wearing this uniform for two years,' Elvis moaned to his buddies. 'Now I have to wear it in a film?'

On 1 March Presley boarded a plane back to the United States. As promised, he hesitated before going on board and waved to Priscilla. He landed at McGuire Field Air Base in New Jersey to a hero's welcome. In front of hundreds of reporters Frank Sinatra's nineteen-year-old daughter Nancy presented him with several lacy dress shirts on behalf of her father, who was to welcome him home on a TV special. Reporters asked Elvis about his relationship with Nancy. 'I just met her,' he replied. 'I think she's engaged to Tommy Sands.'

The Colonel had arranged for Elvis to take a private train back to Memphis so he could make appearances at each station to sign autographs and pose for pictures. He returned to Graceland with mixed feelings. As he had instructed, everything was the same, and the memory of Gladys was everywhere. But, fortunately, Elvis was kept so busy he had little time for tears. He taped Sinatra's TV show, *Welcome Home, Elvis*, performing a great duet with Frank who crooned 'Love Me Tender' to Presley's 'Witchcraft'.

The big news was how much Elvis had changed. He was cool and sophisticated rather than hot and raw. He was still Elvis all right, and the girls screamed and viewers tuned in. The King of Rock 'n' Roll had been away for two years; he had lost his mother and become a model soldier and had now returned home with a touch of humility. His fans didn't know what to make of their idol grown up in a tuxedo, snapping his fingers to the rhythm instead of going into a high-tempo rock 'n' roll number. But when he was linked romantically with Juliet Prowse, his leading lady in *G.I. Blues*, his irresistible image attracted not only screeching teenagers, but their mothers as well.

Elvis and Juliet were seen together on the beach, riding the roller coaster and gambling in Las Vegas. Despite her supposed engagement to Frank Sinatra, she was openly affectionate with Elvis, although he, to no one's surprise, was also seeing other women. Priscilla asked Elvis about Juliet. 'She's a big girl,' he explained. 'Her shoulders are broader than mine. Would I get involved with a woman like that?' Priscilla believed his explanation, as she always did.

When Marlon Brando turned down *Flaming Star*, a picture about a half-breed, Elvis got the part. He was thrilled to find a role that would give him a chance to prove he could act as well as sing. Though all concerned agreed that he was a better actor than expected, songs were added. This was a crushing blow to Elvis, who showed his displeasure on the movie set. Then, in *Wild in the Country*, Elvis played a confused writer torn between three women, Hope Lange, Millie Perkins, and Tuesday Weld – with whom he had a brief but torrid affair.

Though Elvis tried his best not to sing in his movies, box-office receipts were proof that his musicals made more money. He would have to live with the reality that, despite his ability as an actor, the public paid to hear him sing.

In *Blue Hawaii*, one of his best movies, Presley had a very good selection of songs – 'Blue Hawaii', 'Rock-a-Hula Baby', 'Hawaiian Wedding Song', and 'Can't Help Falling in Love'. The soundtrack album was on the

Billboard chart for a year and a half, second only to *G.I. Blues*. There was chemistry between Elvis and his leading lady, Joan Blackman, both on and off the screen. She was one of few actresses worthy of playing opposite Presley in the love department.

While in Hawaii, Elvis gave a concert at the Bloch Arena, Pearl Harbor to fund the building of a memorial to the USS *Arizona*. The necessary funds were successfully raised thanks to his support, along with numerous personal donations.

After making *Follow that Dream*, in 1961, Presley starred in *Kid Galahad* as a boxer harassed by gangsters who want him to rig a fight. Elvis did not like appearing bare-chested, feeling his physique was lacking, especially in the biceps department. But, despite his physical flaws and the increasingly formulaic nature of his movies, everything came together and the film worked.

In December 1962 Priscilla was allowed to visit Elvis in Los Angeles, where she stayed with him in a rented house. Her pleas to consummate their relationship failed again. 'The time will come,' he whispered. Elvis took her to Las Vegas and delighted in her childlike amazement at the casinos, the glittering lights and elaborate stage shows. He bought her expensive evening gowns and jewellery, had her hair dyed black and piled high atop her head, and her face excessively made up.

When Priscilla returned to West Germany, her parents were horrified by her cheap appearance, but they reluctantly allowed her to spend Christmas at Vernon's house in Memphis. Elvis put her luggage in his Rolls-Royce and headed for Graceland, where Grandma Minnie Mae welcomed her warmly. 'If there's anything you need, come to me, honey, and I'll see to it.' That night Elvis gave Priscilla pills to help her sleep, but she blacked out, only waking up two days later. Minnie was furious with Elvis: 'I don't care how many pills you take, but don't you ever give them to this little girl!'

Vernon told Priscilla, 'I wanted to take you to the hospital, but my son wouldn't allow it.'

'That wouldn't be very good publicity, would it, Daddy?' responded Elvis.

'No,' Minnie Mae interrupted, 'but she could have died!'

Elvis made it up to Priscilla at Christmas and, on New Year's Eve, told her that he was going to see to it that she stayed in Memphis for good. 'I'll arrange it. You'll see.'

The Beaulieus absolutely forbade his request, until he offered to fly them to the United States for an 'inspection' tour of his world. Of course, they were in awe of Hollywood, the movie studios and the glamour of it all. In Memphis, Vernon turned on his country charm for the Beaulieus, promising them that Priscilla would live with him and his wife and that she would attend Catholic school. Elvis Presley usually got what he wanted one way or another.

So Priscilla moved to Memphis – and into the King's bed. She was enrolled at the Immaculate Conception, giving Vernon's address as her residence. Elvis was creating the woman he wanted, teaching 'Cilla', as he called her, how to live, dress and act according to his wishes. 'I did what he told me to,' she said. Except to her parents in Germany, it was no secret that Priscilla was living at Graceland, but no one mentioned it, including the press. Because Elvis was a generous benefactor to the city of Memphis, he was given the benefit of the doubt. Officials and residents alike loved and respected him throughout the years and, because of this, he never threatened to relocate.

Priscilla, however, would become a virtual prisoner at Graceland. Colonel Parker was concerned that she might be seen in the grounds, and his fear became a reality when she was spotted taking a stroll in the backyard. He would have preferred her to live with Vernon, according to the agreement with the Beaulieus. But Elvis paid no attention to Parker's fears that his career would be ruined if it became public knowledge that Priscilla was living with him.

In late 1963, Presley had been looking forward to making *Fun in Acapulco* in Mexico until a riot broke out there in a theatre showing *G.I. Blues*. As a result, the Mexican government banned Elvis's movies. So the film was made in Hollywood instead.

Elvis was unimpressed by the uproar over the Beatles when they arrived in the United States in February 1964. They wanted to meet Presley, their idol, but he wasn't interested. Instead the Colonel sent a congratulatory telegram, which Ed Sullivan read on the air when the Beatles appeared on his show. In private, Elvis still referred to them as 'those fucking sons of bitches', but the Colonel was adamant and, on 27 August 1964, he showed the four boys from England into the den of Presley's house in Los Angeles. Elvis played it so cool that there was nothing but silence as Paul McCartney, John Lennon, Ringo Starr and George Harrison ogled him in complete awe. 'Hell,' an exasperated Elvis exclaimed. 'If you guys are gonna sit there and stare at me all night, I'm going to bed. I thought we could sit and talk and jam a little.'

'Yes,' the English four shouted in unison, but no one thought about recording this historic session. John Lennon asked Elvis why he wasn't putting out any new songs. 'Because,' Presley explained with a scowl, 'they have me makin' movies. I don't have time to record anything but the stuff I sing in them.'

'That's sad,' Lennon sighed.

Before the Beatles left at two in the morning, they invited Elvis and his pals to their rented house on Mulholland Drive, but he didn't lower himself by accepting the invitation. People came to him; he did not go to them. John Lennon commented,

> There's only one person in the United States we ever wanted to meet . . . not that he wanted to meet us. And we met him last night. We can't tell you how we felt. We just idolised him so much. When we first came to town, those guys like Dean Martin and Frank Sinatra and all these people wanted to come over and hang around with us at night simply because we had all the women, all the chicks. We don't want to meet those people. They don't really like us. We don't really admire them or like them. The only person that we wanted to meet in the United States of America was Elvis Presley. You can't imagine what a thrill that was last night. Nothing really affected me until I heard Elvis. If there hadn't been an Elvis, there wouldn't have been the Beatles.

MGM press agent George Nichols told me,

> I didn't handle Elvis, but I heard all about him from those who worked with him. He gave MGM a shot in the arm when he started making films at Metro. Elvis did fourteen movies for MGM. He was like a kid in many ways because he was so impressed to be associated with the studio that had stars like Clark Gable, Jimmy Stewart, Spencer Tracy, Lana Turner and the rest. He didn't throw his weight around and was, in fact, very humble. It wasn't like the old days of contract players, of course, but he made his best movies with MGM, like *Viva Las Vegas*.
>
> I overheard him say he was taking diet pills to maintain his weight, and I thought about Judy Garland. Lana took them, Clark took them. It was a way of life in Hollywood. Get fat and your fans won't be interested in you any more. Elvis was hanging on. A little thing like his thirtieth birthday sent him into a tailspin because the press

referred to him as the 'granddaddy of rock 'n' roll'. There he was, an old man already, and along came the Beatles. The pressure was on, but I never heard a bad word said about him. He had a lot of women because he was irresistible – a very handsome guy with charisma – but it was hard for him to live up to his title of King. Clark Gable said it was a burden to wear the crown because any day it could fall off or someone else would claim it. I felt sorry for them in a way because when you reach the top where do you go?

In July 1963 Elvis filmed his fourteenth movie, *Viva Las Vegas*, with the vivacious Ann-Margret. The chemistry between the two stars was instantaneous, and the MGM publicists sharpened their pencils. George Nichols remembered,

They were very shy. Both were extroverts on the outside and introverts at heart. I think the movie spoke for itself, but it took a while before they were alone together off the set. They were very much in love. In public they were with Presley's group known as the Memphis Mafia, but never alone. MGM milked the romance for two reasons – to publicise *Viva Las Vegas* and because their affair was the real thing.
    I knew nothing about his girlfriend Priscilla Beaulieu who, I heard later, was very upset. She went as far as to change her hair colour to match Ann-Margret's.

That's why Priscilla emerged publicly in a *Photoplay* article. The writer claimed she was married to Elvis and published photos of the couple in Germany.
    In an interview for the fan magazine, Ann-Margret said she was going steady with Elvis but was quoted as saying they were engaged. He did not react kindly and was furious that the reporter knew about an enormous round pink bed he had given Ann-Margret. Elvis remained a friend, but the romance was over because she had revealed too much about their relationship. Isn't that just what happened to Lauren Bacall when she told reporters about Frank Sinatra's marriage proposal? Eighteen-year-old Priscilla was more discreet, telling the writer to ask Elvis for the answers to any personal inquiries.
    Ann-Margret wasn't sure what happened. She is, to this day, very careful what she says about Elvis. But his buddy, Lamar Fike, claimed, 'I think he would have married her in a New York second. But he made it clear he'd

do it only if Ann-Margret quit the business. She was very career-oriented. She wouldn't do it.'

Elvis kept in touch with her over the years and sent a horseshoe of flowers each time she opened in Las Vegas. Opinions vary as to whether it was Ann-Margret or Priscilla who was the love of Presley's life.

At the age of thirty, Elvis was the highest-paid entertainer in Hollywood. He spent lavishly, buying cars for friends and strangers alike, but where was he going? In many ways he wanted time to stand still. He wouldn't part with the 1955 pink Cadillac Fleetwood sedan that had belonged to Gladys, or any of her other possessions. He also clung to his favourite gospel music, daring to sing it in Las Vegas despite criticism from both Parker and the hotel bosses. Elvis had the ability to make the right decisions in regard to his career, but was rarely given the chance to prove it. He told a friend he hated musicals. When he saw *The King and I* with Yul Brynner and Deborah Kerr, Elvis wondered, 'Why didn't he say "I love you" without singing it?'

Kissin' Cousins, released in 1964, was a dud, but *Roustabout* with screen legend Barbara Stanwyck went over well. *Girl Happy*, *Tickle Me* and *Frankie and Johnny* were typical Presley films – colourful and entertaining. The silly and forgettable *Harum Scarum* was an embarrassment to Elvis. It had reached the point where his fans would pay to see any of his movies, no matter how bad they were. He wondered why. In fact, Presley wondered about many aspects of his life. Why was he the chosen one . . . ?

Bored, he took prescription drugs to ease the pain of life. Occasionally he tried marijuana, LSD and cocaine, but they did not give him the punch he needed. In fact, he criticised anyone who took hard drugs, and if anyone questioned the way he popped pills he always came back with, 'They are prescribed by doctors so it's OK.'

Like the title of one of his films, it was 'easy come, easy go' for Elvis. He had affairs with most of his leading ladies, and he liked to have 'pyjama parties' with teenage girls wearing white panties, at which he would take pictures of them romping in bed. He took hundreds of Polaroid shots of Priscilla with other girls. Elvis was a voyeur at heart and enjoyed watching his Memphis Mafia pals engage in sex with women. Often it pleased him more to masturbate than to engage in the act itself. He enjoyed dry humping, too, a hangover from his youth. Many of his girlfriends agreed that he tried to avoid penetration.

Meanwhile, Priscilla's father was getting impatient. She had been with Elvis for five years with no talk of marriage, so he put pressure on Colonel Parker who, in turn, told Elvis that he could stall no longer. Getting to the truth of Presley's feelings for Priscilla at this time was frustrating: everyone in his entourage had a different version, but what seems apparent is that neither Elvis nor Priscilla was in control. On Christmas Eve 1966, he went down on his knees, presented her with a three-and-a-half-carat diamond ring, and proposed marriage. Elvis told Marty Lacker that he had no choice. His career would be destroyed if Priscilla's father pressed charges, under the Mann act, for transporting a minor across state lines for sexual purposes. But Elvis spoke the truth when he said, 'I can't do what's expected of me in marriage,' referring to his passion for other women. He went so far as to tell his barber and spiritual advisor, Larry Geller, 'After all, Jesus never got married.'

MGM press agent George Nichols said,

> He would have been happier if Priscilla had walked away. It was a forced marriage and he got the worse of it. Elvis was in no hurry to set a wedding date and planned to postpone it as long as possible. He was getting ready to make *Clambake*, in March 1967, when he tripped over the cord to a television in the bathroom. He fell head first, hit his head on the bathtub and was knocked out cold. Our representatives rushed to his house with the Colonel and found Elvis in bed with a minor concussion. We knew about his drug problem and assumed he was taking diet pills because he was overweight, and sleeping pills to get a good night's sleep. The Colonel asked MGM to postpone *Clambake*, and assured us Elvis would slim down after a much-needed rest.

Parker, who had generally stayed out of Presley's personal life, decided he had to become involved now that it was affecting their association with MGM. He had to clean up his act. The Colonel had a private talk with Elvis, who was meek as a lamb when he and Parker sat down with the Memphis Mafia to straighten out a few matters. Presley's army buddy and loyal friend, Joe Esposito, was put in charge. 'Elvis is not Jesus Christ,' Parker emphasised. 'Take your problems to Joe and he'll get in touch with me.'

The Colonel flew to Las Vegas to make arrangements for Presley's wedding to Priscilla at the Aladdin Hotel. Elvis increased his intake of pills as the date approached.

At 11:41 a.m. on 1 May 1967, the couple were married in an eight-minute ceremony by Nevada Supreme Court Justice David Zenoff. At the wedding reception a hundred guests enjoyed a buffet of ham and eggs, Southern fried chicken, clams casino, oysters Rockefeller, roast suckling pig, poached salmon and champagne. A string trio and a strolling accordionist played romantic ballads that included 'Love Me Tender'.

The newlyweds spent their honeymoon at Presley's home in Palm Springs, returning to Graceland three days later. On 29 May, Priscilla and Elvis wore their wedding outfits at a Graceland reception for Memphis friends.

A week after Presley married, Ann-Margret wed actor Roger Smith, star of 77 *Sunset Strip*, at the Riviera Hotel in Las Vegas on 8 May 1967. Five years later Elvis confessed that he was still carrying a torch for her.

Nancy Sinatra was Presley's leading lady in *Speedway*, a picture about a racing driver whose back taxes are collected by a female I.R.S. agent. Sinatra had recently divorced Tommy Sands and Elvis took the opportunity to engage in his white panty fetish with her. He found Nancy enchanting, but backed off after some heavy petting in her dressing room. Shortly thereafter, Priscilla announced that she was pregnant, and Nancy gave her a baby shower.

Elvis had forbidden his bride to take birth control pills because their long-term effect had not been established. So Priscilla was reliant on the rhythm method, which failed. She contemplated having an abortion because she wanted to spend time with her husband without the burdens of pregnancy. Elvis left it up to Priscilla, who couldn't bear to abort their baby.

With a cast that included Joan Blondell, Burgess Meredith and Katy Jurado, *Stay Away, Joe* should have been a hit – but it was a disaster. *Live a Little, Love a Little* wasn't much better. With the advent of sexually explicit films such as *The Graduate*, the Presley formula had come to appear outdated, and he was equally out of sync with the music world.

In May 1968, the Colonel talked to NBC executive producer Bob Finkel about an hour-long special in which Elvis would sing Christmas songs. The King had other ideas. He told Finkel it was time for a change, that he wanted to do something entirely different. He wanted, in particular, to disconnect himself from his movies. Finkel talked to a young man by the name of Steve Binder, who had directed TV specials with Diana Ross and the Supremes, the Beach Boys, and Petula Clark. Binder met with Presley, who admitted he was terrified of doing live television again, and equally reluctant to face mobs of eager fans once more. Binder knew Elvis had been out of circulation for eight years, but he didn't put this into words. Instead he took a shaken Presley down to Sunset Boulevard, where they waited. 'Prepare yourself,' Elvis warned the director. But no one paid any attention to the King of Rock 'n' Roll. He did everything he could to gain attention, but to no avail. So much for being crushed by adoring fans.

To Parker's dismay, Elvis made his 1968 comeback special using his own ingenuity. On a small stage surrounded by an audience, Elvis, sideburns and all, emerged wearing the famous tight-fitting black leather outfit and opened with 'Heartbreak Hotel'. He ended the show in a white suit and shoes singing 'If I Can Dream', accompanied by a full-scale orchestra. The 76-minute tape was cut to an hour and aired on 3 December 1968 on NBC. One critic said, 'There is something magical about watching a man who has lost himself find his way back home. He sang with the kind of power people no longer expect from rock 'n' roll singers.'

Had Elvis directed one of his lyrics to Priscilla, in the audience but out of camera range? He seemed to look at her and adlibbed, 'You have made my life a wreck' in his rendition of 'Love Me Tender'. He hadn't been intimate with her since the birth of their daughter, Lisa Marie. Though Elvis had told her long ago that he would not have intercourse with a woman who had had a baby, she naturally assumed that, as his wife, she would be the exception. But all her efforts to seduce him were in vain. He believed that making love to her was wrong. Was this temporary, she wanted to know. No, it's forever, he said. Priscilla had become his untouchable Madonna; maybe, he told his buddies, she was his mother reincarnated.

The extraordinary rebirth of Elvis on TV convinced him to return to Las Vegas, the glittering city of lights that had given him such a cool reception in 1956. He would perform at the opening of the International, the largest hotel in Las Vegas at the time, on 31 July 1969. Wearing a black tunic shirt, matching bell-bottoms and black boots, he started with 'Blue Suede Shoes' to a roaring ovation, cheers and the stamping of feet. For his month-long engagement they came from all over the world to see Elvis. Las Vegas had never seen anything like it, and each time he performed there, money poured in as never before.

Presley made close to $1 million for each of his engagements, while the gift shop of the International Hotel overflowed with Elvis photos, buttons, hats and teddy bears. In January 1970, Presley was a bigger hit in Las Vegas than he had been in July. Wearing a white high-collared jumpsuit cut to the waist in front, he was never more handsome or commanding. He sported a karate belt with pearls, and wore diamond rings on eight fingers. MGM filmed his next performance at the International for a documentary, *Elvis – That's the Way It Is*. It featured Elvis rehearsing, showed the spectacular performance that took him, literally, into the arms of the audience and featured footage of him chatting with celebrities like Cary Grant after the show.

Inspired by this remarkable comeback that he found hard to believe, Elvis went on a tour of major cities, including Los Angeles where he was served with legal papers regarding a paternity suit he had been fighting. In a bad mood, he went on stage that night in December and declared how grateful he was to his fans. Not usually known to brag about his accomplishments, he told the audience, 'I've got 56 gold singles and fourteen gold albums. If there's anyone out there who doubts it, if you ever come through Memphis, you can come in and argue about it, 'cause I've got everyone of them hanging on the wall. I'm really proud of it. I outsold the Beatles, the Stones, Tom Jones – all of them put together.'

It was Patricia Ann Parker, a 21-year-old waitress, who had filed the complaint against Elvis in the Los Angeles Superior Court, claiming her pregnancy was the result of a sexual encounter with Elvis in Las Vegas. Though Parker did not prove her case, it was an embarrassment to Presley who feared he might lose the adoration of his fans. He told columnist May Mann he was completely innocent, asking, 'How can anyone do this to me?'

Priscilla stood by Elvis during this difficult time. Well aware as she was of his sexual exploits, the paternity suit came as no surprise to her. As for his lack of interest in her, she blamed the pills he was taking for his mood swings and odd behaviour. But nothing was as bizarre as the occasion when he stormed out of Graceland after an argument over money with his father in December 1970. Elvis simply disappeared. Priscilla said, 'We were mystified. Elvis didn't even know his own phone number.'

Presley, alone for the first time in many years, got in touch with his buddy Jerry Schilling in Los Angeles, and Jerry met him at the airport. 'I need to go to Washington, D.C.,' Elvis said. He wanted to discuss the country's war on drugs with President Nixon and was determined to get a federal narcotics badge. Elvis drafted a letter to Nixon on American Airlines stationery in the scribbled handwriting of a six-year-old, and left it at the northwest gate of the White House.

In the letter he wrote that the drug culture, the hippie element, the S.D.S., Black Panthers, etc., did not consider him as their enemy or, as they called it, the establishment. 'I call it America,' Elvis said, 'and I love it. Sir, I can and will be of any service that I can to help the country out . . . I wish not to be given a title or an appointed position. I can and will do more good if I were made a Federal Agent at Large, and I will help but by doing it my way through my communication with people of all ages. First and foremost I am an entertainer but all I need is the Federal credentials.'

On 31 December 1970, Elvis, wearing a purple crushed velvet suit with a cape, enormous gold belt and flashy rings on his fingers, shook hands with Richard Nixon in the Oval Office. Elvis showed the President some photos of Lisa Marie and Priscilla. They discussed his amazing career and how Presley could get through to his fans about the drug problem. Elvis emphasised the importance of having a badge. Nixon seemed reluctant for a moment before agreeing to get him one. Elvis was so excited he hugged Nixon. The President was stunned by the gesture but patted him on the shoulder and said, 'Well, I appreciate your willingness to help, Mr. Presley.' Elvis received his badge that day, after lunch in the White House mess and a tour of the residence. His gift to President Nixon was a Second World War chrome-plated Colt 45 which is now on display at the Nixon Library.

In Memphis on 9 January 1971, Elvis accepted the Jaycee award given to the nation's Ten Outstanding Young Men of the Year. He was very proud of this honour and appeared shaken when he accepted it:

When I was a child, ladies and gentlemen, I was a dreamer. I read comic books, and I was the hero of the comic book. I saw movies, and I was the hero in the movie. So every dream that I dreamed has come true a hundred times. These gentlemen over here, they are the type who care, are dedicated. You realise it's not impossible that they might be building the kingdom, it's not far from reality. I'd like to say that I learned very early in life that 'Without a song the day would never end/Without a song a man ain't got a friend/Without a song the road would never bend/Without a song . . .' So I keep singing a song. Good night. Thank you.

As he spoke, Elvis had tears in his eyes.

There were further honours. In June, a stretch of Highway 51 South that runs in front of Graceland was officially renamed Elvis Presley Boulevard. Then, during his engagement at the Las Vegas International Hotel from 9 August until 6 September, Elvis was the recipient of the Bing Crosby

Award (later called the Lifetime Achievement Award) from the National Academy of Recording Arts and Sciences.

Overwhelmed by all the applause and adulation, Elvis had not recognised any signs that Priscilla was seeing another man before she left him on 30 December 1971. He said only that she was gone because she didn't love him any more. She turned up on 26 January before his Las Vegas opening in February, and wasn't seen again until the closing night, 23 February. When Priscilla confronted Elvis about a divorce, he responded by raping her. 'This is how a real man makes love to a woman,' he said. When he found out his wife's lover was Mike Stone, his former karate instructor, Elvis tried to hire someone to kill him, but changed his mind. Stone, who was himself married, and Priscilla moved into a tiny hideaway apartment in Belmont Shores, California.

On 18 August 1972, he filed for divorce to save face. On 9 October, Elvis and Priscilla appeared at the Los Angeles County Superior Courthouse, walking out hand in hand twenty minutes later with their divorce decree granted. He kissed her before she walked to her car with a wave. He winked back. Elvis would pay her $275,000 up front and $1.2 million in monthly payments of $6000, in addition to alimony of $1200 and $4000 in child support monthly. That they had left together holding hands was a plus for Elvis fans. He appeared a little bloated, but handsomely gallant under the circumstances. Not many famous divorced couples emerged from a courthouse with such warmth for each other.

Priscilla moved into a Pacific Palisades apartment and opened a dress shop in Beverly Hills called Bis and Beau (her partner's name was Olivia Bis and Beau was taken from her maiden name).

Elvis went home to his new girlfriend, Linda Thompson. They had met in July 1972 at the Memphis Theater, which Elvis rented out for all-night private screenings. Twenty-two years old, Linda was the current Miss Tennessee and had been placed third in the Miss U.S.A. competition. A tall, lovely blonde virgin, she was attending Memphis State University when she was introduced to Elvis by local RCA promo man Bill Browder. When she related their meeting, Linda said that Elvis had sat down next to her and tried the old yawn-and-stretch routine in order to put his arm around her. He was quick to mention that he was no longer married, to which she replied, 'I'm really sorry to hear that, but I could have told you a long time ago you should have married a Memphis girl.' Elvis got a big kick out of that. Linda was a major part of his life for the next four years.

Six days after the granting of his divorce decree, Elvis collapsed at Graceland and was rushed to hospital. His stomach, colon and chest cavity were bloated with oedema, he had hepatitis, a gastric ulcer, and a swollen liver. United Press International reported that Presley was suffering from pneumonia and extreme exhaustion due to his recent tours.

His Memphis doctor, George Nichopoulos, confronted Elvis, who admitted he used Valium occasionally, amphetamines for energy and sleeping pills to get some rest. 'You know what I'm taking,' Elvis said sheepishly. 'You prescribed them.'

'Dr. Nick', as Presley fondly referred to him, made a phone call to a Los Angeles physician, Dr. Leon Cole, who said he had given Elvis shots of Demerol, mild steroids, Novocaine and cortisone to ease the pain in his neck and back. Looking for pills in Elvis's bedroom at Graceland, Dr. Nick and Joe Esposito found 3000 addictive pills such as Seconal, Dexedrine spansules and Placydil. Dr. Nick informed Elvis that he was a drug addict and would be treated with methadone in hospital. When he returned to Graceland, Elvis was almost drug free, but his withdrawal led to severe depression.

Dr. Nick began travelling with Presley on tour. 'Bad things happened when I wasn't around,' he said. He limited Presley's intake of Dreamy, Amatol, Percodan, and Dilaudid, and often substituted placebos or nonaddictive pills. But Elvis's battle with prescription drugs was a roller coaster; he was off and on, but more often the latter. He began talking too much on stage, rattling on and on about whatever crossed his mind. During one show, with Priscilla and Lisa Marie in the audience, he introduced them before saying, 'Our divorce came about not because of another man or another woman but because of the circumstances involving my career. I was travelling too much.' Elvis rambled on about the paternity suit and rumours that he was addicted to drugs: '. . . had the flu, but all across this town – STRUNG OUT! . . . if I find or hear an individual that has said that about me, I'm going to break their goddamn neck, you son-of-a-bitch! . . . I will pull your goddamn tongue out by the roots . . .'

Priscilla was shocked. 'This was out of character for someone who had so much pride, you know — everything that he was against, he was displaying. It was like watching a different person.'

'I'm self-destructive,' he told Linda.

'You do recognise that?' she asked.

'Yeah, I recognise it, but there's not a lot I can do about it.'

*

On 14 January 1973, Elvis made television history with the live satellite broadcast of *Elvis: Aloha From Hawaii*, transmitted at 12:30 a.m. Hawaiian time from the Honolulu International Center Arena. More than one billion people in forty countries watched the show. The tape was shown in the United States on 4 April on NBC. The American eagle design Presley bore on his jumpsuit was his patriotic message to the world. During his final number, 'Can't Help Falling in Love', Elvis tossed his cape into the audience. (It was recovered by Graceland in 1995.) This show is undoubtedly the pinnacle of his superstardom, one of the all-time great moments of his career.

MGM press agent George Nichols said it was an unprecedented honour for Elvis to be given the first TV satellite show. 'It was outstanding,' he remarked.

He was sexy as hell. During the 'Burnin' Love' number, he fucked the microphone. Elvis moved it back and forth like he was making love to it. He gave out coloured scarves to girls who also handed him hankies to wipe off the sweat. You'd think they got the tears of Jesus. Here's a guy who used to throw teddy bears to the audience until a girl swiped a scarf he had around his neck as part of his outfit. That gave Parker the idea to make this a regular part of Presley's performance. One time several girls fought over one scarf and it was torn to shreds. I guess they took the threads home.

Elvis wore lifts, but so did John Wayne. Elvis wore a girdle when he got too paunchy, but Clark Gable did too. It's tough to keep that handsome image but you have to try to earn a living. At the end of the satellite show, they gave Elvis a crown. They saved it and I think it's on display at Graceland. He didn't put it on. He carried it off when he finished the show. He was a humble guy who really didn't know how to play the guitar too well. He relied on backup. He was hooked on karate all his life. Not only did it give him the ability to defend himself, but Elvis considered it a spiritual thing.

In May, Elvis appeared at Lake Tahoe, but this time to bad reviews. *Variety* said, 'Some thirty pounds overweight, he's puffy, white-faced and blinking against the light. The voice sounds weak, delivery is flabby . . . his medley is delivered in listless fashion . . . attempts to perpetuate his mystique of sex and power end in weak self-parody.'

In August Presley appeared at the Hilton International in Las Vegas. The *Hollywood Reporter* described him as indifferent, uninterested, unappealing and fat. 'It is a tragedy, disheartening and absolutely depressing to see Elvis in such diminishing stature.' In one of his appearances, he was angry because the hotel had fired his favourite waiter: '. . . to Hell with the whole Hilton Hotel, and screw the showroom, too.' Near the end of his engagement, though, Elvis told his audience, 'I know we kid around a lot and have fun and everything – but we really love to sing, play music and entertain people. As long as I can do that, I'll be a happy son-of-a-bitch.'

On 28 March 1975, Barbra Streisand attended Presley's performance at the Hilton, and they talked in his dressing room after the show about his co-starring with her in *A Star is Born*, a remake of the Judy Garland film. Elvis was thrilled and accepted her offer of $500,000 plus ten per cent of the gross. The Colonel, however, wanted $1 million and 50 per cent of the profits. Surely, this would have been an ideal movie for Elvis. He was more than capable of playing the part of a doomed singer. When the deal fell through, part of Elvis died – or at least what was left of him.

The *National Enquirer* had taken a shot at Presley when he turned forty in January: 'Elvis at 40 – Paunchy, Depressed & Living in Fear'. Determined to look his best, he had a facelift and cosmetic surgery on his eyes to eliminate the wrinkles and puffiness. When he appeared in Las Vegas he looked and sounded good. But in his appearance on 20 August, he began slurring his words, tried to prop himself up and fell on the edge of the stage, his legs dangling over the side. 'Folks, I'm sorry,' he whispered before collapsing completely. The King was carried off stage, flown to Memphis and admitted to the Baptist Hospital once again. Linda slept on a cot next to his bed. She stayed with him night and day for two weeks.

Elvis could barely make it on to a stage these days. His drummer Ronnie Tutt said, 'I pounded on the drums as hard as possible to wake him up . . . keep him going.'

Linda was responsible for saving Elvis's life on a number of occasions. She was alert even during the night if he wasn't breathing properly. Once he fell asleep at the dinner table and Linda found him drowning in a bowl of chicken soup. As amusing as it sounds, he almost died. Linda almost died, too, when Elvis shot a bullet through the wall of his Las Vegas hotel suite. It barely missed Linda, who was in the bathroom on the other side of that wall.

Dr. Nick was concerned about Elvis's eating habits, not only because of his weight gain, but the effect that the fat intake was having on his heart.

Most of his mother's relatives had died of massive heart attacks before they were fifty. Elvis ate a pound of bacon for breakfast, half a pound of cottage fries and three double cheeseburgers. One of his concoctions, the famous Gold Loaf Special, was a 42,000-calorie sandwich made at the Colorado Gold Mine Company. It consisted of peanut butter, grape jelly, and lean bacon on an entire loaf of Italian bread that had been hollowed out. Once Elvis flew in his private plane *Lisa Marie* from Memphis to Colorado just to pick up 22 of these sandwiches. He used a knife and fork to eat his beloved peanut butter and banana sandwiches. Then there was the Elvis Special, which consisted of peanut butter and cheese on Wonder Bread, and the fried potato and bacon sandwich. His tastes and preferences reflected his humble beginnings; there were few choices in the refrigerator in those days except peanut butter, jelly and potatoes. Not fancy but very, very fattening. 'Eating is the only thing that gives me any pleasure,' he said. It led to his death, too, because he had the arteries of an eighty-year-old man.

On New Year's Eve 1975, at the Silverdome in Pontiac, Michigan, he split his pants bending over to kiss a fan. *Newsweek* referred to him as 'the roly-poly rock 'n' roller'. The *Houston Chronicle* said, 'Attending an Elvis Presley concert these days is like making a disappointing visit to a national shrine.'

In July 1976 Vernon fired long-time members of the Memphis Mafia, Sonny West and Red West, with only a week's severance pay. Hurt and angry, they decided to write a 'tell-all' book about their former boss. To compound Presley's miseries, Linda Thompson left him. 'I finally decided I had to save my own life,' she said. She moved to Los Angeles to pursue an acting career, but she saw Elvis from time to time. She knew about the other women in his life and often stepped aside so he could be alone with them for a day or a week. Her devotion to Presley was beyond love.

Depressed and lonely, Elvis often locked himself in his darkened bedroom with three television sets, trying his best to shut out the rest of the world. He needed a woman, but not for sex, because he had been impotent for some time. He needed a woman by his side at home and on tour. He needed a woman to call 'Mommy' as he had done with Linda. He needed a woman 24 hours a day. On 19 November, his old friend George Klein wanted him to meet the current Miss Tennessee, Terri Alden. She arrived at Graceland with her twenty-year-old sister, Ginger, who caught Elvis's eye. It was love at first sight. The next day they boarded his private jet for Las Vegas where he showered her with gifts. Not knowing what to expect, she was reluctant to spend the night with him, but he promised nothing would happen. She put on a pair of his pyjamas and he fell asleep.

Unlike the sophisticated Linda, Ginger was ill-equipped for life with Elvis Presley. She was very close to her family in Memphis and did not want to leave them for any length of time. Elvis needed her for inspiration, a request she was unable to comprehend. His Memphis Mafia buddies considered her a blessing when she went on tour, but a curse when she refused to accompany him. Elvis's attempts to make her jealous didn't work so he proposed marriage on 26 January 1977, giving her an eleven-and-a-half-carat diamond engagement ring. Ginger would not, however, live at Graceland.

On 3 March, he made out a will, appointing Vernon as executor and trustee of the estate. The three beneficiaries were Vernon, Grandma Minnie Mae Presley, and Lisa Marie. The will provided that Vernon could, at his discretion, disperse funds to other family members should they be in need. Ginger was a witness to the signing of the will, but she was not mentioned in it.

Presley was on a gruelling schedule in the spring of 1977. In Baton Rouge, Louisiana, on 31 March he couldn't locate Ginger at show time. Frustrated and lonely, he took too many drugs. A crowd of 13,000 was told Elvis had the flu and would not be able to perform. He was taken by ambulance to the airport and flown to Memphis, where he was treated for 'a mild case of anemia and gastroenteritis'.

In May Elvis couldn't remember his lines in Philadelphia. After a fight with Ginger in Baltimore, he stumbled on stage and dropped the microphone, but managed to finish the show without his famous gyrations. In June CBS taped his shows in Omaha, Nebraska, and Rapid City, South Dakota. This special, *Elvis in Concert*, was shown in October, two months after his death, and it shocked the country. A bloated and sweating Elvis Presley tried his best and was in good voice, but it was obvious he was suffering. The question raised by everyone was why the Colonel would want to put a sick, confused, fat Elvis on television.

On 26 June, Presley gave what would be his very last concert at the Market Square Arena in Indianapolis, Indiana, his 55th show since January. At the end, Elvis said to the audience, "Til we meet you again, may God bless you. Adios.'

In July Red West's book, *Elvis: What Happened?*, was published. Elvis had tried to talk to Red, explaining he didn't know Vernon was going to fire him and Sonny. Red explained how much they wanted him to get well and that maybe the book would shock him into getting off the pills that were killing him. During these telephone conversations Red was saddened that, even in trying to convince him not to publish the book, Elvis was slurring his words and was obviously spaced out.

Frank Sinatra offered to use his influence to stop publication, but Elvis did not respond. Part of him was sure the book would never be released and part believed he deserved it, like a bad review after a bad concert. He was very concerned how his fans and Lisa Marie would react when they read the truth in black and white. And how would Priscilla react to the revelation that he had planned to kill Mike Stone? Elvis had mixed emotions. He wanted to have Sonny and Red killed. He wanted to defend himself. He wanted to admit the truth that, because of his bad health, he needed medication. 'Well, after the next tour, maybe I'll get myself straightened out.'

But the fact was that he needed the money, while the Colonel had to pay off his gambling debts. Taking time to detox completely would be impossible. The Betty Ford Clinic did not exist at that time, unfortunately, because he might have led the way for other addicts – just as Elizabeth Taylor would do in 1983, with half of Hollywood following her lead.

During the exhausting tour Presley told a friend he was very tired.

'You need some rest.'

'That's not what I mean. I'm just so tired of being Elvis Presley.'

Kathy Westmoreland was his backing singer, introduced by him on stage as the 'little girl with the beautiful high voice'. She toured with Elvis in the seventies, becoming his intimate companion. When he was alone and couldn't sleep, he asked Kathy to spend the night with him, but there was no sex involved. In her 1987 book, *Elvis and Kathy*, she wrote that Presley had an enlarged heart, was a diabetic and suffered from hypertension and glaucoma, and that he had had three unreported heart attacks prior to the one that killed him.

But the most shocking revelation was that Elvis's autopsy revealed he had bone cancer, which had spread throughout his body. Charlie Hodge, who played guitar and sang back-up, wrote in his book *Me 'n' Elvis* that he had been present when Dr. Nick told Vernon Presley about the bone cancer that would eventually have killed Elvis.

Why would this information be kept from the public if it were true? The disclosure would explain Elvis's need for painkillers and other medication. With over 400 books published about Presley, it's difficult to weed out what is true and what is not. The best, without a doubt, are Peter Guralnick's *Last Train to Memphis* and *Careless Love*. He concludes that 'all one has to do is look at Elvis's life, the accelerating dependence on medications available to him in almost unimaginable quantities . . . the medical problems stemming primarily from the use of drugs that Elvis experienced over the last four years [of his life] to understand the causes of his death.'

Lisa Marie arrived at Graceland on 31 July 1977 to spend two weeks with her father. Elvis rallied in her company, but frequently had to push himself to entertain the nine-year-old he so adored. He arranged for a night-time visit to the amusement park when it was closed to the public, and enjoyed spending time with Lisa Marie in her bedroom with its 'hamburger' bed upholstered in white furry material. Though Priscilla had custody of their daughter, she and Elvis never had problems over visitation rights and they frequently had lengthy phone conversations. It was depressing for Priscilla when he was heavily drugged, slurring his words and rambling. She tried to talk to him about the addiction that he swore wasn't real.

The nineteenth anniversary of his mother's death, on 14 August, was as always a difficult day for Elvis, who had arranged to have flowers delivered to her grave weekly over the years. After two months of rest and boredom he was looking forward to leaving for Portland, Maine on the night of the 16th to do a concert. Ginger did not want to go and promised to join him later.

Kathy Westmoreland recalled how lonely Elvis was on one of his last tours. They were sitting on the bed together and he asked, 'What's it all about, Kathy? I'm talking about life . . . and what follows. How are people going to remember me? I've never done a classic film. I've never sung a lasting song.' They meditated and prayed that his good health would be restored. 'I know I look fat now,' he told her, 'but I'm going to look good in my casket.'

Elvis was a religious man in search of his spiritual self. He believed in reincarnation for those who deserved it. Since he was one of the chosen few, Elvis also thought he could heal those who were in pain. Red West recalled in *Elvis: What Happened?* that they had been visiting a hospital to see a friend when a woman in labour was wheeled past Elvis, crying out for relief. He put his hand on her stomach to ease her pain and she swore it worked. He begged to be allowed to see her baby delivered, but the doctors wouldn't allow it.

Presley was intrigued by death and corpses. He witnessed the autopsy of a friend and, on occasion, snuck into mortuaries to view dead bodies.

Linda, taking this in her stride, would listen intently to Elvis's explanations of how autopsies were performed.

On the night of 15 August, Presley went to the dentist to have his teeth cleaned. When he arrived home he called Dr. Nick about getting some Dilaudid for toothache. After playing racquetball for a while, he sat down at the piano and played 'Blue Eyes Crying in the Rain' before going to bed with Ginger around 8:00 a.m. When he couldn't sleep he told her he was going into the bathroom to read for a while.

At 1:30 Ginger woke up, called her mother and put on her make-up. She knocked on Elvis's bathroom door, but got no answer and pushed it open. She found him lying on the floor, his pyjama bottoms down to his ankles and his face buried in vomit on the rug. Elvis had apparently been sitting on the toilet reading *A Scientific Search for the Face of Jesus*.

Ginger called downstairs on the intercom and told bodyguard Al Strada that Elvis was very sick. He ran upstairs followed by Joe Esposito, who tried to revive Presley. Elvis's tongue was half bitten off and his face a deadly purplish colour. The ambulance arrived at Graceland minutes later and carried the lifeless body out on a stretcher. Vernon tried to catch up. 'I'm coming, son!'

If it had been anyone other than Elvis Presley, doctors in the trauma room would not have tried so hard to bring a dead man back to life. At 3:30 Dr. Nick said it was all over. The King of Rock 'n' Roll was dead at the age of 42. It was up to Joe Esposito to face reporters, but he couldn't pull himself together for the 8:00 p.m. press conference.

While the autopsy was still taking place, Shelby County medical examiner Jerry Francisco announced that Presley's death was due to cardiac arrhythmia due to an undermined heartbeat. 'There was severe cardiovascular disease present,' he said. 'He had a history of mild hypertension and some coronary artery disease. These two diseases may be responsible for cardiac arrhythmia, but the exact cause was not determined. Basically it was a natural death. The precise cause of death may never be known.' Francisco added that there was 'no indication of any drug abuse of any kind'. The only evidence of drugs involved those Presley had been taking for his physical condition – mild hypertension and a colon problem. He reported that death had occurred between 9:00 a.m. and 2:00 p.m.

The French headlines read: 'L'adieu à Elvis!' The Soviet newspaper *Pravda* ran a full-page message: 'Elvis Is Dead. The USA Has Given Us Three Cultural Phenomenons, Mickey Mouse, Coke A Cola And Elvis

Presley.' A British front page said simply and sadly: 'King Elvis Dead At 42 And Alone.' Colorado's *Denver Post* wrote, 'Suddenly we feel older . . .'

American flags in Tennessee and Mississippi were lowered to half mast, and ex-President Nixon asked that the same be done nationwide. Eighty thousand people gathered outside Graceland, among them 300 women and children requiring medical attention.

Since Vernon was sick with grief, it was up to Joe Esposito and the Colonel to arrange the funeral. The *Lisa Marie* was sent to pick up Priscilla and her family in California. She did not want Linda on the same plane because 'the *Lisa Marie* was for wives, not girlfriends.' From the minute Priscilla boarded the plane for Memphis, she considered herself Elvis Presley's widow, coiffed, made up and poised, dressed all in black – in contrast to Linda, who wore lavender. Ginger was hardly noticed. At Graceland, Priscilla greeted such celebrities as George Hamilton, Ann-Margret, and President Kennedy's daughter, Caroline, who was working for a New York newspaper.

Originally Elvis had included his ex-wife in his will, as well as members of the Memphis Mafia, but he had changed his mind. It isn't known when Priscilla discovered this. Vernon, who was too shocked to comment on her widow-like performance at the funeral, had resented her from the day she sued Elvis for a fortune when they divorced, but she was the mother of Lisa Marie. That would make a big difference not only in Priscilla's life, but in the memory of the man who bought Graceland for his mama.

Elvis, dressed in a cream-coloured suit, white tie and pale blue shirt, looked handsome in his coffin. During his autopsy, various body parts had been removed and fluids drained and, though his weight remained well over two hundred pounds, his face was not bloated. With an inch of white hair on his sideburns touched up with black mascara, he looked like the young king who won the hearts of people all over the world. The *National Enquirer* managed to get a picture of the famous corpse, thanks to a disloyal cousin who smuggled a camera into Graceland where the funeral services were conducted.

Kathy sang 'Heavenly Father', and the Reverend C.W. Bailey, a family friend, told the gathering of two hundred that Elvis was a frail human being who would be the first one to admit his flaws. He mentioned his meeting with Elvis in Las Vegas and how they had knelt down to pray.Though Presley was known for his gyrations and rock 'n' roll, not many people realise that the only Grammy awards he received were for gospel recordings of 'How Great Thou Art' in 1967, 'He Touched Me' in 1972, and a second version of 'How Great Thou Art' in 1974.

Eighteen white limousines lined up for the three-and-a-half-mile drive to Forest Hill Cemetery. Priscilla told Linda that she was assigned to limousine number sixteen. She hugged Ginger and put her in limousine number five. As the white hearse drove out of the musical gates of Graceland, policemen saluted Elvis in tribute. After a brief service at the mausoleum, members of the family spent time alone with Elvis. Vernon, the last, had to be half-carried to his limousine.

Thousands of Presley fans had viewed his body and went to the cemetery the following day. Hundreds of floral arrangements disappeared as Elvis worshippers hungered for one last souvenir. Not one petal was left behind.

Eleven days later there was an attempt to steal Presley's body from the mausoleum at Forest Hill Cemetery. On 2 October, Elvis and Gladys were reburied in the Meditation Garden at Graceland. Vernon and his mother Minnie Mae were later buried there as well. On 26 June 1979 Vernon died of a heart attack. Upon the death of Vernon's mother, who passed on in 1980 at the age of 87, Lisa Marie was the sole heir, though Vernon realised that it would be in Lisa Marie's best interests to put Priscilla in charge of her estate until she reached the age of 25.

Because Elvis was worth only $1 million when he died, there was a cash flow problem, especially as Graceland cost over half a million dollars a year in maintenance and taxes. Priscilla convinced the executors of Vernon's will to open the house to the public on 7 June 1982. The estate also claimed the rights to Elvis Presley's name and any likeness of him. Graceland hosts over half a million visitors a year, second only to the White House. Today the Elvis Presley Estate is worth over $150 million.

In 1980, executors sued Colonel Tom Parker, who was still receiving 50 per cent of Elvis's earnings after his death according to a contract signed with Vernon. The estate paid Parker $2 million to be rid of him once and for all. After Priscilla refused to pay the mortgage on a house that Elvis bought for Linda Thompson's parents, they were forced to leave. Ginger Alden received the same treatment. Elvis had offered to pay the mortgage on her mother's house and asked for the payment book. When the executors refused to keep up the payments, Mrs. Alden sued. She won in the Tennessee Court of Appeals, but the decision was overturned in the Supreme Court.

Priscilla also refused to allow Elvis's best friend Joe Esposito to use home movies of Elvis for a video he was putting together. Was Priscilla a good businesswoman, or was she simply getting rid of those who loved Elvis more than she did?

On 1 February 1993, Lisa Marie Presley became eligible to receive her inheritance, but she decided to leave it in the hands of Priscilla's management team, although she could reverse the decision at any time. How much money is allotted annually to Lisa and Priscilla, as President of Elvis Presley Enterprises, is not known.

According to *Forbes*, between June 2001 and June 2002 the top five earnings of dead celebrities were Theodor 'Dr. Seuss' Geisel at $19 million, John Lennon at $20 million, Dale Earnhardt, also at $20 million, 'Peanuts' cartoonist Charles Schulz at $28 million – and, topping the list, the King of Rock 'n' Roll, who earned $37 million.

In their 1981 book, *The Death of Elvis Presley: What Really Happened*, authors Charles C. Thompson and James P. Cole concluded that Elvis had died as a result of taking ten codeine tablets, because he was allergic to the drug. Although this wasn't true, the press picked up on it and the question of Presley's drug abuse was opened once again. Memphis medical examiner Dr. Jerry Francisco rejected this theory, insisting that Elvis had died of fatal heart arrhythmia. But the doubt remained and the press harped upon it.

In 1994, the matter was left to the dean of American pathology, Dr. Joseph Davis, a leading expert in forensic sciences and the veteran of 20,000 autopsies. He examined tissue samples, slides and all the other photos from Presley's autopsy. Dr. Davis reported that Elvis could not have died of a drug overdose, or from polypharmacy. 'The position of Presley's body told me that he was about to sit down on the commode when the seizure occurred. He pitched forward onto the carpet, his rear in the air, and was dead by the time he hit the floor.' Davis said that Elvis's weight of 350 pounds would have put a great strain on his heart.

Dr. Nick was charged in 1980 with fourteen counts of illegally prescribing drugs to Elvis, but he was acquitted.

*

Colonel Tom Parker died of a stroke at the age of 87 in January 1997.

Lisa Marie Presley, who bears a strong resemblance to Elvis, married musician Danny Keogh in October 1988. The couple had two children, Danielle and Benjamin, before she divorced him in January 1994. On 26 May 1995, Lisa married singer Michael Jackson. They were divorced in January 1996. In August 2002 she married actor Nicolas Cage, who filed for divorce four months later.

Priscilla Presley had a successful acting career as Jenna Wade in the popular TV soap opera *Dallas*, and appeared in films such as *The Naked Gun*. In 1984 she met the love of her love, businessman Marco Caribaldi, who was eleven years younger than Priscilla. She had a son, Navarone, on 1 March 1987 and, as of this writing, she is still living happily with him. They consider themselves man and wife, but have never married. Obviously, Priscilla has no intention of giving up the Presley name.

Elvis fans are still faithful to him. Every year on his birthday, 9 January, and on 16 August, the anniversary of his death, they hold a candlelight vigil at Graceland that is always reverential and impressive. On the 25th anniversary of the King's death, he was still larger than life when his single 'A Little Less Conversation' went to the top of the charts. Twenty-five years after Presley's death, and 33 years since the Beatles last reached the top of the British charts, Elvis remains the unchallenged king.

> 'The first time I appeared on stage, it scared me to death. I really didn't know what all the yelling was about. I didn't realize that my body was moving. It's a natural thing for me. So to the manager backstage I said, "What'd I do? What'd I do?" And he said, "Whatever it is, go back and do it again."'
>
> – Elvis Presley

About Elvis

'I think Elvis is the sexiest man to ever walk the earth. I love him.'
— Britney Spears

'There was something bordering on rudeness about Elvis. He never actually did anything rude, but he always seemed as if he was going to. On a scale from one to ten, I would rate him an eleven.'
— Sammy Davis Jr

'He was as big as the whole country itself, as big as the whole dream. He just embodied the essence of it and he was in mortal combat with the thing. Nothing will ever take the place of that guy. It was like he came along and whispered some dream in everybody's ear, and somehow we all dreamed it. There have been pretenders. And there have been contenders. But there is only one king.'
— Bruce Springsteen

'Elvis is the sexiest man I've ever seen.'
— Sarah Jessica Parker

'No one, but no one, is his equal, or ever will be. He was, and is supreme.'
— Mick Jagger

'Elvis was God-given, there's no other explanation. A Messiah comes around every few thousand years, and Elvis was it this time.'
— Little Richard

'When I first heard Elvis perform "Bridge Over Troubled Water" it was unbelievable and I thought to myself, how the hell can I compete with that?'

– Paul Simon

'I thought anyone who had been the centre of all that insanity for so long would have some of it rub off on him. But after working in *Change of Habit* with him, I realised I'd never worked with a more gentlemanly, kinder man. He's gorgeous.'

– Mary Tyler Moore

'I love his music because he was my generation, But then again, Elvis is everyone's generation, and he always will be.'

– Margaret Thatcher

'God must have been impatient for some rock 'n' roll in heaven.'

– Jimmy Savile

The Films of Elvis Presley

Love Me Tender (20th Century-Fox, 1956)
Loving You (Paramount, 1957)
Jailhouse Rock (MGM, 1957)
King Creole (Paramount, 1958)
G.I. Blues (Paramount, 1960)
Flaming Star (20th Century-Fox, 1960)
Wild in the Country (20th Century-Fox, 1961)
Blue Hawaii (Paramount, 1961)
Follow That Dream (United Artists, 1962)
Kid Galahad (United Artists, 1962)
Girls! Girls! Girls! (Paramount, 1962)
It Happened at the World's Fair (MGM, 1963)
Fun in Acapulco (Paramount, 1963)
Kissin' Cousins (MGM, 1964)
Viva Las Vegas (MGM, 1964)
Roustabout (Paramount, 1964)
Girl Happy (MGM, 1964)
Tickle Me (United Artists, 1965)
Harum Scarum (MGM, 1965)
Paradise, Hawaiian Style (Paramount, 1965)
Frankie and Johnny (United Artists, 1966)
Spinout (MGM, 1966)
Easy Come, Easy Go (Paramount, 1967)
Double Trouble (MGM, 1967)
Clambake (United Artists, 1967)
Stay Away, Joe (MGM, 1968)
Speedway (MGM, 1968)

Live a Little, Love a Little (MGM, 1968)
Charro (National General, 1969)
The Trouble With Girls (MGM, 1969)
Change of Habit (Universal, 1969)
Elvis, That's the Way It Is (MGM, 1970)
Elvis on Tour (MGM, 1972)

Elvis Presley's Number One Singles

Heartbreak Hotel (1956)

I Want You, I Need You, I Love You (1956)

Don't Be Cruel (1956)

Hound Dog (1956)
Love Me Tender (1956)
Too Much (1957)
All Shook Up (1957)
Teddy Bear (1957)
Loving You (1957)
Jailhouse Rock (1957)
Don't (1959)
Hard Headed Woman (1958)
A Big Hunk O' Love (1959)
Stuck On You (1960)
It's Now or Never (1960)
Are You Lonesome Tonight (1960)
Surrender (1961)
Good Luck Charm (1962)
Suspicious Minds (1969)

Elvis Presley's Number One Albums

Elvis Presley (1956)
Elvis (1956)
Loving You (1957)
Elvis' Christmas Album (1957)
G.I. Blues (1960)
Something For Everybody (1961)
Blue Hawaii (1961)
Roustabout (1964)
Elvis-Aloha From Hawaii (1973)

11

Lest We Forget

Ramon Novarro

Two punks murdered him. It was a horrible death of abuse and torture. But what a shame it is to begin a chapter in this fashion; instead he should be remembered most of all for *Ben Hur* in 1926. He was a handsome and talented homosexual who successfully made the transition from silent films to sound, before bowing out with grace.

I saw Ramon Novarro for the first time on television in *The Barbarian* with Myrna Loy. I was taken by surprise because the film was one of the more erotic and romantic films I have seen. The plot, much like Rudolph Valentino's *The Sheik*, was concerned with a handsome Arab who kidnaps a beautiful white woman, whose hatred for him turns to passionate love. Novarro, who had a beautiful singing voice, finally serenades her into going away with him forever.

But Ramon was less pretentious than Valentino. There was an ease and charm about him that was subtle and yet commanding.

One of thirteen children, he was born Ramon Samaniegos on 6 February 1899 in Durango, Mexico, the son of a prominent dentist. His mother, the beautiful Leonor Gavilan, was of mixed Spanish and Aztec descent, and it was from her that Ramon inherited his operatic voice. As the child of privilege he studied the arts, hoping he had a future in the opera. There was also a time he considered the priesthood. The Mexican revolution, however, forced the Samaniegos family to flee and settle in Los Angeles in 1914. The eldest male of eleven surviving children, Ramon was forced to work at any trade he could find for just a few dollars. He was a singing waiter, theater usher, busboy, grocery clerk, and played bit parts at the Majestic Theater Stock Company for ten dollars a week.

His first break in the silent movies came as an extra in the picture *Joan the Woman*. This opened the door to other bit parts until he came to the attention of director Rex Ingram, who was impressed by the short, handsome, dark-haired young man. Valentino, who had paved the way for the

Latin type that was all the rage in the early twenties, left Metro in 1921 after he asked for more money. It was fate that Novarro came along at that time. As a result Metro signed Novarro to a contract for $100 a week and put him in *The Prisoner of Zenda*. Lewis Stone took the lead part of King Rudolph of Ruritania and Barbara LaMarr played Antoinette de Mauban, with Ramon as the sleek villain, Rupert of Hentzau. Rex Ingram, who had directed *The Four Horsemen of the Apocalypse*, wanted to get even with Valentino for leaving Metro and now set out to replace him with Ramon. He changed his name from Samaniego to Novarro, after the Iberian kingdom of Navarra.

Novarro had become aware of his homosexuality when he was a teenager. He had been intimate with ballet dancer Louis Samuel, who remained a part of Ramon's life for many years. During production of *The Prisoner of Zenda* in the San Bernardino Mountains, Novarro shared a room with the very good-looking actor, Malcolm McGregor, who complained bitterly to Ingram that Ramon had tried to seduce him.

There was little mention of Ramon in the reviews of *The Prisoner of Zenda*. The picture was acclaimed, however, and was listed in fourth place among the best films of 1922.

Although Novarro, had been offered more money by producer Samuel Goldwyn, he decided to stay loyal to Ingram and Metro. He was now making $250 a week, enough to support him and the family to whom he was devoted. Following *Trifling Women* and *Where The Pavement Ends*, in which Ramon caused women to swoon in their seats when he stripped down to his loincloth, he was given the lead in *Scaramouche* opposite Ingram's wife, Alice Terry. *Variety* predicted the picture would do for Novarro what *Four Horsemen* had done for Valentino.

Producer Louis B. Mayer was impressed, too. Though he detested homosexuals, he admired Novarro for his commitment to his mother and sisters who were living in a mansion on West Adams Street in Los Angeles. So what if he was gay? He was humble, sincere, dedicated and discreet. With such devotion to his family, Mayer knew that Ramon would never expose himself to scandal. He felt it an honour to secure him for *Thy Name is Woman* alongside Barbara LaMarr.

Ingram next rushed Ramon into *The Arab*, again with Alice Terry. At the time, thanks again to Valentino, it was the dream of American women to be swept up in the arms of an Arab riding a white stallion, and forced into submission in his desert tent miles from civilisation. But, unlike Valentino, Ramon did not have flaring nostrils, nor was he crass. There was a sense of humour and a hint of dignity in his seduction of Alice Terry. The *New York*

Times described Ramon's character as 'lying but lovable'. By 1924 Novarro had succeeded both in separating himself from Valentino, and in getting his name above the title.

In November 1924 Ramon sailed to France to film exteriors for *The Arab* in Tunisia. On board the *Majestic*, he met fan magazine writer Herbert Howe, who was covering Novarro's trip abroad for Ingram. The two men bonded and were a couple for nearly a decade. His affair with Howe was the only lasting one Ramon had.

The big news in Hollywood was the forthcoming movie *Ben Hur*. Rex Ingram was slated to direct, but screenwriter June Mathis, who had obtained the rights to the film, had changed her mind about Ingram after a lovers' quarrel two years previously. Ingram was angry about this, and was also displeased about the coming merger of the Metro, Goldwyn and Mayer companies. He told *Photoplay*, 'My sympathies are all with those directors who stand or fall on their own merits. I have too often seen a good picture, and the career of a promising director, ruined by so-called supervision.' When Mayer took over editing of *The Arab*, Ingram was outraged. He left Hollywood and soon after had a nervous breakdown.

June Mathis wanted Valentino to play Judah Ben Hur, but he was involved in another contract dispute, this time with the Famous Lasky Players, and was not legally able to work for another studio. June's second choice was her lover, 34-year-old George Walsh, the younger brother of director Raoul Walsh. Francis X. Bushman was slated to play Massala. In February 1924 Mathis, with script in hand and accompanied by her chosen players, sailed for Rome where *Ben Hur* would be filmed for Goldwyn Pictures. Filming moved at a snail's pace and the money allotted to the production was dwindling fast.

In the spring of 1924, the merger of Metro, Goldwyn and Mayer changed the status of *Ben Hur*. It was up to Louis B. Mayer to decide whether the film should be scrapped. He chose to salvage it. MGM needed a blockbuster to prove their worth at the onset. He consulted with Irving Thalberg, who called Novarro to his office on 8 June.

'I want you to make a test for *Ben Hur*,' he told Ramon.

'If you want me to make a test it will be in a hurry and I won't have a chance. You've seen my physique in *When the Pavement Ends*.'

Thalberg agreed. 'You're to tell no one about this, Ramon. You'll leave for Rome tomorrow. If anyone asks, you're going on vacation.'

Thrilled about getting the part of Ben Hur, Novarro sailed with Louis B. Mayer, director Fred Niblo, writer Bess Meredyth and Herbert Howe. June Mathis was fired and George Walsh replaced by Novarro, but Mayer was appalled at the manner in which *Ben Hur* was being handled. Thalberg viewed the film footage and agreed with Mayer. Filming of *Ben Hur* was to be moved to the MGM facilities in Hollywood under his supervision. Though the picture was not Thalberg's forte, he was excited over the challenge.

Novarro returned to Los Angeles and began a regime of physical exercise. At five feet ten, he was in good shape, but needed to build himself up for the rigours entailed in playing Ben Hur.

June Mathis, who had discovered Valentino, never regained her status in Hollywood. When he died suddenly on 23 August 1926, June offered her crypt at Hollywood Forever Cemetery. She died of a heart attack the following year and was buried next to him.

Production of *Ben Hur* resumed on the MGM lot on 18 February 1925. The chariot race brought a day of rare excitement in Hollywood. Forty-two cameras were placed around the arena to catch the action of chariots overturning and crashing into each other, and the final race between Ben Hur and Massala. Thalberg stood in the middle of the arena, checking every detail so they would not have to repeat the race over and over again. Near the end of a gruelling schedule, Thalberg collapsed, but he rallied to edit *Ben Hur* on the ceiling of his bedroom. Production costs came close to an outrageous $4 million, but Mayer and Thalberg considered the expense worth the money.

Ben Hur premiered on 30 December 1925 at the George M. Cohan Theater in New York. Novarro, claiming to have a bad head cold, did not attend. Nor did Thalberg, who was recuperating from his heart attack.

Novarro, now a superstar, was earning $3000 a week. He had his own living quarters, attached to the mansion he had bought for his parents. For privacy, he had his own entrance. His partner George Howe had his own apartment for propriety. Ramon, unlike Billy Haines, was a recluse. He preferred being with his family or with Howe. An honest and religious man, Novarro did not expose himself to the public or pretend he was involved with a woman. But because he kept a low profile, MGM did not push Ramon into getting married.

In 1927 Novarro appeared in *The Student Prince* with Norma Shearer. Unfortunately, none of his later films were to live up to *Ben Hur*. He sang 'The Pagan Love Song' in *The Pagan* and danced the tango in his first talking picture, *Call of the Flesh* with Renee Adoree in 1930. He co-starred with Greta Garbo in *Mata Hari* and with Helen Hayes in *The Son-Daughter*. There were rumours of an affair with Myrna Loy, his leading lady in *The Barbarian*, but they both denied it. Possibly they paired so well together in the film that moviegoers believed they were in love.

There had been rumours about his relationship with Greta Garbo, too. He said in a fan magazine interview, 'Greta is everything that man desires. She has beauty, allure, mystery and an aloofness that only men understand, for it is a quality which is usually to be found in men.' He continued, 'I think everyone should marry. That is, everyone but the artist. He cannot serve two masters – matrimony and art . . . Greta Garbo is first and always the artist and I hope I am that, too. She has promised never to marry and I know that I never shall . . . An actor has no right to marry . . . He is public property.'

In 1933, under a new contract, Novarro would be making $200,000 in a two-picture deal and $1000 a day for retakes. In 1930 he found out that his personal assistant (and former lover), Louis Samuel, had been embezzling his money. Novarro did not prosecute. Losing what might have amounted to approximately $200,000 was a shock, but knowing that a trusted friend had stolen hurt him deeply.

In 1934 L.B. Mayer put Novarro opposite his protégé and lover, Jeanette MacDonald, in *The Cat and the Fiddle*. The film was designed to make Jeanette a star, with Ramon as her leading man.

Novarro began drinking more than usual after the embezzlement and his stagnant movie roles. He lost his 23-year-old brother to cancer in 1929 and his relationship with Howe was winding down. Ramon's attempt to begin a career in opera failed, resulting in a nervous breakdown. Finally MGM released him from his contract on 3 January 1935. The beautiful Novarro was ageing prematurely as a result of his heavy drinking and it showed on the screen. He made *The Sheik Steps Out* for Paramount in 1937, *We Were Strangers* with Jennifer Jones and John Garfield in 1949 for Columbia Pictures, *The Outsiders* with Joel McCrea and Arlene Dahl for MGM in 1950, and *Heller in Pink Tights* with Sophia Loren and Anthony Quinn for Paramount in 1960.

On 18 November 1959 Ramon attended the premiere of MGM's remake of *Ben Hur* with actress Carmel Myers, who had appeared with him in the original version. The movie won eleven out of twelve Academy Award nominations. Ironically, it saved MGM from bankruptcy, just as it had laid the foundation of the newly formed studio in 1925. In the same year Ramon also received the Golden Globe Special Achievement Award for his work in silent pictures.

Novarro appeared on stage, directed several films and attended to his investments. After his mother and father died, he lived in a one-storey Spanish house in Laurel Canyon, took up with gigolos and male prostitutes, and was arrested numerous times for drunk driving.

There were many in Hollywood who knew Novarro was a homosexual, but he was widely considered a gentleman, a class act who kept his private life private – until 30 October 1968.

Twenty-two-year-old street hustler Paul Ferguson was told that Novarro was a 'soft touch' by another male prostitute who had been with the ageing actor the night before. Ferguson called Novarro on the afternoon of 30 October, described himself and was invited to the Laurel Canyon house that evening. Paul asked his nineteen-year-old brother Tom to come along. After dinner and many drinks, Ramon retired to the bedroom with Paul and closed the door. While Novarro was being tortured, probably with a cane to his genitals, Tom made a phone call to his girlfriend in Chicago. He told her they were at Novarro's home and that Paul was trying to find out where the money was. The phone conversation went on for forty minutes. At one point Tom put the phone down, saying he'd better check on Paul to make sure he wasn't hurting Ramon. The girl on the other end could hear screams in the background.

Tom helped the semiconscious Novarro into the shower, assisting him to lie down in bed and then leaving the room. Paul returned, demanding money from Ramon who replied that he had no money in the house. When Tom returned to the bedroom Novarro was on the floor dead.

The following morning Ramon's handyman found the body and called the police, who traced the long-distance phone call made by Tom to his girlfriend. He and Paul were arrested and the case went to trial on 28 July 1969.

The prosecutor, James M. Ideman, described what had taken place as a brutal murder. Paul Ferguson, he explained, had believed there was $5000 hidden in Novarro's house and had become angry when Ramon wanted to pay for sex with a cheque. Paul began hitting him with a cane and put him under a cold shower to revive him. Novarro's hands were bound with an electrical cord to prevent him from warding off the many blows to the most sensitive parts of his body. While Novarro was drowning in his own blood, the Ferguson brothers ransacked the house looking for money.

Tom Ferguson testified that his brother and Ramon had spent an hour in bed while he was on the telephone. After he hung up, he found a bloodied Novarro sitting on the bed. 'I went to urinate,' Tom said. 'When I got back, Paul had beaten Novarro to death.' Paul advised him to confess to the murder since he was under eighteen and, therefore, wouldn't receive the death penalty. Tom agreed but changed his mind when he found out Novarro had been viciously beaten with a cane. He recalled Ramon muttering 'Hail Mary, full of Grace . . .'

In the courtroom, Paul stood up, threw a pen at his brother and screamed, 'Oh, you punk liar son-of-a-bitch! Tell the truth!'

Paul's attorney, Richard Walton, claimed in his summation, 'Back in the days of Valentino, this man who set female hearts aflutter, was nothing but a queer. There's no way of calculating how many felonies this man committed over the years, for all his piety. What would have happened that night if Paul had not gotten drunk on Novarro's booze, at Novarro's urging and at Novarro's behest? Would this have happened if Novarro had not been a seducer and traducer of young men? The answers to those questions will determine the issue and degree of guilt of Tom Ferguson and the issue and degree of guilt of Paul Ferguson.'

The prosecutor, James Ideman, replied that even though Novarro had homosexual tendencies and drank to excess, he was well liked by his associates and had made a great contribution to the entertainment industry. 'I hope sincerely that you will not put Mr. Novarro on trial,' Ideman said. 'He has paid for whatever he did and now it is the Fergusons' turn to pay for whatever they have done . . . They are hustlers . . . That means a male whore. That is what they are. They sell their bodies to other men for money. What kind of person do you think does that? . . . Novarro was trussed up like an animal and beaten to death. I don't think you would treat an animal like that . . . This is deliberate torture. You don't strike a man on his genitals and split his scalp with a cane unless you are torturing him.'

Six weeks later the jury found the Ferguson brothers guilty of murder. They were sentenced to life imprisonment.

Tom Ferguson was paroled in 1977, but sent back to prison for eight years after raping an old woman. He was again paroled in 1990, but returned to prison for failing to register as a sex offender. He is now serving time at the California Medical Facility in Vacaville.

Paul Ferguson was released in 1978, but was convicted of rape and sodomy in 1989 and sent to San Quentin, where he remains as of this writing.

Funeral services were held for Ramon Novarro on 3 November 1969 at the Cunningham and O'Connor Mortuary in downtown Los Angeles. More than a thousand people lined up to pass the bier of the slain idol. Novarro was buried next to his mother at Calvary Cemetery. He left an estate worth $500,000 . . .

'The stars of my day enjoyed a certain privacy. We lived two lives: our film life, and our own private one . . . some of us realised it was necessary in order to sustain the public illusion that made us stars.'

– Ramon Novarro

The Films of Ramon Novarro

Mr. Barnes of New York (Goldwyn, 1922)
The Prisoner of Zenda (Metro, 1922)
Trifling Women (Metro, 1922)
Where The Pavement Ends (Metro, 1923)
Scaramouche (Metro, 1923)
Thy Name is Woman (Louis B. Mayer, 1924)
The Arab (Metro-Goldwyn, 1924)
The Red Lily (Metro-Goldwyn, 1924)
The Midshipman (MGM, 1925)
Ben Hur (MGM, 1925)
The Student Prince (MGM, 1927)
The Road to Romance (MGM, 1927)
Across to Singapore (MGM, 1928)
A Certain New Man (MGM, 1928)
Forbidden Hours (MGM, 1928)
The Flying Fleet (MGM, 1929)
The Pagan (MGM, 1929)
Devil-May-Care (MGM, 1929)
In Gay Madrid (MGM, 1930)
The March of Time (MGM, 1930) Not released.
Call of the Flesh (MGM, 1930)
La Sevillana (MGM, 1930)
Le Chanteur de Seville (MGM, 1931)
Daybreak (MGM, 1931)
Son of India (MGM, 1931)
Mata Hari (MGM, 1931)
Huddle (MGM, 1932)

The Son-Daughter (MGM, 1932)
The Barbarian (MGM, 1933)
The Cat and the Fiddle (MGM, 1934)
Laughing Boy (MGM, 1934)
The Night is Young (MGM, 1935)
The Sheik Steps Out (Republic, 1937)
A Desperate Adventure (Republic, 1938)
La Comidie du bonbeur (Artis Film/Discina, 1940)
La Virgen que forjo una patria (Mundiales, 1942)
We Were Strangers (Horizon/Columbia. 1949)
The Big Steal (RKO, 1949)
The Outriders (MGM, 1950)
Heller in Pink Tights (Paramount, 1960)

Billy Haines

He was the Van Johnson of silent films – handsome, likeable and youthful. But unlike Johnson, he was openly gay. Although Billy Haines might not be a household name like John Gilbert, his story is an interesting chapter in MGM history and well worth telling. From 1928 to 1930 he was the number one box-office draw and easily made the transition from silent films to talkies. In 1934 L.B. Mayer gave Billy a choice between his career and his live-in lover of ten years. Haines chose his 'wife', Jimmie Shields, and as a result was blackballed in Hollywood by Mayer. Yet, with the help of his good friends Carole Lombard and Joan Crawford, Billy became a well-known interior decorator and made millions.

William Haines was born in Staunton, Virginia, on 1 January 1900. His father, Charles, inherited the Haines Cigar Company from his own father, George, an elder statesman of Staunton. Billy's beautiful mother, Laura, who came from an old Virginia family, took up dressmaking when the tobacco business slowed down. Billy worshipped his mother and helped with her sewing while his younger brother and two sisters played outdoors. He also assisted her in the kitchen and became proficient at cooking.

Billy inherited both his father's height and Laura's handsomeness. By the time he was thirteen, he was six feet tall and towered over his classmates, who considered him an oddball. For such a big boy Billy should have taken an interest in sport, but he despised athletics. And he hated Staunton, where nothing exciting ever happened.

At fourteen Billy ran away from home with another boy who was most likely his first lover. The young men found jobs at a Du Pont plant in wild and wicked Hopewell, Virginia for fifty dollars a week. Then they opened a dance hall. It did so well that Billy sent money home to his parents who were going through bad times financially. In 1915, however, the dance hall burned to the ground. Billy headed for New York City, where he got work with the Kenyon Rubber Company for fourteen dollars a week.

In 1917 Laura asked Billy to come home. His father had had a nervous breakdown following bankruptcy. The family moved to Richmond, and Laura was very successful as a dressmaker until she got pregnant. It had been nine years since her last child, George Jr, was born. As the eldest, Billy felt an obligation to his family, but he hated every minute of his two years in Richmond as a department store manager. As soon as his father recovered and found a good job, Billy returned to New York City. At the investment firm of S.W. Straus he worked his way up from salesman to assistant book-keeper, earning twenty dollars a week.

For a while Billy shared an apartment in Greenwich Village with a gay couple, Jack Kelley, a painter from Australia, and seventeen-year-old Archie Leach, a vaudevillian from England. His room-mates would become famous in Hollywood as Orry-Kelly and Cary Grant.

It was through Mitchell Foster, a gay Bostonian, that Billy met rich and influential people. 'It was at this period of my life,' Haines said, 'that I met the woman who played an important part in moulding my existence anew. There have been three women I shall always remember – the ones who have meant the most. The first, of course, was my mother. This woman was the second.' She was twenty years older than Billy and instilled in him an appreciation of the beauty of antiques, priceless paintings, fine furniture and the classics. She demanded so much of his time that he quit his job and luxuriated in the lady's Lower Fifth Avenue apartment for a year. 'I don't know why we parted,' Billy said. 'Maybe I was restless.'

On his own again, Billy thought he'd try his luck at modelling. In 1921 he entered Samuel Goldwyn's 'New Faces' contest and won. He made a screen test and was given a contract paying forty dollars a week. The female winner of 'New Faces' was Eleanor Boardman, who struck up a close friendship with Billy. Together they took the train to Hollywood in March 1922. On the trip Haines caught a cold and a boil erupted on his nose.

Billy feared rejection when he reported to Goldwyn Studios, but instead he was signed to a contract on 10 March 1922 for fifty dollars a week. He was taught some acting techniques, especially how to perform in front of the camera, and assigned as an extra in *Lost and Found on a South Sea Island*. It was filmed on location in Tahiti and there he met scenarist Paul Bern, who introduced him to 'The Girl Who Was Too Beautiful', Barbara La Marr.

Bern was madly in love with her and proposed marriage, though she turned him down. Bern thought it was safe to introduce her to Billy, but he fell in love with La Marr and she with him.

Barbara was the third influential woman in his life. Like Billy, she had left home when she was fourteen; finding herself mixed up with the wrong people, she had landed in juvenile court. Reporter Adela Rogers St. Johns recalled, 'I was there when Judge Monroe told Barbara, "You are too beautiful to be allowed alone in the big city. You are too beautiful to be without protection." I couldn't see the girl but when she turned, I lost my breath.' It was after this that the *Los Angeles Times* labelled her 'The Girl Who Was Too Beautiful'. By the time she was discovered by Douglas Fairbanks and appeared with him in *The Three Musketeers*, she had been married four times.

In 1923, Billy had a small part in *Souls for Sale* alongside Barbara. That same year she adopted a baby boy, though there were rumours that Bern was the father. She would never have married Paul Bern, because she was in love with Billy and wanted to marry him. He returned her love, but marriage was out of the question. After a quarrel, they broke up and she married someone else. But Billy never got over Barbara La Marr, who died from tuberculosis in 1926 at the age of 29.

Billy's seventh film, *The Midnight Express*, was made at Columbia in 1924. He played a lazy son who goes to work in his father's railway yard. After his quick thinking prevents a freight train from colliding with the Express, he marries the engineer's daughter, played by the fading star Elaine Hammerstein. *Variety* said Haines had all the attributes of a leading man. Columbia wanted to buy Billy's contract from Goldwyn, but the asking price of $20,000 was too high.

In April 1924, Metro-Goldwyn-Mayer was born and Haines found himself at the celebration on 26 April at the Goldwyn lot in Culver City. Billy was not as famous as the other stars gathered together that day – Lon Chaney, Norma Shearer, Buster Keaton, Mae Murray, Conrad Nagel, John Gilbert and Eleanor Boardman. Barbara La Marr was there, too, but she refused to talk to Haines.

Billy did not know what to make of the merger, but he hated Louis B. Mayer from the start. He considered the short, pot-bellied, pompous mogul a phony. Perhaps it was Billy's upper-middle-class roots that made him look down on the former junk man who was now master of a Hollywood empire. Billy was a born snob who, through his mother and former 'sponsor', loved and appreciated the finer things in life. He wanted to surround himself with intellectuals and beautiful wealthy people with social standing. He had received his education in New York City by watching them live the good life in style and with grace. L.B. Mayer wasn't Billy's idea of a well-bred magnate. But Irving Thalberg was, and rightly so. Unlike Mayer, Irving was soft-spoken, sympathetic, brilliant – and understanding of homosexuals.

In 1925 Billy was making $250 a week, tax free in those days. Though he regularly sent money to his family in Virginia, he could afford his own apartment on North Western Avenue in Hollywood. Billy's sexuality wasn't a factor at that time. It's doubtful that many people knew he was gay – or cared, for that matter. He led an active social life with men and women. After his affair with actress Norma Shearer, his leading lady in *A Slave of Fashion*, gay director George Cukor said, 'Billy was able to have an affair with a woman if she came on to him and Norma was very flirty and passionate.' 'She was one woman who really got a *rise* out of me,' Billy told Cukor. 'And for me, that's a mouthful!'

At the same time Haines was seeing the handsome Mexican leading man Ramon Novarro. Their relationship is still being debated. Lawrence Quirk claimed they had an affair, as did writer Anita Loos, who is usually a reliable source. According to Loos, Lew Cody, who co-starred with Norma and Billy, was furious over their affair. Billy called him a vain stuffed shirt. Lew responded, 'As if I care what that queer says.' But he did care, reporting to Mayer about Billy's activities with Novarro at a gay bordello on Wilshire Boulevard. Mayer was well aware that Haines was a homosexual, but he did not want the public to get wind of it. Nor did he want Novarro, his popular leading man, involved. Mayer closed down the bordello and was prepared to get rid of Haines before Thalberg stepped in to prevent it. Mayer told Novarro not to see Haines again, but the pair ignored his order.

Though Billy was not intimate with Joan Crawford, they became close friends and co-starred in *Sally, Irene and Mary* in 1925. As Lucille Le Sueur, she came to Hollywood from Kansas City and was the first star 'manufactured' by MGM. Her new name was chosen by a fan magazine contest, but Joan hated it. She told Billy, 'It sounds too much like Crawfish.'

Haines laughed. 'It could have been worse. Suppose they chose "Cranberry" and served you with the thanksgiving turkey?'

Joan was one of the most ambitious young actresses to grace the silver screen. It wasn't beneath her to sleep with an MGM executive if it meant moving up the ladder. Haines helped Joan immensely. He told her to make sure she was seen at nightclubs and to get her name in the newspapers. He took her dancing at Montmartre and the Coconut Grove. A former hoofer, Crawford could do the Charleston better than anybody and won several contests to prove it. When she caught the attention of L.B. Mayer, he was anxious to know what she did after hours. 'I don't care what she does,' he told one of his spies, 'as long as she doesn't get laid on Sunset.'

Haines found out and told Joan, who asked him, 'Did Mayer mean on Sunset or at sunset?'

'He's saying he knows you're sleeping around.'

'Does he know you like boys?'

'Sure,' Haines replied. 'He'll get around to arranging a marriage if there are any concrete rumours.'

'Maybe you and I have a chance,' Joan winked.

'Not unless you're a lesbian. That's how it's done, Cranberry.'

'I like girls occasionally.'

'That isn't good enough,' Haines said.

'Well, if you need a wife to save your ass, I'm available.'

Joan was sincere about marrying Haines if the studio demanded it of him, and it would. By then, though, Joan was divorced from Douglas Fairbanks Jr and engaged to actor Franchot Tone. At the same time she was having a hot affair with Clark Gable, whose star was rising very fast – thanks to Haines, who met him in 1925. Gable had been trying desperately to get hired as an extra at MGM. Where he met Billy isn't known, but their sexual encounter took place at the Beverly Wilshire Hotel. William J. Mann wrote in his wonderful biography of Billy, entitled *Wisecracker*, 'It wasn't a blow job. Billy fucked him in the men's room. Billy was a "fuker", not a "fukee."' Crawford later confirmed this, but since such occurrences were so common in Hollywood, she considered it very amusing.

In 1926 Haines got his big break as the cocky punk turned hero in *Brown of Harvard*. *Variety* said, 'Haines is corking in the name part. He not only looks collegiate and like a halfback, but paces his performance to a nicety, in which glib subtitles are more than the usual help . . . an outstanding performance by Haines.'

After making 23 films, Billy paid a visit to his family in Virginia, stopping off afterwards in New York to see old friends. He met Jimmie Shields on the street. Most likely it was a 'pick-up' and nothing more, but Billy fell in love with the handsome 21-year-old sailor from Pittsburgh. Recently discharged from the Navy after a serious bout of meningitis, Jimmie was at a loose end. Billy offered him work as his stand-in and the two men became lifelong 'companions'. When Jimmie moved into Billy's Hollywood apartment he was indulged like a mistress. Billy would have flings on the side and most likely Jimmie did as well, but nobody could come between them. According to Joan Crawford, Billy and Jimmie had the only solid marriage in Hollywood.

Mike, another successful Haines film, was released at the same time as *Brown of Harvard*. Billy always played the cocky, wisecracking guy who becomes a hero. He was so swamped with fan mail and publicity that fame was beginning to go to his head, but even he had no idea what success lay ahead. *Tell It to the Marines* was a smash and Billy's very best. Lon Chaney was cast as his sergeant and took top billing, but Haines stole the picture.

MGM needed publicity about Billy's social life and the women he was dating. They hinted at a romance with Pola Negri, the lesbian actress who made a spectacle of herself at Rudolph Valentino's funeral, claiming they were engaged to be married. So as to gain more attention, she did not deny her relationship with Billy. MGM wanted him to marry Pola; one fan magazine even published a picture of the bed they would share as man and wife.

Billy wasn't always discreet about his activities. Recognised everywhere, he tried to have sex with a sailor in Pershing Square, a well-known venue for gays looking for a quickie. Mayer suppressed his anger, but made it very clear to Billy that such abandonment would ruin him. 'If I had a son,' he said, 'it would break my heart if he were exposed so please be discreet. I don't care what my stars do in private, but I care very much what they do in public.' Mayer cried, so Billy cried, too.

Haines was earning $1000 a week after *Tell It to the Marines*. He bought a house on North Stanley Drive off Sunset Boulevard and moved in with his beloved Jimmie. They would decorate their new home with prized antiques, Aubusson rugs, Chippendale chairs, Federal beds and original artworks. For Billy, it fulfilled his dream of surrounding himself with the finest furnishings money could buy.

Slide, Kelly, Slide, released in 1927, was another Haines hit. He played the wise guy (what else?) who is tamed by love. Billy had it all now. He was famous and rich and lived in a house that was his pride and joy.

One of Billy's good friends was actress Marion Davies, mistress of newspaper magnate William Randolph Hearst who in 1927 was building his famous mansion, San Simeon. Invited to costume parties there, Billy was amazed that Hearst had so many priceless antiques stored away in the attic.

He thought as many of them as possible should be unpacked and put on display in the great mansion, and the rest catalogued. So Hearst called his good friend Louis B. Mayer about giving Billy time off to do some decorating. 'It was an invigorating three months,' Haines said. 'I was glad to be there for Marion, too. Hearst disapproved of her drinking but I covered for her. He trusted me with his treasures and Marion was one of them.'

Haines was a likeable guy, on and off screen, but the impact Elinor Glyn made on Hollywood in 1927 was not in Billy's favour. Her novel, *It*, and the movie version, were the topic of conversation everywhere. The question was, 'What was "It"?' Glyn said, 'It is a strange magnetism that attracts both sexes. There must be a physical attraction, but beauty is unnecessary.'

And who had 'it'?

'There are only three in Hollywood who have "It",' Glyn said. 'Clara Bow, Tom Mix's horse and the doorman at the Ambassador Hotel.' She went on to name others, such as John Gilbert and Greta Garbo, but her selection of those who did not have 'It' included Ramon Novarro – and Billy Haines.

Though Thalberg liked Glyn, he ignored her rantings as publicity-seeking and nothing more. Mayer, however, was upset that she had said Haines had no sex appeal. And Billy told Glyn to her face, 'You have "It" but you left the "sh" off of it.'

Joan Crawford co-starred with Billy in *Spring Fever* and *West Point* in 1927. Despite Glyn's put-down, he could do no wrong. He was still popular at the box office and this was all that mattered to the powers-that-be at MGM.

Then came the hysteria of the introduction of sound to Hollywood. Haines had a good voice but in the course of taking diction lessons from vocal coach Oliver Hinsdale, he was told, 'The trouble with you, Billy, is you're lip-lazy.'

Haines laughed, 'I've never had any complaints before.'

Leo the Lion roared for the first time from the screen in *White Shadows in the South Seas*. Then in 1929 Thalberg added dialogue to an already completed silent film, *Alias Jimmy Valentine*, a mystery thriller featuring Billy, Lionel Barrymore, and Leila Hyams. The sound portion was filmed at Paramount since MGM did not have the proper equipment. According to Haines, it was horrible working in *Alias Jimmy Valentine*. 'We had to film at night,' he explained, 'because Paramount was busy with their own productions during the day. We had to sit at a table and not move because the microphones were put in vases or plants. It was so hot on the sound stages that our make-up literally melted on our faces.'

Haines performed a skit with Jack Benny in MGM's first all-talkie, *The Hollywood Revue of 1929*. He continued to make good films, but was not comfortable with sound. 'In silents there was more freedom of movement,' he said. 'I could ad lib and make faces to fit the mood, but I couldn't do that with dialogue. There was more to worry about than voice quality. Also, when you make silent pictures you do your work and go out for the evening. When you make talkies, you leave the studio and go home to study your lines for the next day.'

It's possible that Billy realised his future was not in movies when he and Jimmie opened an antique shop on LaBrea Avenue. 'I was besieged by friends who saw my house after my first few housewarming parties,' he said. 'They wanted me to get this, that and the other thing. To help them buy antique furnishings. Some sent interior decorators to me. It interested me, naturally, but I was selfish enough to see that I could turn this hobby into an asset. It seemed a good investment.'

When Joan Crawford married Douglas Fairbanks Jr in 1929, she wanted to change the décor of her home in Brentwood. Anxious for an invitation from her in-laws, Mary Pickford and Douglas Fairbanks Sr, to Pickfair, the White House of Hollywood, Joan asked Billy to redecorate. 'Billy hated my portraits of dancing girls done in black velvet with blonde hair and rhinestones hanging on the wall,' Joan said. 'I also had a collection of dolls that he thought were tacky and childish so we got rid of them. Billy did everything in white and that became my signature.'

Thalberg in the meantime changed Billy's image from cocky college boy to urban playboy. 'In the thirties college boys were out and tough guys were in,' Haines said. He signed a new contract, but it was not a starring one, and he took a pay cut from $3000 to $1500 a week. Billy, who had to rent out his house and move into an apartment with Jimmie, even contemplated getting married to save his movie career. While he was working on *Are You Listening?* opposite Anita Paige, with whom he had already made several films, Billy caught her in the hallway, gave her a big kiss and proposed marriage. But Anita turned him down; she loved him, but only as a friend. And as if Haines did not have enough problems in 1932, his mother suffered a cerebral haemorrhage and died in July.

Fast Life, released in 1932, was the first film Billy made that lost money, and his last for MGM. He might have remained at the studio playing supporting roles had Irving Thalberg not taken leave of absence after a heart attack at Christmas 1932, while Billy committed an indiscretion with a sailor that landed him in jail in early 1933. Mayer gave him a choice. 'Give up your boyfriend and get married or I'll tear up your contract.'

Billy supposedly replied that he was already married.

Had Thalberg not been in Europe recuperating, he would have come to Billy's defence. MGM could not fire Haines because he had a contract, but Mayer could continue to pay him and simply let his contract run out. Unlike John Gilbert, who put an ad in the Hollywood papers to tell the public that MGM would not release him from his contract so he could work for another studio, Haines waited for Thalberg to return. But when he did, he was involved in power battles of his own. Billy was finished.

Carole Lombard was one of the first celebrities to ask Haines to decorate her house. Carole had many gay friends and she adored Billy, who recalled, 'She undressed in front of me. I remember her saying the cutest thing: "I wouldn't do this, Billy, if I thought it would arouse you."'

When Carole began dating Clark Gable in 1936, he asked her why she didn't have any female friends. In typical Lombard fashion she answered, 'Well, there's Billy Haines.'

Lombard's house was the talk of the town. Suddenly Haines was in demand. Claudette Colbert hired him, as did director George Cukor, Jack Warner, Marion Davies, the Mocambo . . . the list goes on and on. Billy was now a highly respected interior decorator and he was held in high regard.

Until Labor Day, 1936, that is . . .

Billy and Jimmie rented a beach house in El Porto, part of Manhattan Beach, thirty minutes from Hollywood. On Thursday, 28 May, Jimmie, who was alone on the beach, approached six-year-old Jimmy Walker and took him home. According to the boy, they showered and got into bed, where Jimmie gave the six-year-old a blow job.

On 31 May, a gang of men approached Billy and Jimmie near their beach house. 'We don't want your kind in El Porto,' one man said. When Billy tried to talk to them, he and Jimmie were beaten up. They barely made it to their car. On 2 June Jimmy Walker's parents sought a morals complaint against Billy and Jimmie. It was a scandal that would not soon be forgotten, if ever. On 4 June, they appeared in court for a closed hearing, but the six-year-old failed to identify Jimmie. In later years Jimmie told author William J. Mann that the lawyer had asked the boy if the man who molested him was sitting in the courtroom. Nobody asked him if he was sitting at the table. Jimmy was about to say, 'The man is sitting right next to you,' but before he could come out with it, the lawyer asked for a dismissal and the judge granted it.

Billy kept a low profile and sent Jimmie to Europe, but the damage was done. He was no longer on Hollywood's elite guest list, although Joan Crawford stuck by him. Then, in 1938, Marion Davies invited him to a gala costume party at her magnificent $7 million beach house in Santa Monica to celebrate William Randolph Hearst's 75th birthday. Hearst made a point of welcoming Billy back into society.

In October 1942, Haines joined the army at the age of 42, and after basic training worked designing netting to camouflage cannons. He was promoted to staff sergeant and honourably discharged in March 1943. He and Jimmie enjoyed orgies at their home with gay friends, but were rarely invited to parties because they became too sexually aggressive after a few drinks.

On 9 May 1955, 'Cranberry' Crawford married Pepsi-Cola tycoon Alfred Steele. Billy gave a gala reception for them in Hollywood with two or three hundred guests in attendance. Crawford hired Haines to decorate her penthouse apartment in New York to the tune of half a million dollars. Four years later Joan found Alfred dead of a heart attack. The first person she called was Haines, who was in Hollywood at the time – a Hollywood he no longer enjoyed. He missed the days of Irving Thalberg, who had died in 1936. Billy had often escorted Irving's sister, Sylvia, to premieres and taken her on holidays in Lake Arrowhead. Irving and his wife, Norma Shearer, had continued to attend Billy's parties when it was no longer fashionable to do so. They were such good friends that Haines thought nothing of 'goosing' Thalberg at a party. 'Oops!' Billy laughed. 'I thought you were Norma.' And he got away with it.

In 1973 Haines was diagnosed with lung cancer. He died at St. John's Hospital on 26 December. As requested, there was no funeral. He was cremated and his ashes interred at Woodlawn Cemetery in Santa Monica. Billy's estate was worth over a million dollars.

Jimmie took an overdose of sleeping pills on 5 March 1974, having left a suicide note that expressed his loneliness. His ashes were placed next to Billy's.

*

Billy Haines proved he could survive without the great MGM. Though he was a good actor, it's doubtful he would have lasted in films. His type was simply outdated – and then there were his indiscretions, and not simply because he was gay. In contrast, Errol Flynn was destroyed, although he was found innocent of statutory rape in 1942. Considering everything, Billy was a lucky guy . . .

'I finally found a way to stop Mayer's tears. I'd start crying too.'
                                                        – Billy Haines

The Films of Billy Haines

Brothers Under the Skin (Goldwyn, 1922)
Lost and Found on a South Sea Island (Goldwyn, 1923)
Souls For Sale (Goldwyn, 1923)
Three Wise Fools (Goldwyn, 1923)
Three Weeks (Goldwyn, 1924)
True As Steel (Goldwyn, 1924)
The Midnight Express (Columbia, 1924)
The Gaiety Girl (Universal, 1924)
Wine of Youth (MGM, 1924)
The Desert Outlaw (Fox, 1924)
Circle the Enchantress (MGM, 1924)
Wife of the Centaur (MGM, 1924)
A Fool and His Money (Columbia, 1925)
Who Cares? (Columbia, 1925)
The Denial (MGM, 1925)
Fighting the Flames (Columbia, 1925)
A Slave of Fashion (MGM, 1925)
The Tower of Lies (MGM, 1925)
Little Annie Rooney (United Artists, 1925)
Sally, Irene and Mary (MGM, 1925)
Memory Lane (First National, 1926)
The Thrill Hunter (Columbia, 1926)
Brown of Harvard (MGM, 1926)
Mike (MGM, 1926)
Lovey Mary (MGM, 1926)
Tell It to the Marines (MGM, 1926)
The Little Journey (MGM, 1927)

Slide, Kelly, Slide (MGM, 1927)
Spring Fever (MGM, 1927)
West Point (MGM, 1927)
The Smart Set (MGM, 1928)
Telling the World (MGM, 1928)
Excess Baggage (MGM, 1928)
Show People (MGM, 1928)
Alias Jimmy Valentine (MGM, 1929)
The Duke Steps Out (MGM, 1929)
A Man's Man (MGM, 1929)
The Hollywood Revue of 1929 (MGM, 1929)
Speedway (MGM, 1929)
Navy Blues (MGM, 1929)
The Girl Said No (MGM, 1930)
Free and Easy (MGM, 1930)
Way Out West (MGM, 1930)
Remote Control (MGM, 1930)
A Tailor-Made Man (MGM, 1931)
The Stolen Jools (National Variety Artists, (MGM, 1931)
Just a Gigolo (MGM, 1931)
The New Adventures of Get-Rich-Quick Wallingford (MGM, 1931)
Are You Listening? (MGM, 1932)
Fast Life (MGM, 1932)
Young and Beautiful (Mascot, 1934)
The Marines Are Coming (Mascot, 1934)

Jimmy Stewart

He won an Academy Award for *The Philadelphia Story*, but is best known for his role as George Bailey in *It's a Wonderful Life*. Moviegoers of all ages recognise Jimmy Stewart. His movies are popular with young and old alike because his type was ageless. His death on 2 July 1997 overshadowed that of Robert Mitchum the day before. Stewart was everything to everybody. He had no distinct image other than his face, but that was good enough for the American public. Six feet three and too thin, he handled his lankiness with ease in both romantic scenes and westerns. He was a war hero, as well, and attained the rank of colonel after many bombing missions over Germany.

Whether it was winning an Oscar or the Distinguished Flying Cross, the Croix de Guerre and seven battle stars, Jimmy accepted with humility and gratitude.

James Maitland Stewart was born in Indiana, Pennsylvania on 20 May 1908, the son of 'Bessie' and Alex, who owned a hardware store. In 1912 a daughter, Mary, was born and in 1914 a second, Virginia. The Stewarts were a God-fearing family. They said grace before every meal and attended the Presbyterian Church on Sundays. Jimmy, an average student, followed in his father's footsteps at Princeton to study engineering but switched to architecture. 'I got to taking the accordion with me whenever there was a party,' he explained in an interview. 'A lot of times they would just ask me to bring it. Almost all the time I'd end up playing all night. When I looked around to find my girl, she was usually gone. I could never understand why. I soon discovered it was better to go to the prom stag, and I generally did. Take a girl and she'd likely be whisked away.'

Stewart, who had done some acting in college for fun, met director Joshua Logan. He was invited to join Logan's repertory company in Falmouth, Massachusetts, a summer theatre group that included Henry

Fonda and Margaret Sullavan, with whom Stewart fell in love. Theirs was a strange relationship that lasted until her suicide in 1960.

In 1932 Stewart shared a room with Fonda in New York City, appearing in small roles in theatre productions of *Carrie Nation*, *All Good Americans* and *Yellow Jack*. In a summer production of *Divided by Three* with Judith Anderson, Hedda Hopper was a member of the cast, and when she returned to Hollywood she spoke highly of him to the MGM casting department. Though he was reluctant to make such a move, Stewart signed a seven-year contract with Metro in 1935 for $350 a week. In his third film for MGM Jimmy played Jeanette MacDonald's fugitive brother in *Rose Marie*; he is taken away in handcuffs as a brokenhearted Jeanette serenades Mountie Nelson Eddy with 'Indian Love Call'.

Margaret Sullavan requested Stewart to play the second lead in Universal's *Next Time We Love*. She had great faith in Jimmy as an actor and predicted a great future in films for him. Divorced from Henry Fonda, and afterwards director William Wyler, Sullavan was married to agent Leland Hayward. It's doubtful whether she and Jimmy had been – or ever would be – intimate, but he never gave up hope.

MGM took notice of him in *Next Time We Love* and co-starred him with Jean Harlow in *Wife vs. Secretary*, followed by *The Gorgeous Hussy* with Joan Crawford. In *Born to Dance* with Eleanor Powell, Jimmy introduced Cole Porter's 'Easy to Love' in an acceptable non-singing voice. He was very good with Margaret Sullavan in *Shopworn Angel* in 1938, and even better alongside Ginger Rogers in *Vivacious Lady* and *You Can't Take It With You*, directed by Frank Capra.

The shy and stuttering Stewart dated a number of girls, including Ginger Rogers, who was described as his 'gal pal'. But if he was smitten with Sullavan, Jimmy didn't know what obsession was until he attended the all-white Mayfair Club Ball in 1938. Irving Thalberg's widow, Norma Shearer, appeared in a red gown and shocked the other guests, to put it mildly. Dressed as a cowboy, Jimmy had too much to drink and told Miss Shearer she was the most gorgeous creature he had ever seen. Eight years older than Stewart, Norma was so flattered that she clung to him like a boa constrictor. Embarrassed to be seen riding around Hollywood in her yellow Rolls-Royce, Jimmy slumped down in the back seat hoping not to be recognised. Norma had given him a gold cigarette case studded with diamonds, but when she asked for a cigarette at parties, instead of using it he fumbled for a pack of Lucky Strikes. After six weeks, they parted company.

Stewart won the New York Film Critics Award for his performance in *Mr. Smith Goes to Washington*. He was also nominated for an Oscar but lost to Robert Donat in *Goodbye, Mr Chips*. Jimmy commented, 'Mr. Smith was a disaster in Washington, D.C. as you can imagine. It opened in Constitution Hall. All the senators were there. Director Frank Capra was there with the vice-president and his wife, and several other senators who became very quiet as the picture got started. Then the film broke and Frank went to fix it. When he got back to his seat, everyone had left. One of the senators considered suing him, but it was a very successful movie.'

Marlene Dietrich, whose career was in a slump, now asked for Jimmy to co-star with her in *Destry Rides Again* at Universal. Once again, an older woman overwhelmed Stewart. Dietrich held on to him as Norma Shearer had, but more privately. So privately, in fact, that she became pregnant the first time they were intimate. Marlene's affairs with men were always romantic and passionate, and it was no different with Stewart, but he wasn't ready to commit himself. He had doubts that he could love a woman for any length of time. Dietrich had an abortion, but her career bounced back with the success of *Destry Rides Again*.

Jimmy was later seen around Hollywood and New York with actress Olivia de Havilland, who said in later years, 'He was just fun to be with, a bit like a grown-up Huck Finn. I think his offer of marriage was a frivolous thing on his part. Jimmy wasn't ready for a wife. I guess he still had some wild oats to sow.'

Or maybe he preferred the company of Margaret Sullavan. They co-starred again in *The Shop Around the Corner*, a delightful movie about co-workers who dislike each other, unaware all the while that they are falling in love as pen pals. Though she was married to Leland Hayward, Jimmy lived close by and was always welcome to drop in, especially if Hayward was out of town. If she and Jimmy were soul mates, it was a bittersweet relationship for him. According to his closest friends, he never got over his feelings for Margaret.

In 1940 Stewart received his one and only Oscar for his portrayal of the cynical reporter in *The Philadelphia Story*, with Katharine Hepburn and Cary Grant. He sent the Oscar to his father who displayed it in his hardware store. That same year his 'gal pal' Ginger Rogers won the Best Actress award for *Kitty Foyle*. About winning the award Stewart characteristically said,

'Waal . . . I never thought much about my performance in *The Philadelphia Story*. I guess it was entertaining and slick and smooth and all that. But *Mr. Smith* had more guts. Many people have suggested that I won it as a kind of deferred payment for my work on *Mr. Smith*. I think there's some truth in that because the Academy seems to have a way of paying its past debts. But it should have gone to Hank [Fonda] that year. That was one helluva performance he gave in *The Grapes of Wrath*.'

Come Live with Me, co-starring Hedy Lamarr, and *Ziegfeld Girl* with Lana Turner were good pictures, but hardly worthy of Stewart's talents. They were the last to be made under his MGM contract.

Stewart had been Louis B. Mayer's ideal contract player – a nice young man from a nice little town in the nice state of Pennsylvania. Like Robert Taylor, who was from a nice little town in the nice state of Nebraska, Stewart did what he was told.

Mayer knew that Jimmy carried a torch for Margaret Sullavan – it was his business to know such things. As far as Mayer was concerned this obsession could be balanced by a worthwhile hobby. For this reason he did not object when Jimmy took flying lessons, just as he had been happy for Robert Taylor to do. He even rewarded Taylor with a Beechcraft. In fact, Mayer had probably been responsible for keeping Taylor out of combat – although Taylor had begged to be allowed on active service, he was relegated to flying instructor and stayed in the U.S. But he was not to succeed in doing the same with Stewart.

While Jimmy was concentrating on his career as an actor, the rest of the world was about to go to war. The German occupation of numerous countries in the early part of 1940 led Congress to pass the Selective Service Bill – the draft – on 16 September. This called for 900,000 men between the ages of 20 and 36 to be drafted that year. When Stewart's number came up he reported to the draft board, but at 138 pounds he was ten pounds under weight. He ate pasta every day and gorged on ice cream and milk shakes until finally he made the grade. According to one friend, Jimmy did not go to the bathroom for 36 hours before weighing in again just to make sure. On 22 March 1941, Stewart was the first leading screen actor to be drafted into the Army.

L.B. Mayer had tried his best to talk him out of it, but failed. So it was a devastated Mayer who gave Jimmy a big going-away party, with every major studio name present. He wanted to fly the flag at half mast when Jimmy was sworn in. His induction was covered by MGM's publicity department, which was allowed to catch Private Stewart on film for as long as possible.

Jimmy, who was dating singer Dinah Shore at the time, hinted that the couple almost got married before he went into the Army. True or not, she eventually sent him a 'Dear John' letter and married the handsome actor George Montgomery.

Stewart had bought a plane when he first arrived in Hollywood, both because he loved aviation and because he wanted to be able to visit his family in Pennsylvania between films. He flew BT-13s at Mather Field, where he was transferred in April 1942 as a flight instructor. He was promoted to lieutenant in July 1942, captain in July 1943, major in January 1944, lieutenant-colonel in August 1944 and colonel in March 1945. For two years Jimmy remained in the United States until he got his wish for combat in late 1943, arriving in Tibenham, England to serve with the 445th Bombardment Group. He flew B17s and B24s.

Stewart's war record included twenty dangerous combat missions as a command pilot and he was awarded the Distinguished Flying Cross with Oak Leaf Clusters, the French Croix-de-Guerre and the Air Medal. After the war he remained active in the U.S. Air Force Reserve, and in 1959 was promoted to brigadier-general.

While he was in the service, Stewart's contract at MGM expired. 'I've always believed that the studio system is the ideal way to make pictures,' he said. 'Everyone calls them the moguls – the Harry Cohns, the L.B. Mayers and the Warner Brothers – and there have been books written about these terrible people that had charge. This is a lie. These people were completely in love with the motion picture. And they *believed* in the motion picture. And worked for quality. They didn't need censorship. They did their own censoring and were very good at it.'

Unsure when he returned from service whether he wanted to sign exclusively with any studio, it was Margaret Sullavan's influence that convinced Jimmy not to go back to MGM. Leland Hayward had told Gregory Peck not to sign with Mayer, who banished Hayward from the MGM lot. Though not obliged to do so, Jimmy had a long talk with Mayer, but the mogul's idea about starring him as a flying ace in *High Barbaree* was unacceptable. Stewart wanted no reference to his accomplishments in the Air Force and he had that condition written into future contracts. One has to wonder if Mayer cried when he said goodbye to

Jimmy, who was a sucker for tears. Mayer usually got his way, but maybe Margaret Sullavan had more influence over Jimmy. He accepted director Frank Capra's offer to star in *It's a Wonderful Life* alongside Donna Reed. At the time the picture was not a commercial success but it has since become a classic. Jimmy was nominated for an Oscar for his portrayal of George Bailey, though he lost to Fredric March in *The Best Years of our Lives*.

About *It's a Wonderful Life*, Jimmy said, 'It was the first picture I did after I got out of the service. Frank Capra called me about it and said the story begins in heaven. "You're in terrible trouble and are about to commit suicide by jumping off a bridge and an angel comes down and he tries to save you, but he can't swim. So you save him. This sounds terrible, doesn't it?"'

In 1949 Stewart made Hollywood history in the film industry. Universal wanted him to make *Winchester '73*, but could not afford his asking price of $200,000. So Stewart's agent, Lew Wasserman, negotiated for a percentage of the profits instead of a salary and Jimmy made a whopping $600,000. Profit aside, this deal established a precedent. Actors, as well as stock holders, began following the trend, whereby they could convert current income into capital gain and thus reduce their tax liability. But more important, it shifted the balance of power from the studio to the star and began the gradual erosion of the studio system.

In 1947 Stewart had been Frank Fay's summer replacement in the Broadway production of *Harvey*. The producers originally asked Bing Crosby, who turned it down because he felt his fans would not appreciate his getting drunk and talking to a six-foot rabbit after his portrayal of a priest in *Going My Way* and *The Bells of St. Mary's*. Jimmy made the movie version of *Harvey* in 1950. 'Was it an escape from reality?' he asked. 'Not at all! The kids said that Harvey was my way of confronting reality. All I was doing was having a friend who I could depend on to face reality with. That's pretty smart of the kids.'

Rope, directed by Alfred Hitchcock, and *Call Northside 777* were released in 1948. This was the year Stewart met the woman he would marry at a dinner party hosted by Mr and Mrs Gary Cooper. Gloria Harrick McLean, who had two sons (Ronald, aged three, and Michael, two) had been divorced for only a year from Edward McLean Jr, a millionaire whose mother owned the Hope Diamond. Gloria came from a prominent family in Larchmont, New York, where she had attended the best schools. Tall and slim, she took up modelling before her marriage to McLean, and received a hefty settlement after he ran off with a Vanderbilt. Divorced from Margaret Sullavan the previous year, Leland Hayward was also a dinner guest at the Coopers' that night and he invited Jimmy and Gloria to join him at Ciro's for some dancing. In a magazine article Jimmy described Gloria: 'She's a little like my mother, who was somewhat domineering but always got what she wanted in a very kindly way.'

And so the elusive Jimmy Stewart married Gloria McLean on 9 August 1949 at the Brentwood Presbyterian Church. They honeymooned in Hawaii. On 7 May 1951 Gloria gave birth to non-identical twins, Kelly and Judy, at the Cedars of Lebanon Hospital. When Jimmy came to take her home he said, 'I'll get the car out of the garage and meet you at the ambulance entrance.' But he forgot to pick her up, and was heading home instead when he realised what he had done. 'Jim had stopped at a photographer's to pick up some pictures,' Gloria explained. 'The photographer asked how I was and that's when Jim ran to the phone.'

The Stewarts settled down in a modest house on North Roxbury Drive in Beverly Hills, where their distinguished neighbours were Lucille Ball, Eddie Cantor, Oscar Levant, Hedy Lamarr and Agnes Moorehead.

Gloria maintained her slim figure and had her face lifted several times. Though a confident woman, she was well aware that her husband was surrounded by beautiful actresses, and though sure of his faithfulness, she was not taking any chances. She was especially concerned when Jimmy worked in *Rear Window* with Grace Kelly, who was known for her affairs with her leading men. One of Gloria's good friends had been married to Ray Milland, who left home for the beautiful and seductive Grace.

In *Rear Window* Jimmy plays a photographer laid up with a broken leg. Out of boredom, he spies on his neighbours and begins to suspect one of them is a murderer. Grace plays the wealthy girlfriend who visits him every night. When asked about Miss Kelly's iciness, Jimmy replied, 'She was anything but cold. Everything about Grace was appealing. I was married but I wasn't dead. She had those big warm eyes and, well, if you had ever played a love scene with her, you'd know she wasn't cold. She had an inner confidence. People who have that are not cold. Grace had that twinkle and a touch of larceny in her eyes.' Jimmy did, in fact, bring fresh flowers from his garden for her every morning.

He wanted very much to work with Grace again in *Designing Woman*, but instead she married Prince Rainier of Monaco. MGM offered Lauren Bacall as a substitute, but Jimmy turned down the project. Gregory Peck stepped in and the film was a hit. Stewart admitted it was one of the few times he had 'let my heart rule my head'.

Gloria said she dreaded the phone call from Jimmy to tell her he would be working late at the studio, so typical of an actor having an affair with his leading lady. But she never got that call, because Jimmy was very much in love with his wife. And, as corny as it sounds, he believed in his marriage vows.

One of Jimmy's best films was *The Greatest Show on Earth*. When he heard that Cecil B. De Mille was directing the picture, he asked for the part of the clown and got it. Jimmy is made up as Buttons throughout the film, but his voice was distinctive enough to identify him.

Stewart returned to MGM for the first time since his departure in 1945 to make *The Stratton Story*. He portrayed baseball player Monty Stratton, who loses his leg in a hunting accident. Though Mayer had cast Donna Reed as his wife, Jimmy requested June Allyson. She was reluctant to do it, but her husband Dick Powell convinced her the film would give her a chance to prove her acting ability, and he was right. She was the perfect wife for Stewart and would follow up in a similar role in *The Glenn Miller Story* (1954), and *Strategic Air Command* (1955). Jimmy then played Charles Lindbergh in *The Spirit of St. Louis* in 1957 before co-starring with Kim Novak in *Vertigo* (1958).

On 1 January 1960 Margaret Sullavan committed suicide. She took an overdose of sleeping pills at the Taft Hotel in New Haven, Connecticut, where she had opened in the play *Sweet Love Remembered* on 28 December 1959. She was 48 years old. It was revealed after her death that Sullavan was almost totally deaf and unable to hear her cues on stage.

In April 1960 Jimmy broke down on national television when he accepted an Oscar on behalf of Gary Cooper, who was dying of cancer. He was a pallbearer at Cooper's funeral. Jimmy was relieved that Gary had not divorced his wife for actress Patricia Neal. Whether the two men discussed it on Jimmy's frequent visits to Cooper on his death bed isn't known, but knowing that Gary was with his family at the end was a blessing as far as Stewart was concerned.

On 11 June 1969, Jimmy and Gloria were getting dressed to attend the funeral of Robert Taylor when they received a call that his 24-year-old stepson, Ronald, had been killed in Vietnam. 'It's a terrible loss,' Jimmy said. 'I think about him every day. But I can't look on it as a tragedy. He was a good boy – not a very good student, but a very good boy. He tried hard, for us, to graduate from college, and when he did, he enlisted in the Marines. And on the field of battle, he conducted himself in a gallant manner. I don't think that's a tragedy.'

*

Stewart had always been a familiar face in westerns, *Broken Arrow* (1950), *Carbine Williams* (1952), *The Naked Spur* (1953), *The Man From Laramie* (1955), *Two Rode Together* (1961), and *How the West was Won* (1963) among them. 'I had the same horse,' he said. 'I rode Pie for 22 years. He was a little quarter horse and Arabian. I could talk to him and he'd do whatever I asked him to. Pie knew the cues and was familiar with the camera. I loved that horse.'

In 1980 the American Film Institute awarded Jimmy the coveted Life Achievement Award: 'In a career of extraordinary range and depth, Jimmy Stewart has come to embody on the screen the very image of the typical American. Whether flying the ocean as Charles Lindbergh, going to Washington as Senator Jefferson Smith, or playing ordinary men who somehow never got around to leaving their hometowns, Stewart has captured the essence of American hopes, doubts, and aspirations. His idealism, his determination, his vulnerability, and above all, his basic decency shine through every role he plays.'

In 1985 the Academy of Motion Picture Arts and Sciences presented Stewart with an honorary Oscar.

The politically conservative Stewart and Henry Fonda, a liberal, remained friends over the years, despite their political differences and even perhaps some touchiness over Margaret Sullavan. In 1982 Fonda was confined to his home with heart problems and other ailments. Jimmy visited him often during Fonda's last days.

Stewart wasn't in the best of health himself. He wore a pacemaker now and was hard of hearing. His friends thought he looked frail, tired and ill, but he went with Gloria to parties, usually sitting quietly by himself.

Gloria was diagnosed with lung cancer in 1993 and died on 16 February 1994. Jimmy was never the same after that and was seldom seen in public. In 1995, on the occasion of his 87th birthday, his hometown of Indiana opened the Jimmy Stewart Museum with his daughters in attendance.

Stewart died of a pulmonary blood clot on 2 July 1997. His funeral was held at the Beverly Hills Presbyterian Church on 7 July. Few of his friends were alive to say goodbye, but Mr. And Mrs. Bob Hope, Nancy Reagan, June Allyson and Esther Williams were there.

Jimmy was buried next to Gloria at Forest Lawn in Glendale. His headstone bears his name and the inscription: 'For he shall give his angels charge over thee to keep thee in all thy ways.'

'You hear so much about the old movie moguls and the impersonal factories where there is no freedom. MGM was a wonderful place where decisions were made on my behalf by my superiors. What's wrong with that?'

– Jimmy Stewart

The Films of Jimmy Stewart

Murder Man (MGM, 1935)
Rose Marie (MGM, 1936)
Next Time We Love (Universal, 1936)
Wife vs. Secretary (MGM, 1936)
Small Town Girl (MGM, 1936)
Speed (MGM, 1936)
The Gorgeous Hussy (MGM, 1936)
Born to Dance (MGM, 1936)
After the Thin Man (MGM, 1936)
Seventh Heaven (20th Century-Fox, 1937)
The Last Gangster (MGM, 1937)
Navy Blue and Gold (MGM, 1937)
Of Human Hearts (MGM, 1938)
Vivacious Lady (RKO, 1938)
Shopworn Angel (MGM, 1938)
You Can't Take It With You (Columbia, 1938)
Made For Each Other (United Artists, 1939)
Ice Follies of 1939 (MGM, 1939)
It's a Wonderful World (MGM, 1939)
Mr. Smith Goes To Washington (Columbia, 1939)
Destry Rides Again (Universal, 1939)
The Shop Around the Corner (MGM, 1940)
The Mortal Storm (MGM, 1940)
No Time For Comedy (Warner Brothers, 1940)
The Philadelphia Story (MGM, 1940)
Come Live With Me (MGM, 1941)
Pot O'Gold (United Artists, 1941)

Ziegfeld Girl (MGM, 1941)
It's a Wonderful Life (RKO, 1946)
Magic Town (RKO, 1947)
Call Northside 777 (20th Century-Fox, 1948)
On Our Merry Way (United Artists, 1948)
Rope (Warner Brothers, 1948)
You Gotta Stay Happy (Universal, 1948)
The Stratton Story (MGM, 1949)
Malaya (MGM, 1949)
Winchester '73 (Universal, 1950)
Broken Arrow (20th Century-Fox, 1950)
The Jackpot (20th Century-Fox, 1950)
Harvey (Universal, 1950)
No Highway in the Sky (20th Century-Fox, 1951)
The Greatest Show on Earth (Paramount, 1952)
Bend in the River (Universal, 1952)
Carbine Williams (MGM, 1952)
The Naked Spur (MGM, 1953)
Thunder Bay (Universal, 1953)
The Glenn Miller Story (Universal, 1954)
Rear Window (Paramount, 1954)
The Far Country (Universal, 1955)
Strategic Air Command (Paramount, 1955)
The Man From Laramie (Columbia, 1955)
The Man Who Knew Too Much (Paramount, 1956)
The Spirit of St. Louis (Warner Brothers, 1957)
Night Passage (Universal, 1957)
Vertigo (Paramount, 1958)
Bell, Book and Candle (Columbia, 1958)
Anatomy of a Murder (Columbia, 1959)
The FBI Story (Warner Brothers, 1959)
The Mountain Road (Columbia, 1960)
Two Rode Together (Columbia, 1961)
The Man Who Shot Liberty Valence (Paramount, 1962)
Mr. Hobbs Takes a Vacation (20th Century-Fox, 1962)
How the West Was Won (MGM, 1963)
Take Her, She's Mine (20th Century-Fox, 1963)
Cheyenne Autumn (Warner Brothers, 1964)
Dear Brigitte (20th Century-Fox, 1965)

Shenandoah (Universal, 1965)
Flight of the Phoenix (20th Century-Fox, 1966)
The Rare Breed (Universal, 1966)
Firecreek (Warner Brothers-7 Arts, 1968)
Bandolero! (20th Century-Fox, 1968)
The Cheyenne Social Club (National General, 1970)
Fools' Parade (Columbia, 1971)
That's Entertainment (MGM, 1974)
The Shootist (Warner Bros., 1976)
Airport 77 (Universal, 1977)
The Big Sleep (Wincast/ITC, 1978)
The Magic of Lassie (Lassie Prod., 1978)

Van Johnson

He had red hair and freckles and wore red socks. He could sing and dance well enough to make him the bobbysoxer's delight. Van Johnson was America's wholesome boy-next-door, the nice young man who wore a uniform and fought in a war. He had a youthful face and a wholesome smile that appealed to both men and women. He had a way about him that was natural and down to earth. And he's still with us as of this writing at the age of 88, despite a serious automobile accident in 1943. He's lived with a steel plate in his head since then and dealt with cancer. He is one of MGM's contract players who survived.

Charles 'Van' Dell Johnson was born on 25 August 1916 in Newport, Rhode Island. His father Charles, a plumber, came to America from Sweden when he was a child and his mother, Loretta, was Pennsylvania Dutch. Bored with married life, she became an alcoholic, and left her husband when Van was three years old. Thereafter he lived with his father in a boarding house at 16 Ayrault Street, not far from the beach. Shortly after his mother deserted him, his paternal grandmother settled in to help with the cooking and housework. Van's father was very strict, religious and a fanatic about physical fitness. He did not believe in showing his emotions. Nor did Van, who was brought up to keep his feelings to himself.

Growing up in Newport, where the very wealthy built their mansions, was a beautiful experience. The Gilded Age began when China trade merchant William Wetmore built Chateau-sur-Mer. Society hostess Alva Vanderbilt's Marble House was magnificent, as was The Breakers, built by Cornelius Vanderbilt II, president and chairman of the New York Central Railroad. Silver heiress Tessie Oelrichs had fabulous parties at Rosecliff, and coal millionaire Edward Berwind's The Elms represented the height of gracious living.

All of these magnificent mansions were there for Van to ogle. He resided on the other side of Newport, where the working class lived, but Charles said Van could have anything he wanted if he earned the money to pay for it. So Van did odd jobs, delivering groceries and shovelling snow. After attending the circus one day he bought a trapeze and rings, hoping to become proficient enough to join. Van was already over six feet tall and muscular with it, but his freckles gave him a boyish appearance. He had no steady girlfriends but was popular because he was a good dancer. There are indications that his first sexual encounter was with a man – most likely with one or more of the sailors who came ashore in the port city. Since Charles and his grandmother never spoke about sex, Van found out about it for himself, as a matter of curiosity, and he wasn't sure about his sexual orientation.

Any form of entertainment attracted Van. He loved the movies and became a Greta Garbo fan. He was a dreamer, but Charles was a realist. In later years Van described his father as 'an awful man'. Maybe he felt this way because Charles was so strict, appalled when his son became interested in acting, which was regarded in the thirties as a profession for sissies. That was what Clark Gable's father called him even when he became a famous movie star. Gable had no respect for his father, but Van was devoted to Charles, and after his grandmother died he had second thoughts about leaving his father alone. He took a job as a waiter at a clam house called the Barnacle, but he was restless and talked to his father about going to New York. Provided he supported himself, Charles agreed to let him go.

Van was nineteen years old when he went off on his own. In New York he contacted his mother, who had remarried and was living in Brooklyn. After sleeping on the floor of her apartment for a few nights, she gave him money to find a place in New York. Van stayed at the Knickerbocker Hotel for nine dollars a week while he made the rounds of theatrical agents. Van met a lot of actors who taught him to fib about his theatrical experience and it finally worked. He auditioned successfully for a show in Greenwich Village called *Entre News*, singing and dancing with eighteen other performers for eighteen dollars a week for a month.

It was producer Leonard Stillman who saw something in Van and hired him for the chorus in his show, *New Faces of 1936*. Van moved into a boarding house with another chorus boy on West Fifty-fifth Street and shared a bathroom with the people on the same floor. Everyone in the show liked Van, who was usually cheerful and friendly though he rarely talked about himself. It was presumed by the other actors that he was gay.

When *New Faces of 1936* closed after forty weeks, Van got a job at the Roxy Theater, which showed films and a stage show five times a day. Just as Radio City Music Hall had the Rockettes, the Roxy had a group of girls called the Roxyettes, backed up by a chorus line of boys. It was hard work, Van said, but he needed the $23.70 a week. After the Roxy he served as master of ceremonies and violinist on the borscht circuit in the Catskill Mountains. But Van's dream finally came true when he auditioned for George Abbott's Broadway musical, *Too Many Girls*, which opened at the Imperial Theater on 18 October 1939. The show starred Eddie Bracken, Richard Kellmar, and a young Cuban dancer, Desi Arnaz. Van did so well that he became the understudy for all three male leads. He danced and sang very well and his smile and exuberance were appealing to the audience.

Feeling ill one night, Van hesitated about whether to go to work – until he got a phone call telling him that he would have to replace Kellmar. Feeling sick, he went on stage in a haze, and he doesn't recall singing 'I Didn't Know What Time it Was'. When the show closed, RKO Pictures bought the movie rights and Van was signed to a contract for $150 a week. He sang, danced and had a few lines of dialogue in the film of *Too Many Girls*. With no other film offers, Van took a job in George Abbot's Broadway musical *Pal Joey*, featuring Gene Kelly and Gypsy Rose Lee's sister, June Havoc. It opened on Christmas Day 1940. Alongside Van in the chorus line was sixteen-year-old Stanley Donen, who would go on to become a director and choreographer in Hollywood. Van soon proved himself, becoming Kelly's understudy for $150 a week.

One of the more interesting friendships he made was with June Allyson, who was appearing next door in *Panama Hattie* as Betty Hutton's understudy. Like Van, June was an avid movie fan and they often sat through a film three or four times. 'We joked about being in a picture together,' she said. 'Van didn't think he photographed that well but I reminded him that not all actors looked like Robert Taylor.' Van made a screen test for Columbia Pictures but was turned down.

When *Pal Joey* closed, he went home to Newport. He had been there only two days when he received word that Warner Brothers wanted to sign him to a contract for $300 a week. He was cast opposite Faye Emerson in a 59-minute programmer, *Murder in the Big House*, but Warners didn't pick up his option. Before leaving Hollywood, though, Van paid a visit to Desi Arnaz, who had recently married Lucille Ball. She got in touch with Billy

Grady, head of talent for MGM. Lucille, who had just signed a contract with the studio, pleaded with Grady. 'Look at those blue eyes and red hair and that smile,' she said. 'Give him a chance.'

After Van did a screen test in 1942 with Donna Reed, he signed a seven-year contract with MGM for $350 a week. He played a soldier in *Somewhere I'll Find You* with Clark Gable and Lana Turner and another soldier bit part in *The War Against Mrs. Hadley*.

On the set of *Somewhere I'll Find You*, Van became friends with comedic actor Keenan Wynn and his wife, Evie. According to fan magazines, the threesome went everywhere together. Though Van liked people and mixed easily, he remained somewhat shy and unsure of himself, whereas Keenan was outgoing, boisterous, and funny. The son of Jewish vaudeville star and movie actor Ed Wynn, Keenan was spoiled and less than ambitious. He took up acting but lived in the shadow of his famous father. Ever craving attention, on one occasion in 1939 he posed on the ledge of a hotel in Boston, but was easily coaxed out of jumping. That same year he married actress Evie Abbot, who gave up her career to become his business manager.

Van was invited to Hollywood parties, but felt very uncomfortable. Not yet an established star, he felt inadequate drinking champagne with Ginger Rogers and her guests and making idle conversation with Jack Benny's famous pals. Van began wearing red socks to establish some sort of identity and they became his trade mark. But he could be himself with Keenan and Evie and he looked forward to their dinner parties. In fact, he was at their house all the time.

Van's break came when Lew Ayres, who played Dr. James Kildare in MGM's popular series, announced himself a conscientious objector because of his religious belief. Louis B. Mayer got rid of Ayres, who entered a labour camp and became a medic in the Army. The Kildare films, like the *Andy Hardy* series, were very popular at the box office. MGM couldn't replace Kildare's character so they invented Dr. Red Adams, one of three young surgeons who would be chosen to take Kildare's place by the wise old Dr. Gillespie, played by Lionel Barrymore. Van was excellent in *Dr. Gillespie's New Assistant* in 1942 and *Dr. Gillespie's Criminal Case* the following year. In between the two Kildare films, Van made *The Human Comedy*, a tearjerker with Mickey Rooney.

'I couldn't wait to get to work in the morning,' Johnson said. 'What a kick it was to drive through those MGM gates in the smog every morning and see that big Leo the Lion looking down at me.' He said he felt at home the first day he arrived at MGM. When he wasn't at the studio, he was at the Wynns' house in Brentwood. Keenan, too, was under contract to MGM and was pressured to 'keep the home fires burning'. Having a son, Ned, helped his image as the happy husband and father, but the neighbours got an earful when the couple had one of their bitter fights. There were rumours that Keenan and Van were gay lovers, although Evie claimed in later years that this was untrue. Peter Lawford's mother wouldn't allow Johnson and the Wynns in her house because, she said, 'they are homosexuals.' The rumours persist to this day.

On Sunday afternoons, Van went to Gene Kelly's house to play volleyball and party with the theatrical crowd, which included June Allyson and Phil Silvers. Keenan spent his spare time racing through the Hollywood hills and the San Fernando Valley on his motorcycle. Nothing was too fast for Wynn. Van owned a Harley himself, but did not risk his life with Keenan. Louis B. Mayer always made it clear that he did not want his male stars to get involved in any sport that was dangerous. Even the big stars like Clark Gable and Robert Taylor obeyed these orders, despite their love for motorcycle racing. And Van wanted, more than anything, to be accepted as a respected member of the MGM family.

In February 1943 Johnson began *A Guy Named Joe* with Irene Dunne and his idol, Spencer Tracy. Van was playing a young aviator who falls in love with a woman mourning the death of her lover, whose ghost returns to help them survive the Second World War. On 30 March 1943, two weeks into filming, Van was driving the Wynns to MGM for the viewing of *Keeper of the Flame*, which starred Katharine Hepburn and Spencer Tracy. As Van drove his DeSoto over the intersection of Venice Boulevard and Clarington Street, another car ran the red light, smashing into Van's convertible and sending it rolling on its side.

'Like a jerk,' Johnson said, 'I put my head forward to brace myself. I remember trying to turn off the ignition to cut down the danger of fire, but I turned on the radio and windshield wiper instead.' Van's head struck the clamp in the middle of the windscreen frame that locked the convertible top when it was up. Thrown from the car, his head hit a kerb and he ended up in the gutter. 'I tried to stand up,' he said, 'but I fell. My face was wet. I thought it was raining, but it was blood.' Van had suffered a fractured skull. Glass punctured his face, neck and head, bone fragments pierced his brain and an artery was severed.

'A cop came over and said he would have to call the Culver City police, since the car had thrown his body to the wrong side of the street,' Johnson said. 'I asked him to show me the right side and I'd crawl there.' By the time the ambulance arrived 45 minutes later, Van had lost three quarts of blood.

Evie suffered a back injury, but Keenan was only shaken up and went to the Hollywood Presbyterian Hospital with Van who was rushed into the operating room. 'They tell me I was almost decapitated,' he said, 'but I never lost consciousness. My nose was up against my eyes, and my scalp had come unstuck. They lifted it up like a flap and poured in handfuls of sulphur.' Doctors told Keenan that Van would never work in films again if he lived. The following morning Spencer Tracy arrived to offer his blood for any transfusions Van might need.

Since filming of *A Guy Named Joe* had just begun, Mayer wanted to replace Van in the picture, but Tracy and Irene Dunne refused to work with another actor in the part so production was shut down for three months.

A metal plate was put into the left side of Van's head and muscle tissue from his right arm was used to rebuild the gash in his forehead. After two months in hospital, Van moved in with the Wynns until he was able to work again. Against doctor's orders, he returned to MGM in late June. 'I owed it to everyone,' he said. 'I'm a man with a debt to pay.' Van was cheerful despite his weakened condition and severe migraine headaches, but his determination paid off. *A Guy Named Joe* was a big success and he was on his way. By the time it was released, news of Johnson's serious car accident had been written about in all the newspapers. Cleverly, MGM did not completely cover the scar on his forehead. Director Victor Fleming explained that it was better for the scars to show than to 'wipe out the boy's personality'. The fascinated public wanted to see for themselves what Van Johnson looked like with a metal plate in his head. One critic said the accident had made him a celebrity, and one particularly popular with women who yearned to mother him back to health.

Van was earning $750 a week by 1943 but he lived modestly. Twenty-seven years old and already a teenager's idol, Van had never been linked with a girl. When he first arrived in Hollywood he had lived in June Havoc's house, but MGM told him to get a place of his own before gossip columnists discovered the arrangement. So he rented a small house near the Wynns in Brentwood, and was still seen almost exclusively in their company.

Van told fan magazines he had been in love with his high school sweetheart, but no such girl had ever existed. He had known many girls, but never been involved with them. Louis B. Mayer told him to date his pal, June Allyson. The pair would frequently go Dutch on evenings out, but June was interested in actor Dick Powell, twenty years her senior. Because Mayer said it would destroy her girl-next-door image if she dated Powell, they saw each other privately before Mayer finally agreed to let them marry in 1945.

'I'm married to MGM,' Johnson said. 'I have one love and it's pictures.' His ideal girl, he said, was the outdoor type. According to MGM press agent George Nichols, however, Van and June did have an intimate relationship, and he would have no reason to lie. But George was only one of a very few who was aware of it and he brushed it off as casual sex. June and Van would nonetheless remain good friends over the years.

In *Three Men in White*, Van again played Dr. Red Adams. This time he is put to the test by Dr. Gillespie, who wants to know if his young assistant can resist temptation when Ava Gardner and Marilyn Maxwell try to seduce him. Dr. Adams comes through with flying colours. Van was very popular as the doctor with a sunny smile and unruly hair. Hollywood columnist Sidney Skolsky wrote, 'He's a hunk of Americana', while the *Los Angeles Times* said, 'He is as American as ice cream, as masculine as a briar pipe, and as cleanly, unaffectedly appealing as a sea breeze in July.'

For Van, it was overwhelming. Suddenly he couldn't leave the studio without being surrounded by eager fans reaching out for a lock of hair or a button from his jacket. He was mobbed wherever he went and deluged with fan mail. Mayer was delighted that Johnson's fans wanted him to marry June Allyson and he encouraged them to date. It was logical to cash in, so MGM put the couple in *Two Girls and a Sailor* with Gloria DeHaven. June was originally supposed to play the pretty sister until Dick Powell suggested she take the role of the plain one. Wealthy sailor Van falls for Gloria who's after his money, but in the end finds love with June, the sincere one. Once again MGM did not completely cover up the scar on Van's forehead. The *Los Angeles Times* said Johnson had audiences applauding 'almost before he is seen on screen'. *Photoplay* wrote, 'Perhaps he fills the empty place in our hearts. He has created so much love in human hearts so badly in need of love.'

After fans broke into his house, though, Van moved into the Beverly Hills Hotel for privacy, looking to the Wynns to provide a home life.

Rumours about Keenan and Van continued to circulate around Hollywood, while there was also speculation that Van and Evie were more than close friends. He regularly escorted her to parties and premieres if Keenan was out of town.

In *Thirty Seconds Over Tokyo*, released in 1944, Van played a pilot whose plane is shot down. His leg amputated, he returns home where he is reunited with his pregnant wife. When she walks into his hospital room, he stands up, forgetting that he has only one leg, and falls down. *Time* described it as 'the most shocking and piteous moment any American war film has yet dared to exhibit'.

It was unusual casting to co-star Van with swimming star Esther Williams in *The Thrill of a Romance*, but their chemistry on the screen was very convincing. 'We were a sweetheart couple who had that MGM look that was so American, with no ethnic traces whatsoever,' Esther said. They became good friends off the set but never dated. About Van she said, 'There was no cuter human being in the world at that time.' The *New York Herald Tribune* described Van in *The Thrill of a Romance* as 'the antithesis of the "wolf" . . . clean cut, amiable, a little shy, and needing aid and comfort.'

Van was again a serviceman in *Weekend at the Waldorf*. Depressed over the loss of his war buddy and without a family, he asks the hotel stenographer, played by Lana Turner, to make out his will. Also in the picture were Ginger Rogers and Walter Pidgeon, who become humorously involved, and Keenan Wynn as a cub reporter. The film broke all records at Radio City Music Hall in New York.

In 1945 Evie had a second son, Tracy, but her marriage to Keenan was already over. As it happened, he was in a serious accident when his motorcycle crashed into a car at the corner of Sunset Boulevard and Hilgard. Wynn suffered a fractured jaw, concussion, a back injury and was in a coma for eleven days. Keenan claimed that in fact his injuries were worse than reported, so Evie didn't leave him. He was warned not to drink, but he was an alcoholic and disobeyed doctor's orders.

Keenan's accident happened during production of *Easy to Wed* (a remake of MGM's 1936 *Libeled Lady* with Myrna Loy and William Powell), starring Van and Esther Williams. Wynn's jaw was wired shut and he had to talk through his teeth. 'I walked out of a door in one scene at 183 pounds,' he said, 'and walked through the door on the other side at 153. I lost thirty pounds in four weeks.'

*

Van invited his father to Hollywood, wanting to entertain him royally. Charles, like every other visitor to MGM, was impressed, but when Van took him to the posh and popular Chasens for dinner, his father ordered a tuna fish sandwich and wouldn't change his mind, despite Van's pleadings. Maybe Charles had had enough of the star treatment. Sightseeing tours in Newport included the boarding house where he lived – 'This was the home of movie star Van Johnson before he became famous . . .' Although proud of his son, Charles was unhappy being a part of his glamorous world.

In MGM's star-studded *Till the Clouds Roll By*, a biography of songwriter Jerome Kern, Van sang and danced with Lucille Bremer to the tune of 'I Won't Dance'. He was wonderful and, for a stocky guy, he was light on his feet. And he had a pleasant voice that reflected his boyish image.

In 1945 Johnson began dating the adorable Sonja Henie, who might be described as Esther Williams on ice. Mayer, though, was not happy with all the publicity they were receiving. Three years older than Van, she was in the process of getting a divorce from millionaire Bob Topping. There was no need to worry, however, because Henie, who needed the publicity to boost her fading box-office appeal, wasn't seriously interested in Van. In fact Mayer should have been grateful for the publicity, because it was becoming increasingly clear that his redheaded boy-next-door was either bisexual or homosexual. Mayer got the first clue when actor Peter Lawford's mother told him her son was gay and reported her suspicions that the Wynns and Johnson were involved in homosexual activities. Since Lady Lawford was, to say the least, a little screwy, Mayer gave her accusations scant credence. But he didn't forget them, either.

And Ed Wynn, returning to New York after a visit to his son, said, 'I can't keep them straight. Evie loves Keenan. Keenan loves Evie. Van loves Evie. Evie loves Van. Van loves Keenan. Keenan loves Van.'

In December 1946 the Wynns announced they were getting a divorce. 'I must have been born to be a bachelor,' Keenan said. 'I never noticed the new drapes or wallpaper or even Evie's new dress, but Van did. I hated shopping trips and I used to ask Van to go along with Evie.'

His father told the press, 'Tonight Keenan and Evie are out together. Tomorrow he's going to put her on a train for Sun Valley to get a divorce.'

Tongues began to wag when Van planned to spend his vacation in Sun Valley, but Keenan said in an interview, 'Van had nothing to do with my wife's decision to divorce me. She sparked my early career, stuck with me when I was hurt, and stood by me during a subsequent mental sickness, when

I tried to corner the highball market and came close to botching everything I had worked for.'

Further evidence comes from gay playwright Arthur Laurents who wrote in his memoirs, 'A sunny male star caught performing in public urinals once too often was ordered by his studio to get married. His best friend, a young comedian and his wife, divorced so he could marry his wife.'

Evie Wynn confirmed this to author David Heymann: 'Mayer decided that unless I married Van Johnson . . . he wouldn't renew Keenan's contract. I was young and stupid enough to let Mayer manipulate me. I divorced Keenan, married Van Johnson, and thus became another of LB.'s little victims.' In later years Evie said she was the only girl Van would consider marrying. He told Lucille Ball he was in love with Evie, but Lucy was disenchanted and thought Johnson had turned from a sweet kid into a selfish egotist.

Four hours after Evie obtained a Mexican divorce, she and Van were married in Juarez on 25 January 1947. 'It was very sudden,' he said. 'We just made up our minds and did it.' In May, they moved into a new house in Santa Monica with the Wynn boys. Though Mayer had saved Johnson's career, the bobbysoxer's delight was not so popular after he married. No longer the leading man, he now took supporting roles in *State of the Union* and *Command Decision*.

Van's social life these days was more exciting than his films. He and Evie remained friends with Keenan, who was invited to Christmas dinner and occasionally attended their A-list parties. But when Evie became pregnant, Keenan tried to keep his distance. On 6 January 1948, a daughter, Schuyler Van, was born. Evie's recovery was a long one. She had been warned not to have another baby, but after a third Caesarian she was weak and sick for months. Van was no comfort to her: he enjoyed the good times but turned his back on the unhappy ones. Evie was on hand, however, when Van put his signature and footprints in cement in the courtyard of Grauman's Chinese Theater in April.

On 11 January 1949, Keenan Wynn married Betty Jane Butler, a 27-year-old model. But they were divorced in June 1953 because, according to Betty Jane, Keenan was too close to his ex-wife Evie.

After making a few forgettable movies, MGM handed Johnson a plum. *In the Good Old Summertime* was a remake of *The Shop Around the Corner*, the Jimmy Stewart picture about two co-workers who dislike each other but, unbeknownst to either of them, are pen pals. The very talented but troubled Judy Garland co-starred. When the film was finished on time,

Mayer asked Johnson how the cast had managed to do it, since Judy was famous for her absences. 'We gave her love,' Van said. 'We made sure she had a fresh rose in her dressing room every day. All she needed was a pat on the back once in a while.'

In 1949 Dore Schary took over production at MGM. Overruled when he wanted to make the war movie *Battleground*, he decided to produce it himself. For realism, director William Wellman put the cast through basic training. Robert Taylor was chosen for the lead but backed out after several days of drilling and crawling on his belly. Despite advice to stay clear of the movie, Johnson agreed to replace Taylor. Schary wanted to shoot *Battleground* in Bastogne, but it proved too expensive so the film was effectively shot on one of MGM's sound stages. Van plays a soldier hungry for scrambled eggs and the part was a good one. He carries the eggs in his helmet during battle until he gets a chance to cook them, but then has to put his helmet back on, scrambled eggs running down his face.

The *New York Times* called *Battleground* the best Second World War movie ever made in Hollywood. In contrast, *The Big Hangover* with Elizabeth Taylor was a bore, but Van said he understood that the star system meant doing mediocre films in between the good ones. Making $5000 a week was incentive enough not to complain. In 1950 Van and Esther Williams teamed up again in *Duchess of Idaho*. Despite the recycled plots, their movies were always popular and well received. *Too Young to Kiss* with June Allyson in 1951 was an amusing film about a young pianist posing as a thirteen-year-old to impress a concert impresario.

Johnson was not as upset with L.B. Mayer's departure from MGM as most of the other stars under contract to the studio. He liked Dore Schary, but was nonetheless unsure of his future. In 1953 he asked permission to perform at the Sands Hotel in Las Vegas. Evie and Keenan were there to support him on the opening night and he played to full houses throughout his engagement.

Easy to Love, again with Esther Williams, was good fun, but both Van and Esther could see the end of the contract system looming at MGM. This was their last film together. Johnson decided to freelance in the summer of 1954 but he signed for two more films at Metro. Esther clashed with Dore Schary the following year, breaking her contract and forfeiting her $3 million pension.

About his twelve years with MGM Van commented, 'I didn't want to go home at night. They were the great years but the studio didn't equip me for facing the real world.'

Brigadoon with Cyd Charisse, Gene Kelly and Van lost much of its hoped-for lustre before a single scene was filmed. Director Vincente Minnelli had planned to make the musical in the mountains of Carmel, California, but MGM could not afford to film it on location so it was shot on a sound stage and in CinemaScope for the regular screen. Van complained that he was having to do everything twice and wanted his salary doubled, but Schary didn't agree.

Perhaps one of Johnson's best films was *The Last Time I Saw Paris* with Elizabeth Taylor. He plays an alcoholic writer who accidentally locks out his wife on a cold snowy night. She comes down with pneumonia and dies. Guilt ridden, he loses custody of his daughter and has to fight to get her back. There was no chemistry between Van and Elizabeth, but he makes up for that in scenes at her death bed and when he pleads with his embittered sister-in-law for custody of his little girl. The theme song, 'The Last Time I Saw Paris', added a memorably bittersweet touch throughout the picture.

Van took whatever movies were offered him, all of them mediocre. His last for MGM was *Slander*, about a TV personality whose career is ruined by a tabloid. He was offered the part of Eliot Ness in the television series *The Untouchables*, but Evie told him to ask for more money and the Ness role went to Robert Stack. Disillusioned by Hollywood, Van and Evie moved to Switzerland. 'I was bored to death most of the time,' he explained. 'I was terribly unhappy . . . The marriage was bad and so was my outlook.' Regarding his move to Switzerland, though, Van said, 'I found out the hard way. Out of sight, out of mind. You have to be where the action is. The phone didn't ring for me.'

When Van became physically violent with Evie she left him, returned to their home in Beverly Hills and filed for divorce. Van, who remained in Europe for six months, told gossip columnist Hedda Hopper, 'What's the good of having a million dollars in a drawer in Switzerland if you can't be with your family and eat an American hot dog once in a while?' He got an offer from producer Ben Segal to play in *Damn Yankees* at a summer theatre in Wallingford, Connecticut for $7500 a week. When Van arrived in New York he called Evie, who agreed to try again.

After *Damn Yankees*, Van opened in *The Music Man* at the Adelphi Theatre in London's West End in March 1961. Although Evie accompanied Van to

England, she left him for good in September, saying he had picked a fight which led to their break-up. 'Van left me for a chorus boy,' Evie told her son, Ned Wynn. She had been warned about her husband's sexuality but refused to believe it. 'I didn't listen,' she said. 'I thought it was just a rumour.' Evie thought she could make him straight, and failed.

During the run of *The Music Man*, Johnson caught his hand in the door of a prop train, severing the top of his middle finger. He was rushed to hospital where his finger was grafted back on. Feeling fit again and ready to tackle Hollywood, Van opened in *The Music Man* at the Coconut Grove in the Ambassador Hotel, Los Angeles for a month. Keenan was there to cheer him on, but Evie was keeping her distance until she and Van appeared in court. The judge awarded her $4000 and ordered Van to pay the mortgages on their homes in Beverly Hills and Palm Beach.

While he was making *Wives and Lovers* with Janet Leigh, Van found a discoloured blemish on his inner thigh that turned out to be cancerous. After minor surgery he left the Cedars of Lebanon Hospital wearing red socks and sporting his all-American smile.

In the summer of 1963 Johnson toured the country in *Bye Bye Birdie, Damn Yankees, The Music Man* and *Guys and Dolls*.

In September 1963 Van's mother Loretta died of a heart attack. She had never seen her granddaughter, Schuyler, because Van had forbidden it. According to Evie, Van hated women because of his relationship with his mother. She had showed up on his doorstep in November 1954 and sued him for support money. The suit was settled out of court, Van agreeing to pay Loretta's past due bills along with $400 a month. It isn't known how long he provided this support. Charles Johnson died the following year at the age of 82. Van was in touch with him during his illness and attended his funeral.

In January 1964, he had another operation to remove a lymph node on his left thigh. 'They cut me wide open,' he told the press, 'and had me on the table for four hours. They went through me with a fine tooth comb and gave me a clean bill of health.'

Van's daughter Schuyler, now sixteen years old, was deeply hurt that her father did not answer her phone calls and letters. Evie was broke and lost both houses, claiming Van owed her $225,000. 'All I have left is a car,' she said. Divorce proceedings dragged on until 1968, when the court awarded Evie 15 per cent of Van's gross income and 50 per cent of their real estate. Calling it the ugliest divorce in Hollywood history, he claimed Evie had wiped him out. 'I make out cheques every week to the dragon lady,' he complained. Evie claimed that Van had lied about his earnings and that she received next to nothing. In order to escape from the state of California and more legal battles, Johnson now bought a penthouse on New York City's East Side.

Like Mickey Rooney, Johnson was popular as an after-dinner speaker. At times he bragged about having a million dollars in a Swiss bank; at other times he complained about having to work for a living.

Keenan Wynn, now 37 years old, was married for the third time in 1954 to 21-year-old Sharley Hudson. They had three daughters in a good marriage that lasted until his death from cancer in October 1986. Johnson said that he and Keenan remained friends until the end: 'He would send me notes, and always thanked me for taking Evie off his hands.'

In 1985 Van performed in *La Cage aux Folles* at the Palace Theater on Broadway. He continued to work in the theatre and in films until a hearing problem slowed him down socially and professionally.

Van Johnson was a delight, both on the screen and in person. I don't know if he still wears his red socks these days but he had them on when I saw him fifteen years ago. He was talking to some little old ladies who were probably bobbysoxers when he was under contract to MGM. They were still showering him with adoration and he was loving every minute of it. I was close enough to see his freckles, and that was good enough. After all, that's what he was all about.

'Let's face it. I was a male Doris Day.'

– Van Johnson

The Films of Van Johnson

Too Many Girls (RKO, 1940)
Murder in the Big House (Warner Brothers, 1942)
Somewhere I'll find You (MGM, 1942)
Dr. Gillespie's New Assistant (MGM, 1942)
The Human Comedy (MGM, 1943)
Pilot No.5 (MGM, 1943)
Dr. Gillespie's Criminal Case (MGM, 1943)
Madame Curie (MGM, 1943)
A Guy Named Joe (MGM, 1943)
White Cliffs of Dover (MGM, 1944)
Three Men in White (MGM, 1944)
Two Girls and a Sailor (MGM, 1944)
Thirty Seconds Over Tokyo (MGM, 1944)
Between Two Women (MGM, 1945)
Thrill of a Romance (MGM, 1945)
Weekend at the Waldorf (MGM, 1945)
Easy to Wed (MGM, 1946)
No Leave, No Love (MGM, 1946)
Till the Clouds Roll By (MGM, 1946)
High Barbaree (MGM, 1947)
The Romance of Rosy Ridge (MGM, 1947)
State of the Union (MGM, 1948)
The Bride Goes Wild (MGM, 1948)
Command Decision (MGM, 1949)
Mother is a Freshman (20th Century-Fox, 1949)
Scene of the Crime (MGM, 1949)

In the Good Old Summertime (MGM, 1949)
Battleground (MGM, 1949)
The Big Hangover (MGM, 1950)
Duchess of Idaho (MGM, 1950)
Grounds for Marriage (MGM, 1951)
Three Guys Named Mike (MGM, 1951)
Go For Broke (MGM, 1951)
Too Young to Kiss (MGM, 1951)
It's a Big Country (MGM, 1952)
Invitation (MGM, 1952)
When in Rome (MGM, 1952)
Washington Story (MGM, 1952)
Plymouth Adventure (MGM, 1952)
Confidentially Connie (MGM, 1953)
Remains to be Seen (MGM, 1953)
Easy to Love (MGM, 1953)
The Siege at Red River (20th Century-Fox, 1954)
Men of the Fighting Lady (MGM, 1954)
The Caine Mutiny (Columbia, 1954)
Brigadoon (MGM, 1954)
The Last Time I Saw Paris (MGM, 1954)
The End of the Affair (Columbia, 1955)
Miracle in the Rain (Warner, 1956)
The Bottom of the Bottle (20th Century-Fox, 1956)
23 Paces to Baker Street (20th Century-Fox, 1956)
Slander (MGM, 1957)
Kelly and Me (Universal, 1957)
Action of the Tiger (MGM, 1957)
The Last Blitzkrieg (Columbia, 1958)
Subway in the Sky (United Artists, 1959)
Web of Evidence (United Artists, 1959)
The Enemy General (Columbia, 1960)
Wives and Lovers (Paramount, 1963)
Divorce American Style (Columbia, 1967)
Yours, Mine and Ours (United Artists, 1968)
Where Angels Go, Trouble Follows (Columbia, 1968)
Company of Killers (Universal, 1970)

The Kidnapping of the President (Sefel, 1980)
The Purple Rose of Cairo (Orion, 1985)
Taxi Killer (IT, 1988)
Clowning Around (Wonderworks, 1991)

Other MGM Guys

Fred Astaire (1899–1987) danced into our hearts with Ginger Rogers during the thirties. He made such MGM classics as *Easter Parade*, *The Barkleys of Broadway*, *Royal Wedding*, *The Band Wagon*, and *Silk Stockings*. A widower, Fred married a female jockey, Robin Smith, in 1980. On his tombstone she inscribed, 'Will Always Love You My Darling. Thank You.'

John Barrymore (1882–1942), known as 'The Great Profile', was from America's Royal Family of Actors and a genius, but he was more interested in drinking and romancing. Among his best-known films were *Grand Hotel*, *Dinner at Eight*, and *Romeo and Juliet*.

Lionel Barrymore (1878–1954), John's older brother, played the gruff Dr. Gillespie in the Dr. Kildare movies.

Freddy Bartholomew (1924–1992) appeared in *David Copperfield*, *Little Lord Fauntleroy*, and *Anna Karenina* with Greta Garbo.

Wallace Beery (1885–1949) won an Oscar for his role as the washed-up prize fighter in *The Champ* in 1931 alongside Jackie Cooper. He appeared in two MGM classics, *Grand Hotel* and *Dinner at Eight*. Beery was excellent with Marie Dressler in *Min and Bill* and *Tugboat Annie*. He was married to Gloria Swanson from 1916 to 1918.

Baritone **Nelson Eddy** (1901–1967) is remembered for his films with Jeanette MacDonald. Their fan clubs refuse to believe they were intimate off the set, but they were indeed very much in love. L.B. Mayer forced her to marry the gay actor Gene Raymond, whom she bailed out of jail several times for sexual offences. Eddy got drunk and remembers nothing about his wedding to Ann Franklin in Las Vegas. He wept when he heard about

Jeanette's death. At his funeral his wife leaned over to Raymond and whispered, 'Now they can sing together forever.'

Director **Victor Fleming** (1883–1949), who was primarily associated with MGM, has been strangely forgotten over the years. He directed such films as *Captains Courageous, Red Dust, The Wizard of Oz, Gone With the Wind*, and *Dr. Jekyll and Mr. Hyde*. Every actress he worked with fell in love with the tall handsome director whom Clark Gable sought to emulate. Fleming had affairs with Norma Shearer, Clara Bow, and Ingrid Bergman, to name only a few. After he impregnated his best friend's wife in 1934 and reluctantly married her, he became a doting father and devoted husband until he fell in love with Ingrid Bergman. Whether he would have divorced his wife for Ingrid isn't known, because he died of a heart attack before a decision was made.

Stewart Granger (1913–1993) was superb in such MGM films as *King Solomon's Mines, Scaramouche, The Prisoner of Zenda*, and *Beau Brummel*. He was married to actress Jean Simmons in 1950, but divorced ten years later when she fell in love with director Richard Brooks.

Van Heflin (1910–1971) won an Oscar for Best Supporting Actor in the 1941 film *Johnny Eager*, which had Robert Taylor in the title role. In June 1971 he was found clinging to the ladder of the swimming pool at his apartment house in Hollywood after suffering a heart attack.

Howard Keel (1917–) had a robust baritone voice which MGM put to good use in *Annie Get Your Gun, Show Boat, Kiss Me, Kate*, and *Seven Brides for Seven Brothers*.

Gene Kelly (1912–1996) had a different style of dancing than the sophisticated Fred Astaire. Kelly was known for his athletic Irish appeal, did his own stunts and often took charge of his films. His best work was in *Anchors Aweigh, On the Town, Summer Stock, An American in Paris*, and *Singin' in the Rain*.

Fernando Lamas (1916–1982) was MGM's Latin lover. He made *The Merry Widow* alongside Lana Turner, with whom he had an affair. She broke it off when he beat her up. He married actress Arlene Dahl in 1954 and had one son, Lorenzo, in 1958. Fernando and Arlene divorced in 1960 and he later married Esther Williams in 1967.

Ricardo Montalban (1920–) appeared in MGM's *Fiesta, On an Island with You, The Kissing Bandit,* and *Across the Wide Missouri.* After Fernando Lamas slapped Lana Turner around, she refused to make *Latin Lovers* with him, and Montalban stepped in.

Robert Montgomery (1904–1981) was atrophied by the studio system, which placed him in a particular screen mould. His best films, *Here Comes Mr. Jordan* and *Mr. and Mrs. Smith,* were made when he was loaned out to other studios. His one good venture for MGM was *They Were Expendable* in 1945.

George Murphy (1902–1992) was a song and dance man, and a good one. His finest films for MGM were *Broadway Melody of 1940, Little Nellie Kelly,* and *For Me and My Gal.* In 1965 he was elected senator for the state of California.

Walter Pidgeon (1897–1984) was reliably good, but usually better when he co-starred with Greer Garson in *Mrs. Miniver, Blossoms in the Dust, Madame Curie,* and *Mrs. Parkington.*

William Powell (1892–1984) is best remembered for the *Thin Man* movies with Myrna Loy. He was engaged to Jean Harlow when she died in 1937.

Franchot Tone (1903–1968) was one of the founders of the Group Theater. His main claim to fame was marrying Joan Crawford in 1935, which is a pity because Tone was a fine actor. After his divorce he became involved with starlet Barbara Payton and was beaten to a pulp by her boyfriend, ex-boxer Tom Neal. Following extensive plastic surgery, he married Payton, but the marriage only lasted a year. Near the end of his life, he again became close to Crawford, who tried to nurse him back to health. One of his best films for MGM was *Three Comrades.*

Robert Walker (1918–1951) was a talented actor, but had to struggle with alcoholism and a broken heart. After his wife Jennifer Jones left him for producer David O. Selznick, Walker was plagued with depression. He did well with Judy Garland in *The Clock,* but Bob's best work was in *Strangers on a Train* at Warner Brothers. In 1951, during a bout with alcohol, doctors injected him with sodium amytol which apparently caused his death.

Johnny Weissmuller (1904–1984) was Tarzan, the Ape Man. He gained a reputation as the fastest swimmer in the world in the early twenties, winning five Olympic gold medals and 52 national championships, and establishing 67 world records. He was married five times before suffering a cerebral stroke, following which he was admitted to the Motion Picture and Television Home for Actors. Johnny was known to give his famous Tarzan yell at all hours of the night and had to be moved elsewhere. Various other actors portrayed Tarzan but none approached Weissmuller.

Robert Young (1907–1998) is probably best known for *Father Knows Best* and *Marcus Welby, M.D.* on television. He was under contract to MGM from 1931 to 1944. What the public did not know about Young was that he was an alcoholic for thirty years. 'I couldn't face the day without two or three martinis,' he said. He conquered his problem with the help of Alcoholics Anonymous.

'At MGM, men are real men.'

– Louis B. Mayer

Bibliography

Allyson, June, with Francis Spatz Leighton, *June Allyson*, Putnam, New York, 1982.

Altman, Dana, Hollywood East, *Louis B. Mayer and the Origins of the Studio System*, Carol Publishing, New York, 1992.

Anger, Kenneth, *Hollywood Babylon*, Straight Arrow Books, San Francisco, 1995.

— *Hollywood Babylon II*, New American Library, New York, 1994.

Anderson, Christopher, *An Affair to Remember*, William Morrow & Co., New York, 1997.

Anderson, Joan Webster, *Forever Young: The Authorized Biography of Loretta Young*, Thomas More, Allen, Texas, 2000.

Bacon, James, *Hollywood is a Four Letter Word*, Henry Regency Co., Chicago, 1976.

Berg, Scott A., *Goldwyn: A Biography*, Knopf, New York, 1989.

Bergman, Ingrid, and Alan Burgess, *Ingrid Bergman, My Story*, Dell, New York, 1980.

Bret, David, *Elvis: The Hollywood Years*, Robson Books, London, 2001.

— *Valentino*, Robson Books, London, 1998.

Brown, Peter Harry and Pat H. Broeske, *Down at the End of Lonely Street: The Life and Death of Elvis Presley*, Dutton, New York, 1997.

Burk, Margaret and Gary Hudson, *Final Curtain*, Seven Locks Press, Santa Ana, CA, 1996.

Carey, Gary, *All the Stars in Heaven*, Dutton, New York, 1981.

Chierichetti, David, *Mitchell Leisen: Hollywood Director*, Photoventures Press, Los Angeles, 1995.

Clarke, Gerald, *Get Happy: The Life of Judy Garland*, Random House, New York, 2000.

Crowther, Bosley, *Hollywood Rajah*, Henry Holt, New York, 1960.

Davidson, Bill, *Spencer Tracy*, E.P. Dutton, New York, 1987.

Davies, Marion, *The Times We Had*, Bobbs Merrill, New York, 1975.

Davis, Bette, *The Lonely Life*, Putnam, New York, 1962.

Davis, Ronald L., *Van Johnson: MGM's Golden Boy*, University Press of Mississippi, 2001.

Deans, Mickey and Ann Pinchot, *Weep No More My Lady*, Pyramid, New York, 1973.

De Mille, Cecil B., *Autobiography*, Prentice Hall, New York 1959.

Lloyd, Ann and Fuller, Graham (Eds.), Desser, Arnold (Consultant Ed.), *The Illustrated Who's Who of the Cinema*, Orbis Publishing Ltd., London, 1983.

Dewey, Donald, *James Stewart*, Turner Publishing, Atlanta, 1996.

Dougan, Andy, *Untouchable: A Biography of Robert DeNiro*, Thunder's Mouth Press, New York, 1996.

Durgnat, Raymond and Scott Simmon, *King Vidor: American*, University of California Press, Berkeley, 1988.

Edwards, Anne, *A Remarkable Woman*, Pocket Books, New York, 1986.

Epstein, Edward Z., *Portrait of Jennifer*, Simon and Schuster, New York, 1995.

Fairbanks, Jr, Douglas, *The Salad Days*, Doubleday, Garden City, New York, 1973.

Finstad, Suzanne, *Child Bride: The Untold Story of Priscilla Beaulieu Presley*, Harmony Books, New York, 1997.

Fisher, Eddie, *Been There, Done That*, St. Martin's Press, New York, 1999.

Fitzgerald, F. Scott, *The Last Tycoon*, Scribners, New York, 1941.

Flamini, Roland, *Thalberg*, Crown, New York, 1994.

Fountain, Leatrice Gilbert, *Dark Star*, St. Martin's Press, New York, 1985.

Fowler, Gene, *Good Night, Sweet Prince*, Viking Press, New York, 1944.

Freedland, Michael, *All The Way: A Biography of Frank Sinatra*, St. Martin's Press, New York, 1997.

Garceau, Jean and Inez Cooke, *Dear Mr. G.*, Little, Brown & Co., New York, 1961.

Gardner, Ava, *Ava: My Story*, Bantam Books, New York, 1990.

Giancana, Sam and Chuck, *Double Cross*, Warner Books, New York, 1972.

Goldman, Albert, *Elvis*, McGraw-Hill, New York, 1981.

Graham, Sheila, *Confessions of a Hollywood Columnist*, William Morrow, New York, 1969.

— *Hollywood Revisited*, St. Martin's Press, New York, 1984.

Guilaroff, Sydney, *Crowning Glory*, General Publishing Group, Santa Monica, California, 1996.

Guiles, Fred Lawrence, *Marion Davies*, McGraw-Hill, New York, 1972.

Guralnick, Peter, *Careless Love*, Little, Brown & Co., New York, 1999.
— *Last Train to Memphis*, Little, Brown & Co., New York, 1994.
Hadleigh, Boze, *Hollywood Gays*, Barricade Books, New York, 1996.
— *Hollywood Lesbians*, Barricade Books, New York, 1994.
— *Conversations with My Elders*, St. Martin's Press, New York, 1986.
— *Bette Davis Speaks*, Barricade Books, New York, 1996.
Halliwell, Ruth and John Walker, *Halliwell's Film Guide*, HarperCollins, New York, 1994.
Harris, Warren G., *Clark Gable*, Random House, New York, 2002.
— *Gable and Lombard*, Simon and Schuster, New York, 1974.
Haver, Ronald, *David O. Selznick's Hollywood*, Knopf, New York, 1980.
Hay, Peter, *MGM: When the Lion Roars*, Turner Publishing, Atlanta, Georgia, 1991.
Heymann, C. David, *Liz*, Coral Publishing, New York, 1995.
Hepburn, Katharine, *Me*, Ballantine Books, New York, 1991.
Higham, Charles, *Ava*, Delacorte Press, New York, 1974.
— *Merchant of Dreams*, David I. Fine, New York, 1993.
Hyams, Joe, *Misled in Hollywood*, Peter H. Wyden, Inc., New York, 1973.
Kelley, Kitty, *His Way: The Unauthorized Biography of Frank Sinatra*, Bantam Books, New York, 1986.
Kobal, John, *People Will Talk*, Alfred A. Knopf, Inc., New York, 1986.
Kotsilibas-Davis, James, and Myrna Loy, *Myrna Loy*, Alfred A. Knopf, Inc., New York, 1987.
Lambert, Gavin, *Norma Shearer: A Life*, Alfred A. Knopf Inc., New York, 1990.
— *GWTW: The Making of Gone With the Wind*, Atlantic-Little Brown, Boston, 1973.
Lamarr, Hedy, *Ecstasy and Me*, Fawcett Crest, New York, 1966.
LaSalle, Mick, *Complicated Women*, Thomas Dunne Books/St. Martin's Press, New York, 2000.
Lawford, Patricia Seaton, *The Peter Lawford Story*, Carroll & Graf, New York, 1988.
Leamer, Laurence, *As Time Goes By: The Life of Ingrid Bergman*, Harper and Row, New York, 1986.
Lewis, Judy, *Uncommon Knowledge*, Pocket Books, New York, 1994.
Linet, Beverly, *Star-Crossed*, G.P. Putnam's Sons, New York, 1986.
Lockwood, Charles, *Dream Palaces*, Viking Press, New York, 1981.
Loos, Anita, *Kiss Hollywood Goodbye*, Viking Press, New York, 1974.
— *The Talmadge Girls*, Viking Press, New York, 1978.

— *Cast of Thousands*, Viking, New York, 1978.

McGilligan, Patrick, *George Cukor: A Biography of a Gentleman*, St. Martin's Press, New York, 1991.

McLellan, Diana, *The Girls*, St. Martin's Press, New York, 2000.

Madsen, Axel, *Stanwyck*, HarperCollins, New York, 1994.

— *The Sewing Circle*, Birch Lane Press, New York, 1995.

Mann, William J., *Wisecracker: The Life and Times of Billy Haines*, Penguin Books, New York, 1998.

Marion, Frances, *Off With Their Heads*, Macmillan, New York, 1972.

Marx, Arthur, *Goldwyn*, Norton, New York, 1976.

— *The Nine Lives of Mickey Rooney*, Berkley Books, New York, 1986.

Marx, Samuel, *Mayer and Thalberg*, Samuel French Trade, Hollywood, California, 1988.

Michael, Paul, *The American Movies Reference Book: The Sound Era*, Prentice Hall, New York, 1969.

Mosley, Leonard, *Zanuck: The Rise and Fall of Hollywood's Last Tycoon*, Little Brown, Boston, 1984.

Paris, Barry, *Garbo*, Alfred A. Knopf, Inc., New York, 1995.

Parish, James Robert and Ronald L. Bowers, *The MGM Stock Company*, Arlington House, New York, 1974.

— *The Hollywood Book of Death*, Contemporary Books, New York, 2002.

Quirk, Lawrence J., *Norma: The Story of Norma Shearer*, St. Martin's Press, New York, 1988.

— *The Films of Robert Taylor*, Citadel, Secaucus, New Jersey, 1975.

— and William Schoell, *Joan Crawford: The Essential Biography*, University Press of Kentucky, 2002.

Porter, Darwin, *Katharine the Great*, Blood Moon Productions, New York, 2004.

Reynolds, Debbie, *Debbie*, Morrow, New York, 1988.

Rich, Sharon, *Sweethearts*, Donald A. Fine, New York, 1994.

Riva, Maria, *Marlene Dietrich*, Alfred A. Knopf, New York, 1993.

Rooney, Mickey, *Life is Too Short*, Villard Books, New York, 1991.

— *I.E. An Autobiography*, G.P. Putnam's Sons, New York, 1965.

Selznick, Irene Mayer, *A Private View*, Alfred A, Knopf, New York, 1983.

Shaw, Arnold, *Sinatra*, Holt, Rinehart and Winston, New York, 1968.

— *Sinatra*, Delilah Books, New York, 1982.

Shipman, David, *The Great Movie Stars of the Golden Era*, Crown, New York, 1970.

— *Judy Garland: The Life of an American Legend*, Hyperion, New York, 1992.

Slatzer, Robert, *The Life and Curious Death of Marilyn Monroe*, Pinnacle Books, Los Angeles, 1975.

Smith, Ella, *Starring Miss Barbara Stanwyck*, Crown, New York, 1974.

Soares, Andre, *Beyond Paradise: The Life of Ramon Novarro*, St. Martin's Press, New York, 2002.

Spada, James, *Peter Lawford: The Man who Kept the Secrets*, Bantam, New York, 1991.

Spoto, Donald, *Blue Angel: The Life of Marlene Dietrich*, Doubleday, New York, 1992.

Stenn, David, *Clara Bow*, Doubleday, New York, 1988.

— *Bombshell: The Life and Death of Jean Harlow*, Lightning Bug Press, Raleigh, North Carolina, 1993.

Swanson, Gloria, *Swanson on Swanson*, Random House, New York, 1981.

Swindell, Larry, *Spencer Tracy*, World Publishing, New York, 1969.

— *Screwball: The Life of Carole Lombard*, William Morrow & Co., New York, 1975.

Teichmann, Howard, *Fonda, My Life*, New American Library, New York, 1981.

Thomas, Bob, *Thalberg*, New Millennium Press, Beverly Hills, 1969.

— *Joan Crawford*, Simon and Schuster, New York, 1978.

— *Selznick*, Doubleday, New York, 1970.

Thomson, David, *Showman: The Life of David O. Selznick*, Alfred A. Knopf, Inc., New York, 1992.

Thompson II, Charles C., and James P. Cole, *The Death of Elvis Presley*, Delacorte Press, New York, 1991.

Turk, Baron Edward, *Hollywood Diva: A Biography of Jeanette MacDonald*, University of California Press, Berkeley and Los Angeles, 1998.

Tornabene, Lyn, *Long Live the King*, G.P. Putnam & Sons, New York, 1976.

Turner, Lana, *Lana: The Lady, The Legend, The Truth*, E.P. Dutton, New York, 1982.

Vickers, Hugo, *Vivien Leigh*, Little, Brown & Co, New York, 1988.

Wayne, Jane Ellen, *Gable's Women*, Prentice Hall, New York, 1987.

— *Crawford's Men*, Prentice Hall, New York, 1988.

— *Ava's Men*, St. Martin's Press, New York, 1990.

— *Lana*, St. Martin's Press, New York, 1995.

— *Robert Taylor: The Man with the Perfect Face*, St. Martin's Press, New York, 1989; Robson Books, London, 1987.

— *Clark Gable: Portrait of a Misfit*, St. Martin's Press, New York, 1993.

— *Marilyn's Men*, St. Martin's Press, New York, 1992.

— *The Golden Girls of MGM*, Robson Books, London, 2002; Carroll & Graf, New York, 2002.

— *Stanwyck*, Arbor House, New York, 1985.

Wellman, William, *A Short Time for Insanity: An Autobiography*, Hawthorn, New York, 1974.

West, Red, Sonny West, Dave Hebler, *Elvis, What Happened?*, Ballantine Books, New York, 1977.

Williams, Esther, *The Million Dollar Mermaid*, Simon & Schuster, New York, 1999.

Yudkoff, Alvin, *Gene Kelly*, Back Stage Books, New York, 1999.